LONDON

SEAN McLACHLAN

LONDON

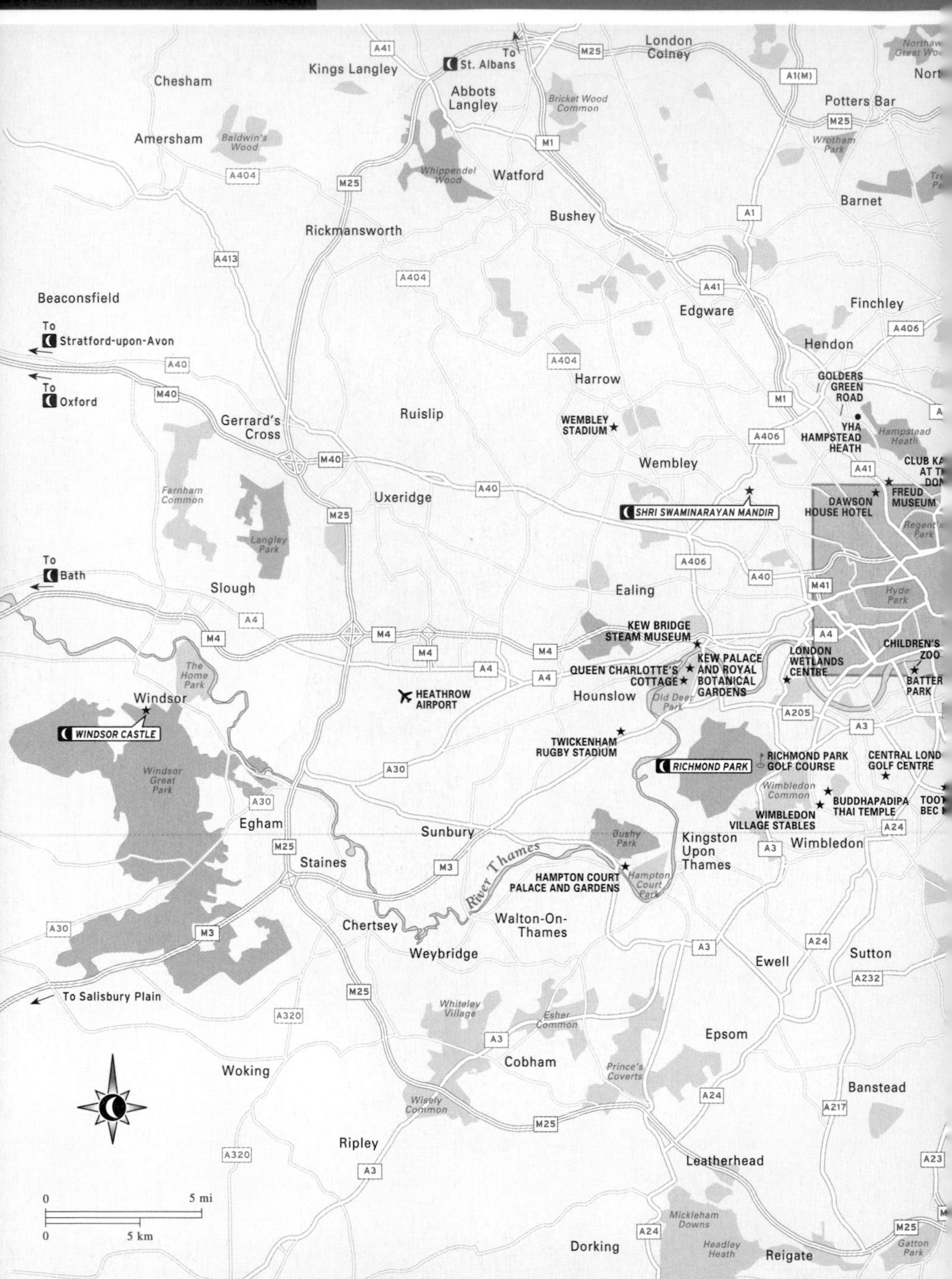

London Colney
St. Albans
Kings Langley
Chesham
Abbots Langley
Bricket Wood Common
Potters Bar
Wrotham Park
Amersham
Baldwin's Wood
Whippendel Wood
Watford
Barnet
Bushey
Rickmansworth
Beaconsfield
Edgware
Finchley
To Stratford-upon-Avon
Hendon
To Oxford
Harrow
Golders Green Road
YHA Hampstead Heath
Hampstead Heath
Ruislip
Gerrard's Cross
Wembley Stadium
Wembley
Farnham Common
Uxeridge
Dawson House Hotel
Freud Museum
Shri Swaminarayan Mandir
Langley Park
Regent's Park
To Bath
Slough
Ealing
Hyde Park
Kew Bridge Steam Museum
The Home Park
Queen Charlotte's Cottage
Kew Palace and Royal Botanical Gardens
London Wetlands Centre
Children's Zoo
Battersea Park
Windsor
Heathrow Airport
Hounslow
Old Deer Park
Windsor Castle
Twickenham Rugby Stadium
Richmond Park
Richmond Park Golf Course
Central London Golf Centre
Windsor Great Park
Wimbledon Common
Buddhapadipa Thai Temple
Wimbledon Village Stables
Egham
Sunbury
Bushy Park
Kingston Upon Thames
Wimbledon
Staines
River Thames
Hampton Court Palace and Gardens
Hampton Court Park
Chertsey
Walton-On-Thames
Weybridge
Ewell
Sutton
To Salisbury Plain
Whiteley Village
Esher Common
Epsom
Woking
Cobham
Prince's Coverts
Banstead
Wisely Common
Ripley
Leatherhead
Mickleham Downs
Headley Heath
Dorking
Reigate
Gatton Park
0 5 mi
0 5 km

MAP 1

To Cambridge
To Salisbury Plain
Cheshunt
Waltham Abbey
Epping
A10
M25
Whitewebbs Park
Epping Forest
M11
Loughton
M25
A12
Enfield
A1023
Chigwell
Weald Park
Brentwood
A10
Chingford
Hainault Forest
Bedford's Park
Thordon Park
A406
M11
Romford
A12
A127
CASTLE CLIMBING CENTRE
A10
Hackney Marshes
M25
Ilford
A12
A406
Dagenham
SEE "LONDON NEIGHBORHOODS" MAP
GEFFRYE MUSEUM
BRICK LANE MARKET, BRICK LANE RESTAURANT, 93 FEET EAST, AND WHITE CHAPEL ART GALLERY
A13
River Thames
A13
THE WAPPING PROJECT
MUSEUM IN DOCKLANDS
Belhus Park
Grays
A13
VIIA THAMESIDE
QUEEN'S HOUSE
Abbey Wood
CUTTY SARK
A205
A1089
NATIONAL MARITIME MUSEUM, OLD ROYAL NAVALCOLLEGE, ROYAL OBSERVATORY & GREENWICH PARK
Bexley
A2
Danson Park
Dartford
Gravesend
Avery Hill
A205
HORNIMAN MUSEUM
A2
A2
Joyden's Wood
Crystal Palace Park
M25
Swanley
Bromley
Petts Wood
A20
Orpington
M20
Croydon
A232
Lullingstone Park
Purley
M25
To Canterbury
Holt Wood
Coulsdon
Warlingham
M26
Borough Green
A22
Caterham
Ightham Common
Mereworth Woods
A21
Seven Oaks
Westerham
Fawke Common
Whitley Forest
© AVALON TRAVEL PUBLISHING, INC.

DISCOVER LONDON

You've saved your money, talked your boss into giving you some time off, and you're all set to head off for a great vacation. You have the world at your feet — Paris, Rome, New York. Why would you pick London? After all, Paris has great cafés and high fashion, Rome has ancient monuments and fine dining, and New York has rocking nightlife. London has none of that, right?

Wrong. London has all that and more.

London suffers from a lot of myths that may have been true 30 years ago (and were probably exaggerated even then) but certainly aren't true now. First, let's tackle the myth of British cooking. Yes, this is the land of jellied eels and mushy peas, but it's also the land of steak and Guinness pie, Sunday roasts, and fine cheese. And even if British cooking doesn't appeal to you, London's replete with restaurants of every nationality. Do you know what Seychellois cuisine tastes like? If a remote archipelago in the Indian Ocean with a population of barely 80,000 can have a culinary outpost in London, you

Royal Albert Hall is a great setting for music lovers.

© VISITLONDON.COM

know you'll find every other type of cuisine here too. Indian, Chinese, French, and Italian are the big draws (oops, you just lost a reason to go to Paris and Rome), but you'll also find Lebanese, Cuban, Thai, Korean, Dutch, Persian, Greek, Afghan. . . well, you get the point.

Another myth is that the English are stodgy, reserved, and generally unfriendly to visitors. Not true. Granted, this is a big city and you'll find a fair amount of big city attitude, but it's nowhere near New York, Los Angeles, or Paris. If you don't come across as crass and boorish yourself (Londoners have to deal with a lot of tourists, after all), you'll find the English to be great conversationalists and helpful guides. If you go on a day trip, you'll find the people in the countryside even nicer. What they lack in American extroverted energy they more than make up with warmth and wit.

Many people say London is dead after dark. This dates to the days when pubs all had to close at 11 P.M. This rule has recently been thrown out, and even if you do hear the bell for last orders (last call) a full hour and a quarter before midnight there are still plenty of other places where you can party all night. The city is full of pubs,

London Black Cabs provide fast, knowledgeable transport.

wine bars, and clubs that stay open late. Since it's a major stop for any band or DJ on a European tour, anyone who wants to go to a concert or rave won't be disappointed.

If you aren't too tired from dancing until dawn or too full from your third helping of curry, you'll want to get down to some sightseeing. Of course, you'll find the obvious – the Changing of the Guard at Buckingham Palace, Big Ben, the Tower of London and. . . why is it that these are the only three universally known sights in London? This city has so much more to offer than Redcoats, chimes, and torture chambers. Some of the best museums and art galleries in the world can be found here. The British Museum has a massive collection of artifacts from all ancient civilizations, and the National Gallery features an impressive array of European art, from the Renaissance to the impressionists. For modern art, head south of the Thames to the Thames Modern, housed in a converted power station. A nice bonus is that all three, and many other museums large and small, are completely free.

While the big attractions are fascinating, what makes London

Across the street from the British Museum stands this elegant Victorian facade.
© SEAN MCLACHLAN

unique are the endless number of interesting little sights and experiences. Stand in the golden light of dusk gazing at Bedford Square, unchanged since America was a British colony, and then quaff an ale in a centuries-old pub. Visit the largest Hindu temple outside India, with its elegant marble sculptures of gods and goddesses, or stand by the Thames watching the boats go by while right next to you towers an ancient Egyptian obelisk covered in hieroglyphs. Or hunt for collectibles at the massive outdoor antique market at Portobello Road, which looks as if 10,000 attics holding bric-a-brac from the past three centuries have been overturned into the innumerable stalls, and then head on over to the chic boutiques of London's wealthy districts for the latest in high fashion.

If the great outdoors is more your style, there's plenty for you here. It does rain a lot in England (which is why so many attractions are indoors), but on a fine day you can enjoy sprawling Hyde Park, with its playing fields and tennis courts, or lush St. James's Park, with its sanctuary for wild birds, both right in the center of London. A little farther out, yet still in the city, are green areas such as Richmond

Farm animals, such as this friendly horse, are a common sight on country walks.

Park, where herds of deer munch on wild grasses; there's even a Wetlands Centre where you can see wildlife you'll find nowhere else in a major city. Or leave the city behind and strike out across the beautiful rolling hills of southern England's countryside.

One of London's major advantages is that it provides easy access to all of southern England. You can visit the mysterious megaliths of Stonehenge, the awe-inspiring cathedral of Canterbury, and the historic university town of Oxford, all within an easy day's journey from the city center. And if you're planning to see more of Europe, London is one of the best places in the world to buy cheap airline tickets.

But why leave? London has everything to offer, all you have to do is come here and start exploring.

An ornate fountain graces Trafalgar Square.

Contents

Shakespeare, Leicester Square

The Tube

Bishops of Winchester

Maps

Front Color Section

Excursions from London

Back Color Section

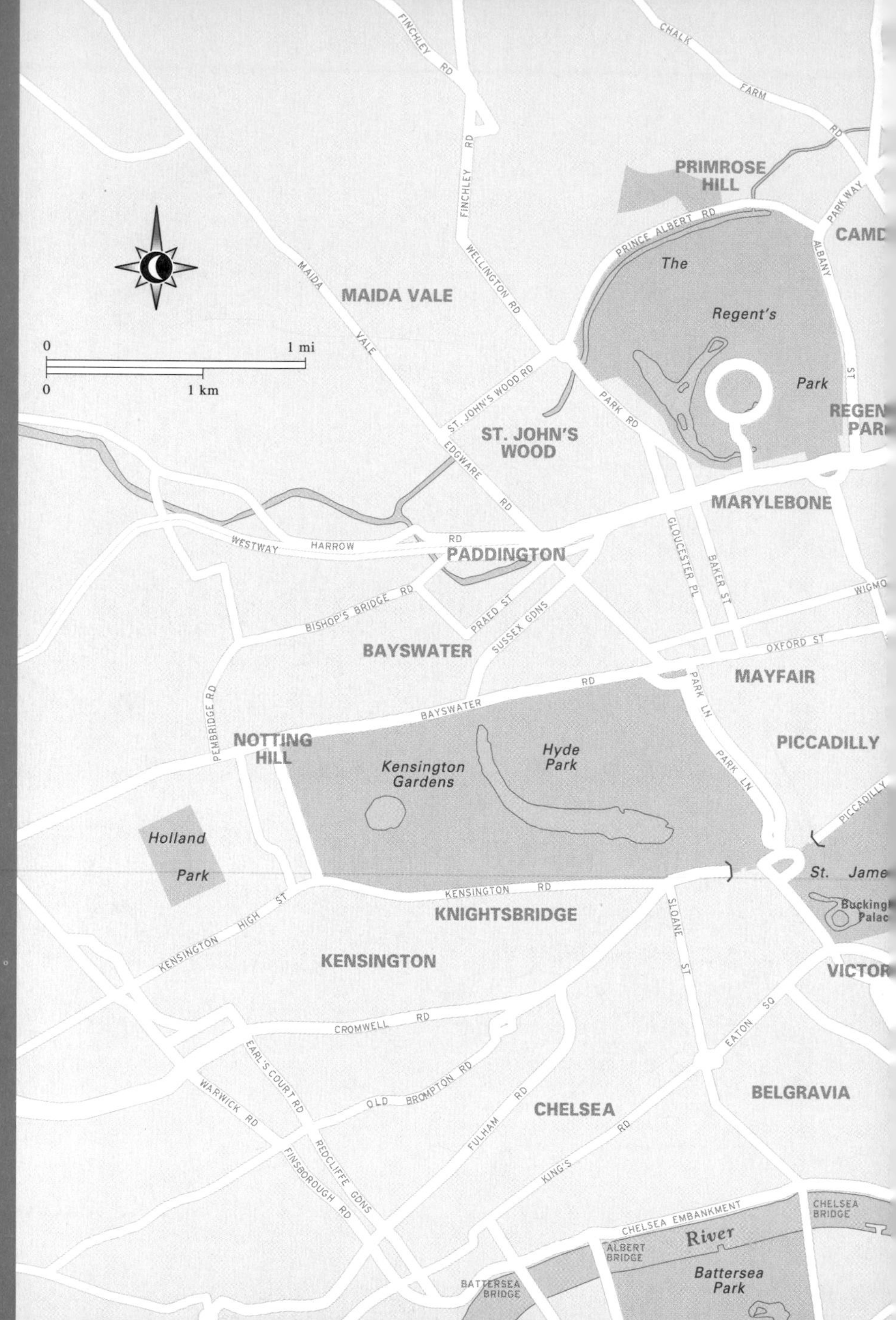
0
1 mi
0
1 km
FINCHLEY RD
CHALK FARM RD
PRIMROSE HILL
PRINCE ALBERT RD
PARKWAY
CAMD
ALBANY ST
The Regent's Park
MAIDA VALE
WELLINGTON RD
ST. JOHN'S WOOD RD
PARK RD
REGEN PAR
ST. JOHN'S WOOD
EDGWARE RD
MARYLEBONE
WESTWAY
HARROW RD
PADDINGTON
GLOUCESTER PL
BAKER ST
WIGMO
BISHOP'S BRIDGE RD
PRAED ST
SUSSEX GDNS
OXFORD ST
BAYSWATER
MAYFAIR
PARK LN
BAYSWATER RD
PEMBRIDGE RD
NOTTING HILL
Hyde Park
Kensington Gardens
PICCADILLY
Holland Park
St. Jame
Buckingh Palac
KENSINGTON RD
KNIGHTSBRIDGE
SLOANE ST
KENSINGTON HIGH ST
KENSINGTON
VICTOR
CROMWELL RD
EATON SQ
EARL'S COURT RD
OLD BROMPTON RD
WARWICK RD
FULHAM RD
CHELSEA
BELGRAVIA
FINSBOROUGH RD
REDCLIFFE GDNS
KING'S RD
CHELSEA EMBANKMENT
CHELSEA BRIDGE
River
ALBERT BRIDGE
Battersea Park
BATTERSEA BRIDGE

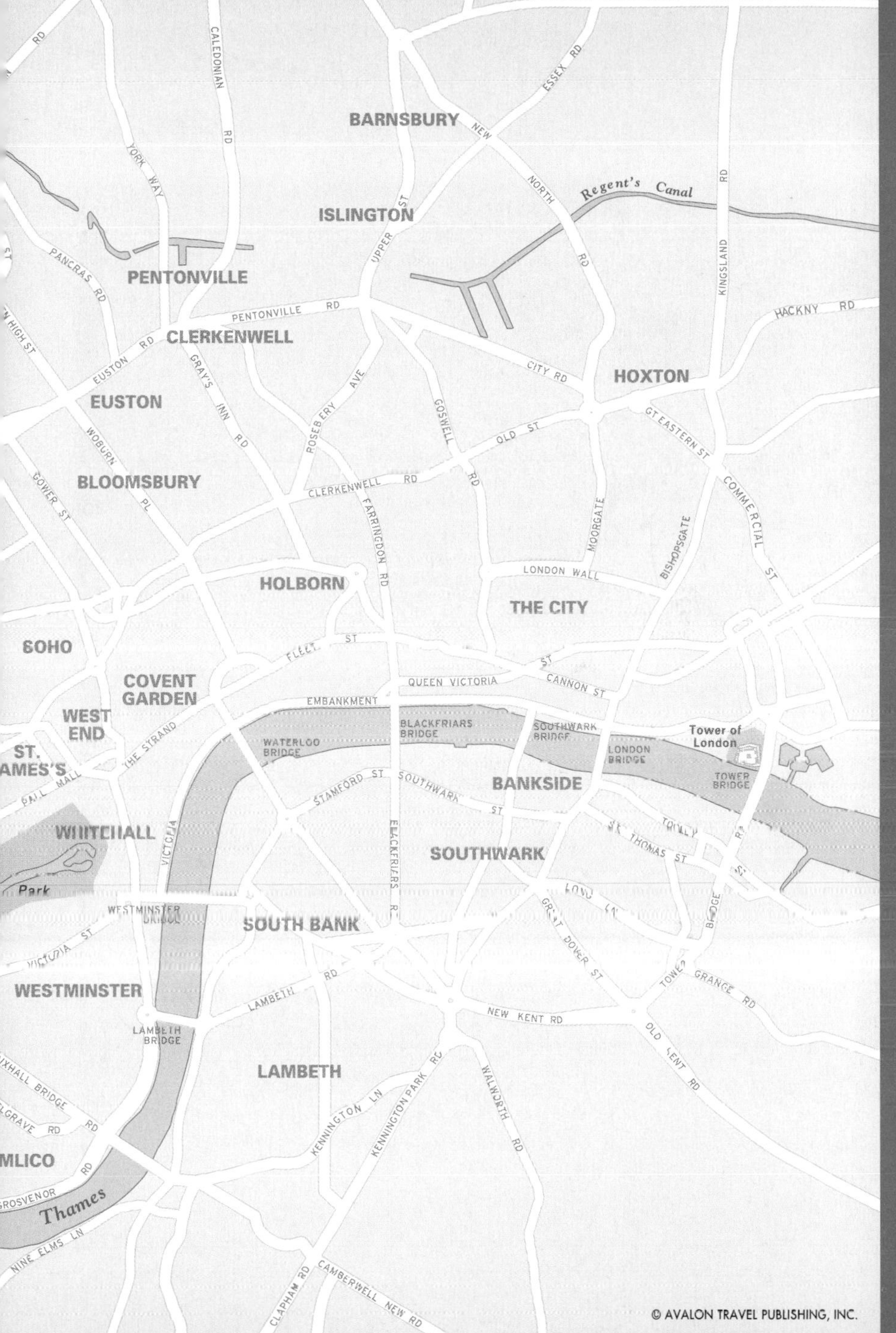
BARNSBURY
ISLINGTON
PENTONVILLE
CLERKENWELL
EUSTON
BLOOMSBURY
HOXTON
HOLBORN
THE CITY
SOHO
COVENT GARDEN
WEST END
BANKSIDE
SOUTHWARK
SOUTH BANK
WESTMINSTER
LAMBETH
Regent's Canal
Thames
Tower of London
CALEDONIAN RD
ESSEX RD
NEW NORTH RD
YORK WAY
UPPER ST
PANCRAS RD
PENTONVILLE RD
KINGSLAND RD
HACKNY RD
EUSTON RD
GRAY'S INN RD
CITY RD
ROSEBERY AVE
GOSWELL RD
OLD ST
GT EASTERN ST
WOBURN PL
GOWER ST
CLERKENWELL RD
FARRINGDON RD
COMMERCIAL ST
MOORGATE
BISHOPSGATE
LONDON WALL
FLEET ST
QUEEN VICTORIA
CANNON ST
EMBANKMENT
BLACKFRIARS BRIDGE
SOUTHWARK BRIDGE
WATERLOO BRIDGE
LONDON BRIDGE
TOWER BRIDGE
THE STRAND
PALL MALL
STAMFORD ST
SOUTHWARK ST
BLACKFRIARS RD
ST THOMAS ST
WESTMINSTER BRIDGE
VICTORIA ST
GREAT DOVER ST
TOWER BRIDGE RD
GRANGE RD
LAMBETH RD
NEW KENT RD
OLD KENT RD
LAMBETH BRIDGE
KENNINGTON LN
KENNINGTON PARK RD
WALWORTH RD
GROSVENOR RD
NINE ELMS LN
CLAPHAM RD
CAMBERWELL NEW RD

London Neighborhoods

London boasts some of the most diverse neighborhoods of any city in the world. From the bustling business center of The City, with its imposing banks and ancient churches, to the relaxed and artsy Camden Town, where you can take a break from shopping to enjoy a canal boat ride, London's neighborhoods offer a full spectrum of experiences to suit any taste. You'll find variety within neighborhoods too. Redcoats guard historic government buildings in Westminster, while just a step away is the soothing greenery of St. James's Park.

WESTMINSTER, VICTORIA, AND PIMLICO

The area of Westminster and Whitehall is the second-oldest inhabited region in the city. In the Middle Ages the elite decided to move away from the old Roman area of Londinium, now called The City, and establish a political and religious base here. With the Houses of Parliament and Westminster Abbey, it remains an important center of power to this day. To the west lies St. James's, with its verdant park and Buckingham Palace. To the south are the transport center of Victoria and the quiet residential district of Pimlico.

MAYFAIR AND PICCADILLY

Art lovers shouldn't miss a day exploring the Victorian streets of Mayfair, where ornate buildings house countless galleries and antique stores, including the famous Sotheby's auction house and the Royal Academy of Arts. Intimate restaurants and lively cafés offer refreshment, while more active visitors may want to party in Piccadilly, the neon heart of modern London. Here the shops, clubs, and bars are packed tight, and something's always going on. Both neighborhoods cater to the fashion-conscious with a variety of chic boutiques.

COVENT GARDEN, WEST END, AND SOHO

Some say London shuts after 11 P.M., but that's not the case here. Covent Garden and the West End are filled with theaters showing the latest plays and musicals, and lots of local pubs, clubs, and restaurants stay open late for the theater crowds. Soho is even livelier. This old bohemian district has great food and a wild nightlife. The area has plenty to offer during the day too, such as the fine art of the National Gallery and Somerset House, classical concerts at St. Martin-in-the-Fields, and the famous Trafalgar Square.

BLOOMSBURY, EUSTON, AND HOLBORN

Breathe in the life of old London with a stroll through the streets of historic Bloomsbury. Georgian town houses, gardens, and squares practically unchanged since the 18th century are the setting for the fantastic collection of the British Museum, itself a product of the Georgian love of beauty and knowledge. Old pubs and quiet restaurants add to the refined atmosphere. It's no wonder so many of the city's famous inhabitants lived here; Dickens and Soane had houses in the area and both houses are now museums. With a good selection of hotels and a generally quiet atmosphere after dark, it's a prime place to spend the night. Farther north lies the University College London district of Holborn and beyond that Euston, home to a major rail center and the British Library.

CHELSEA, KENSINGTON, AND KNIGHTSBRIDGE

For centuries London has been a nexus of power, culture, military might, and, of course, wealth. Nowhere is London's affluence more in evidence than in the neighborhoods to the south of Hyde Park and Kensington Gardens. Ornate Georgian and Victorian mansions line the streets. Fine dining and shopping, including the world-famous Harrods department store, where you can buy anything legal, makes this area a top destination for all London visitors. And a trio of important museums, the Natural History, Science, and Victoria and Albert museums, round out the experience.

NOTTING HILL, BAYSWATER, AND PADDINGTON

Notting Hill has been a center for Afro-Caribbean immigrants for five decades, and the neighborhood is alive with a rich heritage and culture. In the '60s it attracted white bohemians, followed soon by trustafarians and eventually white professionals. Now one of the most chic districts to live, Notting Hill has held onto its roots with an annual carnival and the Portobello Road antiques market. Nearby Bayswater and Paddington are less interesting, but they offer a host of hotels for all budgets and the important transportation center of Paddington Station.

MAIDA VALE, MARYLEBONE, AND ST. JOHN'S WOOD

Unwind in a quiet set of neighborhoods that exude English refinement. Marylebone is home to art galleries and embassies housed in imposing Victorian buildings, while St. John's Wood and Maida Vale are more residential. Marylebone boasts some important attractions, including a stately home-turned-museum called the Wallace Collection. You'll also find 221B Baker Street, home to London's most famous fictional resident. To the north spreads the green expanse of The Regent's Park, crowned by the summit of Primrose Hill, where you can get a panoramic view of London.

CAMDEN TOWN

A day in Camden Town is a lot of fun. With its bustling streets lined with friendly, funky little shops and its sparkling canal, you'll have plenty to see and do. Take a canal boat ride through Little Venice, or sit at a café and watch the world go by. With its laid-back feel and a variety of dining and shopping options, Camden Town has become an increasingly popular place to go. It offers plenty of nightlife too, including some of London's best bars and nightclubs.

THE CITY

As Westminster is the political and religious center of the United Kingdom, The City is its economic heart. The City, also known as Square Mile, used to be all the city there was back in the days of Roman Londinium. In later centuries it became known for its banks and insurance companies, but there are still ample traces of the London that was, including the medieval Guildhall, the house of Dr. Johnson, the Tower of London, and rising above it all the graceful spires of dozens of medieval churches and the baroque splendor of St. Paul's.

ISLINGTON

It happens in every city. There's a poor neighborhood near the center of town where nobody wants to go. Artists move in because they need a cheap place to live. It starts to become trendy, and as housing prices rise, the middle class moves out from the center and begins to colonize the area. The artists move on as the houses are bought, fixed up, and sold at much higher prices. Eventually the rich start moving there to capture the trendiness, but by that time the interesting people have all moved out. Islington is about halfway through this process, so while it's becoming a major destination for nightlife and dining, it's not too expensive yet. Come here for friendly bars, rocking basement concert venues, unusual theater, and some great eating.

SOUTH OF THE THAMES

For centuries London didn't have a wrong side of the tracks; it had a wrong side of the river. An unsavory den of criminals, houses of ill repute, cockfighting rings, and that worst of all sins, the theater, the South Bank of the Thames was also home to much of London's working class and the industries they served. With the industry and shipping all but gone, the area along the river has been refurbished with restaurants and hotels, the Tate Modern, and the HMS *Belfast.* Older buildings, such as Southwark Cathedral and the Imperial War Museum (once, appropriately, Bedlam mental hospital), preserve the history of the area. It's a bit dodgy farther south, but a walk along the riverside is highly recommended.

OUTLYING AREAS

London has never respected boundaries. Archaeologists have discovered evidence of villas and industry outside the Roman city walls. In the Middle Ages London became two cities, the Square Mile and Westminster. During the Industrial Revolution it exploded beyond all control. London sprawls. A visit to this great city isn't complete without a journey to some of its varied outskirts. Downstream lies Greenwich, the zero point for longitude and time and a historic port from the days when Britannia ruled the waves; it's now home to the famous tea clipper *Cutty Sark.* To the southwest lies Richmond with its huge park. Old Kent Road is a center for West African culture, and Brick Lane is the heart of South Asian London. Go out and explore!

Planning Your Trip

WHEN TO GO

One of the most visited cities in Europe, London offers a slightly different experience depending on the season—"slightly" because many of the city's best attractions, such as St. Paul's Cathedral and the British Museum, are indoors. Wintertime visitors can see the top sights without having to worry about the cold and perpetual rains or hordes of tourists. The more inviting warmer months bring greater crowds but also allow for walks and picnics in the many beautiful parks. Airline tickets are more expensive during these times, but there's so much competition among carriers that a little searching can uncover some real deals.

London's weather is always unpredictable, but some times are better than others. Each season has its positive and negative aspects, so consider your plans and needs before deciding on a time to go. Fall and spring tend to be about equally priced, with summer more expensive and winter cheaper. Of course some expenses, such as food, public transport, and shopping stay the same throughout the year, so if you can get a good deal on a flight and accommodation, any time of the year is game. With London being such a popular destination, attractions stay open year-round, closing only for big holidays such as Easter and Christmas and sometimes for the occasional long weekend, called "bank holidays" here. When reading the descriptions below, keep in mind that English weather is known for its variability. The temperatures and weather patterns below are generalizations only, and never, ever, trust a long-range weather forecast while you're in England.

The summer months of June, July, and August can have long stretches of sun, but the city can also be quite hot and sticky. Temperatures are usually in the mid-20s Celsius (high 70s Fahrenheit), but can rise past 32°C (90°F). Since this is the most popular time of year to visit, the masses of tourists won't help your comfort level either, nor will the fact that the Underground and many public buildings aren't air-conditioned (this is a good time to take one of country walks mentioned in the *Excursions* chapter). Away from the concrete and the crowds, you'll beat a bit of the heat, but remember to bring plenty of water. The big plus to summer is that you can have long periods of beautiful weather, sunny and not particularly hot, between hot spells and the occasional rainstorm, and the days seem to last forever, being light by 6 A.M. and not getting totally dark until almost 11 P.M. On the other hand, it's also the most expensive time to go because airlines raise their rates and the lack of room availability may force you to stay somewhere more expensive than you originally planned.

In the fall, September–November, the tourists taper off, especially after the school year starts. Unfortunately, it is often rainy. On the other hand, there can be some lovely days. The weather is at its most unpredictable, so it's best to bring clothes for all temperatures and be flexible with your daily plans, aiming for a mixture of indoor and outdoor destinations. Temperatures range 11–15°C (52–59°F) with September being the best all-around month, after which it gets increasingly dreary. If the weather is good, you can see some wonderful displays of autumn leaves, both in London's parks and tree-lined avenues and out in the countryside.

Winter, December–February, can be quite cold and dark, with only about eight hours of daylight, and usually cloudy daylight at that. You'll find milder times, although there is no way to predict when these will be. Temperatures are generally 1–6°C (34–43°F). With the damp conditions (snow is rare but freezing rain is not), it can feel even colder. One plus is the fewer number of visitors. Since many of London's best attractions are indoors, and hotel and flight availability goes up while prices go down, you shouldn't dismiss winter as a viable time to go. It is the cheapest and the least crowded season, so if you're coming primarily for indoor sights such as museums, galleries, or shopping (especially in the Christmas season), then winter may be your best bet. On the cusp between winter and spring is early March, which can get the weather of either season and attracts some pretty big crowds, thanks to the spring break at U.S. universities. It can be a fun time to go to clubs, but the major sights and budget accommodations can get filled with American backpackers.

Spring, late March–May, is the best all-around time to visit London. The weather is warmer and there is a greater likelihood for sun, although you'll still get rainy spells, especially early in the season. Average temperatures are 11–15°C (52–59°F). May generally has two good weeks, usually later in the month, and it can get up to 18°C (65°F) or even higher. Late spring can be quite warm, with the same downsides as summer. With a good chance for fine weather, and the lull between spring break and the summer crowds, I pick May as the best month to go, but if you don't mind heat and crowds, pick summer because of its higher chances of sun.

WHAT TO TAKE

Luggage

If you are not backpacking it, try to bring luggage that's sturdy and not too big. London streets and public transport can be quite crowded, so if you are going to be doing any amount of walking with your bags, lighter and smaller is always better. Remember that while London may be a long way from your hometown, it's not at the ends of the Earth. You can buy anything here, so you don't have to pack every item you may conceivably need.

Be careful while roving the streets with your luggage. Pickpockets abound, and they love tourists as much as tour operators do. (For more information about bags and security, see *Health and Safety* in the *Essentials* section.)

A day pack is always a good idea for when you are out on the town. You can use it to carry snacks, water, and anything you might end up buying. Try to bring it empty; it will fill up quickly enough.

Clothing

Since London's weather is so unpredictable, it's a good idea to take along clothes for all occasions. The key idea here is *layering*. The temperature and amount of sunlight can change several times in a day, often quite quickly in the spring and fall. You might find yourself taking off your sweatshirt and putting it on again half an hour later. A warm sweater is always a good idea, and comfortable, water-resistant walking shoes are essential. Even if you're visiting in the early spring or late fall, bring some lighter clothes in case you hit a warm spell. If you're visiting in the winter make sure to bring a warm, waterproof jacket or overcoat.

Covent Garden

Trafalgar Square

Piccadilly Circus

Explore London

THE TWO-DAY BEST OF LONDON

If you're in town for only a couple of days, take heart. Most of the key sights are close to the center and within walking distance of each other, and the walks themselves are of great interest. Pick a hotel in one of the central neighborhoods such as Westminster or The City. This provides easy access to the city center, where most of the best sights are congregated. Here's a suggested timetable capturing the highlights of London and a bit of its flavor.

Day 1

Welcome to London! First stop, breakfast. Eat at your hotel or hop on the Tube to Charing Cross Station for the first stop of the day. The exit will put you right in Trafalgar Square. Head over to **St. Martin-in-the-Fields,** the church on the east side of the square, and have a cheap but tasty breakfast downstairs in its Café in the Crypt. After breakfast take a look at the church's attractive interior before walking next door to the National Gallery to soak up one of the finest fine art collections anywhere.

Finish by 11 A.M., walk out of the gallery, across the square, and through Admiralty Arch to The Mall, a long avenue flanked on one side by the priciest real estate in England and on the other by beautiful St. James's Park. At the end is Buckingham Palace, where you can see the **Changing of the Guard** at 11:30 A.M.

After the Redcoats strut their stuff, enter **St. James's Park** and walk along its length, keeping the lake to the north (on the left). After admiring the flocks of nesting wild birds and the surrounding greenery (unless it's winter!), emerge at the other end. Pass between the two large government buildings ahead to Parliament Road. From here you can see the Houses of Parliament and Big Ben rising majestically nearby. Admire their exteriors before breaking for lunch. The Cinnamon Club is a

Horse Guards Parade

good choice for its outstanding Indian cuisine and convenient location. Equally convenient and much cheaper is Pickles Sandwich Bar. Pickles offers takeaway, which is good because it gives you the time to wander a bit in this beautiful neighborhood of Georgian and Victorian period buildings.

After lunch, head to **Westminster Abbey.** This beautiful church, with its storied past and hidden gardens, can easily take up the rest of an afternoon. Consider staying for Choral Evensong at 5 P.M. For dinner, consider Sarastro in the West End, or take your pick from the countless Chinese restaurants on Gerrard Street in Soho. Later in the evening, take in a play in the West End or a bar or nightclub in Soho. The theater venue will depend on what you want to see (book beforehand at www.ticketmaster.co.uk), and for Soho nightlife try the Salisbury Tavern or Madame Jo Jo's.

Day 2

If you're feeling fit and the weather's good, take the Tube to Westminster Station right next to Westminster Bridge. Stay on the Westminster side of the River Thames and follow the **Thames Walk** past Victoria Embankment Gardens, Cleopatra's Needle, Somerset House, and the Temple. At the Millennium Bridge, either go see **St. Paul's** just to the north, stop at the Punch Tavern for lunch, or head over the river to the **Tate Modern,** where you can have lunch in either its restaurant or one of two cafés. After lunch and sightseeing, return to the north bank of the river and continue to the **Tower of London.** The entire walk from Westminster Bridge to the Tower of London is three miles, not including a half-mile side trip for lunch and sights. Spend the rest of the afternoon at the Tower, taking the Yeoman tour.

If the Thames Walk isn't feasible, take the Tube to King's Cross/St. Pancras and the **British Library** next door. After getting your fill of illuminated manuscripts and the Magna Carta, head south to the **British Museum.** The walk takes about 15 minutes, but you can stop at relaxing Russell Square on the way. After the museum, have lunch at Paradiso, just to the northwest. Spend the rest of the afternoon with the museum's mummies, statues, and Hellenic vases. In the evening, cross the street for a pint at the Museum Tavern and then catch the fading light at **Bedford Square** just west of the museum. For dinner, try Archipelago and maybe an after-dinner drink at Na Zdrowie.

British Library

In the evening, you have two options to choose from. First, take the Tube to St. Paul's. From St. Paul's it's less than a 10-minute walk to Ye Olde Cheshire Cheese, where you can dine on excellent pub food and sample a pint or two. Or you can walk about 15 minutes to Charterhouse Street to dine at Abbaye (expensive) or Smith's of Smithfield (moderately priced), before heading to Fabric to dance away your last night in town. Walking to either option takes you past some wonderfully ornate architecture.

A WEEK IN LONDON

With a week in London, you'll be able to see not just major tourist sights but also lesser-known nooks and crannies. This suggested itinerary tours the best London has to offer and will show you many of the highlights and a taste of what lies beyond. Make sure to leave some time for lounging around at a café, pub, or park, or heading down random streets to see what's there. A random walk is especially rewarding in historic areas such as The City, Westminster, and Bloomsbury.

Day 1

Since this is your first day, sleep in and eat a leisurely breakfast at the hotel. Then take the Tube to Charing Cross Station. (If your hotel doesn't offer breakfast, eat at the Café in the Crypt in **St. Martin-in-the-Fields** right next to the Tube exit.) Then take some time to admire the square before heading through Admiralty Arch to The Mall, a long avenue flanked by mansions and St. James's Park. At the end is Buckingham Palace, where you can see the **Changing of the Guard** at 11:30 A.M. Afterward, enter **St. James's Park** and walk along its length, keeping the lake to the north (left). Admire the flocks of wild birds nesting there and the greenery all around you and emerge on the other end. Pass between the two large government buildings ahead of you to Parliament Road. From here you can see the exterior of the **Houses of Parliament** and **Big Ben** before breaking for lunch. Check out the Cinnamon Club for its outstanding Indian cuisine and convenient location. Or pick up some takeaway from Pickles Sandwich Bar, equally convenient and much cheaper. This gives you the time to wander a bit in this beautiful neighborhood of Georgian and Victorian period buildings. After lunch, go see **Westminster Abbey.** This beautiful church can easily take up the rest of your afternoon. Consider staying for Choral Evensong at 5 P.M. For dinner try Bistro 51, especially if it's Sunday when it does a roast, and then head out to the Albert for a drink at a traditional pub.

Day 2

As on Day 1, go to the Charing Cross Tube Station, but this time visit the **National Gallery.** Eat lunch at the gallery café, and then head north to the half-price tickets booth in Leicester Square to find out what plays and musicals are on the day after tomorrow. You won't have many seating options for tonight's or tomorrow's performances, but booking two days in advance gets you plenty of choice. After you've picked a show, walk a couple of minutes east to St. Martin's Lane. Browse the shops as you head north, perhaps stopping for a pint at the Salisbury Tavern. Once you hit Neal Street on your right, go down it until you reach Food for Thought, an awesome vegetarian restaurant. Then head to **Covent Garden,** which always has a lot going on in the evening, especially Saturday.

Day 3

Time for a walk along the Thames, as long as the weather cooperates. Take the Tube to Westminster Station right next to Westminster Bridge. Stay on the Westminster side of the River Thames and follow the **Thames Walk** past Victoria Embankment Gardens, Cleopatra's Needle, Somerset House, and the Temple. At the Millennium Bridge go see

statue of Sir Winston Churchill on Parliament Square

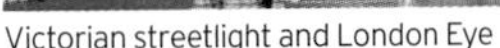
Victorian streetlight and London Eye

guards at Buckingham Palace

Big Ben

St. Paul's just to the north of you, stopping at the Punch Tavern for lunch. Then get back on the Thames Walk and continue to the **Tower of London.** The entire walk from Westminster Bridge to the Tower of London is three miles, not including a half-mile side trip for lunch and sights. Spend the rest of the afternoon at the Tower, taking the Yeoman tour. In the evening, head to The City for dinner. Take the Tube to St. Paul's. From there you have a less than 10-minute walk to Ye Olde Cheshire Cheese, where you can dine on excellent pub food and sample a pint or two.

Day 4

Another day along the Thames! Go to the Blackfriars Tube Station and walk to the Millennium Bridge just a couple of minutes away. Cross the bridge to the **Tate Modern.** For lunch go just behind the Tate to Café 171/Glasshouse. Then get back on the South Bank and head west. Check out the Hayward Gallery on the way, perhaps stopping for a coffee at the National Film Theatre café before continuing to see the Dali exhibition or head up the **London Eye** for an unbeatable view of the city. For dinner and a drink go to Cubana a few minute's walk inland to the east. In the evening take in the show you reserved on Day Two.

Day 5

Now that you're settled in, it's time for a day trip (pick a destination from the *Excursions* chapter). You should pay attention to the weather forecast and try to schedule this trip for when there's going to be good weather, keeping in mind that with the vagaries of British weather, any forecast is dubious. **Windsor** is the most convenient, since it takes less than an hour on the train and you can easily see all the sights in one day. Head out early because the sights all close by about 5 P.M., at which point you can dine in town—Drury House next to Windsor Castle is good—and head back on the train.

Day 6

Take the Tube to King's Cross/St. Pancras and the **British Library** next door. After getting your fill of illuminated manuscripts and the Magna Carta, head south to the **British Museum.** The walk takes about 15 minutes, but you can stop at Russell Square Gardens on the way. From the museum, head to Paradiso, just to the northwest. After lunch spend the rest of the afternoon in the museum and in the evening cross the street for a pint at the Museum Tavern, and then catch the fading light at **Bedford Square** just west of the museum. For dinner try Archipelago and have an after-dinner drink at Na Zdrowie.

Day 7

You have a final day to relax and do some shopping. Check out **Harrods** in the morning and have lunch in the Food Hall, or buy takeaway for a picnic at **Kensington Gardens.** Or you can eat at one of the many posh restaurants in the neighborhood, such as La Bottega del San Lorenzo. Use the afternoon to see **Hyde Park,** especially Speaker's Corner. For dinner walk a few minutes east to True Vert. In the evening take the Tube to St. Paul's and walk to Fabric to dance the night away. You can always sleep on the plane.

LONDON HIGHLIGHTS FOR KIDS

London is a great place to bring children. Because the city is so famous, they'll have already seen pictures of some of the sights and experiencing them in real life will be a thrill. Many museums and other attractions have made an effort to be kid friendly, offering free activity books as well as regular special events. Keep in mind that the little folks get tired easily. Bring snacks and water along and schedule several breaks. Packing a few favorite toys will help the child adjust to the new surroundings. Some of the finer hotels have nanny (babysitter) services and playrooms, which can give you peace of mind if you want to go out late at night.

Educational Yet Interesting

The **Tower of London** is a favorite with kids because it's a castle and has lots of interesting things to see. The Beefeaters, with their colorful costumes, make good photo opportunities and knowledgeable tour guides. Kids will especially like the collection of medieval armor and weapons. At the **British Museum,** children will enjoy the mummies and the sculpture gallery. The museum offers daily activities for children, which you can find out about by calling, checking the website, or asking at the information desk.

For a full day of fun and learning, try Museum Row, where the **Victoria and Albert, Science Museum,** and **Natural History Museum** all cluster together. The last two are the best for little folks. The Science Museum has lots of hands-on displays and the trains, planes, and automobiles are fun to look at. Check out the Apollo Command Module to remind children of what astronauts flew in before the space shuttle. Next door at the Natural History Museum is a four-meter-high moving *Tyrannosaurus rex* and a display called Creepy Crawlies that will give them the willies. If they're not exhausted yet, go to the Victoria and Albert's mazelike sculpture galleries for a world tour of the best classical and medieval art.

Fun and Games

Take in the stunning views of the city from the **London Eye,** also known as the Millennium Wheel. This giant Ferris wheel lifts you 135 meters above the riverside in a glass capsule. While it is ridiculously overpriced, it's an unforgettable sight and a great photo opportunity, unless your child is timid about heights. Right next to it in the County Hall is Namco Station, a giant arcade. An even bigger arcade is the London Trocadero, offering rides, video games, a multiplex cinema, and plenty to eat and drink. While it's not much different from its cousin in your hometown, it's an especially good way to while away a rainy afternoon. Even more memorable is the ***Golden Hinde,*** a reconstruction of Sir Francis Drake's famous ship that hosts parties and special events for kids in which they can dress up like old-time sailors. This is the perfect Birthday in Britain idea.

Cool Things to See

Madame Tussaud's is always popular with the little folk. This wax museum features hundreds of lifelike figures of famous and

London Zoo

the British Airways London Eye, also known as the Millennium Wheel

infamous personages and kids can have their photos taken next to their favorite stars. If you have small children, you might want to think twice about the Chamber of Horrors, as it's quite graphic. The same goes for the **London Dungeon,** a haunted-house–style attraction that takes you through the spooky underside of old London. Actors dressed as nefarious figures from London's past pop out at you and there are gruesome displays of the plague, torture chambers, and other relics of the good old days. Your children might be terrified by all this. On the other hand, they might love it.

You can check out the **London Zoo** in The Regent's Park with its displays of the usual furry, scaly, and slithery friends. Once again, it's not too different from the sights back home, but children often need a bit of familiarity when they're on the road. The park itself makes a nice picnic spot, with beautiful views of London from atop Primrose Hill.

Shopping

Harrods department store has a wonderful toy section, and **Hamleys** sells only toys. Both stock a wide variety of playthings, from detailed model ships to the latest crying, shooting, spinning, racing, mechanical contrivances. Attendants demonstrate various toys and play with your kids. Be prepared to buy something, though, or you'll be in big trouble. The numerous tourist shops clustering around all the major sights can be a bit tacky, but they stock kid-size clothing with British themes, as well as toys such as teddy bears dressed up as Beefeaters or bobbies.

Nighttime Activities

Covent Garden has all sorts of street entertainers and musicians, especially on Saturday evenings. Everything from clowns and magicians to tightrope walkers and jugglers can keep your kids wide-eyed and entertained, and plenty of food stalls and restaurants will keep them fed. Also highly recommended is the Unicorn Theatre, which puts on plays and musicals aimed at children.

OLD BLIGHTY

You just spent more than a few dollars to fly to London. You've picked a nice hotel and have an exciting list of things to see. You're even pleasantly anticipating a long riverside slog along the Thames Walk. But after looking out the front door of the hotel, you see it's pouring rain—or "pissing," as the English call it. You go to the hotel bar and have one of those real ales, popping your head out an hour later. It's still raining, but the wind has picked up and it is coming down at an acute, umbrella-defying angle you never thought possible. So it's back to the bar for another real ale (porter is good on cold, rainy days) and then heading outside an hour later. Yep, it's still raining.

Good news: The bar is still open.

Bad news: Your children are beginning to wonder about your habits and a kind gentleman informs you that the weather could very well stay like this for the duration of your trip.

More good news: Your vacation isn't ruined.

Luckily, and probably not coincidentally, most of London's attractions are indoors. If it's too rainy to go for a long walk, check out a museum, see a play, or warm up at a cozy restaurant. Since most of London's best attractions are close to a Tube station, it's easy to reach them without much exposure to the elements. Buses are a bit more hazardous; the stops, if covered at all, don't provide much protection and one never knows when the next bus is coming. Here's a list of Tube stops that offer a good range of interesting attractions only a splashy sprint away.

Charing Cross

Charing Cross is the best Tube stop for a rainy day: You can eat all your meals, see a historic church, view two premiere art galleries, tour a famous square, and catch a concert or two while spending all of about two minutes outside. The station exit leads right up into Trafalgar Square. On the north side of the square are the **National Gallery** and **National Portrait Gallery,** two world-class art museums that can keep you occupied all day. The National Gallery's café is a good place to get lunch. You can admire **Trafalgar Square** itself, with historic London buildings all around and the Houses of Parliament and the London Eye visible in the distance, by standing on the raised, covered porch of the National Gallery. Right next door to the art museums stands **St. Martin-in-the-Fields,** a beautiful church with lunchtime and evening concerts and choral evensongs. Downstairs is Café in the Crypt, serving breakfast, lunch, tea, and, on concert evenings, a romantic candlelit dinner.

Baker Street

Less than a five-minute walk from the **Sherlock Holmes Museum, Madame Tussauds,** and the **Planetarium,** this is a good option for both kids and adults. Madame Tussauds and the Planetarium are in the same building, and all three attractions are a one-minute walk from The Regent's Park, if you're lucky enough to get a spot of sun. For dining, just a couple of minutes east of Madame Tussauds is Marylebone High Street. Near the north end is Divertimenti, a cooking store/café where you can reserve a cookery class and make your own dinner under the tutelage of an expert chef.

the Great Court of the British Museum

the Enlightenment Gallery at the British Museum

The street is lined with lots of interesting shops and a couple of minutes south from Divertimenti is The Providores and Tapa Room, a fine international restaurant.

Tottenham Court Road

From this Tube stop it's a five-minute walk to the **British Museum.** While that makes it a bit far in a pouring rain, you can spend all day inside. The museum has a café and restaurant, as well as an ongoing series of lectures, films, and free tours. If you begin to get museum fever, pop across the street to the Museum Tavern, or eat at the Bibimbab Café (Korean food), Eve's Sandwich Bar, or Malabar Junction (Indian food), all two minutes from the museum's front door. The streets just south of the museum are filled with bookshops.

Knightsbridge

A good stop for a day of shopping and eating, the Brompton Road exit of Knightsbridge Station is right next to **Harrods,** the greatest department store in London. You can buy literally anything here (as long as it's legal) and the Food Hall serves three great meals a day. If you're dropping from shopping, stop in to the spa on the fifth floor. The Kensington Road exit to Knightsbridge Station gets you right next to **Harvey Nichols** department store and its famous Fifth Floor restaurant, a top spot for chic dining. If you actually want to go outside, both streets and the surrounding ones are lined with fine shops and restaurants.

Other sights, such as Westminster Cathedral, the Houses of Parliament, and the Tower of London, have interesting architecture you'll want to see from the outside on a nice day, so try to go when the sun is peeking out behind those dark British clouds that Constable so loved to paint.

And remember that weather doesn't stop the British from doing anything. There's just too much damp to really be bothered with, so they're perfectly happy to don shorts and play a game of football in the freezing rain. Walking clubs rarely call off a hike because of anything less than a downpour, and sometimes not even then. Just grab a raincoat or umbrella (or both if it's really wretched) and keep on enjoying the holiday.

AFTER HOURS

If you're in London for work, it may be frustrating to find that many of the attractions close by 5 or 6 P.M. Take heart, however, as there's still plenty to do once you get out of the office. Despite rumors to the contrary, London does not die after dark. In fact, it can be at its most alive, with a wealth of places to eat, party, shop, or learn. If work keeps you from seeing London during the day, you can still experience some of the best the town has to offer.

Nightlife

A common stop for office workers are the many pubs, wine bars, and cafés throughout town. While there's much conviviality and a chance to mingle with coworkers in a more relaxed setting, indoor venues can get very loud and crowded at this time of the day. The British tend to let off steam rather than unwind. Even worse, many pubs close at 11 P.M., the relic of a law dating to the World War I, when the government was afraid hung-over munitions workers might cause rather explosive accidents. Since 2006 pubs and bars have been able to apply for an extended license, but the cost and hassle have kept many from doing so. While it's open only until 11 P.M., **Ye Olde Cheshire Cheese** has heaps of antiquarian atmosphere and real pub food. For a later night out on the town, try the **Absolut Ice** bar, where you can impress clients while sharing vodka and conversation amid fantastic ice sculptures. Of course, the nightclubs are all open late, but if you're working you probably can't stay up dancing until 7 A.M. For a not-so-late night out, try the many concert venues in Islington, especially **Embassy, The Warwick Bar,** and **Medicine Bar.**

Portobello Road restaurant

Museums

If you're up for a more relaxed evening, various societies and museums put on lectures, movies, and other special events that are often free. You'll find listings in *Time Out* magazine, available at newsagents, which fortunately stay open far into the night. The major museums often have at least one weekday during which they stay open late. **The National Gallery** is open until 9 P.M. on Wednesdays. This is one of the quietest times to visit and instead of jostling with vast hordes of tourists, you'll be able to relax and enjoy the paintings. Many of the galleries in the **British Museum** stay open until 8:30 P.M. Thursday–Friday. The Great Court stays open until 11 P.M. Thursday—Saturday. There are often concerts or other events at this time, and some ancient sculptures are on display there.

Theater

For theater, your best bet is the **West End.** Before you fly to London, check out what's on at www.ticketmaster.co.uk, where you can also make reservations. Because of its wealth of theaters, the West End has lots of late-night pubs, bars, and restaurants. On the South Bank, **Shakespeare's Globe,** a reconstruction of

Big Ben and Houses of Parliament as viewed from the South Bank

the playhouse where the Bard worked, provides atmosphere and entertainment. Performance times vary, but there are usually a few 6:30 or 7:30 P.M. shows each week. For a more intimate experience, try the **Bookshop Theatre,** a tiny performance space that shows plays only at night, since it's a bookshop by day. You can buy tickets until 7 P.M. at the shop, but since it has a capacity of just 40, you shouldn't expect to see that evening's performance.

Shopping

For some reason the English believe the weekend starts on Thursday evening, and many shops cater to this by staying open to 7, 8, or 9 P.M. on that day. Department stores and shopping malls such as **Harvey Nichols, Selfridges,** and **Whiteleys** stay open until 8 P.M. Monday–Saturday. The famous and well-stocked **Foyles** bookshop stays open until 9 P.M. on those days.

Dining

Of course, the evening is the perfect time to sample London's incredible variety of fine dining. Most restaurants serve dinner until at least 8 or 9 P.M. Excellent eateries such as **Chor Bizarre, Rules, Boisale,** and **Afghan Kitchen,** stay open until 11 P.M. or later. The high concentration of restaurants in many dining areas (see the *Restaurants* chapter), such as **Brick Lane,** guarantees that you will find a place open until at least 10 P.M.

Local Culture

After dark, **Covent Garden** is alive with entertainers, musicians, food vendors, and late-closing shops. Saturday night is busiest as it takes on the atmosphere of a street festival. A walk along **Brick Lane** will take you past dozens of South Asian restaurants and stores selling imports. If Chinese is more your style, head on over to **Gerrard Street** for a great selection of East Asian restaurants and shops. For African foods and imports, go to **Old Kent Road.** All three of these streets are good introductions to the cultures of important immigrant groups. While many of the stores close by 6 P.M. or so, some stay open late and the restaurants usually stay open until 10 or 11 P.M., or in some cases later. For a beautiful view, walk along the **Thames Walk** on either bank to see all of London lit up in the night.

SIGHTS

London is a city steeped in history and tradition. The famous Beefeaters, guardians of the Tower of London and Crown Jewels, wear uniforms unchanged in 200 years. People still worship in medieval cathedrals that have seen the coronation of entire dynasties of monarchs. The chimes of Big Ben have been tolling the hours for more than a century. A walk through London is a walk through the ages.

London's most famous sights follow the city's unstoppable expansion from a riverside village to a massive metropolis taking up hundreds of square miles. The oldest landmarks, such as the Tower of London, next to the Roman city wall, and St. Paul's Cathedral, built on the site of a Saxon church, are at the riverside. The famous London Bridge is only a few meters from where the Romans first spanned the Thames with a wooden bridge to serve ancient Londinium.

Walk away from the Thames to follow the city's expansion through the centuries. Amid the Georgian squares of Bloomsbury, marvel at the British Museum's vast collection of antiquities. Farther away from the river, along bustling Portobello Road, pick up a bit of history yourself at the city's largest antique market.

Then, of course, there's the famous Thames itself. No trip would be complete without a long stroll along the Thames Walk or a boat ride on this timeless river. Cutting through the city, it provides a breath of fresh air and source of commerce as well as picturesque views.

But London does not live solely in the past. The Barbican and the Institute of Contemporary Arts are two of Europe's greatest centers

HIGHLIGHTS

Best Home for Really Rich People: **Buckingham Palace** is the only home you'll ever see with its own regiment of bodyguards. The tour will show you the meeting rooms, banquet halls, and throne room of Britain's royal family (page 35).

Best Government Building: **The Houses of Parliament** and **Big Ben** are both highly photogenic and in the center of Westminster (pages 37 and 38).

Best Church: Across the street from the Houses of Parliament, **Westminster Abbey** is a beautiful cathedral steeped in history (page 39).

Best Art Collection: There are enough da Vincis, Van Goghs, and Monets in the world-class **National Gallery** to keep anyone happy (page 43).

Best Museum: As one of the leading archaeological museums in the world, the **British Museum** houses artifacts from hundreds of cultures. The Egyptian halls alone will give you gold fever, but don't overlook the imposing Assyrian bas-reliefs, classical statues, and dozens of rooms filled with ancient treasures (page 50).

Best Prison: The dank cells in the **Tower of London** once held princes and political dissidents. The walls are covered in mournful graffiti, making a strange contrast with the glittering Crown Jewels (page 64).

Best View: Rising high above the riverside is the **British Airways London Eye,** a futuristic Ferris wheel that offers a stunning view of the city (page 66).

Best Reused Building: Housed in the converted Bankside power station, the **Tate Modern** has a huge collection of modern art. So many styles and techniques are collected here that even those who don't like modern art might be pleasantly surprised. The building alone is worth a visit (page 73).

© SEAN MCLACHLAN

LOOK FOR TO FIND RECOMMENDED SIGHTS.

for cutting-edge art. It is also home to lush and soothing parks, such as Hyde Park, where pontificators and hecklers match wits, and St. James's, where picnicking families can get away from the city while never leaving it. Shoppers will love London for its world-famous stores such as Harrods, where literally everything one could want is for sale.

A nice bonus for visitors is that many of the best sights are free. These include the British Museum, National Gallery, National Portrait Gallery, Southwark Cathedral, and many more sights. Travelers on a budget won't have to skimp on culture to stay within their means.

From the past through the present, London is a thriving city with something to offer everyone. Go out and explore.

Westminster, Victoria, and Pimlico — Map 2

London's governmental center is a lively mix of bustling streets and timeless tradition. The area has some of London's best architecture, with soaring churches and elegant palaces, as well as rows of private buildings from the days of the empire. Apparently all those queens and ministers don't like to walk far for culture, because the neighborhood is filled with world-class galleries, relaxing parks, and centuries-old ceremonies, all close enough that there's no need to use public transport. In fact, the journey is just as interesting as the destinations.

BUCKINGHAM PALACE

Btwn. The Mall and Buckingham Gate SW1, State Room Ticket Office 020/7766-7300, www.the-royal-collection.com

HOURS: Daily 9:45 A.M.-6 P.M. Aug.-Sept. (last admission 3:45 P.M.)

COST: Adults £14, seniors and students £12.50, children under 17 £8, under 5 free, family £36

TUBE: St. James's Park or Victoria

One of the best parts of a visit to this famous royal residence is getting there. Leaving the impersonal government bustle of Whitehall behind, stroll down the tree-lined Mall or better yet, lush St. James's Park, on a relaxing walk that ends at Buckingham Palace.

From late July to late September it is possible to tour 19 of the palace's 661 rooms. The exact dates change from year to year, so check ahead. The highlight of the tour is the throne room, where Queen Elizabeth and her husband Philip, Duke of Edinburgh, sit on ceremonial occasions. You'll also see a spacious ballroom for state banquets and the white drawing room, where the Queen meets with foreign ambassadors. The gold furniture and elegantly painted ceilings are all impressive,

Buckingham Palace hosts the famous Changing of the Guard.

but Queen Victoria's picture gallery is more aesthetically pleasing, having an interesting collection of fine art, including paintings by Rembrandt and Vermeer.

Entrance is by timed ticket, meaning that you buy a ticket with a certain time to enter. If you show up late, you miss out. A visit to the state rooms takes about 2–2.5 hours. You can buy a ticket for a specific time by calling the ticket offices for each attraction, but a £1.25 charge applies. The ticket offices at the palace are open 9:30 A.M.–4 P.M. Audio tours are free with admission.

There are various combination tickets for one or more royal sights, including ones at locations other than Buckingham Palace; check out the website or call the ticket office to find a ticket tailored to what you want to see. Besides the state rooms, at Buckingham Palace you can see the Queen's Gallery (an art gallery) and the Royal Mews (the stables). Some of the more popular combo tickets are: gallery and mews, adults £12, seniors and students £10, under 17 £6.50, under 5 free, family £30.50; state rooms, gallery, and mews, adults £24.50, seniors and students £21.50, under 17 £13.50, under 5 free, family £62.50.

CHANGING OF THE GUARD

At Buckingham Palace btwn. The Mall and Buckingham Gate SW1, 020/7766-7300, www.the-royal-collection.com

HOURS: Daily 11:30 A.M. Apr.-Aug., every other day during other months

COST: Free admission

TUBE: St. James's Park or Victoria

The first thing you'll see when you get to Buckingham Palace is a large roundabout with the Queen Victoria Memorial in the center. If you came to see the Changing of the Guard, this will give you an elevated point from which to look over the crowd of heads. You had better have a zoom lens, though, as you will still be a good way off. To get a front-row look through the iron fence, arrive early to watch the Foot Guards of the Household Regiment change shifts amid pomp and the tunes of a military band. The bright red uniforms and bearskin hats (not made from real bears anymore) make for a colorful display.

QUEEN'S GALLERY

At Buckingham Palace btwn. The Mall and Buckingham Gate SW1, 020/7766-7301, www.the-royal-collection.com

HOURS: Daily 9:30 A.M.-5 P.M. (last admission 4 P.M.) July 26-Sept. 24; Daily 10 A.M.-5:30 P.M. (last admission 4:30 P.M.) the rest of the year

COST: Adults £7.50, seniors and students £6, children under 17 £4, under 5 free, family £19

TUBE: St. James's Park or Victoria

Many works of fine art from the royal collection are on display in the Queen's Gallery. The exhibits are always changing so check to see what's on. The collection varies from Fabergé eggs to royal portraits to Italian masters, so you're never quite sure what you might see.

Entrance is by timed ticket, meaning that you buy a ticket with a certain time to enter. If you show up late, you miss out. A visit to the Queen's Gallery takes about an hour. A free audio tour is included with admission. You can buy a ticket for a specific time by calling the ticket offices for each attraction, but a £1.25 charge applies. The ticket offices at the palace are open 9:30 A.M.–4 P.M.

ROYAL MEWS

At Buckingham Palace btwn. The Mall and Buckingham Gate SW1, 020/7766-7302, www.the-royal-collection.com

HOURS: Open Sat.-Thurs. 10 A.M.-5 P.M. (last admission 4:15 P.M.) July 26-Sept. 24; Sat.-Thurs. 11 A.M.-4 P.M. (last admission 3:15 P.M.) the rest of the year

COST: Adults £6.50, seniors and students £5.50, children under 17 £4, under 5 free, family £17.50

TUBE: St. James's Park or Victoria

If you see anything at Buckingham Palace besides the Changing of the Guard, check out the stables of Buckingham Palace, called the Royal Mews. The guided tour will show you the elegant horse-drawn coaches of monarchs past, as well as the ones still used today. The ornate gilded woodwork of some of the carriages makes them works of art in themselves.

If you're lucky you'll get to see the beautiful Cleveland bays and Windsor grays, the horse breeds favored by British royalty. They are often out training or having exercise, so they're not always around.

THE CHURCHILL MUSEUM AND CABINET WAR ROOMS

Clive Steps, King Charles St.; Enter on Horse Guards Rd. btwn. King Charles St. and Birdcage Walk SW1, 020/7930-6961, www.cwr.iwm.org.uk

HOURS: Daily 9:30 A.M.-6 P.M. (last admission 5 P.M.)

COST: Adults £11, seniors and students £8.50, children under 16 free

TUBE: Westminster

An essential stop for history buffs, this underground bunker, from which Churchill helped win World War II, has been left exactly the way it was on VJ Day. As bombs leveled whole swathes of London, Churchill and his generals worked from this bunker planning British campaigns in Southeast Asia, North Africa, Italy, and Normandy. Walking through here is a bit spooky; you can almost hear the low rumble of the Blitz on the street above and the discussion of strategy among the men and women who worked down here. The map room, Churchill's bedroom, the cabinet room, and the phone room from which the prime minister consulted President Roosevelt are all quite interesting and atmospheric. Included in the ticket is admission to the Churchill Museum here, covering the life of one of Britain's most important prime ministers. An audio tour is included in the price of admission.

HOUSES OF PARLIAMENT

St. Margaret St. at Parliament Sq. SW1, 020/7219-3000, Summer Openings 087/0906-3773, Tours 020/7344-9966, Commons Visitors Gallery 020/7219-4272, Lords Visitors Gallery 020/7219-3107, www.parliament.uk

HOURS: Tours: Mon.-Sat. 9:15 A.M.-4:30 P.M. early Aug.-late Sept.; Commons Visitors Gallery: Mon.-Tues. 2:30-10:30 P.M., Wed. 11:30 A.M.-7:30 P.M., Thurs. 10:30 A.M.-6:30 P.M., Fri. 9:30 A.M.-3 P.M.; Lords Visitors Gallery: Mon.-Wed. from 2:30 P.M., Thurs.-Fri. from 11 A.M.

COST: Tours: Adults £7, seniors, students, and children £5; Free admission to Commons and Lords Visitors Galleries

TUBE: Westminster

A cornerstone of the United Kingdom's government, the Houses of Parliament contain the House of Lords and the House of Commons. It is a vast maze of offices and corridors, with about 1,100 rooms and more than three kilometers (almost two miles) of halls. (For more on how this branch of government works, see *Government and Economy* in the *Background* chapter.)

The core of the building is Westminster Hall, originally completed in 1099 as a royal residence and seat of government that later came to be called the Palace of Westminster. The splendid hammer-beam oak roof, dating to 1397, is a rare and awe-inspiring example of medieval carpentry.

The Palace of Westminster became home to the Lords and Commons in 1512. It went through various rebuildings through the years and managed to survive Guy Fawkes's Gunpowder Plot and the Great Fire of 1666, only to burn down in 1834. Parts of the original Westminster Hall and the Crypt Chapel survived, and the present neo-Gothic building, which encompasses the older building, was finished in 1852. In 1941, the Commons Chamber was destroyed by a German bomb but was soon rebuilt to its former grandeur.

Parliament is primarily a government building, so you have to pass through metal detectors and have your bags X-rayed, and most of the building is off limits to visitors.

If you want to see the government in action, come to an open session and sit in the visitor's gallery. It takes breaks for Christmas, Easter, summer, and sometimes other occasions, so check ahead. Lines can be 1–2 hours long but are sometimes much shorter. Friday mornings are the best time to go and you may not have to wait at all, but the Commons occasionally skips Fridays.

Despite the hassle, it's well worth it. The Commons can get quite lively as ministers shout each other down and engage in near-lethal duels armed only with sharp British wit. The speaker tries to keep order (with varying degrees of success) while the governing party sits to the speaker's right and the opposition sits to the left. Debates at the House of Lords, where the representatives of old money rarely have much at stake, are much tamer. The Commons and Lords keep different hours, and be aware that the debates often end early. The Lords have no set closing time, usually stopping around 10 P.M. Monday–Wednesday and 7:30 P.M. Thursday–Friday. Like the Commons, the Lords do not always meet on Fridays. The notice board in the lobby has a listing of the day's subject of rancor, and many newspapers carry a listing as well.

In August and September Parliament, including the historic Palace of Westminster, opens for guided tours. For U.K. residents, tours are available year-round. Tours do not include the Clock Tower (Big Ben). Entrance for tours and visitors' galleries is at the St. Stephens entrance on St. Margaret Street.

BIG BEN

Houses of Parliament at Westminster Bridge SW1
COST: Free admission
TUBE: Westminster

The most famous part of the Houses of Parliament is Big Ben. The tower is officially called the Clock Tower. Big Ben is the 13.8-ton bell itself, named after Sir Benjamin Hall, chief commissioner of works in 1858, when the bell was rung for the first time. Apparently Sir Hall had a figure like a 13.8-ton bell. It's not the best way to be remembered, but at least he isn't burned in effigy every year like Guy Fawkes.

Big Ben is not open to the public, but its exterior makes it into every photo album. For a nice photo of Parliament with Big Ben rising behind it, go to the little unsigned park across the street from Victoria Tower Gardens, just to the south of Parliament. The Victoria Tower Gardens is worth a visit too, with pleasant views of the Thames and a monument to the Antislavery Society, which succeeded in emancipating all the slaves in the British Empire in 1834. If you are going on the Thames Walk (highly recommended) you can get a good picture from another angle about two-thirds of the way across Westminster Bridge.

Houses of Parliament and Big Ben

ST. JAMES'S PARK

The Mall, Birdcage Walk, and Horse Guards Rd. SW1, 020/7930-1793, www.royalparks.gov.uk
HOURS: Daily 5 A.M.-midnight
COST: Free admission
TUBE: St. James's Park

This lush park is one of the most beautiful in London. Since it stands between the government center of Whitehall and Buckingham Palace, you will probably pass through it at some time during your stay. It is the oldest royal park in London, having been reserved as a game park by Henry VIII in 1532. He built St. James's Palace in the vicinity, which was the royal palace until the royal family moved into Buckingham Palace in 1837.

The park got its present look in the 1830s when landscaper John Nash sculpted the area into a soothing yet tame approximation of nature. The artificial canal at the center was transformed into a lake, complete with Duck Island, where birds of a dozen species find a home amid the city.

As in the other royal parks, a walk here provides a welcome break from big-city bustle, but the thick greenery and pleasing lake make this one of the best spots to get away.

TATE BRITAIN

Millbank at Attorbury St. SW1, 020/7887-8888, www.tate.org.uk
HOURS: Daily 10 A.M.-5:40 P.M. (last admission 5 P.M.); "Late at the Tate" first Friday of the month 6-10 P.M. (last admission 9 P.M.)
COST: Free admission
TUBE: Pimlico

Built on the site of a notorious prison that was a shipping-off point to Australia, the present structure is much more pleasant as a showcase of British art from the year 1500 onward. Seeing the collection can fill an entire day, but even a couple of hours can show you some stunning highlights. Most of the work here is by famous British painters such as Constable, Danby, Millais, and Patterson. You'll also see some interesting portraits of famous people, such as Queen Elizabeth I in Room 2. Room 9 has some large 19th-century paintings with epic themes; Danby's *The Deluge* is especially memorable. Rooms 7, 10, and 11 are devoted to John Constable, who perhaps best of all British artists captures the essence of the English countryside. Rooms 14 and 15 are devoted to the pre-Raphaelites, including Millais's much-reproduced *Ophelia*. Room 28 contains some of Britain's pop art, including an amusing Tube map by Simon Patterson called *The Great Bear* (1992). The station names have been replaced with those of famous people, each line devoted to individuals of different types, from Italian artists to footballers. Attached to the Tate is the Clore Gallery, which showcases the work of famous landscape artist J. M. W. Turner.

If you want to see Tate Britain and the Tate Modern in one day, you might consider taking the Tate Boat, a special river service running every 40 minutes (during gallery opening hours) between the Tate Britain and Tate Modern, with a stop at the London Eye (see *South of the Thames*) and a transfer at the Tate Modern to the Tower of London. This is much faster than walking, since the Tate Modern is downstream from the Tate Britian, and on the South Bank. It's a quick way to get from one spot to another and you'll have nice views on the way. Either get a one-way ticket or a River Roamer, which is valid all day and convenient if you want to see all the sights and return to where you started. Single fares are as follows: adults £4, London Student Card or Travelcard holder £2.65, child under 16 £2, child under 16 with travel card £1.35, families £10. River Roamer tickets are: adults £7, London Student Card or Travelcard holder £4.65, child under 16 £3.50, child under 16 with travel card £2.35, families £16. Check out www.tate.org.uk/tatetotate, call 020/7887-8888, or ask at the information desk of either Tate for the timetable.

WESTMINSTER ABBEY

Broad Sanctuary and Parliament Sq. SW1, 020/7654-4900, www.westminster-abbey.org
HOURS: Mon.-Tues., Thurs.-Fri. 9:30 A.M.-3:45 P.M., Wed. 9:30 A.M.-6 P.M., Sat. 9:30 A.M.-1:45 P.M., open Sun. for worship only

COST: Adults £10, seniors over 60, students, and children under 16 £6, family £22.
TUBE: Westminster

Like many historic buildings, this famous abbey of kings and queens has evolved through time. In A.D. 960 a Benedictine abbey opened on the site, although there may have been a church here even earlier than that. Edward the Confessor finished building a church for the monks in 1065, and much of the present building was erected by Henry III starting in 1245. Later monarchs sponsored their own additions, such as side chapels, stained-glass windows, and elaborate tombs. The two western towers, an imposing part of the London skyline, are based on a design by Christopher Wren and were completed in 1745. The most recent additions are the figures of 10 Christian martyrs over the west door, including Archbishop Oscar Romero of El Salvador and Martin Luther King Jr.

The interior of the abbey is breathtaking with its lofty Gothic ceiling and brilliant stained-glass windows. Since William the Conqueror in 1066, every monarch except Edward V and VIII has been crowned in the abbey. The elegant coronation chair has been used for the crowning of almost every monarch since Edward II in 1307.

Many members of the royal family are buried here. A walk through the abbey is a pageant of royal history and includes the tombs of Queen Elizabeth I, Mary I, and Edward II, to name a few. Also check out the tomb and shrine of Saint Edward the Confessor (reigned 1042–1066), a king who became the country's patron saint until 1415, when he was replaced by St. George. His royal touch was said to cure all types of disease.

England's artistic royalty are buried here too. In Poets' Corner you will find the tombs of more than 100 writers, poets, actors, musicians, and artists, including Geoffrey Chaucer, T. S. Eliot, Lewis Carroll, and Charles Dickens. Scattered throughout the church are other graves of the famous, such as Sir Isaac Newton and Charles Darwin.

Beyond the abbey are the cloisters, which look much the same as they did in the late

© SEAN MCLACHLAN

Westminster Abbey has seen monarchs crowned and buried.

Middle Ages, the Chapter House, with its fine stained-glass windows, and a museum filled with church treasures. Entrance to all of these is included in your ticket. While visitors must pay for admission, the services are free. An uplifting evensong is held at 5 P.M. weekdays and 3 P.M. Saturday and Sunday; it is also free. The abbey is vast and complex, so don't forget to pick up a free map and information guide at the information point.

ST. MARGARET'S

Broad Sanctuary and Parliament Sq. SW1,
020/7654-4900, www.westminster-abbey.org
HOURS: Mon.-Fri. 9:30 A.M.-3:45 P.M., Sat. 9:30 A.M.-1:45 P.M., Sun. 2-5 P.M., may be closed for special services
COST: Free admission
TUBE: Westminster

On the grounds of Westminster Abbey is St. Margaret's Church, popularly known as the "parish church of the House of Commons." Many ministers of Parliament come here for worship and donate to the church. Don't miss the West Window, a stained-glass window commemorating Sir Walter Raleigh, who explored the east coast of North America, and the East Window, a rare example of 16th-century Flemish glasswork. On the exterior of the west wall is a bust of King Charles I, staring toward the lawn of the Parliament building, where stands the statue of the man who had him beheaded, Oliver Cromwell.

WESTMINSTER CATHEDRAL

42 Francis St. SW1, 020/7798-9055,
www.westminstercathedral.org.uk
HOURS: Cathedral: Mon.-Fri. 7 A.M.-7 P.M., Sat. 8 A.M.-7 P.M., Sun. 8 A.M.-8 P.M.; Tower Lift: Daily 9:30 A.M.-12:30 P.M. and 1-5 P.M.
COST: Free admission; Tower Lift: Adults £3, children £1.50, family £7
TUBE: Victoria

Westminster Cathedral is the mother church to the Catholic Archdiocese of Westminster. Consecrated in 1910, it shows an interesting combination of Victorian brickwork exterior and Byzantine mosaic interior. Architect John Francis Bentley (1839–1902) took his inspiration from the Santa Sofia in Istanbul and various other early churches. The influence from the Byzantine period is most noticeable, with brilliant mosaics of church fathers and important biblical figures. The most impressive is the vaulted ceiling of the Lady Chapel, which sports several angels, their wings outspread across a shimmering gold background. The original intention was to cover the entire interior with mosaic, but the money ran out, so the large central domes loom in mysterious darkness. Still, what is here is truly impressive, and may inspire you to explore true Byzantine churches in cities such as Istanbul and Ravenna.

Once you stop being dazzled by the mosaics, you will notice the imposing marble pillars flanking the wide nave. No two pillars are alike, but all hearken to the era of late antiquity. While the interior is what brings the most gasps, take a bit of time to examine the exterior. The patterned brickwork is typical of Victorian style, and the tall St. Edward's Tower juts a cross 284 feet into the sky.

The grand organ, which has an imposing sound that reverberates throughout the roomy interior of the cathedral, is center stage for a regular series of free concerts. The website includes a schedule.

Covent Garden, West End, and Soho — Map 4

If London were a party, this area would be the life of it! Covent Garden has been a major shopping center since the Middle Ages, and Trafalgar Square was the center of the world's largest empire. Not surprisingly, there's plenty to see here, including some of the major attractions that get people to fly for hours and hours just to get here. While the National Gallery and Trafalgar Square are on every visitor's itinerary, make sure to leave time for some of the many lesser-known places of special interest.

COVENT GARDEN

The Piazza and Covent Garden Market,
www.coventgarden.org.uk
or www.coventgarden.uk.com
HOURS: Open 24 hours; shop hours vary
COST: Free admission
TUBE: Covent Garden

In the center of an active shopping and arts district, Covent Garden takes it a notch higher with a wide array of shops and attractions, all housed in a Tudor-period square. Actually, buying and selling has gone on here since at least the time of King John (reigned 1199–1256), when the site first got its name, originally "Convent Garden" for the nearby but now vanished Convent of St. Peter. The present-day Covent Garden was designed by architect Inigo Jones (1573–1652) and has been a thriving center of commerce ever since.

Nowadays the site is popular for theatergoers

because the entrance for the Royal Opera House is here. The shoppers by day and drinkers by night add even more to the crowds. Certain days bring food or antique fairs, and in the evenings, especially on weekends, the square fills with entertainers.

INSTITUTE OF CONTEMPORARY ARTS

The Mall, next to Duke of York Steps SW1, box office 020/7930-3647, www.ica.org.uk

HOURS: Gallery: Daily noon-7:30 P.M.; ICA: Mon. noon-11 P.M., Tues.-Sat. noon-1 A.M., Sun. noon-10:30 P.M.; Box Office: noon-9:30 P.M.

COST: Day membership to the ICA £1.50 weekdays, £2.50 weekends; admission to events varies

TUBE: Charing Cross or Piccadilly Circus

Enjoy cutting-edge shows in a gallery steeped in history. Picasso got his big break in England here. Like the Barbican, the ICA hosts film, live performance, and art exhibitions and strikes a balance between homegrown talent and international productions. While many of the artists use traditional media such as painting and sculpture in innovative ways, others work in New Media, creating their effects with video and computer technology. New Media is a burgeoning medium in the British art scene, and you'll see some of its best practitioners here. The bookshop is a good place to look for art books, DVDs, and magazines. The ICA Bar and Café, open the same hours as the ICA itself, is known for its arty conversation lasting late into the night. A day membership to the ICA or ticket for any ICA event are required to enter.

LONDON TRANSPORT MUSEUM

Covent Garden Piazza Unit 26 at Russell St. WC2, 020/7565-7299, www.ltmuseum.co.uk

HOURS: Mon.-Thurs., Sat.-Sun. 10 A.M.-6 P.M.; Fri. 11 A.M.-6 P.M.

COST: Free admission

TUBE: Covent Garden

As London expanded from the largest city in England to one of the largest cities in the world, the problem of how to get people from one part to another became acute. The story of public transportation in London is surprisingly

FAR FROM THE MADDING CROWD

If you have time to get beyond the usual suspects, or if you just want to see something out of the way, here are a few of London's least visited sights – the sights most people miss. They are all worth a visit and you won't have to beat your way through a hundred tour groups to see them. All are listed elsewhere, as indicated.

Highgate Cemetery: This ornate Victorian burial ground is reminiscent of the aboveground cemeteries of New Orleans. Ornate mausoleums line forested lanes and house famous personages in an atmospheric city of the silent. Very photogenic and peaceful (page 154).

Shri Swaminarayan Mandir: The largest Hindu temple outside India, the Mandir encourages visitors to come learn about this thriving religion and witness rituals dating back thousands of years. Many school groups come here, and it's always nice to see kids learning about the faith of their neighbors, but few tourists make the trip (page 153).

Bramah Tea and Coffee Museum: Where would the British be without tea? Where would the Americans be without coffee? Come here to learn the fascinating history of how two simple drinks changed Western civilization. After seeing the exhibits, sit down in the Tea Room for a cuppa. The gift shop is a good place to pick up something for the folks back home, too (page 137).

Kew Bridge Steam Museum: The United Kingdom became master of the world because it was master of early modern technology. Here, in full working order, are the various steam-driven machines that transformed Britain from a comfy little island into a world power. It's lots of fun for anyone, grown or otherwise, who likes giant, loud machines (page 141).

London Transport Museum

interesting and reveals a lot about the city itself. The various double-decker buses, from toylike examples drawn by horses to the famous red Routemaster, take pride of place in the collection. It also offers information on river transport, the history of bicycles, and every other mode of transport. The museum underwent a £18.6 million expansion and planned to open in spring of 2007 with increased gallery space and more displays for its almost 400,000 objects.

Guided tours, which get you a peek at some of the collection not in the displays, take place at irregular times; check the latest schedule on the website or call the resource desk at 020/7379-6344 for information and booking. Tours cost £10 for adults, £8.50 for seniors, students, and children.

THE NATIONAL GALLERY

Trafalgar Sq. btwn. Whitcomb St. and St. Martin's Ln. WC2, 020/7747-2885, www.nationalgallery.org.uk

HOURS: Daily 10 A.M.–6 P.M., Wed. 10 A.M.–9 P.M.

COST: Free admission

TUBE: Charing Cross or Leicester Square

This is one of the world's great museums of Western art, and a day spent here is a rich experience. It was established in 1824 when the House of Commons bought a private collection for free exhibition to the public. The inventory has grown steadily through the years and now includes about 2,300 paintings. The present building was started in 1832 and has been greatly expanded and modified since. The most recent expansion was the Sainsbury Wing in 1991.

The gallery's focus is on Western European art from about 1250 to the beginning of the 20th century and it covers all the major art movements. To complete your art education, go to the Tate Modern to see 20th century and contemporary art.

The museum is conveniently laid out so that you can see art develop chronologically. Start in the Sainsbury Wing, which is attached to the west wing (left if coming in from the main Trafalgar Square entrance, or go to the separate Sainsbury Wing entrance), for paintings of 1250–1500, including beautiful church art

© LEAH BOYER

A flock of pigeons rises to the sky above the National Gallery and Trafalgar Square.

such as the *Wilton Dyptych* (c. 1395), showing Richard II meeting the Virgin Mary and a crowd of luminous angels, and more secular art such as works by Botticelli. From there head to the west wing to see work of 1500–1600, including some of the masterpieces of the Italian Renaissance, such as the famous study by Leonardo da Vinci of *The Virgin and Child with St. Anne and St. John the Baptist* (c. 1499–1500). Then go north to the extensive collection of works of 1600–1700. The National Gallery's selection of Dutch masters is especially good and includes works by such big names as Rembrandt and Van Eyck. The east wing is devoted to art of 1700–1900, with extensive space dedicated to the impressionists. Manet, Monet, Gauguin, and Van Gogh are all here, as are lesser-known artists who are worthy of hanging next to the greats. Van Gogh's *Sunflowers* gets pride of place and always draws a crowd, as does Monet's famous *Bathers at La Grenouillère.*

Free guided tours depart every day from the information desk at the Trafalgar Square entrance and other locations throughout the gallery. The folks at information can also give you Children's Trails, so that your child can be your guide. Themed audio tours are also available.

After circumnavigating the world of art, you might want to refill at the National Gallery Café on Level 0. A meal for one with a drink usually comes out to less than £10.

The National Gallery is justifiably one of the biggest attractions in London. Because of this it can be terribly crowded. The best time to come is on weekday mornings, when you will mostly have to compete with conveniently short schoolkids, and the late hours on Wednesday evening.

NATIONAL PORTRAIT GALLERY

St. Martin's Place WC2, 020/7312-2463, www.npg.org.uk

HOURS: Daily 10 A.M.-6 P.M., Thurs.-Fri. until 9 P.M.

COST: Free admission; special exhibitions may charge

TUBE: Charing Cross or Leicester Square

One would think that looking at room after

room of portraits of mostly dead people would get dull, but the National Portrait Gallery is a surprisingly interesting stop on the London art circuit. The gallery was established in 1856 to display paintings of leaders and royalty, and the bulk of the collection is of the ruling class from imperial days, so you can attach faces to the names you've been reading about.

But not only kings, queens, and members of government have their pictures here. The only known portrait of Shakespeare taken from life is here, as are portraits of other leading artists. A regular series of temporary exhibitions focus on a theme, such as early explorers, or particular people, such as a recent retrospective on Samuel Beckett.

PICCADILLY CIRCUS

Piccadilly Circus

HOURS: Open 24 hours

COST: Free admission

TUBE: Piccadilly Circus

This busy intersection opened in 1819 to connect Regent and Piccadilly streets and lies at the heart of London's West End theater and dining district. At night Piccadilly Circus lights up with numerous neon signs, but by day it's a bit more traditional with its famous statue of Eros. Actually the statue is titled *The Angel of Christian Charity,* but everyone calls the Hellenic winged archer by the name of Eros, since that's who he looks like. It was erected in 1893 as a memorial to philanthropist Lord Shaftesbury and caused quite a stir since he's seminude. No one seems to mind now and he's a popular meeting point for those who are heading off to a night of fun in Soho. The *Evening Standard* uses the statue as its masthead. Sculptor Alfred Gilbert actually intended the statue to be of Eros's brother Anteros, god of selfless love, in honor of Lord Shaftesbury's donations to charity, which is a bit more appropriate than the mischievous Eros, whose arrows cause so much trouble.

At the northeast side of the Circus is the London Pavilion, with a Victorian-era classical facade. It is a shopping area and part of the London Trocadero, a giant shopping center and amusement park. At the south side of the Circus is the Criterion Theatre (1874), popular for its Reduced Shakespeare Company.

SOMERSET HOUSE

The Strand and Waterloo Bridge, 020/7848-2589, www.somerset-house.org.uk

HOURS: Daily 10 A.M.–6 P.M. (last admission 5:15 P.M.)

COST: Adults £5 each collection, £8 any two collections, £12 three-day pass for all; seniors and students £4, £7 any two collections, £11 three-day pass to all; kids under 18 and U.K. full-time students free; Courtauld Gallery free Mon. before 2 P.M.

TUBE: Temple or Covent Garden

Built by Edward Seymour ("Protector Somerset") in 1547, Somerset House was the first Renaissance building of any scale in England. Somerset later fell out of favor and was executed, and his elegant stone mansion was snapped up by the Crown to be used by queens and their retinues. The building later fell into disrepair before it was extensively remodeled in the 18th century and used by the Royal Academy, Royal Society, and the Society of Antiquaries. Part of it was also used by the Navy Board, and numerous models of old sailing ships still adorn the halls. It now houses three art museums that you can visit separately or together.

A walk around this fine building is a lesson in early British architecture. The terrace gives a wide view of the Thames. Step back a bit and take a look at the broad stone facade, with its subdued but elegant Corinthian columns and pleasing symmetry. Inside, sweeping stairways lit by indirect sunlight bring the visitor to the upper levels, where you can peek out the windows for more views. Take time to visit the courtyard, where a series of fountains jet water from the granite flagstones for a soothing display. In winter the fountains are replaced by an ice rink. At night the whole building and all the fountains are lit up.

While the building itself is an attraction, most people come here to see the three galleries now housed inside. The Courtauld Gallery is the most popular, with a large collection of fine art from early Dutch masters to the impressionists. The Gilbert Collection specializes in decorative arts, and the Hermitage Rooms recreate the famous palace of the czar while hosting temporary exhibitions.

Seeing all three collections can take some time, so you might want to have a bite at the deli on the ground floor. The Courtauld Gallery Café is open on a small terrace during the summer and has table service for a range of hot and cold food. The Courtyard Café is open during summer and offers pleasant views of the sprawling courtyard.

COURTAULD GALLERY

Somerset House, The Strand and Waterloo Bridge, 020/7848-2589, www.somerset-house.org.uk or www.courtauld.ac.uk/gallery/inex.html

HOURS: Daily 10 A.M.–6 P.M. (last admission 5:15 P.M.)

COST: Adults £5 each collection, £8 any two collections, £12 three-day pass to all; seniors and students £4, £7 for any two collections, £11 for three-day pass to all; kids under 18 and U.K. full-time students free; free Mon. before 2 P.M.

TUBE: Temple or Covent Garden

The Courtauld is the most popular of the three galleries in Somerset House. Unlike many museums that group their paintings by period, the Courtauld kept intact the private collections donated to the institution. Gallery I, the Sachler Gallery, contains an interesting collection of early Italian religious paintings. Galleries II–IV contain the Courtauld collection, named after the industrialist and art collector Samuel Courtauld, who brought all these collections together. His family developed rayon, and he used much of his wealth to collect these impressionist and postimpressionist works and encouraged other collectors to pool their collections into this museum. One of the best of his personal collection is Renoir's *La Loge,* painted in 1874 for the impressionists' inaugural group exhibition. The most famous work here is Van Gogh's *Self Portrait with a Bandaged Ear* (1889). The Lee Collection in Gallery V contains Brueghel the Elder's *Landscape with the Flight to Egypt* (1563) and other early Dutch masters. The upper floor houses late 19th- and early-20th-century art. Some interesting Kandinskys are in Gallery XIII, including both his earlier more figurative work and his later abstractions. Room VIII holds several sculptures by Degas and an unfinished yet highly evocative drawing called *Lady with a Parasol* (c. 1870–1872).

GILBERT COLLECTION

Somerset House, The Strand and Waterloo Bridge, 020/7848-2589, www.somerset-house.org.uk or www.gilbert-collection.org.uk

HOURS: Daily 10 A.M.–6 P.M. (last admission 5:15 P.M.)

COST: Adults £5 each collection, £8 any two collections, £12 three-day pass to all; seniors and students £4, £7 any two collections, £11 three-day pass to all; kids under 18 and U.K. full-time students free.

TUBE: Temple or Covent Garden

The Gilbert Collection of decorative arts displays hundreds of objects that once adorned the homes of the rich and powerful. The collection of these everyday objects of the elite is broken down into five main areas. The Enamel Miniatures are delicate and lifelike portraits of nobility, providing a glimpse at faces from the past. The Gold and Treasury section features pompous gold sculptures and tableware made for various emperors and kings. The snuff boxes in the Gold Boxes section are ornate studies in intricate detail, while the silver and gold tableware in the Silver Gallery will almost blind you. My favorite is the Micromosiac section. The inlaid tables and bureaus create little classical scenes out of tiny colored stones. A visit to these rooms will make you feel as if you're living in a palace.

HERMITAGE ROOMS

Somerset House, The Strand and Waterloo Bridge, 020/7848-2589, www.somerset-house.org.uk or www.hermitagerooms.com

HOURS: Daily 10 A.M.–6 P.M. (last admission 5:15 P.M.)

COST: Adults £5 each collection, £8 any two collections, £12 three-day pass to all; seniors and students £4, £7 any two collections, £11 three-day pass to all; kids under 18 and U.K. full-time students free.

TUBE: Temple or Covent Garden

The Hermitage Rooms recreate in miniature the Czar's Winter Palace, now the State

Hermitage Museum in St. Petersburg, Russia, and provide an atmospheric backdrop to a series of visiting exhibitions. The concentration is on older, more established styles in keeping with the ornate setting. Past exhibits have included Byzantine jewelry and luxury art, erotic French art, and Russian avant-garde porcelain. The Learning Centre hosts a regular series of talks and presentations, some of which are free. For more information on what's on at the Learning Centre, call 020/7420-9406 or email education@somerset-house.org.uk.

ST. MARTIN-IN-THE-FIELDS

Trafalgar Sq. WC2, box office 020/7839-8362, Parish office 020/7766-1100, www.smitf.org

HOURS: Open 24 hours

COST: Free admission

TUBE: Charing Cross or Leicester Square

While there are many more elaborate churches in London, St. Martin-in-the-Fields has long been a favorite with tourists and locals alike for its central location, which makes a fine refuge from the bustle in Trafalgar Square outside. Many Londoners come to worship here, including a sizable Chinese congregation that listens to sermons in Mandarin and Cantonese, and many more come to hear the famous series of concerts. Check out the website or call the box office for the schedule as catching one of these is a wonderful way to spend an evening. While admission to the church is free, some concerts have an entry fee. The lunchtime concerts, usually held 2–3 times a week at 1 P.M., are free.

This church is a leading force in liberalizing the Anglican Church. It actively calls for the ordination of women and gays and has a long history of fighting for other causes. In the 1980s the church gave food and a place to sleep to the anti-apartheid protestors picketing nearby South Africa House. Now it spearheads drives to house and employ the homeless. Peter Benenson found the inspiration to create Amnesty International while he sat in one of the pews.

A church has stood here since at least Norman times, but the present structure was built by James Gibbs in 1726. His design might

© DEAN EDWARDS

St. Martin-in-the-Fields at Trafalgar Square offers a famous program of classical music.

seem familiar; many church architects in the United States got their inspiration from Gibbs. The rectangular building, classical facade, and high steeple were imitated throughout New England and beyond.

Downstairs is the crypt. The worn stone slabs of graves making up the floor, with their faded names and dates, are a strange contrast to the gift shop and Café in the Crypt (see the *Restaurants* chapter). You'll also find a brass rubbing center, where children can place a piece of paper over a brass effigy—replicas of famous ones of Shakespeare and various monarchs and knights—and create their own pictures with special metallic waxes. They come out looking very nice and it makes a fun memento. Prices depend on the effigy and range £2.90–15.

Free guided tours of the church are held most Thursdays at 11:30 A.M. and last about 75 minutes. You get to see not only the church but some hidden vaults and the Royal Box, where Hanoveran royalty worshipped. Call or check the website to see if there's a tour when you're in town.

THEATRE MUSEUM

Russell St. at Bow St., Covent Garden WC2, 020/7943-4700, www.theatremuseum.org.uk

HOURS: Tues.-Sun. 10 A.M.-6 P.M. (last admission 5:30 P.M.)

COST: Free admission

TUBE: Covent Garden

After the museum's extensive remodeling in 2006, this collection of theater memorabilia has now reopened. With thousands of posters, handbills, scripts, and costumes from the days of Shakespeare up to the present, the museum gives a comprehensive look at the development of modern stagecraft. The handbills from old Georgian and Victorian plays are amusing for their melodrama and liberal use of exclamation points. A favorite part of the museum is the many colorful costumes, including a Chinese robe designed by Picasso for use in a ballet. Temporary exhibitions showcase famous actors and directors or cover various themes related to the theater arts. The museum hosts regular kids' activities, which are listed on its website.

TRAFALGAR SQUARE

Trafalgar Sq. WC2

HOURS: Open 24 hours

COST: Free admission

TUBE: Charing Cross

London's most famous square lies at the heart of the downtown commercial, arts, and tourist district. It's flanked on the north by the National Gallery, to the east by St. Martin-in-the-Fields, to the west by the gentlemen's clubs of Pall Mall, and to the south by the imposing Canada House and South Africa House, and standing here makes you feel as if you're at the center of the empire.

You would have been 100 years ago. The square was designed in the 1820s by famous architect and landscaper John Nash, who wanted to make a suitable center for what was then the capital of the world's greatest empire. In the center towers Nelson's Column, erected in 1843 to honor the empire's favorite admiral, who defeated the French and Spanish navies in the famous 1805 battle at Trafalgar. Different types of stone from all over the British Isles

Nelson's Column in Trafalgar Square commemorates Britain's greatest admiral.

make up the column as a gesture of unity, and it underwent restoration in 2006 to spruce it up after 150 years of pollution. The edge of the large pool next to the column is a popular sitting place if you don't mind being harassed by flocks of pigeons looking for a handout.

Four plinths mark the corners of the square. Three of them are of old kings and generals, but the fourth remained unoccupied for many years. Now it hosts a series of works by contemporary artists. Some have been controversial, such as Marc Quinn's nude sculpture of a pregnant woman born without limbs titled *Alison Lapper Pregnant*. Some called it exploitation, while others hailed it as a positive image of a strong woman who kept going despite her disability. The bright white sculpture does clash with the traditional spirit of the square, as does the Millennium Wheel arching over the southeast skyline, but the subject matter, celebrating modern courage instead of the victors of centuries-old battles, is spot on.

For a great vista, stand on the steps of the National Gallery on the north of the square. To your right (west) is the 1827 facade of Canada House. The street heading west is Pall Mall, famous for its exclusive gentlemen's clubs and site of aristocratic plotting for generations. To your left (east) stands the church of St. Martin-in-the-Fields, and a little farther to the south is South Africa House. In the 1980s the square was the scene of mass protests against apartheid, and the protestors found a welcoming home in the progressive church. Protests and celebrations are still held in Trafalgar Square, as it is one of the most accessible open areas in central London. To the south Whitehall Street leads down to the Houses of Parliament, Big Ben, and Westminster Abbey, all visible in the distance. To the southwest is Admiralty Arch, a memorial to Queen Victoria erected in 1910.

Most of the architecture you see is Victorian or a little earlier, so if you replace the cars with carriages in your imagination, you can get a good idea of what the older city looked like.

Bloomsbury, Euston, and Holborn — Map 5

One of the most pleasant areas of London, here you will find Georgian facades, towering Victorian buildings, and centuries-old city squares. In among the fine old architecture you will find a wealth of sights. Tranquil, Georgian-era Bloomsbury has long been a center for intellectual activity, and Charles Dickens made his home here for a time, as did the famous architect Sir John Soane. Other learned luminaries have penned great works in the British Museum, or headed north to Euston and its famous British Library, or Holborn and its important university.

THE BRITISH LIBRARY

96 Euston Rd. NW1, 020/7412-7000, www.bl.uk

HOURS: Mon., Wed.-Fri. 9:30 A.M.-6 P.M., Tues. 9:30 A.M.-8 P.M., Sat. 9:30 A.M.-5 P.M., Sun. 11:00 A.M.-5 P.M.

COST: Free admission

TUBE: King's Cross St. Pancras

Like the U.S. Library of Congress in Washington, D.C., the British Library strives to have a copy of every book published in the nation. The stacks are open to researchers only, but there is a fascinating museum filled with treasures of the written word. Many are works of art as well, such as the Lindisfarne Gospels with their intricate Celtic knotwork dating to the late 7th or early 8th century, and several medieval Korans with elaborate gold calligraphy. Don't miss the Sherborne Gospel (c. 1400), one of the most beautiful illustrated manuscripts you will ever see. The showcases of the collection are works of great historical importance, such as the Magna Carta of 1215, which guaranteed the nobility legal rights and was the first written limitation on the power of the King. One display shows the evolution of mapmaking, while another traces the development of printing from its early days in China (the Chinese invented paper, too) to its independent invention by Gutenberg in the 1450s. Gutenberg's first printed work, the famous Gutenberg Bible, shows how people weren't quite accustomed to the new medium. Spaces were left blank so buyers could have them illuminated in the medieval manner. Other high points are pages from the notebooks of Leonardo da Vinci, stamps from the infamous Stamp Act of 1765, and the original handwritten manuscript of *Alice in Wonderland.* A nice treat are some handwritten drafts of famous Beatles songs, complete with scratched-out yet still legible lines that never made it to the recording studio. Also here are a temporary exhibition hall and an extensive stamp collection from around the world. A café and restaurant are on-site.

BRITISH MUSEUM

Great Russell St. btwn. Bloomsbury and Montague Sts. WC1, 020/7323-8299, www.thebritishmuseum.ac.uk or www.british-museum.ac.uk

HOURS: Gallery and special exhibitions: Sat.-Wed. 10 A.M.-5:30 P.M., Thurs.-Fri. 10 A.M.-8:30 P.M., selected galleries open Thurs.-Fri. until 8:30 P.M.; Great Court: Sun.-Wed. 9 A.M.-6 P.M., Thurs.-Sat. 9 A.M.-11 P.M.; Reading Room Library and Information Center: Daily 10 A.M.-5:30 P.M.; Viewing Area: Thurs.-Fri. 10 A.M.-8:30 P.M.

COST: Free admission; some special exhibitions may charge

TUBE: Tottenham Court Road or Russell Square

The British Museum is one of the greatest archaeological treasuries in the world and no visit to London would be complete without seeing it. It opened in 1759 and ever since it has been adding to its vast collections of artifacts from Egyptian, Greek, Roman, Anglo-Saxon, and virtually every other culture. You could spend days walking the galleries and still not get a good look at

The British Museum houses one of the finest archaeological collections in the world.

HIGHLIGHTS OF THE BRITISH MUSEUM

The British Museum is chock-full of fascinating artifacts from virtually every ancient civilization. There's such a wealth of things to see here it can get a little confusing as to what to see first. Here's a guide to some of the highlights of the collection.

From the main entrance, go into the **Great Court.** To the left is Room 4, a grand hall of Egyptian sculpture that makes for great photo opportunities. Make sure not to miss the **Rosetta Stone,** a tablet on which the same decree is written in Greek, hieroglyphics, and demotic (an informal variant of hieroglyphics). When it was discovered in the 19th century, no one knew how to read ancient Egyptian script, but Greek was well known. This discovery unlocked the texts of an entire ancient civilization and profoundly changed our knowledge of history.

Continue to Room 18 to see the sculptures of the Parthenon of Athens, better known as the **Elgin Marbles** after the man who bought them from Ottoman-dominated Greece and brought them to London. Here you'll see scenes of gods and warriors sculpted in the perfect lines of classical Greece. If you have the time, continue through the many other Greek galleries nearby to see everyday objects, busts of famous philosophers, and fine Attic pottery.

On the first floor, called the second floor by Americans, the most popular rooms are Rooms 62 and 63, where the **Egyptian mummies** are kept. Room 62 has a mummy dating to the Roman period with a lifelike portrait mask. Room 63 has an unwrapped mummy that will give your children all sorts of wonderful nightmares and make them become archaeologists (at least that's what it did to me). Be sure to check out the funerary figures, which were supposed to turn into servants in the afterlife and are already arranged into dioramas of daily life, hard at work at their assigned tasks. The artifacts from Sumeria, a civilization predating the glory days of Egypt, are also worth a look, especially the treasures from the **Royal tombs of Ur** in Room 56, including the Standard of Ur familiar from history textbooks.

Some of the most fascinating artifacts in the museum are the most humble. In Room 49 are the **Vindolanda tablets,** common letters from a Roman fort that include military intelligence reports, requests for leave, and even a birthday party invitation by a woman named Claudia Severa to her "sister" (a term of endearment between Roman women) Sulpicia Lepidina. It dates to A.D. 97–103 and is the earliest handwriting from a woman in Latin. All the letters are fully translated and make for great reading. Room 50 houses the **Lindow Man.** This poor fellow was clubbed to death in the 1st century and thrown in a peat bog, which preserved his skin. His stomach contained the remnants of a drink that included mistletoe, a sacred plant of the druids, so he may have been a druid sacrifice.

The British Museum houses a large collection of **African artifacts** in Room 25. African cultures tend to be overlooked by many museums (even here they're relegated to the basement) but they display a wide variety of styles and themes. The high points here are the 16th-century **bronzes from Benin.** Besides the many statuettes, there is an imposing display of plaques showing life in the royal court. The wooden masks and sculptures from West Africa, especially Cameroon, are brilliantly done.

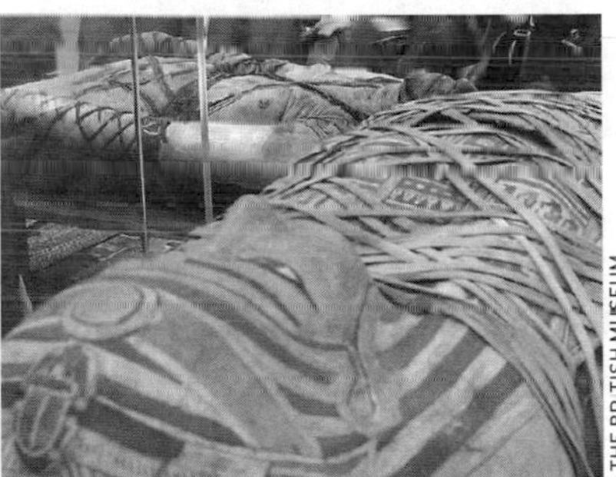

The mummy room at the British Museum is a treasure house of royal remains.

everything. With an inventory of approximately seven million objects, that's not surprising. Come here for a world tour of vanished civilizations.

It is impossible to list all the important artifacts on display, but some of the most important include the Rosetta Stone, which unlocked the mystery of Egyptian hieroglyphics; the Parthenon Sculptures from classical Athens; a room full of mummies; and a vast display of beautiful Greek vessels. The early years of England aren't neglected. From the crude stone tools of the earliest inhabitants to the altars of Romans soldiers guarding Hadrian's Wall, the museum gives a detailed overview of the development of civilization on the island.

The best plan for first-timers is to make your way from the front entrance to the glass-domed Great Court. Opened in 2000, this magnificent glass dome is supported by a large circular area in the center housing the Reading Room, bookshop, temporary exhibition gallery, and restaurant. A slow circuit of the court will reveal several ancient sculptures. Head either left or right from the main entrance to one of the information kiosks. There you can get a free map and information about any special exhibits, tours, or talks. These change regularly and can also be found on the museum's website.

© NIGEL YOUNG

The Great Court of the British Museum is a magnificent dome of glass and metal.

At the center of the court is the Reading Room. Its fine blue and gold ceiling, dating to 1857, has sheltered many aspiring writers, including Oscar Wilde, Algernon Charles Swinburne, Mohandas Gandhi, and Rudyard Kipling. Karl Marx wrote *Das Kapital* here. If learning about the museum is more interesting to you than smashing capitalism, check out the computer terminals with access to COMPASS, the museum's online database of artifacts, which you can also search via its website.

Docents will pass around real artifacts from the collection for you to handle 11 A.M.–4 P.M. daily. Keep an eye out for their tables in selected galleries. Free gallery tours and talks are held throughout the day; check the information desk or website for what's on the day you visit. While these tours tend to clog up already busy galleries, the guides are researchers in their fields and are extremely knowledgeable.

The Court Café in the Great Court and the Gallery Café next to Room 12 serve light meals. In the center of the Great Court, up the sweeping white stairs above the Reading Room, is the full-service Court Restaurant (see the *Restaurants* chapter).

THE CHARLES DICKENS MUSEUM

48 Doughty St. WC1, 020/7405-2127, www.dickensmuseum.com

HOURS: Mon.-Sat. 10 A.M.-5 P.M., Sun. 11 A.M.-5 P.M.

COST: Adults £5, seniors and students £4, children £3, family £14

TUBE: Russell Square or Chancery Lane

While Dickens lived behind this unassuming Georgian facade for only two years, 1837–1839, the prolific author finished *The Pickwick Papers, Oliver Twist,* and *Nicholas Nickleby* during that time. Now a museum, the house has been filled with period furnishings and displays of Dickens's work. Even if you aren't greatly interested in Dickens, a visit will give you a good idea of a moderately wealthy family home of the period. The curators put on a series of special events, including readings and seasonal walks through Dickensian London. The gift shop is loaded with editions of Dickens's books and other items such as quill pens (difficult to use) and busts of the author (inspiring for other writers).

For a special treat, come to the popular performance of *The Sparkler of Albion* on Wednesdays at 7:30 P.M. mid-April–mid-September (£16, bookings 020/7631-1011, www.sparklet.ukf.net). Impersonators put on a great show telling of Dickens's life and art, and free wine and soda are available all evening.

SIR JOHN SOANE'S MUSEUM

13 Lincoln's Inn Fields WC2, 020/7405-2107, www.soane.org

HOURS: Tues.-Sat. 10 A.M.-5 P.M., first Tues. of the month 6-9 P.M.

COST: Free admission

TUBE: Holborn

The 18th-century home of the famous architect who designed the Bank of England shows Soane's wide tastes. Highlights include prints by Hogarth, an Egyptian sarcophagus, and Christopher Wren's watch, but Soane collected just about everything and his house is literally packed with architectural drawings, classical sculpture, casts of famous artwork, Chinese tiles, antique clocks and furniture, stained glass, and on and on and on. Wandering around these cramped halls and packed rooms has been a favorite activity of Londoners for years. It's not surprising—there's plenty to see here, the building, also designed by Soane, is elegant, and the sheer volume and quality of his collection is overwhelming.

Chelsea, Kensington, and Knightsbridge Map 6

It is not surprising that England's most famous department store, Harrods, has had its home here, one of the richest areas of London, for more than a century. Royalty used to live here too, at the elegant Kensington Palace on the west end of the beautiful Kensington Gardens. The contrast between the busy shopping districts and the serene parks make this area a place that everyone can enjoy.

HYDE PARK AND SPEAKERS' CORNER

Btwn. Park Ln. and Knightsbridge W2, 020/7298-2100, www.royalparks.gov.uk

HOURS: Daily 5 A.M.-midnight

COST: Free admission

TUBE: Hyde Park

Covering 350 acres, Hyde Park is one of the larger royal parks and one of the most popular. Made famous by its Speakers' Corner, where anyone can get on a soapbox and pontificate on his or her subject of choice, this park always has something going on. During the reign of Henry VIII (1509–1547), this was a deer park, where the beefy king and his retinue would stalk wild game (or have the peasants flush them out of the underbrush so they could slaughter them wholesale). The park provided a refuge for those fleeing the plague of 1665. People rightly saw that the crowded, filthy streets of London were unhealthy, but one wonders how camping out with a few thousand other people would have been much better. In the happier days of the 1730s, Queen Caroline, wife of George II, built the Serpentine, a long artificial lake taking up the center of the park and dividing it from Kensington Gardens. The most recent addition is the Diana Memorial Fountain, opened in 2004. While it is one of the city's more popular attractions, it is difficult to see why. The oval concrete moat of dubious symbolic value is often clogged up and drained, making it a bit of a disappointment. Lady Di fans will want to see it, but it is of limited interest to anyone else.

Today Hyde Park offers a wide range of diversions. At the northeast corner stands Speaker's Corner, where there's always some sort of debate going on. Feel free to jump in, but be warned that the British are old hands at this and you might get verbally skewered. The rest of the park is devoted to picnicking, sports, or simply walking. Several cafés and restaurants can be found on the shores of the Serpentine, and a walk around the lake makes for a refreshing change from the museums and galleries. If you don't want a change, go to the Serpentine Gallery for some art courtesy of the late Lady Di. This is the park that will get you the farthest away from the blare of traffic.

KENSINGTON GARDENS

Btwn. the Broad Walk and Hyde Park W8, 020/7298-2141, www.royalparks.gov.uk
HOURS: Daily 6 A.M.-dusk
COST: Free admission
TUBE: High Street Kensington or Queensway

This lush, quiet park is a pleasing contrast to the more open and active Hyde Park just to the east. The Italian garden and wealth of trees make a fine setting for Kensington Palace.

The gardens acquired their present configuration in 1728 under Queen Caroline, wife of George II. For many years the park was closed to the public, and then it opened for the "respectably dressed" before becoming a true public park. Queen Victoria added the Italian Gardens, a brilliant display of greenery and flowers, and the elegant Albert Memorial in honor of her husband. This monument is a triumph of the Victorian neo-Gothic style and features detailed carvings reflecting Albert's interests. It is adorned with marble figures representing the various continents (the British had colonies in all of them at the time) and various trades such as engineering and commerce. Farther up are gilded angels, while at the base crowd figures of famous artists. Children will like the Diana, Princess of Wales Memorial Playground, open 10 A.M.–dusk, with its statue of Peter Pan and various imaginative play areas, including tepees and a big pirate ship. A café on-site will allow you to relax while keeping an eye on the kids.

KENSINGTON PALACE

West End of Kensington Gardens W8, 087/0751-5170, www.hrp.org.uk
HOURS: Daily 10 A.M.-6 P.M. Mar.-Oct.,

busy Knightsbridge

10 A.M.-5 P.M. Nov.-Feb. (last admission one hour before closing)
COST: Adults £11.50, seniors and students £9, children 5-15 £7.50, under 5 free, family £34
TUBE: Notting Hill Gate, High Street Kensington, or Queensway

Built around 1605, this was once a country estate until William III bought it in 1689. The king had celebrated architect Christopher Wren turn it into a royal palace. Queen Anne and George I both expanded the palace, but it stopped being used as a residence for the reigning monarch after George II's death in 1760. It was still used by the royal family, however, being the birthplace of Queen Victoria and home to the late Princess Diana. Kensington Gardens was Lady Di's favorite green area, and she could look out her east window, past the statue of Queen Victoria, and see the grass and trees.

An audio tour of the palace is included in the price of admission, and it takes about 1.5 hours. The Victorian Rooms preserve the look of the late 19th century, and a very regal and stuffy look it is, with its patterned upholstery, patterned wallpaper, patterned carpeting, and patterned tablecloths. The king's apartments are truly regal, with chandeliers and ornate carvings everywhere. The Queen's apartments are a bit more sedate and actually more attractive for their refined simplicity. The Royal Ceremonial Dress Collection shows the elaborate attire used in the court from the 18th century to the present day. If you would like to get a bite to eat, no place is nicer in fine weather than the Orangery, built in 1705 and a favorite spot for Queen Anne. The peaceful setting near the Sunken Gardens, also worth a look, comes alive with flowers and trees in the summertime.

NATURAL HISTORY MUSEUM

Cromwell Rd. btwn. Exhibition Rd. and Queen's Gate SW7, 020/7942-5000, www.nhm.ac.uk

HOURS: Mon.-Sat. 10 A.M.-5:50 P.M., Sun. 11 A.M.-5:50 P.M.

COST: Free admission

TUBE: South Kensington

A favorite with kids because of its dinosaur bones and animatronic *T-rex,* this museum has displays on all types of life, both extinct and living. The many interactive exhibits make a visit both educational and fun. This is also the most beautifully housed museum in London. The Victorian-era building is like a Gothic cathedral with biological and botanical motifs instead of saints. The carvings on the columns and the pictures on the stained-glass windows take their inspiration from living forms. Gilded ceiling panels are frames for beautiful paintings of plants. The whole effect is a bit strange but it definitely is memorable and attractive in a unique way.

Once you stop craning your neck to take it all in, check out the section on the human body, which is especially interesting, and don't miss case 9 in gallery 12 of the Fishes section to see some weird deep-sea species that look as if they come from an H. P. Lovecraft story. Kids will also love the giant blue whale in the Massive Mammals section and the various varmints in the Creepy Crawlies room. The display of what can live in the average kitchen is enough to make you give up eating altogether. The Earth Galleries explain the evolution and structure of the world and an earthquake experience takes you inside a Japanese supermarket during the Kobe earthquake. Earth's Treasury is a glittering display of gems. Seeing it all can take the better part of a day, but even a brief visit will show you some of the amazing variety of living forms on the planet.

SCIENCE MUSEUM

Exhibition Rd. btwn. Imperial College Rd. and Cromwell Rd. SW7, 087/0870-4868, www.sciencemuseum.org.uk

HOURS: Mon.-Sun 10 A.M.-6 P.M.

COST: Free admission

TUBE: South Kensington

Right next to the Natural History Museum, this makes a great duo for a day out with your kids. Plenty of interactive displays and videos will keep active minds and hands occupied. Much space is devoted to the development of different branches of science and engineering. For example, you can see the evolution of rocketry from a crude weapon in Napoleonic times up to the space shuttle. Don't miss the Making the Modern World exhibit on the ground floor, which showcases the inventions that made technological civilization what it is. The first floor devotes itself to agricultural and telecommunications displays, while the second floor is devoted to the sea, with lots of ship models. Old planes fill a third-floor gallery, and on the same floor is a recording studio where older children can produce their own radio programs. The medical history section on the fourth floor is a bit creepy. If you think going to the doctor is bad nowadays, here you can see what it was like 50–100 years ago and be grateful. The fifth-floor gallery offers the Science and Art of Medicine.

VICTORIA AND ALBERT MUSEUM

Cromwell Rd. at Exhibition Rd. SW7 020/7942-2000, www.vam.ac.uk

HOURS: Mon.-Sun. 10 A.M.-5:45 P.M., open to 10 P.M. on Wednesdays

COST: Free admission

TUBE: South Kensington

This museum dedicates itself to art and design and while you'll find artifacts going back 3,000 years, the focus isn't on their historical importance but their artistic value and how they were made. The most arresting displays, and the centerpiece of the museum itself, are the cast galleries. Plaster casts of famous statues and monuments, painted to look like the real thing, create a forest of the world's art. While staring up at the magnificent detail of Trajan's Column, which shows the Roman emperor's military feats, be careful not to trip over the art students who come here to draw. Other galleries are organized by medium, such as glass or photography, or origin, such as England or Asia. The British galleries take you through four centuries of British design, with pieces such as the Great Bed of Ware, an imposing four-poster from 1590. The Asian collection displays ancient Japanese bronzes and shimmering kimonos, as well as Chinese Buddhas.

Maida Vale, Marylebone, and St. John's Wood — Map 8

The tree-lined streets and stately homes of this area have sheltered some of London's wealthier residents. Sir Arthur Conan Doyle put his most famous character, Sherlock Holmes, in a house on Baker Street so that his 19th-century readers would know the detective was a respectable gentleman. Other well-heeled (and more real) residents collected vast stores of artwork, such as the Wallace Collection, or created their own, such as the fascinating waxworks at Madame Tussauds.

MADAME TUSSAUDS AND THE PLANETARIUM

Marylebone Rd. btwn. Baker St. and York Gate NW1, 087/0999-0046, www.madame-tussauds.co.uk

HOURS: Mon.-Fri. 9:30 A.M.-5:30 P.M., Sat.-Sun. 9 A.M.-6 P.M.

COST: Adults £22.99, seniors £19.99, children £18.99, under 5 free, family £70

TUBE: Baker Street

Madame Tussaud learned the craft of making wax likenesses from a French doctor, Philippe Curtius, and got a lot of practice during the French Revolution, when she made the death masks of people executed by the guillotine. In 1802 she brought a collection of waxwork figures on a tour of England. She wasn't the only one to do this, as waxwork shows were a popular amusement at the time, but hers were the best. Today Madame Tussauds continues the tradition with an entire population of famous and infamous figures.

The likenesses are simply amazing. Walking through here is definitely one of the stranger experiences you will have in London. Photography is encouraged, although the no-touch rule is strictly enforced, and you can go home with tons of photos of you standing next to the Queen or Tom Cruise.

Some rooms offer you the chance to get onstage for a karaokelike experience and belt out a tune with your favorite star. Others hold interactive games that feel startlingly real. The Spirit of London ride takes you through 400 years of London's history, showing everything from Shakespeare hard at work to the punk scene of the 1970s.

Then, of course, the Chamber of Horrors shows a lovely array of some of England's most famous murderers enjoying their favorite hobby. In Chamber Live, the killers are real (but not real killers). Blood-soaked actors leap out at you from all sides. It's tons of fun if you're into that sort of thing. Chamber Live is not suitable for under-12s, pregnant women, or those with heart conditions, even if they are into that sort of thing.

The state-of-the-art color digital planetarium shows programs about the stars, galaxies, and planets. The crystal-clear projection makes the shows quite entertaining; they're fairly educational, too. Unfortunately, these shows seem to be on the way out in favor of less educational, and less interesting, projected movies.

Many people find Madame Tussauds overpriced. The artistry of the wax figures is beyond doubt, and the gorefest of Chamber Live is full of meaty treats for horror fans, but there are so many interesting free attractions in London that it's kind of hard to justify the expense.

Still, this is one of London's most popular attractions. Lines can be long, so you might want to book through the website. Tickets are discounted after 5 P.M., but you won't have time to see even half of it. Individual tickets are £2 less if you skip Chamber Live. Children under 16 must be accompanied by an adult.

© SEAN MCLACHLAN

The Sherlock Holmes Museum offers a mix of kitsch and literary history.

SHERLOCK HOLMES MUSEUM

221B Baker St. NW1, 020/7935-8866, www.sherlock-holmes.co.uk

HOURS: Daily 9:30 A.M.–6 P.M.

COST: Adults £6, children under 16 £4

TUBE: Baker Street

Many houses of London's famous residents have been turned into museums, but this is the only one for a resident who never existed. While the whole thing is a bit hokey, the curators have done an excellent job of recreating a Victorian gentleman's home. For reasons not entirely clear, Sir Arthur Conan Doyle picked this address for his now famous sleuth, who reportedly lived there 1881–1904. The interior is made up exactly as it is in the stories, so any Holmes fan will have lots of fun picking out the details. Its broader interest lies in that it gives a very good idea of how a well-to-do bachelor lived in those days. The gift shop sells some interesting mementoes.

WALLACE COLLECTION

Hertford House, Manchester Sq. W1, 020/7563-9500, www.wallacecollection.org

HOURS: Daily 10 A.M.–5 P.M.

COST: Free admission

TUBE: Bond Street or Baker Street

The elegant Georgian mansion of Hertford House was finished in 1778 and is one of the more impressive stately homes in London, but what's inside makes this a must-see. The Wallace Collection, gathered by the various marquises of Hertford and Lady Wallace (1818–1890), is one of the best of its kind in the world. Part of the bequest stipulated that the collection couldn't be changed or added to, so it provides a unique look at would interest a rich patron of the arts in the 19th century. The collection includes 775 paintings, mainly from 17th- and 18th-century France and including works by Fragonard and Poussin. Dutch painters are well represented too, with works from Rubens, Van Dyck, and Teniers, to name a few. The famous painting *The Swing* by Fragonard is here, as are Rembrandt's portrait of his son Titus and Venetian scenes by Canaletto. The family also liked to collect gaudy imperial glass, arms and armor, stoneware, porcelain figurines, and much more. The arms and armor collection is the biggest in London (even more so than the Tower of

London's) and second only to the Royal Armoury in Leeds in the nation. The collection of pre-Revolutionary French art is especially good and includes lots of colorful Sevre porcelain (the commodes are a gaudy pink and encrusted with coral) and pieces of furniture once owned by Marie Antoinette and Madame de Pompadour. Quite a lot goes on here, including free classes, family activities, talks, and several major shows a year.

Free and very informative tours start every weekday at 1 P.M., Wednesdays and Saturdays at 11:30 A.M., and Sundays at 3 P.M. The Café Bagatelle in the courtyard is very popular and is open daily 10 A.M.–4:30 P.M., but reservations are required for lunch; call 020/7563-9505.

The City — Map 10

When Londoners talk about "The City" they don't mean London, but rather the area that back in Roman times was encircled by a stout city wall. Even as London blossomed into a major metropolis, this old district, dubbed the "Square Mile," remained a center for commerce, power, and worship, as is evident by its wealth of historic buildings and churches. All the sights are within easy walking distance of each other, but there are so many of them you'll want to work your way systematically through them from one side of The City to the other.

BARBICAN

Silk St. at Whitecross St. EC2, switchboard 020/7638-4141, box office 020/7638-8891, www.barbican.org.uk

HOURS: Mon.-Sat. 9 A.M.-11 P.M., Sun. noon-11 P.M.

COST: Admission varies

TUBE: Barbican or Moorgate

This giant arts center hosts just about every kind of performance, including theater, art, dance, music, and film. The London and BBC symphony orchestras both have their home here, and the Royal Shakespeare Company performs regularly. The acoustics in Barbican Hall are excellent, adding a memorable warmth and depth to classical music. A gallery features daring contemporary and international art and hosts several shows a year. Two cinemas show leading international films and lesser-known gems. The Barbican Gallery is famous for its photographic exhibitions but also shows other media. The center houses various restaurants, cafés, and shops, so you can easily spend an entire day here, and it also offers a wealth of educational programs. Check the website to see what's on at this constantly active venue. The layout is a bit confusing and other visitors are often as confused as you will be, so come early to make sure you find where you need to go.

Outside are a small artificial lake and seating area, popular with the brown-bag lunch crowd. Go along the elevated pathway called Wallside and you can see part of the medieval postern gate, built atop the old Roman gate. In springtime yellow, white, and red wildflowers sprout from its crumbling turret.

DR. JOHNSON'S HOUSE

17 Gough Sq. EC4, 020/7353-3745, www.drjohnsonshouse.org

HOURS: Mon.-Sat. 11 A.M.-5:30 P.M. May-Sept., 11 A.M.-5 P.M. Oct.-Apr.

COST: Adults £4.50, seniors and students £3.50, children £1.50, family £10

TUBE: Blackfriars

The interior of this meticulously restored house, dating to 1700 and once home to the compiler of the first dictionary of English, gives a good idea of what it was like to be a respectable gentleman in the 18th century. Actually, Johnson was an arrogant boozer who chased any female who passed his way, so he wasn't actually *respectable,* but he was respected. He became the subject of James Boswell's *Life of Johnson,* a pioneering work of biography and a great read if you want to get into the spirit of the age. Reading Boswell's vivid descriptions of the chaos of this house, with its many assistants compiling

Dr. Johnson's cat, Hodge, has a statue near his master's home.

the dictionary and the numerous hangers-on, will make a visit to the museum feel like coming home to a fun but dysfunctional family. In the square in front is a statue to Johnson's cat, and around the corner is Ye Olde Cheshire Cheese, one of his favorite pubs.

GEFFRYE MUSEUM

Kingsland Rd. E2, 020/7739-9893,
www.geffrye-museum.org.uk
HOURS: Tues.-Sat. 10 A.M.-5 P.M., Sun. noon-5 P.M.
COST: Free admission
TUBE: Old Street

Many visitors to London miss this museum, set in a beautiful 18th-century collection of almshouses, but that's a shame because it really gives an insight into how middle-class people lived in various periods of London's history. Rooms include spare 17th-century living quarters, becoming more refined as London got richer in the Georgian period, to downright ostentatious (and a bit tacky) in the Victorian period. The 1930s and a contemporary flat are also on display. A period garden, restaurant, and shop are on-site. The restaurant serves contemporary English cuisine with an emphasis on vegetarian dishes. The organic beers are tasty; it also serves English wines.

One of the almhouses, with an interesting herb garden, is open the first Saturday of the month and the first and third Wednesdays of the month. Timed entry is at 11 A.M., noon, 2 P.M., and 3 P.M. Admission for adults is £2, children under 16 are free.

GUILDHALL

Guildhall Yard at Gresham St. EC2, 020/7606-3030,
www.corpoflondon.gov.uk
HOURS: Daily 10 A.M.-5 P.M. May-Sept., Mon.-Sat. 10 A.M.-5 P.M. Oct.-Apr.
COST: Free admission
TUBE: Bank

Standing in the center of the historic Square Mile, the oldest part of London, the Guildhall is home to the city's administration. The building was started in 1411 and is important architecturally in that it is the only secular stone building from before the Great Fire of 1666. An earlier Guildhall probably stood here at least as early as the 12th century. Inside, the Great Hall is where members of the livery guild elect the lord mayor and two sheriffs. The hall is decorated with the emblems of the city's livery companies, a stained-glass window showing the history of London, statues of the giants Gog and Magog, and monuments to important people such as Churchill, Nelson, and Wellington. Below the great hall is a crypt with 19 stained-glass windows showing the coats of arms of the livery companies, but you have to call ahead to book a free tour.

GUILDHALL ART GALLERY

Guildhall Yard at Gresham St. EC2, 020/7332-3700,
www.guildhall-art-gallery.org.uk
HOURS: Mon.-Sat. 10 A.M.-5 P.M., Sun. noon-4 P.M. (last admission 30 minutes before closing)
COST: Adults £2.50, seniors and students £1, children under 16 free; admission is free Fridays and all other days after 3:30 P.M.
TUBE: Bank

Most visitors come to the Guildhall to see the

The Guildhall, built atop a Roman amphitheatre, houses offices for the City of London.

gallery's collection of more than 4,000 paintings amassed over four centuries. The emphasis here is on the glories of the British Empire, with lots of royal portraits and giant scenes of naval battles. John Singleton Copley's *Defeat of the Floating Batteries at Gibraltar, September 1782* (1791) is one of the most impressive of the battle scenes, showing the redcoats taking the important Straits of Gibraltar, which they still control. Many Victorian-era works are on display, such as the allegorical works of Sir John Everitt Millais. *The Woodsman's Daughter* (1851), which seems to extol the virtues and innocence of rural life, is actually based on a cautionary tale about the son of a nobleman who seduced a peasant girl. A number of scenes show early London, such as the beautiful oil painting *The Opening of Tower Bridge* (1895) by William Lionel Wyllie, showing the festive crowds and regattas at the famous tower's grand opening.

While the Guildhall is a medieval building, the area was a meeting place even in Roman times. The remains of an amphitheater, used for all kinds of public functions, were discovered in the Guildhall Yard. A blue arc of tiles in the plaza marks the spot where it once lay, and it is now open as part of the exhibit in the Guildhall Art Gallery. A passage leads you below the yard, where the original ruins and interactive exhibits give you a feel for life in London's earliest period.

MUSEUM OF LONDON

150 London Wall EC2, 020/7600-0807,
www.museumoflondon.org.uk

HOURS: Mon.-Sat. 10 A.M.-5:50 P.M., Sun. noon-5:50 P.M.

COST: Free admission

TUBE: Barbican

Spanning the city's entire history from the first prehistoric inhabitants to the present day, this extensive museum deserves a long visit. Each period has re-created interiors, such as a cramped Roman living room with an uncomfortable-looking toilet and an entire street of Victorian shops. The Medieval Gallery, renovated in 2005, chronicles the bad old days of plague, war, and feudalism in fascinating detail. While the statues, coins, and period garb may be what you expected, you don't often get a chance to see a set of medieval loaded dice. One wonders if the owner died of the plague or by one of the swords hanging nearby. Hands-on displays and computer screens with photos and films make this especially kid friendly. Temporary exhibitions tend to focus on relatively new groups of Londoners, such as the Caribbean and South Asian communities.

The neighborhood is historical too. Right next to the museum is a 13th-century tower and wall built on Roman foundations. If you want to understand how London grew and developed as a city, don't miss this museum.

ST. BRIDE'S

Fleet St. EC4, 020/7427-0133, www.stbrides.com

HOURS: Mon.-Fri. 8 A.M.-6 P.M., Sat. 11 A.M.-3 P.M., Sun. 10 A.M.-1 P.M. and 5-7:30 P.M.

COST: Free admission

TUBE: Blackfriars

This church by Christopher Wren is believed to sit on the site of a Celtic Christian community, perhaps one of the earliest in the British Isles. In the Roman period there was a building with a decorated floor, still visible in the crypt, followed in the 6th century by a Saxon church that was gradually expanded before burning along with 87 other parish churches in the Great Fire of 1666. Christopher Wren largely followed the outlines of the original building. His steeple, famous for the layered design that inspired the wedding cake, was extensively remodeled by the Luftwaffe during the Blitz, but more careful artisans meticulously rebuilt it after the war. St. Bride's was a popular church for journalists working along Fleet Street during its heyday as a center for publishing. Wynkyn de Worde, an assistant of William Caxton, the first printer in England, set up a press here around 1500 to produce schoolbooks and cheap editions of popular works. The area became a center for printers and bookbinders and eventually the famous Fleet Street newspapers. Today it honors this history with an altar dedicated to the memory of reporters who have died in the line of duty. While the public is, to some extent justifiably, cynical about the media, it is good to remember that the nightly news is gathered by regular men and women who go into the worst areas of the world to get the story. During your visit make sure to visit the crypts, where you will get to see not only the Saxon foundations but an interesting exhibit of the development of both the church and the Fleet Street community.

© SEAN MCLACHLAN

The steeple of St. Bride's reputedly inspired the first layered wedding cake.

ST. PAUL'S CATHEDRAL

St. Paul's Churchyard EC4, 020/7246-8348 or 020/7246-8357, www.stpauls.co.uk

HOURS: Mon.-Sat. 8:30-5 P.M. (last admission at 4 P.M.), open Sun. for worship only

COST: Adults £9, seniors and students £8, children 7-16 £3.50, family £21

TUBE: St. Paul's

St. Paul's is one of the landmarks of London and should be on every itinerary. A church has stood here since A.D. 604, a time when much of England was still pagan, and this spot has remained the spiritual center for Londoners ever since. The church was rebuilt several times after being destroyed by fire, the most recent being the Great Fire of 1666.

Christopher Wren, the leading English architect of his day, was commissioned to rebuild it and the present building, finished in 1710, is his masterpiece. St. Paul's quickly became an icon of London, as recognizable to the English as Big Ben and the site of many important events, such as Queen Victoria's Diamond Jubilee and the funerals of Admiral Horatio Nelson, the Duke of Wellington, and Sir Winston Churchill. Martin Luther King Jr. spoke here on his way to collect the Nobel Peace Prize. In 1981, millions watched on television as Charles, Prince of Wales, and Lady Diana Spencer got married here. A solemn ceremony was held here after September 11, 2001, in memory of all those who died in the terrorist attacks, including 67 people from the United Kingdom.

The cathedral is finishing restoration work to remove centuries of accumulated pollution and now stands in its full glory. A complete visit of the cathedral takes at least two hours, preferably three. It's best to make a complete circuit of the nave and various side chapels and then descend to the crypt, where you can rest at the café and browse the gift shop before making your way up a winding staircase 530 steps to the Golden Gallery atop the dome for a magnificent view of London.

© SEAN MCLACHLAN

The Millennium Bridge links the Tate Modern on the South Bank and St. Paul's on the North.

The crypt is the resting place of many memorable people, such as William Blake, John Constable, and, of course, Christopher Wren. In his later years he used to sit in St. Paul's and silently admire his masterpiece. The grave is marked only by a simple plaque, which reads in Latin, "Beneath lies buried the founder of this church and city, Christopher Wren, who lived more than 90 years, not for himself but for the public good. Reader, if you seek his monument, look around you."

Guided tours run four times a day and last 1.5–2 hours. Tours start at 11 A.M., 11:30 A.M., 1:30 P.M., and 2 P.M. and cost £3 for adults, £2.50 for seniors and students, and £1 for children under 16. Space is limited, so arrive early. An audio tour lasting 45 minutes is also available, but the guided tour is much more informative.

The grounds have a nice floral display in summer and are fenced by a very early example of cast-iron work, dating to 1714. Look for the statue of John Wesley (1703–1791), founder of Methodism, in the northern part of the churchyard.

While there is an entry fee to see the church, services are free, as is a free choral evensong Monday–Saturday at 5 P.M. and Sunday at 3:15 P.M. The acoustics in this building are simply wonderful, and respectfully behaved people of all faiths are welcome.

TEMPLE CHURCH

Fleet St. At Middle Temple Ln. EC4, 020/7353-3470

HOURS: Daily (hours vary)

COST: Free admission

TUBE: St. Paul's

Temple Church is one of the oldest churches in London and certainly one of the most fascinating. The round section was built in the 12th century by the Knights Templar in imitation of

© SEAN MCLACHLAN

Templar knights are buried in the beautiful and mysterious Temple Church.

the Church of the Holy Sepulchre in Jerusalem, which is built upon the traditional site of the tomb of Jesus. The Templars were a military religious order dedicated to protecting pilgrims journeying to the Holy Land, and they also became powerful bankers. Tradition had it that coming to this church was as holy an act as going to Jerusalem itself. The long choir was built in the 13th century by Henry III, who intended it to be his mausoleum, but he ended up being interred in Westminster Abbey instead. Like so many churches, it was bombed during World War II. The lead roof caught fire and melted down the stone columns to congeal on the floor among the colored shards of the shattered stained-glass windows.

Luckily the main fabric of the church survived and it has been lovingly restored. Especially notable are the eight stone effigies of Knights Templar on the floor of the round section and the graceful columns and Gothic arches of the choir. Contrary to popular belief, the crossed legs on some effigies do not mean that particular knight went on the Crusades; it's merely a stylistic embellishment. Also check out the gargoyles on the walls of the round section, all different from the others and all rather weird or sinister. In the plaza outside stands a column with a statue of the Templars' emblem, two knights sharing a steed in illustration of their vow of poverty. Individual Templars had only the money and property needed to complete their mission, but the organization itself became vastly wealthy by becoming the major banking concern in Western Europe. It was not to last, however, as the Arabs recaptured Jerusalem and the rest of the Holy Land and the Templars lost their reason for being. But many powerful people still owed them money, and in 1307 King Philip IV of France got the pope to abolish the order. Their assets were seized, in the case of England by the King himself, and some were executed. The temple and the area around it were eventually granted to London's lawyers, and barristers use the surrounding buildings and parks to this day. Their emblems are visible on the exquisite stained-glass windows, a Pegasus for the Inner Temple and a lamb and flag for the Middle Temple.

TOWER BRIDGE

Tower Bridge SE1, 020/7403-3761, www.towerbridge.org.uk

HOURS: Daily 10 A.M.–6:30 P.M. Apr.–Sept., daily 9:30 A.M.–6 P.M. Oct.–Mar. (last admission one hour before closing)

COST: Museum adults £5.50, seniors and students £4.25, children 5–15 £3, children under 5 free

TUBE: Tower Hill

A landmark on the river since 1894, Tower Bridge reflects the architecture of the nearby Tower of London. While the Cornish granite and Portland stone facing makes it look like something out of the Middle Ages, the structure of the bridge is actually of steel, which was just then being used with confidence as a building material. The two towers of Tower Bridge are connected by a glassed walkway providing wonderful views of the Thames and the city. The towers house a museum and the Victorian Engine Rooms, where you can see the massive steam engines that once raised and lowered the bridge, allowing sailing ships to pass underneath. Now they are operated by more modern

© SEAN MCLACHLAN

London's Tower Bridge was built to resemble the Tower of London near its north end.

engines, and it's quite fun to watch them raise and lower. The Tower Bridge website lists the schedule, which varies according to river traffic, but it occurs about 900 times a year. It wasn't so fun for the driver and passengers of a bus in 1952, when the bridge started rising while the bus was going across. The driver, realizing he couldn't stop in time, put the pedal to the metal and jumped the gap! He was honored for his heroism and asked never to do it again.

Many visitors confuse this with London Bridge. Actually, London Bridge is the lackluster concrete construction just to the west of Tower Bridge. The original London Bridge, which was much nicer, was disassembled and moved to Lake Havasu, Arizona.

If you buy a ticket for the museum, you can also get a discount ticket for the nearby Monument, set up in memory of the Great Fire of London just at the north end of the bridge.

TOWER OF LONDON

Tower Hill EC3, 087/0756-6060, booking 087/0756-7070, www.tower-of-london.org.uk

HOURS: Tues.-Sat. 9 A.M.-5 P.M., Sun.-Mon. 10 A.M.-5 P.M. Nov.-Feb.; Tues.-Sat. 9 A.M.-6 P.M., Sun.-Mon. 10 A.M.-6 P.M. Mar.-Oct. (last admission one hour before closing)

COST: Adults £15, seniors and students £12, children £9.50, children under 5 free, family £43.

TUBE: Tower Hill

This World Heritage Site is steeped in history, alive with pageantry, and home to the dazzling Crown Jewels. Reserve at least three hours for your visit as you will want to take your time with what will be one of the most memorable sights during your stay.

When William the Conqueror (reigned 1066–1087) took over England in 1066, he realized London was the key to the kingdom and built a castle to control it. By the late 1070s the famous White Tower was completed. The Tower, 90 feet high, went through several modifications but is still a fine example of Norman architecture. The Tower complex expanded steadily, especially in the 11th–13th centuries, with more walls and towers added as needed.

Being the most secure spot in medieval London, it was an obvious place to keep the Crown Jewels. When Charles I (reigned 1625–1649) was executed at the end of the English Civil

War, most of them were sold. Only the Coronation Spoon and Swords of Temporal Justice, Spiritual Justice, and Mercy remain. When Charles II (reigned 1660–1685) came to the throne and restored the monarchy, new Crown Jewels were made. Some of the high points of the collection include the jewel-bedecked St. Edward's Crown and the quarter-ton, gold-plated Wine Cistern. The Tower's use as a fort is reflected in the Armoury, containing a rather intimidating arsenal of medieval weapons. The swords, crossbows, and cumbersome cannons tell of a brutal age.

Don't miss Traitor's Gate, a gated waterway into the Tower used for political prisoners. Three towers, Wakefield Tower, Lanthorn Tower, and St. Thomas's Tower, were a royal residence and are now called the Medieval Palace. Their reconstructed interiors give a taste of the life of early kings and queens.

Prisoners were mostly kept in Bloody Tower and Beauchamp Tower. The upper chamber of Beauchamp Tower is especially interesting for its many well-preserved inscriptions scrawled on the walls. Despite the crowds of tourists and incessant drone of modern conversation, seeing these desperate messages still gives the visitor an eerie sense of the loneliness and despair the prisoners must have felt.

Some high-ranking inmates recieved more comfortable quarters, but they didn't enjoy them for long. Royal Chancellor Sir Thomas More and Bishop Fisher of Rochester were imprisoned here and executed in 1535 for refusing to acknowledge Henry VIII's divorce and his self-proclaimed role as head of the English Church. Henry's second wife, Anne Boleyn, was executed shortly thereafter followed by another unfortunate Queen, Catherine Howard. Edward Seymour, Protector Somerset and builder of the famous Somerset House was executed in 1552 on a false charge of treason. The following year, Lady Jane Grey tried to take the throne upon the death of Edward VI, but Mary deposed her after only nine days. She was beheaded in 1554.

The Tower is home to the Yeomen Warders, popularly known as Beefeaters. These colorfully clad fellows are responsible for

The Tower of London, built by William the Conqueror, imprisoned both criminals and royalty.

© VISITLONDON.COM

Beefeaters' uniforms were designed centuries ago.

guarding the Tower. Just as famous are the Tower ravens. According to legend, if the ravens ever leave the Tower, the kingdom will perish. The ravens have their wings clipped so as to avoid this possible catastrophe. They're pretty tough, so don't approach or try to feed them.

The best way to learn about the Tower and its traditions is to take a free, one-hour Yeoman Warder tour. The guard will tell you about famous moments in the Tower's history and can answer all your questions. Tours start every half hour throughout the day. Check out the Tower website for more information on several other exhibits inside the Tower, and don't forget to leave lots of time for your visit!

CEREMONY OF THE KEYS

Tower of London, Tower Hill EC3, 087/0756-6060, www.tower-of-london.org.uk

HOURS: Daily 9:30 P.M.

COST: Free admission; Reservations required

TUBE: Tower Hill

For a special treat, try to see the Beefeaters and military guards perform the Ceremony of the Keys at the Tower of London, during which the outer gate is locked and the keys delivered to the resident governor of the Tower. This ceremony has been held every night for more than 700 years and is quite interesting for its traditional fanfare, and it has the added bonus of being free. You must apply for tickets, in writing, at least two months in advance by writing to The Ceremony of the Keys, HM Tower of London, London, EC3N 4AB. Send a self-addressed envelope and two international reply coupons; if you are in the U.K., send a self addressed stamped envelope. If you get a ticket, you will be escorted into the Tower at 9:30 P.M. Don't be late, or you won't get in.

South of the Thames — Map 12

Although the South Bank of the Thames has been connected to the North Bank since Roman times, it has until quite recently been considered a different city, a home of the poor and unsavory that few "real" Londoners would care to visit. English theater was born here, next to the bearbaiting and boxing rings. All these diversions were considered low class, and the few Londoners who decided to slum it on the South Bank carried swords and traveled in groups. Today that's all changed. A whole series of bridges cross the river, linking the two halves of London to each other as never before. Visitors will find a range of attractions that will keep them coming back, and you don't even need to carry a sword any more. Most sights are close to the river, so a walk along the water will give you a chance to see them.

BRITISH AIRWAYS LONDON EYE (MILLENNIUM WHEEL)

Jubilee Gardens btwn. Westminster Bridge and Waterloo Bridge Rds. SE1, 087/0990-8883, booking 087/0500-0600, www.londoneye.com

HOURS: Daily 10 A.M.–8 P.M. Oct.–May, 10 A.M.–9 P.M. June–Sept.
COST: Adults £13, seniors £10 (adult price on weekends and July–Aug.), children £6.50
TUBE: Waterloo

In celebration of the approaching millennium, Prime Minister Tony Blair commissioned a series of grandiose building projects, including the Millennium Dome, Millennium Bridge, and the Millennium Wheel, also known as the London Eye. It is the world's largest observation wheel, basically a glorified Ferris wheel in which the seats have been replaced by roomy observation pods that take you on a "flight" 135 meters (433 feet) up to provide unmatched views of London. It's all quite photogenic and on a clear day you can see the city laid out below you in fantastic detail.

The only downside to the London Eye is the price. If your budget is limited, you can get views almost as good from the top of St. Paul's for less, plus you get to see the cathedral in the bargain.

the London Eye, also known as the Millennium Wheel

Tickets are available in the nearby County Hall or by booking a particular flight time online to beat the lines. Many tour packages also include a prebooked time. Getting a prebooked ticket for a set time before you arrive is a very good idea, especially in high season, as the lines can be dreadfully long.

COUNTY HALL GALLERY

County Hall SE1, 087/0744-7485, www.countyhallgallery.com and www.daliuniverse.com
HOURS: Daily 10 A.M.–5:30 P.M.
COST: Dali Universe adults £11, seniors and students £9.50, children 8–16 £6.50, children 4–7 £5, children 3 and under free, family £28
TUBE: Westminster or Waterloo

This is an often-missed gallery that nevertheless displays some big names, including an extensive Dali collection and works by Picasso and Chagall. The temporary exhibits are also major affairs with extensive collections of famous artists. The location is nice too, in a historic county hall overlooking the Thames, Parliament, and Big Ben. The Dali Universe is a permanent exhibit and a must-see for fans of the eccentric Spanish genius. Works include the famous Mae West Lips Sofa and the *Profile of Time* sculpture. A couple of his crazy bronze sculptures stand outside, their odd dark shapes making a jarring contrast with the white symmetry of the London Eye right next door. The bookshop has a good collection of surrealist literature and art books by Dali. Tickets in the off peak season (October–April) are slightly cheaper, and a combined ticket for the Dali Universe and the current exhibition is slightly higher.

THE *GOLDEN HINDE*

Pickford Wharf, Clink St. SE1, 087/0011-8700, www.goldenhinde.co.uk
HOURS: Vary
COST: Adults £4.50, children £3.50, seniors and students £4, family £15
TUBE: London Bridge

The *Golden Hinde* is a full-scale replica of Sir Francis Drake's galleon that sailed around the globe in 1577–1580. More than a simple museum, the boat is fully seaworthy and has

© SEAN MCLACHLAN

the *Golden Hinde,* a recreation of Sir Francis Drake's ship

circumnavigated the globe just like its predecessor. An informative guided tour is free with admission but you must book it via the website or by phone. Kids especially love the various living-history events that take place throughout the year and the overnight stays, when they get to dress up as Elizabethan-era sailors and go on a pretend voyage.

HMS *BELFAST*

Morgan's Lane, Tooley St. SE1, 020/7940-6300, http://hmsbelfast.iwm.org.uk

HOURS: Daily 10 A.M.-6 P.M. Mar.-Oct. (last admission 5:15 P.M.), 10 A.M.-5 P.M. (last admission 4:15 P.M.) Nov.-Feb.

COST: Adults £8, seniors and students £5, under 16 free.

TUBE: London Bridge

An old World War II cruiser that also saw action in Korea, the HMS *Belfast* is now moored near London Bridge and is open as a museum. Clambering up and down decks and into turrets and engine rooms is lots of fun, and the video displays and signs tell you all about the history of the ship and life on board. If you go in the winter, visit in the afternoon and catch the sunset over the Thames, its bridges, and both its busy banks. Watching nightfall from the prow of this historic ship is a memorable experience.

IMPERIAL WAR MUSEUM

Lambeth Rd. btwn. St. George's and Kennington Rds. SE1, 020/7416-5320/5321, www.iwm.org.uk

HOURS: Daily 10 A.M.-6 P.M.

COST: Free admission; special exhibitions may charge

TUBE: Lambeth North

This museum contains England's largest display of military artifacts, dating from World War I to the present day, and is a must for military history buffs.

The front hall is a vast space under a high glass roof. A German V2 rocket, the terror of the London Blitz, towers over the scene. Around it are lumbering tanks from World War I, intimidating artillery from World War II, and a variety of equipment from several armies. Overhead hang airplanes, including a WWII British Spitfire and a Sopwith Camel.

Beyond the front hall is a wide array of exhibits on several floors. Glass cases display uniforms, documents, and weapons, while films and interactive videos make for an engrossing experience.

Extensive space is given to World War I, a cataclysmic conflict that killed millions in Europe and still looms large in the British consciousness. It was the first truly modern war, as the hundreds of machine guns, grenades, and gas masks attest. The home front is represented too. One amusing artifact is a postcard sent by the leader of a local Girl Scout troop to a railway employee who had failed to enlist. It invited him to join the Girl Scouts, since it was obvious he wasn't a man!

One popular exhibit is the reconstruction of a WWI trench. Mannequins, voice-overs, and sound effects add realistic touches and do an excellent job re-creating the cramped, disorienting life in a ditch so familiar to the soldiers. When one remembers that the real trenches had mud, artillery bombardments, lice, rats,

The cruiser HMS *Belfast* served in both World War II and Korea.

and the stench of dead bodies, one wonders how people were able to stand it for months on end.

The WWII section is equally absorbing. One shows the struggles of the British soldiers in the Burma campaign, including the harrowing experience of being a prisoner in a Japanese POW camp. A recording from a veteran explains how he treated open sores on his legs with tea bags because he had learned that tea is a disinfectant. This trivia saved his legs and probably his life.

The Secret War gallery highlights espionage, and the British cracking of the Nazi Enigma code is given pride of place. This saved countless Allied lives and was a major factor in winning the war. Exhibits also document British spy activities in the Cold War. Other galleries include a reconstructed 1940s house, information on the famous "Desert Rat" Field Marshal Montgomery, and sobering sections on the Holocaust and other crimes against humanity.

While strolling through the museum, pay attention to the conversations of other visitors. The wars of the 20th century affected all British people and many come here to remember. For example, one day by the V2, an old gentleman vividly recalled for his grandson the strange buzzing sound they made as they came down. The first time he heard it he knew instantly that the Germans were using a new kind of weapon, and that he would be hearing it frequently from then on.

A café and bookstore are on-site.

THE LONDON DUNGEON

28-34 Tooley St. SE1, 020/7403-7221, www.thedungeons.com

HOURS: Daily 10 A.M.-5 P.M.

COST: Adults £19.50, seniors £16.25, students £18.25, children £16.95, under 5 free

TUBE: London Bridge

One of the most popular attractions in London takes visitors on a ride through the seamy and bloody underside of London history, with actors playing plague victims, torturers, and Jack the Ripper. It's all good fun in a Halloweenish sort of way, and the kids will probably

THE THAMES WALK

The river Thames has been London's economic lifeline since the Romans first settled here. No visit would be complete without a good walk along this historic river. The most popular route is on either the North or South Bank between **Westminster Bridge** and **Tower Bridge.** The distance between the two bridges is only three miles, and there are plenty of places to stop for a meal, a pint, or shopping along the way. This short walk can easily take all day or you can do it in just a quick afternoon; walk both ways if you're feeling fit, or relax on a boat ride.

Start at **Westminster Tube station,** where you get an excellent view of **Big Ben.** At this point the river is running north, but it will soon curve to the east on its quest for the sea. Cross **Westminster Bridge** to the **South Bank.** This bridge was built in 1854 by Sir Charles Barry, who also designed the **Houses of Parliament** after they burned down in 1834. The present building opened in 1852. As you cross the bridge, the south facade of Parliament comes increasingly into view. About two-thirds of the way across there's a nice photo opportunity for your traveling companions with Parliament and Big Ben in the background.

Surprisingly, what you won't see are many boats. The days of London as the world's biggest port are long past. Most of the vessels plying the river now are either tourist craft or barges of trash, discreetly tucked away in stacks of big yellow containers (the trash, not the tourists). The Docklands farther to the east, however, still attract big freighters from around the world.

Once across, take a left past the old **County Hall** and the **London Eye** to get onto the **Thames Walk,** clearly marked with brown signs. The London Eye lifts visitors 135 meters (433 feet) into the air for an unparalleled view of the city. Or continue on a more terrestrial journey past the London Aquarium and the **Hungerford Railway Bridge,** built in 1863, with its **Diana Memorial Walkways** on either side, built 2000-2001, before the river turns to the east. Though you are now headed toward the sea, the river may be flowing in the opposite direction. The Thames is a tidal river for its last few miles. This made it even more useful for early shipping, because the regular rise and run of the tides helped ships get into and out of the city.

At this curve of the river you'll pass **Waterloo Bridge,** constructed in 1942 using mostly female labor because men were in short supply during World War II, and a modern **cultural center** comprising the Royal Festival Hall, the National Film Theatre, Royal National Theatre, and several galleries. Continue past **Blackfriars Bridge,** an ornate wrought-iron structure built in 1860, and its railway bridge opened two years later, until reaching the **Tate Modern,** housed in an old power plant. Right across the river is **St. Paul's Cathedral,** reachable by the sleek, modern **Millennium Bridge,** opened as part of Tony Blair's grandiose building scheme in celebration of the year 2000. Many people cross at this point to check out one of England's best examples of church architecture, but continue on the South Bank.

Soon you'll pass **Southwark Bridge,** built in 1912, and the **Cannon Street Railway Bridge,** built in 1863. The fact that this and the Hungerford Railway Bridge were opened in the same year, and only three years after the Blackfriars Bridge, shows how important the Victorian railway boom was for industrial London. A little beyond this bridge, detour to see the famous **Clink Prison** (now a museum) and **Southwark Cathedral** before making your way to **London Bridge.** No, London Bridge hasn't fallen down; it was taken down in 1967 to make a bigger one to accommodate London's ever-increasing traffic. The bridge you see here opened in 1972 and is actually the least interesting of London's bridges. Beyond it is the WWII cruiser **HMS *Belfast*,** and a short walk takes you to **Tower Bridge.**

Tower Bridge is one of the landmarks of

London, and it is often mistaken for London Bridge. Built in 1894, its architecture imitates the nearby **Tower of London.** Cross Tower Bridge to the **North Bank** and check out that famous fortress and prison. Now it's time to head west, back to Westminster. Past the Tower, you'll see the **Customs House,** built in 1715 after Christopher Wren's design. You are now in **The City,** the oldest part of London. The Roman city of Londinium was situated here, although there is little to see of it except for bits of city wall, including a large section next to the **City of London Museum,** and the nearby **Temple of Mithras.** After London expanded beyond its ancient boundaries, The City became a center for finance and printing. While most of the publishers have moved on to cheaper quarters elsewhere, it remains the base for many financial institutions.

Soon you'll come upon **St. Paul's,** a magnificent cathedral that you should not miss. After an inspiring tour of the cathedral, get back on the path and continue west. As the river turns to the south, you'll pass the Renaissance-era **Somerset House,** which houses three art galleries that are well worth a look. A little beyond that is **Embankment Gardens,** where you can rest your feet and watch the river go by. Situated right next to the river across the street from the gardens is **Cleopatra's Needle,** given by the sultan of Egypt to the British Empire as a thank-you for kicking Napoleon out of Egypt. This obelisk actually dates from well before Cleopatra and bears the names of the pharaohs Tuthmosis III and Ramses the Great. You can continue on the river or walk through the gardens, which takes you back almost to Westminster before you get back on the path to go through a built-up area.

© LEAH BOYER

Sunset is a good time for a romantic stroll along the Thames.

love it. I found it vastly overpriced and not terribly different from the haunted house my university used to put on for charity, although the production value is certainly higher. Note that children under 16 must be accompanied by an adult.

SHAKESPEARE'S GLOBE THEATRE

New Globe Walk at Bankside SE1, 020/7902-1400, www.shakespeares-globe.org

HOURS: Exhibition daily 10 A.M.-5 P.M. Oct. 1-May 5, 9 A.M.-noon (theater tour and exhibition) and 12:30-5 P.M. (exhibition and Rose Theatre site)

COST: Adults £9, seniors and students £7.50, children 5-15 £6.50, children under 5 free, family £25

TUBE: London Bridge

While the original Globe Theatre, built in 1599 and the site for the performance of many of Shakespeare's plays, has long since vanished, a faithful reconstruction by actor and director Sam Wanamaker stands on the site as a reminder of times past. The theater comes alive with new productions of the Bard's plays and other period pieces and modern works. Even if you don't catch a play here, the tour gives a great feel for life in the Tudor period. It takes you around the theater and then goes underground, where the museum discusses the struggle to reconstruct the theater, finished in 1997, and gives a history of the original. The tour and visit to the exhibition take about 1.5 hours. Tours begin every 15–30 minutes during opening hours and are included in the price of admission.

You can visit the museum and take the tour year-round, even on performance days, but plays only take place May–September because there is no roof. During performances, you don't get to see the theatre area, but instead are taken to the site of the Rose Theatre, another early theater a brief walk away. There are no ruins or reconstruction, so it's best to go when there isn't a play at the Globe.

SOUTHWARK CATHEDRAL

South end of London Bridge SE1, 020/7367-6700, www.southwark.anglican.org or www.dswark.org/cathedral

HOURS: Mon.-Fri. 7:30 A.M.-6 P.M., Sat.-Sun. 8:30 A.M.-6 P.M.

COST: Free admission

TUBE: London Bridge

This church was originally built in 1206 but underwent a major remodeling in 1839. Parts of the exterior are made with flint nodules, their peculiar color giving churches built with them the nickname "puddingstone churches." The interior is inspired by the French Gothic, with an elegant altar screen dating to 1520. The Harvard Chapel is dedicated to John Harvard, who founded the famous American university and was baptized here in 1607. Don't miss the nearby *gisant,* a recumbent stone effigy of an emaciated corpse in a shroud. In past centuries, people didn't flinch away from the unseemly aspect of death. There's also a monument to Shakespeare, who lived in this parish but isn't buried here. One influential writer who does rest here is John Gower, poet laureate to Richard II and Henry IV and dubbed "the first English poet," since he often wrote

Southwark Cathedral is one of the oldest and grandest houses of worship in London.

in English when most only wrote in Latin and French. The stained-glass windows are beautiful even on a cloudy day.

In the new annex is a shop with books on the history of Christianity and an interesting display from archaeological excavations. One notable find is a statue of a Roman hunter god, showing this was a site of worship well before the advent of Christianity. Many original features are visible, including a 1st-century Roman road, the early-12th-century foundations of the Norman priory, and part of a slightly later chapter house and archway. A stone coffin is still in place from the 13th century.

TATE MODERN

The Queen's Walk btwn. Blackfriars and Millennium Bridges SE1, 020/7887-8888, www.tate.org.uk

HOURS: Sun.-Thurs. 10 A.M.-6 P.M., Fri.-Sat. 10 A.M.-10 P.M.

COST: Free admission; special exhibits may charge

TUBE: Blackfriars or London Bridge

The modern art in this museum was originally housed in the Tate Britain until it was moved to the Bankside Power Station. This huge brick and steel edifice was designed by Sir Giles Gilbert Scott, who is also responsible for the red telephone boxes you see everywhere. The remodelers took out all the machinery and left much of the building as a huge open space. This makes for some grandiose installation pieces in the old Turbine Room on Level 1. In 2005, Rachel Whiteread filled it with 14,000 white plastic casts of cardboard boxes. Stacked up every which way in piles several meters high, they made the museum look as if it were haunted by the spirit of a dead moving company. A large gift shop is filled with art and photography books, calendars, and many excellent periodicals.

Level 2 features temporary displays, while Levels 3–5 are set aside for the permanent collection and more visiting exhibitions. Levels 6 and 7 are mostly offices.

In 2006, the collection was reorganized along the lines of the century's four major artistic trends—cubism, futurism, and vorticism; surrealism; abstract expressionism and European informal art; and minimalism. Modern art fans can easily spend an entire day here, but those with less time can still see some of these highlights. Dali is popular for his bizarre imagery and wry sense of humor; his famous lobster phone is on display. Andy Warhol is represented by several pop art pieces, from the playful images of the Marilyn Monroe diptych to a more sobering picture of the Birmingham Civil Rights marchers being attacked by police dogs. Warhol liked to take familiar images from popular media and advertising and rework them into art, hence the term "pop art." Predating him in this idea by the better part of a century was Marcel Duchamp and his "ready mades." To prove that anything could be art, he took to hanging urinals and bicycle wheels on gallery walls, creating the most expensive urinals and bicycle wheels in history. While the bicycle wheels are elsewhere, you'll be relieved to know the Tate Modern has one of the urinals. Small theaters show video art in several spots in the museum.

Each floor has large windows giving sweeping views of the Thames, with the bare metal arch of the Millennium Bridge close at hand and St. Paul's rising above the roofs on the opposite bank. Sit down and enjoy the view at one of three eateries: a café on Level 2, an espresso bar on Level 4, and a restaurant on Level 7. The espresso bar is the least expensive and you get the best views. Not all the tables in the café and restaurant have the views that you get by sidling up to the high counter next to the window in the espresso bar.

If you want to see Tate Britain and the Tate Modern in one day, you might consider taking the Tate Boat (see the *Tate Britain* listing for details).

THAMES CRUISES

Along both banks of the Thames

HOURS: Open at daylight and some nighttime hours; best at sunset or any time during fair weather

COST: See individual listings below

Cutting through the center of London, the Thames is the heart and soul of the city. No trip would be complete without a long look at this river. Try to pick a day with good weather. While that isn't always possible here in Old Blighty, the river and the historic architecture on either bank are lovely in sunshine and make for stunning photographs. Several cruise companies offer boating excursions or shuttle services. Listed are three of the more popular ones.

Catamaran Cruisers: This service runs several types of cruises. The Circular Cruise departs hourly from Westminster Pier and lasts 50 minutes, passing by all the major riverside sights of central London while passengers listen to recorded commentary. Circular Cruises cost adults £9, children under 15 £4.50, children under 5 free, families of up to two adults and three children £22.50. For more flexibility, you can take a Point-to-Point Cruise departing regularly throughout the day from Embankment, Waterloo (London Eye), Bankside, Tower, and Greenwich piers. You can buy either a single or return fare and costs depend on which two piers you are traveling between. The maximum distance and cost is between Waterloo and Greenwich piers; a one-way ticket costs adults £6.80 and children £3.40, while a return trip costs adults £8.60 and children £4.30. Seniors, students, and groups of more than 15 get 10 percent off on all tickets. Catamaran Cruises offers discount tickets to major sights if you combine them with a cruise, and it runs a variety of entertainment and dining cruises. These vary from season to season, as can its more regular cruises, so call ahead or check out www.catamarancruisers.co.uk for details. Its offices are on Embankment Pier, Victoria Embankment, WC2. For information or reservations call 020/7987-1185.

City Cruises: City Cruises offers daily sightseeing cruises as well as nighttime dinner, dance, and cabaret cruises. Cruises depart from Westminster Pier, Waterloo Millennium (London Eye) Pier, Tower Pier, and Greenwich Pier daily. Time between each pier is 20 minutes to an hour, and the entire round-trip is 2.5 hours. London Travelcard holders get one-third off (family cards not included), student card holders get 30 percent off, and London Freedom Pass holders get half off adult tickets. Besides simple transportation, City Cruises offers sightseeing tours that include meals, as well as nighttime entertainment cruises. Times and costs vary, but they are in most cases identical or within a few pence of Catamaran Cruisers' rates. Coincidence? Probably not. Call 020/7740-0400 or check out its website at www.citycruises.com.

Tate Boat: If you are visiting either the Tate Britain or Tate Modern, you can take a shuttle boat between the two (see listing for *Tate Britain* for details).

Outlying Areas — Map 1

London is vast, and while many visitors are content to stay in the center, there's plenty to see beyond it. Luckily the Tube can get you most anywhere you want to go, and light rail and buses take up where the Tube leaves off. The jewel of outer London is the old tea clipper *Cutty Sark,* made famous in bars worldwide. Now you can see the real ship for yourself. Be sure not to miss Hampton Court Palace either, a stately royal home with a beautiful garden. Both the *Cutty Sark* and Hampton Court are easy to reach by rail.

CUTTY SARK

King William Walk, Greenwich SE10, 020/8858-2698, www.cuttysark.org.uk

HOURS: Daily 10 A.M.–5 P.M.

COST: Adults £5, seniors and students with ID £3.90, children under 16 £3.70, children under 5 free, family £12.50

DOCKLANDS LIGHT RAILWAY: Cutty Sark

Commissioned in 1869, the *Cutty Sark* is the last tea clipper in existence. It was built for John Willis, who decided to make a name for himself by winning the annual race from China

© SEAN MCLACHLAN

The *Cutty Sark* is a lovingly restored nineteenth century tea clipper.

to London. Tea was all the rage in England and he got rich off shipping between London and China. The *Cutty Sark* never won the race, and the tea trade stopped using sailing vessels when the Suez Canal opened. The narrow canal was safe only for steam ships, which could go straight ahead without having to worry about the wind blowing them to the side.

The ship shifted to the Australian wool route in the 1880s and broke the speed record on that route, becoming one of the most famous vessels on the high seas. By 1895 the age of sail was on the wane, and the clipper was sold to a Portuguese company, making various trips and becoming run-down until it was bought by an admirer in 1922 and restored to its former glory. It opened to the public in 1957.

Nothing is quite like standing on the main deck of an old sailing ship. The towering masts, fine woodwork, and timeless flow of the Thames are sure to stay vivid in your memory for many years. The ship is on dry land now, but stand on the prow and look beyond the narrow bit of concrete between you and the river. It won't take much imagination to feel as if you're on the water.

Sailing ships were incredibly complicated pieces of engineering. This one has three masts, the mainmast being 47 meters (152 feet) tall, which could support 43 sails covering the area of 10 tennis courts. The rigging extends more than 18 kilometers (11 miles). Sailors had to know how best to arrange every rope and sail to catch the slightest breeze. The poop deck houses the officers' quarters, which look fairly nice until you realize the master, mate, and second mate had to share this space for months. The two deckhouses for petty officers and apprentices are even more claustrophobic. The ship had a crew of 28 at most, but when journeys lasted up to six months, it is not surprising that discipline had to be harsh to keep order.

Below the main deck is the tween deck, which held the cargo. On the way to China and Australia, the *Cutty Sark* carried English manufactured goods and it returned with more than one million pounds (weight, not money) of wool for England's garment industry or tea for its breakfast tables. Now this deck is a museum outlining the history of the ship and the industries it served. Kid-friendly panels below the main ones give the little folks a chance to learn too. The lower hold has a colorful collection of ship figureheads and an interpretive video center.

Free tours are run on a first-come, first-served basis throughout every weekday and last half an hour.

HAMPTON COURT PALACE AND GARDENS

East Molesey, Surrey, 087/0752 7777, bookings 087/0753-7777, www.hamptoncourtpalace.org.uk

HOURS: Daily 10 A.M.–6 P.M. Mar. 26–Oct. 28, daily 10 A.M.–4 P.M. Oct. 29–Mar. 25

COST: Adults £12.30, seniors and students £10, children £8, family £36.40

BRITISH RAIL: Hampton Court Palace

Thomas Wolsey, archbishop of York, finished this sumptuous Tudor mansion in 1525 but gave it to Henry VIII three years later in an ultimately fruitless attempt to curry his favor. The king's son Edward was born here in 1537, and one of his many wives, Jane Seymour, died a few days after giving birth to him. Another of his wives, number five Catherine Howard, still haunts one of the galleries—she ran screaming down it as she tried to escape execution. In 1604 James I authorized the King James Bible here, and the palace continued to be a royal favorite well into the 18th century. There's a lot to see, so schedule at least half a day not including travel. The high points include Henry VIII's Great Hall adorned with original tapestries, the Chapel Royal, with its ornate blue vaulting, and the well-preserved Tudor kitchens that give a glimpse of how the commoners lived and worked. In the warmer months the gardens are breathtaking, with neatly sculpted shrubbery laid out in a formal pattern. Kids will love puzzling through the complex hedge maze. The garden is home to the world's oldest vine, planted in 1768 and still producing up to 318 kilos (700 pounds) of grapes every year. To avoid the queue, it's best to book your tickets in advance or buy them at any staffed South West Trains station. Costumed guides give regular, informative tours that are entertaining for adults and kids alike, and there are numerous special events throughout the year. Check the website for details.

Getting to Hampton Court is pretty straightforward. The train, operated by South West Trains, runs from Waterloo to Hampton Court Station and takes a little more than half an hour; the palace is a two-minute walk across the bridge from the station. The train service passes through Wimbledon station, where the London Underground District Line begins. Hampton Court is in Travel Zone 6.

RESTAURANTS

Once notorious for mushy peas and blood pudding, British food has become much more pleasant in recent years. The infusion of foreign influences has also made it more cosmopolitan, and a new emphasis on healthy eating has lightened the dishes without sacrificing taste.

While traditional English fare is still popular, it's impossible to overestimate the effect that Asian cooking, especially South Asian cooking, has had on the national palate. Recently, chicken tikka masala has overtaken fish-and-chips as England's favorite food, and all those lovely kormas, vindaloos, and *jalfreezis* seem to be getting only more popular. It may sound strange, but you haven't really sampled British cuisine until you've eaten at an Indian restaurant, usually packed with locals of all ethnicities and social classes. And "South Asian" does not mean just Indian. Many of the cooks in Indian restaurants are in fact Bengali, and Pakistanis are well represented too. The subcontinent has a rich variety of regional cuisines—from the sweet Kashmiri to the fiery vindaloo—so there's something to please every palate.

Thanks to its huge immigrant population, London is famous for having some of the most eclectic dining options in the world. You'll have plenty of choices, whether you're tucking into a roast goose (what the English used to have for Christmas before they started importing turkeys from the United States) or sizzling your taste buds with some rich curry. There are more unusual offerings too, such as savory Ethiopian food, where the waiter roasts the coffee right in front of you—wafting the aroma in your face

HIGHLIGHTS

Best Exotic Date: Feast like a maharaja in **Chor Bizarre,** an elaborately decorated Indian restaurant. To really impress your date, ask for your food "extra spicy" (page 81).

Best Way to Feel Like Aristocracy (until the bill comes): During High Tea at the **Savoy,** guests sip tea and nibble scones amid refined surroundings in one of London's grandest hotels (page 86).

Best Game: The most traditional of traditional British restaurants, **Rules** has been in business since 1798. Pricey, but oh-so-good (page 88).

Best Vegetarian/Best Value: Food for Thought is hands down the cheapest, most central, and simply the best vegetarian restaurant in London. Even meat eaters are regulars here (page 88).

Best Fine Dining for Men Who Wear Skirts: If you're Scottish by blood or inclination, head to **Boisdale** and splurge on a rich, hearty meal of fresh game, haggis, or beef. Don't forget to help your meal settle with some aged whiskey and a cigar (page 92).

Best Place for Cheap Eats in The City: In the heart of The City yet still affordable, the historic **Punch Tavern** has an excellent salad bar and original 19th-century decor (page 97).

Best Hard-to-Find Cuisine: There aren't many Afghan restaurants around, and that's a shame. Fortunately there's **Afghan Kitchen** where hearty portions, an interesting blend of spices, and rock-bottom prices could make this the fast food of the future (page 99).

LOOK FOR TO FIND RECOMMENDED DINING.

in traditional Ethiopian hospitality. Or perhaps you'd prefer to dig into a plate of hearty pasta courtesy of an Italian cook, or some heavily seasoned goat meat cooked in traditional Nigerian style. East Asian cuisines, such as Chinese and Japanese, are well represented right next to the hopping nightlife of Soho.

Concern about genetically modified food, and the pesticides, hormones, and other toxins found in most prepared food, has led to a boom in organic and GMO-free eating in the United Kingdom. Many restaurants proudly proclaim their dedication to serving their patrons healthier fare, and there are a number of vegetarian restaurants for those who would prefer to avoid meat. But don't let the term "vegetarian" limit you; meat eaters often dine at vegetarian restaurants in London because the cooking is so good.

Whatever your tastes, you will have no problem satisfying your hunger in London. Now loosen your belt and dig in!

PRICE KEY

£	Entrées under £7
££	Entrées £7-15
£££	Entrées more than £15

Westminster, Victoria, and Pimlico — Map 2

London's center is full of restaurants of many styles, and being close to some of the major sights makes them convenient as well. As it's the governmental center of the United Kingdom, most of the clientele have lots of money to spend, and the prices on the menus are set accordingly, but the restaurants here are of top quality and there *are* a few budget options.

CONTEMPORARY BRITISH

TATE GALLERY RESTAURANT ££

Tate Britain, Millbank at Atterbury St. SW1, 020/7887-8825, www.tate.org.uk

HOURS: Mon.-Fri. 11:30 A.M.-5 P.M., Sat.-Sun. 10 A.M.-5 P.M.

TUBE: Pimlico

After browsing the fine collection of British paintings in the Tate Britain, top off your day with lunch at the museum's very own restaurant. The restaurant serves traditional British fare enlivened with modern flair, and the wine list is impressive. Have a glass while enjoying fine British art such as Rex Whistler's appropriately placed 1925 painting *The Expedition in Pursuit of Rare Meats*. It's best to make reservations before visting the gallery, as spaces fill quickly.

DELI

PICKLES SANDWICH BAR £

6 Old Queen St. W1, 020/7222-8749

HOURS: Mon.-Fri. 7 A.M.-4 P.M., Sat. 8 A.M.-2:30 P.M.

TUBE: St. James's Park

It's hard to find cheap eats in London's tourist and governmental center, but Pickles has kept its prices low for years, becoming something of a local institution. Here you can find freshly made sandwiches, homemade cakes, and the usual assortment of hot and cold drinks. There are a few tables in the small, sparsely decorated interior, but most diners get takeaway and munch while wandering through one of London's most scenic areas.

EUROPEAN

R. S. *HISPANIOLA* ££

Victoria Embankment WC2, 020/7839-3011, www.hispaniola.co.uk

HOURS: Daily 11 A.M.-11 P.M.; Lunch: Noon-3 P.M.; Dinner: 6:30-11 P.M.

TUBE: Embankment

Moored along Victoria Embankment next to the Hungerford Railway Bridge, this converted boat has a view of the river that's hard to beat. The main restaurant is open for lunch, afternoon tea, and dinner, and serves European cuisine such as medallions of pork fillet with fresh apples and pink peppercorn and tagliatelle with stir-fried vegetables and parmesan shavings. Several options are vegetarian and vegan meals can be made on request. Tapas are available throughout the day (11 A.M.–11 P.M.) or enjoy a Light Bite, such as bangers and mash or chili con carne with rice, until 5 P.M. There's outdoor seating, but full meals aren't served outside. The cocktail lounge next door has live piano music Thursday–Saturday evenings.

FRENCH/ TRADITIONAL BRITISH

BISTRO 51 ££

54 Buckingham Gate SW1, 020/7963-8325, www.bistro51.co.uk

HOURS: Mon.-Sat. noon-3 P.M., 6-11 P.M., Sun. noon-3 P.M.

TUBE: St. James's Park

A bright, relaxed restaurant attached to the Crowne Plaza Hotel, Bistro 51 offers traditional dishes both from Britain and France and caters to a mixture of hotel guests, tourists, and local professionals who dine in a choice of several small rooms. The menu is heavily French with lots of good seafood, but it also serves British standbys such as lamb shank. On Sundays there's a traditional Sunday roast with all the trimmings. The wine list is well chosen and there's al fresco dining in warm weather in the nearby courtyard garden.

INDIAN

CINNAMON CLUB £££

42 N. Audley St. W1, 020/7491-9988, www.truevert.co.uk

HOURS: Mon.-Fri. 7:30-11:30 A.M., noon-3 P.M., 6-9 P.M., Sat. 7:30-11:30 A.M., noon-4 P.M., Sun. 9 A.M.-4 P.M.

TUBE: St. James's Park or Westminster

The bookshelves lining the walls remind diners that this was once a public library, but I'm willing to bet the fountain is a later development. The chefs cook some fine Indian dishes; the curry spices are flown in specially from India. The Cinnamon Club is one of the few Indian restaurants that serves breakfast, but it passes up the many fine Indian breakfast foods for English breakfasts and one "Anglo-Indian" dish, kedgeree with smoked haddock and poached egg.

INTERNATIONAL

BANK WESTMINSTER £££

45 Buckingham Gate SW1, 020/7379-9797

HOURS: Mon.-Fri. noon-2:45 P.M., 5-10:30 P.M., Sat. 5-10:30 P.M.

TUBE: St. James's Park

International twists on familiar favorites make this a popular place for downtown business types, but you'll see families here too. The seafood selection is especially good, with offerings such as roast monkfish with cracked coriander, tabbouleh, and Swiss chard roulade and *tzatsiki*. Landlubbers who want something a bit more traditional should try the Cumberland sausages with swede (rutabaga) and black peppercorn mash and red onion jus. Attached is the Zander bar, which has live jazz and DJs, and the longest bar in the United Kingdom.

TRADITIONAL BRITISH

FOOTSTOOL £££

St. John's Church, Smith Sq. at Gayfere St. SW1, 020/7222-2779

HOURS: Mon.-Fri. 11 A.M.-3 P.M., open evenings and weekends during events

TUBE: St. James's Park or Westminster

This is a popular spot for concertgoers attending shows in St. John's, or for those wishing to have a lunch in a quiet neighborhood. Enjoy the buffet before the show, or reserve a table for the set-menu dinner afterward. The food is traditional British, and the setting is atmospheric; patrons dine under the brick vaulting of the 18th-century church cellar. For a starter, highly recommended is the wild boar terrine with apricots. One of the best things about dining in London is that wild game is so often found on the menus of finer restaurants.

Mayfair and Piccadilly — Map 3

As it's one of London's nicer residential areas, it is not surprising to find a wide variety of good dining here, with an emphasis on British and Continental cuisine, and interesting fusions of various styles. While most restaurants are in the higher price categories, catering to the well-heeled art aficionados trolling the local galleries, there are a few less expensive options.

FRENCH

SKETCH GALLERY — £££

9 Conduit St. W1, 087/0777-4488

HOURS: Lecture Room: Tues.-Fri. noon-2:30 P.M., 7-10:30 P.M., Sat. 7-10:30 P.M.; Gallery: Tues.-Sat. 7 P.M.-midnight

TUBE: Oxford Circus

This is fine dining at its finest, with a menu that has the reputation for being the most expensive in London. Whether it is or not is a matter of some dispute in this city of overpriced eateries, but when the average entrée costs more than £30, it is certainly a serious contender. Still, the decor in both the Lecture Room and Gallery are sedate but elegant, and the food is everything one would expect. The fillet of beef with cuttlefish carpaccio made my taste buds abandon me for a millionaire.

TRUE VERT — ££

42 N. Audley St. W1, 020/7491-9988, www.truevert.co.uk

HOURS: Mon.-Fri. 7:30-11:30 A.M., noon-3 P.M., 6-9 P.M., Sat. 7:30-11:30 A.M., noon-4 P.M., Sun. 9 A.M.-4 P.M.

TUBE: Marble Arch

Bare wooden floors and rustic furnishing lend this café a Continental charm. The walls are decorated with the works of local artists (for sale) and bottles of French wine (also for sale). The menu varies with what the chef could get fresh that morning, but it always concentrates on French cuisine served in an unpretentious style. It's popular for breakfast among local professionals who come to sip their coffee, munch on great pastries, and read the paper.

HIGH TEA

THE RITZ — £££

150 Piccadilly W1, 020/7493-8181, www.theritzlondon.com

HOURS: Daily seatings at 11:30 A.M., 1:30, 3:30, 5:30, 7:30 P.M.

TUBE: Green Park

High tea at the Ritz has been a tradition of the London elite for a century. Tea is served five times a day in the Palm Court, an ornate room that resembles the banquet hall of a French chateau. The tea, served in delicate china, includes a choice of sandwiches, scones, and pastries. On weekdays a pianist plays in the background, replaced on weekends by a harpist. Afternoon tea is £35 per person, and at 7:30 P.M. there's a champagne tea available, the price of which depends on the champagne. Book at least six weeks in advance. It's that popular. Formal dress is required.

INDIAN

CHOR BIZARRE — ££

16 Albemarle St. W1, 020/7629-9802/8542, www.chorbizarre.com

HOURS: Daily noon-3 P.M., 6-11:30 P.M.

TUBE: Green Park or Piccadilly

A recipient of numerous awards, Chor Bizarre serves North Indian cuisine and heaps of atmosphere. The emphasis is on Kashmiri, but there are dishes from all over India and plenty of vegetarian options. The best are the *thalis,* platters with a sampling of several different dishes that provide what the restaurant calls a "gastronomic journey." The platters provide a good introduction to a sampling of various regional styles. The interior is sumptuous with elegant inlaid furniture and art objects all around, many of which are for sale. Regular wine tastings are held, unusual for an Indian restaurant.

CURRY: HOW SOUTH ASIA TRANSFORMED THE WAY THE BRITISH EAT

South Asian immigrants first started coming to London in significant numbers as students in the late 19th century. In the mid-20th century the trickle of immigrants became a flood. While places such as Brick Lane are famous for their curry houses, South Asian restaurants can be found everywhere in London and even in the smaller country towns. While there was initially some resistance on the part of the English to the cuisine and the immigrants themselves, Asian culture – or more particularly Indian culture – is now seen as trendy. Even the grumpiest old folks will dig into a good curry every now and then, and a visit to London would not be complete without a meal at one of its innumerable curry houses.

South Asian cuisine could be found in England long before it became trendy. British officers and bureaucrats often returned from the colonies with servants in tow to cook them the meals they had learned to love while abroad. In the 1960s curry restaurants began to open in London and smaller towns such as Canterbury and St. Albans. Some of these places still survive and tend to be the best around, having learned through trial and error how to cook for the Western palate while keeping true to the original spirit of the cuisine. The current boom began in the 1980s and has been going strong ever since. Even small towns and outlying neighborhoods of London will have a curry house or two.

The first thing to know about curry is that there's no such thing; it is in fact a general term for any number of combinations of certain spices, most important among them turmeric, cardamom, chili, cinnamon, coriander, fennel, ginger, red and black pepper, and saffron, among others. Back in India, curry is mixed fresh for each meal; however, this is too time-consuming for a fast-paced Western lifestyle. Instead, most restaurants have a "red" pot (a tomato-based curry) and a "black" pot (a pepper-based curry) – two basic mixes that can be added to for different dishes.

And what a variety of dishes they can make! India has a population of more than one billion, a history stretching back to the beginnings of civilization, and a diverse population made up of a myriad of ethnic, religious, and cultural groups, yielding numerous regional cuisines. Many menus actually contain brief descriptions of the restaurant's particular regional cuisine, and the waiters can always answer any questions.

One thing to keep in mind is that observant Muslims and Hindus frown upon alcohol, so some of the more traditional restaurants do not serve it. Since Hindus are not supposed to eat meat (another rule broken by many individuals) some restaurants don't serve that either. This can actually be a plus, as you are more likely to find traditional cooking in such a place than in one catering more to Western habits.

INTERNATIONAL

RICHOUX £££

41a S. Audley St. W1, 020/7629-5228, www.richoux.co.uk

HOURS: Mon.-Fri. 8 A.M.-11 P.M., Sat. 8 A.M.-11:30 P.M., Sun. 9 A.M.-11 P.M.

TUBE: Marble Arch or Bond Street

A traditional French patisserie, Richoux also serves full meals in an elegant but relaxed atmosphere. The menu is international and eclectic, offering everything from seared teriyaki salmon to Welsh rabbit. Late starters can take advantage of the all-day breakfast menu featuring both continental and full English. The afternoon cream teas are wonderful and a great way to refuel before hitting the gallery trail. The dessert list may keep you there for a while, however, as may the selection of Godiva chocolates.

LEBANESE

JOURY BISTRO AND LOUNGE £

72 Duke St. W1, 020/7493-8555

HOURS: Mon.-Sat. noon-11 P.M.
TUBE: Marble Arch or Bond Street
If you want to eat cheaply in Mayfair, there's not much choice beyond sandwich shops and boring chain stores, so Joury comes as a refreshing surprise with its combination of presentation and value. The open kitchen is garlanded with strings of onion, while the dining room features tiled tables and couches covered with colorful blankets. The ceiling supports what could be the most hanging lamps of any restaurant in London. The menu lists Middle Eastern favorites, such as falafel and shish kebab, and lots of Arab desserts too, such as fresh baklava. For a drink, try *ayran,* a refreshing thin yogurt mixed with salt that is excellent for rehydrating after a hot day. The lunch specials are an especially good value.

TRADITIONAL BRITISH

BENTLEY'S OYSTER BAR AND GRILL ££

11-15 Swallow St. W1, 020/7734-4756, www.bentleysoysterbarandgrill.co.uk
HOURS: Oyster Bar: Daily noon-midnight; Restaurant: Daily noon-3 P.M., 6-11 P.M.
TUBE: Piccadilly Circus
Bentley's, opened in 1916, is one of London's oldest oyster bars, and it underwent a complete renovation in 2005. The curved oyster bar is a perennial favorite, where diners sup on hot, fresh bivalves. You can also eat upstairs in the formal dining room, but the oyster bar is more social and fun. For those who don't like bottom feeders, there's Dover sole and cured herring as well as plenty of other seafood dishes. Give at least two days' notice for reservations.

Covent Garden, West End, and Soho Map 4

This is *the* place to eat in London. Not only are you close to the nightlife, especially London's world-famous theaters, but you can get some wonderful dinners at rock-bottom prices. Head on over to Chinatown in Soho for cheap Asian cooking. The streets get so packed at night you'll think half the city is there, but don't despair; there are plenty of places to choose from.

AMERICAN

HAMBURGER UNION £

25 Dean St. W1, 020/7379-6004
HOURS: Mon.-Tues. 11:30 A.M.-9:30 P.M., Wed.-Sat. 11:30 A.M.-10:30 P.M., Sun. 11.30 A.M.-9:30 P.M.
TUBE: Covent Garden
Gourmet hamburger bars have become popular in London of late, which is a good thing considering the quality of the average burger here 10 years ago. Hamburger Union's free-range char-grilled beef should keep any meat lover happy, but there are vegetarian dishes too. When the British say hamburger *bar,* they mean it literally. A full selection of drinks is available.

ASIAN

GERRARD ST. W1

Gerrard St. and streets immediately adjacent
TUBE: Piccadilly Circus or Leicester Square
If you like Asian food and don't want to spend a lot, London's Chinatown is where you want to be. I tried counting the number of restaurants in this area and soon had to give up. Much of the clientele is Chinese, which is reassuring, and most menus are bilingual. Ducks hang in the windows, and the smell of cooking wafts through every street in the neighborhood. The majority of the restaurants are reasonably priced, but you'll also see a few places where you can splash out for a grand, multicourse banquet, something the Chinese do very well. A sprinkling of Japanese, Korean, and Vietnamese restaurants add variety to the majority Chinese businesses.

NEW WORLD ££

1 Gerrard Pl. W1, 020/7734-0677
HOURS: Daily 11 A.M.-midnight
TUBE: Piccadilly Circus or Leicester Square
Big Chinese lanterns and lacquered screens

decorate this two-story Chinese restaurant that's been a local favorite for more than 20 years. The menu offers Cantonese and provincial food and lots of dim sum, which is what many of the regulars come here for. The dim sum are served the traditional way by carting them around the restaurant, making for a constant parade of tempting delicacies. New World also serves entrées such as fried crispy noodles with mixed seafood and brisket of beef in curry sauce with rice.

CAFÉS

BAR ITALIA £

22 Frith St. W1, 020/7437-4520
HOURS: Open 24 hours
TUBE: Leicester Square

Opened in 1959 by the Polledri family, this bustling café in the heart of Little Italy is still in the same hands and serves great coffee, *panini,* pizza, bagels, and breakfasts. The fact that Italian is spoken here and euros are accepted currency lend to the Italian feel. It's perfect for early-morning or late-night refuels. Upstairs used to be the workshop of John Logie Baird, who transmitted the first television images in 1925 (of an office boy named William Taynton who worked downstairs). His term for the invention, "noctovision," never caught on but the BBC became the first TV broadcaster in 1932.

CAFÉ IN THE CRYPT £

St. Martin-in-the-Fields Trafalgar Sq. WC2, 020/7839-4342, www.smitf.org
HOURS: Mon.-Wed. 8 A.M.-8 P.M., Thurs.-Sat. 8 A.M.-10:30 P.M., Sun. noon-8 P.M.
TUBE: Charing Cross or Leicester Square

Dine amidst the dead in this atmospheric café below St. Martin-in-the-Fields. The flagstones are centuries-old graves, but the food is fresh and reasonably priced. For breakfast, choose between a full English or the healthier home-made muesli. Lunch offers soups, salads, and sandwiches, and there's a daily tea from 2–6 P.M. For a truly romantic experience, come to see one of the church's famous nighttime concerts and enjoy a pre- or post-concert candlelit dinner with a variety of traditional English dishes. Because the gift shop and brass rubbing center are down here too, this café can get pretty busy and loud at times, but it's more sedate at dinnertime.

St. Martin-in-the-Fields, famous for classical concerts, houses a reasonably priced café in its crypt.

EXOTIKA £

7 Villiers St. WC2, 020/7930-6133
HOURS: Mon.-Thurs. noon-11 P.M., Fri.-Sat. noon-midnight, Sun. noon-10 P.M.
TUBE: Charing Cross

This is mostly a takeaway joint for the office workers in the neighborhood, but there are some seats. Exotika specializes in quickly prepared fajitas, noodles, and other power foods that will fill you up without emptying your wallet. It's great for a pit stop while walking from one sight to another. The constant coming and going of patrons on the run makes it a bit of a hectic place to eat, but this is the sort of restaurant people go to in a hurry.

MAISON BERTAUX £

28 Greek St. W1, 020/7437-8382/6007
HOURS: Mon.-Sat. 9 A.M.-11 P.M.
TUBE: Tottenham Court Road or Leicester Square

This little French café and patisserie has been serving customers since 1871. An old photo behind the counter shows the window display from that period, and it seems the selection of gooey cakes, tasty pies, and filled (and filling) croissants hasn't changed much—nor does it need to. The food is great (no full meals here, just snacks), the coffee is done properly, and the staff is matronly and personable. You can't go here twice without being remembered. There's some sidewalk seating, or stay inside on one of two floors that exude shabby gentility.

PATISSERIE VALERIE £

44 Old Compton St. W1, 020/7437-3466, www.patisserie-valerie.co.uk
HOURS: Mon.-Fri. 7:30 A.M.-8:30 P.M., Sat. 8 A.M.-8:30 P.M., Sun. 9 A.M.-6:30 P.M.
TUBE: Leicester Square

One of London's older patisseries, this longtime favorite of Soho bohemians started in 1926 on

LONDON'S CHEAP EATS

If you want to save money and don't mind a bit of grease, there are plenty of budget eating options in London. Restaurants can be expensive, and Londoners are always on the go, so the city is filled with takeaway places to serve their needs. Many stay open late to catch the postpub crowd.

The most famous cheap meal in town is fish-and-chips. Choose from various types of fish – cod, haddock, and plaice (some of the most popular) – which are then fried in batter and served with chips (french fries) for a tasty and filling meal. Lunch or dinner at a traditional fish-and-chip shop, called a chippery or "chippie," will put you back only a few pounds. Although fish-and chips-are available in pubs and many restaurants, these places are often cooking frozen, prepared meals and there is definitely a difference.

Doner kebab is a relatively recent import from Turkey. Purportedly made of lamb, beef, or chicken (but usually lamb), *doner kebabs* consist of slabs of meat glopped onto a vertical spit half enclosed by a heater. The cylindrical mass rotates day and night, and pieces are shaved off with a long knife and served in a pita with tomatoes, lettuce, onions, and seasoning. Kebab stands are everywhere and do a brisk business at pub closing time, when the dozen pints in your stomach are calling for some absorbing fat. Like fish-and-chips, kebabs will put you back only a few pounds but typically contain almost twice as much fat.

For more Western fare, go to one of the fried-chicken joints that seem to be on every street in the country. These vary widely in quality, from reasonably good to dangerously inedible, so look before ordering. Many of these places also serve hamburgers – but they don't hold a candle to the burgers back in the States. A meal of fried chicken generally goes for less than £5 and comes with chips and a drink.

Sandwiches are a healthier alternative. Prewrapped sandwiches are available in supermarkets, at most newsstands, and in special sandwich shops, and they run £2-4. They come in an endless variety, from traditional bacon sandwiches to chicken vindaloo. The sandwich shops are an old British favorite, and neighborhood shops can be good places to meet folks. (Some favorite shops are listed in this chapter).

To save money in a regular, sit-down restaurant, order water. Make sure to ask for "tap water" to avoid being served (and charged for) mineral water. Further savings can be found in the budget restaurants listed in this chapter; they all manage to serve inexpensive meals without sacrificing quality.

Frith Street before the Luftwaffe convinced it to relocate here by the rude, but very effective, method of blowing up its building. The heaping and reasonably priced breakfasts and lunches, and the wonderfully sweet pastries and good coffee, keep both floors bustling at all times of the day. The upstairs retains classic 1950s "modern" wall art in the form of geometric green guitars and less identifiable shapes. The owners have opened several other branches, but this is the original.

CARIBBEAN

MR. JERK £

189 Wardour St. W1, 020/7287-2878

HOURS: Mon.-Sat. 10 A.M.-10:30 P.M., Sun. 10 noon-8 P.M.

TUBE: Tottenham Court Road

With such a large Afro-Caribbean population, London offers a great selection of island cooking. Mr. Jerk fulfills a need for good Caribbean cooking close to the center, and it is great value for money too. Crowds pack the simple wooden tables during lunch and dinner, so it's best to come a bit between. Try the jerk chicken with hard food, which is chicken with a spicy sauce served with a side of yams, dumpling, and fried banana. Spiced mutton and oxtail are also popular. The portions are hefty, so come with a good appetite.

CONTEMPORARY BRITISH

ANDREW EDMUNDS ££

46 Lexington St. W1, 020/7437-5708

HOURS: Mon.-Fri. 12:30-3 P.M., 6-10:45 P.M., Sat. 1-3 P.M., 6-11 P.M., Sun. 1-3 P.M., 6-10:30 P.M.

TUBE: Oxford Circus or Piccadilly Circus

In a city where fine restaurants are often stuffy, Andrew Edmunds's relaxed atmosphere is a welcome change. This cozy, candlelit restaurant serves organic produce and wonderfully flavored British cuisine. Families dine here as do high-powered business types. The handwritten menu varies every morning depending on what's available, but the meat and fish dishes are always a safe bet. (I especially liked the rabbit stew with white wine cream.) An extensive and well-chosen wine list rounds out the menu. Reservations for both lunch and dinner are advisable.

CUBAN

CASA DEL HABANO £

100 Wardour St. W1, 020/7314-4001

HOURS: Mon.-Sat. 10 A.M.-11 P.M.

TUBE: Tottenham Court Road

Cuban-style sandwiches and seafood are the main attractions here, as is the opportunity to smoke a real Havana cigar. Lots of people order the crayfish, which are supposed to be the best in town since they're flown in direct from the island. It also serves vegetarian meals. The daiquiris will get you in the mood for even the worst play the West End has to offer. Its slightly more expensive sister, Floridita, is at the same address.

FLORIDITA £

100 Wardour St. W1, 020/7314-4000

HOURS: Mon.-Wed. 5:30 P.M.-2 A.M., Thurs.-Sat. 5:30 P.M.-3 A.M.

TUBE: Tottenham Court Road

Live Cuban music may tempt you out onto the dance floor, but the Cuban rum keeps you in your seat at this popular restaurant and nightspot. The meals are hearty and include lots of meat and seafood dishes as well as vegetarian options. The same management owns the more laid-back Casa Del Habano at the same address with a similar drink menu.

HIGH TEA

SAVOY £££

Savoy Pl. btwn. Savoy Hill and Savoy St. WC2, 020/7420-2669, www.fairmont.com/savoy

HOURS: Mon.-Sat. 8 A.M.-11 P.M., Sun. 9 A.M.-11 P.M.

TUBE: Charing Cross

Enjoy high tea at one of London's oldest and most famous luxury hotels. With an elaborate plaster ceiling and French porcelain rose chandeliers, the Thames Foyer at the Savoy really captures the fin-de-siècle charm of the grand hotels of ages past. Everything is served on fine china and with glittering silverware—choose between Earl Grey or the Savoy's own blend. Teas cost £28 or £35.50

for the champagne tea. A pianist plays 2:15–5:30 P.M. Monday–Friday and 2–6 P.M. Saturday–Sunday. Reservations and "smart casual" attire are required.

INTERNATIONAL

AXIS RESTAURANT AND BAR £££

1 Aldwych WC2, 020/7300-1000, www.onealdwych.com

HOURS: Mon.-Fri. noon-2:45 P.M., 5:45-10:45 P.M., Sat. 5:45-11:30 P.M.

TUBE: Covent Garden or Temple

This basement eatery is popular with professionals trying to impress clients or dates. The menu offers a variety of international dishes such as pan-fried red mullet with pancetta, asparagus, and pea puree, or venison with truffled potato cake, vincotto onions, and caramelized tomato jus. On Fridays and Saturdays, the restaurant hosts "Give Me Movies," a three-course dinner and a movie in a private screening room for £38.50 per person. Screening times vary so check ahead. And it's "Give Me Jazz" 8–11 P.M. Tuesdays and Wednesdays with live jazz to accompany your meal.

ITALIAN

REZ'S ££

17-21 Tavistock St. WC2, 020/7379-9992, www.rezs.co.uk

HOURS: Mon.-Fri. noon-midnight, Sat. noon-11 P.M.

TUBE: St. Paul's

Subdued lighting and large windows make this an ideal place to watch passersby on Tavistock Street. The food is traditional Italian, made with quality ingredients and brought with quick service. The pizzas are especially popular with the lunch crowd. Since it's close to the Royal Opera House and many theaters, it is popular with the arts crowd and has a loyal local following. Sit at tables set on the sidewalk outside; Tavistock Street is never terribly busy, so it's nicer than it sounds.

MEDITERRANEAN

SARASTRO ££

126 Drury Lane WC2, 020/7836-0101, www.sarastro-restaurant.com

HOURS: Daily noon-11:30 P.M.

TUBE: Covent Garden

Step inside this Victorian town house and you'll think you've stepped onto an opera stage. Golden drapery, ornate statuary, frescoed ceilings, elaborate mosaics, and props from old operas adorn every square inch of the interior. Even many of the seats are actually refurbished opera boxes. It's no surprise that directors and actors come here for their opening and closing nights. Opera performances are often given Sunday and Monday evenings. And the food's good too, with Mediterranean dishes such as lamb Anatolian style, Mediterranean prawns, and fettucine with cream, mushrooms, and Parma ham. With everything to look at, you can easily forget what you're eating!

THAI

BUSABA EATHAI ££

106-110 Wardour St. W1, 020/7255-8686

HOURS: Mon.-Thurs. noon-11 P.M., Fri.-Sat. noon-11:30 P.M., Sun. noon-10 P.M.

TUBE: Goodge Street or Tottenham Court Road

Come for communal seating, friendly fellow diners, and fantastic Thai food at this noisy, busy restaurant. The extended hours and fast service (both somewhat rare in this town) make it convenient for visitors who need to make time to refuel between wanderings. The food's quite good, with a mixture of the usual Thai favorites emphasizing noodles and curry and coming in heat levels from mild to volcanic. In general, it's best in Thai restaurants not to brag about how much spice you can take, as the staff will assume you have a tongue of asbestos and a stomach of iron. You've been warned.

TRADITIONAL BRITISH

THE GRAND DIVAN, SIMPSON'S-IN-THE-STRAND £££

100 Strand WC2, 020/7836-9112, www.fairmont.com/svy/simpsons

HOURS: Breakfast: Mon.-Fri. 7:15-10:30 A.M.; Lunch: Mon.-Sat. 12:15-2:30 P.M., Sun. 12:15-3 P.M.; Dinner: Mon.-Sat. 5:45-10:45 P.M., Sun. 6-9 P.M.

TUBE: Charing Cross

For traditional British fare in an equally traditional setting, it's hard to beat this restaurant owned by the prestigious Savoy hotel and dating to 1828. Breakfast, lunch, and dinner all are served here, featuring such favorites as marbled goose liver terrine, roast rib of Aberdeen Angus beef, and roast saddle of lamb. It's filling stuff, but the height of satisfaction for any meat lover. After eating, retire to the art deco Knight's Bar, which retains the feel of the restaurant's original purpose—to serve a chess club that used to meet here.

ROCK AND SOLE PLAICE £££

47 Endell St. WC2, 020/7836-3785

HOURS: Mon.-Sat. 11:30 A.M.-11 P.M., Sun. noon-10 P.M.

TUBE: Covent Garden

Claiming to be the oldest fish-and-chip shop in London, the Rock and Sole Plaice has been serving Britain's artery-hardening favorite since 1871. In nice weather sit outside at the picnic tables; in foul weather choose the basic interior. It offers more than a dozen types of fish to choose from, and all are cooked in the open kitchen before your eyes. Many aficionados say that this is the best chippery in town.

RULES £££

35 Maiden Lane WC2, 020/7836-5314, www.rules.co.uk

HOURS: Mon.-Sat. noon-11:30 P.M., Sun. noon-10:30 P.M.

TUBE: Covent Garden

The oldest restaurant in London, Rules has been in business since 1798 and the decor shows it. Dine on excellent traditional dishes amid antique furniture and paintings. Dickens, Thackeray, and H. G. Wells all ate here, as have a slew of royals and other famous and not-so-famous people. In autumn, the menu features fresh game, such as grouse, caught on the Rules estate in the Pennines. The baked toffee apples are a great way to finish off. If you are a meat lover and plan to splash out just once during your stay, come here. Make reservations well in advance.

VEGETARIAN

FOOD FOR THOUGHT £

31 Neal St. W1, 020/7836-9072

HOURS: Mon.-Sat. noon-8:30 P.M., Sun. noon-5 P.M.

TUBE: Covent Garden

English breakfasts, fish-and-chips, and pints of ale are great stuff, but after a while they can make you feel a bit greasy. Purify your body and pamper your palate at this homey little vegetarian favorite. The basement dining area is crowded with plain wooden tables and communal seating. It's very friendly and is a social center for vegetarians and vegans. The menu changes daily depending on what ingredients are fresh that morning, but there are always several vegan and gluten- and wheat-free options. Portions are always generous and the food is always good. Take advantage of the pretheater three-course meal 5:30–8 P.M. Monday–Saturday for under £6.50.

Bloomsbury, Euston, and Holborn — Map 5

After perusing the British Museum, you won't have a shortage of nearby dining choices. This is a good area to find less expensive dining options; the general rule is that the farther away from the museum and its tourist hordes, the better the value and quality of the meal. The slew of restaurants just south of the museum tend to be mediocre, but are all decent enough when in a hurry, and there are a few good options.

CAFÉ

CAFÉ IN THE GARDENS £

Northeast corner of Russell Square W1, 020/7637-5093

HOURS: Mon.-Fri. 7 A.M.-6 P.M., Sat.-Sun. 8 A.M.-5 P.M.

TUBE: Russell Square

The main attraction at this café is its location, on the northwest corner of historic Russell Square. The menu includes sandwiches, *paninis,* pizza, full English breakfasts, and desserts. The prices are reasonable and while the food isn't anything outstanding, it's enlivened by the outside seating, where you can take in the fine views of the Victorian facade of the Hotel Russell and the lush trees and lawn of the square itself. It's perfect for a quick or lazy stop while exploring Bloomsbury.

INDIAN

MALABAR JUNCTION £££

107 Great Russell St. WC1, 020/7580-5230

HOURS: Daily noon-3 P.M., Mon.-Sat. 6-11:15 P.M., Sun. 6-10:45 P.M.

TUBE: Tottenham Court Road

Tasty and authentic Keralan cuisine in a convenient location—what more can you want? Informal and cheap lunches are served downstairs on metal trays that seem to be ubiquitous in eateries on the subcontinent. Upstairs there's a more formal dining room, set under a glass roof and tastefully decorated with flowers. Kerala is the richest of the Indian provinces and its cuisine features sweet flavors as well as seafood. You'll notice lots of Indian families eating here, usually a good sign.

INTERNATIONAL

ARCHIPELAGO £££

110 Whitfield St. W1, 020/7383-3346

HOURS: Mon.-Fri. noon-3 P.M., Mon.-Sat. 6-11 P.M.

TUBE: Warren Street or Goodge Street

Famished for frog's legs? Craving crickets? Wild for wildebeest? This is the restaurant for you. All those things are really on the menu, as are even more unfamiliar offerings such as chocolate-covered scorpion. If you're asking *why?,* then you should probably go somewhere else. But those willing to take a chance should come here for an adventurous experience. You may end up not liking your kangaroo fillet, but you'll certainly come away with a good story. As expected, the menu varies with availability. The decor is also unusual, with palm trees and golden Buddhas.

MY OLD DUTCH ££

121 High Holborn WC1, 020/7242-5200

HOURS: Daily 11 A.M.-11:30 P.M.

TUBE: Tottenham Court Road

This popular eatery offers Dutch-style *pannekoeken*—large, flaky pancakes stuffed with anything and everything under the sun. Try the Amsterdammer, with smoked bacon, apple slices, and maple syrup. There's even some Asian fusion, such as a chicken curry pancake with basmati rice, mango chutney, and yogurt. The lack of atmosphere in this modern and functional restaurant is more than made up for by the huge portions and a well-stocked bar. It can be quite lively on weekend nights as Londoners fill up before a night on the town.

ITALIAN

PARADISO ££

35 Store St., 020/7255-2554, www.ristoranteparadiso.co.uk

HOURS: Lunch: Mon.-Sat. noon-4 P.M.; Dinner: Mon.-Fri. 6-11 P.M., Sat. 5:30-11 P.M., Sun. 5-11 P.M.

TUBE: Goodge Street or Holborn

Sicilian-owned since 1934, this popular Italian eatery offers subdued lighting, simple decor, and first-rate food. The homemade pasta is prepared daily and cooked to perfection. While you won't get the heaping portions of many cheaper Italian restaurants, you will savor every bite. A nice selection of Italian wines rounds out the evening. The walls are decorated with pictures of the various screen stars who have come here. It's said the Marx Brothers, on their only trip to London, insisted on dining at Paradiso.

KOREAN

BIBIMBAB CAFE £

37 Museum St. WC1, 020/7404-8880, www.bibimbabcafe.com

HOURS: Daily 10:30 A.M.-7 P.M.

TUBE: Tottenham Court Road or Russell Square

Among the overpriced and frankly mediocre restaurants that cluster in the streets south of the British Museum, this unpretentious Korean eatery stands out for its unusual cuisine and rock-bottom prices. The dish that lends the restaurant its name is a mixture of fresh vegetables and a fried egg, making for a filling meal for a fiver. It also serves noodle dishes

RESTAURANTS

and unusual imported drinks such as aloe vera juice. The menu isn't very long, but it's all rather unfamiliar so that doesn't really matter. For the less adventurous there are *ciabattas* and a good selection of teas, coffee, and sodas. There's free wireless Internet too.

POLISH

NA ZDROWIE: THE POLISH BAR £

11 Little Turnstile WC1, 020/7831-9679

HOURS: Bar: Mon.-Fri. 12:30-11 P.M., Sat. 6-11 P.M.; Restaurant: Mon.-Fri. 12:30-10 P.M., Sat. 6-10 P.M.

TUBE: Tottenham Court Road

A crowded little restaurant and bar with filling Polish dishes and more than 40 varieties of vodka, Na Zdrowie offers good value for the money with filling dishes such as *bigos* (a stew with sauerkraut, fresh cabbage, mixed meats, smoked meats, red peppers, mushrooms, and seasonings). Another filling favorite is pierogi, a plate of 10 handmade ravioli-style dumplings with various fillings of your choice, such as cabbage or roasted minced meat. And, of course, it has great kielbasa. There isn't much seating, so if you want to eat on a weekend night, come early because the bar gets packed.

TRADITIONAL BRITISH

EVE'S SANDWICH BAR £

108 Great Russell St. WC1, 019/1636-9949

HOURS: Mon.-Sat. 8 A.M.-5 P.M.

TUBE: Tottenham Court Road

A traditional sandwich shop is always a good option for cheap eats, especially when it's so close to the British Museum and other Bloomsbury sights. Typical of sandwich shops, there aren't many seats, and there's a small extra charge for eating in. If the weather is fine, the best option is to get takeaway, sit on the front steps of the British Museum, and admire the Victorian facades across the street. There are the usual offerings of sandwiches, jacket potatoes, English breakfasts, and the not-too-traditional but still tasty *paninis.*

VEGETARIAN

PLANET ORGANIC £

20 Torrington Pl. WC1, 020/7436-1929

HOURS: Mon.-Fri. 8 A.M.-9 P.M., Sat. 10 A.M.-7:30 P.M., Sun. noon-6 P.M.

TUBE: Goodge Street or Holborn

Who says the English don't know how to eat healthy? At this supermarket/café/restaurant, one can find all things organic: produce, bread, snacks, cereal, beer, even cruelty-free beauty products. At the front of the store is a café and restaurant serving good coffee and homemade organic dishes such as vegetarian lasagna. The meals are reasonably priced and come in takeaway packets. For drinks, the smoothies are recommended. One wall holds health and exercise magazines and a notice board for those into healthy living.

Chelsea, Kensington, and Knightsbridge Map 6

After a long day of shopping, reenergize with some of London's top dining. You don't even have to leave the shops; many department stores have excellent dining halls with fine food from around the world. Though most of the choices here are a bit more expensive on average, you'll also find some cheaper options.

ASIAN

JENNY LO'S TEA HOUSE £

14 Eccleston St. SW1, 020/7259-0399

HOURS: Mon.-Sat. 11:30 A.M.-3 P.M., 6-10 P.M.

TUBE: Victoria

Enjoy good Cantonese cooking in this friendly, understated neighborhood restaurant. Jenny Lo's has been a local institution for more than 50 years and is still owned by the same family. Besides various soups, noodles, and rice dishes, there are a few Thai and Vietnamese selections too. Tea connoisseurs will enjoy the extensive choice, with dozens of varieties on the menu. The service is quick too, and with such low prices, you can't really go wrong.

NAHM £££

5 Halkin St. SW1, 020/7333-1234, www.halkin.co.uk

HOURS: Mon.-Fri. noon-2:30 P.M., 7-11 P.M., Sat. 7-11 P.M., Sun. 7-10 P.M.

TUBE: Hyde Park Corner

Attached to the exclusive Halkin hotel, this popular Thai restaurant imitates the hotel's clean lines and modern Asian style. The menu is traditional Royal Thai, with artfully presented dishes that vary constantly depending on what has been flown in fresh from Bangkok. Famous chef David Thompson does such an excellent job recreating the cuisine of Southeast Asia that this was the first Thai restaurant in Europe to be awarded a Michelin star. If you are new to Thai cuisine, or just want to try a variety of flavors, try getting the fixed-price menu, which serves four courses with eight dishes in total. Reservations are recommended.

EUROPEAN

FIFTH FLOOR, HARVEY NICHOLS £££

Harvey Nichols, 109-125 Knightsbridge SW1, 020/7235-5250

HOURS: Mon.-Fri. noon-3 P.M., 6-11 P.M., Sat. 11:30 A.M.-11 P.M., Sun. 11:30 A.M.-3 P.M.

TUBE: Knightsbridge

This is the perfect place to go after shopping at the famous department store, assuming you still have credit left on your plastic. The decor is minimalist, with lots of white; this, and the subdued conversation, makes the restaurant a welcome relief after the consumer feeding frenzy downstairs. At night it gets a bit trippy when the walls start changing color, thanks to special fiberoptic lighting. The kitchen serves the best in modern European cuisine, such as salmon fillet with Tarbais beans ragout, confit tomato, and *piquillo* peppers. To save money for more shopping, head to the café, which serves sushi and Mediterranean snacks. It's a bit crowded and noisy, but the food is just as good and the prices are more reasonable.

FOLIAGE £££

Mandarin Oriental Hotel, 66 Knightsbridge SW1, 020/7235-2000 or 020/7201-3723

HOURS: Mon.-Sun. noon-2 P.M., 7-9:30 P.M.

TUBE: Knightsbridge

True to its name, Foliage's tables are bedecked with leaves and there's a fantastic view of the trees and grass of Hyde Park. For those who don't fret over cost, this is one of the more relaxing restaurants in London. The menu is an interesting selection of European cuisine, including rabbit and foie gras, and several vegetarian options. A set-lunch menu is a bit more reasonably priced and always well chosen for quality. The nearby hotel bar is elegant and a bit more boisterous.

INTERNATIONAL

HARRODS FOOD HALL ££

Harrods, 87-135 Brompton Rd. SW1, 020/7730-1234, www.harrods.com

HOURS: Mon.-Sat. 10 A.M.-8 P.M., Sun. noon-6 P.M.

TUBE: Knightsbridge

Harrods' famous food hall offers just about anything you might want to sink your teeth into, and a few things you probably wouldn't. If calf's brain and veal heart aren't up your alley, try the fine deli or the freshly prepared pizza or sushi. There's nowhere to eat in the actual hall; instead, get a meal boxed up and enjoy a fine picnic at Hyde Park across the street. The food hall also sells beer, wine, and champagne—all of which are perfectly legal to drink outdoors.

ITALIAN

LA BOTTEGA DEL SAN LORENZO ££

23 Beauchamp Pl. SW3, 020/7591-0074

HOURS: Mon.-Sat. 10 A.M.-5 P.M.

TUBE: Knightsbridge

Those into the Slow Food movement, which emphasizes local, organic materials rather than the processed slop in fast food, should try this tiny little Italian eatery. La Bottega offers a fine variety of *paninis, piadinas,* and salads, as well as Italian wines. The walls are lined with shelves filled with olive oil and preserves for sale. There are only four tables overlooking busy Beauchamp Place, so many locals get takeaway. There's a proper sit-down restaurant owned by the same people next door, but I prefer the lunchtime casual feel of this lucky find.

SCOTTISH

BOISDALE £££

15 Eccleston St. SW1, 020/7730-6922

HOURS: Mon.-Fri. noon-2:30 P.M., Mon.-Sat. 7-11 P.M.

TUBE: Victoria

Come to Boisdale to enjoy hearty Scottish fare such as beef, haggis, and wild game lathered in rich sauces. The smoked salmon is also excellent. Cigars and whiskey are the rule here, which fits well with the crowd of affluent business types who frequent this comfortable, clublike restaurant. Expect red-paneled walls, a dark wood floor and furniture, and paintings of Highland scenes on the walls. If you can't make it to Scotland this trip, you'd have a hard time doing better than this.

Notting Hill, Bayswater, and Paddington Map 7

This area has long been famous for its ethnic diversity. Caribbean immigrants started settling here in the 1950s, and now many Arabs and Persians live here too. British cuisine can still be found, though, and there are many different styles and price ranges to choose from.

ASIAN

ROYAL CHINA RESTAURANT £££

13 Queensway W2, 020/7221-2535, www.royalchinagroup.co.uk

HOURS: Mon.-Thurs. noon-11 P.M., Fri.-Sat. noon-11:30 P.M., Sun. 11 A.M.-10 P.M.

TUBE: Queensway

Black furnishings, Chinese art, and big mirrors give a classy feel to this popular Chinese eatery. The emphasis here is on Cantonese cuisine and dim sum, and it does the latter extremely well. The regular menu is quite long and has everything from noodle dishes to meats and soups. Everything is made with fresh, quality ingredients and while dinner can be a bit pricey, the dim sum lunch is cheaper. Reservations are recommended.

CAFÉ

CAFÉ DIANA £

5 Wellington Terrace W2, 020/7792-9606, www.cafediana.com

HOURS: Daily 8 A.M.-11 P.M.

TUBE: Notting Hill Gate

An Arab-owned café that serves falafels and full English breakfasts and has walls covered in photos of Princess Diana? Well, this *is* London, after all. The much-loved princess actually stopped by a few times, and photographs of the beaming owners next to their object of adoration get pride of place. The food's good too. Besides the usual café food such as pastries and breakfast plates, there are "Diana's Dishes"—a selection of Middle Eastern staples such as hummus and kebabs. Vegetarians can try "Diana's salads."

DELI

TOM'S DELICATESSEN ££

226 Westbourne Grove W11, 020/7221-8818

HOURS: Mon.-Sat. 8 A.M.-6 P.M., Sun. 9 A.M.-5 P.M.

TUBE: Notting Hill Gate or Bayswater

Tom's has been a local favorite for years, and the two floors of gourmet food are the reason. Tom's carries everything from fine cheese to seasonings and meat, but the real draw for out-of-towners is the cheap meals. The freshly made pizzas—such as ham, parmesan, and artichoke hearts—are very popular and creative, and the heaping sandwiches are also good. The choice of salads is rivaled only by Punch's Tavern in The City. Eat in or get takeaway and munch while window shopping. Generous portions and a modest price (considering the neighborhood) make this a great value for the money.

PERSIAN

COLBEH ££

6 Porcester Pl. W2, 020/7706-4888/7772, www.colbeh.co.uk

HOURS: Daily noon-midnight

TUBE: Marble Arch

Persian cuisine has been developing for

Tom's Delicatessen, a local favorite

millennia and shows Middle Eastern and Indian influences. The Colbeh serves a wide range of traditional dishes to a loyal following of local Persians and Anglos. A waiter cooks naan bread in an oven in the front room and then walks over to your table to serve it piping hot. Try the special naan, covered in sesame seeds and big enough for two. The main dishes use a blend of spices and usually a rice base to highlight a choice of meat, but there are a few vegetarian options. Try the Zereshk Polo, sweet and sour berries cooked with saffron and chicken on a bed of rice. The desserts are goopy and delicious, but the meal portions are so large you might not have room. Highly recommended.

TRADITIONAL BRITISH

S&M CAFÉ £

268 Portobello Rd. W10, 020/8968-8898, www.sandmcafe.co.uk

HOURS: Mon.-Thurs. 9 A.M.-11 P.M., Fri.-Sat. 9 A.M.-11:30 P.M., Sun. 9 A.M.-10:30 P.M.

TUBE: Ladbroke Grove

Get your mind out of the gutter! S and M stand for "sausage and mash," Britain's ultimate comfort food—although chicken tikka masala is giving it a run for its money. Sausages, mashed potatoes, and gravy... that's what you'll get here, but the sausages come in every variety, from Italian to vegetarian, and the dinerlike atmosphere may make you wax nostalgic for that favorite truck stop back home. It's a good place to go for those who need to take care of a hangover.

Maida Vale, Marylebone, and St. John's Wood Map 8

This is one of London's more exclusive areas, and it offers a great variety of international cuisine at a full range of prices. Perhaps all the embassies and consulates in the area have had an effect, because this is one of the more cosmopolitan neighborhoods for dining in the city.

CAFÉ

DE GUSTIBUS £

53 Blandford St. W1, 020/7486-6608

HOURS: Mon.-Fri. 6:30 A.M.-4 P.M.

TUBE: Baker Street or Bond Street

This bakery/café has won awards for its dozens of varieties of fresh-baked breads, and it gets points from me for friendly service and cheap but hearty fare. There aren't very many seats in the bare interior, but most people get a takeaway sandwich or a loaf to bring home. The breads include Arabian flatbread, San Francisco sourdough, *panini*, olive or rosemary focaccia, Black Forest rye, and many more, and they can be stuffed with several varieties of meat, seafood, or vegetarian fillings. There's no need to slow down your sightseeing; grab a sandwich here and keep on going!

DIVERTIMENTI £

33-34 Marylebone High St. W1, 020/7935-0689,

www.divertimenti.co.uk
HOURS: Mon.-Fri. 9:30 A.M.-6 P.M., Sat. 10 A.M.-6 P.M., Sun. 11 A.M.-5 P.M.
TUBE: Baker Street or Regent's Park
Attached to a cooking school and shop, Divertimenti offers hearty and well-made sandwiches, salads, soups, and cheese platters in the Mediterranean style. A cappuccino and snack here makes a nice pick-me-up while shopping along Marylebone High Street or after browsing the utensils at the cook shop (see *Shopping*). The dining area is informal and decorated in modern Italian design. Oh, and the cakes are astounding.

INTERNATIONAL

THE PROVIDORES AND TAPA ROOM £££

109 Marylebone High St. W1, 020/7935-6175, www.theprovadores.co.uk
HOURS: Tapa Room: Mon.-Fri. 9 A.M.-10:30 P.M., Sat. 10 A.M.-10:30 P.M., Sun. 10 A.M.-10 P.M.; Providores: Daily noon-2:45 P.M., Mon.-Sat. 6-10:30 P.M., Sun. 6-10 P.M.
TUBE: Baker Street or Bond Street
For a menu that's truly international, with dishes from Italy, Spain, and across North Africa, come to this Kiwi-owned, two-story restaurant. On the ground floor, a reasonably priced café and wine bar serves a traditional English fry up along with a good cup of coffee (refuge from the swill served in many cafés). The "tapa" of the name isn't a misspelling of tapas, the Spanish snack that few London restaurants are capable of doing right, but refers to the painted Polynesian cloth decorating the walls. Upstairs is a fine dining experience with international dishes such as seared kangaroo fillet with Greek yogurt or plantain and quinoa dolmades with sesame tofu puree. Come here for unusual dishes in a relaxed setting and the excellent range of New Zealand wines.

VILLANDRY ££

170 Great Portland St. W1, 020/7631-3131, www.villandry.com
HOURS: Mon.-Sat. noon-3 P.M., 6-10:30 P.M., Sun. 11:30 A.M.-4 P.M.
TUBE: Baker Street or Regent's Park
A relaxed, open space allows for comfortable dining on Villandry's popular international cooking. The menu changes from month to month depending on what's in season, but the cuisine is always as refined yet unpretentious as the atmosphere. The seafood is especially good here, with a char-grilled fish of the day and other options. Landlubbers will have a choice of duck or steak, and vegetarians are catered to with healthy creations such as artichoke heart with fresh herbs.

SEAFOOD

BACK TO BASICS ££

21a Foley St. W1, 020/7436-2181, www.backtobasics.uk.com
HOURS: Mon.-Sat. noon-3 P.M., 6-10:30 P.M.
TUBE: Oxford Circus
Fresh fish is the specialty at this bright and informal café with simple wooden floors and tables. The extensive seafood menu changes from day to day depending on what was fresh at the market before opening. The kitchen cooks everything to perfection and this, plus the generous portions, makes the restaurant one of the most popular spots in town for seafood lovers. There's also a lovely wine list with more than 50 vintages from all the major regions. In fine weather, there are also a few outdoor tables. Reservations are recommended.

TRADITIONAL BRITISH

THE HONEST SAUSAGE £

The Broadwalk, The Regent's Park NW1, www.honestsausage.com
HOURS: Daily 8:30 A.M.-6 P.M.
TUBE: Baker Street or Regent's Park
After walking around The Regent's Park, fill up on free-range meat and organic, homemade bread at this little kiosk. The menu features basic burgers and sandwiches, with a few salads for the vegetarians. The meat comes from small British farms and any imported materials are Fair Trade. A favorite selection is the "Park Porker," a pork sausage on an organic bun. There's some indoor seating in rather

uninspiring and crowded surroundings, so a much better option is to sit outside and admire the park from a shaded table.

VEGETARIAN

EAT AND TWO VEG £

50 Marylebone High St. W1, 020/7258-8595

HOURS: Mon.-Sat. 9 A.M.-11 P.M., Sun. 10 A.M.-10:30 P.M.

TUBE: Baker Street

The name of this popular vegetarian eatery is a play on the expression "meat and two veg," the traditional British meal and a general term for anything old-fashioned. But old-fashioned this place definitely is not. The trendy decor and healthy but satisfying fare is just the thing after spending too much time in the pub subsisting on lager and crisps. Vegetarian food has been catching on in London in recent years, and this is one of the best places to get it.

Camden Town Map 9

This artsy and well-off area is home to lots of different restaurants, offering everything from British to Asian and more. Innumerable eateries lie along Chalk Farm Road and Camden High Street, but a select few of London's old favorites are listed here, plus a couple of promising newcomers.

CARIBBEAN

COTTONS £

55 Chalk Farm Rd. NW1, 020/7485-8388, www.cottons-restaurant.co.uk

HOURS: Rhum Shack: Mon.-Thurs. 5 P.M.-midnight, Fri. 5 P.M.-1 A.M., Sat. noon-1 A.M., Sun. noon-11 P.M.; Restaurant: Mon.-Thurs. 6-11 P.M., Fri. 6-11:30 P.M., Sat. noon-4 P.M., 6-11:30 P.M., Sun. noon-11 P.M.

TUBE: Chalk Farm or Camden Town

Cottons features three dining rooms, all decorated with island themes, where patrons fill up on exciting Caribbean favorites such as curry goat and rum-and-ginger marinated grilled swordfish. There's a short but interesting menu of vegetarian options too, such as jerked tofu. The bar features 150 varieties of rum in various forms, from straight up to mixed in elaborate cocktails, making this a good place to take a drinking date. A happy hour 9 P.M.–1 A.M. Fridays and Saturdays features DJs playing groove, R&B, reggae, and '80s hits.

INDIAN/SEYCHELLOIS

KAZ KREOL ££

35 Pratt St. NW1, 020/7485-4747

HOURS: Mon.-Fri. noon-3:30 P.M., 7-11 P.M.

TUBE: Camden Town

The Seychelles are a group of about 150 islands in the Indian Ocean, and their cuisine is like South Asian food with an island twist. In what Indian restaurant could you find papaya chutney and octopus curry? There's a lot of seafood, of course, but also various land critters such as chicken and goat, and some vegetarian options as well. Kaz Kreol opened in 2006 and is the only Seychellois (you learn a new adjective every day!) restaurant in town. It also offers a good value £8 all-you-can-eat lunch buffet with dessert and coffee included.

INTERNATIONAL

CAMDEN LOCK MARKET £

Chalk Farm Rd. at Camden Lock Pl., 020/7284 2084, www.camdenlockmarket.com

HOURS: Daily until sundown

TUBE: Camden Town

Camden Lock is filled with boutiques selling fashion, accessories, and weird gifts, and a whole alley of restaurants keeps shoppers energized for more browsing. The emphasis is on international food and you can find just about anything here, including pizza, sushi, curry, Vietnamese soups, Mexican burritos, crepes, pasta, and egg rolls—all served cheap and quick. It's not fine dining, just convenience and instant satisfaction. There's some seating in front of some of the stalls, and an overcrowded seating area, so many people prefer to eat as they walk or sit on the curb.

Camden Lock Market has an alley of restaurants to keep shoppers fueled.

MEDITERRANEAN

CAFÉ CORFU £££

7 Pratt St. NW1, 020/7267-8088, www.cafécorfu.com

HOURS: Tues.-Thurs. noon-10:30 P.M., Fri. noon-11:30 P.M., Sat. 5-11:30 P.M., Sun. noon-11:30 P.M.

TUBE: Camden Town

Cuisine straight from the Greek islands is what's on here. In the brightly colored dining room, tuck into some great seafood such as the *tsipoura,* grilled sea bream shipped fresh from Greece. There are dishes for landlubbers too, such as *arni youvetsi,* a slow-roasted lamb shank with an unusual but tasty cinnamon and tomato broth. The drink menu offers an interesting selection of Greek wines and beers, which you can sample in the restaurant or in a separate cocktail bar. You'll find belly dancing and DJs playing Greek hits from 9 P.M. on Friday and Saturday nights.

VEGETARIAN

GREEN NOTE ££

106 Parkway NW1, 020/7485-9899, www.greennote.co.uk

HOURS: Tues. 6-10:30 P.M., Wed.-Thurs. 6-11 P.M., Fri. 6-midnight, Sat. noon-midnight, Sun. noon-10:30 P.M.

TUBE: Camden Town

This vegetarian restaurant/café/bar/music venue opened in 2006 and is a lot of fun. The interior is just bare wooden floors and tattered, overstuffed couches, lending the place a student's living-room feel. That's not a bad thing, because the laid-back atmosphere suits it. The menu is a varied mix of dolmades, tapas, and salads, with a hearty weekend brunch for the hangover crowd. There's live music, usually acoustic, most nights, and the place is becoming an increasingly popular venue for independent musicians. Check the website for a schedule.

The City — Map 10

At lunchtime, London's financial center is abuzz with people going out to eat. The streets empty out at night, but not everyone goes home; many linger to enjoy the fine dining that caters to wealthy bankers and other business types. Lots of wealth in the vicinity means there are some really exclusive places, but there are also cheaper options for the rest of us. The proximity to so many important sights such as St. Paul's means that sightseers have only a short walk for lunch or dinner.

ASIAN

K-10 ££

20 Copthill Ave., 020/7562-8510, www.k10.net

HOURS: Mon.-Fri. 11:30 A.M.-3 P.M.

TUBE: Bank

The soothing blue interior of this chic basement

restaurant serving sushi and other Japanese favorites is popular with The City lunch crowd, which eagerly orders flavorful sushi and sashimi as well as modern Japanese cooked dishes. The rice dishes and salads are moderately priced, but start ordering the sushi and it will add up quickly. The takeaway service is especially popular, and you might want to consider it so you can sit in a park or churchyard and eat. It's not as if the sushi is going to get cold.

BELGIAN

ABBAYE £££

55 Charterhouse St. EC1, 020/7253-1612

HOURS: Mon.-Fri. noon-10:30 P.M.

TUBE: Farringdon

This is a good high-end bar and restaurant for diners with hearty appetites. You can wash down filling Belgian dishes with a variety of excellent Trappist ales, some of the most respected microbrews in the world. The mussels are served with a huge variety of sauces, popular with the crowds of City workers who flock here. While happy little bivalves dominate the menu, there are vegetarian sausages, king prawns, and a number of other meat and fish dishes. Sometimes you'll find jazz performances in the evenings.

DELI

PUNCH TAVERN £

99 Fleet St. EC4, 020/7353-6658

HOURS: Daily for breakfast 7:30-11:00 A.M., lunch 11:30-3:00 P.M., dinner 3-10:30 P.M.

TUBE: Temple

The famous magazine *Punch,* which satirized generations of British politicians, was created here in the 1840s, and cartoons from the magazine adorn the art deco walls. This pub seems to be in the process of transforming itself into a restaurant, although a fully licensed one, as the emphasis is more and more on inexpensive meals for City workers. The best deal is the salad bar, where diners can choose between heaping helpings of 15 different prepared salads, all of which are made from fresh and quality ingredients.

INTERNATIONAL

JUST THE BRIDGE ££

1 Paul's Walk, Millennium Bridge north side EC4, 020/7236-0000, www.justthebridge.com

HOURS: Lunch: Daily noon-3:30 P.M.; Dinner: Mon.-Sat. 6-11 P.M.; Brunch: Sat.-Sun. 11:30 A.M.-5 P.M.

TUBE: Blackfriars or Mansion House

International cooking and a great view of the Millennium Bridge combine to make a fun place to eat, especially as a stop for lunch between seeing the Tate Modern and St. Paul's. Most of the dishes are inspired by Asian cuisine, with selections such as slow-roasted duck with wild cherries, seafood and vegetable tempura, and Mongolian lamb with rice wine and black bean. It offers several vegetarian options for the health conscious and a long cocktail list for the rest of us. There's also a bar and an outside terrace.

LEON £

12 Ludgate Circus EC4, 020/7489-1580, www.leonrestaurants.co.uk

HOURS: Mon.-Fri. 7 A.M.-11 P.M.

TUBE: Blackfriars

The emphasis at Leon is on healthy food, fast service, and long hours—making it a sharp contrast to most other dining spots in the City. It's become quite popular too. The menu is international in flavor with a Moroccan influence and plenty of vegetarian and dairy-, wheat-, and lactose-free options. Breakfasts include power smoothies or grilled mushroom sarnie (sandwich) with roast tomatoes. Lunch and dinner vary from roasted sweet-potato falafel to chili chicken shish.

SEAFOOD

GOW'S RESTAURANT AND OYSTER BAR ££

81 Old Broad St. EC2, 020/7920-9645, www.ballsbrothers.co.uk

HOURS: Mon.-Fri. 11 A.M.-11 P.M.

TUBE: Liverpool St.

A relaxed and friendly restaurant popular with business people, Gow's is the place for oyster

IN DEFENSE OF BRITISH COOKING

A common misperception is that British cooking is all boiled vegetables, soggy toast, and poisonous meat. That's only partially true. While there's a good amount of bad food in Britain, the culinary arts have come a long way in recent years. The British, especially fashion-conscious Londoners, have woken up to the need for a healthier, less fatty, and tastier diet. Greasy standbys such as fish-and-chips are still popular, but there are plenty of options to try without upsetting your stomach and expanding your girth.

One traditional food that's experiencing a bit of a revival is oysters. Oyster bars were once ubiquitous in London, back in the day when oysters could be plucked from the mouth of the river itself. The bars were frequented by all social classes, but now they are mainly popular among wealthier diners, who combine oysters with high-priced spirits. Oysters are served raw or cooked and usually come with a bit of salt and butter. Seafood lovers will enjoy a good tuck-in at a British oyster bar and can relax in the knowledge that a dozen raw oysters have only 110 calories but are a good source of vitamin A, calcium, zinc, and iron.

Another popular British institution is the breakfast café. Frequented by everyone from professionals to construction workers, these places offer crowded and noisy sociability along with gut-busting breakfasts. A full English breakfast usually includes sausages, bacon, eggs, baked beans, fried mushrooms, toast, and tea. Quality is generally good and prices hover around £5 for a meal that will keep you going until dinner. Breakfast cafés offer smaller meals as well, and some have bowed to modern dietary sensibilities by offering vegetarian breakfasts. These cafés can be found in all areas of London; a few favorites are listed in this chapter. Many stay open all day because the English can have breakfast any time. In fact, Somerset Maugham once quipped that to eat well in England, one should have three breakfasts a day.

Sad to say, independent cafés are on the wane in London, pushed out by larger chains offering a quick bagel and overpriced coffee. On April 20, 2006, the *Daily Telegraph* reported the number of independent cafés in London had dropped by 40 percent since the year 2000. A campaign called Save the Proper British Café raised some money for a few endangered establishments, but they seem to be fighting a losing battle.

Another staple of traditional eating are the pie shops, serving hot pies filled with various combinations of meat and vegetables. These, too, are an endangered species and vary widely in quality. Tastes in dining have moved on, and the pie shops seem to have been left behind. Some even still serve that nadir of British cuisine – jellied eels. I have yet to meet an English person who eats jellied eels, and the squishy mass I tried told me why. The horror... the horror....

Some of the more expensive restaurants offer refined dining, and those who can afford it will be in for a treat. Traditional British restaurants usually offer fresh game such as venison, pheasant, grouse, and many others. The quality of the meat is exceptionally high and will be cooked to perfection. But the pinnacle of British culinary achievement has to be the Sunday roast, served with a variety of sides such as vegetables and chips. Make sure to go to a good restaurant or a pub that cooks its own food, and you'll have a meal to remember.

Many restaurants call themselves "contemporary British." This term is used by all sorts of establishments and it's often hard to tell what it means. Usually a contemporary British restaurant offers new twists on old favorites, such as adding chutney to a traditional meat dish, or having Continental meals along with British ones.

The main problem with British cuisine is that it is so often done badly. Avoid the cheaper restaurants and pubs, and go hunting for real British fare!

lovers. Oysters have long been a staple of London cuisine, and Gow's serves them in a traditional English setting with lots of dark wood and oil paintings. It offers other dishes too, mostly seafood, such as grilled Dover sole and seared blue tuna, and seasonal dishes using fresh local produce, all washed down with a selection of more than 100 fine wines. Check the website for regular wine tastings complete with dinner specifically matched to the vintage.

SOUTH AMERICAN

GAUCHO £££

125-126 Chancery Lane WC2, 020/7242-7727, www.gaucho-grill.com

HOURS: Mon.-Fri. noon-11:30 P.M.

TUBE: Chancery Lane

Meat lovers know that Argentina makes some of the best steaks in the world, and here they get to try them in the cowboy (or *gaucho* in Argentina) tradition at this modern and stylish eatery. The steaks come in a variety of cuts and with a choice of seasonings; if you're bewildered by the wide choice, the steak experts will be happy to help you decide. For those not into steak, it serves wood-roasted salmon, shrimp enchiladas, and mushroom *parpadelle* (one of the few vegetarian options on the entrée list).

TRADITIONAL BRITISH

SMITHS OF SMITHFIELD ££

67-77 Charterhouse St. EC1, 020/7251-7950, www.smithsofsmithfield.co.uk

HOURS: Ground Floor Café: Mon.-Fri. 7 A.M.-5 P.M., Sat. 10 A.M.-5 P.M., Sun. 9:30 A.M.-5 P.M.; Dining Room: Mon.-Fri. noon-3 P.M. and 6-11 P.M., Sat. 6-10:45 P.M.; Top Floor: Mon.-Sun. lunch, dinner, and weekend brunch

TUBE: Farringdon

Bare brickwork, high ceilings, and spacious seating give an industrial feel to this popular four-story restaurant that serves breakfast, brunch, and Saturday dinner; the late hours are reserved for the bar. The meat dishes such as the braised lamb are especially good here, which is not surprising considering the restaurant is right next to Smithfield Central Markets, London's only commercial meat market. Favorites include the chunky sandwiches and the variety of salads. There's also a juice bar for the more health conscious.

YE OLDE CHESHIRE CHEESE £

145 Fleet St. EC4, 020/7353-6170

HOURS: Mon.-Sat. 11 A.M.-11 P.M., Sun. noon-10:30 P.M.

TUBE: Blackfriars

A wonderful old 17th century pub frequented by great writers such as Boswell, Johnson, and Dickens, the Cheshire Cheese has long been a City institution. Lots of barristers and tourists come here for the drinks and the atmosphere, but it's also one of the best places to get real pub food. All the old favorites such as fish-and-chips and steak and kidney pie are cooked fresh on the premises, not from prepared frozen dinners as in so many other pubs. The downstairs dining area features Johnson's favorite seat. The upstairs is roomier but almost as atmospheric.

Islington Map 11

While this neighborhood is a little farther out from the center, that means there are some good deals on dining, and the eclectic mix of cultures means there are some unique restaurants here. Islington has become known for its bars and clubs, and plenty of restaurants have appeared in recent years to feed people before they head off for a night of fun.

AFGHAN

AFGHAN KITCHEN £

35 Islington Green N1, 020/7359-8019

HOURS: Tues.-Sat. noon-3:30 P.M., 5:30-11 P.M.

TUBE: Angel

Afghan cuisine tastes like a mixture of Middle Eastern and Indian cooking, and this popular restaurant serves it just right. The dishes, such as the *lavan-e-murgh* (chicken in yogurt), all come heavily spiced, but more for flavor than for heat. Meat eaters will also find lamb, and there are vegetarian options such as *borani kado* (pumpkin with yogurt). Sides include rice or a large loaf of Afghan bread (the bread is unique and good for sopping up all the yogurt and sauce). To drink, try the freshly squeezed carrot juice. All the dishes are great, the portions huge, and the prices dirt cheap. The decor, a spare modern interior without a hint of Afghan artistry, could be a little more in keeping with the cuisine. For Afghan arts, head next door to Rau, a well-stocked store of Afghan arts and crafts.

ASIAN

ART TO ZEN CAFÉ GALLERY £

27 Upper St. N1, 020/7226-5300, www.art2zen.co.uk

HOURS: Daily 10:30 A.M.-10:30 P.M.

TUBE: Angel

This combination art gallery, café, and restaurant has a subdued interior. With oil lamps made out of bottles and modern paintings by the resident artist on the walls, it makes for a relaxing dinner. The menu concentrates on Asian and Asian fusion with dishes such as Japanese fried chicken with spring onion, sesame sauce, and rice. There are several vegetarian options such as linguine with pesto sauce, sun-dried tomatoes, capers, parmesan flakes, and tomato *concassée.* Another favorite is the deep-fried tofu with sake and ginger dressing and stir-fried julienne of vegetables. Most dishes are GMO-free and the prices are quite reasonable. Reservations are recommended.

© VISITLONDON.COM

Art to Zen combines art and food.

VIET GARDEN ££

207 Liverpool Rd. N1, 020/7700-6040

HOURS: Daily noon-3:30 P.M., and Mon.-Thurs., Sun. 5:30-11 P.M., Fri.-Sat. 5:30-11:30 P.M.

TUBE: Angel

This good-value Vietnamese eatery is on the site of a former Italian restaurant, and the interior still looks formal and Western. The food's authentic though, and the soups are recommended, especially the hot and sour soup. The Vietnamese are masters at blending various sauces into soups to make a filling and tasty meal. It's not exactly hot-weather food, though, so in summer try some of the seafood or vegetarian dishes.

EUROPEAN

LOLA'S £££

The Mall Building, 359 Upper St. N1, 020/7359-1932, www.lolas.co.uk

HOURS: Mon.-Fri. noon-2:30 P.M., 6-11 P.M., Sat. noon-3 P.M., 6-11 P.M., Sun. noon-3 P.M.

TUBE: Angel

The unusual, glass-roofed building that houses this restaurant used to be a tram shed for London Electricity. The upper level is now devoted to the restaurant with an antique market downstairs, making this the perfect place to stop for a bite after doing a bit of shopping. A seasonal menu features European dishes from both land and sea, with choices such as Welsh black sirloin steak and organic salmon with asparagus and Jersey Royals (potatoes). Everything is of excellent quality, and the setting is interesting, but the prices may curtail your antiquing a bit.

ITALIAN

METROGUSTO £££

11 Theberton St. N1, 020/7226-9400, www.metrogusto.co.uk

HOURS: Mon.-Thurs. 6:30-10:30 P.M., Fri.-Sat. 12:30-2:30 P.M., 6:30-11 P.M., Sun. 12:30-5 P.M.

TUBE: Angel

Classy Italian cooking in a subdued and cozy oak and walnut dining room make for a nice dinner for two. The pasta *del giorno* is always a good bargain, and the regular entrées are all done with flair. The menu has a good selection of seafood, with creations such as almond-crusted tuna steak with licorice sauce, but landlubbers might want to try the veal scallops, mustard seeds, and marsala wine with fried leeks. An impressive wine list rounds out the evening. Reservations are recommended.

OREGANO £

18-19 St. Albans Place N1, 020/7288-1123

HOURS: Tues.-Thurs. 5:30-11 P.M., Fri. 5:30-11:30 P.M., Sat. 12:30-11:30 P.M., Sun. 12:30-10:30 P.M.

TUBE: Angel

Oregano's rather unassuming interior is the locale for great wood-fired pizzas and the standard pasta favorites. The restaurant is on a quiet side street, which makes for a nice change from the often chaotic Upper Street, and it is becoming popular with locals for its no-nonsense Italian cooking. This isn't high cuisine, but the generous portions of quality food will get you ready for a night on the town, and it's a very good option for filling up for cheap.

RESTAURANTS

South of the Thames Map 12

The area south of the Thames is home to a multinational population that works hard for a living. The result is a wide range of dining options that won't break your budget. Those willing to splash out, so to speak, can eat right next to the river and enjoy the view.

AFRICAN

OLD KENT ROAD

Old Kent from Bricklayer's Arms to Trafalgar Ave. SE1

TUBE: Elephant and Castle or Borough

Those looking for something really different should head down to Old Kent Road, a center for African immigrants and lined with inexpensive restaurants, bars, and takeaway fast food. Most of the restaurants are Nigerian, but there's a sprinkling of Ethiopian eateries as well. Favorite Nigerian dishes include *suya,* a variety of shish kebab, and goat's meat soup. The fried yams are savory too. Nigerian cuisine is generally quite spicy and heavy, so it makes good after-bar eating. Many restaurants have attached clubs serving palm wine and featuring live African bands. Though many white Londoners may say this area is dangerous, this may say more about the way the area is perceived by a small minority than its actual reality.

CAFÉS

CAFÉ 171/GLASSHOUSE £

171 Union St., Bankside SE1, 020/7654-0100, www.jerwoodspace.co.uk

HOURS: Mon.-Fri. 8 A.M.-3 P.M.; Breakfast: 8-11 A.M., Lunch: noon-2:30 P.M.

TUBE: Borough or Southwark

The popular Jerwood Space gallery and rehearsal area offers two options for dining. Café 171 is a brightly lit area just next to the gallery, which makes for a nice stop after seeing the art. Café 171 serves beer, wine, snacks, and breakfast. The Glasshouse is a full restaurant set farther back in the building and serves an international menu in a great atmosphere. The restaurant features a high glass roof so diners can enjoy eating al fresco even when it's pouring rain.

CAFÉ ROSSI £

57 Borough High St. SE1, 020/7407-3718

HOURS: Daily 6 A.M.-7 P.M.

TUBE: Borough

This bustling, friendly little place is popular with local workers and apparently every cop on the South Bank. Nothing highbrow, just good, honest full English breakfasts and hot tea and coffee at a decent price, served all day. It also offers a selection of sandwiches and pastries. This is the place to go for breakfast when staying in one of the nearby hostels; experience how hard-working Englishmen and women fill up before the start of their day.

NATIONAL FILM THEATRE CAFÉ £

National Film Theatre SE1, 020/7928-3232, www.bfi.org.uk

HOURS: Daily 9 A.M.-9 P.M.

TUBE: Waterloo

While this café's menu isn't particularly notable, it has a very convenient location just under Waterloo Bridge on the South Bank of the Thames. Sit at the windows and watch people go back and forth along the Thames Path, or check out the book fiends browsing the stacks at the South Bank Book Market. Decent coffees, a deli, and a selection of beers on tap makes this popular with a mix of path walkers and moviegoers at the National Film Theatre.

PATISSERIE LILA £

1 Bedale St. SE1, 020/7403-6304, www.patisserielila.com

HOURS: Mon.-Sat. 8 A.M.-6 P.M.

TUBE: London Bridge

This informal little patisserie, with bare brick walls decorated with assorted antique bric-a-brac, feels as if it's been taken straight out of Paris. The cakes and pastries are phenomenal, especially the various chocolate creations, and the coffee is well prepared. It even makes a type of chocolate cake layered with thin sheets of gold. I'm not sure what the Recommended Daily Allowance of gold is, but it will definitely fulfill your chocolate quota.

The National Film Theatre Café has a convenient South Bank location.

TATE MODERN CAFÉ £

Tate Modern btwn. Bankside and Sumner St. SE1, 020/7887-8000, www.tate.org.uk

HOURS: Daily 10 A.M.-6 P.M.

TUBE: Southwark or London Bridge

There are actually two cafés in this major art museum—one on the second floor and one on the fourth. The café on the second floor offers quick drinks. The upper café is by far the better, with amazing Thames views and a variety of simple British meals, salads, and drinks. The food isn't anything terribly special, but the coffee is good and its convenient location and fabulous view make it worth a stop. There's an outside porch where patrons can sit and get some great photos of the Millennium Bridge, the river, and St. Paul's.

CONTEMPORARY BRITISH

BANANA STORE ££

1 Cathedral St. SE1, 017/1357-9795

HOURS: noon-3 P.M., 6:30-9 P.M.

TUBE: London Bridge

If you didn't fill up at Borough Market, walk

around the corner and down into this little cellar eatery. The menu changes regularly depending on what's fresh and available, but it features a range of familiar dishes such as chicken Caesar salad and more unusual offerings such as pan-fried chorizo with new potatoes and red onion salad. It also serves a good selection of canapes. A bar is attached, and the walls are devoted to the paintings and photographs of local artists. While the menu lacks a bit of imagination, you can get a good value meal served quickly in a relaxed atmosphere.

CUBAN

CUBANA £££

48 Lower Marsh SE1, 020/7928-8778, www.cubana.co.uk

HOURS: Mon.-Tues. noon-midnight, Wed.-Thurs. noon-1 A.M., Fri. noon-3 A.M., Sat. 5 P.M.-3 A.M.

TUBE: Waterloo

Cubana is an upbeat restaurant serving "prerevolutionary" Cuban food. It's unclear how prerevolutionary Cuban cuisine is different from postrevolutionary Cuban cuisine, unless bourgeois decadence is a seasoning. If so, Cuban has added a lot of it to its cocktails, which are some of the best in town. Happy hour runs Mon.–Sat. 5–6:30 P.M. and Mon.–Tues. 10 P.M.–midnight, and sees the crowd really pick up. Despite the prerevolutionary culinary ideals, the walls are adorned with Kalashnikovs and pictures of Che and Castro. I won't hazard a guess as to the symbolism of having Cuban election posters in the bathroom.

INTERNATIONAL

GABRIEL'S WHARF £££

Gabriel's Wharf, 56 Upper Ground SE1, 020/7401-2255, www.gabrielswharf.co.uk

HOURS: Daily until late

TUBE: Waterloo or Southwark

Conveniently situated along the Thames Path, this is a lively place to stop and rest your feet before continuing. The House of Crepes offers tasty, flaky treats, and Sarnis is good for a quick, quality sandwich. Riviera Restaurant has a nice terrace overlooking the Thames

Gabriel's Wharf has several restaurants to choose from.

where you can sample the Mediterranean cuisine and fine wine list. Gourmet Pizza Company offers heartier face while Studio Six is a good place for a quick beer and a snack. All offer both outside and inside seating.

OXO TOWER RESTAURANT, BAR, AND BRASSERIE £££

OXO Tower, Barge House St. at Upper Ground SE1, 020/7803-3888

HOURS: Mon.-Sat. noon-2:30 P.M., 6-11 P.M., Sun. noon-3 P.M., 6:30-10 P.M.

TUBE: Waterloo

The menu here takes its inspiration from Asia, France, and the Mediterranean, but you'll take inspiration from the views of the Thames from this eighth-story restaurant. The meals are pricey—even the three-course prix-fixe lunch will set diners back £30—but this is the best mealtime view of the river, unless you picnic along the Thames walk. The cocktail list is impressively long and occasionally there's live music in the evenings. Reservations are required.

OXO Tower offers great views of the Thames.

DELFINA ££

50 Bermondsey St. SE1, 020/7357-0244, www.delfina.org.uk

HOURS: Mon.-Thurs. noon-3 P.M., Fri. noon-3 P.M., 7-10 P.M.

TUBE: London Bridge

Delfina is an informal spot popular with the artistically oriented lunchtime crowd and the artists-in-residence at the attached studio space. The menu offers international dishes with an Asian slant, with selections such as miso-glazed aubergines with sesame sticky rice, pickled ginger, and cucumber salad. There's a lot of fish on the menu, and one particularly good dish is the char-grilled Australian fish of the day (quite fresh considering how far it had to travel) with mixed-leaf salad and organic lemon. The well-lit and family-friendly eating area makes for lively conversation and the walls are decorated with contemporary art. Reservations are recommended. There's also a café open 8 A.M.–noon and 3–5 P.M. Monday–Friday.

TRADITIONAL BRITISH

THE COUNTY HALL RESTAURANT ££

County Hall on Thames Walk SE1, 020/7902-8000

HOURS: Daily 12:30-10:30 P.M.

TUBE: Waterloo

Set in historic County Hall, this is a quiet refuge from the chaos just outside and affords a fine view of the river, Thames Walk, and the London Eye. The interior has a lofty ceiling and big windows that bring in a lot of light. The menu includes British favorites with a Continental twist, such as slow roasted English pork with apple, white pudding, and cider, and salmon fish cake with poached egg and hollandaise sauce. Vegetarians should try the lemon thyme gnocchi with broccoli, goat cheese, and walnut sauce. Attached to the restaurant is the Rotunda Lounge, offering slightly cheaper burgers and salads. Reservations are required, but not for the Rotunda Lounge.

Outlying Areas — Map 1

London's suburbs need to eat too, so those staying farther from the city center won't go hungry. Many of the city's minority communities live outside central London where rents are more reasonable, so there is a wide variety of food choices from around the world.

KOSHER

GOLDERS GREEN ROAD

Golders Green Rd. btwn. Brent St. and North End Rd. NW11

The Jewish community of London, especially the Orthodox community, is centered around Golders Green Road, a long, busy street lined with kosher restaurants, bakeries, butchers, and groceries. There are plenty of Judaica shops too. Those who keep strictly kosher will want to frequent this area, as no other part of London—not even the old Jewish district of the East End—can match it for variety and value. Out-of-town Jewish travelers have been known to be scooped up for Shabbat dinner by friendly strangers.

SOUTH ASIAN

BRICK LANE

Brick Lane btwn. Bethnal Green and Whitechapel Rd.

London's most famous South Asian street features countless restaurants to satiate any curry cravings. Many people call this Indian food, but in fact a good number of the chefs are Bengali, and there are Pakistani restaurants as well. There's so much choice that the best approach is to stroll down the street reading menus. Touts will approach offering discounts and will often throw in a free drink if you come to their restaurant. To get what you've been offered, make sure they accompany you to the restaurant and relay the deal to the waiters.

A GUIDE TO KOSHER AND HALAL FOODS

London has had a Jewish population since medieval times. It's said the first Jews came over with William the Conqueror in 1066, but there may have been a small community even earlier than that. The bulk of the Jewish population gathered in London and has established numerous restaurants and groceries to serve those who would like to keep kosher.

Muslims are more recent arrivals. While there have always been a (very) few in the country, the mass immigration started in the late 19th century, increasing steadily into the 20th century and today. In London, Muslims now far outnumber Jews and have established their own halal restaurants and shops to cater to those who wish to follow that religion's dietary rules.

The best source of information on kosher eating in London is the **London Beth Din Kashrut Division** (735 High Rd. N12, 020/8343-6246, www.kosher.org.uk). The website contains a huge amount of information and is updated regularly. The center for kosher shopping is Golders Green Road and the surrounding neighborhood. The road itself has numerous shops and restaurants offering the best selection in the country. The neighborhood of Hendon, especially around Brent Street, has another concentration of shops and restaurants. For more information, check the website www.somethingjewish.co.uk, which lists kosher establishments in London and across the United Kingdom.

With many Muslims going into the restaurant trade, it's easy to find halal meals. Many takeaway places, and an increasing number of sit-down restaurants, have the word halal written in Arabic on the front of their businesses. Indian restaurants are often halal because many are run by Bengalis; Brick Lane is a good place to go for lunch or dinner. There are so many Muslims in London that you can find halal restaurants and shops just about anywhere, yet for some reason there is no central resource that lists them all. A good place to start is the **Islamic Cultural Centre and Central London Mosque** (146 Park Rd., 020/7724-3363, www.iccuk.org).

ARTS AND ENTERTAINMENT

There are no end of things to do in London. While some visitors flock to the biggest attractions, such as the National Gallery and the British Museum, many lesser-known places are still worthy of a look. Lovers of the fine arts have hundreds of galleries, theaters, and museums to explore, and the smaller galleries are often more interesting since they take chances on emerging young talent. London's many little museums focus on more specific topics than the larger, general institutions while others focus on celebrities from the past.

Be sure to take advantage of London's nightlife! The city has an undeserved reputation as a sleepy town, but there are plenty of places to keep clubgoers happy until the wee hours, especially those into indie music or the rave scene. Many venues charge a cover price—sometimes quite steep—so check ahead. A night out clubbing can really bust your budget! If dancing the night away isn't your style, catch a play or a musical at one of the many theaters. London is one of the leading cities in the world for drama and music, and performances of all types abound.

London is also home to a thriving gay and lesbian community. Venues catering to gay and lesbian visitors, and dance and live-music venues in general, come and go with the tastes of the crowd. One year a place may be hot; the next it might be dead. Focus instead on "old standbys," businesses that have maintained their popularity for several years.

HIGHLIGHTS

Coolest Bar in London: The combination of ice walls, an ice bar, and even ice glasses at **Absolut Icebar** create a beautiful if somewhat chilly place to have a drink (page 108).

Best Mixed Drinks and Best All-Around Feel: The laid-back **Warwick Bar** serves that essential elixir, the Dalek, and no attitude (page 111).

Best Nightclub: Awesome DJs, packed dance floors, and a hypnotic light show make **Fabric** a place to lose yourself all night (page 113).

Best Art Gallery: Like the Tate, **The Wapping Project** is a converted power station. Unlike the Tate, it lacks pretension and contains art that is both beautiful and accessible (page 134).

Best Way to Experience India Without Leaving London: **Shri Swaminarayan Mandir** is a stunning white-marble Hindu temple where millennia-old rituals take place daily (page 153).

PHOTOBYTE / ALAMY

Shri Swaminarayan Mandir

LOOK FOR TO FIND RECOMMENDED ARTS AND ENTERTAINMENT.

London is host to innumerable special events and annual festivals, so be sure to see what's going on while in town. Attending a gala event such as the Notting Hill Carnival or Rise Festival is loads of fun and offers the opportunity to see a part of London visitors coming at other times will miss.

As might be expected in the computer age, the best help for planning a trip (besides this book, of course) is the Internet. Most galleries, nightclubs, and theaters have websites listing what's going on. Also check any of the city's major newspapers, or the very useful magazine *Time Out,* for listings and events.

Nightlife

London has an undeserved reputation of being dead after dark. True, many of the pubs still close at the traditional 11 P.M., but others have gotten one of the new late licenses that the government introduced in 2006, and the clubs never stop. Venues come and go, especially for live music and nightclubs, so stick to the more established places here. For a more relaxed evening, try a café or wine bar.

BARS

The British like to drink, and there are plenty of places for them to do it. For a change from the traditional pubs (see the *Pubs* section), try this list of good spots varying from the ultra-trendy to the laid-back.

Mayfair and Piccadilly Map 2

ABSOLUT ICEBAR

31-33 Heddon St. W1, 020/7478-8910,
www.belowzerolondon.com
HOURS: Sun.-Wed. 12:30-11:45 P.M., Thurs.-Sat. 12:30 P.M.-12:40 A.M.
TUBE: Piccadilly Circus or Oxford Street

The Below Zero Lounge Bar and Restaurant is inviting with its squishy leather seats and unusual nibbles such as the kangaroo, ostrich, and fois gras sampler plate, but for a unique experience head to the Absolut Icebar within the same premises, kept at a constant minus 5°C and sculpted entirely out of ice. The ice sculptures are quite beautiful in the soft blue light, and the drinks, all of which contain Absolut vodka, come in a sculpted ice glass. A smart dress code is required and reservations are recommended. A cover charge of £12 includes the first drink and an essential thermal cape.

MACANUDO FUMOIR

Claridge's Hotel, 55 Brook St. W1, 020/7629-8860,
www.claridges.co.uk
HOURS: Mon.-Sat. noon-midnight; Sun. noon-11 P.M.
TUBE: Bond Street

An elegant cigar bar, all dark leather and marble, Macanudo Fumoir in the exclusive Claridge's hotel is the place to be to enjoy a fine cigar with your drink. While the Macanudo brand is given pride of place on the cigar menu, there's a good selection of other brands, including Havanas and vintage cigars. The bar is fully stocked and has an especially good selection of cognacs and ports to sip with your stogie. An excellent stop after dinner is Gordon Ramsey's in the same building. Smart attire is required.

Covent Garden, West End, and Soho Map 3

GUANABARA

Parker St. at Drury Ln. WC2, 020/7242-8600,
www.guanabara.co.uk
HOURS: Mon.-Sat. 5 P.M.-2:30 A.M., Sun. 5 P.M.-midnight
TUBE: Covent Garden or Holborn

Guanabara is named after the bay at Rio de Janeiro. Except for the slicing rain outside, you'll think you're really there. You'll find strong Brazilian drinks, including a huge selection of *cachaca,* and beautiful people on the small dance floor. This bar hosts Brazilian bands and DJs so there's music and dancing every night. For some extra energy, try the Brazilian snacks such as cassava chips. What more could you want?

THE *QUEEN MARY*

Waterloo Pier, Victoria Embankment WC2
020/7240-9404, www.queenmary.co.uk
HOURS: Vary
TUBE: Embankment

A pleasure-cruise boat built in 1933, the *Queen Mary* now rests at dock but is still the site for daily festivities. Catch some rays (if there are any to catch) on the Sun Deck bar, or hide in the Ward Room (drinks noon–8 P.M. daily) if the weather's foul. The Hornblowers Nightclub (8 P.M.–2 A.M. Friday and Saturday) makes for a fun place to socialize. The views of the lights over the river are magical and it's a popular place to bring a date, but you might have trouble finding a dark corner that isn't already occupied.

Chelsea, Kensington, and Knightsbridge Map 5

BLUE BAR

The Berkeley, 1 Wilton Pl. SW1, 020/7235-6000

HOURS: Mon.-Sat. 4 P.M.-1 A.M., Sun. 3 P.M.-midnight

TUBE: Knightsbridge or Hyde Park Corner

An upscale hotel bar in the Berkeley, part of the Savoy group, the Blue Bar gets its name from its calming blue interior, done in a strange, almost purplish shade rarely seen. The leather floor and white onyx bar make the visuals even stranger. There are tapas to nibble and a Grape and Smoke menu that pairs up the best stogie for your favorite vintage. The bar seats only 60, so it has an exclusive, private club sort of feel. Smart casual dress required.

Maida Vale, Marylebone, and St. John's Wood Map 7

MATCH

37-38 Margaret St. W1, 020/7499-3443, www.matchbar.com

HOURS: Mon.-Sat. 11 A.M.-midnight

TUBE: Oxford Circus

Don't let the posh interior or rich punters turn you away; there's no dress code here and an interesting variety of people to watch. The champagne list is impressive both in variety and price, and there's a good selection of mixed drinks. The food menu combines comfort foods such as burgers and macaroni and cheese with unusual offerings such as Cornish squid fritters. A DJ spins everything from jazz to garage, depending on the mood of the crowd.

SOCIAL

5 Little Portland St. W1, 020/7636-4992, www.thesocial.com

HOURS: Mon.-Fri. noon-midnight, Sat.-Sun. 1 P.M.-midnight

TUBE: Oxford Circus

Very hip but surprisingly down to earth, Social puts on DJs and/or live music nightly, playing house, soul, acid rock, funk, old school rave, and more. Sometimes there are surprise

The *Queen Mary*, an old pleasure boat, is now a popular bar.

concerts by various independent bands. The interior is crowded and a bit plain, with photo and art exhibitions adding a bit of life to the walls. Some events have a cover charge, but most are free. It's a fun venue and a good place to meet people, but does the world really need hip-hop karaoke?

Camden Town Map 9

BARFLY

49 Chalk Farm Rd. NW1, 020/7691-4244, box office 087/0907-0999, www.barflyclub.com

HOURS: Opening times vary

TUBE: Chalk Farm or Camden Town

This popular indie club has rather spare decoration and a good but not outstanding drink menu. The focus here is the music, which attracts both younger and older rockers. Lots of successful bands such as Death in Vegas and Coldplay performed here before they got big. With stages both upstairs and downstairs hosting a nightly selection of rock, electronic, funk, and more from London favorites, it might just produce a few more stars. Visitors from outside London probably won't have heard of most of these bands, but the quality is generally good and the atmosphere fun.

BARTOK

78-79 Chalk Farm Rd. NW1, 020/7916-0595, www.bartokbar.com

HOURS: Mon.-Thurs. 5 P.M.-3 A.M., Fri. 5 P.M.-4 A.M., Sat. 1 P.M.-4 A.M., Sun. 1 P.M.-3 A.M.

TUBE: Chalk Farm

Bartok has taken the old rave concept of a chill-out room and made it highbrow, with sofas, chandeliers, long red curtains, and a mix of contemporary and classical music. The bar itself is named after a famous Hungarian composer. Besides classical music and vocalists, Latin and technopop DJs play regularly. The menu is a mixture too, with Thai appetizers and a selection of British, almost publike fare.

The City Map 10

THE DRUNKEN MONKEY

222 Shoreditch High St. E1, 020/7392-9555, www.thedrunkenmonkey.co.uk

HOURS: Mon.-Fri. noon-12:30 A.M., Sat. 6 P.M.-12:30 A.M., Sun. noon-11:30 P.M.

TUBE: Liverpool Street

This bar, lit with giant red Chinese lanterns, has an unusual atmosphere that mainly draws a mixed crowd—an older clientele who come for the dim sum, and younger folks who come for the DJs playing funk, hip-hop, house, and more. The bar has the usual beers, shots, and a good selection of cocktails. Early in the day, the crowd is older and more laid-back, with a lot of City workers playing hooky. At night it gets more energetic as the crowd gets younger.

Islington Map 11

EMBASSY

119 Essex Rd. N1, 020/7226-7901, www.embassybar.com

HOURS: Mon.-Thurs. 4 P.M.-midnight, Fri.-Sat. 4 P.M.-2 A.M., Sun. 4 P.M.-1 A.M.

TUBE: Angel

Embassy is famous for its top DJs playing Thursday–Saturday in two bars. The ground floor is a laid-back bar with leather seats and red and gold decor. The basement is more energetic, with a small and usually full dance floor where pulsing DJ music incorporates a fair amount of Latin beats into the usual mix. The crowd is young and trendy, but relaxed; you won't get attitude if you're a little older and don't spend hundreds of pounds on your wardrobe. A small cover charge applies after 9 P.M. on Fridays and Saturdays.

KINKY MAMBO

144-145 Upper St. N1, 020/7704-6868, www.kinkymambo.co.uk

HOURS: Tues.-Sun. 5 P.M.-2 A.M.

TUBE: Angel or Highbury and Islington

Kick back in a comfortable booth under the rosy light of 1950s chandeliers while sipping one of about 150 cocktails with names such as Mambo Moonshine and Neutron Lover. The Thai cocktail even comes with an edible flower. There's music every night (usually a DJ but sometimes a live act), and it changes constantly—jazz, Brazilian, disco, and even the occasional stand-up comic. Some nights have a modest cover charge. A cool place, but the young and wild should head to the nearby Warwick Bar.

THE WARWICK BAR

45 Essex Rd. N1, 020/7688-2882, www.thewarwickbar.com

HOURS: Mon.-Thurs. 5 P.M.-midnight, Fri. 5 P.M.-1 A.M., Sat. 2 P.M.-1 A.M., Sun. 2 P.M.-midnight

TUBE: Angel

The poorly signed exterior is easy to miss, but the owners care so little that they even make fun of the fact in their promotional literature. Apparently you just have to be in the know. Behind what looks like an abandoned storefront is a laid-back lounge with leather couches and a cool bar area. The jukebox plays a mixture of old and new rock Monday–Wednesday, while DJs spin the platters 8 P.M.–closing Thursday–Sunday. I love this place for its fun crowd, friendly management, and lack of attitude. It has a good range of real ales and some interesting mixed-drink creations, including the Dalek, made with Jägermeister, butterscotch schnapps, and Tabasco sauce. You will be exterminated!

COMEDY CLUBS

The famous dry British wit takes a back seat at comedy clubs, where the monologues are roaringly funny. A lot of the humor is pretty racy, but it isn't much worse than what audiences in the United States or Canada are used to. The easily offended should probably avoid these stand up routines anyway.

Covent Garden, West End, and Soho — Map 4

COMEDY CAMP

3-4 Archer St. W1, 020/7734-3342, bookings 087/0060-0100, www.comedycamp.co.uk

HOURS: Tues. 7:30 P.M. for 8:30 P.M. start and usually finishes 10:50 P.M., bar closes 1 A.M.

TUBE: Piccadilly Circus or Leicester Square

Bar Code, a mostly gay bar in Soho, hosts a comedy night every Tuesday. The show is mostly gay- and lesbian-themed, but the comedians and crowd are both mixed. Some famous gay comedians have performed here, such as flamey TV staple Graham Norton, whom even the archbishop of Canterbury thinks is funny. The bar itself is cool and trendy in typical Soho style. While the food is a bit pricey, there are special £2 drinks on Tuesdays.

COMEDY STORE

1A Oxendon St. SW1, Club 020/7839-6642, Tickets 087/0060-2340, www.thecomedystore.co.uk

HOURS: Nightly at 6:30 P.M. or 11 P.M. for late shows

TUBE: Piccadilly Circus or Leicester Square

Let no one say the British don't have a sense of humor. At the Comedy Store, irony, understatement, and reserve are set aside in favor of slapstick, rants, and potty humor. A lot of the nights feature group shows, offering a sample of some of the best in British humor. The Comedy Store started in a tiny space above a strip club in 1979, and this is now one of the best-known comedy venues in the country. The spacious theater seats up to 400, and the BBC occasionally records comedy shows here. A bar and reasonably priced diner are on-site.

COMEDY THEATRE

6 Panton St. SW1, box office 087/0060-6637

HOURS: Box office open Mon.-Sat. 10 A.M.-7:30 P.M.

TUBE: Piccadilly Circus or Leicester Square

Here's something a bit unusual for London—an old-time theater dedicated entirely to comedy. The Comedy Theatre has earned its reputation as one of the best venues in London by staging some very well-received and long-running performances. The focus is on comedic plays; in 2006, it started a successful run of *Donkey's Years*, which traces one man's chaotic midlife crisis through situational comedy and slapstick. While you might miss some of the cultural references, there's still plenty to laugh at.

DANCE CLUBS

Some people never run out of energy. If walking around the city all day hasn't tuckered you out, get out and dance. On weekends these clubs get packed, and many feature top DJs. During the week it's a bit less crowded but no less fun. Cover charges and opening times change depending what's on, but most open in early evening and go until dawn. Many clubs offer free or discounted entry for early guests, depending on the DJ and the night. Check the websites for details.

Mayfair and Piccadilly Map 3

BAR BOLLYWOOD

34 Dover St. W1, 020/7493-0200, www.barbollywood.net

HOURS: Thurs.-Sat. 7 P.M.-1:20 A.M.

TUBE: Green Park

Bar Bollywood is one of the biggest and most popular hot spots for the South Asian music community. The music, played by DJs or live performers, varies from traditional bhangra to the latest in South Asian hip-hop. A lot of Bollywood stars mingle with their fans here. While the crowd is mostly South Asian, all are welcome and after a couple of the elaborate cocktails you'll feel right at home. Since many South Asians do not drink, the bar also offers a variety of nonalcoholic cocktails. Each night is a theme night that changes often, but entry requires being on the membership list or in a mixed-sex group. The door charge is £10 before 10 P.M. and £15 after.

Covent Garden, West End, and Soho Map 4

MADAME JO JO'S

8-10 Brewer St. W1, 020/7734-3040, www.madamejojos.com

HOURS: Vary according to performance

TUBE: Piccadilly Circus or Leicester Square

This basement club used to be a strip club and retains the plush red velvet decor and secretive booths. (It appeared in Stanley Kubrick's film *Eyes Wide Shut,* which should give an idea of the ambience.) The club attracts an interesting mix of people who come for the DJs and live bands playing hip-hop, rock, electronic music, disco, and funk in a series of weekly and monthly club nights. Kitch Caberet, a dinner show that starts at 7 P.M. Saturdays, features the torch songs of yesteryear. For something a little more mainstream, try the Deep Funk Fridays. Other nights are filled with guest performers and DJs, and there always seems to be something interesting going on.

Chelsea, Kensington, and Knightsbridge Map 6

PACHA

Terminus Pl. SW1, 020/7833-3139, www.pachalondon.com

HOURS: Vary

TUBE: Victoria

If you can't make it to Ibiza, home of the first of the famous Pacha club chain, you can still check out this oak-paneled club and rave through the night. The stained-glass ceiling makes for a trippy view—if you can tear your eyes away from the young and beautiful crowd long enough to look up. The two dance floors showcase various house DJs, including some from Ibiza. The club is very trendy and unusually well lit, so you can't wear just anything the way you can in the dark, smoky industrial clubs such as Fabric.

Camden Town Map 9

EGG

Corner of York Way and Vale Royal N7, 020/7609-8364, www.egglondon.net

HOURS: Vary according to performance

TUBE: King's Cross/St. Pancras

A rocking nightclub with great DJs on two dance floors, Egg has become one of the epicenters for the London rave scene. The chill-out areas are quiet enough to actually talk to people, making this a bit more social than blaring clubs such as Fabric. Another nice touch is the open courtyard, which allows people to cool off and get away from the fog, lasers, and throbbing music for a while. A lot of singles come here looking to meet someone. This is far from a laid-back club, however; the dance floors are some of the most alive around. There's a guest list, but if it's not too busy—or you're good at fast-talking bouncers—it's not too hard to get in. Getting there involves walking up a long and lonely industrial street with a fair number of disreputable types, so it's best not to walk alone.

The City — Map 10

FABRIC

77A Charterhouse St. EC1, 020/7336-8898,
www.fabriclondon.com

HOURS: Vary

TUBE: Chancery Lane or St. Paul's

The best DJs in London regularly play to Fabric's three packed dance floors connected by dark corridors and several bar areas. A few things stick out in my memory: beautiful forms silhouetted in red haze, a dictatorial but efficient bouncer presiding over unisex toilets, pounding bass beats, and walking out at closing time into broad daylight. Unlike a lot of clubs, this is not a meat market; it's too loud to have a conversation and everyone's here for the music. People don't care how you look, since they can barely see you anyway. While it's one of the more expensive nightclubs (up to £15 depending on the show), it's well worth it.

TURNMILLS

63B Clerkenwell Rd. EC1, 020/7250-3409,
www.turnmills.co.uk

HOURS: Vary but usually closes 6 A.M.

TUBE: Farringdon

This is one of the largest of London's many rave clubs, with three dance floors (one large, two medium) and lots of winding hallways, bars, and chill out areas in between. Upstairs is a quieter restaurant/bar, good for chatting with whomever you met on the dance floor. The crowd are dedicated ravers, with a bit of a rougher element mixed in. The security's good though, and medics wander around all night in case someone takes more than he or she can handle. Good music, lots of beautiful people, and plenty to explore.

Islington — Map 11

ELECTROWERKZ

7 Torrens St. EC1, 020/7837-6419,
www.electrowerkz.com

HOURS: Vary according to performance

TUBE: Angel

A gloomy warehouse interior and a throbbing sound system make for a great atmosphere for dancing, if not conversation. There are DJs or live bands most nights. The most popular show is 100 percent Dynamite, a famous DJ duo that appears every other Saturday to play a mix of reggae, funk, hip-hop, dubstep, soul, and jungle. During the day, there are paintball battles (see *Urban Paintball Games* in the *Recreation* chapter for more information).

South of the Thames — Map 12

MINISTRY OF SOUND

103 Gaunt St. SE1, 087/0060-2666,
www.ministryofsound.com

HOURS: Vary according to performance

TUBE: Elephant and Castle

Famous DJs play on three dark, industrial dance floors at arguably the most popular venue in London. What else could get hundreds of people walking through Elephant and Castle late at night? The Saturday Sessions get the top DJs and the biggest crowds, but there's plenty going on the other nights of the week too. The crowd is mostly younger, with regular clubbers dancing side by side with country kids coming to the big city to have fun. The well-stocked bar is a haven after a long session out on the floor, and it comes with its own DJ.

Outlying Areas — Map 1

93 FEET EAST

150 Brick Lane E1, 020/7247-3293,
www.93feeteast.co.uk

HOURS: Vary

TUBE: Aldgate East

93 Feet East is an unpretentious club with heavy security and a college-style crowd. The front dance floor and bar doesn't have the greatest sound system, but the system in the back dance floor, which has good DJs and a nice light show, more than makes up for it. Beyond this room is a cool candlelit chill-out bar. There's often a barbecue and outdoor bar early in the evening, making this a popular transition venue between the drinkers and the ravers.

GAY AND LESBIAN

Oscar Wilde was prosecuted 100 years ago for what he called "the noblest of Greek traditions." Luckily for those following in his footsteps,

London has become much more tolerant of the gay lifestyle. Clubs and pubs seem to start up or go in and out of favor all the time, but these seasoned favorites draw a loyal following. Most are in Soho, and if you're gay, that's the place to be. Pick up one of the many free gay magazines out there; there's usually a voucher for discounted entry to one of these hot spots.

Covent Garden, West End, and Soho — Map 4

BAR CODE

3-4 Archer St. W1, 020/7734-3342,
www.bar-code.co.uk

HOURS: Mon.-Sat. 4-1:30 P.M., Sun. 4-10:30 P.M.

TUBE: Piccadilly Circus or Leicester Square

This hip, mostly gay bar with lots of mood lighting and a raucous clientele has become one of the major social centers for the Soho crowd. Happy hour is 4–7 P.M. daily, with £2 drinks, and extends to 9 P.M. on Mondays in a successful attempt to get people to party on the first workday of the week. The happy hour extends all Tuesday night for Comedy Camp, a popular gay/lesbian/mixed stand-up night. Many nights, especially weekends, bands and DJs play until late.

CANDY BAR

4 Carlisle St. W1, 020/7494-4041,
www.candybar.easynet.co.uk

HOURS: Vary

TUBE: Tottenham Court Road

Candy Bar, the first full-time women's bar in the United Kingdom, opened in 1997 and has become a major destination for London lesbians. Men are allowed only as guests of women in a largely successful bid to keep out straight men harboring unrealistic fantasies. The management prides itself on showcasing the best female DJ talent, which is otherwise underrepresented in the all-too-male–dominated club scene. Weekends are the best time to hear DJs, and there are various drink specials and events throughout the week.

CLUB G-A-Y AT ASTORIA

157-165 Charing Cross Rd. WC2, 020/7434-9592,
www.g-a-y.co.uk

HOURS: Mon., Thurs., Fri. 11 P.M.-4 A.M., Sat. 10:30 P.M.-5 A.M.

TUBE: Tottenham Court Road

This centrally situated concert hall brings in lots of DJs and pop stars for its regular gay club nights, called G-A-Y, and it is the busiest gay venue in London. The very campy atmosphere can turn some people off, but most think it's a lot of fun. Mondays feature '90s music on the main (and crowded) dance floor, while the bar has Camp Attack, with '70s and '80s music. Thursdays a DJ plays hard rock on the floor and pop at the bar. Fridays is more Camp Attack, with '70s, '80s, and '90s music. Saturday is the biggest night with live performances by big names in pop.

HEAVEN

Arches, Villiers St. WC2, 020/7930-2020,
www.heaven-london.com

HOURS: Vary

TUBE: Charing Cross

Entering the arches under the Hungerford Railway Bridge to reach the front door sets the mood for this dark, cruisy dance venue. Pulsing lights, lasers, smoke, loud music, and an even louder crowd make an over-the-top evening. Mondays is "Popcorn" with DJ dance mixes; Wednesdays is "FM" with house, R&B, and pop. Fridays and Saturdays are the big nights, with loud dance music on all three floors. You can buy tickets at the door but it's better to get them ahead of time, especially on weekends.

MOLLY MOGGS

2 Old Compton St. W1, 020/7437-1786,
www.mollymoggs.co.uk

HOURS: Mon.-Sat. noon-midnight, Sun. noon-11:30 P.M.

TUBE: Leicester Square

This unassuming little club at the gateway to the Soho gay district is home to a regular series of free drag shows. The crowd is straight-friendly, but the drag queens complain about gawking tourists peering through the windows from Charing Cross Road. It gets pretty packed for the shows, which happen Sunday through Thursday. Showtime is 3:30 and 8 P.M. Sundays, and 8:30 P.M. during the week. The name of the pub comes from an 18th-century barmaid whose beauty was the subject of a popular ballad. The lyrics are on the website and are quite funny, although not as funny as the wisecracks you'll hear at the show.

THE RETRO BAR

2 George Ct. WC2, 020/7321-2811
HOURS: Vary according to performance
TUBE: Charing Cross

Dip back into the '80s and '90s in this gay but straight-friendly bar. Posters of old Brit Pop stars adorn the walls and there's lots of Smiths and Morrisey on the jukebox. A number of theme nights include live DJs on Mondays, What's in Your Record Bag on Thursdays (you get to spin your cool and/or embarrassing old vinyl), and Twin Peaks Sundays (showing episodes and serving doughnuts, coffee, and cherry pie).

Outlying Areas — Map 1

CLUB KALI AT THE DOME

The Dome, 178 Junction Rd. N19, 020/7272-8153, www.clubkali.com
HOURS: First and third Fri. of the month, 10 P.M.-3 A.M.
TUBE: Archway

Club Kali bills itself as the biggest South Asian gay and lesbian dance club in the world. One wonders how it can be sure, but it is certainly a big night. The Dome gets jammed with people gyrating to bhangra, Hindi, and Arabic mixes as well as Western music. You'll see lots of traditional music and dress here; people are sticking to their roots and embracing the gay lifestyle at the same time. Club Kali also runs events at various other venues. Check the website to see what's on where.

JAZZ CLUBS

London isn't the first town that comes to mind when one thinks of jazz, but the jazz scene here has been going strong since black GIs discovered they could get into a lot more clubs here than they could back home. In addition to the dedicated jazz venues listed below, check out other concert venues and church music series for more jazz performances.

Covent Garden, West End, and Soho — Map 4

JAZZ AFTER DARK

9 Greek St. W1, 020/7734-0545, www.jazzafterdark.co.uk
HOURS: Vary
TUBE: Oxford Circus or Leicester Square

This cocktail bar/restaurant/music venue comprises a front bar area and a red-lit restaurant serving tapas in the back. The crowd is a mix of young and old and it can get quite packed and boisterous as everyone imbibes the bar's limited but choice selection of shooters, wines, and cocktails. There's live music every night, with blues and Latin filling in for the jazz occasionally. A lot of performers play only a single night, so be sure to book in advance to catch them.

RONNIE SCOTT'S

47 Frith St. W1, 020/7439-0747, www.ronniescotts.co.uk
HOURS: Vary
TUBE: Tottenham Court Road or Leicester Square

This famous jazz venue has an incredible history, starting in 1959 as a meeting ground for British jazz musicians to get together and jam. Since then it's seen a host of stars, and it hasn't limited itself just to jazz either. Jimi Hendrix made his last appearance here, and Tom Waits and Mark Knopfler have both been on stage. Nowadays there's a full lineup of jazz performances, with each group usually playing for a few nights in a row. A short but decent food menu, with dishes such as crispy roast duck and leek and mustard crumble, allows guests to dine while listening.

Camden Town — Map 9

JAZZ CAFÉ

5 Parkway NW1, box office 087/0534-4444, restaurant reservations 020/7534-6955 or 020/7916-6060 on Sundays
HOURS: Daily 7 P.M.-2 A.M.
TUBE: Camden Town

One of the more popular jazz clubs in town, the Jazz Café is neither a café nor exclusively devoted to jazz. Latin, soul, and funk bands also play here. For a full night out, reserve a table at the balcony restaurant, which serves favorites such as sirloin steak and pan-fried trout and affords a good view of the stage. The lineup of performers is truly impressive, and there's something on every night. Book well in advance, as this is a very trendy place to be.

LIVE-MUSIC VENUES

Every band comes through London on its world tour, and local acts often play nowhere else. Most of these places have a cover charge, which varies depending on the venue and the performance. It's best to check ahead of time how much it is, as prices can range from nominal to extortionate.

Covent Garden, West End, and Soho — Map 4

12 BAR CLUB

Denmark St. WC2, 020/7240-2622

HOURS: Café: Daily 9 A.M.-9 P.M.; Bar: Daily 11 A.M.-11 P.M.; Music: Mon.-Thurs. 7:30 P.M.-1 A.M., Fri.-Sat. 7:30 P.M.-3 A.M., Sun. 7 P.M.-12:30 A.M.

TUBE: Tottenham Court Road

This is the smallest venue listed, but I love it! The folks here manage to run a bar, café, and club hosting up to four acts a night every night of the week, in a space smaller than the average American duplex. While one could forgive some shoddy entertainment in such a place, the performers are of consistently high quality. Singer-songwriters are the main fare, with styles including folk, "antifolk," acoustic, and even punk, which despite rumors to the contrary is anything but dead. The café serves cheap sandwiches, soups, and salads, and the bar has a limited but select choice of drinks.

BLOW UP METRO

Metro Club, 19-23 Oxford St. W1, 020/7437-0964, tickets 020/7734-8932, 020/7403-3331, or 087/0060-0100, www.blowupmetro.com

HOURS: Vary

TUBE: Tottenham Court Road

This little basement club hosts live rock most nights and enjoys a reputation as one of the most popular places to go for gigs. Of course, this means get tickets in advance or take your chances with the long queue that appears early in front of the door. DJs do their stuff after most shows, playing a mixture of indie, post-punk, nu-metal, retro, and more. It's a cool place that's totally about the music.

Bloomsbury, Euston, and Holborn — Map 5

100 CLUB

100 Oxford St. W1, 020/7636-0933, www.the100club.co.uk

HOURS: Vary

TUBE: Tottenham Court Road

Britain's longest-running live-music venue has been packing them in since 1942, when American GIs jitterbugged with the local lasses and Englishmen complained that the Americans were "overpaid, oversexed, and over here!" The 100 Club has tons of history, from its jazz origins through the heady punk days of the 1970s, and it has seen early appearances by performers such as Glenn Miller, The Sex Pistols, and the Rolling Stones. Today, lots of good jazz, blues, soul, and indie bands play here. DJs play Friday and Saturday, and there's usually a live act. There's plenty of music during the week too, heavy on the jazz but with other styles well represented.

Notting Hill, Bayswater, and Paddington — Map 7

NOTTING HILL ARTS CLUB

21 Notting Hill Gate W11, 020/7460-4459, www.nottinghillartsclub.com

HOURS: Vary

TUBE: Notting Hill Gate

This is one of the smaller venues, with a capacity of just more 200 and a postage-stamp–sized stage, but it's a fun one. The bare concrete cellar serves strong, reasonably priced drinks and features bands from all over the map, who play here because the club gives unusual acts and unknown talent a chance. Experimental film and graphic arts exhibitions get their time too. It's hard to summarize this club since you can see just about anything here. In one week it featured electronica, Scandinavian films, South Asian mixes, funk, a fanzine convention, and a klezmer concert. With this sort of variety you'll have to pick and choose your days, but there's bound to be something on the calendar you'll like.

Camden Town Map 9

DUBLIN CASTLE

94 Parkway NW1, 020/7485-1773

HOURS: Daily 11 A.M.-midnight

TUBE: Camden Town

What looks like a typical local pub by day is transformed at night into a showcase for new talent by unknown bands. There's not much decor here—in fact this used to be a wonderfully filthy dive before it was fixed up into a moderately shoddy dive, but the music is good and the people are usually attitude-free. You'll see live bands with a thankfully low cover charge every night but Sunday. Fridays and Saturdays are pretty busy, so get there early to avoid queuing up. While you'll never see most of these bands again, Blur did some early concerts here so you just might catch a rising star.

JONGLEURS CAMDEN

11 East Yard, Camden Lock 17, off Chalk Farm Rd. NW1, 020/7428-5929, www.jongleurs.com and www.dingwalls.com

HOURS: Vary

TUBE: Camden Town

A mixture of live music and comedy makes for a venue to suit any mood. Fridays and Saturdays are comedy nights, with the well-connected Jongleurs chain of comedy clubs pulling in some major acts. The other nights feature a mix of DJs and live music, varying from island rhythms to jazz to new rock. The bar serves comfort food such as burgers and chili and the usual selection of drinks. It's a fun place to go after enjoying the canal at Camden.

Islington Map 11

THE HOPE AND ANCHOR

207 Upper St. N1, 020/7700-0550, www.bugbearbookings.com

HOURS: Vary

TUBE: Angel or Highbury and Islington

Several times a week, this rock venue in the basement of a pub showcases up-and-coming (at least they hope so) acts trying to make it to the big time. The quality of the bands can vary quite a bit, but the cover charge is cheap, the beer is good, and since on any given night there will usually be at least three bands playing, it's hard to complain. Expect uninspiring surroundings, loud music, a raucous crowd, and a generally good time.

MEDICINE BAR

181 Upper St. N1, 020/7704-9536, www.medicinebar.net

HOURS: Mon.-Tues. noon-midnight, Wed.-Thurs. noon-1 A.M., Fri. noon-2 A.M., Sat. noon-3 A.M., Sun. noon-12:30 A.M.

TUBE: Angel or Highbury and Islington

This old pub has bay windows fronting Upper Street, making it a good place to people-watch while lounging in one of the tattered yet still comfy leather chairs. The walls are decorated with giant acupuncture charts and there's a theaterlike section in the back that hosts DJs most nights. This was one of the first bars to offer DJ nights and it draws a young crowd that really packs the place on weekends. Talking to anyone is a bit difficult given the volume of the sound system, so it's more of a drinking-while-being-thumped-by-the-bass-beat sort of place.

PUBS

Pubs are a cornerstone of English culture. That's not to say anything about English drinking habits, but rather that the pub has a special place in the national culture as a communal area for socializing. More than simply providing a venue to drink with friends, the pub is one of the few public places where the somewhat reserved English will mingle with strangers, making it a perfect place to meet English people and sample the country's finest product: real ale. Many pubs are centuries old and have fascinating histories, so they're worth a visit even for those who don't drink.

Westminster, Victoria, and Pimlico Map 2

THE ALBERT

52 Victoria St. SW1, 020/7222-5577

HOURS: Sun.-Wed. 11 A.M.-11 P.M., Thurs.-Sat. 11 A.M.-midnight; Carvery: Daily noon-2:30 P.M., 5:30-10 P.M.

TUBE: St. James's Park

Quaff a pint amid the somewhat faded elegance of this fine pub dating to 1852. Brass chandeliers, period prints, hand-cut windows, and an unusual leaf design on the ceiling make for an interesting atmosphere. It's a bit too popular with the tourists, but after seeing the decor you'll know why. Lots of Londoners come here too, though, including politicians who head upstairs to a carvery serving succulent meat dishes. The "division bell" will occasionally ring to send them back to Parliament to vote. Three tasty courses with coffee will put you back £16.50.

Mayfair and Piccadilly Map 3

THE ARGYLL ARMS

18 Argyll St. W1, 020/7734-6117

HOURS: Mon.-Sat. 11 A.M.-11 P.M., Sun. noon-10:30 P.M.

TUBE: Oxford Circus

Step out of the busy shopping district around Oxford Circus and into the elegant Victorian Age. One of London's best-preserved Victorian pubs, the Argyll Arms actually dates to 1742 and sports Georgian architecture. The inside was completely refurbished in 1897 to appeal to Victorian sensibilities, with deep red molded walls and ceiling and private compartments screened with cut glass. The glasswork, mirrors, counter, back bar, and wood paneling are all original. The selection of real ales is good too! It tends to be quite busy with tourists and locals alike, but find a seat in one of the compartments and you'll have a true old-time pub experience.

Covent Garden, West End, and Soho Map 4

LAMB AND FLAG

33 Rose St. WC2, 020/7497-9504

HOURS: Mon.-Sat. 11 A.M.-11 P.M., Sun. 11 A.M.-10:30 P.M.

TUBE: Leicester Square or Covent Garden

Visitors could easily miss this pub hidden at the end of Rose Street (which is really no more than an alley at that point), but they shouldn't. Licensed in the reign of Elizabeth I, it is the oldest pub in Covent Garden. Charles Dickens and Samuel Butler drank here and the ground floor was used for cockfights and bare-knuckle boxing. In the nearby alley, the poet John Dryden was nearly clubbed to death by rogues who were probably hired by the Earl of Rochester—a satire suspected to have been written by Dryden attacked Rochester and the court. The rambling layout, low beams, and 19th-century decorations make this a true pub experience.

SALISBURY TAVERN

90 St. Martin's Lane WC2, 020/7836-5863

HOURS: Mon.-Fri. 11 A.M.-11 P.M., Sat. noon-11 P.M., Sun. noon-10:30 P.M.

TUBE: Leicester Square or Covent Garden

For a taste of Victorian England, check out the interior of the Salisbury Tavern. It's pretty much unchanged since 1892, with ornate woodwork, etched glass, and brass lamps. It's quite popular and is crowded most nights; try to get a seat at one of the plush red couches in the front room. This is one of the more atmospheric pubs in London, and it can be surprisingly quiet in the daytime, so that's often the better time to go.

THE SHERLOCK HOLMES PUBLIC HOUSE AND RESTAURANT

10-11 Northumberland St. WC2, 020/7930-2644

HOURS: Mon.-Sat. 11 A.M.-11 P.M., Sun. noon-10:30 P.M.; Food served daily noon-11 P.M.

TUBE: Charing Cross

This friendly pub fills quickly in the evenings with both tourists and local workers. The main attraction is the upstairs, where there's a faithful if somewhat dusty recreation of the famous sleuth's living room designed for the Festival of Britain in 1951. The upstairs also has a restaurant serving traditional English fare. The bar downstairs serves sandwiches and sides, as well as several guest ales, including its very own (and quite good) "Sherlock Holmes Ale." Holmes fans will want to see the more extensive reconstruction at 221B Baker St., but since there's no ale over there you might want to do both.

TOM CRIBB

36 Panton St. WC2, 020/7747-9951

HOURS: Mon.-Sat. 11 A.M.-11 P.M., Sun. noon-10:30 P.M.

TUBE: Piccadilly Circus or Charing Cross

It's unclear just when this pub, originally called the Union Arms, was founded but it was taken over in 1820 by the famous boxer Tom Cribb. Cribb lost only one fight in a career of more than 80 matches, this at a time when boxers didn't wear gloves and fought until they dropped. His first fight lasted 76 rounds! Not surprisingly, the pub became a popular hangout for prizefighters and their rich patrons and fans; it's mentioned in Thackeray's *Vanity Fair* and the Sherlock Holmes story "Rodney Stone." The cozy interior is decorated with boxing memorabilia and there's good pub food on the menu.

Bloomsbury, Euston, and Holborn Map 5

BRADLEY'S SPANISH BAR

42-44 Hanway St. W1, 020/7636-0359

HOURS: Mon.-Sat. 11 A.M.-11 P.M., Sun. noon-10:30 P.M.

TUBE: Tottenham Court Road

OK, so this is a bit of a hole—literally, since most patrons sit in the dark and cramped basement—but this is the most lovable hole in all of England. The vinyl jukebox plays '60s Brit Pop

REAL ALE: BEER AS IT SHOULD BE

A trip to the pub is a quintessentially British experience, and if you're a beer snob, you'll insist on drinking real ale.

The term "real ale" is reserved for beer that's brewed using traditional ingredients and secondary fermentation. "Traditional ingredients" means there are no artificial clarificants, preservatives, or other additives. "Secondary fermentation" means that the yeast is still alive in the cask, so that fermentation continues, providing a fuller, fresher taste. (Don't worry, the yeast all settles to the bottom and never gets in the glass.) Because of this process, such beers are often called "cask conditioned" or simply "cask ales."

The British take their beer seriously – so seriously that they have a full-time lobbying organization to ensure that real ales don't disappear under the onslaught of tasteless lagers. The **Campaign for Real Ale** (CAMRA, www.camra.org.uk) is a national organization that promotes the brewing and, of course, the drinking of real ales. It also supports traditional pubs on the basis that they're an important aspect of British culture and must be preserved in the days of theme pubs, big chains, and plasma-screen televisions.

One of its current campaigns is for an honest pour. A pint glass is a full pint only if the contents come to the bottom of the lip. While this makes it a little hard to carry the glass back to the table without sloshing on the ground, patrons are getting what they paid for. (Try taking a sip before leaving the bar!) Legally, up to 5 percent of the glass can be head, so don't get too picky. CAMRA also sponsors real-ale festivals across the United Kingdom (see *Festivals and Events*).

While constant vigilance is the price of good beer, traditional brewing is actually enjoying a heyday. More than 600 breweries in the United Kingdom are brewing an estimated 2,500 ales. Many of these are small, local operations and you won't find their product except in a few nearby pubs as a "guest ale."

Another important organization is **Cask Marque** (www.cask-marque.co.uk), a body that reviews how pubs serve their cask ales and rates them on variety, serving temperature, and overall quality. Those with high marks are awarded a Cask Marque sticker (a blue sign with the symbol of a beer tap) on their window. Rest assured that within there are quality ales served the proper way. Most of the pubs listed here have received Cask Marque approval; those that haven't are listed because of their historic importance.

Oh, and a word of warning: Remember that British beer, especially some of the real ales, tends to be stronger than American and Canadian brews.

the Cask Marque sticker

ARTS AND ENTERTAINMENT

and Motown, and the bathroom was dubbed "the smallest loo in London" by *Smoke* magazine. (It's unclear why it's called the Spanish Bar, unless it's for the Mexican beer on sale.) If the description hasn't sold you, just trust that it's more than the sum of its parts. Don't come right after the surrounding offices let out, or you'll never get in.

THE LAMB

94 Lamb's Conduit St. WC1, 020/7405-0713
HOURS: Daily 11 A.M.-midnight
TUBE: Holborn

This atmospheric old pub dates from the Victorian era, with old-style seats of green leather and dividing boards, side rooms, and outside seating in a small backyard. Photos of Victorian stage heartthrobs and sirens line the walls. Hear the "polyphon," an old music machine that plays a metal disc, for a small donation to the pub's charity of the moment.

MUSEUM TAVERN

49 Great Russell St. WC1, 020/7242-8987
HOURS: Mon.-Thurs. 11 A.M.-11 P.M., Fri.-Sat. 11 A.M.-midnight, Sun. noon-10 P.M.
TUBE: Tottenham Court Road or Russell Square

There's been a tavern here since at least the 1720s, but the etched glass mirrors and fine wooden bar date to the 1880s. If you're wondering why there are four doors leading inside, that's because Victorian pubs used to be divided, so this was originally four pubs in one. As it sits right across from the British Museum, it's not surprising that this pub is crawling with tourists. Still, there's beer aplenty, and in the evenings it turns into a neighborhood pub where the Queen's English is heard more often than American and Japanese.

PRINCESS LOUISE

208-209 High Holborn WC1, 020/7405-8816
HOURS: Mon.-Fri. 11 A.M.-11 P.M., Sat. noon-11 P.M., Sun. noon-10:30 P.M.
TUBE: Holborn

This pub was built in 1872, redecorated in 1891, and hasn't changed much since. Ornamental carved glass mirrors line the walls and an ornate molded ceiling hangs overhead. Even the bathrooms are preserved from the period, although they have been cleaned since installation. Because of its central location and reputation as one of the historic drinking houses of London, it gets packed after the nearby offices let out and is equally busy on weekends.

Chelsea, Kensington, and Knightsbridge — Map 6

GRENADIER

18 Wilton Row SW1, 020/7235-3074
HOURS: Mon.-Sat. 11 A.M.-11 P.M., Sun. noon-10:30 P.M.
TUBE: Hyde Park Corner

The Duke of Wellington's Grenadier Guards used to drink and sup here when this was an officer's mess, exchanging tales of Waterloo and other victories. The building dates to 1818 and is steeped in history and atmosphere; fans of British military history will not want to miss having a pint and admiring military bric-a-brac on the walls. The dining room sells good pub grub and there's even a ghost on the premises, apparently some poor officer who was flogged to death for cheating at cards.

Maida Vale, Marylebone, and St. John's Wood — Map 8

THE BARLEY MOW

8 Dorset St. W1, 020/7935-7318
HOURS: Mon.-Sat. 11 A.M.-11 P.M., Sun. noon-10:30 P.M.
TUBE: Baker Street

It doesn't get much more authentic and atmospheric than this old pub. The building dates to 1718, when it quenched the thirst of local farmers at a time when the area was still mostly fields. The interior was reworked in the Victorian era and has retained most of its features, including two very rare drinking boxes—little private rooms open only to the bar where Victorian gentlemen could drink and do business in private. Most of these boxes were done away with early in the 20th century because of fears that their privacy encouraged immorality. Old brass plates show the price list from a time when rum was 15 shillings a gallon. It's a truly historical drinking experience, despite the TV.

PONTEFRACT CASTLE

71 Wigmore St. W1, 020/7486-4941
HOURS: Mon.-Sat. 11 A.M.-11 P.M., Sun. noon-10:30 P.M.
TUBE: Bond Street

Set among the fine Georgian facades of Wigmore Street, the Pontefract Castle is an open, well-lit pub with bay windows looking out onto the street. It's fun to sit here and people-watch along the busy shopping district. An iron spiral staircase twists up to a restaurant serving the usual pub fare. The pub, named after a castle in West Yorkshire where Richard II was murdered in 1400, attracts a mix of tourists and locals, both gay and straight.

The City — Map 10

THE BLACK FRIAR

174 Queen Victoria St. EC4, 020/7236-5474
HOURS: Mon.-Sat. 11 A.M.-11 P.M., Sun. noon-10:30 P.M.
TUBE: Blackfriars

An art nouveau wonder, the Black Friar was built in 1905 on the site of the Dominican friary that gives the pub and nearby bridge their names. The interior is decorated with bas-reliefs of the merry friars at work and play, and many of the seats are original little cubbyholes. The pub owes its odd triangular shape to the fact that it was built in the spare space between earlier buildings. The other buildings are now gone, and the pub juts toward the traffic from the north end of Blackfriars Bridge.

THE OLD BELL

95 Fleet St. EC4, 020/7583-0216
HOURS: Mon.-Sat. 11 A.M.-11 P.M., Sun. noon-10:30 P.M.
TUBE: Blackfriars

This pub, originally called "The Swan," burned down in the Great Fire of 1666. Nobody knows just how old the first pub was. In 1678, the famous architect Christopher Wren rebuilt it for the masons who were rebuilding St. Bride's and St. Paul's. Early printer Wynkyn de Worde, one of Caxton's assistants and "the father of Fleet Street printing," had his press on this site. Today it is a favorite for lawyers and judges working in the nearby courts, and journalists still come here to relive the glory days of Fleet Street. With its fireplaces and black-oak fittings, and St. Bride's churchyard right next door, it's a great place to soak in the atmosphere of old London. The interior was greatly remodeled in Victorian times, but the staircase is original from the 17th century.

THE TIPPERARY

6 Fleet St. EC4, 020/7583-6470
HOURS: Mon.-Fri. 11 A.M.-11 P.M., Sat.-Sun. noon-6 P.M.
TUBE: Temple

The Tipperary was built on the site of an early-14th-century monastery that brewed ale, and it's been served on this spot ever since. Around the year 1700, S. G. Mooney and Son Brewery of Dublin bought the site and it became the first Irish pub outside Ireland—and the first to serve Guinness. Both the downstairs and upstairs bars retain much of their original character, although they have been extensively restored. The pub, called by various names through the years, was renamed "the Tipperary" in 1918 in honor of Irish Fleet Street printers returning from the front. The site used to be an island between the Thames and Fleet Rivers, and now the Fleet, much reduced in size but still lending its name to the street, flows right underneath the building. Oh, and the folks here know how to pour a Guinness.

YE OLDE CHESHIRE CHEESE

145 Fleet St. EC4, 020/7353-6170, www.yeoldecheshirecheese.com
HOURS: Mon.-Sat. 11 A.M.-11 P.M., Sun. noon-10:30 P.M.
TUBE: Blackfriars

This is the way pubs used to be: smoky, tiny little rooms with dim lighting and great beer. Aspiring writers should come here to soak up the history and a couple of ales while working on the Next Big Thing. Boswell drank with Dr. Johnson here as he worked on Johnson's

© SEAN MCLACHLAN

The George in Southwark is a well-preserved pub dating to Shakespeare's day.

famous biography, and Dickens and Chesterton drank here too. The crowd is a mixture of tourists and City barristers, so it's unclear why this is one of the cheaper pubs in town, but patrons should be grateful. Look for the alley of Wine Office Court to find the entrance.

YE OLDE WATLING

Corner of Bow Lane and Watling St. EC4, 020/7653-9971

HOURS: Mon. -Fri. 11 A.M.-11 P.M.

TUBE: St. Paul's or Bank

When Sir Christopher Wren was rebuilding St. Paul's after the Great Fire of 1666, he wanted his workers to have a place to relax, so he built this pub out of the beams of old ships. Many of the exposed beams are visible today, with cut marks from the craftsmen plainly visible. The bar staff serves real ales in a jovial atmosphere of mostly City workers. Outside is Watling Street, an old Roman road that used to run from St. Albans all the way to Wroxeter. Stand just outside the front door to catch a great photo of the dome of St. Paul's jutting above the narrow lane.

South of the Thames Map 12

THE GEORGE

77 Borough High St. SE1, 020/7407-2056

HOURS: Pub: Mon.-Sat. 11 A.M.-11 P.M., Sun. noon-10:30 P.M.; Restaurant: Mon.-Sat. 5-10 P.M.

TUBE: Southwark

This is one of the oldest and best-preserved pubs in London; it's actually managed by the National Trust because of its cultural significance. The present building was rebuilt in 1677 after a fire, but there has been a pub on this site since the medieval period; both Dickens and Shakespeare drank here. Notice the arcade (the only one left in a London pub), the thick beams on the low roof, and the small-paned windows, and imagine Elizabethan gentlemen and rogues quaffing ales in the galleries. Also note the selection of real ales at the bar.

THE GLOBE

Green Dragon Court SE1, 020/7407-0043

HOURS: Mon.-Sat. 11 A.M.-11 P.M., Sun. noon-10:30 P.M.

TUBE: Southwark

The Globe makes a good place to sneak away

from the tourist crowd on the Thames Walk. Built in 1872 in Gothic Revival style by Augustus Pugin (who also helped design the new Parliament after it burned down in 1834), the pub features original fittings such as a pressed-design ceiling and drinking stalls. A scene from *Bridget Jones's Diary* was filmed here. The Globe is so named because it was once thought to stand on or near the site of the famous theater. It was actually built on the site of a 15th-century inn.

WINE BARS

If beer isn't your drink of choice, and the bars and clubs are too raucous, have a more refined night out at one of London's elite wine bars. Many host tasting nights that familiarize guests with the culture, and they often serve meals specially cooked to complement the wine list. Since wine bars are generally the domain of City workers and other such well-heeled spenders, "smart casual" dress is generally required.

Westminster, Victoria, and Pimlico — Map 2

EBURY WINE BAR AND RESTAURANT

139 Ebury St. SW1, 020/7730-5447,
www.eburywinebar.co.uk

HOURS: Mon.-Sat. 11 A.M.-11 P.M., Sun. 6-10:30 P.M.

TUBE: Sloane Square or Victoria

A classy wine bar with traditional British furnishings and lots of flowers, the Ebury is a good choice for a romantic night out. The wine list is well chosen but not confusingly encyclopedic, and the prices are much more reasonable than in some of those expense-account travesties in the City. In addition to wine and the usual bar snacks, the restaurant features a full menu of contemporary European cuisine, including dishes such as English new season lamb cutlets and roasted guinea fowl breast. Entrées run a few pounds to either side of £14 and are nicely done, although there's virtually nothing for vegetarians.

If you drink at Ebury Wine Bar and stay at the Lime Tree, it's just a short stagger home.

Mayfair and Piccadilly Map 3

FINO'S WINE CELLAR

123 Mount St., Grosvenor Sq. W1, 020/7491-1640, www.finos.co.uk

HOURS: Mon.–Fri. 11 A.M.–11 P.M.

TUBE: Bond Street

This family-owned restaurant and wine bar offers intimate surroundings and an extensive wine selection served from its long wooden bar. The wine list includes some of the best vintages from Italy, France, Spain, Australia, South Africa, and California, with an emphasis on the Continental. Bottles range from £17 on up to more than £200, and the staff can direct you to the best vintage in your price range. Private rooms are available for a quiet evening. The restaurant features British and Continental favorites such as roast fore ribs of Scots beef with Yorkshire pudding (£14.50) or veal scaloppine with lemon sauce (£13.90). Ask about the daily specials, which often include fresh game.

The City Map 10

THE JAMAICA WINE HOUSE

12 St. Michael's Alley (off Cornhill) EC3, 020/7929-6972

HOURS: Mon.–Fri. 11 A.M.–11 P.M.

TUBE: Bank

Hidden in a little back alley, this wood-paneled wine bar, with an unusual Victorian tiled ceiling in one room, is a favorite among City business types who like to take time off to chat with colleagues over a bottle of wine. The building stands upon the site of Pasqua Rosee's Head, London's first coffeehouse, built in 1652. Back then coffeehouses were an important meeting place for City professionals, and things haven't changed much around here. The bar serves a good selection of wines from all major wine-growing regions at City prices. There's also a decent beer selection and English food is available noon–3 P.M.

The Arts

London is filled with things to do, from highbrow culture to low humor and just plain fun. Music abounds, both in professional venues and in churches, or head on over to a museum or art gallery for more culture. Many of these listings are of specialized interest and can satisfy a variety of passions, whether for Sherlock Holmes or contemporary art.

Remember that art galleries are closed between shows. It takes several days or even weeks to set up an exhibition, so check before heading out. The quietest time to visit is usually weekday mornings, when you can have the space more or less to yourself. School groups tend to come in the afternoons, and everybody seems to show up on weekends. The same holds true for museums.

CINEMA

Catch everything from the latest blockbuster to an interesting art film at one of London's movie houses. After all the touring and traffic, a couple of hours spent watching a film in a darkened theater may be just the ticket.

Covent Garden, West End, and Soho Map 4

PRINCE CHARLES

7 Leicester Pl. WC2, 020/7494-3654, www.princecharlescinema.com

TUBE: Leicester Square

This movie theater screens interesting independent and progressive films from around the world as well as the edgier mainstream offerings. It's also one of the cheapest movie theaters in London, with tickets never more than £4. The "Feel Good Fridays" series offers £1 films and munchies. It manages to turn a profit in this high-rent area through volume and drink sales, so get in line early for the movie and expect it to be crowded in the bar right after performance time.

The City Map 10

BARBICAN

Silk St. at Whitecross St. EC2, switchboard 020/7638-4141, box office 020/7638-8891, www.barbican.org.uk

HOURS: Mon.-Sat. 9 A.M.-11 P.M., Sun. noon- 11 P.M.

TUBE: Barbican or Moorgate

The Barbican's sprawling arts center includes two movie theaters that show leading international films and lesser-known gems. They often have themed seasons of classic movies, such as the German Expressionist series in 2006, which offers a chance to see movies rarely shown anywhere else. Lectures and workshops for budding filmmakers happen regularly.

South of the Thames Map 12

BFI LONDON IMAX CINEMA

Waterloo Bridge and Stamford St. SE1, 087/0787-2525, www.bfi.org.uk/imax

COST: Adults £7.90, seniors over 60 and students £6.50, children £4.95

TUBE: Waterloo

If you're a film junkie, or just have footsore children in tow, drop in to see the latest blockbusters and special features on the biggest screen in London. While viewing the latest Hollywood extravaganza on IMAX is an experience, even better are the films specially made for the larger format. Former features include an amazing undersea voyage, as well as a 3D safari and a journey on the moon. The theater is run by the British Film Institute, which also hosts films at the National Film Theatre.

NATIONAL FILM THEATRE

Waterloo Rd. at Upper Ground SE1, 020/7928-3232, www.bfi.org.uk

COST: Varies depending on screenings

TUBE: Waterloo

Just a few steps from the Thames Walk is this relaxing stop for weary feet. The National Film Theatre is owned by the British Film Institute, which also runs the IMAX Cinema, curates a National Film and Television Archive, and hosts several film festivals. Between the three theaters at this site and the IMAX down the road, it shows more than 3,000 films to more than six million people every year. With screenings of classic, current, and experimental movies every day of the week, there's always something good to watch. Check the website for listings of regular talks and workshops.

CLASSICAL MUSIC

Home to several major symphony orchestras, London is a top destination for those interested in classical music. An interesting feature of the city's nightlife are the church concerts, held in many of the city's historic houses of worship, offering beautiful architecture, fine acoustics, and cheap or even free admission.

Covent Garden, West End, and Soho Map 4

ST. MARTIN-IN-THE-FIELDS

Trafalgar Sq. WC2, box office 020/7839-8362, parish office 020/7766-1100, www.smitf.org

HOURS: Box office open Mon.-Sat. 10 A.M.-5 P.M. by phone; in person Mon.-Wed. 10 A.M.-5 P.M., Thurs.-Sat. 10 A.M.-8 P.M.

TUBE: Charing Cross or Leicester Square

This popular church runs one of the best-loved concert series in the city. Atmospheric Concerts by Candlelight are held at 7:30 P.M. on Tuesdays, Thursdays, Fridays, and Saturdays. The performers conduct a variety of early music, classical, baroque, chamber, world, and piano and song recitals. In addition, there's a regular series of jazz nights, usually held twice a month. The lunchtime concerts, usually held 2–3 times a week at 1 P.M., cover a similar range and are free.

Chelsea, Kensington, and Knightsbridge Map 6

ROYAL ALBERT HALL

Kensington Gore at Exhibition Rd. SW7, 020/7589-8212, www.royalalberthall.com

HOURS: Box office open daily 9 A.M.-9 P.M.

TUBE: South Kensington

You might recognize this theater's stately galleries and vast stage from its Proms, an annual classical music concert broadcast across the world, or any of the many other concerts

© SEAN MCLACHLAN

The Royal Albert Hall is an elegant music venue and a jewel of Victorian architecture.

it holds. With more than 300 events a year, it's one of the busiest venues in London. The emphasis is on classical music, with contemporary composers all fighting to have their pieces staged here. A night at the Royal Albert is considered a major career coup. Jazz, rock, and other music styles get stage time too; Dylan and the Who both had important performances here. The Royal Albert isn't the type of place to do things moderately; it has no fewer than 13 bars and three restaurants open during performances.

ROYAL COLLEGE OF MUSIC

Prince Consort Rd. SW7, 020/7591-4314, www.rcm.ac.uk

HOURS: Box office open Mon.-Fri. 10 A.M.-4 P.M.

TUBE: South Kensington

Founded in 1882, this music school venue is primarily for students to show off what they've learned. You wouldn't know they're still in training from the quality of the performances, though; they're incredible. There are lunchtime and evening concerts and recitals and the prices are quite reasonable, making this a good bargain for cash-strapped classical-music lovers. The performances reflect the variety of music the students are learning, with classical, opera, and chamber music most prominent. For those with a musical bent extending beyond simple appreciation, there is a regular series of workshops and lectures.

The City — Map 10

GUILDHALL SCHOOL OF MUSIC AND DRAMA

Silk St., Barbican EC2, 020/7628-2571, www.gsmd.ac.uk

HOURS: Hours and prices vary

TUBE: Moorgate

The Guildhall School puts on an impressive series of concerts and plays. Concerts tend toward the classical and opera, with jazz thrown in to liven up the mix. The plays are generally reworkings of old favorites, often in contemporary settings. While everything is performed by students, the quality of work is exceptionally high and you might see some future stars here; Noel Coward and Ewan McGregor are both graduates. Tickets are generally cheaper than those of professional performances, although there is no noticeable difference in quality—another bonus. The performances can be either at the school or at other venues, so be sure to check first.

ST. LUKE'S

161 Old St. EC1, box office 084/5120-7593,
church 020/7490-3939, www.lso.co.uk/lsostlukes

HOURS: Box office open daily 9 A.M.–8 P.M. for phone reservations only

TUBE: Old Street

This elegant church was finished in 1733 by Hawksmoor, one of the leading architects in English history. Beneath its soaring steeple is one of Hawksmoor's signature classical facades hiding an elegant interior. The main reason to visit this church, however, is the varied musical program put on throughout the year (St. Luke's and the Barbican are the twin homes of the London Symphony Orchestra). The emphasis is on classical, but there also are folk, jazz, and world music concerts. Hawksmoor must have had an ear for music, because the acoustics are wonderful. Especially popular are the free BBC Radio 3 lunchtime concerts broadcast across the nation. The Crypt Café opens one hour before most performances and serves drinks and snacks, and it serves full meals during the BBC 3 concerts.

ST. SEPULCHRE-WITHOUT-NEWGATE

10 Giltspur St. EC1, 020/7248-3826,
www.st-sepulchre.org.uk

TUBE: St. Paul's or City Thameslink

Admiring 400-year-old stained-glass windows while listening to Mozart or other fine works of classical music is a memorable way to spend an evening. One window depicts Captain John Smith, the first governor of the colony of Virginia, who was saved by Pocahontas (Smith is interred in the south aisle). The church, like so many others in the City, was rebuilt by Wren after the Great Fire; unlike most of these other churches, Wren worked with the original exterior, which was built around 1450 and had partially survived the conflagration. Free classical concerts are at 1 P.M. every Wednesday, and a series of other classical and organ concerts (usually free) are held throughout the year.

TEMPLE CHURCH

Fleet St. at Middle Temple Ln. EC4, 020/7353-8559,
www.templechurch.com

TUBE: Temple or Blackfriars

Free Wednesday lunchtime organ recitals and Sunday morning chorus performances enliven this atmospheric church built in the 12th century by the Knights Templar. The organ recitals are generally at 1:15 P.M. and are free, but it's good to check ahead. The excellent free choral service at 11:15 A.M. on Sundays takes advantage of the unusual acoustics of the round church. Various other concerts (some of which cost a fee) are performed throughout the year.

South of the Thames — Map 12

ROYAL FESTIVAL HALL

Belvedere Rd. at Concert Hall Approach SE1,
087/0163-3899, www.rfh.org.uk

HOURS: Box office open daily 11 A.M.–6 P.M.

TUBE: Waterloo

The Royal Festival Hall is part of the South Bank Centre, built in 1951 during the postwar gala Festival of Britain. Some of the best orchestras and dance troupes in the world perform in its spacious facilities. Three million people attend the performances here every year, taking their pick from numerous offerings of homegrown and international talent. There's also an ongoing series of free music and events, including many for children.

CONCERT HALLS

London's concert halls are often historic structures that are architectural marvels to behold and well worth a visit to treat the eyes as well as the ears. The emphasis is usually on classical and jazz, but all kinds of music is played here. (For more modern fare, check out *Live-Music Venues* in the *Nightlife* section.)

Chelsea, Kensington, and Knightsbridge — Map 6

CADOGAN HALL

Sloane Terrace SW1, 020/7730-4500, www.cadoganhall.com

HOURS: Box office open Mon.-Sat. 10 A.M.-7 P.M.

TUBE: Sloane Square

Home to the Royal Philharmonic Orchestra, Cadogan Hall features wonderful acoustics in a beautiful space. The gleaming white walls and large windows provide a bright atmosphere for daytime concerts, and the Oakley Room Bar, with its elegant Georgian-style molded ceiling, offers pre- and postconcert drinks, as well as at intermission. Besides the Royal Philharmonic, which has been entertaining audiences since 1946, many guest soloists and orchestras make their appearance in a very full concert schedule. Fans of classical music should not miss seeing a performance here.

Maida Vale, Marylebone, and St. John's Wood — Map 8

ROYAL ACADEMY OF MUSIC

Marylebone Rd. NW1, 020/7873-7373, www.ram.ac.uk

HOURS: Box office open Mon.-Fri. 10 A.M.-noon, 2-4 P.M.; Museum: Mon.-Fri. 12:30-6:30 P.M., Sat.-Sun. 2-5:30 P.M.

TUBE: Baker Street or Regent's Park

Arguably the most prestigious school for music in the United Kingdom, the Royal Academy puts on regular performances throughout the year in which students show off their considerable classical and jazz talents. Some of these folks will be big names one day. When school is not in session, the academy fills its halls with guest performers. The Musical Theatre (020/7873-7300) also hosts occasional musicals. Shows vary in price and some are free. Check the website for a full schedule. The building houses a free musical museum with old instruments, including a violin made by the master Stradivarius.

WIGMORE HALL

36 Wigmore St. W1, 020/7935-2141, www.wigmore-hall.org.uk

HOURS: Box office open Mon.-Sat. 10 A.M.-8:30 P.M., Sun. 10:30 A.M.-5 P.M.

TUBE: Oxford Circus or Bond Street

This elegant venue was built in 1901 by the Bechstein Piano Company. Painted above the stage is a glorious art nouveau cupola of the Soul of Music gazing up at the golden-rayed Genius of Harmony. The hall is host to more than 400 shows a year. It's the premier venue for chamber music, but the schedule also includes classical, song and piano recitals, early music, and jazz. The fine lineup and great acoustics make this a favorite recording location for the BBC. It also hosts a lot of talks and family activities.

DANCE

Talented dance troupes—modern to ballet—abound in London, which has long held a reputation as an important center for the art. Most spaces are devoted exclusively to dance, but many concert venues, especially the Barbican, also put on regular dance performances.

Covent Garden, West End, and Soho — Map 4

PEACOCK THEATRE

Portugal St. WC2, 020/7863-8198, www.peacocktheatre.com or www.sadlers-wells.com

TUBE: Holborn

The smaller cousin of Sadler's Wells, the Peacock Theatre attracts a similar series of performers but from lesser-known companies thanks to its smaller, more intimate venue. That's OK because the performances are still good and the space is more intimate. Occasionally it gets big names too, such as the Shaolin Monks. (Kung fu isn't exactly dance, but after watching the monks break stuff with their hands, feet, and heads, no one would argue their right to be here.)

Bloomsbury, Euston, and Holborn — Map 5

THE PLACE

17 Duke's Rd. WC1, 020/7121-1100, www.theplace.org.uk

TUBE: Euston

The Place is one of London's leading contemporary dance performance centers and the training ground for some of the country's best dancers. The performances are by both in-house and guest artists and push the boundaries of what can be expressed by the human body. Some of these folks are truly stunning to watch in action; give this a try even if contemporary dance usually isn't your thing. The Robin Howard Dance Theatre, where performances take place, has a little more than 300 seats so everyone gets a good view.

Islington — Map 11

SADLER'S WELLS

Rosebery Ave. EC1, 020/7863-8000,
www.sadlers-wells.com
TUBE: Angel

Sadler's Wells, one of the most popular dance venues in London, attracts a steady series of major international performers. Styles vary from classical to experimental, with an emphasis on more modern styles, including Latin and ballet. While this is primarily a dance venue, there's also a regular opera series. Its 2006 season provides an example of its eclecticism; included, among others, were the Ballet Nacional de Cuba, the Australian Bangarra Dance theater doing aboriginal contemporary dance, and the samba dancers of Brasil Brasileiro. A very cool café is on-site.

GALLERIES

London is a major center for art. The impressionists came to paint the fog and the Thames, and contemporary artists jockey for prestige in a chaotic world of patronage, grants, and gallery openings. Art lovers will have a great time sampling the innumerable galleries displaying works from all regions and eras. While most galleries are free, they occasionally have special exhibitions that charge a fee. Note that while there are a lot of galleries in Mayfair, only a tiny minority is listed. A walk through this affluent neighborhood will discover many, many more.

Mayfair and Piccadilly — Map 3

ART FIRST

9 Cork St., 1st Floor, W1, 020/7734-0386,
www.artfirst.co.uk
HOURS: Mon.-Fri. 10 A.M.-6 P.M., Sat. 11 A.M.-2 P.M.
COST: Free admission
TUBE: Green Park

On gallery-heavy Cork Street, Art First distinguishes itself with established and emerging contemporary artists working in painting and sculpture, with a special focus on art from Scotland and South Africa. Much of the work is abstract and conceptual, but there's representative art as well. The gallery has a simple, spacious, open floor plan; visitors won't be distracted by the building itself, as in some other gallery spaces, and can concentrate on the art.

FRANCIS KYLE GALLERY

9 Maddox St. W1, 020/7499-6870/6970,
www.franciskylegallery.com
HOURS: Mon.-Fri. 10 A.M.-6 P.M., Sat. 11 A.M.-5 P.M.
COST: Free admission
TUBE: Oxford Circus

This traditional gallery showcases contemporary artists who paint pictures that are beautiful, rather than bizarre and pretentious (no unmade beds or footballs covered with Bible pages here!). These fine works of landscape and portraiture show real evidence of talent, despite being so conservative that the subject matter is recognizable. It's a relief to see there's still a place for craft, technique, and aesthetic sensibility in the contemporary art world. The artists portray a remarkable variety of styles and themes, and with a new show every month or so there's always something worth seeing.

HAMILTONS

13 Carlos Pl. W1, 020/7499-9493,
www.hamiltonsgallery.com
HOURS: Mon.-Fri. 10 A.M.-6 P.M.
COST: Free admission
TUBE: Green Park or Piccadilly Circus

Hamiltons is a well-designed basement space flooded with light through a large sun roof. On a good day it's absolutely brilliant inside, which shows off the selection of contemporary art to good effect. It hosts a variety of painting, sculpture, and photography exhibits by leading artists such as Andy Warhol, Richard Caldicott,

Robert Mapplethorpe, and Jedd Novatt. The shows are almost always good and attract consistent praise in the notoriously fickle London art scene. Exhibits change approximately once a month.

MARLBOROUGH FINE ART

6 Albemarle St. W1, 020/7629-5161, www.marlboroughfineart.com

HOURS: Mon.-Fri. 10 A.M.-5:30 P.M., Sat. 10 A.M.-12:30 P.M. (closed Saturdays in August)

COST: Free admission

TUBE: Green Park

Marlborough has been in business since 1946. This famous fine-art dealer runs some of the most popular exhibitions in the city, showing work by top international painters, printmakers, and sculptors that tend toward the representational rather than the obtuse. It puts on 6–8 shows a year and they generally cause quite a stir. The shop also has an extensive collection of prints for sale.

REDFERN GALLERY

20 Cork St. W1, 020/7734-1732/0578, www.redfern-gallery.com

HOURS: Mon.-Fri. 11 A.M.-5:30 P.M., Sat. 11 A.M.-2 P.M.

COST: Free admission

TUBE: Green Park or Piccadilly Circus

On gallery-rich Cork Street, the Redfern Gallery manages to distinguish itself from the crowd by exhibiting a combination of modern and contemporary art that has stood the test of time. By concentrating on artists with solid reputations for setting trends and making enduring art, the gallery has made each visit here an education. Since opening in 1923, it has shown such luminaries as Corot, Pissaro, Nash, and Gear. It also introduced Paul Delvaux and Jun Dobashi to the London public. The exhibit space is roomier than in many galleries, so allow for some extra time to get a good look.

ROYAL ACADEMY OF ARTS

Burlington House, Piccadilly at Burlington Arcade W1, 020/7300-8000, tickets, 087/0848-8484, www.royalacademy.org.uk

HOURS: Royal Academy: Mon.-Fri. 10 A.M.-6 P.M., Sat.-Sun. 10 A.M.-10 P.M. (last admission half an hour before closing); John Madejski Fine Rooms: Tues.-Fri. 1-4:30 P.M., Sat.-Sun. 10 A.M.-6 P.M., free guided tour Tues.-Fri. 1 P.M.

COST: Admission costs vary

TUBE: Green Park

The academy was founded in 1768 and is Britain's oldest and most prestigious school for the arts. Because of this, aspiring artists either love it or hate it and spend their careers trying to get in it or overthrow it. Nobody, however, can ignore it. Its gallery includes works by such greats as Constable and Reynolds and it puts on major shows every year. Check out the website to see what's on, because there's a good chance you'll want to add it to your list of things to do. The academy also hosts a series of evening lectures, which can be rather pricey but are always informative, and there are equally informative free lunchtime lectures 1–2 P.M. A complete listing can be found on the website.

Covent Garden, West End, and Soho — Map 4

PHOTOGRAPHERS' GALLERY

5 & 8 Great Newport St. WC2, 020/7831-1772, www.photonet.org.uk

HOURS: Mon.-Sat. 11 A.M.-6 P.M., Sun. noon-6 P.M.

COST: Free admission

TUBE: Covent Garden

When it opened in 1971, this gallery was the first independent gallery in Britain devoted exclusively to photography, and it has a long history of displaying some of the best contemporary photographers. In addition to a series of yearly exhibitions that always get a lot of notice in the arts press, the Photographers' Gallery hosts the annual Citibank Photography Prize—one of the most prestigious photography contests in the world. You'll find an inexpensive café where patrons can sit and admire the work over an espresso and a shop with a good collection of prints and books for sale.

PROUD GALLERY

32 John Adam St. at corner of Buckingham St. WC2, 020/7839-4942, www.proud.co.uk

HOURS: Mon.-Thurs. 10 A.M.-7 P.M., Fri.-Sun. 11 A.M.-6 P.M.
COST: Free admission
TUBE: Charing Cross

Carling, the British equivalent to Budweiser both in popularity and quality, sponsors this two-story gallery exhibiting pop culture–related photography. Leading photographers show off their snaps of movie stars, fashion models, and rock bands, and the little shop does a brisk business in related CDs, posters, postcards, and T-shirts. In 2006 it had a retrospective of the Ramones, with Carling flowing free at the opening. The boys would have been proud.

Bloomsbury, Euston, and Holborn Map 5

FOUNDLING MUSEUM

40 Brunswick Sq. WC1, 020/7841-3600, www.foundlingmuseum.org.uk
HOURS: Tues.-Sat. 10 A.M.-6 P.M., Sun. noon-6 P.M.
COST: Adults £5, seniors and students £4, children under 16 free
TUBE: Russell Square

Until the advent of social services in the 20th century, abandoned children had to survive on the street or in dismal workhouses. In 1739, Captain Thomas Coram created the Foundling Hospital, the first such institution in the country, and saved thousands of children from poverty, despair, and early death. Coram also enjoyed hanging out with artists, and soon the hospital became Britain's first public art gallery. William Hogarth sat on the board of governors and encouraged artists to donate their works to attract wealthy sightseers, who could then be hit up for a donation. The museum tells the story of this great charitable institution; the gallery showcases the art collection, including paintings by famous British artists, such as Hogarth and Reynolds, displayed in a restored 18th-century interior. The Coram Café serves light meals and drinks.

GETTY IMAGES

46 Eastcastle St. W1, 020/7291-5380, www.gettyimages.com
HOURS: Mon.-Wed., Fri. 10 A.M.-6:30 P.M., Thurs. 10 A.M.-7:30 P.M., Sat. noon-6:30 P.M.
COST: Free admission
TUBE: Oxford Circus

Getty Images is world famous as a major source for photojournalism and creative photography. Its bright and roomy Soho storefront offers many famous photos—and surprising ones you haven't seen before—at a reasonable price (starting at £65). Alongside pictures of Muhammad Ali and various movie stars hang creative pieces of landscapes and daily life. With one of the world's largest stocks of images to draw from, you're sure to find something suitable for any wall.

OCTOBER GALLERY

24 Old Gloucester St. WC1, 020/7242-7367, www.octobergallery.co.uk
HOURS: Tues.-Sat. 12:30-5:30 P.M., closed in August
COST: Free admission
TUBE: Holborn or Russell Square

Showcasing the transvangarde (meaning the "transcultural avant-garde"), the October Gallery brings in work from the Horn of Africa to Mongolia. It's inspiring to see talented artists pushing the limits in countries that almost never make it into the mainstream media—all areas of the world are dynamic and changing. You'll definitely see art here you won't see anywhere else. For example, 2006 saw an exhibit of the work of an Australian aboriginal community that, although numbering only 600 people, has produced several accomplished painters. A gallery café is open 12:30–2 P.M. Tuesday–Friday.

Chelsea, Kensington, and Knightsbridge Map 6

SERPENTINE GALLERY

Kensington Gardens W2, 020/7402-6075, www.serpentinegallery.org
HOURS: Daily 10 A.M.-6 P.M.
COST: Free admission
TUBE: Knightsbridge

This converted 1934 tea pavilion in the heart of Kensington Gardens takes the prize for best gallery setting in London. A visit here is an enjoyable addition to a walk through the gardens, especially if the unpredictable English weather takes a turn for the worse. The Serpentine hosts various temporary exhibits throughout the year, with an emphasis on modern and contemporary. Many big-name artists have exhibited here, including Andy Warhol and Man Ray. Lady Diana was a patron and helped fund a £4 million renovation in 1998.

Maida Vale, Marylebone, and St. John's Wood — Map 8

RIBA

66 Portland Pl. W1, 020/7307-3770, www.riba.org

HOURS: Mon.-Fri. 10 A.M.-6 P.M., Sat. 10 A.M.-5 P.M.

COST: Free admission

TUBE: Oxford Circus

The Royal Institute of British Architects (RIBA) runs this gallery featuring photos and scale models of great architectural works. Detailed texts on the walls explain the projects as well as the architects' careers. Even the building, designed by Grey Wornum in the 1930s, is notable. Anyone interested in architecture will have a fascinating time here. A café and bookshop are on-site, and a regular lecture series keeps budding architects educated and social.

The City — Map 10

THE CHAMBERS GALLERY

23 Long Lane EC1, 020/7778-1600, www.thechambersgallery.co.uk

HOURS: Mon.-Fri. 10 A.M.-6 P.M.

COST: Free admission

TUBE: Barbican

Opened in 2004, this relative newcomer to the London art scene has made a name for itself with exhibitions of 20th-century painting and sculpture, concentrating on artists from Britain and Eastern Europe. The Russian and Ukrainian works are especially interesting, with styles varying from neoimpressionism to Soviet realism, proving that while the region lacked democracy, it didn't lack artistic ability or a cultural life. The exhibitions change monthly, making this a good gallery to visit regularly when popping in and out of London.

GUILDHALL ART GALLERY AND ROMAN AMPHITHEATER

The Guildhall, Guildhall Yard at Greshman St. EC2, 020/7332-3700, www.guildhall-art-gallery.co.uk

HOURS: Mon.-Sat. 10 A.M.-5 P.M., Sun. noon-4 P.M.

COST: Adults £2.50, seniors and students £1, children free; free admission after 3:30 P.M. and on Fri.

TUBE: Bank

Set in the historic Guildhall, this gallery showcases leading British artists from the past and the present day. Lots of battle scenes portray victorious redcoats, and there are scenes of London and country life as well. While many of the paintings aren't terribly famous, they do give a good impression of how the British liked to think of themselves. One, called *The Heart of the Empire,* shows the city itself as it was in the 19th century and pretty much sums up the mood. In the basement are the remains of part of a Roman amphitheater built in A.D. 70 to host gladiator games. The fights must have been popular, because it was expanded in A.D. 200 to hold 6,000 people at a time when the population of Londinium numbered about 30,000.

Islington — Map 11

ESTORICK COLLECTION OF MODERN ITALIAN ART

39A Canonbury Sq. N1, 020/7704-9552, www.estorickcollection.com

HOURS: Wed.-Sat. 11 A.M.-6 P.M., Sun. noon-5 P.M.

COST: Adults £3.50, seniors and students £2.50, children free

TUBE: Highbury and Islington

This elegant Georgian mansion has a comprehensive collection of Italian futurist paintings. Futurism was an art style born out of the havoc of industrialization and the carnage of World War I and emphasized the speed and technological advance of modern society. Typical of this style is the study for *The City Rises* (1910) by Umberto Boccioni, in which people and buildings seem to be swept along by a windstorm of colored motion. Others show futurism's trading of ideas with cubism, such as Gino Severini's *Portrait of Eric Estorick* (1956), which is more of a study in angles and shading than an actual image of the man. There's also a good collection of sculpture and paintings by other famous Italian artists such as Modigliani. The café will give you a taste of Rome with real cappuccinos (tough to find in London) and light lunches.

South of the Thames Map 12

BANKSIDE GALLERY

48 Hopton St. SE1, 020/7928-7521,
www.banksidegallery.com
HOURS: Daily 11 A.M.-6 P.M.
COST: Free admission
TUBE: Blackfriars or Waterloo

Most tourists miss this little gallery next to the Tate Modern, but it's well worth a visit. Here the members of the Royal Watercolour Society and the Royal Society of Painter-Printmakers display their best work, with styles from the traditional to the experimental. There are rotating exhibitions and society members offer their work for sale, including a fair amount of affordable art that can make a unique personal memento or a gift for someone back home.

BEACONSFIELD

22 Newport St. SE11, 020/7582-6465,
www.beaconsfield.ltd.uk
HOURS: Thurs.-Sun. noon-6 P.M.
COST: Free admission
TUBE: Vauxhall

Artists—not curators or wannabes—run this gallery and it shows. The art is rebellious and hard to pigeonhole, which is probably why it doesn't make it into other spaces. That doesn't mean it's bad, however. The way the art scene goes in this town, it could end up winning the Turner Prize any day. It's a very social place, where artists hang out and mingle with visitors. A nice bonus is the café, which has a coffee machine from the 1950s.

DANIELLE ARNAUD

123 Kennington Rd. SE11, 020/7735-8292,
www.daniellearnaud.com
HOURS: Fri.-Sun. 2-6 P.M.
COST: Free admission
TUBE: Lambeth North

Danielle Arnaud is one of the London art scene's leading ladies, and her beautiful Georgian home doubles as an art gallery. It's strange to walk through someone's house looking at her art—this gallery is so private there isn't even a sign—but Arnaud's welcoming manner soon gets you over it. She likes to sponsor relatively unknown international contemporary artists, who aren't so relatively unknown after she's done with them. The artists have lots of fun making installation pieces that reflect the domestic nature of this gallery and are quite creative making art that fits the space.

HAYWARD GALLERY

South Bank Centre, Belvedere Rd. near Royal Festival Hall SE1, 020/7921-0813, ticket office 087/0169-1000,
www.hayward.org.uk
HOURS: Mon., Thurs., Sat.-Sun. 10 A.M.-6 P.M., Tues.-Wed. 10 A.M.-8 P.M., Fri. 10 A.M.-9 P.M.; Waterloo Sunset Pavilion daily 10 A.M.-6 P.M.
COST: Adults £7.50, seniors 60 and older £6, children 12-16 £3, under 12 free out-of-school hours, Mondays half price
TUBE: Waterloo

The concrete monstrosity that houses this gallery is a typical example of brutalism, an architectural style that ravaged the British landscape in the 1960s. This particular example has sharp angles of concrete reminiscent of a ship ready to launch into the Thames. Fortunately, the interior is much more pleasing, with various temporary exhibitions usually featuring contemporary artists with a political bent. The Waterloo Sunset Pavilion, a glass and steel semicircle stuck on one end of the gallery, affords nice views and has touch screen monitors with classic cartoons and artist's videos.

JERWOOD SPACE

171 Union St., Bankside SE1, 020/7654-0171,
www.jerwoodspace.co.uk
HOURS: Mon.-Fri. 9 A.M.-6 P.M., Sat.-Sun. 10 A.M.-6 P.M.
COST: Free admission
TUBE: Southwark or Borough

This gallery, housed in a converted Victorian school, exhibits artists sponsored by the Jerwood Foundation and includes winners of its various competitions for drawing, sculpture, painting, and photography. The emphasis is on contemporary art that takes chances. The Jerwood Foundation also provides rehearsal space at a reduced cost for young artists, as well as for theater and dance companies; however, these rehearsals are generally not open to the public. Café 171 and the Glasshouse offer satisfying cuisine in an artsy setting at a moderate cost. Gallery hours can vary depending on the exhibit, so check the website before visiting.

PURDY HICKS GALLERY

65 Hopton St. SE1, 020/7401-9229, www.purdyhicks.com

HOURS: Mon.-Tues., Thurs.-Fri. 10 A.M.-5:30 P.M., Wed. 10 A.M.-7 P.M., Sat. 11 A.M.-5 P.M.

COST: Free admission

TUBE: Southwark or London Bridge

Tucked away on a little side street behind the Tate Modern is an interesting gallery that's easy to miss. The converted Victorian industrial building, with its brickwork and steel beams left intact, makes for an interesting space for contemporary art. The gallery showcases a lot of rising talent, and the artists' desire to "make it" into the Tate Modern is obvious. Two shows often run simultaneously, one on the ground floor and another in the basement.

Outlying Areas — Map 1

THE WAPPING PROJECT

Wapping Hydraulic Power Station, Wapping Wall E1, 020/7680-2080, www.thewappingproject.com

HOURS: Mon.-Sat. noon-10:30 P.M., Sun. noon-6 P.M.

COST: Free admission

TUBE: Wapping

This is a unique arts space in London and a personal favorite. The space is set in a converted power station, similar to the Tate Modern, and the curators left much of the original machinery intact. In addition to the vast open spaces harbored in the Tate, the original fabric of the Wapping building lends it a ghostly atmosphere and postindustrial charm. Some top artists have done a great job adapting their work to the surroundings. Angus Boulton's video installation of derelict Soviet sports facilities and military bases turned the looming dark interiors into eerily similar spaces from the other side of Europe. Wapping Food (open noon–3:30 P.M., 6:30–11 P.M. Mon.–Fri., 10 A.M.–3:30 P.M., 7–11 P.M. Sat., 10 A.M.–3:30 P.M. Sun.) takes up part of the old station and serves a variety Continental dishes, including braised octopus and veal involtini.

WHITECHAPEL ART GALLERY

80-82 Whitechapel High St. E1, 020/7522-7888, www.whitechapel.org

HOURS: Tues.-Sun. 11 A.M.-6 P.M., Thurs. 11 A.M.-9 P.M.

COST: Free admission

TUBE: Aldgate East or Whitechapel

One of London's leading independent galleries, the Whitechapel hosts temporary exhibits in a variety of media and emphasizes contemporary art. It was founded in 1901 and was the first major gallery in London's working-class East End. Works by such big names as Picasso, Kahlo, Pollock, and Rothko have hung from these walls. The gallery's influence has been major, and Whitechapel is now an important center for the contemporary art scene. The gallery's café was designed by Turner Prize nominee Liam Gillick and offers snacks and lunches in an open, chic, and modern atmosphere.

MUSEUMS

Here are the very best of all the many museums in London, dealing with practically every topic under the sun. Some are tiny, while others are so large you might want to divide a visit over a couple of days.

Westminster, Victoria, and Pimlico — Map 2

THE GUARDS MUSEUM

Wellington Barracks, Birdcage Walk SW1, 020/7414-3271/3428, www.theguardsmuseum.com or www.guards-shop.com

HOURS: Daily 10 A.M.-4 P.M.

COST: Adults £3, seniors and students £2, children under 16 free

TUBE: St. James's Park

Military history fans will love this detailed museum tracing the development of the five regiments of the Foot Guards units, some of the most elite fighting forces of the United Kingdom. The Grenadier, Coldstream, Scots, Irish, and Welsh guards have fought in many of the major battles of the past three centuries and continue on active service today. Uniforms, artifacts, and dioramas bring the history to life and make an interesting historical primer before watching them march at the Changing of the Guard. The shop sells an amazing variety of model soldiers that should keep the young on your list happy.

JEWEL TOWER

Old Palace Yard SW1, 020/7222-2219

HOURS: Apr.-Oct. 10 A.M.-5 P.M., Nov.-Mar. 10 A.M.-4 P.M.

COST: Adults £2.60, under 16 free.

TUBE: Westminster

This stout tower is one of the few surviving parts of the medieval palace at Westminster and dates to 1365–1366. Outside you can still see part of the original moat. The ground floor is the best preserved, with a vaulted ceiling and sculpted bosses dating to 1365. Originally the clerk's office, it's now a café and gift shop. The first floor contains an informative history of Parliament that is helpful to read before visiting that famous building across the street. The second floor covers the history of the Jewel Tower, begining with its construction by Edward II to hold his personal wealth. The Crown Jewels were, and still are, held in the Tower of London since they are property of the kingdom. In the 17th century the building was used as an archive and later as the Board of Trade Standards Department.

Mayfair and Piccadilly — Map 3

THE HANDEL HOUSE MUSEUM

25 Brook St. W1, 020/7495-1685, booking 020/7399-1953, www.handelhouse.org

HOURS: Tues., Wed., Fri., Sat. 10 A.M.-6 P.M., Thurs. 10 A.M.-8 P.M., Sun. noon-6 P.M.

COST: Adults £5, seniors and students £4.50, children £2

TUBE: Bond Street

This restored Georgian house was the place George Frideric Handel called home from 1723 until his death in 1759. He wrote *Messiah* and *Fireworks Music* here, among other pieces. (Another great composer, Jimi Hendrix, lived next door 1968–1969.) The house has been refurnished with period furniture and paintings and contains a collection of Handel's personal items. The museum hosts many special events and concerts throughout the year, including weekly recitals at 6:30 P.M. on Thursdays. There's also a small gift shop. If you like classical music, attending a live show in Handel's own home will be the high point of your trip.

Covent Garden, West End and Soho — Map 4

BENJAMIN FRANKLIN HOUSE

36 Craven St. WC2, 020/7839-2006, www.benjaminfranklinhouse.org

HOURS: Wed.-Sun. 10 A.M.-5 P.M.; also open Mondays June-Sept.

COST: Adults £9, seniors, students, and children £6

TUBE: Charing Cross

Famous as one of the Founding Fathers of the United States, Benjamin Franklin was a devoted Anglophile and lived at this house for almost 16 years—from 1753 until the outbreak of the American War of Independence in 1775. During that time he wrote his autobiography, made many innovations in science and technology, and tried to bring peace between the empire and its dissatisfied colony. The museum uses voice-overs and period displays to show how London shaped this remarkable man's career.

Bloomsbury, Euston, and Holborn — Map 5

THE CARTOON MUSEUM

35 Little Russell St. WC1, 020/7580-8155, www.cartoonmuseum.org

HOURS: Tues.-Sat. 10:30 A.M.-5:30 P.M.

COST: Adults £2.50, seniors £1.50, students and under 18 free

TUBE: Tottenham Court Road or Russell Square

The British are known for their wit, and none are wittier than their political cartoonists. From Hogarth's 18th-century tirades against the evils of gin to modern skewerings of Tony

Blair, this museum follows the development of the cartoon as a medium to inform and entertain. Many turn their crosshairs on American politicians, so if you object to your government's being made fun of by educated foreigners, by all means come here. The upstairs is devoted to nonpolitical comics such as the *Artful Dodger,* which became *Dennis the Menace* in the United States. One room is set aside as a place for kids to draw, with books and posters illustrating how.

PERCIVAL DAVID FOUNDATION OF CHINESE ART

University of London School of Oriental and African Studies, 53 Gordon Sq. WC1, 020/7387-3909, www.pdfmuseum.org.uk

HOURS: Mon.-Fri. 10:30 A.M.-5 P.M.

COST: Free admission

TUBE: Russell Square or Euston Square

Anyone interested in Asian art should catch this museum showcasing the work of one of the world's greatest ceramic traditions. About 1,700 Chinese ceramics are here, including many owned by important emperors. The styles vary from simple, harmonious bowls to vases decorated with intricate scenes of daily and court life. The upper floor has some of the best works, with delicate designs painted on tiny snuff bottles that seem almost to move with life. You could spend quite a lot of time examining the details of these elegant pieces, and the explanatory notes are helpful to those who aren't students of Chinese art.

PETRIE MUSEUM OF EGYPTIAN ARCHAEOLOGY

University College London, Malet Pl. at Torrington Pl. WC1, 020/7679-2884, www.petrie.ucl.ac.uk

HOURS: Tues.-Fri. 1-5 P.M., Sat. 10 A.M.-1 P.M.

COST: Free admission

TUBE: Goodge Street or Euston Square

With more than 80,000 objects from ancient Egypt and Sudan, there's enough to sate the appetite of even the greatest mummy fan. The Sudanese exhibits are especially interesting, representing a culture just south of Egypt that had a great influence on its northern neighbor. In the Egyptian collection, treasures include a fragment from the earliest list of Egyptian pharoahs and the oldest examples of metalwork, the oldest wills, the oldest gynecological essay, and the only papyrus written by a veterinarian. The more usual suspects of mummies, bas-reliefs, and statues are well represented here too, and all the periods of Egypt's history from the predynastic to the Islamic period are explained.

Camden Town — Map 9

THE JEWISH MUSEUM

Raymond Burton House, 129-131 Albert St. NW1, 020/7284-1997, www.jewishmuseum.org.uk

HOURS: Mon.-Thurs. 10 A.M.-4 P.M., Sun. 10 A.M.-5 P.M. (last admission half an hour before closing)

COST: Adults £3.50, seniors £2.50, students and children £1.50

TUBE: Camden Town

England's Jewish community has a long and interesting, although not always happy, history. The collection here, housed in a pleasing early Victorian structure, highlights the life of English Jews. The collection of religious artifacts is especially good and a series of rotating exhibits focus on various aspects of Jewish life. If you have time, visit the other Jewish museum in Finchley (Sternberg Center, 80 East End Rd. N3, 020/8349-1143, 10:30 A.M.–5 P.M. Mon.–Thurs., 10:30 A.M.–4:30 P.M. Sun., Tube: Finchley Central,). While it's a bit out

The Jewish Museum

of the way of the city center, the Finchley museum focuses more on Jewish life in London as opposed to the country in general. Tickets covering both museums cost adults £4.50, seniors £3, and students and children £2.

The City Map 10

BANK OF ENGLAND MUSEUM

Bartholomew Ln. at Threadneedle St. EC2, 020/7601-5545, www.bankofengland.co.uk/museum

HOURS: Mon.-Fri. 10 A.M.-5 P.M.

COST: Free admission

TUBE: Bank

Money makes the world go 'round, and for three centuries London has been one of the greatest centers of capitalism in history. The Bank of England was founded in 1694 and became the empire's official bank, controlling interest rates and issuing currency. Its museum traces the development of banking and commerce through four centuries and provides an important insight into how a little island kingdom became a world superpower. Coin collectors will enjoy the displays showing changes in England's currency through the years, and the gold bars, both Roman and modern, will dazzle even the most jaded eyes. Because it's in the Bank of England building, it's probably one of the best-guarded museums in the world, so don't get any ideas.

THE CLOCKMAKERS' MUSEUM

Guildhall Library, Aldermanbury btwn. Gresham St. and Love Lane EC2, 020/7332-1868, www.clockmakers.org

HOURS: Mon.-Sat. 9:30 A.M.-4:30 P.M.

COST: Free admission

TUBE: Bank

You don't have to be a horologist to appreciate the craftsmanship that has gone into the 500 years worth of clocks here. The collection of the Worshipful Company of Clockmakers of London includes a German wall clock from the 15th century, one of the earliest examples of a domestic timepiece, and the marine chronomers that made it possible to determine longitude. A curio cabinet contains miniature clocks, astronometric clocks that show the relative position of the planets, and a watch in the form of a skull to remind you that your time is limited. If this doesn't sate your appetite for timepieces, visit the British Museum's collection.

PRINCE HENRY'S ROOM AND SAMUEL PEPYS EXHIBITION

17 Fleet St., 020/7936-4004

HOURS: Mon.-Fri. 11 A.M.-2 P.M.

COST: Free admission

TUBE: St. Paul's

This fine example of Tudor architecture somehow survived the flames of 1666 and is now a museum to London's most famous diarist of the period, Samuel Pepys. The building was a tavern in his day and served various functions through the years until the Samuel Pepys Club opened a museum in his honor here in 1975. Among the collection are various articles showing his life and times. Note the fantastic molded plaster ceiling bearing the feathered device of Prince Henry. It's a bit of a mystery why this royal symbol is here, since there's no evidence that this was ever owned by the royal family; in fact, it was an inn since the 15th century. For a while the inn was called "The Prince's Arms."

South of the Thames Map 12

BRAMAH TEA AND COFFEE MUSEUM

40 Southwark St., SE1, 020/7403-5650, www.bramahmuseum.co.uk

HOURS: Daily 10 A.M.-6 P.M.

COST: Adults £4, seniors and children £3.50, family £10

TUBE: Tower Hill

Discover the fascinating history of tea and coffee, two drinks that have transformed the Western world. The English didn't always drink tea, but when the first tea ships came in from China they got hooked. Soon tea was being planted in other parts of the empire, such as India and Ceylon, and it went from being the exclusive preserve of the upper class to the daily drink of just about everybody. Displays examine how tea and coffee became part of our daily lives, changing how we live, work, trade, and interact. A tea room is on-site, of course, serving traditional British leaf tea and tasty scones, and the coffee is excellent. A shop sells a wide variety of teas and coffees, and all the paraphernalia to accompany it; they're great gifts for the caffeine junkies on your list.

CLINK PRISON MUSEUM

Clink St. SE1, 020/7403-0900, www.clink.co.uk
HOURS: Mon.-Fri. 10 A.M.-6 P.M., Sat.-Sun. 10 A.M.-9 P.M.
COST: Adults £5, under 16 or over 60 £3.50, students £3.50, family £12
TUBE: London Bridge

The Clink was the most infamous prison in London, and it gave its name to all others. It was burned down in the Gordon riots of 1780, but now there's a delightfully cheesy tourist trap where the prison once stood. Mannequins tell the story of what it was like to be stuck in this hellhole for debt, prostitution, or being a Catholic. The guided tours are replete with grisly details and there are plenty of props, such as a pillory and a chopping block, to handle and take photographs with. Highbrow it's not, but you'll actually learn a few things—that the bishop of Winchester, who owned the prison, also gave licenses to local brothels, or the fact that the old ball and chain was considered a privilege, because it meant you could go out onto Clink Street to beg for money.

DESIGN MUSEUM

Shad Thames SE1, 087/0833-9955, www.designmuseum.org
HOURS: Daily 10 A.M.-5:45 P.M.
COST: Adults £7, seniors and students £4, kids under 12 free
TUBE: London Bridge

The Design Museum makes for an interesting stop if you're continuing the Thames Walk past the south side of Tower Bridge. Dedicated to the history and further development of British interior design, the museum displays all sorts of styles, from the cool to the downright bizarre. One wonders how many giant test tubes filled with waterproof light bulbs ever made it into homes and offices. A lot of the latest designers' work is on display, as are cool classics from bygone decades. The website lists classes and talks, and the bookshop has a treasure trove of design books and funky gifts.

FLORENCE NIGHTINGALE MUSEUM

St. Thomas's Hospital, 2 Lambeth Palace Rd. SE1, 020/7620-0374, www.florence-nightingale.co.uk
HOURS: Mon.-Fri. 10 A.M.-5 P.M., Sat.-Sun. 10 A.M.-4:30 P.M.
COST: Adults £5.80, seniors, students, disabled, and children £4.80, family £16
TUBE: Westminster or Waterloo

This interesting museum is dedicated to one of the great names in medical science. Nightingale helped provide clean and well-aired hospitals while in charge of a nursing contingent during the Crimean War. At that time most soldiers died of disease, not by violence, so this was a great step toward reducing overall mortality in the armed forces. After returning from the front, she worked tirelessly to promote sanitary conditions in hospitals and to make nursing a respectable job for women. The collection, housed in Nightingale's original nursing school, includes her personal belongings, correspondence, and artifacts from the Crimean War. The shop stocks some of the 200 books and reports she wrote in her lifetime.

MUSEUM OF GARDEN HISTORY

St. Mary-at-Lambeth Church, Lambeth Palace Rd. at Lambeth Rd., SE1, 020/7401-8865, www.museumgardenhistory.org
HOURS: Daily 10:30 A.M.-5 P.M.
COST: Adults £3, seniors and students £2.50
TUBE: Lambeth North

Green-thumbed visitors will love this museum's displays of the development of the garden, including the ancestors of the various tools that are used today. It's housed in the historic St. Mary-at-Lambeth Church, and on fair days the displays glow with color as the sun shines through stained-glass windows. One window shows a curious image of a traveling peddler and his dog. According to legend, a peddler and his pet dog rested here in the 16th century and were taken in by the priest. The peddler never forgot the act of charity, and when he became rich later in life he offered an acre of land to the church if it would put up a stained-glass window to him and his dog. That acre is now the site of the County Hall and the Millennium Wheel. As is appropriate considering its location in the neighborhood's historic church, a 14th-century building extensively remodeled in the 19th century, the museum also has a multimedia display on the history of Lambeth. Of course, there's a garden too—an Elizabethan-style knot garden filled with beautiful plants. A café and shop are on-site.

THE OLD OPERATING THEATRE

9A St. Thomas's St. SE1, 020/7188-2679, www.thegarret.org.uk

HOURS: Mon.-Sat. 10:30 A.M.-5 P.M.

COST: Adults £4.95, seniors and students £3.95, children £2.95, family £12.50

TUBE: London Bridge

Hidden in the garret of St. Thomas's church, the house of worship for old St. Thomas's Hospital, is a perfectly preserved 19th-century operating theater—the only one in the country. The displays trace the development of medicine from folk cures and rough hackwork to more modern methods, including anesthesia and disinfectant. Part of the garret was used as a herb garden, and various medicinal plants such as opium are on display. There are a preserved brain and heart too, remnants of old operations. Best, however, are the old surgery tools: bone saws, tonsil guillotines, and an eight-pronged cervical dilator. Good old days? Think again.

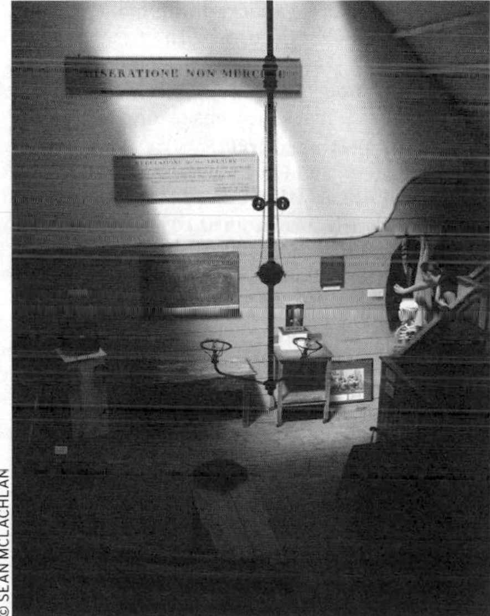

The Old Operating Theatre is the only preserved 19th-century surgery room in England.

WINSTON CHURCHILL'S BRITAIN AT WAR EXPERIENCE

64-66 Tooley St. SE1, 020/7403-3171, www.britainatwar.co.uk

HOURS: Daily 10 A.M.-6 P.M. Apr.-Sept., 10 A.M.-5 P.M. Oct.-Mar.

COST: Adults £9.50, seniors and students £5.75, children £4.85, under 5 free, family £25

TUBE: London Bridge

The Blitz, what Londoners call the campaign of bombing that the German Luftwaffe inflicted on London during World War II, was one of the greatest periods of the city's history. Thousands of people lost their lives and hundreds of irreplaceable buildings were destroyed, but through it all Londoners kept their chins up and went on to win the war (with a little help from several other nations). Through audiovisual displays and reconstructed air shelters, this museum helps visitors understand a little of what it was like living under regular bombardment. It's all quite impressive and kid friendly, but the Imperial War Museum does it almost as well (and with more historical information) for free.

Outlying Areas — Map 1

FREUD MUSEUM

20 Maresfield Gardens NW3, 020/7435-2002, www.freud.org.uk

HOURS: Wed.-Sun. noon-5 P.M.

COST: Adults £5, seniors and students £3, children under 12 free

TUBE: Finchley Road

Sigmund Freud fled his native Vienna to escape the Nazis, setting up his home and psychoanalysis business here. This pleasant house is preserved as Freud left it, with his books and

WEIRD LONDON: THE CITY'S MOST OFFBEAT ATTRACTIONS

A city as massive as London is never without its freakier side. Luckily the British penchant for creating museums out of everything means you can visit the bad old days in modern comfort. It won't stop the shivers up your spine, but you can be thankful you were born in the modern era.

The Hunterian Museum at the Royal College of Surgeons (35-43 Lincoln's Inn Fields WC2, 020/7869-6560, 10 A.M.-5 P.M. Tues.-Sat., free admission, Tube: Holborn) is a gruesome collection of anatomical and pathological specimens. The history of surgery from its early, barbaric years to its relative modernity today makes for a fascinating if stomach-churning lesson in the blessings of modern technology. Check out the pickled samples from old operations.

The Old Operating Theatre (9A St. Thomas's St. SE1, 020/7188-2679, www.thegarret.org.uk, daily 10:30 A.M.-5 P.M.) is the only preserved pre-20th century operating theater in England. Displays explain how hospitals worked back then, and there's a wonderful collection of torture instruments masquerading as medical equipment.

Highgate Cemetery (Swain's Lane N6, 020/8340-1834, www.highgate-cemetery.org, opens weekdays 10 A.M., weekends 11 A.M., £2) is a beautiful and surprisingly peaceful cemetery. Started in the 19th century when the old graveyards in the center of town were getting full and stinky, Highgate was for upper-class people who didn't want to be buried with the unwashed rabble. They tried to immortalize themselves with elaborate gravestones, including weeping statues and Egyptian pyramids.

A special treat is the **Enlightenment Gallery** in the east wing of the British Museum (Great Russell St. WC1, 020/7323-8299, www.thebritishmuseum.ac.uk, 10 A.M.-5:30 P.M. Sat.-Wed., 10 A.M.-8:30 P.M. Thurs.-Fri., free admission), preserved in the eclectic manner of 18th-century museums. There are many unusual displays here, but a favorite is Case 20, "Magic, Mystery, and Rites" – a collection of magical paraphernalia including the crystal ball of the astrologer and mystic Doctor John Dee, a magician favored by Queen Elizabeth I. While the queen herself had a law against consulting practitioners of the mystical arts, she is said to have consulted Dr. Dee and his crystal ball three times: once to find out what would happen in the showdown against the Spanish Armada; again when the Duc de Alençon was asking for her hand in marriage; and a third time when she wanted to know the best cure for her toothache. The crystal ball apparently said that the Spanish Armada would be no problem and that she should stay single, but it's not recorded what the spirits prescribed for the toothache.

The Grant Museum (Department of Biology, Darwin Building, University College London, Gower St. WC1, 020/7679-2647, www.grant.museum.ucl.ac.uk, 1-5 P.M. Mon.-Fri., free admission, Tube: Euston) is a small lab in the basement simply packed with biological samples from every ecozone. The cases full of articulated skeletons and pickled critters staring out mournfully can be a bit creepy, but kids love it. Check the website for its many children's educational events.

To really feel some pain, head to the **British Dental Association Dental Museum** (64 Wimpole St. W1, 020/7935-0875, www.bda.org/museum, 1-4 P.M. Tues. and Thurs., free admission, Tube: Baker St.). Ah yes, the good old days... when cavities meant a trip to the marketplace where a guy with a grimy pair of pliers who hadn't washed his hands in three months yanked out the rotting stump with nothing but brute force and a good swig of rum (usually for him; victims had to supply their own). Displays show early drills, toothbrushes, and the dentures of royalty.

(For more weirdness, check out the *Walking Tours* section in the *Recreation* chapter for ghost walks, Jack the Ripper tours, and other creepy crawls through London.)

remarkable collection of antiquities all in place; the famous couch still sits in the same spot where his patients poured out their childhood secrets for his scrutiny. There are also important exhibits about his daughter, Anna, who made major contributions to the field although she has been overshadowed by her father's fame.

HORNIMAN MUSEUM

100 London Rd., Forest Hill, 020/8699-1872, www.horniman.ac.uk

HOURS: Daily 10:30 A.M.-5:30 P.M.

COST: Free admission; special exhibitions may charge

BRITISH RAIL: Forest Hill

Though a bit distant from central London, the Horniman Museum houses an impressive collection of art and natural wonders. Luckily, it's right near Forest Hill Train Station so it's actually quite simple to get there. (Direct services from London Bridge station depart appoximately every 10 minutes and take 13 minutes.) The World Cultures collection is the third-largest ethnographic collection in the United Kingdom, after the British Museum and the Pitt-Rivers Museum. Highlights include mummy cases, African masks, and a colorful statue of the goddess Kali trampling the body of Shiva. There's also a collection of European folk art. The Natural History collection has more than a quarter of a million (dead) specimens, including lots of little creepy crawlies for kids to enjoy. The Musical Instrument collection features more than 7,000 instruments from around the globe, including a pair of 1,500-year-old bone clappers from Egypt in the form of human hands. Sound recordings bring the displays alive.

KEW BRIDGE STEAM MUSEUM

Green Dragon Ln. and Kew Bridge Rd. TW8, 020/8568-4757, www.kbsm.org

HOURS: Tues.-Sun. 11 A.M.-5 P.M.

COST: Cornish Engine Steaming (weekends): Adults £7.50, seniors and students £6.50; Rotative Engine Steaming (weekends): Adults £6.50, seniors and students £5.50; Weekdays (engines not running): Adults £4.25, seniors and students £3.25; children under 15 free, but must be accompanied by an adult

TUBE: Gunnersbury or Kew Gardens

The Kew Bridge Pumping Station, built in 1838, once supplied water and power to London though massive steam engines. The British were masters of transforming simple water into power by heating it into steam. This unusual museum shows how it was done, as well as the immense variety of machines invented to run the Industrial Revolution. The museum has collected rotative engines from pumping houses across the country. They heated up water to produce steam, which the engine then used to rotate a beam. The Cornish engines are in their original engine houses and were also used to pump water. Steam is generated by a 1927 Lancashire boiler.

Note: The machines run only on weekends. Visit then to see the rotative engines puffing away as if they were still powering the empire. On special weekends the caretakers start up the Cornish engines too. They're all quite loud with massive moving parts, making them popular with kids.

MUSEUM IN DOCKLANDS

West India Quay E14, 087/0444-3856, www.museumindocklands.org.uk

HOURS: Daily 10 A.M.-6 P.M.

COST: Adults £5, seniors over 60 £3, kids under 16 free

TUBE: Canary Wharf

This museum chronicles the United Kingdom's interaction with the rest of the world by examining the trade that passed through its greatest port, the Docklands area of London. The story of how a little island kingdom was able to dominate the world through good seamanship and business acumen is a fascinating one, and the walk-through reconstruction of an 1850s sailor's neighborhood is a must-see if you enjoyed the similar displays in the Museum of London. There are lots of interactive displays and special events for kids, making it a good place to take little ones.

NATIONAL MARITIME MUSEUM

Romney Rd., Greenwich SE10, 087/0781-5189, www.nmm.ac.uk

HOURS: Daily 10 A.M.–5 P.M., 6 P.M. July–Aug.

COST: Free admission

DOCKLANDS LIGHT RAIL: Cutty Sark

The only way a little island kingdom could ever grow into an empire was to become a master of naval technology. This large and well-organized museum traces the development of Britain's maritime might with interactive displays, films, artifacts, even whole ships. You'll see an ornate gilded royal barge, a weird-looking metal speedboat from the 1930s, and a spinning lighthouse lamp. Sections on explorers, traders, passengers, and sailors show how the experience of empire was different for different people, along with a sobering exhibit on the slave trade. The museum also has a good planetarium, with shows at various times (£4). A café and gift shop are on-site.

OLD ROYAL NAVAL COLLEGE

2 Cutty Sark Gardens, Greenwich SE10, 020/8269-4799, www.greenwichfoundation.org.UK

HOURS: Grounds: Daily 8 A.M.–6 P.M.; College: Daily 10 A.M.–5 P.M. (chapel opens Sun. 12:30 P.M.)

COST: Free admission

DOCKLANDS LIGHT RAIL: Cutty Sark

Founded by a royal grant in 1694, these grand classical edifices were originally a hospital and old-age home for sailors before becoming a naval college. Besides soaking up the elegance of the grounds and imposing buildings, visit the Painted Hall, completed by James Thornhill in 1726 as a formal dining room. The ceiling and walls are elaborately painted in the baroque style with images of William and Mary ruling the waves, accompanied by ancient gods and warships. Think the Sistine Chapel with an imperial theme. Equally elegant is a chapel completed by Thomas Ripley in 1751, with ornate molded balconies and ceiling in bright blue and pink, and an altar dwarfed by Benjamin West's 1789 painting of *St. Paul's Shipwreck and Subsequent Reception on the Island of Malta.* The informative Greenwich Visitor's Centre, with a shop and café attached, is on-site.

© SEAN MCLACHLAN

The beautifully preserved chapel at the Old Royal Naval College dates to 1751.

QUEEN'S HOUSE

Romney Rd., Greenwich SE10, 087/0781-5189, www.nmm.ac.uk

HOURS: Daily 10 A.M.–5 P.M.

COST: Free admission

DOCKLANDS LIGHT RAIL: Cutty Sark

Back in the 17th century, Greenwich was a little town far from London and a quiet refuge from the crowding and stench of the city. Queen Anne and James I started building a palace here, which was finished in 1635 by Inigo Jones during the reign of Charles I and Henrietta Maria. It was one of the first buildings in the classical style in the country and caused quite a controversy when it was first built. Few of the original furnishings remain, but it now houses a small but interesting collection of royal portraits and paintings of naval battles, as well as a display of artifacts from the *Mary Rose,* the flagship of Henry VIII that sank in 1545 and was marvelously preserved in silt.

ROYAL OBSERVATORY

Greenwich Park, Greenwich SE10, 087/0781-5189, www.nmm.ac.uk

HOURS: Daily 10 A.M.-5 P.M., until 6 P.M. July-Aug.

COST: Free admission

DOCKLANDS LIGHT RAIL: Cutty Sark

Atop a lofty hill in the center of Greenwich Park stands one of the most historically important observatories in the world. For three centuries, royal astronomers have mapped the heavens and studied the motions of the planets. The observatory was also instrumental in the research to determine longitude, crucial for a seafaring nation that needing efficient shipping. Displays discuss the life and research of the various royal astronomers and the quest for the secret to determining longitude. In honor of this important achievement, Greenwich is the spot for the zero degree of longitude, so you can stand on a line and have one foot in the Western Hemisphere and another in the Eastern. It's an attractive building too, especially the observation room, one of the only surviving interiors by the famous architect Sir Christopher Wren.

OPERA

Lavish scenery, thunderous orchestras, and ear-splitting arias make for a memorable night's entertainment and a classy date. While not as famous as Vienna or Rome's, London's opera scene has no shortage of performances and can stand up to the best the continent has to offer.

Covent Garden, West End, and Soho — Map 4

LONDON COLISEUM

St. Martin's Lane at William IV St. WC2, 020/7632-8300, ENO 087/0145-1700, www.eno.org

TUBE: Leicester Square or Charing Cross

The English National Opera performs here, which is good news for opera fans who don't understand Italian; the performers sing entirely in English. In addition to an impressive opera series, there are ballet performances in the summer and winter seasons. The interior is everything one would expect from a major European opera house—a late-Victorian masterpiece with a sweeping semicircle of red cushioned seats facing an elegantly framed, massive stage that puts on sumptuously decorated performances. With 2,354 seats, it's the largest theater in London, so the singers really have to belt out those tunes!

ROYAL OPERA HOUSE

Floral and Bow Sts. WC2, 020/7304-4000, www.roh.org.uk

HOURS: Box office open Mon.-Sat. 10 A.M.-8 P.M.

TUBE: Covent Garden

This grandiose opera house hosts both the Royal Opera and the Royal Ballet. The interior is vast and the performances are sumptuous, with leading stage designers and artists working together to make some of the highest of high art ever seen. Other highbrow acts in opera and classical music play here as well. The £10 Monday special is a good way to beat the usually high ticket prices, but seats are given out on a ballot system via the website, so space isn't guaranteed.

Chelsea, Kensington, and Knightsbridge — Map 6

OPERA HOLLAND PARK

Holland Park btwn. Holland Walk and Abbotsbury Rd. W8, 084/5230-9769, www.operahollandpark.com

HOURS: Box office open Mon.-Sat. 1-6 P.M.

TUBE: Holland Park

This modest stage in the center of beautiful Holland Park is one of the least pretentious venues for catching an opera. It operates in the summer only, and the audience sits in the open enjoying the lazy warmth of the evenings as the cast performs various operas in the original languages with subtitles. You'll find a bar and two restaurants on-site, or book a picnic when booking tickets and dine al fresco.

THEATER

England in general, and London in particular, have been instrumental in developing drama into a fine art. This is the city where Marlowe, Shakespeare, Osborne, and countless others made their mark. Catch at least one show while in town, and don't worry about the expense. While some productions are ridiculously overpriced, cheap seats are easy to find and many of the smaller theaters are quite reasonable. London has hundreds of theaters; go to any of them and pick up a free *Official London Theatre Guide,* printed every two weeks, which offers listings of what's on.

Covent Garden, West End, and Soho — Map 4

DONMAR WAREHOUSE

41 Earlham St. WC2, 087/0060-6624, www.donmarwarehouse.com

HOURS: Box office open Mon.-Sat. 10 A.M.-7:30 P.M.

TUBE: Covent Garden

One of London's most famous cutting-edge theaters, the Donmar Warehouse produces many of its own plays and has earned a slew of awards. Older plays from greats such as Molière are performed with new twists. Its *Don Juan in Soho* is a typical example, with the famous lover trying to find his way in Soho's frantic nightlife. The theater's reputation attracts many Hollywood stars eager to improve their street credibility. The theater gets its name from the building's original purpose—it was a vat room and hop warehouse for an old brewery.

PALACE THEATRE

Shaftesbury Ave. at Cambridge Circus and Charing Cross Rd. W1, 24-hour booking 087/0895-5579, www.palace-theatre.co.uk

TUBE: Leicester Square or Tottenham Court Road

This towering Victorian landmark in the heart of the tourist area is extremely popular and puts on mostly popular musicals such as *Monty Python's Spamalot* and Andrew Lloyd Webber's *Whistle Down the Wind.* Webber owns the theater, so there's usually one of his musicals being performed. The massive facade is hard to miss as it looms over Cambridge Circus. It's worth a look just to see what the Victorians could achieve with colored bricks and a lot of pomposity.

ST. MARTIN'S THEATRE

West St. at Upper St. Martin's St. WC2, 087/0162-8787, www.stmartinstheatre.co.uk

HOURS: Box office open Mon.-Sat. 10 A.M.-8:30 P.M.

TUBE: Leicester Square

Agatha Christie's *The Mousetrap* has been playing since 1952, making it the longest-running show in the world. The plot has Christie's usual amusing characters and unpredictable twists and turns, and it is a must for any mystery fan. The theater itself was built in 1916 and has an attractive exterior and interior. An earlier restoration kept true to the original design and so coming here is a bit of a historical experience. It remains one of the only privately owned theaters in the West End.

THEATRE ROYAL, DRURY LANE

Catherine St. WC2, 24-hour booking 087/0890-1109, www.theatreroyaldrurylane.co.uk

TUBE: Covent Garden

Drury Lane has been associated with the theater since the beginning. In 1660, a theater was built upon this site, one of only two officially sanctioned playhouses. It's been an institution in the London drama scene ever since. The present building dates to 1812 and while it lacks the imposing facade of the Theatre Royal, Haymarket, it certainly has a beautiful interior. It tends to show modern hits such as Mel Brooks's *The Producers.*

THEATRE ROYAL, HAYMARKET

Haymarket SW1, 24-hour booking 087/0901-3356, general enquiries 020/7930-8890, www.trh.co.uk

TUBE: Piccadilly Circus or Leicester Square

The repertoire at the Theatre Royal, Haymarket, tends toward traditional works, as befits its splendid neoclassical building, designed by John Nash in 1821 as part of his rebuilding of Regent's Park and Regent Street. This leading theater attracts such stage luminaries as Judi Dench. Apparently the shows are worth sticking around for; 19th-century manager John Buckstone still haunts the auditorium and the dressing room.

Bloomsbury, Euston, and Holborn — Map 5

CAMDEN PEOPLE'S THEATRE

58-60 Hampstead Rd. NW1, 087/0060-0100, www.cptheatre.co.uk

HOURS: Box office open 24 hours

TUBE: Warren Street or Euston Square

This popular venue supports newer production companies with innovative takes on contemporary plays. They emphasize movement, gesture, and visuals in a way that makes seeing a performance here feel quite different from the usual dialog-driven stage managing. May and June brings the Sprint festival, showcasing "physical, visual, and unusual theatre." A dozen companies put on as many plays, each showing only a couple of days, and the experimental productions get a lot of buzz in the theater press.

DRILL HALL THEATRE

16 Chenies St. WC1, 020/7307 5060, www.drillhall.co.uk

HOURS: Box office open daily 10 A.M.–9:30 P.M., until 6 P.M. Sun.

TUBE: Goodge Street

The Drill Hall is a noted gay and lesbian theater that hosts both British and international performances, with numerous jazz concerts, comedy shows, and poetry recitals throughout the year. Plays and musicals touch on aspects of homosexual, bisexual, and transgendered life in modern Britain. There's also an extensive program of children's shows, classes, and workshops. BBC Radio regularly records comedy and quiz programs here.

Chelsea, Kensington, and Knightsbridge — Map 6

ROYAL COURT

Sloane Sq. at Cliveden Pl. SW1, 020/7565-5000, www.royalcourttheatre.com

HOURS: Box office open Mon.–Sat. 10 A.M.–6 P.M. or until performance time

TUBE: Sloane Square

The Royal Court is one of the major playhouses in London and concentrates on new work by leading playwrights—or those who will be leading playwrights after getting their work into such a prestigious venue. In 1956 it garnered notoriety with a production of Osborne's *Look Back in Anger,* a play about an alienated generation that met with howls of derision by critics and is now considered a classic. In the 1960s the theater waged an epic battle against the Lord Chamberlain, who held the power to censor whatever he found offensive, and eventually won a victory for art over stuffiness. It's been pushing the limits ever since with innovative plays on contemporary issues. A bookshop and bar are on-site.

Notting Hill, Bayswater, and Paddington — Map 7

GATE THEATRE

The Prince Albert, 11 Pembridge Rd. W11, 020/7229-0706, www.gatetheatre.co.uk

HOURS: Box office open Mon.–Fri. 10 A.M.–6 P.M.

TUBE: Notting Hill Gate

This little space shows some interesting experimental theater. The capacity is only 70, so the Gate provides a more intimate experience than most theaters, and it's very good at transforming its tiny space into whatever the production requires, giving you the feeling that you're actually in the play. Tickets are £15, or £10 for seniors and students, making this one of the more affordable theater options. Even more affordable are the "Happy Mondays," when the first 20 tickets sold at the door cost whatever you can afford (don't be *too* stingy; the arts need support).

Maida Vale, Marylebone, and St. John's Wood — Map 8

OPEN AIR THEATRE

Inner Circle, The Regent's Park NW1, 0870/060 1811, www.openairtheatre.org

HOURS: Box office open Mon.–Sat. 10 A.M.–6 P.M. late Mar.–May; Mon.–Sat. 10 A.M.–8 P.M., Sun. noon–8 P.M. May–early Sept. (performance days only)

TUBE: Baker Street or Regent's Park

Sitting under the stars to watch a play or concert is a great way to cap off a day lounging in The Regent's Park. The theater, set amid trees, flowers, and singing birds, puts on a varied run of new plays and musical revues in the summer. While the theater is open to the elements, it boasts that 94 percent of its performances are completed every year. It stops the show only if it's pouring, and if rained out you can exchange your tickets for another performance.

LONDON THEATER ON THE CHEAP

London is rightfully famous as a major center for the theatrical arts. On any given night there are hundreds of plays and musicals performed on the city's innumerable stages. The only problem is, full-price tickets can put theatergoers back £20, £40, or even £60! When world-class cultural attractions such as the British Museum and National Gallery are free, why do theatrical pleasures have to come at such a cost?

But don't despair, a cheaper way is possible. Several theaters offer discounts. If you are a senior citizen, a student, or if you're under 26 (or, in some theaters, under 25), many theaters will offer a significant reduction on tickets. Buying tickets the same day can also get you reduced rates, as the theaters desperately try to fill all their seats. Check with your hotel and tour company to see if they offer discounts. You can find out more about what's on and what's cheap by picking up a free copy of the *London Theatre Guide,* available at theaters, hotels, and various other attractions, or online (www.officiallondontheatre.co.uk).

Another popular option is the half-price TKTS booth on Leicester Square, run by the Society of London Theatre, the theaters' official marketing organization. While it may not always have seats to all the shows, there are some good deals here. You'll find a host of other "half-price" ticket vendors, especially in Soho, but beware. These vendors add a commission to the price, so sometimes you aren't getting as good a deal as they lead you to believe. The best thing to do is to go to the actual theater, find out how much seats are, and then go to one of these businesses and see how much it charges.

Some venues regularly offer cheap tickets. If you don't mind standing, you can see a play at Shakespeare's Globe Theatre in the "groundlings" section for only £5. Show up at the National Theatre, the Royal Court, or the Donmar Warehouse an hour before showtime on a night when they are sold out, and you can get standing-room-only tickets for a few pounds or even less. The National Theatre's Travelex £10 season offers good seats (although not the best seats) to a series of plays in the spring and summer for less than the price of an entrée at most restaurants. Travelex also sponsors £10 Mondays at the Royal Opera House, but you must apply online several weeks in advance (www.travelex.roh.org.uk). The Bridewell Theatre is also known for putting on shows at very low rates. The Royal Court's Monday shows are only £7.50, a smart way for it to fill the theater on the slowest night of the week. Booking online can also reduce ticket costs at many theaters.

If you are an avid fan and plan to see a bunch of shows, consider joining the Theatregoers' Club (www.whatsonstage.com). For £30 a year, members can go on the club's Outings, which feature discounted tickets and special bonuses such as drinks or backstage tours.

And don't forget the little theaters. Check the newspaper or magazines such as *Time Out* for what's going on in London's innumerable student or alternative venues. You'll be amazed at the variety and scope of the performances, and sometimes you can even find free shows.

A few caveats are in order. Scalpers (called "touts" here) are rife, and some even set up their own official-looking booths or websites. It's best to buy direct from the theater, TKTS, or other established shops. If you buy from a tout, you might end up with a fake ticket or one to a worse seat than you thought you were getting. Also be aware that some seats are "limited visibility." Reputable vendors will always tell you if a seat is limited visibility, and these should be the cheapest seats in the house. Ask to see a seating plan so you know where you'll be, and ask to see the face value of the ticket, since vendors should charge no more than 25 percent of the face value. Also avoid signing any forms, as these could nullify your legal rights and set you up for getting ripped off.

The key to getting cut-rate tickets is flexibility. You may not see what you want to see when you want to see it, but a bit of research can get you into some quality shows at very reduced rates.

The City Map 10

THE BARBICAN

Silk St. at Whitecross St. EC2, switchboard 020/7638-4141, box office 020/7638-8891, www.barbican.org.uk

HOURS: Mon.-Sat. 9 A.M.-11 P.M., Sun. noon-11 P.M.

TUBE: Barbican or Moorgate

The Barbican's spacious theater is popular with Londoners looking for innovative takes on classic plays or a sampling of new international works from underrepresented countries such as Iceland and Iran. Workshops and lectures are held on a regular basis for those who want to look beyond the performance.

BRIDEWELL THEATRE

Bride Lane at New Bridge St. EC4, 020/7353-3331, www.bridewelltheatre.org

TUBE: Blackfriars

This community theater seats only 134, making for an intimate theater experience, and features many classic plays, often reworked to fit modern themes. It is also one of the most affordable theaters in London; tickets to many shows in the 2006 season went for only £5, and there are popular Lunchbox performances of short plays for the same price. A bar is on-site. Since all the performances are put on by outside companies, there is no box office in the building. Call the theater or check the website for booking information for particular performances.

Islington Map 11

ALMEIDA THEATRE

Almeida St. N1, 020/7359-4404, www.almeida.co.uk

HOURS: Box office open Mon.-Sat. 10 A.M.-7:30 P.M.

TUBE: Angel or Highbury and Islington

A mixture of plays, opera, and community theater projects makes a season at the Almeida a big draw. It's no surprise that leading playwrights such as Charlotte Jones and Frank McGuinness put on their latest works here. In addition to new plays, the theater showcases more established works such as those by Maxim Gorky. The opera season, again a mixture of the old and new, has been going strong since the 1980s. School groups and local writers also work with more established theater artists to put on their own productions. A bar serving light meals and drinks is on-site.

KING'S HEAD THEATRE

115 Upper St. N1, 020/7226-1916, www.kingsheadtheatre.org

HOURS: Mon.-Thurs. 11 A.M.-1 A.M., Fri.-Sat. 11 A.M.-2 A.M., Sun. noon -12:30 A.M.

TUBE: Angel

Enjoy a play in a small theater situated in a 19th-century pub. The King's Head puts on a combination of new works and classics, and it boasts that more than 30 of its plays have transferred to the West End—a sure sign it's doing something right. What's nice about this theater is that it's small (no opera glasses are necessary and there are no nosebleed seats) and the working glass lamps appeal to my love for the historic. The special pretheater menus are a good bargain and let you sip a pint or a glass of champagne while watching the performance.

South of the Thames Map 12

BOOKSHOP THEATRE

At The Calder Bookshop, 51 The Cut SE1, 020/7593-1520

HOURS: Box office open Mon.-Sat. 9 A.M.-7 P.M.

TUBE: Waterloo

Tucked away in the back room of an independent bookstore is a small stage. In the evenings the bookshelves are cleared away and seats are set up for performances of leading modern plays. As it has a capacity of only 40, it's best to book ahead but you'll be rewarded with an intimate theater experience, great acting, and a chance to browse the shop's excellent selection of theater books. With prices below £10, this is one of the best deals in the whole theater scene.

NATIONAL THEATRE

Upper Ground at Waterloo Rd. SE1, 020/7452-3000, www.nationaltheatre.org.uk

HOURS: Box office open Mon.-Sat. 10 A.M.-8 P.M.

TUBE: Waterloo

The three stages housed in this unattractive concrete mass along the South Bank host new dramas and old favorites, as well as musicals, workshops, films, and talks. On any particular day there are several things to see. The National is home to the spring and summer Travelex £10 season, at which selected seats will put you back only 10 bob, a great deal considering the quality of the performances. Book well in advance, because tickets go fast.

OLD VIC THEATRE

The Cut at Waterloo Rd. SE1, 087/0060-6628, www.oldvictheatre.com
HOURS: Box office open Mon.-Fri. 10 A.M.-6 P.M.
TUBE: Waterloo

The attractive 200-year-old interior, with its elegant staircase and gilt decoration, make for a classy evening out. Kevin Spacey is the artistic director and he puts on a mixture of classics and modern favorites. Spacey himself occasionally takes the stage, as he did in the 2006 season when he played Jim Tyrone in *A Moon for the Misbegotten.* If visiting in October, try to get into the 24 Hour Plays Gala, for which a surprise cast of stars write, direct, rehearse, and perform a play in just 24 hours. It's on for one night only (the poor actors couldn't survive more than one of these a year) and all the proceeds go to charity.

SHAKESPEARE'S GLOBE THEATRE

New Globe Walk at Bankside SE1, 020/7401-9919 or 020/7850-8590, www.shakespeares-globe.org
HOURS: Box office open mon-Fri. (weekends in spring and summer) 10 A.M.-6 P.M.
TUBE: London Bridge

Not even Stratford-upon-Avon can compete with the Globe for making the world of Shakespearian theater come alive. In a reconstructed Globe Theatre that looks just as it did when the Bard was director (except that it's much cleaner and members of the audience have bathed and retained most of their teeth), costumed actors prance the stage performing Shakespeare's plays and works by his contemporaries. The theater comes alive May–September with new productions of the Bard's plays, as well as other

Shakespeare's Globe Theatre

period pieces and modern works. Seats vary £15–31, or stand in the yard as the commoners did for only £5.

UNICORN THEATRE

147 Tooley St. SE1, box office 020/7645-0560, 020/7645-0500, www.unicorntheatre.com
HOURS: Box office open Mon.-Fri. 9:30 A.M.-6 P.M., Sat. 10 A.M.-6 P.M., Sun. noon-5 P.M.
TUBE: London Bridge

The Unicorn Theatre has been putting on plays and musicals just for kids since 1947. Both the acting and the venue (completed in 2005) are first rate and the production quality is quite high. The performances are a mix of old and new, with the new emphasizing multiculturalism. The website lists upcoming performances with a handy age guide so you can pick the best one for your child. The theater does not admit children under four, for reasons obvious to anyone with a child under four.

Architecture

HISTORIC BUILDINGS

Despite the Great Fire, many lesser fires, the Luftwaffe, and the even more destructive Blitz of "urban development," London has retained many fine historic homes. A visit to one or more of these beauties will give you a taste of the London that was and an insight into people's lives centuries ago.

Westminster, Victoria, and Pimlico — Map 2

BANQUETING HOUSE

Whitehall SW1, 087/0751-5178, www.hrp.org.uk

HOURS: Mon.-Sat. 10 A.M.-5 P.M.

COST: Adults £4.50, seniors and students £3.50, children £3

TUBE: Westminster or Embankment

The only surviving fragment of the Palace of Whitehall after a calamitous fire in 1698, the Banqueting House gives a good idea of the glory of England's former palace. This section was designed in 1619 by the famous architect Inigo Jones and was one of the first classical buildings in the country. Charles I had Rubens paint the elegant ceiling of the main hall; 14 years later, it was one of the King's last sights as he stepped from the room onto the scaffolding outside the window, where he was beheaded before a gaping crowd.

Covent Garden, West End, and Soho — Map 4

SOMERSET HOUSE

The Strand and Waterloo Bridge, 020/7845-4600, www.somerset-house.org.uk

HOURS: Daily 10 A.M.-6 P.M.

TUBE: Temple or Covent Garden

This impressive old stately home facing the Thames was built by Edward Seymour "Protector Somerset" in 1547 and was the first grand Renaissance building in England. After Somerset fell out of favor, his elegant stone mansion was used by queens and their retinues. The building was extensively remodeled in the 18th century and used by the Royal Academy, Royal Society, Society of Antiquaries, and the Navy Board. It features an ice rink in winter and concerts in the summer. It's a soothing place to sit and relax, whether inside the stately courtyard, or on the patio overlooking the Thames.

Outlying Areas — Map 1

KEW PALACE

Kew Gardens, by the Main Gate, Richmond TW9, 087/0751-5179, www.hrp.org.uk

HOURS: Tues.-Sun. 10 A.M.-6 P.M. late Apr.-Sept. (last admission 5 P.M.)

COST: Adults £5, seniors and students £4, children 5-16 £3, under 5 free

TUBE: Kew Gardens

This residence of the royal family provided a refuge for aristocratic bluenoses away from the stink of London 1728–1818. The building, an imposing brick structure surrounded by beautifully manicured gardens, was built in 1631 and is known as "The Dutch House" because it was originally built by a wealthy Flemish family in the style of their country. King George III lived here for some time, and many other members of the royal family have visited. Queen Charlotte, George III's wife, died here in 1818 and it ceased to be used as a residence. Inside, visit the many rooms filled with 18th- and 19th-century furniture, including the princesses' dollhouse and George III's collection of curios. The palace finished a 10-year restoration project in 2006 and is in pristine condition.

QUEEN CHARLOTTE'S COTTAGE

Kew Gardens, Richmond TW9, 020/8332-5655, www.hrp.org.uk

HOURS: Sat.-Sun. 10 A.M.-4 P.M.

COST: Free admission

TUBE: Kew Gardens

This little cottage was built by Queen Charlotte sometime before 1771 (nobody's quite sure when) as a home away from her home-away-from-home. It was popular with the royal family as a summerhouse and as a place to have tea and picnics. It was also a welcome refuge for Queen Charlotte and her daughters during King George III's periodic bouts of madness. The cottage is nestled among trees and a garden, making for an excellent photo opportunity. Entrance to the cottage is free, but nearby Kew Palace charges a fee. The two buildings are best seen in unison since they are part of the same complex.

HISTORIC CHURCHES AND HOUSES OF WORSHIP

No visit to London would be complete without seeing some of its fantastic church architecture. While Southwark Cathedral and Westminster Abbey are major tourist destinations, these churches are less well known to the casual visitor. Keep in mind that visitors are not permitted during services, but they are more than welcome to attend as worshippers. Churches are generally open early morning to early evening, with services at various times of the day. Many are closed on Saturdays. Call ahead to be sure, but since so many of the historic churches are clustered in The City, if one is closed there are usually a half dozen more just a short walk away. Most offer concerts during the year (the best of these are listed in the *Classical Music* section).

Bloomsbury, Euston, and Holborn Map 5

ST. GEORGE'S

7 Little Russell St. WC1, 020/7405-3044, www.stgeorgesbloomsbury.org.uk

COST: Free admission

TUBE: Tottenham Court Road or Russell Square

While Sir Christopher Wren is the most famous of British architects, his pupil Nicholas Hawksmoor (1661–1736) is considered by many to be equally accomplished. Hawksmoor's main contribution was six London churches, of which this was the last. Consecrated in 1730, it shows Hawksmoor's characteristic blending of Roman and Gothic styles, with influences from his teacher. The stepped tower is inspired by the Mausoleum of Halicarnassus, one of the seven wonders of the ancient world. Behind a conservative classical entrance is a bright plastered interior with gilded Corinthian columns. The church was undergoing restoration in 2006, but even so is strikingly beautiful.

ST. PANCRAS

Euston Rd. and Upper Woburn Pl. NW1, 020/7388-1461, www.stpancraschurch.org

COST: Free admission

TUBE: King's Cross/St. Pancras

Legend says this is the site for the first church in England, founded in A.D. 313—the year that the Emperor Constantine made Christianity legal in the Roman Empire—making this the oldest church site in London. St. Pancras opened in 1822 and is immediately recognizable by its unusual design, funded by the Duke of York. The duke was a fan of classical architecture; thus caryatid columns mark the entrance to the catacombs. These graceful female figures, holding a ewer in one hand and an inverted torch in the other (a symbol of death), are an imitation of the Erechtheum in Athens. The Temple of the Winds, by Pericles, was the model for the steeple although it's surmounted by a cross instead of a triton. Impressive stained-glass windows illuminate the interior. Free classical music recitals are held at 1:15 P.M. Thursdays.

Maida Vale, Marylebone, and St. John's Wood Map 8

ALL SOULS CHURCH

Langham and Regent St. W1, 020/7580-3522, www.allsouls.org

COST: Free admission

TUBE: Oxford Circus

The odd circular spire of All Souls is immediately noticeable at the north end of Regent Street. This is the crowning glory of the famous architect John Nash, who finished the street and the church in 1824. The interior is rectangular and rather spare, with golden Corinthian columns and large windows that let in plenty of light and make this a pleasing venue for the regular classical and organ concerts. Check the website for the current schedule. Like so many churches, it was bombed out during the Blitz and had to be extensively remodeled.

ISLAMIC CULTURAL CENTRE AND LONDON CENTRAL MOSQUE

146 Park Rd. NW8, 020/7724-3363,
tours 020/7725-2212, www.iccuk.org
HOURS: By reservation
COST: Free admission
TUBE: Baker Street

This mosque and cultural center has been a leading force in the Islamic community since 1944, and the worshippers here spend a great deal of energy on outreach. The mosque, with its towering white minaret and golden dome, is visible from the western edge of The Regent's Park and is one of the largest mosques in Europe, able to house 5,000 worshippers inside. The Cultural Centre runs a continuing series of classes and events, and guided tours are available by reservation. A bookstore is on-site.

The City — Map 10

ST. BARTHOLOMEW THE GREAT

Little Britain at West Smithfield EC1, 020/7606-5171,
www.greatstbarts.com
COST: Free admission
TUBE: Barbican or St. Paul's

This fantastic medieval church is one of the most atmospheric in The City. Built by a courtier to King Henry I in 1143, it was the center of a large complex of church buildings before the Dissolution of Henry VIII took away most of its lands and two-thirds of the church itself. What remains, however, is grandiose, with high Gothic vaulting, a semicircular aisle going around the nave, and numerous old graves. A brown marble example shows the busts of Percival and Agnes Smallpace (died 1558 and 1588), complete with frilled collars, and the inscription, "Behowlde youre selves by us sutche once were we as you and you in tyme shalbe even duste as we are now." Food for thought.

ST. CLEMENT DANES

The Strand opposite Royal Courts of Justice WC2,
020/7242-8282
COST: Free admission
TUBE: St. Paul's

This church, set incongruously upon a traffic island, has a tumultuous history. Originally constructed by the Danish Viking community in the 9th century, St. Clement was rebuilt by William the Conqueror, only to be destroyed by the Great Fire of 1666 and rebuilt again by Wren in 1681. The soaring steeple was added by James Gibbs in 1719. Predictably, it was gutted by German incendiary bombs and only the hollow shell of the walls and steeple remained. Pockmarks from shrapnel can still be seen on the outside walls. The walls of the crypt display ornate metal funerary plaques from the 18th and 19th centuries. The church was adopted by the Royal Air Force in 1956 and restored by Anthony Lloyd. It is now the central church of the RAF, evident from the two air marshal statues in front and the banners and Roll of Honour inside.

© SEAN MCLACHLAN

the gateway to St. Bartholomew the Great Church

ST. DUNSTAN-IN-THE-WEST

186-187 Fleet St. WC2,
Anglican Church 020/7405-1929,
Romanian Church 020/7735-9515
COST: Free admission
TUBE: St. Paul's

Built in 1832, St. Dunstan is one of the newer churches in The City. While it lacks some of the baroque grace of the Wren churches, it still sports a fabulous octagonal tower; there is a statue of Queen Elizabeth I below. It's interesting to note that it acts as both an Anglican and a Romanian Orthodox Church; the Anglican Church has created close ties with the Orthodox and other Christian communities. Also look for the clock tower, which has two cavemen-looking figures that strike the bells every hour. They are Gog and Magog, legendary giants who lived in England before humans arrived.

ST. MAGNUS THE MARTYR

Lower Thames St. EC3, 020/7626-4481,
www.stmagnusmartyr.org.uk
COST: Free admission
TUBE: Monument

St. Magnus was a Christian Viking who has been honored here since about 1100. The present church was designed by Wren after the Great Fire, but subsequent fires, bombings, and remodelings have altered it greatly. Of special interest are a stained-glass window in the northwest corner, dating to 1671 and showing the emblem of the Worshipful Company of Plumbers, and a shrine along the north wall containing a fragment of the True Cross. On the south wall, a shrine to St. Magnus shows him wearing a historically inaccurate horned helmet, an invention of Victorian romanticism. A beam from the Roman wharf found under Fish Street stands on the church porch.

ST. MARTIN-WITHIN-LUDGATE

40 Ludgate Hill EC4, 020/7248-6054
COST: Free admission
TUBE: Blackfriars

This is one of the many churches rebuilt by Sir Christopher Wren after the Great Fire of 1666, and it is a fine example of Wren's use of symmetry. The square nave is divided into a cruciform pattern with pillars and lowered ceilings in the corners. The soothing lines of the church provide a welcome contrast to the rumble of traffic outside. Even in Wren's day the traffic was loud, so he added an entryway between the street and the main part of the church to lower the noise. Free music recitals are held 1:15–2:15 P.M. most Wednesdays. This is the official church of the Knights of the Round Table—not the original knights, but a later example of English eccentricity.

ST. MARY-LE-BOW

Cheapside EC2, 020/7248-5139,
www.stmarylebow.co.uk
COST: Free admission
TUBE: St. Paul's or Mansion House

St. Mary's is one of the best-loved churches in London. It is said that you can't call yourself a real cockney unless you were born within earshot of its bells. The 11th-century Norman church originally on this site was destroyed by the Great Fire of 1666 and rebuilt by Sir Christopher Wren. After the Luftwaffe wrecked it again in 1941, it was rebuilt according to Wren's plan. The steeple largely escaped damage, although it had to be taken off the unstable structure and stored for many years. Its graceful spire is now back in place and is a testament to Wren's genius. The church holds a free series of classical concerts at 1:05 P.M. most Thursdays.

ST. MARY-LE-STRAND

The Strand at Surrey St., 020/7836-3126,
www.stmarylestrand.org
COST: Free admission
TUBE: Temple or St. Paul's

St. Mary, like St. Clement Danes, is set upon a traffic island. James Gibbs completed it in 1724 and it is notable primarily for its ornately molded ceiling, apse, and Corinthian columns of white plaster enlivened with cherubs and gold leaf. The interior is a rare original; the church was lucky enough to escape the Blitz pretty much unscathed. It is the official church of the Women's Royal Naval Service and includes several monuments to important members of that organization. Classical music recitals are held at 1:05 P.M. every Wednesday.

ST. SEPULCHRE-WITHOUT-NEWGATE

10 Giltspur St. EC1, 020/7248-3826, www.st-sepulchre.org.uk

COST: Free admission

TUBE: St. Paul's

The largest church in London, St. Sepulchre was built around 1450 and, like so many churches, was burned in 1666 and rebuilt by Sir Christopher Wren. Check out the stained-glass window on the south wall showing John Smith, the first English governor of the Virginia colony, and Pocahontas. Smith's grave is in the south aisle. While the church has been extensively remodeled through the centuries, the 17 carved bosses on the porch are from the original design. There are also many monuments to the Royal Fusiliers, City of London regiment, as this is their affiliate church. Check the website for the schedule of St. Sepulchre's famous and long-running music series.

Outlying Areas Map 1

BUDDHAPADIPA THAI TEMPLE

14 Calonne Rd. SW19, 020/8946-1357, www.buddhapadipa.org

HOURS: Mon.-Fri. 6 A.M.-6 P.M., Sat.-Sun. 6 A.M.-4 P.M.

COST: Free admission

TUBE: Wimbledon Park

The first Buddhist temple in the United Kingdom, the Wat Buddhapadipa is a striking Thai monastery and temple and is home to several monks. The grounds cover four acres and include a beautiful garden, pond, and soothing meditation area. Inside there are a golden Buddha and some brilliant murals portraying the life of the Buddha. Classes on Buddhism and meditation are ongoing. This is one of the most relaxing places in London and a great refuge from all the chaos of the big city.

SHRI SWAMINARAYAN MANDIR

105-119 Brentfield Rd., Neasden, 020/8965-2651, www.mandir.org

HOURS: Mandir and Haveli: Daily 9 A.M.-6:30 P.M.; Understanding Hinduism Exhibition: Daily 9 A.M.-6 P.M.

COST: Mandir and Haveli: Free; Understanding Hinduism Exhibition: Adults £2, seniors and children 6-16 £1.50

TUBE: Neasden or Stonebridge Park

Consecrated in 1995, this is the largest Hindu temple outside of India. The temple is faced with brilliant white Italian marble and the seven pinnacles are elaborately carved, as are the walls and columns. Visitors must go on a tour, which is very informative about the various shrines and rituals. An Understanding Hinduism exhibition describes the beliefs and development of one of the world's oldest religions. An excellent vegetarian shop is on-site. Check the website to see if one of the numerous Hindu festivals is happening during your stay, as some are closed to visitors.

Note: You must remove shoes before entry, and no shorts or skirts shorter than knee length (although security can provide guests with a sarong) are allowed, nor is photography.

MONUMENTS

Being such a historic city, London has gathered a whole army of monuments to heroes and events. Everywhere you look, memorials to past tragedies and glories abound. Literally thousands of monuments are in the city, but here's a list of the most, um, monumental.

Covent Garden, West End, and Soho Map 4

CLEOPATRA'S NEEDLE

Embankment btwn. Waterloo and Hungerford Bridges, SW1

HOURS: Open 24 hours

COST: Free admission

TUBE: Embankment

Most visitors don't expect to see ancient Egyptian monuments in London, but right along the Thames Walk stands an obelisk covered in hieroglyphics. It was originally erected at Heliopolis by the Pharaoh Thothmes III around 1500 B.C.; two centuries later, Ramses the Great added some inscriptions boasting of his military prowess. When Cleopatra was redecorating Alexandria in 12 B.C., she had the obelisk moved there. It was donated to the British

© SEAN MCLACHLAN

Cleopatra's Needle on the Thames Path dates to 1500 B.C.

nation in A.D. 1819 by Mahommed Ali, viceroy of Egypt, after the English kicked Napoleon's troops out. Getting it to England, however, proved a bit problematic. The obelisk was encased in a metal cylinder and towed away, but it was lost in a storm in the Bay of Biscay—only to be spotted by another ship, floating along unharmed. The chips out of its bottom are courtesy of German bombing.

NELSON'S COLUMN

Trafalgar Sq. WC2

HOURS: Open 24 hours

COST: Free admission

TUBE: Charing Cross

Probably the most famous and recognizable monument in London, Nelson's Column was erected in 1843 to commemorate the empire's greatest admiral. Admiral Horatio Nelson (1758–1805) joined the Navy at the tender age of 12 and rose through the ranks to become a captain by the time he was 20. He lost an eye in one battle, an arm in another, and finally his life at the Battle of Trafalgar, where his famous command, "England expects every man to do his duty" so fired up his fleet that it broke Napoleon's naval power and saved England from invasion. The old boy stands 169 feet (51.5 meters) from his base to the top of his jaunty hat; in 2006 the whole thing underwent a meticulous £420,000 restoration and cleaning. His pedestal is cast from the bronze of captured French guns and depicts his four greatest victories.

Camden Town Map 9

HIGHGATE CEMETERY

Swain's Lane, Hampstead and Highgate, N6, 020/8340-1834, www.highgate-cemetery.org

HOURS: Eastern cemetery opens Mon.-Fri. 10 A.M., Sat.-Sun. 11 A.M. (last admission 4:30 P.M. Apr.-Oct., 3:30 P.M. Nov.-Mar.)

COST: Admission £2, camera permit £1, standard tour £5, special tour £70, £7 for each person over 10 people

TUBE: Highgate

Early-19th-century London was dirty and crowded, and not just for its living inhabitants. It was getting to the point that if you wanted to bury someone, you had to dig someone else up. To relieve the congestion in London's public burial grounds, Parliament approved the creation of private cemeteries. Highgate Cemetery opened in 1839 and proved so popular among the city's well-to-do—who didn't want to be buried among the common rabble—that the owners created an East Cemetery in 1854. Highgate eventually filled up and started to wear down. The West Cemetery shut down and was in danger of becoming derelict when a band of volunteers decided to preserve the unique funerary architecture. A tour or solitary stroll through the ornate mausoleums will reveal the resting places of many famous people, such as Karl Marx, George Eliot, six lord mayors of London, and several hundred other notables. Though visitors can see the East Cemetery on their own, a tour is required to visit the West Cemetery.

Please remember that this is still a functioning cemetery. Visitors are asked to dress and act accordingly and video cameras, picnics, and smoking are not allowed.

The City — Map 10

GOLDEN BOY

NW Corner of Giltspur and Cock Lane
HOURS: Open 24 hours
COST: Free admission
TUBE: St. Paul's

This fat little naked guy commemorates the Great Fire of London, caused, according to the plaque, by the "sin of gluttony." The fire stopped just short of here, which is too bad, because the old Inn that sat on this site was the scene for sins far more serious than gluttony. At a time when the only bodies a surgeon could get to practice on were those of the executed, "resurrection men" would steal the newly dead from graveyards and lay them out for sale in the upper floors. The practice was so widespread that graveyards had to post armed guards.

© SEAN MCLACHLAN

The Golden Boy commemorates the Great Fire of 1666, caused by the "sin of gluttony."

MONUMENT

Monument St. at Fish St. Hill EC3, 020/7626-2717, www.towerbridge.org.uk
HOURS: Daily 9:30 A.M.-5 P.M.
COST: Adults £2, children £1
TUBE: Monument

Just opposite Monument Station stands a 202-foot column commemorating the Great Fire of London. The height is significant; it's the exact distance from the pillar to the house in Pudding Lane where the fire started. The column, designed by Sir Christopher Wren and completed in 1677, sports a bright golden flame at the top and an observation tower with splendid views reachable by 311 steep steps. Making it all the way up the steps earns you an official certificate proving your accomplishment. The platform became a popular place for distraught Londoners to hurl themselves to their deaths; more people died at the Monument than from the fire itself until a protective screen was put up. The inscription at the base blamed the Catholics for the fire, but The City changed it in 1831.

TEMPLE BAR

Entrance to Paternoster Square just north of St. Paul's EC4
HOURS: Open 24 hours
COST: Free admission
TUBE: St. Paul's

Temple Bar is the last surviving old London gatehouse, unless you count the old medieval postern at the Barbican. Unlike that crumbling but atmospheric ruin, the Temple Bar is preserved in all its baroque splendor. It was designed by Wren, erected in 1672, and stood at the conjunction of Strand and Fleet streets, marking the boundary between The City and Westminster. By 1878 traffic had become too busy and the city management deemed it a nuisance; it was moved to private land until 2004, when it was placed here.

Festivals and Events

In addition to its regular attractions, London plays host to many annual festivals and special events. Attending a festival can give a unique twist to your trip and since many are sponsored by the diverse ethnic communities that make up the fabric of London, they are also a good way to appreciate the city's amazing multiculturalism.

Since the actual dates and even the locations for most events change year to year, be sure to check the event website or call the information number for details for the time you plan to visit. There are also a large number of one-shot or irregular festivals. For information on these and other events, check the entertainment listings in one of the local newspapers or magazines to find out what might be on. Good sources of information include *Time Out* magazine and the London Tourist Board's *Totally London* booklet, or its monthly *London Planner*. Most events are free but some, such as the beer festivals and Chelsea Flower Show, charge a fee.

JANUARY

CHINESE NEW YEAR

www.chinatown-online.co.uk

London has long had a vibrant Chinese community. The Chinese New Year celebrations are justifiably famous, with lots of parades and fireworks as well as colorful performances you won't usually see at other times of the year, such as the dragon parade. After watching the parade, head on over to Soho for some authentic and affordable Chinese cuisine. Since the Chinese have a different calendar from the West's, the time for their New Year changes in relation to the Western one. Check out the website to find out when it is each year.

During Chinese New Year, Chinatown hosts dazzling parades with fireworks.

NEW YEAR'S DAY PARADE

www.londonparade.co.uk

If you've recovered enough from New Year's Eve, head down to Parliament Square and watch this huge parade, with marchers and floats representing each borough and various organizations. It's lots of fun and a big fundraiser for charity.

FEBRUARY

LONDON FASHION WEEKEND

087/0890-0097, www.londonfashionweek.co.uk

Billed as "four days of pure retail therapy," this is an annual get-together of more than 100 designers selling their collections at a cut rate to make way for this year's new arrivals. You can also get beauty and makeup tips from the experts. Tickets start at £10 and must be booked by phone or through the website.

MARCH

LONDON DRINKER BEER AND CIDER FESTIVAL

www.camranorthlondon.org.uk

Brought to you by those nice folks from the Campaign for Real Ale, this three-day festival is smaller and more laid-back than its annual Great British Beer Festival. Sample real ales, cider, and perry (a cider made from pears instead of apples). There's good home cooking too.

ST. PATRICK'S DAY

St. Paddy's Day is a great time to head on over to one of London's many Irish pubs and raise a glass to the Emerald Isle. Check out the entertainment listings in *Time Out* and other magazines for the many Irish folk and rock music concerts held around this time. While lots of events are held on the day, also keep an eye out for events on the closest weekend.

APRIL

THE BOAT RACE

www.theboatrace.org

If you have to ask which boat race, you aren't English. Every April sees the rivalry between Oxford and Cambridge played out in a grueling race between the two universities' rowing teams. It's been going on since 1829 and starts near Putney Bridge (accessible from the Tube stop of the same name) and ends near Chiswick Bridge (near Chiswick Rail Station). The best vantage points are at the Surrey Bend of the river in Hammersmith (Ravenscourt Park Tube Station).

FLORA LONDON MARATHON

www.london-marathon.co.uk

Tens of thousands of runners from around the world converge on London every year for one of the leading marathons. Some famous athletes run here, but even more inspiring are the hordes of regular people who through sheer determination have trained themselves to run 26 miles through London's less-than pristine air. Some even dress up in bizarre costumes to raise money for charity.

INTERNATIONAL GUITAR FESTIVAL

www.igf.org.uk

Music lovers won't want to miss this annual showcase of talent that's been going on since 1994. All styles and traditions of guitar playing are represented, such as jazz, rock, and classical, and there are chances for audience participation as well in the festival's hands-on workshops. Some of the biggest names in the guitar world make an appearance here. Prices vary but there are some free events.

INTERNATIONAL JAZZ WEEKEND

www.britishjazzfoundation.co.uk

The British Jazz Foundation is a major force in promoting jazz in this country. Its annual jazz festival, held on Easter weekend, brings in dozens of the best performers from around the world to play at a variety of venues.

ST. GEORGE'S DAY

St. George was a Roman soldier who was also a Christian. When ordered to persecute his fellow

Christians he refused and was martyred in A.D. 303. He became the patron saint for medieval knights and King Edward III (reigned 1327–1377), who loved all things knightly, made him patron saint of England. On April 23, England's patron saint is celebrated all over town with special concerts, club nights, and other events. Many pubs and clubs have drink specials, and there are usually lots of folk-music events going on.

SCIENCE FICTION FILM FESTIVAL

www.sci-fi-london.com

Get a taste of the future at this massive showcase of science-fiction films. There are plenty of British entries, but many more from around the world, varying from independent shorts and anime to potential blockbusters. Some old favorites make it back on the big screen too.

VAISAKHI FESTIVAL

www.london.gov.uk

London has a thriving Sikh community numbering in the tens of thousands. Sikh New Year is on April 14, and the community comes out to celebrate for a free, daylong event at Trafalgar Square. There are prayers and speeches by prominent Sikhs and performances of traditional music and dance as well as modern DJs.

MAY

CHELSEA FLOWER SHOW

Royal Hospital, Royal Hospital Rd., 087/0906-3781, www.rhs.org.uk/chelsea

Royal Horticultural Society holds this event lasting five days every May. Started as the Great Spring Festival in Kensington in 1862, the flower show has been at this location since 1913. Exhibitors from around the world show off their best flowers in colorful displays, making for great photos. Gardeners will love this show. Those being dragged along against their wills can still enjoy a day out in the sun (weather permitting) along with some lobster and champagne.

COVENT GARDEN MAY FAYRE AND PUPPET FESTIVAL

St. Paul's Church Garden WC2, 020/7375-0441, www.stpauls.co.uk

Every year St. Paul's Church hosts a traditional festival that's fun for the whole family. This is one of the city's biggest folklore events and is an interesting glimpse at old-time English culture. Check out the *Punch and Judy* show, which famous diarist Samuel Pepys saw in 1662.

ENCOMPASS

www.encompass-london.com

One of London's hippest annual events, Encompass brings together dozens of artists performing electronic music for three days of parties, concerts, and a lot of behind-the-scenes business and talent scouting. The festival features techno, break beat, house, electro, grime, hip-hop, and much more, with concerts at several different venues. Workshops for wannabe DJs explain how to break into the scene.

THE LITTLE CHILLI FESTIVAL

020/8742-9911, www.amc.org.uk

This music festival, held for two weeks in late May and early June, celebrates musical traditions from all over Asia. Past performers have included music and dance troupes from Japan, Java, China, and plenty from India. Ticket prices, locations, and contact information varies, so check the website for details. The festival is sponsored by the Asian Music Circuit, which hosts concerts all year.

JUNE

CHELSEA FESTIVAL

020/7351-1005, www.chelseafestival.org.uk

This 10-day extravaganza features all types of performing arts, such as dance, contemporary and classical music, and plenty of art. Some events are free, but others cost various prices.

CITY OF LONDON FESTIVAL

www.colf.org

The City of London Festival is a city-sponsored festival of the arts that usually takes place for two weeks in late June and early July and attracts worldwide talent. The theme for the 2006 festival was Japan, with Japanese film, music, and art, including an installation piece by Yoko Ono in St. Paul's. There also are always events that don't adhere to the annual theme, such as art and city walks.

COIN STREET FESTIVAL

020/7401-2255, www.coinstreetfestival.org

More like a season of entertainment than a festival, the neighborhoods along the South Bank host a variety of events June–September. Many of them are one- or two-day festivals celebrating a particular ethnic group making up London's rich tapestry, whether it be Turkish, Cuban, or Brazilian.

HAMPTON COURT PALACE FESTIVAL

020/8233-6400, bookings 087/0060-2338, www.hamptoncourtfestival.com

Enjoy a summer evening listening to music and gazing at beautiful Hampton Court as it glows

THE FOLK SCENE: MUSIC, DANCE, AND STORYTELLING

English culture is rich in folklore. For much of its history, England was a conservative, rural, and provincial society that tended to preserve the ways and stories of the past, including many traditions that stretched back to pagan times.

One of the oddest survivals is Morris dancing, in which grown men prance around waving handkerchiefs and thwapping one another with sticks to the tune of a pipe, tabor, or fiddle. Nobody really knows what it all means, but it's great fun to watch. It seems to have originated as part of the celebrations of Whitsunday, the seventh Sunday after Easter (also called Pentecost), but may date to pre-Christian times. The most accomplished Morris dancer of them all was William Kempe, one of Shakespeare's comedic actors who Morris-danced from London to Norwich in 1600, a distance of 100 miles. Variants of Morris dancing include military-style processions; the dance may be related to the sword dances of the Highlands. During the Whitsun season, Morris dances are performed in London and across the country. Other folk dances, especially Irish jigs and Highland dancing, are also popular.

Folk music has never really disappeared from the English consciousness. Since the '60s it has been enjoying a renaissance, with regional styles and old songs being preserved while bands create new sounds by fusing folk with newer styles such as rock and electronic music. London has a thriving folk music scene. Perhaps because of the city's rootless nature, Londoners feel the need to get back to the soil with folk music.

The **English Folk Dance and Music Society** (2 Regent's Park Rd. NW1, 020/7485-2206, www.efdss.org) has been preserving and promoting traditional folk arts for more than a century. The society runs a series of concerts, festivals, and classes at its London office, highlighting not only British folk arts but also those from other countries.

There are several good Internet resources for finding out what's playing. *Folk London* (www.grove-cottage.demon.co.uk/folklon) is a print magazine that includes a good listings page. *Folk and Roots* (www.folkandroots.co.uk) has listings for all of the United Kingdom, which is useful when traveling beyond London.

Unfortunately, there are no exclusively folk-music venues in town, unless you count the space at the EFDSS office, but there are a few clubs that do host a lot of folk events. The **Islington Folk Club** (http://web.ukonline.co.uk/martin.nail/Islington/IFCintro.htm) meets every Thursday evening (except in summer) at various spots around Islington. Its website has a listing of upcoming events. The tiny **12 Bar Club** (see *Live-Music Venues* under *Nightlife*) has lots of very good folk performers. The **Greenwich Traditional Musicians Co-Operative** puts on weekly events in Greenwich, if you're willing to travel a bit. The events were being held at the Lord Hood pub (300 Creek Rd., Greenwich SE10, 020/8858-1836, Docklands Light Rail: Cutty Sark) but the pub was sadly under threat of demolition – another old local in the jaws of "developers" – so check the website (www.greentrad.org.uk/) to see where they'll be. **Power's Bar** (332 Kilburn High Rd. NW6, 020/7372-3112, Tube: Kilburn) has various folk and acoustic performances throughout the week, including an Irish music jam 4-7 P.M. every Sunday.

with colored lights. In 2006, the stage featured Eric Clapton, Van Morrison, the Glyndebourne Festival Opera, and many others. Food is available but many choose to pack a picnic instead. Ticket prices vary according to performance.

ROYAL ACADEMY OF THE ARTS SUMMER EXHIBITION

087/0848-8484, www.royalacademy.org.uk

The prestigious Royal Academy of the Arts hosts the world's largest open-submission contemporary art show mid-June–mid-August. The Royal Academy has been running this show since 1769. Tickets are adults £7, seniors £6, students £5, children 12–18 £3, children 8–11 £2, children under 7 free.

TROOPING THE COLOUR

Horse Guards Parade SW1, 020/7414-2479

For the Queen's birthday, observed on a Saturday in mid-June, traditional England pulls out all the stops for a gala parade. The massive numbers of people who show up for this might block your view, but any kids on your shoulders will have a great time.

JULY

CROYDON MELA

020/8686-4433, www.croydon.gov.uk/summerfestival

Since 1996 the Croydon Mela (*mela* is Sanskrit for "meeting" or "festival") has been one of Europe's biggest Asian festivals. Four stages of live music showcase everything from traditional bhangra to the latest Asian rap. For the kids there are a fun fair and special activities. Food stalls serve up heaps of great curry.

EUROPRIDE PARADE

www.europride.com

Every year across Europe, the GLBT community takes to the streets to celebrate its community and demand equal rights. London's parade is the biggest, with tens of thousands of people marching to Trafalgar Square and carrying a massive rainbow flag. Soho's gay district becomes one huge party afterward.

JAZZ ON THE STREETS MIDSUMMER FESTIVAL

www.jazzonthestreets.co.uk

Enjoy a week of jazz at more than a dozen venues in Soho and the West End. An outdoor stage is at Soho Square and some years there's one at Trafalgar Square too.

LONDON UNITED/RISE FESTIVAL

www.risefestival.org

The Rise Festival was started to make a stand against racism and highlight the efforts of trade unions, community, and charity groups to bring the diverse peoples of London together; the London United moniker was attached after the Tube bombings. A week of exhibitions, films, neighborhood celebrations, music, poetry slams, and theater culminate in a one-day music bash of rap, reggae, soul, and more. There's also a special play zone for the kids.

THE PROMS

Kensington Gore at Exhibition Rd. SW7,
020/7589-8212, www.bbc.co.uk/proms,
box office open daily 9 A.M.–9 P.M.

The famous BBC Proms, beloved by public television fans, is more than tuxedos and classical music; more than 70 concerts are held in prom season (lasting mid-July–early Sept.) for a wide range of tastes, if your tastes are for classical, opera, choral, and baroque. There's always a free day of live music on Trafalgar Square for those who don't want to cough up the £6–73 a ticket to go see it in the Royal Albert Hall.

AUGUST

GET LOADED IN THE PARK

www.getloadedinthepark.com

London's famous club scene comes into the daylight of Clapham Common for one day in August with famous DJs and rising stars. Official and unofficial after-parties happen at various clubs in case you didn't get enough tunes during the day. Tickets cost £30 at the gate, or less when you buy early but advance tickets sell out quickly. Tickets are available from

Ticketmaster (087/0060-1801) and at various music stores in town.

GREAT BRITISH BEER FESTIVAL

www.gbbf.org

Sponsored by the Campaign for Real Ale, this festival showcases the best beer England has to offer and has served a quarter million pints over five days. Guest beers from other countries are on tap as well.

LONDON MELA

www.ealing.gov.uk/ealingsummer

Join throngs of people at Europe's massive Asian festival. Tons of live music, traditional arts and crafts, food stalls, and a "Magic Mela" for children make this a fun day out for the whole family.

NOTTING HILL CARNIVAL

www.lnhc.org.uk

Europe's largest street festival was started by Trinidadian immigrants back in 1964 to bridge the gap between black and white. Steel bands, a Carnival parade, good food, and fun-loving people make Notting Hill the place to be the last weekend in August. It's hot and crowded—half a million people gathered in 2005—but where else can you see face-painted London bobbies dancing in the street?

SEPTEMBER

BRICK LANE FESTIVAL

020/7655-0906, www.bricklanefestival.com

The area around Brick Lane has always attracted immigrants—from the Huguenots in the Middle Ages to the Bengalis and Somalis of today. That diversity is celebrated in a festival combining outdoor music, an arts and crafts fair, and lots of activities for the kids. The festival coincides with the Banglatown International Curry Festival, so you can enjoy a curry and a coffee at a streetside café while the kids attend stilt-walking and face-painting workshops. History tours and open houses explain the background of the neighborhood.

THE GREAT RIVER RACE

020/8398-9057, www.greatriverrace.co.uk

The biggest and most colorful rowing race in Europe, this 22-mile challenge from rural Surrey to the London Docklands attracts a wide range of traditional vessels. Past contestants have included a replica Viking longship, a Hawaiian outrigger war canoe, and a replica 54-foot Bronze Age Greek galley. Tower Bridge, four miles from the finish line, is a good place to watch the race.

THE MAYOR'S THAMES FESTIVAL

www.thamesfestival.org

This annual free festival takes place on and around the Thames between Westminster and Tower bridges. For one weekend in September, Londoners celebrate their famous river with parades, live entertainment, children's activities, a circus, and fireworks.

RAINDANCE FILM FESTIVAL

www.raindancefilmfestival.org

One of the best showcases of independent and cutting-edge films anywhere, Raindance has become a leading contender to the ever-more-commercialized Sundance. The festival lasts several days and includes workshops for budding filmmakers. Opening and closing night films are shown at Cineworld Haymarket Cinema (63–65 Haymarket, 020/7287-3833, £15). Festival screenings are held at Cineworld Shaftesbury Avenue, The Trocadero Centre (7–14 Coventry St., 087/1200 2000, £8.70). An all-festival pass is a bit steep at £80, but you get days of entertainment and, for struggling directors, a lifetime of inspiration.

RIVERFRONT JAZZ

www.riverfrontjazz.co.uk

For 11 days in late September and early October, Greenwich becomes a cold-weather New Orleans with a series of jazz performances in various restaurants and bars around town. Some are free; others have a cover charge.

OCTOBER

PEARLY KINGS AND QUEENS HARVEST FESTIVAL

St. Martin-in-the-Fields, Trafalgar Sq. WC2, 020/7766-1100, www.smitf.org

An interesting product of cockney folklore survives in central London. In early October, the Pearly Kings and Queens, so named because of their suits covered in buttons, gather at St. Martin-in-the-Fields to celebrate a rather pagan harvest festival. Men and women parade in traditional cockney costumes covered in mother-of-pearl buttons stitched into elaborate designs. These volunteers spend much of their time throughout the year raising money for various local charities.

THE TIMES BFI LONDON FILM FESTIVAL

www.lff.org.uk

This is a more mainstream film festival than Raindance and shows hundreds of films from around the world during the course of two weeks, so it's a great place to see the "next big thing" in international cinema. Screenings, lectures, and workshops are divided among several venues. Prices depend on the location and number of activities.

NOVEMBER

ASIAN ART IN LONDON

020/7499-2215, www.asianartinlondon.com

This weeklong celebration of Asian art and antiques is held in more than 50 galleries and art dealer shops and includes a wide array of special exhibitions and lectures. All events are free, but much of the art on display is museum quality and unaffordable for all but the fattest of wallets.

LONDON JAZZ FESTIVAL

www.serious.org.uk

This multivenue event features lots of headliners from the jazz world, and many of the shows are free—a nice plus. Serious sponsors many other concerts throughout the year, so check out the website for some good music, or call the BBC Radio 3 information line (087/0010-0300) for a free brochure.

LORD MAYOR'S SHOW

www.lordmayorsshow.org

Every year since 1215, the newly elected lord mayor of the City of London has proceeded from The City to Westminster to present himself or herself to the reigning monarch. It's always done in high style to impress one's boss/rival, and while the relationship is smoother than it was in the Middle Ages, the lord mayor still pulls out all the stops. Expect lots of pomp and circumstance and about half a million spectators.

REMEMBRANCE SUNDAY CEREMONY

The Cenotaph and Westminster Abbey

Dignitaries from several countries and hundreds of veterans gather at the Cenotaph to pay their respects to those who died defending the United Kingdom. The ceremony is held the Sunday closest to Armistice Day, November 11th, and includes a parade of veterans and a wreath-laying ceremony by the Queen.

DECEMBER

CHRISTMAS LIGHTS AND TRAFALGAR SQUARE TREE

Trafalgar Sq. and Oxford St.

Trafalgar Square lights up for the holidays with a massive Norwegian pine draped with decorations. Oxford Street is garlanded with lights and tinsel and many stores across town, especially the big department stores such as Harrods, pull out all the stops for their window displays.

SHOPPING

Napoleon once scoffed that England was a nation of shopkeepers. It is, and just as England conquered Napoleon, it conquered the world with its financial acumen (and a little help from the Royal Navy). London rivals any city in the world for its number and variety of shops. Whatever you want to buy, you will find it here.

Although London doesn't have a defined shopping district, it does have several major shopping areas. Bloomsbury is known for its bookshops, while Knightsbridge is famous for its high-end fashion. While these are the best spots to find a large concentration of these shops, London is so vast and varied that good shopping can be found everywhere.

Shopping in London can be expensive, with prices rivaling those in New York, but a closer look will reveal many bargains. London's charity shops not only have an interesting selection, but they support good causes as well. The ubiquitous Oxfam shops are a favorite haunt for bargain books, and it's a welcome thought that your money is going toward sustainable development and famine relief. Scouring the markets and smaller independent shops can also save money. What's more, you'll find items such as antiques or liquor that would go for twice as much back home.

Like any city, London has its specialties: Tea, books, prints, and antiques are all good buys here. London is especially strong in fashion for both men and women. Much of this is high end, but those with smaller budgets can make some fun finds in the vintage shops and larger department stores. If you want to splurge, try the "bespoke" service, which

© VISITLONDON.COM

HIGHLIGHTS

Best Open-Air Market: Wandering through **Portobello Road Antiques Market** is a bit like rummaging through the nation's attic. Most of the stuff on sale is too new or too banged up to make it into a proper museum, but having it all collected here creates a kind of museum in itself, one dedicated to the household items past generations of English lived with and used (page 166).

Best Unaffordable Browsing: Christie's and **Sotheby's** sell the finest antiques, ranging from Tudor furniture to rare wines and cigars. Most of it is completely out of the question for a normal bank account, but they offer constantly changing exhibits of what's for sale (pages 169 and 171).

Best Bookstore: Rare, used, and remaindered books on the Humanities are the mainstay on the packed shelves of **Unsworths,** located opposite the British Library. With a knowledgeable staff and a stunning collection, your main problem will be trying to limit your purchases (page 174).

Best Department Store: Harrods sells just about anything you can think of and a few things you can't. It's a great place to buy souvenirs and gifts for the folks back home (page 186).

Best Food Market: A market since the Middle Ages, **Borough Market's** many stalls stock fresh produce, hard-to-find imports, and takeaway meals (page 189).

Best Design Shop: Too many design shops in London are either overpriced, cutesy, or trying too hard to be chic and modern, but not **Beyond the Valley,** a collective featuring the work of young, offbeat artists (page 192).

© JO JACKSON, BEYOND THE VALLEY

LOOK FOR TO FIND RECOMMENDED SHOPS.

means getting clothing or jewelry custom-made to your exact specifications. The term originated when periwigged gentlemen in the 18th century used to "speak for" a particular length of cloth. That cloth was then "bespoken for" and would end up as a coat or trousers. Availing yourself of a bespoke service at one of the city's many fine tailors will ensure that you have the best fit possible.

Some of the best shopping can be found in London's lively markets. Portobello, the great Saturday antiques market, is the most famous. Camden Market offers arts and crafts in relaxing surroundings, while the city's many farmers markets provide a healthy and refreshing change from eating at restaurants. Several shopping districts are famous for one particular type of shop, such as Cecil Court Road where the scores of shops are famous for books, stamps, prints, and other paper collectibles. And don't miss the various little specialty shops sprinkled throughout the city, selling everything from Indian art to whiskey. These places are preferable to the big name stores because they better capture the spirit, variety, and friendly service that is London at its best. Chatting with a shopkeeper while rummaging through collectable coins or Cuban cigars is a great way to spend an afternoon.

Shopping Districts

In the Middle Ages, vendors selling similar types of merchandise tended to cluster together. The guilds encouraged this as it made it easier to control their particular trades. Like many formerly medieval cities, London has kept this tradition and many streets have several or even dozens of similar stores. This makes it easy for the time-pressed traveler to find exactly what's desired.

Covent Garden, West End, and Soho — Map 4

BERWICK STREET

Berwick St. W1

HOURS: Usually 9 A.M.–6 P.M.

TUBE: Tottenham Court Road

For vintage vinyl and used CDs, this is the place to be. The dozen or so little shops that line Berwick Street sell every type of music imaginable, but they concentrate on rock, soul, jazz, R&B, and rap. You can find lots of British titles here and learn about the local music scene. The area also has a good selection of skate and clothing shops for the younger crowd. Be sure to check out Reckless Records (26 Berwick St., 020/7434-3362), which sells secondhand vinyl and CDs in the basement and the latest rock, pop, reggae, jazz, folk, experimental, and classical CDs on the ground floor. Note: South of Broadwick the street descends into a less-desirable area and the record shops disappear, so it's best to approach Berwick Street from the north.

CECIL COURT ROAD

Btwn. Charing Cross Rd. and St. Martin's Lane, www.cecilcourt.co.uk

HOURS: Usually 9 A.M.–6 P.M.

TUBE: Leicester Square

Tucked behind the National Gallery is a Victorian street that is closed to traffic, making for a pleasant and atmospheric place to window-shop at storefronts that have changed little in 100 years. Cecil Court Road specializes in printed matter, whether books, engravings, stamps, or old magazines. At number 3 is Storey's Ltd. (020/7836-3777, www.storeysltd.co.uk), which has been in business since 1929 and sells antiquarian prints and maps. The Cecil Court Stamp Shop (020/7240-1051) at number 6 has a vast collection of stamps to satisfy any collector. Number 11 is home to David Drummond at Pleasures of Past Times (020/7836-1142), which has an amazing collection of old circus advertisements, theater playbills, antique Christmas and Valentine's Day cards, postcards, and children's books. The famous occult and esoteric bookshop Watkins (020/7836 2182, www.watkinsbooks.com) is at numbers 13, 15, 19, and 21. Watkins was founded in 1894 and is one of the oldest bookstores of its kind in the world. Many more shops are on this street, and browsing here will teach you as much about old England as any museum.

© VISITLONDON.COM

Postcards come in all varieties and are sold everywhere.

COVENT GARDEN

Btwn. Covent Garden Market and the Piazza to Long Acre, Floral St., and Neal St. WC2, 020/7839-3220, www.coventgarden.uk.com

HOURS: Usually 9 A.M.-8 P.M.

TUBE: Covent Garden

The mostly pedestrian streets of this shopping district have plenty of boutiques and big-name outfits to keep you browsing the better part of a day. This is one of London's older shopping districts. What used to be a garden owned by Westminster Abbey (when it was called "Convent Garden") became a covered shopping center when Inigo Jones designed a covered piazza in imitation of Italian markets in 1630. Under its great metal and glass arch you can jostle with the crowds to examine the many souvenir shops. While it's incredibly touristy, it can be a lot of fun as many street performers strut their stuff here.

GERRARD STREET

Gerrard St. W1

HOURS: Usually 9 A.M.-6 P.M.

TUBE: Piccadilly Circus or Leicester Square

The heart of London's Chinatown offers a myriad of shops. The imported books and movies are mostly in Chinese only, but some shops sell items in both Chinese and English. Martial-arts enthusiasts will like the shops selling training manuals and equipment, and those in the know about Chinese medicine will find the selection as good as in any other city in the Western world. For those with less specialized interests, plenty of shops sell statues, cookware, and various knickknacks. After your hunger for shopping is satisfied, take care of your other hunger at one of the area's innumerable Asian restaurants.

Chelsea, Kensington, and Knightsbridge — Map 6

KING'S ROAD

Kings Rd. from Sloane Sq. to the Thames

HOURS: Usually 9 A.M.-6 P.M.

TUBE: Sloane Square

A bit more affordable than the other shopping districts of Knightsbridge, King's Road also boasts more variety. You'll find fashion here, but you'll also find antiques, vintage clothing, and the famous Chelsea Farmers' Market (listed under its own heading). For fashion, stop by number 72, where Diesel (020/7225-3225, www.diesel.com) sells the latest urban trends. If you have kids in tow, take them to Daisy and Tom, a department store for the wee folk. It's at 181–183 (020/7349-5800, www.daisyandtom.com) and has lots of clothing and toys, as well as its own hair salon. A traditional carousel (rides 11 A.M., 1 P.M., 3 P.M., 5 P.M. Mon.–Sat., 1 P.M., 3 P.M. Sun.) and a puppet theater running every half hour will keep them occupied if they don't share your love of shopping.

SLOANE STREET

Btwn. Knightbridge and Kings Rd. and btwn. Brompton Rd., Sloane St., and Beauchamp Pl./Pont St.

HOURS: Usually 9 A.M.-6 P.M.

TUBE: Knightsbridge or Sloane Square

Sloane Street's windows are packed with designer fashion displays, so even if you can't afford anything you can always grab some food at Harrods' Food Halls and window-shop à la *Breakfast at Tiffany's*. But if you are feeling flush, try designer Karl Lagerfeld's outfits at Fendi at numbers 20–22 (020/7838-6288, www.fendi.com), or Phoebe Philo's designs at Chloe at numbers 152–153 (020/7823-5348, www.chloe.com). For something a little different, try the Asian styles of Shanghai Tang at number 6A/B (020/7235-8778, www.shanghaitang.com) Once you've found the perfect outfit, match it with a pair of shoes at one of Sloane Street's innumerable shoe shops.

Notting Hill, Bayswater, and Paddington — Map 7

PORTOBELLO ROAD ANTIQUES MARKET

Portobello Rd. btwn. Chepstow Villas and Colville Terr. W11, 020/7229-8354

HOURS: Shop hours vary; open all day Saturday

TUBE: Notting Hill Gate

If there's good weather on a Saturday, head on

over to this bustling antiques market. Antique shops line both sides of Portobello Road, but on Saturdays hundreds of stalls open to sell their wares. A visit here is like rummaging through London's attic. Old woodworking tools are piled next to brass telescopes, the lenses of which catch the gaudy colors of art nouveau jewelry. In a side alley, suits of armor and the weapons of half-forgotten battles rust in quiet dignity. Not far away is a row of stalls selling old prints and postcards, telling of sights and vacations long past. Occasionally you'll be startled by something more recent, such as memorabilia from Charles and Diana's wedding or a Beatles' lunchbox. Seeing these things amid the World War I medals, Victorian cookbooks, and bowler hats makes one realize the vast amount of material the multitudes of London use and discard in their lives. Over the course of the generations, the market ends up with a whole history in objects, some useless, some charming, others edifying. Farther up the road the antiques start giving way to discount modern goods, mostly new clothing with some retro stuff thrown in. Note of caution: Portobello Road can be extremely crowded and pickpockets are more interested in studying the inside of your wallet than browsing the stalls.

WHITELEYS

Queensway btwn. Westbourne Grove and Porchester Gardens, 020/7229-0044, www.whiteleys.com

HOURS: Center: Mon.-Sun. 8:30 A.M.-midnight; Shops: Mon.-Sat. 10 A.M.-8 P.M., Sun. noon-6 P.M.

TUBE: Queensway, Royal Oak, or Bayswater

If you're feeling guilty about spending all your time shopping and not seeing anything historical, come here. Whiteleys opened as a shopping center in 1912 and has kept its Edwardian decoration. The interior is of marble, with a sweeping ironwork staircase, illuminated by a soaring glass dome, leading to the second level. Since this is a shopping center, you'll find a lot of chain stores here, but there are also several good cafés, a kids' play area, and a spa, making this a bit different from most malls back home.

Camden Town — Map 9

CAMDEN LOCK

Camden Lock Pl., Chalk Farm Rd. NW1, 020/7485-7963, www.camdenlockmarket.com

HOURS: Usually 10 A.M.-6 P.M.

TUBE: Waterloo or Southwark

Set in the old T. E. Dingwells Timber Yard, where large river barges unloaded their cargoes to the smaller boats that plied the waters upstream, Camden Lock Place is the center for shopping for many area residents. With almost 50 shops specializing in everything from clothing to home furnishings, you're sure to find something to please. My favorites are Celtic Dawn, 35 Middle Yard (020/7284-3940), which sells exquisite Celtic art and jewelry, and Lock One Batik Gallery, 6B Upper Market Hall (020/7267-4458), selling handmade batiks from Java. There are also many smaller stalls and the sidewalks really fill up for the weekend market.

© DEAN EDWARDS

Camden offers a funky and eclectic shopping experience.

The City Map 10

THE ROYAL EXCHANGE

Threadneedle, Cornhill, and Gracechurch Sts., 020/7623-3857, www.theroyalexchange.co.uk

HOURS: Shops: Mon.-Fri. 10 A.M.-6 P.M.; Grand Café and Bar: Mon.-Fri. 8 A.M.-11 P.M.

TUBE: Bank

The Royal Exchange got its name when Queen Elizabeth I set aside this spot for business in 1566. The present building dates to 1844 and consists of four levels of shopping around a large covered courtyard. The high-end restaurants and shops within its stately interior offer a pleasurable if wallet-draining shopping experience, with well-known names such as Cartier, Bulgari, and De Beers. A restaurant and bar are in the courtyard, sheltered by a glass dome. The prices and quality are both high, and you can order a £120 plate of caviar if you like. Be sure to see the series of 24 large paintings on the walls of the ambulatory illustrating the history of commerce in Britain, done by Sir Frederic Leighton in 1895.

Islington Map 11

CAMDEN PASSAGE

Camden Passage, off Upper St. N1, 020/7359-0190, www.themallantiques.co.uk or www.camdenpassageislington.co.uk

HOURS: Usually 9 A.M.-6 P.M.

TUBE: Angel

A little lane lined with antique shops, Camden Passage is one of the more interesting antique markets in the city. At number 12 is Anne's Vintage Costume and Textiles (020/7359-0796), which, unlike many of the other vintage clothing shops of Camden, reaches way back for some real style. Wandering through here is like seeing an attic that hasn't been cleared in a very long time, with uncomfortable-looking dresses from the 1890s, slinky flapper wear from the 1920s, and grandma clothes from the 1950s. Camden Passage has an old Victorian tram station at 359 Upper Street, now home to The Mall (020/7351-5353), housing 35 stalls for porcelain, silver, art deco, clocks, glassware, and more. Wednesdays and Saturdays are the big days, with all the shops open and stalls spilling out into the street. Other days can be a bit dead, so try to come on those two days. Another caveat: This is one of the more overpriced of London's generally overpriced antique markets, so haggle hard.

South of the Thames Map 12

GABRIEL'S WHARF

56 Upper Ground SE1, 020/7401-2255, www.gabrielswharf.co.uk

HOURS: Tues.-Sun. 11 A.M.-6 P.M.

TUBE: Waterloo or Southwark

If you're walking along the Thames path on the South Bank, you might want to stop at the more than a dozen little shops and boutiques specializing in fashion and accessories for yourself and your home. Ganesha (020/7928-3444, www.ganesha.co.uk) offers furnishing and decorations from India, while Vivienne Legg Ceramics (020/7401-2240) sells wheel-formed, hand-painted ceramics. Julie Clark (020/7249-2403, www.julieclark.com) offers fashions for women and children made of natural fibers, and David Ashton (020/7401-2405, www.davidashton.co.uk) sells handmade jewelry and offers a bespoke service. Other options are London Bicycle Tour Company (020/7928-6838, www.londonbicycle.com), offering bike hires and tours, and Riverside Therapies (020/7401-9528, www.riversidetherapies.co.uk), which offers backrubs, aromatherapy, and other treatments.

HAY'S WHARF

Tooley St. and Thames River

HOURS: Daily 9 A.M.-6 P.M.

TUBE: London Bridge

Wharves and warehouses have been in this area since the Middle Ages, but the area got its present name when Alexander Hay founded the Hay's Wharf Company in 1651. He eventually owned most of the area between London and Tower bridges. The present buildings date to 1856, just before Hay's Wharf became London's first cold-storage area. "London's Larder," as it was called, supplied most of the meat and dairy for the city. Now that refrigerated trucks prowl the streets, Hay's Wharf is a shopping area and a convenient stop along the Thames path. The Hay's Gallery (020/7403-0933) sells cool postcards and posters of movie stills. Choose from formal and semiformal wear for men and women at Next (087/0386-5529), or shoes at Carducci Shoe Company (020/7357-6751). There's a Christmas Shop (020/7378-1998, www.thechristmasshop.co.uk) for English-style ornaments, and little kiosks sell jewelry and women's accessories. The high glass arch makes for dry shopping no matter what the weather and a good sanctuary if you get rained off the Thames path.

OXO TOWER WHARF

Barge House St. SE1, 020/7401-3610, www.oxotower.co.uk

HOURS: Usually Tues.-Sun. 11 A.M.-6 P.M.

TUBE: Waterloo

Highly visible with its tall tower blazoned with OXO in bright red letters, the Oxo Tower Wharf is home to a diverse collection of design and art studios, cafés, galleries, and restaurants. Several good jewelers are here, and the design shops sell a wide range of ceramics, glassware, furnishings, and accessories. The nice thing about the shops here is that they are almost all owned by independent artists, so your money goes straight to the source and you get a chance to meet them in person.

Outlying Areas — Map 1

BRICK LANE MARKET

Brick Lane, Cheshire St., and Sclater St. E1, www.eastlondonmarkets.com

HOURS: Sun. 6 A.M.-2 P.M.

TUBE: Aldgate East

You probably didn't fly several thousand miles to go to a flea market, but the main attraction of this weekly market is the mix of people in the crowd. Brick Lane is at the heart of what's locally called Banglatown, London's biggest Bengali neighborhood. Amid the stalls selling secondhand clothing, cheap imports, old junk, and bootleg DVDs is a swirling crowd of Bengalis, blacks, Anglos, and Orthodox Jews. The Anglos first created this neighborhood hundreds of years ago, and it became a center for the Jewish community in the 19th and 20th centuries. Now it's mostly black and Bengali. Besides the merchandise, these streets are lined with enough South Asian eateries to satisfy even the biggest curry craving, and there are still some bagel shops too.

Antiques and Auction Houses

As it's been a major metropolis for centuries, it hardly comes as a surprise that London is one of the best places to buy antiques in the world. Antique shops abound, with items to suit all budgets. An antique can make a unique gift or a treasured keepsake from your vacation. Antique shops tend to cluster together (see the *Shopping Districts* section for more listings). Those with bigger bank accounts can check out the auction houses. Even if you don't buy anything, auction houses are still worth a visit. The displays of items up for bid are constantly changing, the quality of the art and antiques is often equal to anything in a museum, and since they mostly end up in private collections, chances are you won't see them again.

Mayfair and Piccadilly — Map 3

CHRISTIE'S

8 King St. SW1, 020/7389-9060, www.christies.com

HOURS: Mon.-Fri. 9 A.M.-5 P.M.

TUBE: Green Park or Piccadilly Circus

This famous auction house is a delight to see. Of course, only the wealthiest travelers will actually be able to buy anything, but the auctions are fascinating to watch and the presale displays are art shows in themselves. Christie's is one of the oldest of London's many auction houses, dating to 1766, and it has made an international name for itself by selling some of the best in fine art, antiques, and wine. One recent coup was the sale of the collection of Barons Nathaniel and Albert von Rothschild for $90 million, a record for any single-owner European collection.

GRAY'S ANTIQUE MARKET

58 Davies St. and 1-7 Davies Mews W1, 020/7629-7034, www.graysantiques.com

HOURS: Mon.-Fri. 10 A.M.-6 P.M.

TUBE: Bond Street

One of the best antique malls in London, Gray's has dozens of stalls selling every type of antique and collectible imaginable, from royal mementoes to fine china to samurai armor. Wandering through this shopping mall of the past is fascinating, and there are plenty of affordable items, such as postcards and coronation mugs,

GIFTS THEY'LL APPRECIATE

OK, all those folks back home are expecting you to bring them something, but do they actually *want* the stuff that's in most tourist shops? Will they really treasure that plastic model of the Tower of London? Is that shot glass with Big Ben on it really unique? (It isn't. Go to Paris and you can get the same shot glass adorned with the Eiffel Tower.) If you want to get souvenirs your friends will thank you for behind your back, here are some ideas.

Cheap antiques. London's many open-air markets are great for this. Get a Queen Elizabeth coronation mug, or a newsmagazine from World War II. The variety is endless, so it's quite easy to get an individualized present with a British theme.

Coffee-table books. London's bookshops abound in handsomely produced books with beautiful photographs. Whether the subject is famous paintings, aristocratic homes, the English countryside, or London itself, there's sure to be something to furnish every living room on your list.

Old prints. Before the advent of photography, books, magazines, and newspapers were illustrated with engravings. The image was etched onto a metal plate, daubed with ink, and could be reproduced an almost unlimited number of times. Since London printed more books in the 17th–19th centuries than any other city in Europe, it's not surprising that it was at the forefront of the engraver's art. Luckily, so many prints were made that most are reasonably priced. Specimens that are especially old or by famous artists such as Hogarth can be quite pricey, but it is easy to find an attractive 19th-century print, suitable for framing, for under £20. Shop around; you'll find plenty of selection.

Fine tea. If you know a tea drinker, you can't go wrong with some high-quality tea from one of London's many tea shops. If you want to get a bit fancier, buy a teapot or an entire tea set. You'll find an infinite variety to choose from, from British traditional to Asian to ultramodern.

Arts and crafts. London is just as much Bengali as it is English, so head on down to the shops on Brick Lane and get some silk or artwork. In the Afro-Caribbean sections of Brixton and Notting Hill, you can buy island crafts and African clothing. The city is so cosmopolitan, you can find items from just about anywhere.

Music. London is alive with music. Artists from around the United Kingdom and Europe come here to make their fortunes. The folk scene is strong, with many local bands and imports. London's large black community produces a huge number of good artists in reggae, hip-hop, African, and jazz. Institutions such as the London Symphony Orchestra are world leaders in recording classical music. Whatever your friends' taste in music may be, you will be able to find CDs that are difficult or impossible to find back home.

Fashion. If you really like that person on your list, go to one of the city's top fashion stores and deck him or her out in the latest trends. This can get expensive, and you'll want his or her measurements beforehand because you won't be able to return anything from across the sea, but for the fashion-conscious you can't go wrong in London.

among the high-priced rarities, such as Regency furniture. Not all the stall attendants are always there, especially early in the morning, but someone from the information desk can usually open a stall and handle any transactions. Note that Gray's takes up two adjacent buildings.

SOTHEBY'S

34-35 New Bond St. W1, 020/7293-5000, www.sothebys.com

HOURS: Mon.-Fri. 9 A.M.-4:30 P.M., Sat.-Sun. noon-4 P.M.

TUBE: Bond Street or Oxford Circus

Like its equally famous and only slightly younger rival, Christie's, this auction house specializes in the best antiques and fine art. It has been a London institution since 1744. While most things here are out of many people's price range, the auctions are open to the public and the items are on show in a constantly changing display. Sotheby's is especially strong in 20th-century British art, but it sells art and antiques from all nations and periods. Watching the bidding, and the collectors discussing their next purchase in the galleries, is a cultural experience in itself.

Covent Garden, West End, and Soho — Map 4

GROSVENOR PRINTS

19 Shelton St. WC2, 020/7836-1979, www.grosvenorprints.com

HOURS: Mon.-Fri. 10 A.M.-6 P.M., Sat. 11 A.M.-4 P.M.

TUBE: Covent Garden

The 18th and 19th centuries saw a florescence of the printmaker's art, and no shop in London stocks more of their art than Grosvenor Prints. With prints on all subjects, and many by famous artists such as Roberts, Hogarth, and Piranesi, its collection is unparalleled. Most of the prints are rare, and prices are in the dozens if not hundreds of pounds, so the shop is more for collectors or those who are willing to spend a little extra for a work of art that can be passed down through the generations. Every conceivable subject is represented, so you are sure to find something to fit with your decor and interests. It also stocks a small amount of ephemera such as broadsheets and silhouettes.

South of the Thames — Map 12

BERMONDSEY ANTIQUE MARKET

247 Long Lane SE1, 020/7969-1500

HOURS: Fri. 4 A.M.-2 P.M.

TUBE: Borough or London Bridge

The opening time for this antique market should clue you in that this is a place for pros. Many antique dealers from across the city and beyond come here looking for stock for their own stores, and designers looking for vintage styles come here for inspiration. The best deals go in the early mornings, so set your alarm and you might come away with something special. As in other leading antique markets such as Gray's, you can find just about anything in the chaotic piles of aged bric-a-brac.

Bath and Beauty

In the days before interior plumbing, regular bathing, and toilet paper, refined ladies and gentlemen used to hide their noxious vapors with scented soaps and perfumes. While you're no doubt familiar with the three modern conveniences listed above, you'll still love the various scents and toiletries offered in these stores. Clothing stores are another good place to look for perfumes and toiletries.

Covent Garden, West End, and Soho — Map 4

PENHALIGON'S

41 Wellington St. WC2, 020/7836-2150, www.penhaligons.com

HOURS: Mon.-Tues. 10 A.M.-6 P.M., Wed.-Sat. 10 A.M.-7 P.M., Sun. 11 A.M.-5 P.M.

TUBE: Covent Garden

A traditional perfumery that makes all its own scents, Penhaligon's was founded in 1870 to serve the gentlemen of London. Women's perfumes weren't added to its stock until 1976! In this elegant store you can sample its many scents, some dating to the foundation of the business. They are subtly strong without being overpowering, and there are various accessories to choose from, such as leather goods, brushes, and jewelry boxes, all made exclusively for the store. Apparently its stock meets with approval at the palace, since it has a Royal Warrant as manufacturers of "toilet requisites."

Maida Vale, Marylebone, and St. John's Wood — Map 8

DANIEL GALVIN

58-60 George St. W1, 020/7486-9661, www.danielgalvin.com

HOURS: Mon.-Wed., Sat. 8:30 A.M.-6 P.M., Thurs.-Fri. 8:30 A.M.-8 P.M.

TUBE: Baker Street or Bond Street

This beauty salon specializes in giving your hair just that right tint, and it'll do your eyelashes and eyebrows too. If you already like your color, go in for a beauty treatment such as hair detox, facials, dermabrasion, and hand and nail treatments. The famous stylist Daniel Galvin does personal makeovers, but the waiting list is long. His list of famous clients is a who's who of London glitterati, but that doesn't mean he won't do normal folks too. You can make appointments up to eight weeks in advance, and it's best to make them as early as possible.

SPACE NK APOTHECARY

83A Marylebone High St. W1, 020/7486-8791, www.spacenk.co.uk

HOURS: Mon.-Wed., Fri. 10 A.M.-6:30 P.M., Thurs. 10 A.M.-7 P.M., Sat. 10 A.M.-6 P.M., Sun. noon-5 P.M.

TUBE: Baker Street or Regent's Park

In addition to its own brand of beauty products, Space NK also sells a wide range of lines from around the world, such as the popular Yu-Be skin treatments from Japan. Its stock covers aromatherapy, antiaging treatments, fragrances, bath oils, and sun care. It sells special products for babies too, including a handy baby traveling kit if you have your tyke in tow. Since it offers such a range of lines all under one roof, this shop makes a good destination if you're looking for gifts for someone hard to please.

Books and Music

If you're a book lover, you're going to have a hard time getting out of London with your bank account intact. The city has literally hundreds of great bookshops, from the big but quality chains to cramped little neighborhood stores filled with the scent of dust and leather bindings. The independent shops are listed here because of their intellectual, unhurried atmosphere and their good selection of hard-to-find new and used titles the bigger guys don't carry. With the advent of online shopping and supermarket bookshelves, independent booksellers are an endangered species. Don't let them become extinct!

BOOKSTORES

Covent Garden, West End, and Soho — Map 4

FOYLES

113-119 Charing Cross Rd. WC2, 020/7437-5660, www.foyles.com

HOURS: Mon.-Sat. 9:30 A.M.-9 P.M., Sun. noon-6 P.M.

TUBE: Tottenham Court Road or Leicester Square

This large, rambling bookshop is very browsable and much more organized now that it's reorganized its infamously labyrinthine collection. Other recent changes include an art gallery, café, and a very cool piranha tank in the kids' section. The music section is enlivened by

Ray's Jazz, a popular independent music store that has since moved here. Jazz musicians occasionally play at the café, and there's a busy author-signing schedule throughout the year. Foyles has been a London institution since 1903, and a look through the shelves is amply rewarded.

STANFORDS

12-14 Long Acre WC2, 020/7836-1321,
www.stanfords.co.uk
HOURS: Mon.-Wed., Fri. 9 A.M.-7:30 P.M., Thurs. 9 A.M.-8 P.M., Sat. 10 A.M.-7 P.M., Sun. noon-6 P.M.
TUBE: Covent Garden

Claiming to be the biggest travel bookshop in the world, Stanfords backs up its boast with a massive stock of guidebooks and travelogues from all publishers in many languages. If you can't find it here, it's probably out of print. A browse through the packed shelves will make you realize just how much of a world there is to see out there. The map section is a gold mine of information and the staff doesn't mind if you stand around planning out treks to strange, far-off places.

Bloomsbury, Euston, and Holborn — Map 5

ATLANTIS BOOKSHOP

49A Museum St. WC1, 020/7405-2120,
www.theatlantisbookshop.com
HOURS: Mon.-Sat. 10:30 A.M.-6 P.M.
TUBE: Tottenham Court Road or Holborn

Founded in 1922, Atlantis is an occult bookshop steeped in history. Gerald Gardner lived nearby and collaborated with the former owner to publish Gardner's groundbreaking *High Magic's Aid.* Alistair Crowley perused the shelves and it seems every major name in British and European occult circles has passed through these doors. It has been owned by the same family, with a brief ownership by another, for three generations. The shop stocks books and magazines on a wide array of practices, including small-press titles that are impossible to find in the United States.

BOOKMARKS

1 Bloomsbury St. WC1, 020/7637-1848,
www.bookmarks.uk.com
HOURS: Mon.-Fri. 10 A.M.-7 P.M., Sat. 10 A.M.-6 P.M.
TUBE: Tottenham Court Road

Bloomsbury has always been home to London's radicals. Marx studied at the British Museum reading room, and generations of suffragettes, anarchists, Gordon rioters, squatters, and other activists have raised their fists at the system in this neighborhood. Bookmarks continues this tradition by stocking one of the best selections of socialist and activist books in England. You'll find titles on communism, socialism, women's liberation, black history and politics, developing nations' issues, kids' books, and a large stock of hard-to-find periodicals. Notices announce upcoming events and demonstrations.

GAY'S THE WORD

66 Marchmont St. WC1, 020/7278-7654,
www.gaystheword.co.uk
HOURS: Mon.-Sat. 10 A.M.-6:30 P.M., Sun. 2-6 P.M.
TUBE: Russell Square

London's leading gay and lesbian bookshop has been in business since 1979, a time when the gay-rights movement was just picking up steam. The bright blue storefront has provided a focus point in London that has helped the movement considerably, and it continues to act as a meeting place today. It stocks a good selection of fiction and nonfiction, as well as British and international queer film. Readings and other events take place throughout the year, and the local gay writers group and lesbian discussion group have been meeting here for years.

GOSH!

39 Great Russell St. WC1, 020/7636-1011
HOURS: Mon.-Wed., Sat.-Sun. 10 A.M.-6 P.M., Thurs.-Fri. 10 A.M.-7 P.M.
TUBE: Tottenham Court Road

Comics have come a long way from the spandex-clad superheroes of earlier years. Current comic books (called "graphic novels" by defensive aficionados) use a variety of styles, from journalistic works about the troubles in Palestine and the Balkans to bizarre experiments with visuals and plot. Artistic comics from around the world are on display here, with an emphasis on famous and unknown British artists, and down a narrow spiral staircase is a large collection of manga. Vintage comics adorn the walls.

LONDON REVIEW BOOKSHOP

14 Bury Place WC1, 020/7269-9033, www.lrb.co.uk

HOURS: Mon.-Sat. 10 A.M.-6:30 P.M., Sun. noon-6 P.M.

TUBE: Tottenham Court Road

Being owned by the leading literary review, *The London Review of Books,* this shop can attract the biggest names in literature to do readings. Check out the website for a schedule of who is coming next. While there's a cover charge for such events, you get wine and nibbly bits, so consider it an evening's entertainment. Aside from the literary stars, this is quite a good bookshop too, extending over two well-stocked floors with especially strong sections on London history, contemporary literature, poetry, and literary magazines.

QUINTO BOOKSHOP

63 Great Russell St. WC1, 020/7430-2535

HOURS: Daily 10 A.M.-6:30 P.M.

TUBE: Tottenham Court Road

One of the best used bookstores in London, Quinto also has one of the best locations, being right opposite the British Museum. You can find every subject imaginable amid the rather chaotic bookshelves that rise from floor to ceiling. The history and art sections are especially well stocked. In the back room are antiquarian books. With 50,000 titles in stock at any one time, this is said to be the largest secondhand bookstore in London. There's a smaller branch at 48A Charing Cross Road WC2, 020/7379-7669.

UNSWORTHS

101 Euston Rd. NW1, 020/7383-5507, www.unsworths.com

HOURS: Mon.-Sat. 10 A.M.-6:30 P.M., Sun. noon-5 P.M.

TUBE: Euston or King's Cross/St. Pancras

Strategically placed opposite the British Library, Unsworths is one of London's most respected booksellers and specializes in the best remaindered and secondhand titles in classics, history, and humanities—it stocks the complete line of the Loeb Classical Library and a stunning selection of antiquarian titles. One time I saw a 1729 edition of Buddeus's *Historia Ecclesiastica* and a 1533 Galen of Pergamum's *De Victus Ratione in Morbis Acutis.* If you understood the previous two sentences you know just what I'm talking about—caviar for the mind.

Notting Hill, Bayswater, and Paddington — Map 7

BOOKS FOR COOKS

4 Blenheim Crescent W11, 020/7221-1992, www.booksforcooks.com

HOURS: Tues.-Sat. 10 A.M.-6 P.M.

TUBE: Ladbroke Grove or Notting Hill Gate

The name pretty much says it all. You can find cookbooks on every type of cuisine imaginable here. Something is hunger-inducing about seeing more than 8,000 cookbooks lining the walls. Luckily, celebrity chefs often cook up wonders in the back and serve them at tables set within the store or conduct workshops where you can learn expert tips. Workshops are taking place constantly, so check the website for a current schedule.

Maida Vale, Marylebone, and St. John's Wood — Map 8

DAUNT BOOKS

83-84 Marylebone High St. W1, 020/7224-2295, www.dauntbooks.com

HOURS: Mon.-Sat. 9 A.M.-7:30 P.M., Sun. 11 A.M.-6 P.M.

TUBE: Baker Street or Regent's Park

Browse the latest titles within this refined Edwardian bookshop with elegant wood facade and cheerful skylights. Much of the stock is organized by country, so that guidebooks, nonfiction, and fiction are all in one place for a literary journey around the world. You'll find secondhand books and a well-stocked children's section too. This is one of the more inviting bookshops in the city, and famous authors regularly do readings here.

BEYOND BLOOMSBURY: HIDDEN GEMS ON THE BOOKSTORE TRAIL

While the shopping chapter lists several of the most popular bookshops in areas frequented by tourists, here are some of my favorite places for fellow book lovers who want to trek the byways of London in search of rare titles or specialist tomes. Check the websites before your trip as many of these stores have regular readings by important authors.

Bookartbookshop (17 Pitfield St. N1, 020/7608-1333, www.bookartbookshop.com): A visit to this shop showcasing the work of the best publishers of artist's books will expand your ideas as to what a book can be. Artist's books are publications in which the book itself is a work of art. They are often hand-printed on handmade paper or feature innovative typesetting or binding. Despite this, many titles manage to be reasonably priced. You'll find a lot of experimental prose and poetry here, as well as richly illustrated works you'll probably never see elsewhere. It's open 1-7 P.M. Wednesday-Friday, 1-6 P.M. Saturday.

Calder Publications (51 The Cut SE1, 020/7620 2900, www.calderpublications.com): John Calder is a legend in British publishing. He started his publishing house in 1949, when much of London was still in ruins and paper was scarce. Calder published many blacklisted American writers during the McCarthy era, giving them important exposure abroad, and championed names such as Miller and Burroughs, who, while they weren't named as Communists during the witch hunt of the 1950s, were still too wild for American publishers. He also published controversial British authors, including all of Samuel Beckett's novels. His book stock has an especially strong theater section. (See the *Arts and Entertainment* chapter for the tiny Bookshop Theatre he runs in the back room.) It's open 9 A.M.-7 P.M. Monday-Saturday.

Forbidden Planet (179 Shaftesbury Ave. WC2, 020/7420-3666, www.forbiddenplanet.com): This is a huge science-fiction, fantasy, and horror bookshop that also sells comics, figurines, and DVDs. The American imports are a bit expensive, but it's an excellent source for British titles that are hard to find in the United States. It stocks an extensive manga section and a selection of videos of British TV series. It's open 10 A.M.-8 P.M. Monday-Saturday, noon-6 P.M. Sunday.

Souls of Black Folks (407 Coldharbour Ln. SW9, Brixton, 020/7738-4141): A bookstore focusing on the literature, history, politics, and culture of black people around the world, Souls of Black Folks has been a Brixton institution for years. Its selection of English authors is especially good, and you'll find a lot of works other bookstores don't stock. The café is always lively with conversation, and there's a well-attended series of readings. It's open 10 A.M.-11 P.M. Monday-Saturday.

Treadwell's (34 Tavistock St. WC2, Covent Garden, 020/7240-8906, www.treadwells-london.com): A friendly little bookshop that opened in 2003, Treadwell's has quickly gained a reputation as one of the leading occult and esoteric bookshops in London, with an incredible variety of quality used (and some new) titles packed into its overflowing shelves. Downstairs is a meeting room that is commonly used for talks and workshops on various esoteric subjects. In 2006 it dedicated some of its space to the Offstage Theatre Bookshop (020/7240-3883). It's open noon-7 P.M. daily.

Don't forget museum bookshops. The British Museum is a good stop for history and archaeology buffs. The National Gallery's art-book collection is extensive, and smaller museums feature specialist volumes on their particular subjects.

And don't miss the book fairs! London is host to many book fairs every year and most bookshops will have flyers announcing them. The Provincial Booksellers Fairs Association puts on a monthly antiquarian book fair in Bloomsbury that is especially good. Its website at www.pbfa.org lists locations and dates.

South of the Thames Map 12

SOUTH BANK BOOK MARKET

Waterloo Bridge, on the South Bank

HOURS: Daily all day, weather permitting

TUBE: Waterloo

If you're strolling along the Thames Walk on the South Bank, this book market, which has been going on longer than anyone can remember, makes for a nice stop. The books are all used and vary from the classics to last year's bestsellers, and there's a good selection of nonfiction. They're all jumbled together on long tables in no particular order, but browsing is half the fun. This is a good place to find a used novel to read as you travel. There's also a selection of videos and old prints.

MUSIC

London is a music capital. The city's large Afro-Caribbean community is famous for many musicians playing in a variety of styles. Too few of these artists are well known overseas so a trip to a music store will result in some incredible discoveries. Brit Pop is a world of its own too; it's very different than North American pop music and many of the bands don't get much coverage outside the country. If the nightclubs leave you hungry for more, drop in to these shops and pick up tunes you'll have a hard time finding back home.

Covent Garden, West End, and Soho Map 4

SOUNDS OF THE UNIVERSE

7 Broadwick St. W1, 020/7494-2004

HOURS: Mon.-Fri. 11:30 A.M.-7 P.M., Sat. noon-6:30 P.M.

TUBE: Piccadilly Circus

A popular store for fans of rare roots, reggae, house, break beat, and more, Sounds of the Universe stocks many of its titles in vinyl as well as CD to please the many DJs who come here. There are good sections for hip-hop, Latin, postpunk, African, funk, and northern soul, as well as plenty of hard-to-find tracks at good prices. The listening stations can lead you in the right direction if you're unsure of what to buy, and it usually havs something great playing over the sound system. Highly recommended.

Notting Hill, Bayswater, and Paddington Map 7

DUB VENDOR

150 Ladbroke Grove W10, 020/8969-3375, www.dubvendor.co.uk

HOURS: Mon.-Sat. 10 A.M.-7 P.M.

TUBE: Ladbroke Grove

The bright mural outside makes it easy to spot this store from way off. Go inside the bright orange interior to check out what London's thriving Jamaican music community is mixing up these days. It stocks plenty from the Old Country too. You can find reggae, rasta, ska, soul, and soca here, both in vinyl and CD. It offers a modest selection of DVDs too and the store is a good place to find out what's happening in the local music scene.

Islington Map 11

FLASHBACK

50 Essex Rd. N1, 020/7354-9356, www.flashback.co.uk

HOURS: Mon.-Sat. 10 A.M.-7 P.M., Sun. noon-6 P.M.

TUBE: Angel or Highbury and Islington

A well-stocked shop selling new, used, and vintage music, Flashback is one of those places that it's hard to get out of without buying something. The ground floor is mostly new and used CDs, with a good selection of most types of music, while the basement is given over the vintage vinyl and DVDs. It also carries video games. The staff is well hooked into the London music scene and can point the way to cool clubs and up-and-coming local bands.

HAGGLE VINYL

114-116 Essex Rd. N1, 020/7704-3101, www.hagglevinyl.com

HOURS: Mon.-Sat. 9 A.M.-7 P.M., Sun. 10 A.M.-5:30 P.M.

TUBE: Angel or Highbury and Islington

London used to be a great city for buying used vinyl, but the garrulous owner of this shop said that in 2005 an average of one shut down every month, and the trend shows every sign of continuing. One hopes his business will survive, because it's jam-packed with more than 40,000 albums of rock, reggae, soul, jazz, folk, hip-hop, house, garage, and more. Lots of this stuff never made it onto CD, so here's your only chance. He's also got a huge rarities section for the collectors.

Clothing and Accessories

For the fashion conscious, London is one of the top cities to be, trailing only New York and Paris for variety and style. It offers shops for all ages and sizes, and while many are expensive, a diligent search can uncover some bargains. Many shops are predominantly for either men or women and are listed accordingly, but they'll often have a line for the other sex as well, so your significant other won't be bored.

CHILDREN'S CLOTHING

London's designers don't just limit themselves to outfitting adults; they create fashions for the little folks too. Kids' stores will often have toys and games, since they have yet to learn the inherent joys of shopping.

Mayfair and Piccadilly — Map 3

TARTINE ET CHOCOLAT

66 S. Molton St. W1, 020/7629-7233, www.tartine-et-chocolat.fr

HOURS: Mon.-Sat. 10 A.M.-6 P.M.

TUBE: Bond Street

If your toddler throws a tantrum if you dress him or her in anything less than the latest French fashions, this Paris-based chain can help you out. It offers clothes for boys and girls from newborns to 10 years. While some of it is a little on the froufy or formal side for everyday wear, there are lots of good garments for everyday use too. It changes its stock according to season just like grown-up stores do, so your child won't be out of step with the times.

Chelsea, Kensington, and Knightsbridge — Map 6

RACHEL RILEY

14 Pont St. SW1, 020/7259-5969, www.rachelriley.com

HOURS: Mon.-Sat. 10 A.M.-6 P.M.

TUBE: Knightsbridge

Rachel Riley has dedicated her career to making babies and children look trendy. The designs are colorful and a bit formal—lots of collared shirts for the boys and sundresses and frills for the girls—and the shop is a veritable palette of pastels. The style carries over to its teens' and ladies' lines too. You'll find everything from play clothes to wedding outfits here, but with prices that equal those of adults' top fashions, don't give them any chocolate ice cream.

JEWELRY

While fashions come and go, good jewelry always stays in style (if vintage is more your look, check the *Vintage Clothing* and *Antiques and Auction Houses* sections). Clothing and department stores often have excellent choices in jewelry too.

Mayfair and Piccadilly — Map 3

ANGELA HALE

5 Royal Arcade, 28 Old Bond St. W1, 020/7495-1920, www.angela-hale.co.uk

HOURS: Mon.-Sat. 10 A.M.-6 P.M.

TUBE: Green Park

This boutique specializes in antique and modern costume jewelry. Every purchase is packed into its trademark little pink boxes, convenient if you're shopping for gifts. Admirers of art deco will love the variety of antique and reproduction jewelry and picture frames. You can find some very individual pieces here to set off your outfit, and with customers such as Kate Moss and Stella McCartney, you'll be in good company.

Covent Garden, West End, and Soho — Map 4

THE BEAD SHOP

21A Tower St. WC2, 020/7240-0931, www.beadshop.co.uk

HOURS: Mon. 1-6 P.M., Tues.-Fri. 10:30 A.M.-6 P.M., Sat. 11:30 A.M.-5 P.M.

TUBE: Covent Garden or Leicester Square

Design your own jewelry amid this vast stock of beads. The beads are made of everything from Swarovski crystal to carved wood and include many imports from all over the world. The more expensive beads are made from gold, silver, pearls, and a dazzling array of precious and semiprecious stones. More modest spenders can outfit themselves with lacquered beads and those made from Chinese enamel, glass, bone, and much more. Tools and space are provided to let you create your own designs, and the staff are always happy to give suggestions.

Chelsea, Kensington, and Knightsbridge — Map 6

DOWER AND HALL

60 Beauchamp Pl. SW3, 020/7589-8474, www.dowerandhall.com

HOURS: Mon.-Sat. 10:30 A.M.-6:30 P.M.

TUBE: Knightsbridge

Some of London's best jewelry designers showcase their work here, including Dower and Hall themselves. The style is predominantly contemporary, with an emphasis on silver and colored gemstones, but the shop also sells gold and platinum pieces. Unlike in many other jewelry stores in the area, there are plenty of options for shoppers who don't have unlimited funds. If you don't quite like an arrangement of stones on a pendant or set of earrings, it has a quick bespoke service that can get you exactly what you want in a matter of hours.

Notting Hill, Bayswater, and Paddington — Map 7

DINNY HALL

200 Westbourne Grove W11, 020/7792-3913, www.dinnyhall.com

HOURS: Mon.-Wed., Fri.-Sat. 10 A.M.-6 P.M., Thurs. 11 A.M.-7 P.M., Sun. noon-5 P.M.

TUBE: Notting Hill

From the affordable to the astronomical, Dinny Hall creates interesting designs using various metals to accentuate precious and semiprecious stones. One of its lines is made of laboratory-created gemstones, allowing for some interesting experiments in color at a reduced price. If you want to propose in London, you could do worse than buy one of its engagement rings, either premade or bespoke. The shop also sells a signature line of bath oils, perfumes, and scented candles.

MEN'S CLOTHING AND ACCESSORIES

The English are a strange lot. Walking the streets you'll see some of the worst- and best-dressed people in the world, and how they clothe themselves seems to have little to do with their income. If your fashion sense needs a pick-me-up, try some of the many men's clothing stores, most of which also stock accessories. If you want to splurge, bespoke services can give you a suit fit for a prince (they have experience with outfitting royalty), while many stores offer fine fashion at reasonable prices.

Mayfair and Piccadilly — Map 3

BRIONI

32 Bruton St. W1, 020/7491-7700, www.brioni.it

HOURS: Mon.-Fri. 9 A.M.-6 P.M., Sat. 10 A.M.-6 P.M.

TUBE: Green Park

Brioni is Italy's oldest tailoring firm, with retailers around the world. If you want a tailor-made, excellently cut suit and don't care how much it costs, come to this tailor, where the subdued lighting and leather chairs make it seem as if you're in a gentleman's club on Pall Mall. It also sells accessories and some women's clothing. Pierce Bronson got suited up here for his James Bond role, but don't expect any gadgets from Q Division—all you get is a very nice suit.

DUNHILL

48 Jermyn St. SW1, 084/5458-0779, www.dunhill.com

HOURS: Mon.-Fri. 9:30 A.M.-6:30 P.M., Thurs. 9:30 A.M.-7 P.M., Sat. 10 A.M.-6:30 P.M.

TUBE: Green Park or Piccadilly Circus

Dunhill is one of the most luxurious London stores for men and is on the exclusive Jermyn Street, a center for elite fashion for many decades. In the roomy shop, you'll find leather bags, belts, wallets, gloves, ties, cuff links, lighters, and much more. Bespoke services are available if you're in the market for a suit. It's all a bit pricey, as are most things in this section of town.

GIEVES AND HAWKES

1 Saville Row W1, 020/7434-2001,
www.gievesandhawkes.com
HOURS: Mon.-Thurs. 9:30 A.M.-6:30 P.M., Fri. 9 A.M.-6 P.M., Sat. 10 A.M.-6 P.M.
TUBE: Green Park or Piccadilly Circus

One of the older and finer tailors in London, Gieves and Hawkes used to make uniforms for the Royal Navy back when the military wore their best suits into battle. Its clientele is a bit more peaceful now than in the 18th century when the business started, and it includes royalty and celebrities who want a traditional English cut that remains forever stylish. In addition to bespoke tailoring, it stocks a full range of menswear, including knitwear and shoes.

TURNBULL AND ASSER

71-72 Jermyn St. SW1, 020/7808-3000,
www.turnbullandasser.com
HOURS: Mon.-Sat. 10 A.M.-6 P.M.
TUBE: Green Park or Piccadilly Circus

This famous tailor and shirtmaker has been outfitting English notables since 1885. Past clients have included Winston Churchill and Prince Charles. If you decide to join their ranks you'll find more than 1,000 materials that can be tailor-made into men's shirts, its specialty. It is also famous for its ties, but it actually provides all items of male clothing and has a section for female clothing too. Besides the Jermyn Street address, it operates a counter at Harrods.

Notting Hill, Bayswater, and Paddington — Map 7

ARMAND BASI

189 Westbourne Grove W11, 020/7727-7789,
www.armandbasi.com
HOURS: Mon.-Sat. 10 A.M.-6 P.M., Sun. noon-5 P.M.
TUBE: Notting Hill Gate or Bayswater

The Spanish are known for their chic clothing, and Armand Basi is one of their more popular labels. This is its only store in London, so if you want to look Spanish, you'll have to go either here or Madrid. Expect lots of black as well as tight cuts and Mediterranean styling. The ground floor is for women and includes a line of scents to go along with the clothing, while the basement is a metrosexual's paradise of sheer shirts, tight pants, and more black. The guys get accessories too, including a choice of attractive leather belts.

The City — Map 10

LIPMAN AND SONS

44 Fleet St. EC4, 020/7353-1731,
www.lipmanandsons.co.uk
HOURS: Mon.-Fri. 9 A.M.-6 P.M.
TUBE: Temple

If you are looking for a formal night on the town but didn't bring a suit or tux, come here for some excellent service and a wide variety. Suits come in single- or double-breasted, two- or three-piece, and you'll find morning suits and tuxedos in various colors. This being England, you can even get a top hat. It also sells the suits it hires, and while they are used they are in very good condition. If you decide to buy the suit you just rented, half the rental fee will be deducted from the price. Group rates are available.

T. M. LEWIN

59 Ludgate Hill EC4, 017/0242-1611, www.tmlewin.co.uk
HOURS: Mon.-Fri. 8 A.M.-6 P.M., Sat. 11 A.M.-6 P.M.
TUBE: Cannon Street

T. M. Lewin has been making men's shirts since 1898, when Victoria was Queen and men wore suits on all occasions. The shirts are all of cotton and come in a bewildering array of cuts, styles, and patterns. You can find formal shirts to go with your best suit or casual wear for lounging in the park. It also sells shoes, accessories, and a range of women's clothing. While the off-the-rack products are all of high quality, there's a full bespoke service to ensure a perfect fit. This store is the most convenient for stylish City workers, but check the website for other locations throughout London.

Islington — Map 11

THE AFRICAN WAISTCOAT COMPANY

33 Islington Green N1, 020/7704-9698,
www.africanwaistcoatcompany.com
HOURS: Wed. and Sat. 10 A.M.-5:30 P.M., Thurs.-Fri. 10 A.M.-4 P.M., Sun. 10 A.M.-2 P.M.
TUBE: Angel

Here's something you'll find nowhere else—traditional English bespoke waistcoats tailored from Yoruba fabrics from Nigeria. All the fabrics are handwoven of silk or cotton and vary from brilliantly colored to more subdued. In keeping with Yoruba decorative tradition, they are of thin strips of differently colored material sewn in vertical strips, giving a strong African effect that blends remarkably well with a Western suit. The owner makes frequent trips to Nigeria to oversee the production of the fabric, and he does the tailoring himself in this little shop next to Camden Passage.

SHOES

Is all this walking around town making your shoes look like a pair of voles put through the washing machine? Look no farther. London is full of shoe stores catering to the trendy and the practical, and most clothing stores also carry shoes.

Mayfair and Piccadilly — Map 3

GINA

9 Old Bond St. W1, 020/7409-7090, www.gina.com

HOURS: Mon.-Sat. 10 A.M.-6 P.M., Thurs. 10 A.M.-7 P.M.

TUBE: Green Park or Piccadilly Circus

This pricey shoe store is a favorite for models and actresses. Madonna's a customer, and it's had plenty of cover shots on leading fashion magazines. Established in 1954, it specializes in women's handmade leather shoes that are fashionable without being flashy. Most are high heels, but there are some flats and boots, and the bridal section can get you fitted out for that walk down the aisle. The dainty handbags are equally stylish and expensive.

Covent Garden, West End, and Soho — Map 4

OFFICE

57 Neal St. WC2, 020/7379-1896, www.postemistress.co.uk

HOURS: Mon.-Sat. 10 A.M.-6 P.M., Thurs. 10 A.M.-7 P.M.

TUBE: Leicester Square or Covent Garden

A wide variety of men's and women's shoes, and boots and sandals, are available here for all occasions. The emphasis is on the casual, with bright colors and bold but not overblown designs. The men's selection is a bit more conservative than the women's, with plenty of leather shoes you could wear to the office alongside the hiking boots and beach sandals. The selection of sports shoes for both sexes is quite good.

VINTAGE CLOTHING

Londoners have been fashion conscious since the days of cloaks and codpieces, so there's a thriving trade in vintage clothing. Some of this stuff is really vintage from the horse-and-carriage days, but there are plenty of bellbottoms (called flares here) and miniskirts too.

Westminster, Victoria, and Pimlico — Map 2

CORNUCOPIA

12 Upper Tachbrook St. SW1, 020/7828-5752

HOURS: Mon.-Sat. 10 A.M.-6 P.M.

TUBE: Victoria

Noticeable by its bright red paint and retro signage, Cornucopia is packed with vintage clothing and accessories from all eras, with everything you need to compose a complete retro outfit. The dim interior is packed with clothing and you have to push your way through rows of old suits, dresses, and pants. Stuff even hangs from the ceiling.

Bloomsbury, Euston, and Holburn — Map 5

LAURENCE CORNER

62-64 Hampstead Rd. NW1, 020/7813-1010, www.laurencecorner.co.uk

HOURS: Mon.-Sat. 9:30 A.M.-6 P.M.

TUBE: Warren Street or Euston

With England's epic struggles through the centuries, it is not surprising that there's a whole shop dedicated to old uniforms. The workwear selection includes outfits for medical and emergency personnel and there's a large modern military-surplus section stocking backpacks, sleeping bags, and a limited amount of other camping gear. Those with a flair for the historical can find uniforms from all eras, including quite expensive ones from Napoleonic times. The clothes are available for rent or purchase and make impressive costumes for a fancy dress party.

Notting Hill, Bayswater, and Paddington Map 7

THE ANTIQUE CLOTHING SHOP

282 Portobello Rd. W10, 020/8964-4830

HOURS: Fri.-Sat. 9 A.M.-6 P.M.

TUBE: Ladbroke Grove

Going through this store is like rummaging through the attic of a family that has lived in the same house for generations. In addition to fabric-wasting bell-bottoms, the stock goes all the way back to stodgy Victorian dresses. You might be surprised how reasonable the prices are for most items, but keep in mind that a lot of people have been living in London for a long time, which means there's no shortage of old clothes lying around.

WOMEN'S CLOTHING AND ACCESSORIES

From funky to formal, few places can beat London for its quality and range of clothing stores. All budgets are catered to (for retro fashions check *Vintage Clothing*). The majority of the stores listed here stock mostly or exclusively women's clothing and accessories, but some have menswear sections... or at least a nearby pub. (Also see the *Shopping Districts* section for streets that house numerous boutiques.)

Mayfair and Piccadilly Map 3

BROWNS

23-27 S. Molton St. W1, 020/7514-0016, www.brownsfashion.com

HOURS: Mon.-Wed., Fri.-Sat. 10 A.M.-6:30 P.M., Thurs. 10 A.M.-7 P.M.

TUBE: Bond Street or Oxford Circus

This very trendy shop is always up on the latest styles from the big names. While everything goes for designer prices, it stocks only the more wearable items as opposed to the impractical shockers designers use to get on television. A good selection of handbags, shoes, and accessories will round out your outfit. Also check out its Labels for Less store just down the road at 50 South Molton for slightly older but much cheaper designer clothes. If you don't mind wearing last year's fashions (which will probably be this year's fashions back home), it makes for an affordable option.

BURBERRY

157-167 Regent St. W1, 020/7839-5222, www.burberry.com

HOURS: Mon.-Sat. 10 A.M.-7 P.M., Sun. noon-6 P.M.

TUBE: Oxford Circus

A few years ago my wife bought me a Burberry toiletry bag in its trademark brown tartan. It's been quite durable and survived several camping trips and about a dozen countries without any noticeable signs of wear. Now every time I see that famous pattern—and I see it everywhere in London, on purses, on jackets, and especially on umbrellas—I think of brushing my teeth. Burberry has a range of fashion and accessories for men and women from the traditional to the modern. The store, founded in 1856, has a good stock of accessories as well.

HOUSE OF CASHMERE

8-9 Burlington Arcade W1, 020/7495-7385, www.house-of-cashmere.co.uk

HOURS: Mon.-Sat. 10 A.M.-5:30 P.M.

TUBE: Piccadilly Circus or Green Park

Forgot to pack a sweater? Head over to House of Cashmere, a well-stocked little shop in the exclusive Burlington Arcade. All items are of high quality and are sure to shelter you from the nastier meteorological aspects of any trip. They offer a remarkable range of styles and colors to choose from, as well as scarves and other accessories for both men and women.

MULBERRY

41-42 New Bond St. W1, 020/7491-3900, www.mulberry.com

HOURS: Mon.-Wed., Fri.-Sat. 10 A.M.-6 P.M., Thurs. 10 A.M.-7 P.M.

TUBE: Bond Street or Oxford Circus

Some of the finest leather bags in the city are

CHARITY SHOPS: GOOD BARGAINS AND WORTHY CAUSES

If you're a bargain hunter, be sure not to miss London's many charity shops. These are stores run by nonprofits that sell donated used merchandise for low prices. Since the shops are run by the organizations themselves, all the profits go to the charity. The Oxfam shops are especially good for used books, and they are actually Europe's largest retailer of secondhand books. Their selection of secondhand clothing and household items is also good.

Charity shops abound in London and other major towns, so only a few are listed here. As you wander around the streets you will discover many more. Shops that specialize in a particular item are noted. Give them a try. You'll walk away with some bargains and the knowledge that your money is going to a good cause.

Oxfam

One of the leading charities in England, Oxfam sponsors programs such as emergency relief, environmental preservation, arms control, and sustainable development projects, putting millions of pounds a year into countless projects in dozens of countries.

12 Bloomsbury St. WC1, 020/7637-4610 (books)
22 Earlham St. WC2, 020/7836-9666 (clothing)
23 Drury Lane, Covent Garden WC2, 020/7240-3769
52 Goodge St. W1, 020/7636-7311 or 020/7636-7311
34 Strutton Ground, Victoria SW1, 020/7233-3908
76 Marylebone Lane W1, 020/7487-3852
15 Warwick Way, Pimlico SW1, 020/7821-1952
91 Marylebone High St. W1, 020/7487-3570 (books)
29 Islington High St., Islington N1, 020/7837-2394
240 Edgware Rd., Paddington W2, 020/7724-0332
89 Camden High St., Camden NW1, 020/7387-4354

Cancer Research UK

The world's leading independent organization dedicated to cancer research, Cancer Research UK funds innovative treatments and trains specialists in the battle to beat one of the world's toughest and deadliest diseases. In 2004-2005 it spent £217 million on research, much of it coming through its charity shops, which sell used clothing, housewares, books, and music. You can learn more by going to the website at www.cancerresearchuk.org. These folks need your support – sooner or later you or someone you love might need theirs.

24 Marylebone High St., Marylebone W1, 020/7487-4986
7 Butterfly Walk, Camberwell Green SE5, 020/7701-2500
393 King's Rd., Chelsea SW10, 020/7352-4769
34 Upper St., Islington N1, 020/7226-8951
81 Camden High St., Camden NW1, 020/7383-5910
83 St. John's Rd., Clapham SW11, 020/7223-5349
350 North End Rd., Fulham SW6, 020/7381-8458
168 Balham High Rd., Balham SW12, 020/8675-0515
187 Kilburn High Rd., Kilburn NW6, 020/7625-8515
123A King St., Hammersmith W6, 020/8563-0440

Marie Curie Cancer Care

The main focus of this organization is to care for those dying of cancer, whether in one of its 10 free hospices or through a free private nurse at home. This allows patients to live their final months in dignity, and its research institute looks for ways to beat the disease. The charity shops are a major money earner for the organization and sell the usual assortment of used goods.

169 Haverstock Hill, Belsize Park NW3, 020/3204-2081
27 Junction Rd., Upper Holloway N19, 020/7272-7631
32 Topsfield Parade, The Broadway Crouch End N8, 020/8341-2779
318/320 St. Paul's Rd., Highbury N1, 020/7226-0565
114 Ladbroke Grove, Notting Hill W10, 020/7229-9512
18 The Broadway, Mill Hill NW7, 020/8959-4238
59 Chaseside, Southgate N14, 020/8886-5433
54 Golders Green Rd., Golders Green NW11, 020/8457-5859

Trinity Hospice

Offering expert and caring care in hospices or private homes in central and southwestern London, Trinity was founded in 1891 and is the oldest hospice in the United Kingdom. It helps out about 2,000 people a year free of charge.

107 Balham High Rd., Balham SW12, 020/8673-9441
283 Lavender Hill, Battersea SW11, 020/7228-4737
389 Kings Rd., Chelsea SW10, 020/7352-8507
124 Clapham High St., Clapham SW4, 020/7498-7400
40 Northcote Rd., Clapham SW11, 020/7924-2927
9 Old Town, Clapham SW4, 020/7498-2349
785 Fulham Rd., Fulham SW6, 020/7736-8211
31 Kensington Church St., Kensington W8, 020/7376-1098
16 Bute St., South Kensington SW7, 020/7589-2234
20 Notting Hill Gate, Notting Hill W11, 020/7792-2582
206 Upper Richmond Rd., Putney SW15, 020/8785-3201 (books)
147 Putney High St., Putney SW15, 020/8780-0737
158 Queensway, Queensway W2, 020/7229-8291
124 Streatham High Rd., Streatham SW16, 020/8769-7703
77 Streatham Hill, Streatham SW2, 020/8674-6787
9 Tooting High St., Tooting SW17, 020/8767-9111
25 Turnham Green Terr., Turnham Green W4, 020/8742-3036
85 Wilton Rd., Victoria SW1, 020/7931-7191
393 Walworth Rd., Walworth SE17, 020/7703-8607
106 The Broadway, Wimbledon SW19, 020/8543-8349

available at this prominent British design company. With prices at £300 and up, they had better be some of the finest. In addition to its signature bags, its sells luxury luggage, organizers, and wallets. The women's wear covers all seasons and tends toward a vintage look with lots of tans and browns for a stylish yet informal outfit. While most of the products are for women, the room downstairs features a line for guys.

STELLA MCCARTNEY

30 Bruton St. W1, 020/7518-3100, www.stellamccartney.com

HOURS: Mon.-Fri. 9 A.M.-6 P.M., Sat. 10 A.M.-6 P.M.

TUBE: Green Park

This converted Georgian town house is home to a cruelty-free fashion line. Stella and her father, Paul (yes, *that* Paul), are longtime vegetarians and committed to protecting the animals of the world. None of these good-quality clothes, shoes, or accessories uses animal products or animal testing, and therefore are made without causing harm to other living creatures.

TOP SHOP

36-38 Great Castle St. at Oxford Circus W1, 020/7927-7863, www.topshop.co.uk

HOURS: Open 24 hours

TUBE: Oxford Circus

This purports to be the largest fashion store in the world. Just paying the rent for this huge chunk of real estate in such an expensive neighborhood means it must be one of the most successful too. You'll find everything here, from inexpensive accessories to top-of-the-line designer labels, for everyone in the family. Most of the clothes on offer are priced at levels that normal people can actually afford, and judging from the crowds swirling through its four floors on a weekday morning, it's a popular idea.

Covent Garden, West End, and Soho — Map 4

AGENT PROVOCATEUR

6 Broadwick St. W1, 020/7439-0229, www.agentprovocateur.com

HOURS: Mon.-Wed., Fri.-Sat. 11 A.M.-7 P.M., Thurs. 11 A.M.-8 P.M., Sun. noon-5 P.M.

TUBE: Oxford Circus or Tottenham Court Road

The famous (or infamous) window displays for this shop pretty much say it all. Agent Provocateur sells lingerie, shoes, and accessories that manage to be stylish while being not much at all. The shop is tasteful, however, so no one has to feel funny about going in here. Styles vary from classic silk pajamas to indescribable creations best left to personal observation. In addition to lingerie, it sells a signature line of beauty products that include perfume, bubble bath, and oils.

Chelsea, Kensington, and Knightsbridge — Map 6

ANYA HINDMARCH

15-17 Pont St. SW1, 020/7838-9177, www.anyahindmarch.com

HOURS: Mon.-Sat. 10 A.M.-6 P.M., Wed. until 7 P.M.

TUBE: Sloane Square

Anya Hindmarch's stylish handbags make great gifts for a friend or for yourself. With prices running into the hundreds of pounds, they are a bit expensive, but they are a definite fashion statement. There are bags for all occasions, from formal leather ones to go with evening wear to straw baskets for the park. You can also Be a Bag, putting a photo of your choice onto a handbag. In case you don't have anything to put *in* your bag, pick up one of its quality leather day planners or journals.

LULU GUINNESS

3 Ellis St. SW1, 020/7823-4828, www.luluguinness.com

HOURS: Mon.-Fri. 10 A.M.-6 P.M., Sat. 11 A.M.-6 P.M.

TUBE: Sloane Square

Lulu Guinness is a trendy handbag designer's shop frequented by people who like bold statements in their accessories. Its business material declares that its style "blends schoolgirl, vamp, and granny." Madonna's a customer, so you get the idea. The bags are adorned with funky art or statements such as "You can be too rich and too thin," which counts as controversial in this neighborhood! Guinness is the designer who made the famous flowerpot design, helping the green-thumbed English take their gardens with them. The scarves, made with equally bright designs, go well with the bags.

PHILIP TREACY

69 Elizabeth St. SW1, 020/7824-8787,
www.philiptreacy.co.uk
HOURS: Mon.-Fri. 10 A.M.-6 P.M., Sat. 11 A.M.-5 P.M.
TUBE: Sloane Square

If you've ever seen pictures of the races at Ascot, you know British women like to make a statement with their hats. Well, Treacy is one of the people who's responsible for the elaborate lids society ladies wear. One hat looks like a purple feather duster arching over the head like a balding man's combover. A visit here certainly offers an insight into the tastes of the British elite. Treacy also designs similarly over-the-top handbags. On the more practical side, there's a good line of streetwear with floral patterns or solid colors. Many of Treacy's products can be found at the major department stores such as Selfridges and House of Fraser, but you get the full selection here.

RIGBY AND PELLER

2 Hans Rd. SW1, 020/7589-9293,
www.rigbyandpeller.com
HOURS: Mon.-Sat. 9:30 A.M.-6 P.M., Wed. until 7 P.M.
TUBE: Knightsbridge

This elegant lingerie shop has the distinction of being awarded a Royal Warrant, which means it supplies the palace with "women's necessaries," as they used to say in the Army. (Yes, the palace has an official lingerie store.) It's certainly elegant stuff, varying from simple but quality underwear and swimwear to sensuous lingerie. It also has a bespoke service to provide undergarments that will be perfectly fitted. And no, they won't tell you what the Queen wears.

Notting Hill, Bayswater, and Paddington — Map 7

THE DRESSER

10 Porchester Pl. W2, 020/7724-7212,
www.dresseronline.co.uk
HOURS: Mon.-Fri. 11 A.M.-6 P.M., Sat. 11 A.M.-5 P.M.
TUBE: Marble Arch

If you've been window-shopping at all the posh boutiques but haven't been able to afford to step inside, come here for lightly used top-of-the-line fashion and accessories at cut-rate prices. Both men and women can find bargains here, but since it's a used-clothing store, you can't go in with a certain outfit in mind; you have to browse instead and hope for the best. "The Best," if you're a guy, is to find some of Eric Clapton's cast-offs. He regularly donates his old clothes here and the proceeds go to help the Crossroads Antigua Foundation, an alcohol- and drug-abuse treatment center. Clapton's stuff goes for a wee bit more than the usual offerings, but it's for a good cause and you'll earn loads of cool points.

HEIDI KLEIN

174 Westbourne Grove W11, 020/7243-5665,
www.heidiklein.co.uk
HOURS: Mon.-Sat. 10 A.M.-6 P.M., Sun. noon-5 P.M.
TUBE: Notting Hill Gate

A swimwear boutique may look a bit out of place in Old Blighty, but if you are continuing to the English coast or the Mediterranean, you can check out the selection of bathing suits and bespoke service for the perfect fit. Its salon also offers a tanning bed in the likely event of Brighton being rained out, and waxing and beauty treatments just in case. Its line of skincare products will keep you from showing the worst effects of the sun.

Maida Vale, Marylebone, and St. John's Wood — Map 8

LONG TALL SALLY

19-25 Chiltern St. W1, 020/7487-3370,
www.longtallsally.com
HOURS: Mon.-Wed. 9:30 A.M.-5:30 P.M., Thurs. 10 A.M.-7 P.M., Fri.-Sat. 9:30 A.M.-6 P.M., Sun. 11 A.M.-4 P.M.
TUBE: Baker Street

This shop is dedicated to fashions for tall women of all ages. It stocks a full range of outfits, including jeans, casual wear, office and formal wear, and bathing suits, and its large selection of fashion in hard-to-find sizes makes this a good stop for women who have trouble finding anything decent-looking that fits them. It also stocks accessories, shoes, and maternity clothes.

Department Stores

If you're pressed for time, you can get all your shopping done in one dizzying stop with a visit to one of London's famous department stores. Since they cater to various budgets all under one roof, you'll be able to find just the thing in your price range. Harrods has a famous sale in January and July and spectacular window displays at Christmas time. Many other department stores follow suit.

Mayfair and Piccadilly Map 3

FORTNUM AND MASON

181 Piccadilly SW1, 020/7734-8040, www.fortnumandmason.co.uk

HOURS: Mon.-Sat. 10 A.M.-6:30 P.M., Sun. noon-6 P.M.

TUBE: Green Park or Piccadilly Circus

Starting as a grocer's shop in 1707, Fortnum and Mason soon gained a name for itself as the place to buy exotic imports from Britain's global empire. Talk of its selection of delicacies trickled up the social ladder until it became a supplier for the royal family, a distinction it keeps to this day. Much of it is very British, with offerings such as marmalade and tea given generous space, but keeping with tradition it also carries international goods, such as Florentine biscuits and rare Russian caviar. The wine section is well stocked with Continental bottles and even some English wine (try the mead instead). The wicker gift hampers filled with goodies are a surefire hit for the people back home. Please note that on Sundays only the Food Hall and Patio Restaurant are open.

SELFRIDGES

400 Oxford St. W1, 087/0837-7377, www.selfridges.co.uk

HOURS: Mon. 10 A.M.-8 P.M., Tues.-Wed., Fri.-Sat. 9:30 A.M.-8 P.M., Thurs. 9:30 A.M.-9 P.M., Sun. 11:30 A.M.-6 P.M.

TUBE: Marble Arch or Bond Street

Selfridges is a vast department store rivaling its older and more elegant cousin Harrods for top place among London shopping centers. You can buy just about anything here, from designer brands to perfume to household ware. The technology section sells high-tech gadgets, from digital cameras to stylish portable speakers for your MP3 player. The dining area offers a great variety of cuisines to choose from. Selfridges often hosts special themed events with DJs or live music.

Chelsea, Kensington, and Knightsbridge Map 6

HARRODS

87-135 Brompton Rd. SW1, 020/7730-1234, www.harrods.com

HOURS: Mon.-Sat. 10 A.M.-7 P.M., Sun. noon-6 P.M.

TUBE: Knightsbridge

In an era of Super Wal-Marts and giant retail outlets, this famous department store proves that bigger *can* be better. There's really no point listing what you can buy in this London landmark, because it sells everything—yes, pretty much everything. No guns—this is England—but if it's legal you can find it here in one of the more than 300 departments. Suffice it to say that it is all high quality and there's something for every budget. Its logo, "everything for everybody everywhere," pretty much says it all.

Harrods started in the East End in 1834 as a grocer and tea seller; it still sells these two items in abundance. It quickly expanded and became one of London's main stores. During the wealthy imperial era of the late 19th century, Londoners wanted a store that could offer all the products of the empire, and Harrods could deliver. It attracted attention by installing the world's first escalator in 1898, providing brandy at the top for those who were less than enthusiastic about the concept of a moving staircase. In the 1930s it stocked the first television sets, when BBC started experimental broadcasts.

The building itself is an attraction, with its

Harrods department store is renowned for selling literally everything.

ornate Victorian facade dating to 1901. Decorated with art nouveau windows, cherubs, and a grand dome, it was designed by C. W. Stephens, who also designed Claridge's Hotel. Curiously enough, at 4.5 acres it covers the exact same area as historic Borough Market, south of the Thames (see *Food and Drink*). While Borough Market has satisfied Londoners' stomachs since the beginning of recorded history, Harrods has catered to their other appetites, taking a profitable share of the retail market by selling anything people wanted to buy. Alfred Hitchcock, missing its fresh herrings, had them shipped to him while directing movies in Hollywood. Author A. A. Milne found a teddy bear for his son here that inspired *Winnie-the-Pooh*. Their funerary service even embalmed Sigmund Freud.

The interior is made up of a series of themed halls. The Egyptian Hall is a funky but historically inaccurate depiction of a temple interior. ABC Carpet on the second floor has Persian rugs you can't buy in the United States. Urban Retreat is a health and beauty spa taking up the entire fifth floor. The vast Food Halls on the ground floor are a great place to sit and munch or buy takeaway for the nearby parks (see also the *Restaurants* chapter).

HARVEY NICHOLS

109-125 Knightsbridge SW1, 020/7235-5000, www.harveynichols.com

HOURS: Mon.-Sat. 10 A.M.-8 P.M., Sun. noon-6 P.M.

TUBE: Knightsbridge or Hyde Park Corner

This department store is a good place to go for the latest London fashions, which means trendy as well as expensive. With three of its seven floors given over to women's fashion, and two more for men's, the selection is hard to beat. Like its rival Harrods, it stocks more than just fashion, with departments for beauty, home, and gifts. The spacious floors are a little less claustrophobic than Harrods, but they lack the older store's elegance. The fifth floor has a café, sushi bar, restaurant, food market, and wine shop.

Food and Drink

FARMERS MARKETS

If restaurant food is getting a bit tiring, go to one of the many farmers markets around town. Here you can buy fresh fruit, vegetables, and farm products at fair prices. The farmers markets are a great way to save on food if your budget is tight, and you can sample some excellent British and foreign produce. The imports, however, are a bit pricier. Especially good are the cheeses and organic food. For a more limited but markedly cheaper selection, keep an eye out for the many small produce stands throughout the city. And if the weather doesn't cooperate, don't worry; several of the markets listed here are covered.

Westminster, Victoria, and Pimlico — Map 2

PIMLICO ROAD MARKET

Orange Sq., corner of Pimlico Rd. and Ebury St. SW1, 020/7833-0338, www.lfm.org.uk

HOURS: Sat. 9 A.M.-1 P.M.

TUBE: Sloane Square

A pleasant, shady square hosts the smallest of the markets listed here. A visit here will give you a taste of a typical neighborhood market, for a rich neighborhood anyway. Sample the fresh breads, produce, and organic food in stalls that cluster around a statue to Mozart. It recalls the brief period in 1764 when the eight-year-old, who was already performing on stage and was considered a prodigy, lived at 180 Ebury Street with his sick father. Not wanting to disturb him, Amadeus didn't play for a while and composed his first two symphonies instead.

Chelsea, Kensington, and Knightsbridge — Map 6

CHELSEA FARMERS MARKET

Park St. SW3, 020/7515-7153, www.chelseafarmersmkt.org

HOURS: Sat. 8 A.M.-noon May-Oct.

TUBE: South Kensington

A highbrow market in the exclusive SW3 postcode, this weekly gathering nevertheless keeps its neighborly feel and features organic produce, gourmet foods, and arts and crafts. Florists come out and have some colorful bouquets on offer. Another nice touch is the ongoing chefs' series, in which master chefs demonstrate their thing and give you tips. The demonstrations start at 10:30 A.M. Usually there is a live music troupe or two to liven things up a bit.

Notting Hill, Bayswater, and Paddington — Map 7

NOTTING HILL MARKET

Car park behind Waterstones, access via Kensington Pl. W8, 020/7833-0338, www.lfm.org.uk

HOURS: Sat. 9 A.M.-1:30 P.M.

TUBE: Notting Hill Gate

This is one of the city's largest farmers markets and it stocks a good selection of organic produce. Being in one of the ritzier areas of town, it's a bit pricier than some, but you can find lots of good imports and specialty goods here. Go here in the morning and Portobello Road in the afternoon for a satisfying if exhausting all-day wander.

Camden Town — Map 9

CAMDEN MARKETS

Chalk Farm Rd. from Camden Town Station to Hartland Rd. NW1, 020/7284-2084, www.camdenlockmarket.com

HOURS: Daily until sundown

TUBE: Camden Town

The area along Chalk Farm Road in Camden is lined with funky shops announcing themselves with garish signs and giant fish and frogs hanging onto the walls. Four markets lie along this road. Camden Market at Buck Street is packed tight with discount clothing, accessories, and music. Camden Canal Market at Castlehaven Road is the liveliest of the four with street fashion and hip-hop music stalls standing cheek by jowl with flowery hippie gear—everyone mingles here. Farther north on Chalk Farm Road at Camden Lock Place is a more upscale market selling arts, crafts, and fashion, and the plaza behind has cheaper clothes and lots of food stalls. The last market is Stables, at Hartland Road. Beyond a large section with food and clothing stalls is an extensive and reasonably priced antiques market. Because of increased popularity, many stalls are now staying open throughout the week. While you won't get to sample everything, you will beat the crazy weekend crowds. A lot of the market is covered, so rain won't be much of a problem.

South of the Thames Map 12

BOROUGH MARKET

8 Southwark St. SE1, 020/7407-1002, www.boroughmarket.org.uk

HOURS: Open 24 hours; retail foods for sale Fri. noon-6 P.M., Sat. 9 A.M.-4 P.M.

TUBE: Borough

This historic market is mainly used by the city's restaurant owners and grocers and really gets busy after 2 A.M., but it is open for the general public during more civilized hours. Much of the space is devoted to wholesale fruit and vegetables, but there are plenty of retail stalls devoted to fine foods. The market's history shows the curious continuity of London's establishments. The Romans discovered a market in the area when they arrived. Its location astride the meeting point of their roads leading from London to the southern part of the country and coastline was probably a big reason why they built the first bridge across the Thames where they did. London Bridge is close to the site of the old Roman bridge and directly north of the market. Farmers continued selling their produce here into the Middle Ages and a document dating to 1276 complains that the crowds coming here were blocking the old London Bridge. While London's rulers moved the market several times through the years, it's always been in the same general area and has been at its present 4.5-acre site (1.8 hectare) since 1756.

GOURMET FOOD

If you've trembled to horror stories of the foulness of British food, fear not; you've been fooled. These fair isles produce some of the best cheeses and meats in the world, and for the rest, well, they import it! Here you can find delicacies from the continent and beyond, flown in fresh for the insatiable appetites of this giant metropolis (also see the *Farmers Market* section for shopping al fresco).

Mayfair and Piccadilly Map 3

PAXTON AND WHITFIELD

93 Jermyn St. SW1, 020/7930-0259, www.paxtonandwhitfield.co.uk

HOURS: Mon.-Sat. 9:30 A.M.-6 P.M.

TUBE: Green Park or Piccadilly Circus

The United Kingdom is justifiably famous for its cheeses. From pungent stiltons to sharp cheddars, you'll find it all here. This shop started as a stall in Clare Market in 1742 before becoming a brick-and-mortar shop several years later. This was followed by the honor of becoming a supplier to Queen Victoria in 1850. Since then its success has been assured and the list of famous and royal patrons has lengthened considerably. It moved to its present location in 1896 and still supplies Buckingham Palace. The staff is, of course, highly knowledgeable, and if you ask enough questions you'll feel like an expert by the time you get out the door. The custom-made hampers make great gifts, but make sure to tell the staff you're taking an international flight so they can give you prewrapped cheeses that can make it through customs. Check out the website to find out if there's going to be a cheese tasting. It has other locations at Bath (1 John St., 012/2546-6403) and Stratford-upon Avon (13 Wood St., 017/8941-5544).

Covent Garden, West End, and Soho Map 4

CARLUCCIO'S

28A Neal St. WC2, 020/7240 1487, www.carluccios.com

HOURS: Mon.-Fri. 8 A.M.-8 P.M., Sat. 10 A.M.-7 P.M., Sun. noon-6 P.M.

TUBE: Covent Garden

If English food is getting you down, either go for a curry or browse this Italian-owned deli and gift shop selling tasty Italian imports such as crostini spreads, pasta, olive oil, wine, and meat. Its mushroom selection is the biggest I've ever seen. You can have a sandwich made to order that you can munch on while watching the chaotic action in Covent Garden. The Neal Street Restaurant next door is under the same management.

Maida Vale, Marylebone, and St. John's Wood — Map 8

VILLANDRY

170 Great Portland St. W1, 020/7631-3131, www.villandry.com

HOURS: Mon.-Sat. 7:30 A.M.-10 P.M., Sun. 9 A.M.-4 P.M.

TUBE: Baker Street or Regent's Park

While locals come to this large gourmet shop to buy supplies for their own cooking, you might want to stop in to get one of Villandry's hampers before heading off for a picnic at nearby Regent's Park. The staff can pack you a picnic for any number of people. Prices start at £25. The meals include a starter, a main dish, and a dessert and you can even get breakfast and afternoon tea hampers. The cuisine is unpretentious and international, with tandoori chicken and mezes sharing the list with quiche and roast leg of lamb. The massive all-day hamper, costing £45 per person, includes breakfast, lunch, and afternoon tea and can keep you out in the park from sunup to sundown.

Camden Town — Map 9

FRESH AND WILD

49 Parkway NW1, 020/7428-7575

HOURS: Mon.-Fri. 8 A.M.-9 P.M., Sat. 8 A.M.-8 P.M., Sun. 10 A.M.-7 P.M.

TUBE: Camden Town

This great organic store carries just about everything you could want, including fresh produce, prepared food, pasta, meat, and more. The food is mostly from British organic farmers and isn't horribly overpriced as in North America. Enough people are selling, and buying, organic food that an economy of scale has lowered the prices. A beauty and health section sells stuff for parts of your body other than your stomach, and a counter offers takeaway sandwiches and salads. It has another store at 208–210 Westbourne Grove, Notting Hill, 020/7229-1063.

South of the Thames — Map 12

KONDITOR AND COOK

10 Stoney St. SE1, 020/7407-5100, www.konditorandcook.com

HOURS: Mon.-Fri. 7:30 A.M.-6 P.M., Sat. 8:30 A.M.-5 P.M.

TUBE: London Bridge

One of London's most respected bakers specializes in cakes baked with free-range eggs and natural butter. A small number of tables allows you to sit in or on the street outside and view bustling Borough Market while sampling some of the best cakes you'll ever have. While they are loaded with sweetness, they manage to be flavorful as well as rich, showing the bakers use technique as well as mountains of sugar. The bakery operates a bespoke service if you want to plan a special birthday or anniversary celebration while you're in town.

LIQUOR

Besides the real ales in its pubs, London is a good place to sample fine liquors. A bottle of vintage stuff makes for a great gift, one you might even be generous enough to give to someone else. Whiskeys are in abundant supply, and imports round out the selection. If only someone could do something about the English wine industry.

Bloomsbury, Euston, and Holborn — Map 5

ROYAL MILE WHISKIES

3 Bloomsbury St. WC1, 020/7436-4763, www.royalmilewhiskies.com

HOURS: Mon.-Sat. 11 A.M.-7 P.M., Sun. noon-5 P.M.

TUBE: Tottenham Court Road

Named after its parent store on the Royal Mile in Edinburgh, this shop stocks a fine selection of Scottish whiskeys and is conveniently situated just around the corner from the British Museum. There is something for all budgets here, from regular brands to offerings from small distilleries and whiskeys from before the World War (the *first* World War!). The staff are experts and can steer you to just the right bottle. The shop also stocks a wide range of cigars, fine beers, and accessories.

South of the Thames Map 12

VINOPOLIS

1 Bank End SE1, 087/0241-4040, www.vinopolis.co.uk

HOURS: Mon., Fri.-Sat. noon-9 P.M., Tues.-Thurs., Sun. noon-6 P.M.

TUBE: London Bridge or Southwark

In a perfect example of London's ability to maintain its identity through the centuries, the site of a 2nd-century Roman wine warehouse is now home to London's most famous wine shop. The stock is huge and includes wines from all around the globe (even England) available at all price levels. It also sells whiskeys and other spirits. Part of the original warehouse, including amphorae (ancient wine jugs) and the timber floor, are visible through a glass floor. The Southwark Tourist Information Center is also housed in this building. Self-guided wine-tasting tours will increase your expertise on vintages from every major region. The tours cost £15 and up and reservations are recommended, especially on Saturdays.

SWEETS

Indulge yourself with some fine chocolate or Asian treats at these two delicious stores. If you're still not glutted, head to the tempting candy section at Harrods.

Mayfair and Piccadilly Map 3

LA MAISON DU CHOCOLAT

46 Piccadilly W1, 020/7287-8500, www.lamaisonduchocolat.com

HOURS: Mon.-Sat. 10 A.M.-7 P.M., Sun. noon-6 P.M.

TUBE: Piccadilly Circus

You don't want to miss this one. The selection of handmade French chocolates is almost impossible to beat outside of France or Belgium. Besides a quality assortment of caramels, truffles, milk and dark chocolates, it sells various creations such as Habanera, a collection of dark chocolate perfumed with vine-ripened peaches and milk chocolate infused with mirabelle plums. It offers gift boxes for all budgets too, from modest £10 affairs to over-the-top hedonistic packages for close to £200. It's perfect as a gift for that special someone, especially if you've been away from home too long writing a guidebook.

MINAMOTO KITCHOAN

44 Piccadilly W1, 020/7437-3135

HOURS: Sun.-Fri. 10 A.M.-7 P.M., Sat. 10 A.M.-8 P.M.

TUBE: Piccadilly Circus

This small storefront draws you in with colorful Japanese kites in the shape of fish and a beautiful Edo-period painted screen, but the candy on display is even more pleasing to the eye. The Japanese are masters of artful presentation, and these sweets are as attractive as they are tasty. The Kohakukanume is a plum-wine jelly sprinkled with gold powder encasing a whole plum, while the Kibimochi are little rice cakes filled with strained bean paste and powdered with soybean flour. While it's all quite sweet, the ingredient list shows Japanese candies are healthier than the usual Western fare. It's great for someone with a sweet tooth looking for a new experience.

TEA AND COFFEE

London, of course, is a great place to buy tea. England has been importing tea for centuries and in the colonies of the empire the British combined traditional methods with imperial efficiency to create many fine blends and flavors. Coffee drinkers aren't forgotten either. You can find even the rarest of beans here.

Mayfair and Piccadilly Map 3

H. R. HIGGINS (COFFEE-MAN)

79 Duke St. W1, 020/7629-3913, www.hrhiggins.co.uk

HOURS: Mon.-Fri. 9:30 A.M.-5:30 P.M., Sat. 10 A.M.-5 P.M.

TUBE: Bond Street

H. R. Higgins has been supplying tea and coffee to Londoners since 1942, a particularly gutsy year to open a business. It's still owned by the same family and offers a wonderful assortment of teas and coffees, including rare varieties. It's the only supplier besides Harrods where I could find Yemeni coffee, for example. A small café in the basement gives you a chance to try a cup of something unfamiliar to see if you want to get some more to take away.

Covent Garden, West End, and Soho — Map 4

THE TEA HOUSE

15A Neal St. WC2, 020/7240-7539

HOURS: Mon.-Sat. 10 A.M.-7 P.M., Sun. 11 A.M.-6 P.M.

TUBE: Covent Garden

Among the abundance of London's tea shops, The Tea House stands out. Among its well more than 100 hundred varieties from all over the world, you'll be sure to find the tea that's right for you, from soothing Darjeeling to the explosive taste of Gunpowder tea (it's not really made from gunpowder, although it looks as if it is). The shop also stocks a variety of interesting teapots, from the traditional to the modern and avant-garde, and all the tea accessories you'll ever need.

Camden Town — Map 9

CAMDEN COFFEE SHOP

11 Delancey St. NW1, 020/7387-4080

HOURS: Mon.-Fri. 9:30 A.M.-5:30 P.M. (closes Thurs. at 2:30 P.M.), Sat. 9:30 A.M.-5 P.M.

TUBE: Camden Town

This popular neighborhood shop stocks coffee from around the world, including the excellent, full-bodied varieties from Cuba, which are legal everywhere except the United States. It's a very basic place—no trendy art on the walls, no frappuccinos costing more than a daily wage in the developing world—just old-fashioned grinding and roasting equipment and sacks of coffee beans everywhere. The variety is good and the owners really know their coffee. The prices are good too. Note that this shop doesn't serve coffee; it just sells beans.

The City — Map 10

TWININGS TEA AND COFFEE MERCHANTS

216 Strand WC2, 087/0241-3667, www.twinings.com

HOURS: Mon.-Fri. 9:30 A.M.-4:45 P.M.

TUBE: St. Paul's

Thomas Twining (1675–1741) founded the House of Twining by buying Tom's Coffee House at the back of the present site in 1706. Coffee was already the rage, and Twining started serving tea too. In 1717 he opened the Golden Lyon here as a shop to sell tea leaves and coffee beans. In 1787 his grandson, Richard Twining (1749–1824), built the doorway at the front, incorporating the Golden Lyon symbol and two Chinese figures. Twinings claims, and it may well be true, that it's the oldest company in London to operate continuously on the same site with the same family since its foundation. It carries the complete (and considerable) range of Twinings teas, a selection of coffee, and accessories, and it has a free little museum at the back.

Gift and Home

Gifts come in all shapes, sizes, and tastes, so here's a catch-all for the myriad of stores that defy categorization, along with those that sell items for the home. British homes are cozy and comfortable, perhaps as a way for the inhabitants forget the inclement weather outside their doors.

Mayfair and Piccadilly — Map 3

BEYOND THE VALLEY

2 Newburgh St. W1, 020/7437-7338, www.beyondthevalley.com

HOURS: Mon.-Sat. 11:30 A.M.-6:30 P.M., Sun. noon-5 P.M.

TUBE: Oxford Circus

After the stultifying sameness of Carnaby Street, and the cutesy preciousness of so many London design stores, the cool and edgy items at Beyond the Valley come as a gratifying relief. This nonprofit arts collective featuring art, clothing, and design objects by young artists is simply filled with cool stuff—some examples are the egg holder made of green Army men and the six-pack T-shirt. Some of

© JO JACKSON, BEYOND THE VALLEY

Beyond the Valley is an artist cooperative offering funky clothes and home decorations.

the wall hangings and furniture are unique and sure to make your home much more interesting to look at.

SMYTHSON

40 New Bond St. W1, 020/7629 0550, www.smythson.co.uk
HOURS: Mon.-Wed., Fri. 9:30 A.M.-6 P.M., Thurs. 10 A.M.-7 P.M., Sat. 10 A.M.-6 P.M.
TUBE: Bond Street or Oxford Circus

Smythson is an interesting shop specializing in stationery, making for a unique gift for that favorite letter writer back home. The art of writing letters has declined in the age of email, but with this beautiful stationery you might just inspire people to head to the post office again. The shelves are stuffed with an overwhelming variety, but you can also buy some personalized stationery, which Smythson can make in all sorts of styles. It also sells men's and women's leather goods such as handbags, wallets, and diaries. There's so much leather in this store that it's one of the best-smelling shops in London!

SWAROVSKI

137-139 Regent St. W1, 020/7434-2500, www.swarovski.com
HOURS: Mon.-Wed., Fri.-Sat. 10 A.M.-7 P.M., Thurs. 10 A.M.-8 P.M., Sun. noon-6 P.M.
TUBE: Oxford Circus or Piccadilly Circus

The major crystal designers Swarovski has many outlets throughout the city and the world, but this is its flagship store. Stepping in here makes it seem as if the entire world has been crystallized. Sparkling glass encrusts handbags, watches, and lamps, and crystal lions and toucans peer out at you from their cases. The selection of jewelry is almost blinding, and if for whatever reason you are in the market for a tiara, it can supply those too.

THOMAS GOODE

19 S. Audley St. W1, 020/7499-2823, www.thomasgoode.co.uk
HOURS: Mon.-Sat. 10 A.M.-6 P.M.
TUBE: Bond Street or Green Park

Thomas Goode has been famous for its silverware, bone china, and crystal since 1827. Nowadays it continues to sell some of the best of these luxuries, as well as hand-embroidered bed and table linen. Needless to say, it knows the business and has a fine stock. The style leans toward the traditional, but there are also more modern items. A museum in the shop shows off some of the commissions it's done in its long history, including many pieces for royal families. Other antiques are for sale, such as a hand-painted coffee set from France from the 1820s.

Bloomsbury, Euston, and Holborn — Map 5

HABITAT

196 Tottenham Court Rd. W1, 020/7631-3880, www.habitat.net
HOURS: Mon.-Wed., Fri. 10 A.M.-6:30 P.M., Thurs. 10 A.M.-8 P.M., Sat. 9:30 A.M.-6:30 P.M., Sun. noon-6 P.M.
TUBE: Tottenham Court Road

One of the larger interior design and home stores in London, Habitat is filled with furniture and accessories for every room in your house. Designer furniture takes up much of the space, but there are plenty of home accessories as well, with an especially good selection of glassware and linens. While this is not exactly a shop catering to tourists, it's a good destination if you're fitting out a short-term flat in London. The prices are low and the style, with lots of bright colors and funky designs, will cheer up your interior.

PURVES AND PURVES

222 Tottenham Court Rd. W1, 020/7580-8223, www.purves.co.uk

HOURS: Mon.-Fri. 9:30 A.M.-5:30 P.M., Sat. 10 A.M.-5 P.M.

TUBE: Goodge Street

Funky, modern furniture and home accessories are what's on sale here, with an emphasis on bright colors and a quirky style. The store is very browsable, with all sorts of strange things on the shelves. While the furniture isn't exactly the easiest thing to bring onto a plane, you can outfit a stylish flat here if you're staying awhile. For more temporary visitors, its selection of home accessories, such as colorful balloon mobiles for your baby and bouncing rubber vases, are much more packable.

Notting Hill, Bayswater, and Paddington — Map 7

COCO RIBBON

21 Kensington Park Rd. W11, 020/7229-4904, www.cocoribbon.com

HOURS: Mon.-Fri. 10 A.M.-6:30 P.M., Sat. 10 A.M.-6 P.M., Sun. 12:30-5:30 P.M.

TUBE: Ladbroke Grove

This luxury boutique for women in the heart of Notting Hill carries just about everything you could want if you want to create a high-class room. It sells antique French furniture and hand-printed silk curtains, and you can even buy a chandelier if you're willing to trust the airline with it. Once the room is decorated, you can decorate yourself with lingerie, jewelry, beauty products, and fashion accessories. The store tries to offer everything for the person seeking a luxury lifestyle, and it certainly carries an unusual selection.

Maida Vale, Marylebone, and St. John's Wood — Map 8

DIVERTIMENTI

33-34 Marylebone High St. W1, 020/7935-0689, www.divertimenti.co.uk

HOURS: Mon.-Fri. 9:30 A.M.-6 P.M., Sat. 10 A.M.-6 P.M., Sun. 11 A.M.-5 P.M.

TUBE: Baker Street or Regent's Park

Aspiring chefs will love the trendy assortment of Italian goods for sale here, from high-quality cookware to linens, tableware, and more. The styles vary from retro to rustic to ultramodern, but it's all good quality and the selection changes with the seasons. Divertimenti hosts the popular Cookery Theatre, in which you make your own dinner under the tutelage of master chefs. The café (see the *Restaurants* chapter) is a good pit stop after shopping if you want someone else to do the cooking.

SKANDIUM

86 Marylebone High St. W1, 020/7935-2077, www.skandium.com

HOURS: Mon.-Wed., Fri.-Sat. 10 A.M.-6:30 P.M., Thurs. 10 A.M.-7 P.M., Sun. 11 A.M.-5 P.M.

TUBE: Baker Street

A popular center for Scandinavian design, this two-story emporium offers everything for the home from famous and not-so-famous designers. If you're fixing up a flat in town, it's a good choice for the clean lines and quality material that Scandinavia is known for. It's not as cheap as Ikea, but you don't have to build it yourself and it's better made. It also handles shipping if you don't mind the expense.

The City — Map 10

BBC SHOP

Bush House Arcade, The Strand WC2, 020/7557-2576, www.bbcshop.com

HOURS: Mon.-Fri. 10 A.M.-6 P.M., Sat. 10 A.M.-5:30 P.M., Sun. noon-5 P.M.

TUBE: St. Paul's

BBC fans won't want to miss this shop at the back of the headquarters for the famous broadcast company's World Service. It sells everything from episodes of *Fawlty Towers* to radio-controlled Daleks and all the back episodes of your favorite shows that you missed on public television. The BBC is rightfully famous for its film adaptations of classic works of literature, so snapping up some of these is a quick and painless way to be introduced to the likes of Dickens and Austin, and it might inspire you to pick up the books too. The latest programs are all here, both in audio and video, along with the books that accompany many series. American formats are available, but be sure to specify before you buy.

IAN LOGAN DESIGN SHOP

42 Charterhouse Sq. EC1, 020/7600-9888, www.ian-logan.co.uk
HOURS: Mon.-Fri. 10 A.M.-6:30 P.M., Sat. 11 A.M.-5 P.M.
TUBE: Barbican

Billing itself as a toy shop for grown-ups, Ian Logan carries a large number of interesting widgets such as large tin biplanes, papermaking kits, pocket microscopes, wooden pull toys, and other bric-a-brac. The pinhole photography kit allows you to turn a box into a camera. Logan himself is often away on one of his buying junkets around Europe, but he's an interesting chap to talk to with a taste for the obscure and offbeat.

South of the Thames — Map 12

RADIO DAYS

87 Lower Marsh SE1, 020/7928-0800, www.radiodaysvintage.co.uk
HOURS: Mon.-Thurs., Sat. 10 A.M.-6 P.M., Fri. 9 A.M.-7 P.M.
TUBE: Waterloo

The spot for one-stop shopping for your nostalgia fix, this jam-packed shop offers detritus from the past 80 years. Fix your house up the way grandma used to have it (assuming grandma was British) or dress up in the fashions of the '60s and '70s. A visit will turn up some truly weird items. My favorite was a clock that looked like the wheel of an old sailing ship, with a glass center filled with coral and seahorses, but my taste battled my sense of irony, taste won, and I didn't end up buying it. Who knows? Maybe it's still there.

Specialty

CERAMICS

Get a souvenir you can eat from at one of London's fine ceramic or china shops. Besides the shops listed here, department stores usually have excellent selections. The British have been making fine china for centuries, and it shows in the quality.

Mayfair and Piccadilly — Map 3

CONTEMPORARY CERAMICS

7 Marshall St. W1, 020/7437-7605, www.cpaceramics.com
HOURS: Mon.-Sat. 10:30 A.M.-6 P.M. (open Thurs. until 7 P.M.)
TUBE: Oxford Circus or Piccadilly Circus

This gallery store is run by the Craft Potters Association and showcases the work of its members, some of the leading ceramic artists working in the United Kingdom today. Their range is truly impressive, with simple but stylish tableware next to unique sculptures. It hosts regular exhibitions of famous ceramicists or recent graduates from art schools, with all the items for sale. The staff is used to traveling customers, so they will bundle up your purchase for a safe ride home.

WEDGWOOD

158 Regent St. W1, 020/7734-7262, www.wedgwood.co.uk
HOURS: Mon.-Wed., Fri.-Sat. 10 A.M.-7 P.M., Thurs. 10 A.M.-7:30 P.M., Sun. noon-6 P.M.
TUBE: Oxford Circus

This well-known distributor of fine china has its own shop in the West End filled with its trademark traditional styles, including the often-seen white-on-blue design with classical motifs, and plenty of more modern looks as well. The large showroom is like a museum of ceramics and the quality of the merchandise is really first-rate. Unlike a lot of posh stores in the area, it carries items to suit all budgets.

CIGARS

If you're from the United States, chances are you've never smoked a real Cuban cigar (those fake ones from Mexican border towns don't count). Now's your chance. Havanas are legal here, just as they are everywhere else in the world outside the United States. Sautter is the best source, but any decent cigar shop will stock them.

Mayfair and Piccadilly — Map 3

SAUTTER OF MAYFAIR

106 Mount St. W1, 020/7499-4866

HOURS: Mon.-Fri. 9 A.M.-6 P.M., Sat. 9 A.M.-4:30 P.M.

TUBE: Bond Street or Green Park

This little cigar shop has a humidor stuffed with a dizzying variety of Havanas, famous for their aromatic smoke and smooth taste. Virtually all the stock is from Cuba, but it carries a few from other nations. Keep in mind that Cuban products are illegal to bring back to the United States, but you can buy singles to enjoy here. The shop also stocks a full range of smoking accessories.

IMPORTS

Cosmopolitan London's many nationalities have always set up shops to cater to their homesick brethren. A look through these stores is like a global journey and can net you some great meals, mementoes, and ideas for your next trip.

Covent Garden, West End, and Soho — Map 4

AFRICAN ENTERPRISES

Unit 3, The Arches Shopping Centre beneath Hungerford Railway Bridge WC2, 020/7839-5707

HOURS: Mon.-Fri. 9:30 A.M.-7 P.M., Sat. 10:30 A.M.-6 P.M., Sun. 11 A.M.-5 P.M.

TUBE: Charing Cross

South Africans will feel right at home in this little emporium tucked under the arches of the Hungerford Railway Bridge. Radio South Africa plays on the sound system, and the shelves are full of S.A. beauty products, snacks, frozen foods, drinks, and a good selection of wine. There's also a selection of national team gear, books, and DVDs. If you're thinking of visiting the country, the rack of guidebooks will be helpful. The African sculptures are worth picking up too.

AUSTRALIA/CANADA/NEW ZEALAND/SOUTH AFRICA SHOP

27 Maiden Lane WC2, 020/7836-2292, www.australiashop.co.uk, www.canadashop.co.uk, www.newzealandshop.uk.com, and www.southafricashop.co.uk

HOURS: Mon.-Fri. 10:30 A.M.-6:30 P.M., Sat. 11 A.M.-6:30 P.M., Sun. 11 A.M.-5:30 P.M.

TUBE: Covent Garden

Four shops in one serve Her Majesty's subjects away from home with all the things they miss from home. Vegemite, Tim Tams, Moosehead, Jungle Oats, Bluebird Biguns—it's all here in a veritable comfort-food heaven. In addition to the food and drink, it stocks DVDs, bath products, books, and maps. If you're heading to one of these countries for the first time, a visit here will familiarize you with the things the natives can't do without. It's also a bit of a social center for homesick people working in London.

TIBET DREAMS

50A Earlham St. WC2, 020/7836-5445, www.tibetdreams.co.uk

HOURS: Daily 11 A.M.-7 P.M.

TUBE: Covent Garden

The smell of incense will draw you into a cluttered little shop full of prayer flags, jewelry, and men's and women's clothing. Tibetan jewelry is generally larger and heavier than what Westerners are used to, but it's of an attractive style that stands up to years of wear. The clothing is equally durable—Tibet's a rough climate, after all—so its fashions make a good choice if you plan to do some cold-weather hiking. There's a small selection of books and music as well. The staff is a good source of information for Tibetan cultural and political events in town.

Islington — Map 11

RAU

36 Islington Green N1 020/7359-5337

HOURS: Wed. 10 A.M.-5 P.M., Thurs. 11 A.M.-5 P.M., Sat. 10 A.M.-6 P.M.

TUBE: Angel

While the daily news makes Afghanistan look like a miserable war zone creating nothing but terrorists, it's actually a land of ancient culture with a rich arts and crafts tradition. The owner of this two-story shop has been going to Afghanistan for more than 30 years and brings back an amazing variety of richly woven wall hangings, elaborately embroidered clothing, heavy silver jewelry, and carved wooden furniture. If the selection here whets your appetite for more Afghani experiences, head next door to the Afghan Kitchen for an authentic meal.

OUTDOORS

With the much-mourned passing of the YHA Adventure Shop, outdoor stores in London are now completely dominated by chains. I've listed my favorite here but be warned that it's cheaper to buy outdoors equipment and clothing in the United States or Canada.

Westminster, Victoria, and Pimlico — Map 2

NOMAD ADVENTURE TRAVEL

52 Grosvenor Gardens SW1, 020/7823-5823, www.nomadtravel.co.uk

HOURS: Mon.-Fri. 9:30 A.M.-7 P.M., Sat. 9:30 A.M.-6 P.M., Sun. noon-5 P.M.

TUBE: Victoria

Convenient one-stop shopping for your outdoor needs, Nomad Adventure Travel has a huge stock. Besides the usual sleeping bags, tents, and backpacks, it carries a good choice of knives, compasses, cooking gear, and just about everything else. It even has its own line of travel health products, such as insect repellents and first-aid kits. The staff are generally knowledgeable, especially the travel-health nurses who can tell you how to stay healthy when you head off to remote corners of the world.

UMBRELLAS AND CANES

You can find umbrellas anywhere in London, but for real style in a museum piece of a shop, there's only one place to go.

Bloomsbury, Euston, and Holborn — Map 5

JAMES SMITH AND SONS

53 New Oxford St. WC1, 020/7836-4731

HOURS: Mon.-Fri. 9:30 A.M.-5:25 P.M., Sat. 10 A.M.-5:25 P.M.

TUBE: Tottenham Court Road

This shop is worth a look just for its admirably preserved early-19th-century storefront, which gives you an idea what the "nation of shopkeepers" looked like back then. Established in 1830, it has been selling umbrellas and canes ever since, from the utilitarian to the elegant, and in every price range. If you forgot your umbrella at home (or less likely, your cane), come here for a historic and rewarding shopping experience, and keep the business alive for another 175 years.

Toys and Collectibles

The British are great collectors. It seems every home has a little museum of stamps, coronation spoons, dolls, or some other commonplace item imbued with an almost mystical importance. If you are a collector, or have come to the point in your life when you really must have a complete set of Princess Diana commemorative plates, you're in luck. London has it all. Antique shops and markets are another good place to look for collectibles.

Shopping is also hard work on the wee ones, so stop in at a toy store and reward their fortitude. The selection at these stores is truly incredible, especially for the latest electronic gadgets and handmade toys that can be hard to find back home.

Mayfair and Piccadilly Map 3

HAMLEYS TOYS

188-196 Regent St. W1, 087/0333-2455, www.hamleys.com

HOURS: Mon.-Sat. 10 A.M.-8 P.M., Sat. 9:30 A.M.-8 P.M., Sun. noon-6 P.M.

TUBE: Oxford Circus

A truly outstanding toy store, Hamleys has seven floors of playthings for kids of all ages. There's everything from a baby's first toys on up to scale models and art supplies for tweens. It has a large video-games section, of course, but it leaves plenty of space for traditional board games and toys for the imagination. At The Bear Factory, your child can pick a style of bearskin and then stuff it, add a heart, a name, and even a voice, and suit it up as a one-of-a-kind companion. There's something heartening in bringing a teddy bear to life. A big candy section and a café will get you refreshed for more adult shopping along Regent Street. If you forget to pick up something for the little folks back home, don't sweat it; it also has stores in Heathrow and Stansted.

TRADITION OF LONDON

5A Shepherd St. W1, 020/7493-7452, www.traditionoflondon.com

HOURS: Mon.-Fri. 9 A.M.-5:30 P.M., Sat. 9:30 A.M.-4:30 P.M.

TUBE: Green Park or Piccadilly Circus

Tradition is one of the most respected manufacturers of metal model soldiers in the world. These aren't little green Army men but miniature works of art with accurate uniforms and equipment, making them collectibles rather than toys. You can get them unpainted or painted by Tradition's excellent staff. You can even order bespoke soldiers painted to represent a particular regiment. While this shop is already overrun with tiny armies, take a look through the catalog for even more sets. It also sells antique soldiers, painted sets, and military books and magazines.

Covent Garden, West End, and Soho Map 4

THE CINEMA STORE

4B Orion House, Upper St. Martin's Lane WC2, 020/7379-7838, www.the-cinema-store.com

HOURS: Mon.-Wed., Sat. 10 A.M.-6:30 P.M., Thurs.-Fri. 10 A.M.-7 P.M., Sun. 11 A.M.-5 P.M.

TUBE: Leicester Square or Covent Garden

This shop carries an incredible collection of movie DVDs, books, posters, scripts, lobby cards, and other memorabilia. Most of it is new, but it also carries a good collection of vintage movie magazines and posters. The employees are all film nuts so you can get into some great conversations here. Between hanging out here and the British Film Institute (see the *Arts and Entertainment* chapter), you can find out all you'll ever need to know about British cinema.

DRESS CIRCLE

57/59 Monmouth St. WC2, 020/7240-2227, www.dresscircle.com

HOURS: Mon.-Sat. 10 A.M.-6:30 P.M.

TUBE: Leicester Square

If you like showbiz, you'll love this shop stocking soundtracks and sheet music of all the major and most minor musicals, as well as a host of other mementoes such as T-shirts, books, videos, DVDs, posters, and various other knickknacks. The staff really knows and loves the musical theater, so if you're trying to track down something that's hard to find, you can do no better than to come here. Its website is a good place to catch up on the latest West End stage gossip.

FRASER'S/STANLEY GIBBONS

399 Strand WC2, 020/7557-4408, www.frasersautographs.com and www.stanleygibbons.co.uk

HOURS: Mon.-Fri. 9 A.M.-5:30 P.M., Sat. 9:30 A.M.-5:30 P.M.

TUBE: Embankment or Covent Garden

Two leading collectors' shops in one building

should satisfy your craving. On the ground floor is Stanley Gibbons, which deals exclusively in stamps from the latest first-day covers to the rarest of the rare. Given that it stocks an estimated three million stamps, the notice behind the counter declaring "We Sell Stamps" is the most unnecessary sign in London. Upstairs is Fraser's, which deals in autographs. It sells signed photographs of just about everybody and every purchase comes with a lifetime guarantee of authenticity

THE TINTIN SHOP

34 Floral St. WC2, 020/7836-1131,
www.thetintinshop.uk.com
HOURS: Mon.-Sat. 10 A.M.-5:30 P.M.
TUBE: Covent Garden

Here's a shop devoted entirely to the famous Belgian comic-strip reporter/crime fighter. Not only does it carry the books, but also T-shirts, coffee mugs, umbrellas, key chains, towels, and anything else you can imagine. You can even get a Snowy duvet cover. If it's about Tintin (or Snowy, or Captain Haddock, etc.) this store has it. Only Brussels has another store like this.

Bloomsbury, Euston, and Holborn — Map 5

MODEL ZONE

202 High Holborn WC1, 020/7405-6285
HOURS: Mon.-Sat. 9:30 A.M.-6 P.M., Sun. 11 A.M.-5 P.M.
TUBE: Tottenham Court Road

Model Zone's vast stock of model trains, planes, cars, tanks, and boats will keep any modeler happy. If you don't have the patience for dealing with 100 little pieces and glue sticking to your fingers, try out some of the radio-controlled models or model soldiers. It stocks all the biggest brands and many smaller European ones that are hard to find in the United States, along with a complete range of accessories for dioramas and train sets.

PLAYIN' GAMES

33 Museum St. WC1, 020/7323-3080
HOURS: Mon.-Wed., Fri.-Sat. 10 A.M.-6 P.M., Thurs. 10 A.M.-7 P.M., Sun. noon-6 P.M.
TUBE: Tottenham Court Road

If your kids are getting bored with the museums, take them into this shop for some welcome diversions. Among its more than 1,000 games, you should be able to find something to entertain the little ones, or yourself. It's crammed with board games, collectible card games, role-playing games, and just about everything else except computer and electronic games. It stocks a huge variety of chess sets, including handy magnetic travel sets and elaborate (and expensive) tabletop ones.

Maida Vale, Marylebone, and St. John's Wood — Map 8

THE BEATLES STORE AND GALLERY

231 Baker St. NW1, 020/7935-4464,
www.beatlesstorelondon.co.uk
HOURS: Daily 10 A.M.-6:30 P.M.
TUBE: Baker Street

One-stop shopping for all things Beatles, this shop has a gallery where for £1 you can see original posters, autographs, film cells, and sketches by Stuart Sutcliffe. The store itself is practically a museum of Beatlemania, selling everything from reproduction gold singles to the usual posters, T-shirts, coffee mugs, and original rarities. A TV plays nonstop Beatles videos and films. If you have a Fab Four fan waiting at home, here is where to go to do your shopping.

RECREATION

London is more than museums and fine dining; it is a city of parks and plazas, walks and waterways, sports and sanctuaries for wildlife. Lovers of the outdoors and an active lifestyle will find no shortage of things to do here.

Considering that this is such a sprawling metropolis, there are a surprising number of wildlife sanctuaries and preserved natural areas within its boundaries. Some of the larger parks, such as Greenwich Park, have "wild" areas, parts that are not maintained and get overgrown with flowers and bushes. Herds of deer graze on the grass, while countless species of birds flutter about. There's even a preserved wetlands sanctuary. Leaving the city behind can be a great break from shopping and sightseeing.

For those who like to keep fit, the better hotels often have their own gyms or offer reduced rates for guests at the local gym, and there are some gyms that offer short-term memberships for visitors. If you prefer breaking a sweat outdoors, play football or throw a Frisbee around in one of the many open green areas in this vast city, or go horseback riding or roller-skating through Hyde Park. For sports fans, there are plenty of opportunities to see some great games and lots of places to play one of your own. Football (soccer in the United States) and cricket are the big draws in England, but just about every other game is well represented too, especially the rough-and-tumble sport of rugby.

But probably the best exercise to engage in here is a good long walk. Several tour companies will take you on themed walks to see any-

HIGHLIGHTS

Best Gym: The **YMCA** is still cheap, still clean, still well equipped with everything you need to stay fit. But please, please don't start singing the Village People song (page 204).

Best Bit of Nature in the Heart of London: A lush refuge for waterfowl sitting in the middle of an artificial lake, **St. James's Park** brings a glimpse of wildlife to the city. For some more wildlife, go clubbing in Soho (page 206).

Best Picnic Spot: Sit on Primrose Hill in **The Regent's Park,** the highest point in London, and enjoy sweeping views of the city while playing Spot the Landmark (page 208).

Best Escape from London While Still Being in It: Herds of deer graze amid trees and waving fields of wild grass in lush, almost wild **Richmond Park** (page 211).

Best Place to Soak Up the Atmosphere of Old London: Unspoiled **Bedford Square** features a verdant garden at its center. The sounds of the nearby cars will fade away and you can almost hear the creak of carriage wheels and the clop of hooves (page 212).

Best Way to See Hyde Park: Visit **Hyde Park Stables** and join in a centuries-old tradition by parading through Hyde Park on horseback, sneering at the commoners who have to slog along on foot (page 216).

LOOK FOR TO FIND RECOMMENDED ACTIVITIES.

thing from where Jack the Ripper ripped to where Johnson and Dickens wrote. And don't forget to strike out on your own by taking a relaxing stroll through one of London's many lush parks or historic squares to soak up the scenery and breathe in some (relatively) fresh air. There's no better way to catch the feeling of London than exploring on foot. Even more opportunities for some good hikes await outside of London (see the *Excursions* chapter) for those who want to get out into the English countryside, which even in bad weather is incredibly beautiful. Hikers, nature lovers, and bird-watchers should not miss a chance to see the country beyond the city limits.

But even if you don't get out of the city, London is truly an eclectic place and has more to offer than anyone can experience in one lifetime. Since you can't do it all, and you're on vacation anyway, don't wear yourself out trying to see everything. Take a day off to watch some cricket or see some rare birds in a wetlands preserve. It will put your trip in a whole new light.

Family Fun

AQUARIUMS AND ZOOS

At the beginning of the 20th century, the Thames was so polluted that it was all but dead. A vigorous cleanup campaign in recent years has helped dramatically, bringing fish back into the waters. It still needs some work, however, and it's so murky you can't see anything anyway, so head on over to London's only major aquarium to examine the creatures of the deep up close. Landlubbers can visit two zoos or go and see wild deer in many of the larger parks.

Maida Vale, Marylebone, and St. John's Wood — Map 8

LONDON ZOO

Outer Circle, The Regent's Park, 020/7722-3333, www.zsl.org/london-zoo

HOURS: Daily 10 A.M.-4 P.M. in winter, 10 A.M.-5:30 P.M. in summer

COST: Adults £14.50, seniors and students £12.70, children £11.50, children under 3 free

TUBE: Baker Street or Regent's Park

While it's a bit pricey, the London Zoo is a fun place to take the kids and see the usual lions and tigers and bears. The fuzzy little squirrel monkeys are amusing to watch, and the various educational programs are enlightening. The zoo is part of a network that's breeding endangered species in captivity, and London is home to many such projects, including one for the fearsome-looking Komodo dragons. All the animals are in areas built to reproduce their natural habitat. A shop and café are on-site.

South of the Thames — Map 12

LONDON AQUARIUM

County Hall, Riverside Building, Belvedere Rd. SE1, 020/7967-8000, www.londonaquarium.co.uk

HOURS: Daily 10 A.M.-6 P.M. (last admission 5 P.M.)

COST: Adults £11.75, students 15-18 and seniors £9.50, children 3-14 £8.25, family £36

TUBE: Westminster or Waterloo

An educational and fun stop along the South Bank Thames Walk just east of Westminster Bridge, the London Aquarium offers 50 displays of all sorts of life from the sea, displays that transport you from the bustle outside to the quiet submarine world that more than 80 percent of the globe calls home. The kids especially like the sharks and feeding time for the piranhas. The octopi and jellyfish are cool in a squishy sort of way. Reserve about two hours for your visit, because there's lots to see and watching the brilliantly colored tropical fish swim around can be very soothing.

Outlying Areas — Map 1

BATTERSEA PARK CHILDREN'S ZOO

Btwn. Albert Bridge Rd., Queenstown, and Battersea Park Rd., 020/7924-5826, www.batterseaparkzoo.co.uk

HOURS: Daily 10 A.M.-dusk (weekends only in winter)

COST: Adults £5.95, children 2-15 £4.50, family £18.50

BRITISH RAIL: Battersea Park

This small zoo is designed just for kids and offers a lot of fun activities for them, making a welcome diversion from the usual tourist sights. Part of it is a petting zoo, where they can get acquainted with farm animals. There are more exotic critters as well, such as emus and lemurs, although the population isn't as diverse or interesting as in the London Zoo. Various activities and special events take place constantly.

ENTERTAINMENT CENTERS

Video games, bowling, slot machines, and bars sit side by side in London's entertainment centers, which try to appeal to the whole family.

Covent Garden, West End, and Soho — Map 4

FUNLAND

Trocadero, Piccadilly Circus W1, 020/7395-1704, www.funland.co.uk

HOURS: Sun.-Thurs. 10 A.M.-midnight, Fri.-Sat. 10 A.M.-1 A.M.
TUBE: Piccadilly Circus
Flee the chaos of Piccadilly Circus into the chaos that is the Trocadero. As one of London's most popular shopping malls/tourist traps, it gets jammed with people rummaging through overpriced clothes and souvenirs. Flee farther! Head up the neon-lit escalators to Funland, an indoor entertainment center for the whole family. You can gamble at the fruit machines (a milder British version of the slot machine) or drink at the bar while your children can enjoy video games, bumper cars, and a large bowling alley. This is a great remedy for your child's museum fatigue.

South of the Thames — Map 12

NAMCO STATION COUNTY HALL
County Hall, Westminster Bridge Rd. SE1, 020/7967-1067, www.namcoexperience.com/countyhall
HOURS: Daily 10 A.M.-midnight
TUBE: Waterloo
In the basement of County Hall is an extensive entertainment center with video games, bumper cars, and six lanes of bowling. Fruit machines (a sort of slot machine) and a bar entertain the adults while the kids spend all their coins. Namco also hosts birthday parties and special events, so if your little guy or gal is turning a year older while you're in town, this is a good gift idea.

Health and Fitness

DAY SPAS

Important tip: You're on vacation; don't forget to relax. If sightseeing is making you bleary-eyed and footsore, unwind for an hour or a day at a spa. While spas are generally thought to be a woman's domain, many cater to guys too, and you can get everything from a facial and a plunge in a whirlpool bath to traditional Asian treatments and expert massages.

Mayfair and Piccadilly — Map 3

ELEMIS DAY SPA
2-3 Lancashire Ct. W1, 087/0410-4210, www.elemis.com
HOURS: Mon.-Thurs. 9 A.M.-9 P.M., Fri.-Sat. 9 A.M.-8 P.M., Sun. 10 A.M.-6 P.M.
TUBE: Bond Street or Oxford Circus
Hidden on a quiet little side street, Elemis provides a vacation from your vacation with full spa facilities for both men and women. It offers a whole menu of treatments from facials to foot massages and everything in between, including several exotic ones such as coconut-milk baths. The suites take you on a voyage around the world, with a Moroccan steam bath, a Balinese suite with a hot spice ritual, and a Thai suite for couples where you can get spa treatments and a full meal. The spa shop sells treatments you can take home with you.

Camden Town — Map 9

ACUMEDIC CENTRE
101-105 Camden High St. NW1, 020/7388-5783/6704, www.acumedic.com
HOURS: Shop: Mon.-Sat. 9 A.M.-6 P.M., Sun. 10 A.M.-5 P.M.; Clinic: Mon.-Sat. 10 A.M.-7 P.M., Sun. 10 A.M.-5 P.M.
TUBE: Camden or Mornington Crescent
A popular emporium offering natural health and beauty products as well as traditional treatments such as herbalism, massage, and acupuncture, Acumedic has been dispensing Chinese treatments since 1972. The store has an extensive stock, but it's a bit baffling to those unfamiliar with Chinese medicine. A good book section, however, can illuminate the uninitiated, and the music and tea sections are equally accessible. The clinic offers advice and treatments for skin, muscle, and joint complaints. It also has several treatments designed to relieve stress, such as acupressure massage to untie those tension knots in your back.

FITNESS CENTERS

Walking all day not enough exercise for you? Work up a sweat in a fitness center. Those listed here all have daily memberships ideally suited to the short-term visitor. Many of the better hotels have their own fitness centers or offer discounts to local ones, so if you must exercise every day, it might be cheaper to stay at one of them. London's many municipal centers are often crowded, but they're cheap; a couple of the better ones are listed here. If you're staying in London for a while, ask at your local municipal fitness center about the Wellness Card, which offers discounts to regular users.

FITNESS FIRST

Locations vary, 087/0898-8080, www.fitnessfirst.co.uk

HOURS: Vary by location

This international fitness chain has almost 50 branches in London, including a women's-only club at 81–84 Chalk Farm Road (020/7284-0004). While the facilities vary from center to center, they generally have a wide range of classes such as aerobics, yoga, and martial arts in addition to the usual workout room, games areas, and fitness instructors. You can get a free one-day guest membership by applying online. It offers various other types of membership, with a minimum of a three-month contract, so this is an option only if you are going to be staying in town awhile.

Covent Garden, West End, and Soho — Map 4

OASIS SPORTS CENTRE

32 Endell St. WC2, 020/7831-1804, www.camden.gov.uk/sport

HOURS: Mon.-Fri. 6:30 A.M.-10 P.M., Sat. -Sun. 6:30 A.M.-6 P.M.

TUBE: Tottenham Court Road or Covent Garden

This popular and centrally situated municipal fitness center gets pretty crowded, but that's because it offers great facilities in the center of town with no membership required. The big draws are the heated indoor and outdoor pools, but it also features a workout room, squash courts, and numerous classes such as judo and step aerobics to get you fit. If you're feeling lazy, try the sauna, steam room, or sun bed. Locker rooms and a café are on-site, and there's good access for those with disabilities. Charges vary depending on what you do, but the prices are quite reasonable.

Bloomsbury, Euston, and Holborn — Map 5

YMCA

112 Great Russell St. WC1, 020/7343-1700, www.ymcaclub.co.uk

HOURS: Mon.-Fri. 11 A.M.-7 P.M., Sat.-Sun. 11 A.M.-4 P.M.

TUBE: Tottenham Court Road

Fitness junkies staying in Bloomsbury won't have far to go to work up a sweat. It's the oldest YMCA in the world, founded in 1844 by Sir George Williams in response to the unhealthy and temptation-filled life of the city, and has a large weight room, lap pool, climbing wall, more than 100 classes every week from yoga to aerobics, and personal trainers on staff to help you get your body the way you want it to be. While memberships are sold on a yearly basis, you can buy a day pass for £10 and a weeklong membership for £45.

Notting Hill, Bayswater, and Paddington — Map 7

LAMBTON PLACE HOTEL

Lambton Pl. W11, 020/7229-2291, www.lambton.co.uk

HOURS: Mon-Fri. 6:15 A.M.-11 P.M., Sat.-Sun. 8:30 A.M.-9 P.M.

TUBE: Notting Hill Gate

For those with money and calories to burn, this exclusive fitness club is in a hotel but open to the general public. Each member gets his or her own fitness instructor and lots of personal attention. The workout room is small but fully equipped, and you'll find a climbing wall, free weights, pool, and a very soothing eucalyptus steam room. After your workout you can take advantage of the free Internet access or a wide range of spa treatments such as facials, deep massage, and acupuncture. The daily rate is £40, half price for guests of the nearby Portobello Hotel.

Camden Town — Map 9

TALACRE COMMUNITY FITNESS CENTRE

Dalby St. NW5, 020/7974-8765, www.camden.gov.uk/sport

HOURS: Mon.-Fri. 9 A.M.-10 P.M., Sat. 9 A.M.-6 P.M., Sun. 9 A.M.-8 P.M.

TUBE: Kentish Town

Opened in 2002, this is one of the newest municipal fitness centers in town and is well equipped with an outdoor football pitch, a large workout area, a gymnastics hall, and locker rooms. An indoor sports hall is used for a variety of games and has well-attended basketball and badminton clubs, and an outdoor paved area can be used in good weather. There's also Treetops, a fun multilevel soft play area for kids that is available for hire for children's parties. A snack bar and juice bar are on-site. Charges vary depending on what you do, but are generally low.

Parks and Scenic Squares

The crowded and winding streets of London can get to be too much sometimes, so it's a relief to know the city's beautiful parks are always close to hand. Many have wild areas filled with birds, waterfowl, and even deer. The English are masters at screening off parks with trees and other greenery so that you don't see that you're in the middle of the city. Kids will love the chance to run around on the grass, fly a kite, or have a picnic. Most parks offer deck chairs April–September, usually costing a couple of pounds an hour. Entry to all parks is free unless otherwise noted.

PARKS

Westminster, Victoria, and Pimlico — Map 2

COLLEGE AND LITTLE CLOISTER GARDEN

Westminster Abbey, Dean's Yard entrance SW1, 020/7654-4900, www.westminster-abbey.org

HOURS: May-Sept. Tues.-Thurs. 10 A.M.-6 P.M. and Oct.-Apr. Tues.-Thurs. 10 A.M.-4 P.M.

COST: Admission included with Abbey ticket (adults £10; seniors over 60, students, and children under 16 £6; family £22)

TUBE: Westminster

Visitors to Westminster Abbey often miss the two peaceful little gardens just next door. The Little Cloister was created in the 18th century and features a burbling fountain at its center. Through a 14th-century doorway you can catch a glimpse of the Chapel of St. Catherine, built in the mid-12th century. These picturesque ruins were once the infirmary chapel and many early bishops were consecrated there. It was also the scene of King Henry III's swearing to uphold the Magna Carta in 1253. Farther on is the more spacious College Garden, a sanctuary of peace and quiet in the heart of London that was started as a garden for medicinal herbs

© MOIRA ALLEN

Bright floral displays are one of the many attractions of St. James's Park.

in the 11th century. Sit on a bench and admire the floral displays, and snap a great photo of Parliament towering above the garden wall.

ST. JAMES'S PARK

The Mall, Birdcage Walk, and Horse Guards Rd. SW1, 020/7930-1793 or 020/7298-2000, www.royalparks.gov.uk

HOURS: Daily 5 A.M.-midnight

TUBE: St. James's Park

A lovely park between the attractions of Trafalgar Square and Buckingham Palace, this lush patch of greenery makes for a relieving breath of fresh air while you go from one to the other. Thick foliage and a pond full of ducks, swans, and more than a dozen other species of birds make you feel as if you've stepped out of London. It's great for romantic strolls in the evening. What it lacks in size (only 23 hectares/58 acres), it makes up in beauty.

Mayfair and Piccadilly — Map 3

GREEN PARK

Wellington Arch, Piccadilly, and Constitution Hill W1, 020/7930-1793 OR 020/7298-2000, www.royalparks.gov.uk

HOURS: Daily 9 A.M.-8 P.M. in summer, 10 A.M.-4 P.M. in winter

TUBE: Green Park

The 16-hectare (40-acre) patch of land now called Green Park has been a magnet for people wanting to get away from the crowding, noise, and pollution of the city for more than 400 years. It's set between St. James's Park and Hyde Park just north of Buckingham Palace, making it the middle section of a relaxing, although long, park walk. It's mostly open, with long lines of tree-lined walkways, and is a good place for a picnic. A beautiful monument/fountain to Canadian war dead stands at the south end near the palace.

Covent Garden, West End, and Soho — Map 4

VICTORIA EMBANKMENT GARDENS

Savoy Pl. and Victoria Embankment WC2, 020/7641-5264, www.westminster.gov.uk

HOURS: Daily 7:30 A.M.-9:30 P.M.

TUBE: Charing Cross

This strip of greenery doesn't quite block all the noise and sight of the river road, but it's the closest thing to quiet relief in this part of town. It was originally suggested by Sir Christopher Wren when he was rebuilding London in 1666, but work didn't start until 1864. The 15 hectares (37 acres) are filled with flowers and greenery in the warm season, and numerous benches offer relief for office workers who want to eat lunch outside their cubicles. Statues to various worthies adorn the park, including an unusual one to the Imperial Camel Corps. A bandstand occasionally hosts concerts; check the website for details.

Chelsea, Kensington and Knightsbridge — Map 6

CHELSEA PHYSIC GARDEN

66 Royal Hospital Walk SW3, 020/7352-5646, www.chelseaphysicgarden.co.uk

HOURS: Wed. noon-5 P.M., Sun. noon-6 P.M. Apr.-Oct. Tues. and Thurs. noon-5 P.M. July 18-Sept. 7

COST: adults £6.50, students and children 5-15 £3.50, children under 5 free

TUBE: Sloane Square

This 1.6-hectare (4 acres) garden is an oasis of calm and natural beauty in the center of Chelsea. It was founded by the Royal Society of Apothecaries in 1673 for training apprentices in the knowledge of healing herbs. Guides offer free tours explaining the garden's history and the uses of the various plants. You'll see a pleasant lily pond and a greenhouse, as well as some wonderful floral displays in season. A café and a gift shop are on-site.

HOLLAND PARK

Btwn. Holland Walk and Abbotsbury Rd. W8, 020/7602-2226, www.rbkc.gov.uk

HOURS: 7:30 A.M.-dusk

TUBE: Holland Park

One of the more pleasant parks in London is this 21-hectare (54-acre) gem situated in the heart of an affluent neighborhood. Paved and unpaved paths wind their way through the trees, almost giving the impression that you're in the countryside. More than 30 species of birds are regularly seen here, making it one of the best places to go bird-watching in the city. The Kyoto Gardens, a Japanese-style sanctuary with a waterfall, is one of the more pleasant places to sit for awhile, but there are plenty of other secluded spots. The park also features a playground, six tennis courts, two squash courts, a football pitch, and an opera house (for information on tennis and opera, see the appropriate listings).

HYDE PARK AND SPEAKERS' CORNER

Park Ln. and Knightsbridge W2, 020/7298-2100 or 020/7298-2000, www.royalparks.gov.uk

HOURS: Daily 5 A.M.-midnight

TUBE: Hyde Park

This 142-hectare (350-acre) stretch of green is the biggest of the three royal parks cutting through the center of the city. What it lacks in wild patches it makes up in size and a range of activities. Here you can get the farthest away from the blare of traffic and enjoy the water at The Serpentine, an artificial lake. You'll find several places to eat or have a coffee by the water, and you can also hire boats. Horse rides are available through Hyde Park Stables (see *Sports* in this chapter). This park is popular with Londoners who want to get out and throw a Frisbee or kick a football, and cultural activities take place here too. To the west is Kensington Palace, and to the northeast is the famous Speaker's Corner, where pontificators hold forth on whatever strikes their fancy.

SPEAKERS' CORNER: AN INTERACTIVE LONDON TRADITION

In the northeast corner of Hyde Park is a space where anyone who has something to say can get up and start holding forth on his or her subject of choice. On any given day you may see Socialists, conspiracy theorists, espousers of obscure religious beliefs, and a good many people who just have something to gripe about, all standing on boxes or other makeshift platforms trying to make themselves heard. Because the English are generally quick of wit, the speeches can be quite amusing and, occasionally, edifying.

The space was given over to public speaking in 1872, when the Royal Parks and Gardens Act made it the park's decision whether to allow public meetings. This was done after years of agitating by members of the working class, who had only recently gotten the vote and demanded that they be guaranteed freedom of speech. They had been meeting at Hyde Park on a semi-regular basis, but they wanted their presence to be legalized so they wouldn't have to fear the police.

Most major parks in London have a speakers' corner, but Hyde Park is the most famous because it has been the scene of so many major events. Marx and Lenin used to come here, and in 2003 it was the meeting place for the largest demonstration in British history, when more than one million people called for an end to the war in Iraq. Fearing the ramifications of such a huge gathering, the park managers tried to forbid the protest, but the right to gather in Speakers' Corner was too ingrained. Fiery editorials appeared in the press and the park had to let the gathering happen.

While freedom of speech in Speaker's Corner is greatly respected, that doesn't mean the speakers are. Speakers are often heckled, especially by regulars – generally little old men with nothing better to do and who think of the event as a sort of game. Woe betide the speaker who gets his facts mixed up or doesn't have a bulletproof defense for his point of view. The whole interchange is lots of fun and a good way to learn about the various factions in British society. Be careful with trying out heckling yourself, though. Punters who aren't up on the issues get verbally torn to shreds within a matter of seconds, to the general derision of the assembled masses.

You are, of course, perfectly welcome to stand up and say something yourself. I've never done this, nor seen any tourist who had sufficient guts, but it could be an interesting experiment. If you do decide to give it a try, drop me a line and I'll come along and heckle you.

Maida Vale, Marylebone, and St. John's Wood — Map 8

THE REGENT'S PARK

North of Marylebone Rd. NW1, 017/1486-7905 or 020/7298-2000, www.royalparks.org.uk

HOURS: Daily dawn-dusk

TUBE: Baker Street or Regent's Park

Designed in 1811 by the architect John Nash for his patron the Prince Regent, this is one of the largest and most popular of London's parks. On a nice summer weekend hundreds of people will be here, but the 166 hectares (410 acres) of grass, sports fields, and gardens never feel crowded. Queen Mary's Gardens in the Inner Circle are outstandingly beautiful with 30,000 roses. Avid gardeners can quiz each other about the 400 varieties grown here, and there are acres upon acres of other flowers, trees, and bushes to keep you busy too. Babbling fountains and even an artificial waterfall provide soothing background noise. Head to the north end of the park and climb Primrose Hill for a panoramic view of London. If you want to have a picnic while you're in town, wait for a nice day and come here. Several cafés and ice-cream stands are in the park in case you forget to pack a lunch.

© SEAN MCLACHLAN

The many fountains at The Regent's Park offer cool sanctuary on a hot day.

The City — Map 10

POSTMAN'S PARK AT ST. BOTOLPH-WITHOUT-ALDERSGATE

Aldersgate St. EC1, 020/7283-2231, www.stbotolphsaldersgate.org.uk

TUBE: Barbican

This church was finished in 1791 upon much older foundations, and while it lacks the baroque grace of the many Wren churches, it more than makes up for it with its peaceful garden, called Postman's Park, containing flowers, grass, park benches, even a fountain with a koi pond. One interesting feature is the Watts Memorial, erected in 1900 by a parishioner who wanted to create a monument to those who had given their lives while trying to save others. Each is given a plaque briefly telling the person's story, and the accumulated effect is moving.

Islington — Map 11

NEW RIVER WALK

Junction of Canonbury Rd. and Canonbury Grove to St. Paul's Rd. N1, 020/7527-4953/4971

HOURS: Mon.-Fri. 8 A.M.-dusk, Sat. 9 A.M.-dusk, Sun. 10 A.M.-dusk

TUBE: Highbury and Islington

The "New River" flowing through the area is actually an aqueduct built in 1613 to bring drinking water from Hertfordshire south into the burgeoning city of London. This impressive feat of early engineering ran 38 miles and still acts as one of the city's water supplies. About half a mile has survived being paved over and has been lined with trees and flowering bushes to make a park. The walk is easy (stroller and wheelchair friendly) and makes for a shady and quiet refuge. Little waterfalls and park benches provide added relaxation. While it's not as grandiose as the famous parks farther

© SEAN MCLACHLAN

The plaques at Postman's Park honor those who died while saving others.

south, it's as good as it gets in a built-up area such as Islington.

Outlying Areas Map 1

BATTERSEA PARK

Albert Bridge Rd., Queenstown, and Battersea Park Rd., 020/8871-7530, www.wandsworth.gov.uk/sport

HOURS: Daily 8 A.M.–dusk

BRITISH RAIL: Battersea Park

If you get ambitious and find yourself walking this far west on the Thames Walk, you've earned a rest in one of London's largest and most pleasant parks. Built in 1853, it was the site of the first match under the Football Association rules 10 years later. A boating lake with swans and other waterfowl cavorting on lush little islands offers pleasant diversion with paddleboats and rowboats. Adults pay £3 for half an hour or £4.50 for an hour, while children 14 and younger pay £1.50 for half an hour and £2.50 for an hour. Rowing lessons are available. Kids can also hire a recumbent tricycle at £5 an hour to take a spin through the park's many meandering paths, which make their way through open sports areas and little forests. Facing the river is a giant Chinese peace pagoda with four golden Buddhas. The only off-note is the looming stacks of the defunct Battersea Power Station, which are in the process of being transformed into flats, a shopping area and, on top of one of the stacks, a one-table restaurant.

GREENWICH PARK

Greenwich, 020/8858-2608, www.royalparks.gov.uk

HOURS: Daily dawn–dusk

DOCKLANDS LIGHT RAIL: Cutty Sark

This 74-hectare (183-acre) park set just south of most of the attractions of Greenwich makes for a perfect place to relax after sightseeing. In fact, you'll probably pass through it anyway because the Royal Observatory is on a hill right at its center. From there, and from other hills in the park, you can get a magnificent view of the Thames, the Millennium Dome, and distant landmarks in the center of town

© SEAN MCLACHLAN

The Royal Observatory stands on the meridian line atop a hill in Greenwich Park.

such as the BT Tower and Centrepoint. You'll find a sizable playground, a small boating lake for rowboats and paddleboats (020/7262-1330, 10:30 A.M.–5 P.M. Easter–Oct., adults £2.50, children £1.50 for 20 minutes), but the best part is the wild areas in the northern edge, where a herd of fallow and red deer graze on wild grass.

HAMPSTEAD HEATH

North End Way and Highgate NW3, 020/8348-9908, www.cityoflondon.gov.uk/openspaces

HOURS: Daily dawn–dusk

TUBE: Hampstead or Belsize Park

Of all of London's open areas, the 324 hecatres (800 acres) of this wild heath have the most rural feel. The land was actually considered waste in earlier times, because it was formed by a glacier that left a sandy and gravelly lump that was no good for growing anything, and it was thus left alone in a near-pristine natural state. The park's ponds are one of the sources for the Fleet River, which flows underneath The City. Also on the grounds is Kenwood House, a 17th-century mansion with concerts in the gardens. You can hear them quite well for free by sitting outside the fence. Go up Parliament Hill to get a commanding view of the London skyline. Unfortunately, your hike starts with the long walk from the Tube.

KEW GARDENS AND ROYAL BOTANIC GARDENS

Kew Gardens, Richmond TW9 020/8332-5655, www.kew.org

HOURS: Mon.–Fri. 9:30 A.M.–6 P.M., Sat.–Sun. 9:30 A.M.–7 P.M. Apr.–Aug. (closes progressively earlier in fall and winter)

COST: Adults £9.50, seniors and students £6.50, children under 17 free

TUBE: Kew Gardens

Founded in 1759, this is one of London's most popular getaway spots, thanks to the breathtaking array of plants on display here. Of the many great botanical gardens of Europe (something the Europeans have been doing very well

© VISITLONDON.COM

Sundial in Kew Gardens

for centuries) this is by far the best. The rose gardens are as good as in The Regent's Park, and the orderly rows of other flowers and plants from around the world make for a relaxing and interesting stroll. This is not just a pleasure garden, but an important research and educational center. Check the website to see what's happening in the ongoing calendar of events. Couple this with a visit to the nearby Kew Palace and Queen Charlotte's Cottage, and you have a full day out.

LONDON WETLAND CENTRE

Queen Elizabeth's Walk SW13, 020/8409-4400, www.wwt.org.uk/visit/wetlandcentre/

HOURS: Daily 9:30 A.M.-6 P.M., until 5 P.M. in winter

COST: Adults £7.50, seniors and students £6, children £4

BRITISH RAIL: Barnes

Here's something you wouldn't expect so close to the city: 43 hectares (108 acres) of thriving wetlands with large populations of fish and waterfowl. The education center is informative and the paths run through beautiful scenery, but the most remarkable thing about this lush ecological sanctuary is that it didn't exist until 2000. This is all reclaimed industrial riverfront, carefully managed into a real wetland that attracts migratory birds from all over Europe. The world could use a few thousand more of these projects.

Take a train from Waterloo, Clapham Junction, or Richmond to Barnes. The Centre is a 10-minute walk from the station. Several buses leave from the station to the park, bearing the destination Richmond.

RICHMOND PARK

Petersham Rd. and Kingstone Hill TW10, 020/8948-3209 or 020/7298-2000, www.royalparks.org.uk

HOURS: Summer 7 A.M.-dusk, winter 7:30 A.M.-dusk

TUBE: Richmond

Richmond Park is more than 1,000 hectares (about 2,500 acres) of hills, meadows, woodland gardens, and ponds. Swans, mallards, pike, 650 roaming deer, cycle and jogging paths, and ancient oaks all combine to make it my favorite park in London. If you don't have the time to go on a country hike (see the *Excursions* chapter) but you still want to get away from it all, come here. It has been a reserved area since medieval times and is now an official National Nature Reserve. While much of it makes you feel as if you're out in the sticks, you'll find places to eat, a playground, and golf.

From Richmond Station it is a 1.5-km (1 mile) walk to the park, or you can take one of the many Richmond-marked buses from the station.

SCENIC SQUARES

Starting in the 18th century, builders began to make whole neighborhoods centered around squares. Many of these exist today with their architecture intact, providing a glimpse of Georgian or Victorian London. Sit on a bench, listen to a burbling fountain or admire an old building, and watch the world go by.

Covent Garden, West End, and Soho Map 4

COVENT GARDEN

Covent Garden Market and the Piazza to Long Acre, Floral St. and Neal St. WC2, 020/7839-3220, www.coventgarden.uk.com

HOURS: Daily 9 A.M.-8 P.M.

TUBE: Covent Garden

Covent Garden gets its name from "Convent Garden," referring to a time in the Middle Ages when it was one of the gardens owned by Westminster Abbey. After the dissolution of church property, Henry VIII gave it to the Earl of Bedford, and subsequent earls maintained it as a garden until it was turned into a piazza in the 1630s by Inigo Jones. It remains a center for shopping and eating for crowds of tourists, but it's most fun as a place to see street entertainers. High-wire acts, jugglers, and comedians vie for your attention. There's always something going on, and plenty of benches and curbs to sit on and watch the action. Though shop hours can vary, street entertainers stay late, especially on weekends.

SOHO SQUARE

SW of Oxford St. and Charing Cross Rd. W1, 020/7641-5264

HOURS: Daily 10 A.M.-dusk

TUBE: Tottenham Court Road

This little park makes for a nice getaway from the hectic crowds in the nearby Charing Cross shopping district. Grab a takeaway from one of the nearby restaurants or sandwich bars and have your lunch amid trees, grass, and flowers. The space isn't terribly large and it can be crowded at times, but it's much quieter than the surrounding area and has plenty of park benches. This is one of the older squares in town, having been laid out in the 1680s, and a statue to Charles II, sculpted by Caius Gabriel Cibber in 1681, still stands near the center.

Bloomsbury, Euston, and Holborn Map 5

BEDFORD SQUARE

Gower St. and Tottenham Court Rd. WC1

HOURS: Open 24 hours

COST: Free admission

TUBE: Tottenham Court Road or Russell Square

Soak up the atmosphere of Georgian London in this unspoiled 18th-century square. On all sides stand Georgian arcades spotted with blue signs commemorating the many famous people who have lived here. To name a few, on the east side at number 6 lived Lord Eldon (1751–1838), who served as lord chancellor, and at number 41 on the south side lived Sir Anthony Hope Hawkins (1863–1933), the famous author who wrote as "Anthony Hope." A beautiful garden in the center bursts with color in the spring, but it's open only to residents. Still, the wrought-iron fence and flowers make a nice backdrop to this picturesque square.

LINCOLN'S INN FIELDS

New, Little, and Great Turnstile On High Holborn WC2, 020/7974-1693, www.camden.gov.uk/parks

HOURS: Daily 7:30 A.M.-dusk

TUBE: Holborn

Lincoln's Inn Fields has been a meeting place for Londoners since Inigo Jones designed it in the 17th century and it is the largest of London's city squares. It wasn't always friends meeting up, though—for many years it was a popular dueling spot. Now the only duels going on are at the public tennis courts. To rent one of the three tarmac courts, call 077/1751-6371 or go to the booth next to the courts 10 minutes before or after the hour. It costs £6.90 for adults, £2.60 for seniors and under 16s. There's plenty of grass to sit on, too, if all you want to do is eat some lunch and relax.

RUSSELL SQUARE

Russell Sq. (north of the British Museum) WC1, 020/7974-1693, www.camden.gov.uk/parks

HOURS: Daily 7 A.M.-10 P.M.

TUBE: Russell Square

This broad square is surrounded by a mixture of Georgian, Victorian, and modern buildings, encompassing almost the entire architectural history of the city. All that is lacking is a Tudor frame house and a section of the Roman wall to create a complete panorama of London history. The best view is on the east side, where the

SHHH... PLACES FOR QUIET CONTEMPLATION

London is a hectic place, so sometimes you just need some peace and quiet. Luckily, there are several places you can get away from it all and still enjoy the atmosphere of this wonderful city. Here are a few of them. Wander around enough and you'll find more on your own.

Parts of the Thames Walk: While the Thames Walk can get a little crowded on weekends and during the peak tourist season, it's long enough that you can get away from the crowds. One of the main attractions of the Thames is that it is the largest open space you will see in central London. After the crush of Tottenham Court Road or Piccadilly Circus, it's a profound relief to bring a lunch, sit down on a bench, and watch the boats go by as the sunlight plays on the water.

The British Museum Reading Room: Under a towering gilt dome in the Great Court of the British Museum is a circular reading room that has attracted scholars for generations. You can sit and read the books, mostly on art and archaeology, or write quietly and enjoy the fact that many other writers have been here before you.

Churches: London is filled with historic, beautiful churches, and everyone is welcome to sit for a while and enjoy the peaceful atmosphere. Nobody will bother you or expect you to be praying. Professionals have been known to go to churches on their lunch breaks and do *sudoku* puzzles. You can, of course, come to worship, and with the Anglican Church being so welcoming, you don't even have to be Anglican (or straight) to join in the services.

Parks: Some parks are more peaceful than others, but they all offer respite from the chaos that is London. Richmond Park or The Regent's Park are good choices for their wide-open spaces. Hyde Park is less peaceful but more central. St. James's is a favorite for its beautiful lake alive with waterfowl, which turns into a magical sight in the golden light of evening.

Temple Yard and Gardens: The most peaceful place is, strangely, right in the middle of The City. The area around the old Templar church is owned by barristers, and they have a series of peaceful yards and gardens with shady trees, lush grass, sparkling fountains, and convenient benches. It never seems to be terribly busy, and everyone maintains a hushed silence, as if in unconscious respect of the one peaceful spot in the heart of the financial district.

Oh, and one more tip, although it's more of a request. Please keep these places *peaceful*. There's a severe shortage of quiet spots in London, so come and be still.

stately Hotel Russell raises its redbrick Victorian spires, making for a nice background to a photo. Lots of grass, flower beds, park benches, trees, and a playful fountain at the center make it a nice place to relax after visiting the area's attractions. Bring a picnic or go to the café on the northeast corner. The square was finished in 1814 and the paths still trace the outlines of the original garden.

TAVISTOCK SQUARE

Tavistock Sq. off Woburn Pl. WC1, 020/7974-1693, www.camden.gov.uk/parks

HOURS: Daily dawn-dusk

TUBE: Tottenham Court Road or Russell Square

Like Bedford Square, this is another well-preserved Georgian square filled with history. The shady trees and Georgian row houses encircling it offer a pleasant view. A statue of Gandhi stands in the center. While Gandhi helped the British lose their biggest and richest colony, even at the time many in the British government admired him. Nearby is a memorial to the victims of Hiroshima. Dickens used to live at Tavistock House on the east side and come here to escape his writing, but that building has been replaced. At number 33 on the west side lived Ali Mohammed Abbas (1922–1979), one of the founders of Pakistan. An evening stroll through this and Bedford and Russell squares, especially as the sun is setting and turning the pale gray Georgian bricks to gold, will evoke a London long passed.

Walking Tours

The best way to see London is to get out and walk, and it really helps to bring a knowledgeable guide along. Luckily, guided walking tours tend to be modestly priced, with only a couple of hours of walking and the chance to end the tour at a pub or restaurant, so anyone in reasonable shape will be able to do them. One thing to look for is a qualified guide accredited by the London Blue Badge or City of London Guide schemes. All of the businesses below hire such guides or ones with academic qualifications.

ANGEL WEEKEND WALKS

Angel, Highbury, and Islington Tube Stations N1, 020/7226-8333, www.angelwalks.co.uk

COST: Adults £5, seniors, students, and children £4

Learn all about the historic Borough of Islington from Peter Powell, an actor and local historian who's been leading walks since 1985. Dickens, Orwell, Paine, and Marx all lived in the borough, and Powell has no end of stories about them. Powell used to be on the Islington council and knows the place inside and out, so if you are interested in learning about the historical and literary legacy of this underrated borough, his is the walk to pick.

BISHOPSGATE INSTITUTE

230 Bishopsgate EC2, 020/7932-9200, www.bishopsgate.org.uk

COST: Prices vary

TUBE: Liverpool Street

This respected arts institute offers a few guided walks every season, usually concentrating on music, theater, and film. The guides are very knowledgeable and the institute also offers talks. Some are one-off tours, while others are longer courses with regular walks during the course of several weeks. Long-term visitors should try the latter, as the courses are very informative and are a nice opportunity to meet Londoners with similar interests.

CULTURAL HERITAGE RESOURCES

Locations vary, 020/8806-4325, www.chr.org.uk/walks.htm

COST: Prices vary

CHR is a heritage and museum management company and has been organizing cultural, historical, and literary walks since the 1970s. The guides really know their stuff, being professional archaeologists, historians, or museum curators. Their most popular is a theaterland walk that takes you around Covent Garden and the West End and explains how what used to be pasture and gardens became one of the foremost theater venues in the world. They also occasionally run some very informative architectural walks. Because this is a nonprofit, these are some of the cheapest tours you'll find.

LONDON HORROR TOURS

Locations vary, 077/7969-1026, www.londonhorrortours.co.uk

COST: £6 per person

The slightly spooky John Pope-de-Locksley will lead you through the bloody back streets of London to uncover murders, hauntings, and even vampires. He is one of the many Rippologists who is convinced he knows who Jack the Ripper was, and he'll tell you all about his theories while you're on the trail of London's most famous serial killer. The vampire tour is also interesting, uncovering rumors of a vampire living in Highgate Cemetery and the facts behind local Satanists.

THE ORIGINAL LONDON WALKS

Locations vary, 020/7624-3978 or 020/7794-1764, www.walks.com

COST: Adults £6, seniors and students £5, children under 15 free if accompanied by parent

Although the big tour companies tend to just shuttle vast hordes of people about, one major tour company *does* give you an in-depth, personalized insight to the city, offering a dizzying array of themed tours conducted by very qualified guides. The theater tours, for example, are led by actors and actresses from the

London stage, while the historical walks are done by historians, not just some bloke who's read a couple of books. Tours have set meeting times and spots and you don't have to book—just show up on time. Visit the website or look for the ubiquitous white pamphlets.

Sports

BOATING

You're in the middle of the city, but you can still get out onto the water. Not only are there are a wealth of options for exploring the Thames, but the inland waterways and lakes also beckon. If it's a bright day, be sure to put on some sunscreen; the water reflects the light and you'll get burned more quickly than you think. Londoners often forget this and end up looking like lobsters.

Maida Vale, Marylebone, and St. John's Wood — Map 8

THE BOAT HOUSE AT THE REGENT'S PARK

The Boating Lake, Hanover Gate, The Regent's Park NWI, 017/1486-7905, www.royalparks.org.uk

HOURS: Daily 10:30 A.M.-5 P.M., weather permitting

TUBE: Baker Street or Regent's Park

Cutting through the southern part of The Regent's Park is a beautiful boating lake complete with lush islands inhabited by swans and other waterfowl. Getting out onto the water is relaxing and romantic. You can hire rowboats for an hour for adult £6.30 and child £4.25, or for a half hour for adult £4.75 and child £3.25. A family ticket, for up to two adults and three kids, is £20 per hour—a small discount applies before noon. Next to the lake is a shallow kid's paddle lake where the little guys and girls can have their very own yellow Pedalo for £3 for 20 minutes.

Camden Town — Map 9

NARROWBOAT TO LITTLE VENICE

London Waterbus Company, 58 Camden Lock Pl. off Chalk Farm Rd. NW1, 020/7482-2660, www.londonwaterbus.com

HOURS: Vary by tour

TUBE: Camden Lock

A relaxing cruise on a historic riverboat along the canals of Camden may be just the thing after wearing out your feet shopping. The canals date to the 19th century and were essential for transporting goods in the days before trucks. The company offers several tours, including one that skirts the open green area of The Regent's Park, another going between the arty Camden Lock district and Little Venice, and several more options. You can also take a full-day trip starting at Camden Lock at 9:30 A.M. and getting back at 6 P.M. Fares depend on which trip you take, but they are quite reasonable.

CLIMBING

This is the big city, so there aren't any real rock routes to clamber up, but most large gyms have climbing walls. Below is the best center devoted to climbing. If you want real rock, head on up to Scotland.

Outlying Areas — Map 1

CASTLE CLIMBING CENTRE

Green Lanes N4, 020/8211-7000, www.castle-climbing.com

HOURS: Mon.-Fri. 2-10 P.M., Sat.-Sun. 10 A.M.-7 P.M.

TUBE: Manor House or Finsbury Park

Indoor climbing can't beat getting out onto natural rock, but since you aren't going to get to do that here in the big city, this is your best chance to be on the ropes. It has several different walls to challenge climbers of all abilities and experienced staff to help out if needed. To be allowed to climb on your own, you must pass a basic proficiency test, which will be no problem for anyone with a bit of experience. Kids can climb with a registered adult or join the Geckos, a climbing school just for them, which you must book by calling 020/8806-5914. A café and shop are on-site.

GOLF

London isn't exactly the greatest golfing destination around, the game actually having been invented in Scotland, but you can find a couple of greens if you want to putt your vacation away. Unfortunately, London's congestion means you'll have to head out of the center to do so. The courses listed here are open to the general public. The several other private clubs do not offer temporary memberships to visitors.

Outlying Areas — Map 1

CENTRAL LONDON GOLF CENTRE

Burntwood Ln. SW17, 020/8871-2468, www.clgc.co.uk

HOURS: Course: Daily dawn-dusk; Driving Range: Mon.-Thurs. 9 A.M.-10 P.M., Fri.-Sun. 9 A.M.-8 P.M.

COST: 9 Holes, weekdays £11, weekends £13.50; 18 Holes weekdays £17, weekends £27, driving range £5.25

TUBE: Balham

This popular golf center features a nine-hole course, driving range, shop, and clubhouse and is open to everyone on a pay-and-play basis. It offers classes and one-on-one tuition if you want to improve your game and numerous special events and competition if you want to meet other golfers. There are special classes and events for kids too. Clubs and trolleys are available for hire. While you can just show up anytime, booking is essential for weekends and bank holidays.

THE PRINCE'S AND DUKE'S GOLF COURSES AT RICHMOND PARK

Roehampton Gate at Richmond Park btwn. Petersham Rd. and Kingstone Hill, 020/8876-1795, www.richmondparkgolf.co.uk

HOURS: Daily dawn-dusk

COST: Weekdays £19, weekends £23, £9 last three hours of daylight

TUBE: Richmond

Two 18-hole golf courses and a driving range in the midst of London's most beautiful park—what more could you ask for? Well, it features a large pro shop, café, and clubroom too. Please note that the park was looking for a new management company for the golf courses, so things might change before you go there. Call ahead for more information. "Smart casual" dress and golf shoes are required. Shoes, clubs, and buggies are available for hire.

From Richmond Station it is a 1.5-km (1 mile) walk to the park, or you can take one of the many Richmond-marked buses from the station.

HORSEBACK RIDING

You'll not find many places to ride in the city, but you have the choice of central and convenient or outlying and beautiful. There's no better way to see the land than from the back of a horse. In the countryside, beware of fox hunters and the people who oppose them. They've been having bitter fights for years now and it's a good time to be a neutral tourist.

Notting Hill, Bayswater, and Paddington — Map 7

HYDE PARK STABLES

63 Bathurst Mews W2, 020/7723-2813, www.hydeparkstables.com

HOURS: Mon.-Fri. 7:15 A.M.-5 P.M., Sat.-Sun. 9 A.M.-5 P.M.

COST: £45 per hour

TUBE: Lancaster Gate

Enjoy Hyde Park's five miles of bridleways atop a horse or pony. Lords and ladies used to trot along the unfortunately named Rotten Row (it's cleaner than in previous centuries) while socializing and gossiping, and a group outing on a fine day can make for a memorable experience. Don't worry if you've never ridden before; the horses are very docile and you'll be provided a quick lesson. The stable also offers more serious one-on-one lessons if you want to improve your style.

Outlying Areas — Map 1

WIMBLEDON VILLAGE STABLES

24 A/B High St. Wimbledon SW19, 020/8946-8579, www.wvstables.com

HOURS: Office open Mon.-Fri. 9 A.M.-5 P.M.

COST: Weekdays: £38 for one-hour lesson/ride, £70 for two-hour ride; Weekends: £43 for one-hour lesson/ride

TUBE: Wimbledon

While this is mostly a members-only stable, it does have some facilities for riding on weekdays for nonmembers, and it's good that it does. It's just next to the large, grassy Wimbledon Common, which connects to the semiwilderness of Richmond Park and Ham Common to provide excellent countryside to explore, so even though it's a bit of a hike from the center, it will be well worth it. Lessons are available, and the staff will assess your riding ability before you set out.

PAINTBALL

Guns are rare in England, which has led to a much lower murder rate than in the United States (fancy that!) but if you really feel like shooting someone, don some camo and get into a paintball match.

Islington Map 11

URBAN PAINTBALL GAMES

7 Torrens St. EC1, 020/7837-6419, www.urbanpaintballgames.com

HOURS: Mon.-Fri. 6-10:30 P.M., Sat. 11 A.M.-4 P.M., 5-9 P.M., Sun. 3-7:30 P.M.

COST: Prices vary

TUBE: Angel

A converted warehouse is host to a popular dance club at night, but by day it is transformed into a multilevel urban jungle with lots of hidey holes to spring out from and blast your friends and enemies. The place really does a good job at creating a complex (and occasionally confusing) combat space. Think Mad Max in the city. There's a bar on-site, but that will just lower your level of combat readiness and make it easier for your friends to kill you. Protective clothing, headgear, and weapons are provided. You must be over 16 to play.

SKATING

Both roller- and ice-skating are widely popular in London. If you have your skates with you, head on over to one of the larger parks to have a good time. Hyde Park is the most popular, with people of all ages swooping along the paths. A good website is www.londonskaters.com, run by an informal group of folks who share the same sense of fun. Their website is full of information for skaters and will give you some valuable contacts for get-togethers, lessons, shops, places to hire skates, and product reviews.

Mayfair and Piccadilly Map 3

LONDON SKATE

Serpentine Rd. near Bandstand, Hyde Park W1, 020/7870-5934, www.londonskate.com

HOURS: Wed., starting time generally 8 P.M.

COST: Free admission

TUBE: Hyde Park Corner

This city-sponsored mass skate takes place every Wednesday in Hyde Park, attracting 200–800 people. Marshals are on hand to keep everything orderly and safe and to direct traffic. From Hyde Park to route heads out to various routes across London. It's lots of fun and a unique way to see the sights, and it is a very friendly and social event. Kids welcome. You must provide your own skates.

Covent Garden, West End, and Soho Map 4

SOMERSET HOUSE

The Strand and Waterloo Bridge WC2, 020/7848-2589, www.somerset-house.org.uk

HOURS: Daily 10 A.M.-10 P.M.

COST: Admission (including skate hire) adults £8, children £6

TUBE: Temple or Covent Garden

In winter the courtyard of beautiful Somerset House becomes a large and popular ice rink. This is a perfect way to keep the kids occupied while you go see the three art museums inside the house, or you can all skip the museums and enjoy the ice instead.

The City Map 10

BROADGATE ICE RINK

Broadgate Centre, Eldon St. EC2, 020/7505-4608, www.broadgateice.co.uk

HOURS: Mon.-Thurs. noon-2:30 P.M., 3:30-5:30 P.M., Fri. noon-2:30 P.M., 3:30-6 P.M., 7-9 P.M., Sat.-Sun. 11 A.M.-1 P.M., 2-4 P.M., 5-7 P.M.

COST: Adults £6, children £4

TUBE: Liverpool Street

This little outdoor ice rink just a short walk from Liverpool Street Station is perfect for a quick break from sightseeing. While it's not terribly big, it is very popular with families and it gives your kids a chance to meet British kids. You can hire skates for adults £2 and children £1. The rink is open October–early April only.

SWIMMING

While the weather isn't always conducive to outdoor swimming, the English have circumvented that by building numerous indoor pools in their capital city. Of course, the nicer hotels have pools too, so if you must have a dip on your trip, you can save time by getting a hotel with a pool. If you want to do laps in an Olympic-size pool, you'll have to go to one of the fitness centers.

Chelsea, Kensington, and Knightsbridge — Map 6

THE SERPENTINE LIDO AND PADDLING POOL, HYDE PARK

South end of the Serpentine, Hyde Park W2, 020/7706-3422, www.royalparks.org.uk

HOURS: Daily dawn-dusk mid-June-mid-Sept.

COST: Adults £3.50, children £0.80

TUBE: Hyde Park Corner

Part of the artificial waterway cutting through Hyde Park is roped off for swimming, with a separate wading area and playground for kids. It can get pretty full when school lets out, but your child won't mind splashing about with a bunch of little English people and the occasional duck. There's a grassy area nearby so you can spread out a towel and sunbathe. This is probably the oldest swimming area still in use in London, the Serpentine having been built by Queen Caroline in 1730 for her royal yachts. People used to swim in the Thames too, but it's not recommended.

Outlying Areas — Map 1

HAMPSTEAD HEATH PONDS

Hampstead Heath

HOURS: Daily dawn-dusk

COST: Adults £2, seniors, students, and children £1

BRITISH RAIL: Hampstead Heath

Lakes are really the best way to swim, with no river murk, no salt from the sea, and much less toxic than public pools. The only place I know of to go lake swimming in London is the wild park of Hampstead Heath. The ponds aren't very big, but they're refreshing and you can spread a towel out on the grass and catch some rays afterward. One is for men only, another for women only, and the third is mixed. Swimmers must pass an easy test before being allowed to bathe, and no children under eight are allowed.

TOOTING BEC LIDO

SE Corner of Tooting Common SW16, 020/8871-7198, www.wandsworth.gov.uk

HOURS: Daily 6 A.M.-8 P.M. May 27-Aug. 31, 6 A.M.-5 P.M. Sept.

COST: Weekdays: adults £2.60, seniors, students, and children £2.10; Weekends: adults and students £3.10, seniors £2, children £2.25, children under 5 free

TUBE: Balham or Tooting Bec

One of the largest open-air pools in Europe has been a favorite of water-loving Londoners for generations. Opened in 1906, it's also the oldest public pool in London. It offers a 90-meter pool for adults, a paddle pool for the kids, and a grassy area for sunbathing. Despite its age, the facilities are modern and showers, changing areas, and toilets for people with disabilities make this a very accessible place to go for a dip. A café is on-site.

TENNIS

The city that hosts Wimbledon is not without its tennis courts. Some private, residential gardens have courts, and if you are staying in a nearby hotel you may be allowed access. If not, head over to one of these courts in London's beautiful parks. For more locations, go to www.londontennis.co.uk.

Chelsea, Kensington, and Knightsbridge — Map 6

THE HYDE PARK TENNIS CENTRE

South Carriage Dr., Hyde Park W2, 020/7262-3474, www.willtowin.co.uk

HOURS: Daily dawn-dusk

COST: One hour weekdays £11.50, weekends and after 5 P.M. on weekdays £12.50

TUBE: Hyde Park Corner

If you feel like something a bit more active than lazing in the sun or heckling the pontificators at Speaker's Corner, rent one of the six tennis courts in Hyde Park. The Tennis Centre also offers a hitting wall, clubroom, café, shop, showers, changing area, and two minicourts for the kids. Will to Win, which also runs the tennis courts in The Regent's Park, offers professional coaching for children and adults and a regular series of classes. Reserving a court is recommended, especially on weekends. Equipment rental costs £5 an hour.

TENNIS AT HOLLAND PARK

Btwn. Holland Walk and Abbotsbury Rd. W8, 020/7602-2226, www.rbkc.gov.uk

HOURS: Open 7:30 A.M.-dusk

COST: One hour £5

TUBE: Holland Park

Six tarmac tennis courts and two squash courts are set in beautiful Holland Park. You can rent courts for an hour, on the hour, throughout the day by calling the number above. Note that courts must be reserved; no walk-ins are accepted. Two of the courts are floodlit. Courses and personal instruction are available for all levels, including for children. Equipment is available for rent and balls are for sale at the park office.

Maida Vale, Marylebone, and St. John's Wood — Map 8

THE REGENT'S PARK TENNIS CENTRE

York Bridge Rd., the Inner Circle, The Regent's Park NW1, 020/7486-4216, www.willtowin.co.uk

HOURS: Daily dawn-dusk

COST: One hour weekdays £11.50, weekends and after 5 P.M. on weekdays £12.50

TUBE: Baker Street or Regent's Park

Catch a game in beautiful Regent's Park at one of 12 tennis courts. The Tennis Centre also offers a clubroom, café, shop, showers, changing area, and two minicourts for the kids. Will to Win, which also runs the Hyde Park tennis courts, offers professional coaching for children and adults. Reserving a court is recommended, especially on weekends. Courts are booked for 60 minutes on the hour. Equipment rental costs £5 an hour.

Outlying Areas — Map 1

WIMBLEDON

The All England Lawn Tennis Club on Church Road, 020/8971-2473 or (44) 20/8971 2473 (overseas), www.wimbledon.org

HOURS: Ticket office: Mon.-Fri. 9 A.M.-5 P.M.

See the stars of the tennis world square off at its greatest competition. The famous tennis championship takes place every year at Wimbledon Park for two weeks late June–early July. Ticket prices depend on the day and seat location and range £23–83, with standing-room tickets as low as £4.

Spectator Sports

The Brits are big sports fans. Their favorites are football (soccer to Yanks) and cricket. Rugby is an unabashedly violent game similar to American football, but without the wimpy padding. For some reason you can pass only backward, but strangely that doesn't slow down the momentum of the game.

BOXING

You'll find no shortage of other spectator sports in town, but a unique attraction has to be the amateur boxing at the Real Fight Club. If that doesn't appeal, you can find plenty of amateur, and less violent, games going on in the neighborhood parks.

THE REAL FIGHT CLUB

Office at 11 Plough Yard EC2, box office 070/9239-0390, www.therealfightclub.co.uk

HOURS: Box office open Mon.-Fri. 9 A.M.-5 P.M.

COST: Ticket prices vary

Inspired by the movie of the same name,

self-styled White Collar Warriors get trained in the gym and then go toe-to-toe with other cubicle slaves for three, two-minute nondecision rounds to hash out their aggressions and go for the glory. The level of the fighting varies from amateurish to semipro, and there's a real kick in seeing how normal the fighters look. They could be (and sometimes are) the guy next to you on the Tube. Their office mates cheering them from the bleachers are almost as entertaining. While it's mostly men, some women fight too. Of course, all you need to do is go out late on a Friday and Saturday night and you can see this in the streets for free. Locations vary.

CRICKET

If you want to feel very English during your stay in London, how about going to a cricket match? Two of the most important pitches in the cricket world are right here in town. The players wear semiformal white attire and play on well-manicured fields. They even break for tea! Professional play is in the summer, but you'll see amateur matches in the parks at all times of the year.

Maida Vale, Marylebone, and St. John's Wood — Map 8

LORD'S CRICKET GROUND

St. John's Wood Rd. NW8, switchboard 020/7616-8500, tickets 020/7432-1000, tours 020/7616-8595 or 8596, www.lords.org

HOURS: Tours Apr.-Sept. daily at 10 A.M., noon, and 2 P.M. (except during major matches and on preparation days); Oct.-Mar. daily at noon and 2 P.M.

COST: Adults £8, seniors and students £6, children £5

TUBE: St. John's Wood

Considered by many to be the home of cricket, Lord's hosts some of the most important matches in the country and has heaps of history. The tour of the grounds and museum, including a viewing of the famous "Ashes" urn, is quite interesting and a good way to learn about the history and rules of this complicated game. The tour guides are used to curious and clueless overseas visitors and can answer all your questions. They might even shoot back some questions about baseball. You cannot buy tickets for games in person, but via the Internet and phone only.

South of the Thames — Map 12

THE OVAL CRICKET GROUND

Kennington Oval SE11, 087/1246-1100, www.surreycricket.com

HOURS: Box office open 24 hours

TUBE: Oval

Home to the Surrey County Cricket Club and close to the center of town, this is a good place to catch a cricket match. Some historic matches have happened here, the most recent being England's winning the Ashes in 2005. The grounds are huge, so you might want to spend a little extra to get a good seat. The home team is one of the better teams in England and has a good collection of trophies in its long history, which stretches back to 1845.

FOOTBALL

Called "soccer" in North America, football easily beats Anglicanism as England's official religion. Talk to any English fan and you will be regaled with football trivia and detailed conspiracy theories as to why the national team hasn't won a World Cup since 1966. The best teams are organized into the Premier League (often called the Premiership), and below them are the Football League, which is divided into The Championship, League 1, and League 2. Below these are several leagues for lesser or amateur teams. Depending on how they do, teams can get promoted up to a higher league or relegated to a lower one.

Islington — Map 11

ARSENAL FOOTBALL CLUB

Emirates Stadium, Drayton Park N5, 020/7704-4000, box office 020/7704-4040, www.arsenal.com

HOURS: Box office open Mon.-Fri. 9:30 A.M.-5 P.M., Sat. 9:30 A.M.-noon

TUBE: Arsenal

One of the biggest and best known of London's many football clubs, Arsenal has a reputation for winning. It's racked up numerous trophies, including being Premier League champion several times, most recently 2001/2002 and

2003/2004, and it won the Football Association (FA) Cup in 2002, 2003, and 2005, and several other times in the past century. Nicknamed "The Gunners," the team was formed by workers at the Royal Arsenal in 1886. Its huge following buys out home games very quickly, so if you want to see a game, book way in advance. This advice applies to all the teams listed here, but especially for Arsenal.

Outlying Areas — Map 1

CHARLTON ATHLETIC

The Valley, Floyd Rd., Charlton SE7, 020/8333-4000, box office 087/1226-1905, www.cafc.co.uk

HOURS: Box office open Mon.-Fri. 8 A.M.-8 P.M., Sat. 9 A.M.-1 P.M.

BRITISH RAIL: Charlton

This southeast London team, nicknamed "The Addicks," plays at The Valley in Charlton. The Addicks have had their ups and downs, doing well in the '30s–late '50s, and then being relegated to lower leagues several times before clawing their way up to the Premiership in 1998. This checkered record hasn't damped the fans' spirits, and Charlton has rewarded this loyalty by taking the rare step of having an elected fan sit on the board of directors.

CHELSEA FOOTBALL CLUB

Stamford Bridge, Fulham Rd. SW8, 087/0300-1212, tours 087/0603-0005, www.chelseafc.co.uk

HOURS: Box office open Mon.-Fri. 9 A.M.-5 P.M., Sat.-Sun. 10 A.M.-2 P.M.

TUBE: Fulham Broadway

Another popular football club, Chelsea had its most memorable season in 2004/2005, when it won the Premiership, the League Cup, and the Community Shield. The last, although not the most prestigious, led to huge celebrations since it beat archrivals Arsenal. The club won the Premiership again in the 2005/2006 season. Its ads boast that the stadium has the largest number of pubs within a mile radius of any football stadium in town. Note that in the 2006 season, tickets were not available over the phone, but you had to buy them in person or through the website.

FULHAM

Craven College, Stevenage Rd., Fulham, box office 087/0442-1234, www.fulhamfcfc.com

HOURS: Box office open 24 hours

TUBE: Putney Bridge

The oldest professional football team in London, Fulham was founded in 1879 but hasn't won any major honors. It's been in an FA Cup final only once, in 1975, and slipped down to the Third Division for a few years in the 1990s, but still has a loyal fan base. A turnaround came in 1998 when Mohammed Al-Fayed, the millionaire owner of Harrods, bought the team and got it back up into the Premiership. Fans often call the team "The Cottagers" or "The Whites."

TOTTENHAM HOTSPUR

Park Ln., Tottenham, 087/0420-5000, www.tottenhamhotspur.com

HOURS: Box office open Mon.-Fri. 9:30 A.M.-5 P.M.

BRITISH RAIL: White Hart Lane

A Premiership team with a huge rivalry with Arsenal, the Spurs were founded in 1888 and are one of the oldest professional teams in London. Fans often call the Spurs the "Lilywhites" because of their white home jerseys. They've been in the Premiership since the League began in 1992 and have earned many honors, including eight FA Cups (the latest in 1990–1991) and three League Cups (the latest in 1998–1999). They've never placed higher than fifth in the Premiership, however, and a win is the fans' greatest dream.

WEMBLY STADIUM

Stadium Way, Wembley HA9, 020/8795-9000, www.wembleystadium.com

TUBE: Wembley Park

England's national football ground opened in 1923 but closed in 2000, was demolished, and is in the process of being rebuilt. This project has gotten a lot of fire from the press because of delays and cost overruns. It was due to reopen in 2007, but that isn't written in stone. Recent FA Cups have been held at Millennium Stadium in Cardiff, Wales.

The stadium is full of history, having

© DEAN EDWARDS

The popular Tottenham Hotspur is in the Premier League.

sponsored every FA Cup while open in addition to countless other important events. Its brightest moment came during the 1966 World Cup, when the English national team beat West Germany 4-2 in extra time. The stadium also hosts rugby games and concerts, and it will be one of the sites for the 2012 Summer Olympics.

WEST HAM UNITED

Boleyn Ground, Green St., Upton Park E13, 020/8548-2748, box office 087/0112-2700, www.whufc.com

HOURS: Box office open Mon.-Fri. 9 A.M.-5 P.M., nonmatchday Sat. 9 A.M.-1 P.M., matchday Sat. 9 A.M.-kickoff, matchday Sun. 10 A.M.-kickoff

TUBE: Upton Park

This Premier League team is a three-time FA Cup winner, most recently in 1980. The club was founded in 1895 by ironworkers and it's still nicknamed "The Irons" and "The Hammers." The team has had its ups and downs in recent decades but has done well in the past couple of seasons, being runners-up for the 2006 FA Cup and winning the 2004/2005 Football League Championship Playoff. The team runs a popular youth-development program that brings in a lot of young talent from around the world.

RUGBY

While football is the most popular game in England, you might also appreciate the rough-and-tumble sport of rugby. An honest violence to this game is mixed with complex tactics and unusual rules, such as the fact that players can't pass the ball forward, and there's no padding as in American football. Numerous amateur teams play in the larger parks, so if you're up for it, try to get in a game.

Outlying Areas — Map 1

TWICKENHAM RUGBY STADIUM

Rugby Rd., tickets 087/0902-0000, tours 087/0405-2001, www.twickenhamstadium.com or www.rfu.com

HOURS: Box office: Open 24 hours; Museum: Tues.-Sat. 10 A.M.-5 P.M., Sun. 11 A.M.-5 P.M.

COST: Ticket prices vary, tour including museum entry adults £9, seniors, students, and children £6, family £30

TUBE: Hounslow East

Some of the top matches take place at this impressive stadium, the home of England rugby and the Rugby Football Union, and it is holy ground for rugby fans. A Museum of Rugby is on-site and you can take a guided tour of the museum and stadium any day of the week except Monday by reserving online or calling the number above. The museum features displays on rugby heroes from the past and present and houses the famous Calcutta Cup, awarded to the winner of the annual England versus Scotland match.

ACCOMMODATIONS

Finding a good place to stay in London can be a bit tricky, especially if you don't have bottomless pockets and are coming in the high season. It's best to make reservations in advance rather than risk a long slog around town to find a roof to put over your head.

North American visitors are often surprised at how much smaller rooms are in Europe. While some may be used to vast rooms for a reasonable price by the side of the interstate, you will not find them here. Bathrooms are often small, and they may not include a tub with the shower. Some rooms don't even have a bathroom; the term "en suite" means that a room does. Also note that many hotels do not have air-conditioning, which isn't a problem except during a hot summer. "Listed" buildings, meaning those that have historic value, make for an atmospheric stay but they are not allowed to make any major changes, such as providing access for those with disabilities. Those with mobility issues should call ahead to see if their needs can be accommodated.

You'll find that many hotels, especially outside of London, are decorated in a typical English style: patterned bedspreads, wallpaper, and upholstery, and paintings of traditional English scenes such as foxhunting. The nicer rooms come with four poster beds, antique prints, and fine wood furniture. Some hotels take it a bit far though, and all the froofy floral patterns can become a bit much for the eyes.

Many hotels also include breakfasts of varying quality. A continental breakfast can mean anything from a huge buffet in the better hotels, to toast and jam in the youth hostels. Other

HIGHLIGHTS

Best Budget Hotel: A friendly and knowledgeable staff, central location, and low prices make the **Luna and Simone Hotel** a good option for those who want to save their money (page 225).

Best Fancy Hotel That's Not Too Expensive: Stay in refined elegance without blowing your bank account. The **Hotel Russell** features an ornate Victorian facade, marble reception area, park views, and is close to the British Museum (page 233).

Best Luxury Hotel: Small yet elegant, peaceful yet central, **The Montague on the Gardens** is the place to stay if money's no object. Guests can sip tea while looking out onto the Duke of Bedford's private garden (page 233).

Best Location for a Youth Hostel: This is a *youth hostel!?* An elegant mansion built in 1607, the **YHA Holland House** is set amid the greenery of one of London's best parks, providing cheap accommodation in a matchless setting (page 234).

Weirdest Hotel Decor: The **Pavilion Fashion 'Rock N' Roll Hotel** features disco balls, tigerskin rugs, and a manager who dresses as Elvis and drives a purple Lamborghini. Need I say more? (page 237)

Holland Park

LOOK FOR TO FIND RECOMMENDED LODGING.

hotels may offer a full English breakfast—if they do, they may also offer the healthier alternative of a good continental breakfast.

CHOOSING AN ACCOMMODATION

While budget travelers and backpackers have plenty of youth hostels to choose from, these can fill up fast; it's best to make reservations in advance. Be aware that most youth hostels have few single and double rooms, if any. More likely you will be in a room with 4–12 people. The good news is that there are dozens of hostels in or near the center of town. There are also some cheap hotels (£40 or less for a single) in the center of town. Remember, however, that "cheap" has two meanings; most of these will not have private bathrooms, will be on noisy streets, and may be several rather grungy floors up with no lift (elevator).

In the £40–80 range, the availability and quality increases markedly. The nicer places in this bracket tend to lie away from the center, which increases their appeal for visitors who want relaxing surroundings. Only those close to a Tube station, making them convenient for out-of-town visitors, are included here.

For £80–150 you have your run of the town. London is filled with fine hotels and the more you're willing to spend, the more choices you have. What you get for your money depends on the neighborhood. A Notting Hill hotel in this price bracket won't be as nice as a similarly priced one South of the Thames, but you get the bonus of being in a better neighborhood.

For those with robust bank accounts, London offers a splendid variety of elite hotels priced from the expensive to the appalling. These places are often historic and architectural attractions in themselves. Since most travelers cannot afford to stay in such luxury, only a few of the most famous are listed here.

Package tours will often provide accommodation, but most of the time there is little or no choice of where you get to stay. Closely check out the hotels offered, as a bad room in a distant neighborhood can sour your whole visit.

Westminster, Victoria, and Pimlico — Map 2

Accommodation in central London is notoriously expensive, but a bit of searching can find little places on out-of-the-way streets that are more reasonable. You might have to compromise on room size or amenities such as a television, but how much time are you going to spend in your room anyway? Most of the reasonably priced beds are in quieter neighborhoods such as Pimlico, but if you don't mind paying a bit (or a lot) more, there are plenty of options closer to the major sights.

UNDER £40

ASTOR VICTORIA HOSTEL

71 Belgrave Rd. SW1, 020/7834-3077, www.astorhostels.com

TUBE: Pimlico or Victoria

A great option if you want to be close to the sights of Westminster and the transport hub of Victoria, this hostel is part of the Astor chain and combines its usual friendly service and somewhat chaotic clientele. Amenities include a TV lounge, Internet access, and kitchen facilities, and it serves a continental breakfast. The hostel is for 18- to 35-year-olds only (but I've seen older people there).

ROSEDENE HOTEL VICTORIA

119 Ebury St. SW1, 020/7730-4872

TUBE: Victoria

It's hard to find cheap accommodations in this neighborhood, but Rosedene delivers with basic but livable dorms and private rooms. Some rooms are en suite and all come with tea- and coffee-making facilities. A big draw for budget travelers is the free Internet, rare in a hotel this cheap, and there are kitchen and laundry facilities too. It's nothing to write home about, but it's close to the sights, the Victoria train and bus transport hub, and will save money. Stay here if you can't get into Astor's Victoria Hostel.

£40-80

LUNA AND SIMONE HOTEL

47/49 Belgrave Rd. SW1, 020/7834-5897, www.lunasimonehotel.com

TUBE: Victoria

This family-owned hotel offers a good location and great value for the money. The rooms are simply decorated in the English style and come with a TV, hair dryer, and tea- and coffee-making facilities, and a full English breakfast is included. With the exception of two singles, all rooms are en suite. You have free wireless Internet access on the ground and first floors. The staff is superhelpful and quite knowledgeable. All in all, this is a good, basic bed-and-breakfast that will make any stay in London a pleasant and affordable one.

MORGAN GUEST HOUSE

120 Ebury St. SW1, 020/7730-2384,
www.morganhouse.co.uk
TUBE: Victoria

Small but cozy are the keywords for this little hotel. The rooms are small even by English standards but are clean and comfortable and the staff is very helpful. Not all rooms are en suite. A full English breakfast is included in a pleasantly rustic dining room. A garden out back can be quite relaxing in fine weather, and it gives an illusion of privacy in this busy neighborhood. It wins high points for charm and location, but be prepared for a rather cramped stay.

NEW ENGLAND HOTEL

20 St. George's Dr. SW1, 020/7834-1595
TUBE: Victoria or Pimlico

This refurbished Georgian town house has a homey feel with a friendly and helpful staff, showing how good a family-run hotel can be when the family knows the town and how to make guests happy. All rooms are en suite and include TV, hair dryer, and Internet access, and come decorated in a flowery English style. There's an elevator too—rare and very welcome in such an old building. A full English breakfast is included.

VANDON HOUSE HOTEL

1 Vandon St. SW1, 020/7799-6780,
www.vandonhouse.com
TUBE: Victoria or St. James's Park

A small but clean hotel close to Victoria Station and the parks, the Vandon offers surprisingly spacious rooms and bathrooms considering the location and price bracket. Not all of the 32 rooms are en suite, but they do come with a TV, and the staff is pleasingly helpful. A few rooms on the interior look out onto an airshaft and aren't nearly as nice as the ones facing the street, so try to get one of the latter. There's a cozy lounge/library too. A continental breakfast is included.

£80-150

THE GRANGE ROCHESTER HOTEL

69 Vincent Sq. SW1, 020/7828-6611,
www.grangehotels.com
TUBE: Victoria or St. James's Park

Relax in four-star English ambience. The marble bathrooms, hand-carved rosewood fittings in the bedrooms, and general decor of the Grange Rochester all give the place a traditional feel. There's a laid-back wine bar on the ground floor, as well as a lounge bar and restaurant. The rooms are quite spacious by London standards, and they all are en suite and come with Internet access, tea- and coffee-making facilities, and a hair dryer. While it is a bit far from the nightlife, it is close to Victoria, a major transit hub that can get you anywhere you need to go.

LIME TREE HOTEL

135/137 Ebury St. SW1, 020/7730-8191,
www.limetreehotel.co.uk
TUBE: Sloane Square or Victoria

Close enough to the Victoria Coach and Rail Station to be convenient, but far enough away to be in a decent neighborhood, this family-owned bed-and-breakfast is a good option for those who want to balance value and location. All rooms are en suite and come with a safe, TV, and wireless Internet. There's a beautiful (and aromatic) rose garden out back. What makes this hotel especially good, however, is the friendly and helpful staff. Many smaller hotels do not have someone at the front desk 24 hours, but the Lime Tree does. A full English breakfast is included.

MORGAN GUEST HOUSE

120 Ebury St. SW1, 020/7730-2384,
www.morganhouse.co.uk
TUBE: Sloane Square or Victoria

Like the Lime Tree Hotel just across the way, the Morgan House offers good value and a reasonably central location. The rooms are traditionally furnished and come with a TV and a sink. Not all rooms are en suite and they can be a bit small; a nice bonus for families is a family room with bunk beds. A full English breakfast served in a cheery yellow dining room is included. Since the Morgan and the Lime Tree are within sight of each other, it begs for comparison; although the Lime Tree is the slightly better deal, the Morgan is also perfectly acceptable.

SANCTUARY HOUSE HOTEL

33 Tothill St. SW1, 020/7799-4044, www.fullershotels.com

TUBE: St. James's Park

It's not surprising that this hotel, owned by the Fullers brewery, has a welcoming pub on the ground floor of this beautiful Victorian building. The traditionally decorated rooms are all en suite and have air-conditioning, TV, and a hair dryer. The location earns high marks—it's just a few minutes' walk to Westminster, St. James's and the connecting parks, and Buckingham Palace. Though the Sanctuary is on the higher end of this price bracket, the location and general atmosphere make it well worth it.

WINDERMERE HOTEL

142-144 Warwick Way SW1, 020/7834-5163

TUBE: Victoria or Pimlico

A very nice bed-and-breakfast close to the transport hub of Victoria and the sights of Westminster, the Windermere offers friendly service and good-size rooms individually decorated in the English style. All rooms are en suite and come with tea- and coffee-making facilities, hair dryer, safe, and TV. A full English breakfast is included. The Pimlico Room restaurant downstairs offers English and European dining and is worth eating at, unlike so many hotel restaurants. This hotel has only 22 rooms, so many of the restaurant clientele are actually locals.

£150 AND UP

51 BUCKINGHAM GATE

45-51 Buckingham Gate SW1, 020/7769-7766, www.51-buckinghamgate.com

TUBE: St. James's Park or Victoria

You can't really ask for a more prestigious location. Just a few minutes from Buckingham Palace, this hotel sits behind a wrought-iron fence like many of the stately homes in the neighborhood, and once you're inside there's nothing to reduce that first impression—think giant windows, vases stuffed with flowers, and lots of marble. It has no rooms per se, only 84 suites and apartments, all spacious and including meticulous room service. A bistro and bar are on-site, and there's a twice-daily shuttle to the shopping areas of Kensington and Bond Street. The hotel's spa, featuring chemical-free Sodashi treatments, will relax you if you somehow weren't already.

CITY INN

30 John Islip St. SW1, 020/7630-1000, www.cityinn.com/london

TUBE: Pimlico

This large hotel next to the Tate Britain and the Thames is a good location for those looking to explore Westminster in detail. The decor incorporates clean lines and minimalism, making for a modern feel. The upper stories have great views of the Thames and Westminster. All rooms are en suite and come with TV, CD/DVD player and free video library, and Internet access. You'll also find a fitness room, a bar, and a café with a large vegetarian menu. This is a modern hotel with great location and service, but it's lacking in traditional atmosphere.

Mayfair and Piccadilly Map 3

Mayfair and Piccadilly are some of the more expensive areas of London to live and shop, and hotel rooms are priced accordingly. In return are peaceful residential lanes, a thriving arts and dining scene, and easy access to wonderful parks, perfect for romantic evening strolls.

£40-80

EDWARD LEAR HOTEL

28/30 Seymour St. W1, 020/7402-5401,
www.edlear.com

TUBE: Marble Arch

This hotel is the former home of Victorian writer and artist Edward Lear, who was known for his nonsense poetry and bizarre drawings. It's just a short walk from Oxford Street and within easy walking distance of the theater district. The staff is friendly and helpful, but the beds aren't the most comfortable and it's not always as clean as it should be. Still, this is a convenient location at a good price. Not all rooms are en suite, but all include TV and tea- and coffee-making facilities. There's Internet access in the lounge and a full English breakfast is included.

£80-150

FOX CLUB

46 Clarges St. W1, 020/7495-3656,
www.foxclublondon.com

TUBE: Green Park

This little bed-and-breakfast has only nine rooms, a restaurant and bar, and exudes the air of a private club, which, in fact, it partially is. Shelling out a hefty membership fee gets reduced rates, not a bad idea if you fall in love with the place and want to return regularly—something that could very well happen. The Georgian building is beautifully furnished and decorated in a traditional English style, providing heaps of atmosphere and a real sense of class. The en suite rooms are bright and come with a TV and free wireless Internet. The rates are cheaper for nonmembers alike on weekends, which means this hotel just manages to squeeze into the top of this price bracket.

HOLIDAY INN MAYFAIR

3 Berkeley St. W1, 087/0400-9110,
www.holidayinn.co.uk

TUBE: Bond Street or Green Park

One of the few midpriced options in the area is this member of the Holiday Inn chain. It's pretty much what you'd expect from a Holiday Inn: efficient service, clean rooms, decent price, and uninspiring decor. Still, you get to be in a wonderful part of town without spending all your shopping money. All rooms are en suite and come with air-conditioning, Internet access, hair dryer, and tea- and coffee-making facilities. It's a good place to stay in a rich neighborhood without being rich yourself.

MILLENNIUM HOTEL LONDON MAYFAIR

44 Grosvenor Sq. W1, 020/7629-9400,
www.millenniumhotels.com

TUBE: Bond Street or Green Park

Overlooking classy Grosvenor Square, this hotel is ideally situated for exploring the neighborhood and offers historic charm. The building was the 18th-century home of the Duchess of Kendel. Its other claim to fame was that it was the spot for the official announcement that the Duke of Wellington had won the Battle of Waterloo, ending Napoleon's dreams of conquest. The hotel itself has tons of facilities, including a helpful concierge service, fitness room, and a lounge and bar onsite. All rooms are en suite and come with TV, tea- and coffee-making facilities, Internet access, and air-conditioning.

£150 AND UP

CLARIDGE'S

55 Brook St. W1, 020/7629-8860,
www.claridges.co.uk

TUBE: Bond Street

If you want to splash out for a fine hotel in London but don't like the overblown feel of the Ritz or the Savoy, try the elegant but relaxed experience of Claridge's. From the start,

Claridge's has catered to long-stay visitors, such as country aristocrats in London for "the season." Because of this emphasis, all the art-deco elegance somehow has a homey feel to it, although no home I ever got to live in! The service is, of course, impeccable; there are even personal butlers for hire. Rooms are individually decorated in a range of styles, and there are two bars and a spa on-site. Star chef Gordon Ramsay serves fine cuisine at Gordon Ramsey's, deservedly the most famous of the hotel's three restaurants. The Macanudo Fumoir's smoking room is stocked with rare cigars (see the *Arts and Entertainment* chapter).

THE RITZ

150 Piccadilly W1, 020/7493-8181, U.S. toll-free 877/748-9536, www.theritzlondon.com

TUBE: Green Park

Situated in an imposing late-Victorian edifice, this luxury hotel has been a favorite of the rich and famous for generations. It's easy to see why. The building is designed to look like a French country estate, and the long hallways, ornate statues, and glittering chandeliers surround guests with Continental opulence. The rooms continue the motif, with soft blues, pinks, and yellows, French-style furnishings, and embellishments in gold leaf. Pay a little extra for a room with a fine view of Green Park. Please note that there's a formal dress code in the hotel's public areas. The ornately decorated hotel restaurants require men to wear jackets, a good idea anyway since it feels as if you're dining in Versailles. The hotel is also home to one of London's most ornate and exclusive casinos.

Covent Garden, West End, and Soho — Map 4

To be right in the middle of the action, stay here. You'll have to pay for the convenience, or be willing to take a less-than-wonderful room in cramped quarters, but the reward is the best nightlife that London has to offer. You may never sleep in your room! This area tends to be noisy at night and early in the morning, so those who do want to sleep should try to get a room on an upper floor that doesn't face the street.

UNDER £40

YHA OXFORD ST.

14 Noel St. W1, 087/0770-5984, www.yha.org.uk

TUBE: Oxford Circus or Tottenham Court Road

Budget travelers who want to be in the middle of Soho's nightlife come to this raucous and centrally situated youth hostel. It's a bit of a party place, so be warned/advised. The hostel is within walking distance of many of London's most popular sights and neighborhoods, which means this is a good place to save money on transport too. You'll find a kitchen, laundry, and TV lounge on-site. Unlike most other YHA hostels, there is no breakfast included. For non-YHA members, there's an extra £3 a night to stay.

£40-80

MANZI'S

1-2 Leicester St. WC2, 020/7734-0224, www.manzis.co.uk

TUBE: Leicester Square

The Manzi's rooms are basic and a bit small, but they're clean and cheap considering the hotel's great location in the theater district. To save money for the shows, consider this hotel. A continental breakfast is included; for later meals try the excellent seafood restaurant, a London favorite that's been run by the same Italian family since 1928. The hotel has been in operation since the 19th century—Johann Sebastian Strauss stayed here in 1838.

£80-150

THE FIELDING HOTEL

4 Broad Ct., Bow St. WC2, 020/7836-8305, www.the-fielding-hotel.co.uk

TUBE: Covent Garden

You can't find a much better location to take advantage of London's thriving theater scene. In the center of the theater district on a quiet pedestrian street right opposite the Royal Opera House, the Fielding serves a mixture of professionals and tourists in a 19th-century building. All rooms are en suite (shower only) and come with a TV, telephone, and tea- and coffeemaker. It's very popular, so book well in advance. Please note that this hotel does not accept children under 13 nor does it have an elevator, so those with mobility issues may want to reconsider a stay here.

KINGSWAY HALL HOTEL

66 Great Queen St. WC2, 020/7309-0909

TUBE: Holborn

Upon arrival at this hotel, guests are in for a visual treat. The classical facade hides an art deco foyer with lots of white marble and a funky spiral staircase. The rooms are less impressive but perfectly livable and simply decorated in the English style. Amenities include a TV, hair dryer, iron, and air-conditioning and downstairs there are a gym, steam room, and whirlpool bath. A great location near the theater district and the rather theatrical decor combine to make this a fun stay for those into the arts. Try to get a room in the back to avoid overlooking Kingsway, a busy and noisy thoroughfare.

RATHBONE HOTEL

30 Rathbone St. W1, 020/7636-2001, www.rathbonehotel.com

TUBE: Tottenham Court Road

The Rathbone is a comfortable and efficient hotel in a convenient and central location, but because of the area there can be a bit of traffic noise. It's not too bad, but it's something to keep in mind for light sleepers who want to sleep past rush hour. All the rooms in this well-appointed hotel are en suite, decorated in a modern style, and are generally larger than what's usually offered in London. Amenities include TV, free wireless Internet, and air-conditioning. A restaurant and bar are on-site.

ROYAL ADELPHI HOTEL

21 Villiers St. WC2, 020/7930-8764, www.royaladelphi.co.uk

TUBE: Charing Cross or Embankment

This serviceable but unspectacular hotel with faded carpets has few facilities, but it is in a convenient location at a good price. Not all the rooms are en suite, but the communal bathrooms are kept clean. Amenities include a TV and there's Internet access in the small but comfortable lounge. The hotel bar is open 24 hours, as is the reception, where you'll find friendly and knowledgeable staff. There is no elevator in the hotel, and the long flight of stairs makes it almost impossible for those with mobility issues to stay here. All in all, it's a great deal for service and location over beauty and facilities.

THISTLE CHARING CROSS

The Strand WC2, 087/0333-9105, www.thistlehotels.com

TUBE: Charing Cross

The Thistle Charing Cross is the old railway hotel for Charing Cross Station and has seen lots of travelers pass through its doors. This luxury hotel is at the top of this price bracket and in high season rooms can run higher than £150. Still, a reduced rate can make a stay here worthwhile for its supercentral location (two minutes' walk to Trafalgar Square with many rooms overlooking St. Martin-in-the-Fields) and great service. All rooms are en suite and come with TV, Internet access, and air-conditioning. A restaurant, bar, café, and lounge are on-site.

£150 AND UP

SAVOY

Savoy Pl. btwn. Savoy Hill and Savoy St. WC2, 020/7836-4343, www.fairmont.com/savoy

TUBE: Charing Cross

With a sweeping view of the river, an all-star guest list that has included painters and princes, and a sterling reputation as one of the finest luxury hotels in London, the Savoy has been a meeting place for the city's elite for generations. It was built in 1889 to cater to the wealthy who wanted to enjoy London's cultural

© SEAN MCLACHLAN

The grand entrance to the Savoy hints at the elegance inside.

life. Some of Monet's famous paintings of the Thames were done from the upper floors, and one of the rooms he used has been turned into the "Monet Suite." The art deco–style rooms, with all marble bathrooms and cream walls, captures some of that history. The crowd is a mixture of professionals and well-heeled travelers who come to enjoy the hotel's restaurants, bars, fitness area, and spa. Note: The building was undergoing a massive refurbishment, which should be completed by the time this book goes to press.

Bloomsbury, Euston, and Holborn — Map 5

Historic buildings, major attractions, and some surprisingly good deals on rooms makes this my favorite place to stay in London. Bloomsbury is the best part of this area, since Euston and Holborn get progressively dodgier as you head north toward the major train stations. Still, if you are brave or very large, there are some rock-bottom deals in Euston, and all are right next to a major transport center.

UNDER £40

ASHLEE HOUSE

261-265 Grays Inn Rd. WC1, 020/7833-9677, www.ashleehouse.co.uk

TUBE: King's Cross/St. Pancras

A friendly and well-managed hostel, the Ashlee House is well hooked up to the travelers' circuit and offers good advice for tours and things to see. It's a quick walk to King's Cross/St. Pancras, which means it's convenient for Tube and rail connections. Unfortunately, this also means it's in a bit of a run-down area so solo female travelers may want to think twice about staying here. The hostel attracts a mostly younger crowd, but it's generally quiet. Internet access, kitchen facilities, job-search assistance, travel information, laundry facilities, lounge, and a continental breakfast are provided.

ASTOR MUSEUM INN

27 Montague St. WC1, 020/7580-5360, www.astorhostels.com

TUBE: Russell Square

Cramped bathrooms and old carpet keep this from being the best of London's youth hostels, but its location can't be beat—directly opposite the British Museum in the heart of historic Bloomsbury. Many of London's sights are within easy walking distance, saving guests lots of public transportation and making a stay here a good value. A nice mix of young backpackers and older travelers stay here, as do people seeking work. Though the hostel is open to 18- to 35-year-olds only, it hasn't refused a room to anyone older than 35 that I know of. Amenities include Internet access, kitchen facilities, TV room with DVD library, beer for sale at reception, and a continental breakfast.

YHA ST. PANCRAS

79-81 Euston Rd. NW1, 020/7388-9998 or 087/0770-6044, www.yha.org.uk

TUBE: Euston or King's Cross/St. Pancras

What this YHA branch lacks in character it sure makes up for in convenience. The clean, spacious youth hostel is right across from the British Library and close to two major public transport hubs and several tourist destinations. Breakfast is included, and there's a big lounge area with TV and Internet access, laundry and kitchen facilities, and tons of visitor information at reception. For non-YHA members, it's an extra £3 a night to stay here.

£40-80

ALBANY HOTEL

34 Tavistock Place WC1, 020/7837-9139, www.albanyhotelwc1.co.uk

TUBE: Russell Square or Euston

The first thing to notice about the Albany Hotel is the bright-green paint and veritable jungle of flowers and plants in front. Behind this award-winning display hides a cramped but cozy hotel. None of the rooms is en suite, but there is a sink in each and a bath and shower on every floor. A full English breakfast is included. With only 11 rooms, a gregarious Spanish host, and a communal breakfast table, there's plenty of conversation. The hotel is across the street from a police station, so this has got to be the safest of spots in a generally safe neighborhood.

ALHAMBRA HOTEL

17-19 Argyle St. WC1, 020/7837-9575, www.alhambrahotel.com

TUBE: King's Cross/St. Pancras

This 52-bedroom establishment has been a hotel since the 1840s. It's a friendly, family-owned place, with free wireless Internet and a full English breakfast included. Some rooms share bathrooms, but en suite rooms are available. All the rooms are a bit small, but clean. Note: There are no lifts. The Alhambra is only a couple of minutes' walking distance of King's Cross/St. Pancras Tube and Rail Station, but despite this it still manages to have a quiet location. The station links with several Tube lines.

AROSFA

83 Gower St. WC1, 020/7636-2115, www.arosfahotel.com

TUBE: Goodge Street or Russell Square

This friendly little bed-and-breakfast in a Georgian town house is close to all the sights of Bloomsbury. The en suite rooms are pretty small, especially the bathrooms, but how much time are you going to spend in them anyway? Plus, there are only 15 of them, so guests are assured lots of individual attention from the helpful staff. There's a small private garden and a full English breakfast is included. Try to get a room in the rear to avoid hearing the traffic on busy Gower Street.

AVALON PRIVATE HOTEL

46-47 Cartwright Gardens WC1, 020/7387-2366, www.avalonhotel.co.uk

TUBE: Russell Square or Euston

Set in the sweeping Georgian frontage on Cartwright Gardens, this makes for a picturesque yet quite affordable accommodation choice. In many ways this is a slightly scaled down and cheaper version of the Harlingford, just a few doors down at numbers 61–63. The Avalon offers the same great location and views, the same access to the private garden and tennis courts, and the same bed-and-breakfast feel, but the interior and rooms are a little less ornate. The Harlingford may be preferable for its atmosphere and excellent service—but to save about £20, stay here.

MABLEDON COURT HOTEL

10-11 Mabledon Pl. WC1, 020/7388-3866, www.mabledonhotel.com

TUBE: Euston Square or King's Cross/St. Pancras

Among the many affordable hotels in the immediate vicinity, the Mabledon Court stands out because of its pleasant sunroom, which is a lovely place to lounge in fair weather. The rooms are a bit basic, but they receive lots of sun and come with a TV, hair dryer, and tea- and coffee-making facilities. A full English breakfast is included and is served in the bright dining room. The Mabledon really seems to be trying to maximize England's feeble light here! Though the hotel is close to the rather noisy Euston Road, it's on a quiet street.

£80-150

HARLINGFORD HOTEL

61-63 Cartwright Gardens WC1, 020/7387-1551, www.harlingfordhotel.com

TUBE: Russell Square or Euston

Staying in this Georgian listed building designed by famous architect James Burton in 1807 really gives guests a feel for old Bloomsbury. Despite the age of the building, all the rooms have spacious bathrooms, are fixed up in a modern style, and are supplied with a TV and tea- and coffee-making facilities. There's wireless Internet access in the lounge and guests have access to the private Cartwright Gardens just in front. The hotel has a supply of rackets and balls and for £5 an hour guests can use the tennis courts. A full English breakfast is included. This is one of the more family-friendly hotels in town.

HOTEL RUSSELL

1-8 Russell Square WC1, 020/7837-6470, www.principal-hotels.com

TUBE: Russell Square

The ornate Victorian facade rising above scenic Russell Square harkens to an earlier time, but inside the Hotel Russell are the results of a recent £12 million effort to modernize the hotel's 373 rooms to a four-star standard. All rooms are en suite, air-conditioned, and are of either traditional or modern style. Amenities include a TV, fridge, broadband, a safe large enough for a laptop, and 24-hour room service. Downstairs, off the marble-columned reception area, are a restaurant, bar, and lounge that used to be the hangout of Virginia Woolf. Seven rooms for those with disabilities are available, rare in a Grade II listed building.

£150 AND UP

THE MONTAGUE ON THE GARDENS

15 Montague St. WC1, 020/7637-1001, U.S. toll-free 877/955-1515, www.montaguehotel.com

TUBE: Russell Square

This four-star deluxe hotel is set in a Georgian

The Montague on the Gardens

building right next to the British Museum; for those willing to splash out, it's hard to imagine a better place to stay in London. The ornate and traditional decor is enlivened with plenty of plants, and each individually decorated room comes with broadband and wireless Internet. The Chef's Table restaurant offers fine English cuisine and there's afternoon tea in the richly furnished lounge. In back are two conservatories overlooking a lush garden owned by the Lord Bedford.

Chelsea, Kensington, and Knightsbridge Map 6

If your idea of a good vacation is to be weighed down with shopping bags at the end of the day, consider staying in London's best shopping district. There are some cheap rooms here—although space and amenities might be sacrificed—but it frees up more money for the shops. Of course, for those who don't mind spending some of that shopping money on a better room, the sky's the limit on luxury and refinement.

UNDER £40

ACE HOTEL

16-22 Gunterstone Rd. W14, 020/7602-6600, www.ace-hotel.co.uk

TUBE: Barons Court or West Kensington

While the Ace Hotel (actually a youth hostel) is not within easy walking distance of any notable sights, it is close to a Tube station and offers a great value for the price. A favorite among budget-conscious travelers, the hotel is situated in four converted Victorian town houses and the bar, TV and Internet lounges, game room, and barbecue area make for a very social stay. Most rooms have shared bathrooms, but en suite rooms are available. A continental breakfast is included. It's a few pounds more expensive than some of the shoddier hotels in other neighborhoods, but it makes up for it in style and fun.

YHA EARLS COURT

38 Bolton Gardens SW5, 087/0770-5804, www.yha.org.uk

TUBE: Earl's Court

An old stately home is the venue for a fun crowd of young international travelers looking to explore London on the cheap. You'll find a small courtyard garden for staying in, and plenty of local shops, pubs, and restaurants for going out. To head out farther afield, consider hiring a bike for £1.50 an hour. The hostel has a kitchen, laundry, Internet access, TV lounge, and a continental breakfast is included. For non-YHA members, it's an extra £3 a night to stay here.

YHA HOLLAND HOUSE

Holland Walk in Holland Park W8, 087/0770-5866, www.yha.org.uk

TUBE: Holland Park

This has got to be the best setting for a youth hostel—a 17th-century mansion in the middle of beautiful Holland Park. The interior is clean (as is usual for YHA hostels) and spacious (a bit more rare), but given that it's in one of London's best parks, you won't be inside for long. Hire a bike for £1.50 an hour to explore the local area, or simply go for a shady walk along one of the many paths that meander through the park. The hostel has a kitchen, laundry, Internet access, TV lounge, and a continental breakfast is included. For non-YHA members, it's an extra £3 a night to stay here.

£40-80

ABBEY HOUSE

11 Vicarage Gate W8, 020/7727-2594, www.abbeyhousekensington.com

TUBE: High Street Kensington

This family-run bed-and-breakfast is modestly priced for this part of town. Like many smaller places in London, it's in a converted town house dating to about 1860, and it has been able to maintain its homey atmosphere. There's a TV in each room, but none of the rooms are en suite. This is offset by comfortable surroundings and fine decoration; it really feels like staying in some rich relative's house. Another plus is the short walk to Kensington Gardens. A full English breakfast is included.

LONDON TOWN HOTEL

15 Penywern Rd. SW5, 020/7370-4356

TUBE: Earl's Court

A converted Victorian town house close to Earl's Court Tube Station, the London Town Hotel offers no-frills accommodation at a good price in a central location. If you're looking for swank, look elsewhere, but for convenience and value, look here. All rooms are en suite and are clean but rather simply decorated; some come with a TV and hair dryer. A ground floor lounge offers free coffee and tea and a continental breakfast is included. The neighborhood has lots of shops, restaurants, and pubs and makes a good base from which to explore the rest of the city.

MERLYN COURT HOTEL

2 Barkston Gardens SW5, 020/7370-1640, www.merlyncourthotel.com

TUBE: Earl's Court

The Merlyn is a small, quiet, family-run bed-and-breakfast in a brick Victorian building. Its 20 rooms include triples and quads in addition to singles and doubles, which makes it a good option for small groups traveling on a budget. The decor is rather plain but the rooms get a lot of light. Most, but not all, rooms are en suite. No phones or TVs are in the rooms, but there's a TV in the lounge. A continental breakfast is included. Be advised there is no elevator, which might be a bit of a problem if you're staying on the sixth floor. While it's not in the center of the action, the location is quiet and it's an easy walk to the western edge of Kensington Gardens and Harrods; it's also very close to Earl's Court Tube Station.

£80-150

THE DIPLOMAT HOTEL

2 Chesham St. SW1, 020/7235-1544, www.btinternet.com/~diplomat.hotel

TUBE: Knightsbridge

A Victorian mansion-turned-hotel, the Diplomat offers surprisingly good value and location. A sweeping staircase is lit by a lofty glass dome, and the 26 rooms offer comfortable accommodation and individual service. All rooms are en suite and come with satellite TV. A buffet breakfast is offered in the mornings, and breakfast and lunch on the patio in fair weather. The neighborhood is nice with lots of similarly grandiose buildings, making for pleasant surroundings. Unlike in so many listed hotels, there's actually a lift.

WINCHESTER HOTEL

17 Belgrave Rd. SW1, 020/7828-2972, www.winchester-hotel.net

TUBE: Victoria

Set close to London's best parks, attractions, and shopping, the Winchester offers good value for the money with somewhat small double rooms at the low end of this price range. Unlike many hotels in the neighborhood, the Winchester is family-run, which makes for more personable service. Each room is individually decorated with ornate, traditional European patterns. All rooms are en suite and come with a TV. A full English breakfast is included.

£150 AND UP

THE HALKIN HOTEL

5 Halkin St. SW1, 020/7333-1000, www.halkin.co.uk

TUBE: Hyde Park Corner

The 41 spacious rooms in this elegant hotel are individually designed in a contemporary Italian style with Asian touches. It's all a bit sleek and minimalist, which comes as a relief after the over-the-top floral prints of many British hotels. The hotel's location right between Hyde and Green Parks makes for nice evening strolls, and the hotel itself is quiet and relaxing. Unlike many hotels set in Georgian buildings, the Halkin manages to be completely wheelchair-accessible. It offers a large free breakfast, a bar, and the in-house restaurant, Nahm, is excellent for Thai food (see the *Restaurants* chapter).

Notting Hill, Bayswater, and Paddington — Map 7

This relaxing residential district has some fine hotels and is a good place to stay and unwind at the end of the day. There are some truly beautiful hotels here, and they're not far from the action. More budget-conscious travelers may want to stay in Paddington or Bayswater, where the rooms are cheap and close to Hyde Park and Paddington Station.

UNDER £40

ASTOR'S LEINSTER INN

7-12 Leinster Sq. W2, 020/7229-9641, www.astorhostels.com

TUBE: Queensway or Bayswater

This hostel in the Astor chain isn't as well situated as its Museum Inn, but it is much roomier and offers everything from single en suite rooms to eight-bed dorms. Up to 360 people may be staying here at any one time, which makes it very social if a bit noisy, but then again most hostels are noisy. The TV lounge, game room, Internet access, kitchen facilities, and night bar make this a place where lots of backpackers hang out before and after their daily tour of the city. A continental breakfast is included. The hostel caters to 18- to 35-year-olds only, but those older than 35 have stayed here.

SMART HYDE PARK VIEW

11 Craven Hill Gardens Bayswater W2, 020/7262-3167, www.smartbackpackers.com

TUBE: Queensway

A clean and friendly youth hostel very close to Hyde Park, the SMART Hyde Park View makes a good choice for backpackers who want to enjoy the greenery while staying close to the center of everything. There are single rooms and dorms of up to six beds. Facilities include a laundry room, bar, TV room, games room, and a 24-hour reception desk. Note that there are no kitchen facilities, a negative if cooking is part of your budget requirements, but there's a microwave to heat up food.

£40-80

BARRY HOUSE HOTEL

12 Sussex Pl., Hyde Park W2, 020/7723-7340, www.barryhouse.co.uk

TUBE: Lancaster Gate or Paddington

A bed-and-breakfast in a town house dating to 1840, the Barry House is close to both the transportation hub of Paddington and the greenery of Hyde Park. This is a good option if you want to be in the center of everything but still stay on a quiet residential street. The decor is a bit spartan and it's a bit cramped, but it's so close to the park you'll want to spend more time among the grass and trees than in a bedroom. A full English breakfast is included, there's free wireless Internet, and families are welcome.

GARDEN COURT HOTEL

30-31 Kensington Gardens Sq. W2, 020/7229-2553, www.gardencourthotel.co.uk

TUBE: Bayswater

This nice Victorian hotel has a friendly staff and a good central location. The decor is traditional English, with lots of cushy chairs and patterned wallpaper. One of the best features is the lush little garden where guests can sip free hot drinks. The hotel has an elevator, rare in an old building such as this, and some rooms are en suite; all have TVs and hair dryers. A continental buffet breakfast is included and there's free Internet access in the lounge. All in all, it's a great value for the money.

NOTTING HILL HOTEL

2 Pembridge Sq. W2, 020/7727-1316, www.nottinghillhotel.com

TUBE: Notting Hill Gate

You must make some sacrifices to stay cheaply in this part of town. The sacrifice here? Old furnishings, cheesy wood paneling, and general dreariness. But in return, you get an affordable place to stay on a quiet street in the exclusive neighborhood of Notting Hill. All rooms are en suite and a continental breakfast is included. If cost and location are more important than style, this may be worth a try.

£80-150

ASHLEY HOTEL

15 Norfolk Sq. W2, 020/7723-3375, www.ashleyhotels.com

TUBE: Lancaster Gate or Paddington

Situated in three Victorian town houses in a garden square with no through traffic, this bed-and-breakfast gets high marks for location and even higher marks for its superhelpful management, which is full of advice on where to go and what to see. The rooms themselves are mostly en suite, and all have TVs and tea- and coffee-making facilities. The decor is a bit plain, but the tranquility outside more than makes up for it. If you don't mind trudging up four flights of steps, there's a reduced "alpine rate" for those staying on the top floor. A full English breakfast is included.

AVERARD HOTEL

10 Lancaster Gate W2, 020/7723-8877, www.averard.com

TUBE: Lancaster Gate

Like many hotels in the area, the Averard is in a converted Victorian town house. While the exterior could use some replastering and a paint job, the interior of the ground floor is very elegant; the ornate statues and chandeliers make it seem as if you're checking into a deluxe hotel. The lounge continues this illusion with its antique furniture, piano, and paintings. The rooms are more in keeping with this price bracket—comfortable if not terribly large or modern—rooms are all en suite, come with a TV, and are decorated in a traditional English style. Another plus is that the hotel is within sight of Hyde Park. A full English breakfast is included.

CARDIFF HOTEL

5, 7, 9 Norfolk Sq., Hyde Park W2, 020/7723-3513/9068, www.cardiff-hotel.com

TUBE: Lancaster Gate or Paddington

A nice bed-and-breakfast on the low end of this price range, the Cardiff has been family-owned for more than 40 years. It's on the same garden square as the Ashley and housed in a trio of converted Victorian town houses. While the decor is modest and the rooms rather small, it's a clean and pleasant place to stay. Most rooms are en suite and all include TV and tea- and coffee-making facilities. A full English breakfast is included.

PAVILION FASHION ROCK 'N' ROLL HOTEL

34-36 Sussex Gardens W2, 020/7262-1324, www.pavilionhoteluk.com

TUBE: Paddington

For something a little different, stay at one of the 30 themed rooms in the Pavilion Fashion Rock 'N' Roll Hotel. Concepts include Honky Tonky Afro, with lime-green wallpaper, a disco ball, and a tiger skin rug. Another is Flower Power, a weird mix of hippie crash pad and English country cottage. The website features pictures of each room so request the one best suited to your strangeness. Lots of bands, artists, and celebrities like to stay here because of the decor and the attitude. All rooms are en suite and come with a TV. A continental breakfast is included.

ST. DAVID'S HOTEL

14-20 Norfolk Sq. W2, 020/7723-3856/4963, www.stdavidshotels.com

TUBE: Lancaster Gate or Paddington

Situated in the hotel-rich Norfolk Square, St. David's has been family-run for more than 30 years. The staff is very friendly and the welcoming atmosphere maintains a homey feel that's very pleasant at the end of the day. The Duke of Windsor used to house his valet at number 18 when he was in town for "the season," but now the building caters to a mostly tourist crowd. All rooms have TV and Internet access. A full English breakfast is included.

£150 AND UP

THE LENNOX HOTEL

34 Pembridge Gardens W2, 087/0850-3317, www.thelennox.com

TUBE: Notting Hill Gate

Stay in style at this restored 19th-century town house, now a four-star hotel. The neighborhood is quiet and residential, but you won't have to walk too far to get to all the fun Notting Hill has to offer. All 20 rooms are en suite, air-conditioned, and come with satellite TV, safe, and wireless Internet. The decor is what makes this hotel; the place still retains traditional furnishings and period prints so that it feels as if you're staying in the home of an unusually large family. A bar and comfortable lounge are on-site.

THE PORTOBELLO HOTEL

22 Stanley Gardens W11, 020/7727-2777, www.portobello-hotel.co.uk

TUBE: Holland Park and Notting Hill Gate

An ornate white-columned facade hides this little gem of a hotel. Many of the rooms and bathrooms are small (even by English standards) but they are attractively decorated in various themes, such as the Japanese Room and the Colonial Room. The designers seem to have had a lot of fun going overboard in decorating the rooms; some have round beds, while others have old-style clawfoot tubs. Call ahead for descriptions of which rooms are available. The hotel has its own bar and restaurant open 24 hours. A continental breakfast is included.

Maida Vale, Marylebone, and St. John's Wood Map 8

While this area is a bit away from the center, it's quiet at night and the streets are lined with some fantastic architecture. This has been a residential district for centuries, so hotels can be a bit thin on the ground, but those that are here blend well with the neighborhood. Many are actually old homes, so you can enjoy a quiet drink by the fire with the ghost of some Victorian gentlefolk.

£40-80

THE NEW INN

2 Allitsen Rd. NW8, 020/7722-0726

TUBE: St. John's Wood

Here's something special: a little five-room inn in charming St. John's Wood above a pub dating to 1810. The en suite rooms are a bit spare but a decent size, and they come with TV, wireless Internet, hair dryer, and tea- and coffee-making facilities. The real plus here is the neighborhood (trendy, residential, quiet) and the atmosphere (cozy Englishness and a thankfully quiet pub downstairs). It's surprising it's so cheap. Book well in advance.

£80-150

HOTEL 82

82 Gloucester Pl. W1, 020/7486-3679, www.hotel82london.com

TUBE: Marble Arch or Baker Street

Of the three hotels on Gloucester Place listed, Hotel 82 is at the higher edge of this price bracket; the other two are at the lower edge. As with the other buildings on this street, the hotel is from the Georgian period but has some modern decorating in the interior—lots of light wood and white walls to make it pretty cheery. All rooms are en suite and air-conditioned. An on-site spa offers massages, aromatherapy, a sauna, and a whirlpool bath for an extra charge. A continental breakfast is included.

LINCOLN HOUSE HOTEL

33 Gloucester Pl. W1, 020/7486-7630, www.lincoln-house-hotel.co.uk

TUBE: Marble Arch or Baker Street

Set in a converted Georgian town house cheerfully decorated with flowers and close to the theater and shopping districts, this hotel has a very friendly and helpful staff, free wireless Internet in rooms, and free access through the hotel computer in the lobby. The rooms are all en suite and include TV, hair dryer, and tea- and coffee-making facilities. All rooms except the budget singles include a small refrigerator. A full English breakfast is included. If you like the location but the Lincoln House is full, try the Wigmore just down the street—but try here first.

ST. GEORGE'S

14-15 Langham Pl. W1, 020/7580-0111,

www.stgeorgeshotel.com
TUBE: Piccadilly
Its site at the top of Regent Street makes this a good base for shopping expeditions, and it is also popular with business travelers. The modern-style rooms are all en suite and come with TV, free wireless Internet, tea- and coffee-making facilities, hair dryer, and safe. While the streets down below are constantly busy, the windows are double-glazed to ensure you get some sleep. A restaurant/bar/lounge on the 15th floor provides nice city views. It's good value for the money in a good location, but with only 87 rooms in such a central location, book well in advance.

WIGMORE COURT HOTEL

23 Gloucester Pl. W1, 020/7935-0928,
www.wigmore-court-hotel.co.uk
TUBE: Marble Arch or Baker Street
This converted Georgian town house has lots of history and a good location. The rooms come with TV and tea- and coffee-making facilities, and all are designed in a traditional English style in keeping with the general feel of the house and neighborhood. A free, self-serve kitchen and laundry facilities are available, something rare and welcome in this price bracket. A full English breakfast is included. Try to get a room facing away from the street, as Gloucester Place can get pretty busy.

£150 AND UP

DURRANTS HOTEL

Corner of George St. and Spanish Pl. W1,
020/7935-8131, www.durrantshotel.co.uk
TUBE: Marble Arch
Durrants is a good choice for art lovers; it's right next to the Wallace Collection and a few minutes' walk from the gallery district. It's set in a converted row of Georgian town houses, and the aesthetics within the public areas and rooms are pleasing with lots of antique furniture and prints in the classic British style. The beds are handmade and are extremely comfy. Not all rooms have air-conditioning, so double-check when booking if this is an issue. There are a traditional British bar and restaurant on-site. While this isn't as sumptuous as many other luxury hotels, it's on the low end of the price range and gets good marks for decor and atmosphere.

Camden Town Map 9

You could do worse than staying in Camden Town, a hopping neighborhood cut through by a scenic canal. Sorry to say, most hoteliers haven't figured that out yet so there are few options to choose from, but you get to be close to some nice shopping, dining, and nightlife.

UNDER £40

SMART CAMDEN INN

55-57 Bayhem St. NW1, 020/7388-8900,
www.smartbackpackers.com
TUBE: Camden Town
This clean, popular hostel in Camden Town offers a range of dorms accommodating 4–14 people. The place is pretty much what one would expect from a youth hostel in London—lots of young backpackers and the usual facilities (kitchen, laundry facilities, TV room, games room, 24-hour reception, and continental breakfast). What makes it stand out is its cleanliness and the fact that quality budget accommodation in Camden Town is a bit scarce.

ST. CHRISTOPHER'S CAMDEN

48-50 Camden High St. NW1, 020/7407-1856,
www.st-christophers.co.uk
TUBE: Camden Town or Mornington Crescent
This Camden branch of the popular St. Christopher's chain has all their its usual lively atmosphere and helpful service. Dorms hold 6–10 people and are clean and well maintained by an efficient and knowledgeable staff full of information on local nightlife. The crowd is social and fun, but a bit young. Some rooms are

en suite. Facilities include a lounge, bar, games room, restaurant, Internet access, and laundry facilities. A continental breakfast is included.

£40-80

CAMDEN LOCK HOTEL

89 Chalk Farm Rd. NW1, 020/7267-3912, www.camdenlockhotel.co.uk

TUBE: Chalk Farm or Camden Town

This rather basic hotel is unfortunately the only option in Camden Town in this price bracket. The rooms are small and there's a bit of a noise issue because of its location on Chalk Farm Road, but it's livable. All rooms are en suite and come with a TV and tea- and coffee-making facilities. A full English breakfast is included. (This isn't the ravest review, but if you want your own room on a budget, this isn't bad—and it's the sole option in Camden Town.)

£80-150

HOLIDAY INN LONDON-CAMDEN LOCK

30 Jamestown Rd. NW1, 020/7485-4343, www.holidayinn.co.uk

TUBE: Camden Town

If you want to combine Holiday Inn familiarity with Camden Town partying, this modern chain hotel in the heart of Camden Town's dining, nightlife, and shopping district is a good choice. All rooms are en suite, air-conditioned, and come with Internet access, TV, tea- and coffee-making facilities, and hair dryer. The decor is modern and rather uninspiring, but it's clean and well maintained. Try to get a room looking out over Camden Lock Canal. You'll find a cocktail lounge and restaurant on-site, but dozens of better options are within a few minutes' walk.

The City — Map 10

London's business center is not known for its hotel population, being mostly abandoned at night by workers and tourists alike. However, one can still find some nice rooms here, with the advantage of a short walk to some of London's greatest sights. In the early evening, socialize with all the bankers and insurance agents who just got off work and flock to centuries-old pubs to unwind. Most of the hotels cater to the business crowd, but they welcome vacationers as well.

UNDER £40

YHA CITY OF LONDON

36 Carter Lane EC4, 020/7236-4965 or 087/0770-5764, www.yha.org.uk

TUBE: St. Paul's

It's hard to beat the location of this budget accommodation, housed in a historic building that used to be the choirboys' school for St. Paul's. Go out the front door, walk a few steps, turn a corner and presto! St. Paul's is looming up before you. The carpets are a bit scary, but who cares? Breakfast is included, and

The YHA City of London is set in an old outbuilding of St. Paul's.

you'll find a no-commission currency exchange at the reception desk, laundry facilities, and a big lounge with a pool table, book exchange, and Internet access. For non-YHA members, it's an extra £3 a night to stay here.

£80-150

CLUB QUARTERS GRACECHURCH

7 Gracechurch St. EC3, 020/7666-1620, www.clubquarters.com

TUBE: Monument

This Edwardian edifice used to be a bank and is still in the financial district, which means that the surroundings are safe, clean, and pretty dead at night and on weekends. The front-area concierge and lounge is simply beautiful with lofty ceilings, comfortable leather furniture, and cool marble walls and floors. All rooms are en suite and air-conditioned with modern decor; amenities include a TV, hair dryer, and tea- and coffee-making facilities. A traditional English restaurant is on-site, but with all the fine dining available in the immediate area there are plenty of other options. Note: The Club Quarters Gracechurch is a "members only" hotel on weekdays, as this hotel primarily caters to companies. It's still a good deal and close to everything, so it's well worth it for weekend-only stays.

£150 AND UP

GREAT EASTERN HOTEL

40 Liverpool St. btwn. Great Eastern Walk and Bishopsgate Arcade EC2, 020/7618-5000, www.great-eastern-hotel.co.uk

TUBE: Liverpool Street

The Great Eastern is one of London's historic grand hotels and has been serving guests since 1884. The redbrick Victorian facade hides a modernist foyer and 271 rooms. The rooms on the lower floors are more traditional in design, with dark wood furnishings. The two upper floors are brightly colored and full of light. Four restaurants and two bars will keep body and soul together and the original architectural features are historic sights in themselves. While it is right next to Liverpool Street Station, the design keeps this in mind and guests won't hear a thing. The hotel is also popular with celebrities.

THREADNEEDLES

5 Threadneedle St. EC2, 020/7657-8080, www.theetoncollection.com

TUBE: Bank

You'd never expect to find a luxurious modern hotel tucked behind this nondescript exterior. The building used to be Midland Bank, which opened in 1856, and it contains many original features such as a beautiful painted-glass ceiling in the forecourt and the original tellers' counter, which now serves as a bar. The 69 rooms are decorated in a modern style and reached by soothingly lit, quiet corridors. The amenities reflect the fact that this is a favorite hotel for well-heeled business visitors to The City; there are phones in the bedroom and bathroom, and a cordless for in-between. Spacious desks and wireless Internet help you work while plasma TVs and comfy beds help you relax. The Bonds Bar and Restaurant offers a good place to meet with clients.

Islington — Map 11

This neighborhood is a little far away from the center of town, which means finding rooms that are nicer than usual for their price bracket. Unfortunately, as in Camden Town, there's a shortage of options. Islington is an oasis in a region that's otherwise a bit decayed, and it boasts a fun nightlife, especially for dining and clubbing. If you don't mind having to hop on the Tube or bus every morning and evening to see the sights, this is a good choice.

£40-80

ELENA HOTEL

366 Essex Rd. N1, 020/7359-4118, www.elenahotel.net

TUBE: Highbury and Islington

LONG-TERM STAYS

If you plan to stay in London for a while, you have plenty of options to choose from. Youth hostels often give discounts for weekly rates and generally cost £60-150 a week, with most being on the lesser end of the spectrum. Several agencies offer house and flat shares, starting around £65 a week for a shared room. You can also get a bedsit, meaning your own room in a house, from around £150 a week. You will usually have to share a bathroom and kitchen. Newspapers and expat magazines carry classified ads for individuals who are looking for a housemate/flatmate, but they will be less flexible if you are staying only a short time. Good places to look for accommodation are www.thegumtree.com, www.tntgrapevine.com, and *Loot* magazine.

Several companies offer house shares, in which you either get your own room or you share with one or more people. The Dover Castle youth hostel (6A Great Dover St. SE1, 020/7403-7773, www.dovercastlehostel.com, tube: Borough) offers flats at weekly rates in Zones 1 and 2. They're cheap and mostly include utilities and wireless Internet, but they tend to be in bad areas or a bit too far from the center. London Up! (84 Kingsway WC2, 020/7404-1372, www.londonup.com) offers shared houses all across London where you can live with other international visitors; this offers more choice.

A similar but option is Your London Place (accommodation@london.com), which manages two houses in Southwark near Old Kent Road. I stayed at one of them while researching this book – the houses are well maintained, considering they're shared by up to a dozen people. Most tenants are in their 20s or early 30s and get along remarkably well. Minimum stay is two weeks, and average stay is about three months. Utilities and wireless Internet are included, and the management takes care of cleaning and maintenance. If you're the type of person who can deal with living in such a crowded house, it's a good place to find your feet.

If you're looking to rent for the long term, newspapers and expat magazines list numerous flats for rent for all budgets (well, not the lowest budgets, this being London) and they're a good place to start. Rental agencies can also hasten your search. Reputable ones won't charge a fee to the tenant, instead making their money by charging the landlord. Before getting a flat, it's best to familiarize yourself with London a bit, finding out what neighborhood you'd like to live in and how convenient the public transportation is to get to work.

Before you sign a lease, know your rights. A landlord can ask for a maximum of only two months' rent for a security deposit, and those who rent by the week should ask for only two weeks' worth. Make sure to find out which utilities are included. Landlords are not allowed to retain your passport or any other official document. While most landlords in London are honest, there are a few nasty slumlords and cheats so keep your wits about you and read your contract carefully before you sign.

The Elena Hotel is a clean, cheap, albeit somewhat noisy bed-and-breakfast. Not all rooms are en suite, but all come with TV and tea- and coffee-making facilities. The cool purple decor in the rooms is soothing and maximizes London's often dim natural light. A full English breakfast is included. A traditional British restaurant and bar is on the ground floor and is quite good, but Islington is filled with dining options. Note that the nearest Tube station is nearly a mile away, so a taxi is recommended.

KANDARA GUEST HOUSE

68 Ockendon Rd. N1, 020/7226-5721, www.kandara.co.uk

TUBE: Highbury and Islington or Old Street

This little bed-and-breakfast on a quiet residential street has been in business for more than half a century. The Kandara Guest House is family-owned and family friendly, and it's convenient for exploring Islington's nightlife. The main sightseeing areas are quickly reached on public transport. None of the 11 rooms are en

HOME STAYS

Visitors to London sometimes complain that they can't meet any English people. Locals can be rather reserved, and if you aren't good at striking up conversations with strangers, then you may spend your entire vacation without actually having a real conversation with a Londoner. One way to avoid this problem is to stay with some. Many private homes offer spare rooms to visitors. While living with a stranger for a few nights can be a hit-or-miss experience, most travelers report that they had a wonderful time and gained a better insight into the country and culture.

Most home stays require a minimum of one week and payment in advance. Some don't take credit cards, but the majority of host families have been doing this to supplement their income for years and are as professional and well prepared as London's hotels, meaning that quality and service can vary widely but is generally decent. Some advertise in the same periodicals and websites as flats do, and you'll find agencies (listed below) that handle home stays as well as more usual accommodation.

Facilities vary widely. Some rooms are en suite, but most aren't. Most include utilities and free access to kitchen and laundry, but it's good to check. You may be sharing the house with other visitors, or you may be the only one. Some offer breakfast or complete board for an extra charge. Some hosts are very sociable, while others run their places like a hotel. Houses that are big enough to rent out rooms, and whose owners are needy enough to do so, tend to be farther out from the center, so while you get to live with an English family, you'll have to commute to the sights. Look around and see what's available; you'll find plenty to choose from.

Amber Accommodation Agency (020/7624-4231, www.amberaccommodation.com) offers home stays to students in all areas in London, including some in Zone 1. A single room costs £115-160 depending on location and whether meals are included.

Hosts International (76-78 Mortimer St. W1, 020/7323-5244, www.hosts-international.com, Tube: Oxford Circus) lists more than 600 host families in London and other southern English towns and cities. A large and experienced company, it mainly serves overseas students coming here to study. Prices range £105-220 depending on location and whether meals are included.

London Up! (84 Kingsway WC2, 020/7404-1372, www.londonup.com, Tube: Holborn) offers home stays with prices ranging about £80-120 for a single-occupancy room, utilities included.

UK Homestay (36-38 Hanway St. W1, 020/7436-7738, www.uk-homestay.com, Tube: Tottenham Court Road), run by Britannia Student Services, offers home stays to both students and the regular traveler. Its homes are in all zones, including Zone 1, and range in price £115-215 for a single depending on location and whether meals are provided.

suite, but they come with TV, wash basin, and tea- and coffeemakers. A full English breakfast is included.

£80-150

HILTON HOTEL

53 Upper St. N1, 020/7354-7700, www.hilton.co.uk

TUBE: Angel

A well-managed, modern hotel close to Islington's nightlife, this Hilton features the clean, spacious, and rather uninspiring rooms you've come to know and expect. All rooms come with air-conditioning, TV, hair dryer, tea- and coffee-making facilities, and video games. A very nice modern restaurant has a breakfast buffet in the mornings and Mediterranean dishes at night, but there are plenty of other dining options close by. The bar is pretty good too, but it has to deal with even more local competition.

JURYS INN

60 Pentonville Rd. N1, 020/7282-5500,

www.jurysinns.com
TUBE: Angel
Accommodation choices are rather slim in Islington, but this chain hotel is a decent value for the money and quite close to all the action on Upper Street. The modern rooms are of a good size and come with the typical TV, hair dryer, and coffee- and tea-maker. It has a restaurant and pub too, but with all the great dining and drinking nearby it's doubtful you'll need them. The discounted pass to a nearby gym might be useful for shedding some calories after a night on the town, however. Check the website for regular specials that can save a considerable amount on a room.

South of the Thames — Map 12

London's South Bank has become the number 1 choice for budget-conscious travelers. With easy access to the river and some popular sights, as well as lots of nightlife, it's the new place to be. The nightlife does get a bit rowdy farther south, however, so for a quiet evening consider picking a place in the nicer districts close to the river. While there's a good selection of youth hostels, you'll find few independent hotels and there's a shortage of midpriced hotels, so chains provide some other options.

UNDER £40

DOVER CASTLE AND BAR

6A Great Dover St. SE1, 020/7403-7773,
www.dovercastlehostel.com
TUBE: Borough
This friendly, social hostel attracts a young crowd. The bar on the ground floor is open until 2 A.M., so this is more of a party place than a sleeping place. The fact that you get a free drink at check-in should give you a head's up. Still, the staff is courteous and efficient, and while Southwark is not the nicest of neighborhoods, the hostel is right next to the Borough Tube Station so you won't have to be in it long. The hostel also offer flats at weekly rates in Zones 1 and 2. There is Internet access and a continental breakfast is included.

ST. CHRISTOPHER'S ORIENT ESPRESSO

58 Borough High St., 020/7407-1856,
www.st-christophers.co.uk
TUBE: Borough
Guests must check in at St. Christopher's Village just up the street before heading up here. The rooms at the Orient Espresso are just as good, but there is a coffee shop and Internet café on the ground floor instead of a bar, thus it ends up being a bit quieter. Guests here also have access to all the facilities at the much more social and louder St. Christopher's Village down the street. A continental breakfast is included.

ST. CHRISTOPHER'S VILLAGE

165 Borough High St., 020/7407-1856,
www.st-christophers.co.uk
TUBE: Borough
St. Christopher's Village is one of the most popular hostels in London and can often be full. It's a friendly place and great for meeting fellow backpackers who pack the pub downstairs. The Village attracts a mainly younger crowd, but some older folks come here too. The facilities are clean and include a large chill-out room with video games and beanbags, rooftop sauna, hot tub, overpriced Internet access, lots of free travel information, and a free tour of central London every Friday afternoon. A continental breakfast is included.

£80-150

MAD HATTER HOTEL

3-7 Stamford St. SE1, 020/7401-9222,
www.fullershotels.co.uk
TUBE: Southwark
This hotel, above a pub, is owned by Fullers Brewery but is a quiet and relaxed place to stay in any case. The location is quite good—just

a few minutes' walk away from Blackfriars Bridge and many South Bank sights—and the rooms are clean and reasonably sized for this price range, although the bilious purple walls leave something to be desired. Still, for a decent hotel in a good location, this is a viable option. The 30 rooms fill up quickly, so it's best to book well ahead.

PREMIER TRAVEL INN LONDON SOUTHWARK

Anchor, Bankside 34 Park St. SE1, 087/0990-6402, www.premiertravelinn.com

TUBE: London Bridge

While this hotel chain lacks atmosphere, the Southwark branch has an excellent location and offers surprisingly good value for the money. All rooms are en suite and come with air-conditioning, TV, tea- and coffee-making facilities, wireless Internet, and that ubiquitous chain hotel decor. A nice bonus is the small discount offered Friday–Sunday. A pub and restaurant are on-site, and there are family rooms and good access for those with disabilities. Though the hotel itself may be boring, it's a dozen steps from the Thames Walk so what does it matter?

RIVERBANK PARK PLAZA

18 Albert Embankment SE1, 020/7958-8000, www.parkplaza.com

TUBE: Vauxhall or Waterloo

A modern four-star chain hotel that caters to professionals and tourists alike, the chic and modern Riverbank Park Plaza is just a quick walk across the river to Westminster. The spacious rooms are all en suite and come with Internet access, TV, tea- and coffee-making facilities, and hair dryer. Make sure to get a room facing the Thames to be treated to an almost impossibly great view of the river and Parliament. (The hotel will charge an extra £40 for it, though—enough to knock a room up to the luxury price bracket.) The back rooms have an uninspiring view of a train line. Though the hotel is short on atmosphere (except for the river view), it's long on comfort and service.

SOUTHWARK ROSE HOTEL

43-47 Southwark Bridge Rd. SE1, 020/7015-1480, www.southwarkrosehotellondon.co.uk

TUBE: London Bridge

This hotel has one of the best locations for a South Bank accommodation. A quick walk over the river drops you into The City and all its attractions, or head west along the South Bank to see the Globe Theatre and Tate Modern. The hotel is chic, modern, and clean and the rooms are all en suite with air-conditioning, TV, safe, and tea- and coffee-making facilities. It's on a busy street and while it's well insulated against the traffic, those with sensitive ears may want to request a room in back. A restaurant and bar are on site and a continental breakfast is included.

ACCOMMODATIONS

£150 AND UP

MARRIOTT COUNTY HALL

County Hall at Westminster Bridge Rd. SE1, 020/7928-5200, www.marriott.co.uk/lonch

TUBE: Waterloo

Enjoy excellent views of the Houses of Parliament and the London Eye from the historic County Hall, home of the municipal government 1922–1986. For South Bank hotels it's impossible to beat this location. The London Eye, London aquarium, Dali exhibit, and access to Westminster Bridge are just downstairs from your room. The rooms are comfortable and well kept (what one would expect from the Marriott chain). It's really worth spending the extra money for a view of the Thames, as the south-facing view looks over the rather unattractive skyline of Southwark. The fitness center, open around the clock, is the largest I've seen in a London hotel, and an alluring spa offers a wide range of services.

MERCURE LONDON CITY BANKSIDE

71-79 Southwark St. SE1, 020/7902-0800, www.mercure.com

TUBE: Southwark or Borough

Popular among business travelers, this French chain is well situated for professionals visiting South Bank offices. Its location right behind the Tate Modern and the Millennium Bridge makes it good for travelers too. The double-glazed windows in the rooms facing Southwark Street, which can be filled with traffic, help ensure a good night's sleep. The double rooms are a bit small, but upgrade to the larger and better-fitted superior rooms for a few extra quid. A big bonus here is the Loft Bar and Restaurant, a trendy in-house eatery decorated in bright colors, soaked with sunshine from large skylights, and featuring a special selection of wines shipped from Paris. The basement has a gym open around the clock.

Outlying Areas — Map 1

The farther away from central London, the more you get for less. Even the budget places are better, and the Tube serves the whole city. It's a longer trip (a commute, really) to go see the sights, but if where you stay is important, consider these more remote options. In high season it's much easier to find a room away from the center than it is close to the sights.

UNDER £40

YHA HAMPSTEAD HEATH

4 Wellgarth Rd. NW11, 087/0770-5846, www.yha.org.uk

TUBE: Golders Green

To get away from it all while on a budget, try this youth hostel right on the edge of the spacious Hampstead Heath park. The basic hostel accommodations are clean and functional in typical YHA style, and the location is relaxing. If you're feeling lazy, unwind in the enclosed garden. Breakfast is included and you'll find Internet access, a TV lounge, kitchen, and laundry room on-site. Bicycles are available for hire (£1.50 an hour). For non-YHA members, it's an extra £3 a night to stay here.

YHA THAMESIDE

20 Salter Rd. SE16, 087/0770-6010, www.yha.org.uk

TUBE: Rotherhithe or Canada Water

This clean, modern hostel is halfway between central London and Greenwich, just moments from the Thames. That's not a problem as long as the Tube is running, but after a night out you'll be returning on one of the night buses. This means the Thameside hostel doesn't fill up as fast as the others and is a good option if budget accommodations can't be found elsewhere. Unusually for a youth hostel, all rooms are en suite. Breakfast is included and you'll find Internet access, a TV lounge, kitchen, and laundry room on-site. Bicycles are available for hire (£1.50 an hour). For non-YHA members, it's an extra £3 a night to stay here.

£40-80

DAWSON HOUSE HOTEL

72 Canfield Gardens NW6, reservations 020/7624-0079, guest number 020/7328-4857, www.dawsonhousehotel.com

TUBE: Finchley Road

This restored Victorian town house, part of the great suburban sprawl of the 19th and early 20th centuries, makes for a pleasant stay. The lush back garden is excellent for relaxing after a long day tromping around the city. All rooms are en suite, with a TV, telephone, and coffee- and tea-making facilities. An English- or Dutch-style breakfast is included and vegetarian breakfasts are available on request. Though Dawson House is a bit far from the center, just a few minutes' walk will lead to either West Hamstead or Finchley Road Tube stations. Camden Market, the Freud House, and the Freud Museum are also a short walk from here.

EXCURSIONS

London offers so much that it would be easy to spend an entire vacation here. That would be a mistake, however, because southern England offers even more. From the dreaming spires of Oxford to the mysterious monuments of Salisbury Plain, from the lofty towers of Windsor Castle to the quiet streets of St. Albans, endless diversions are just a day trip away.

England's countryside is worth at least one day's excursion. There is so much to England beyond its capital, and some of the best attractions are an easy day's trip or a relaxing overnight stay. Haven't gotten your fill of history and beautiful architecture? Try Oxford or Cambridge. Both of these university towns are jewels of architectural brilliance and have great restaurants, museums, and shops.

To get farther afield, try punting up the Cam to Grantchester, where Rupert Brooke and Virginia Woolf used to take tea and talk about writing, or hire a bike and cycle to Blenheim Palace near Oxford. To get out into the wild, try one of the country walks. There's really no beauty that can match the English countryside on a fine day. Take a breath of fresh air and see some of the nature that inspired Constable and Turner. Take in some history along with your vistas; stand atop the towers of Windsor Castle and look out over the rolling hills of England, or drink in the ancient atmosphere of Salisbury Plain, with its mysterious megalithic ruins of Stonehenge and Avebury.

While the major tour operators all run regular excursions to these locations, independent travelers should leave the tour bus behind and strike out on their own. Traveling at your own

© MOIRA ALLEN

HIGHLIGHTS

Best Roman Remains: In Bath, a remarkably preserved Roman bathhouse has been converted into the **Roman Baths Museum and Pump Rooms,** a museum explaining the history of the building and town. The highlight is the main pool, which still retains the atmosphere of ancient times (page 252).

Best Country Ramble: Traipse through rolling hills and ancient ruins along the **Bath Skyline** while the medieval towers of Bath loom in the distance (page 253).

Best Place to Fall Asleep in the Shade: Lawn chairs, a sparkling stream, and high tea under the shade of trees at **The Orchard at Grantchester** make for the perfect place to dream your vacation away (page 261).

Best Pilgrimage Site: A pilgrimage destination for centuries, the massive **Canterbury Cathedral** is a treasure house of art and history. Don't forget to see the atmospheric crypts and stay for the enchanting Choral Evensong (page 266).

Best Architecture: At **Magdalen College** the dreamiest of Oxford's dreaming spires rise up in Gothic splendor, providing a suitable backdrop to 1,000 years of learning (page 273).

Best Museum in All England: For an intimate and eclectic look at how people play music, cast spells, go to war, build houses, and do any number of other things around the world, explore the crowded collection of anthropological specimens at the **Pitt Rivers Museum** in Oxford. Keep an eye out for the shrunken heads! (page 273)

Best Old Rocks: There are a lot of old rocks in England. In fact, they're all old. But if you're interested in rocks that have been carved by people – people from a very long time ago – don't miss the famous megalithic monument of **Stonehenge** (page 277).

LOOK FOR TO FIND RECOMMENDED SIGHTS, ACTIVITIES, DINING, AND LODGING.

Best Historic Building: An often-overlooked house of worship, the **Cathedral and Abbey Church of St. Alban** has been standing since Anglo-Saxon times – and there may have been a pagan temple on the site before that. The building is a jumble of different architectural styles and the interior boasts some rare medieval paintings (page 281).

Best Place to Capture the Spirit of the Bard: Shakespeare is alive and well in his hometown of Stratford-upon-Avon; the Bard's most famous plays are performed several times daily by a small army of actors. But for something unique, visit **Shakespeare's Birthplace,** the lovingly preserved house where he was born, to see how he lived before becoming famous. (page 292).

Best Royal Residence: If you were a bit underwhelmed by Buckingham Palace, come to **Windsor Castle** for some real royal style. This medieval castle used to guard kings and queens in more turbulent days, but is now a comfortable home-away-from-home for the queen (page 296).

© MOIRA ALLEN

Bath Abbey towers above the Roman baths and Georgian homes nearby.

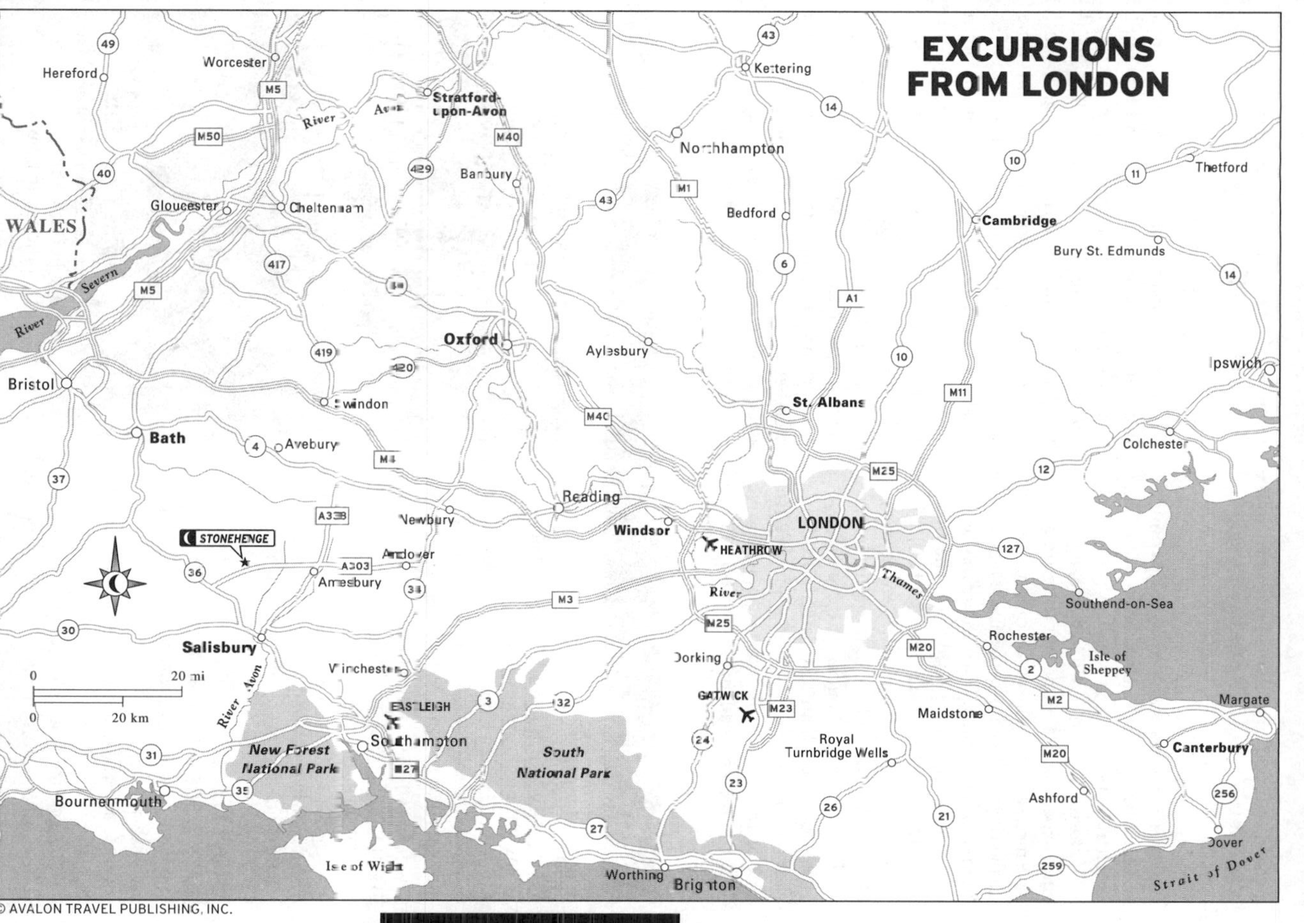
EXCURSIONS FROM LONDON
Hereford
Worcester
Stratford-upon-Avon
River Avon
Kettering
Northampton
Thetford
Banbury
Gloucester
Cheltenham
WALES
Severn
River
Bedford
Cambridge
Bury St. Edmunds
Oxford
Aylesbury
Ipswich
Bristol
Swindon
St. Albans
Bath
Avebury
Colchester
Reading
Newbury
Windsor
LONDON
HEATHROW
STONEHENGE
Andover
Amesbury
Thames
River
Southend-on-Sea
Salisbury
Rochester
Dorking
Isle of Sheppey
Winchester
GATWICK
EASTLEIGH
Margate
Maidstone
Southampton
New Forest National Park
South National Park
Royal Turnbridge Wells
Canterbury
Ashford
Bournemouth
Isle of Wight
Worthing
Brighton
Dover
Strait of Dover
0
20 mi
20 km
M1
M2
M3
M4
M5
M11
M20
M23
M25
M40
M50
A1
A303

pace allows you to see what you want to see and to make discoveries that you might not otherwise. The tourist information centers listed for each town make getting there easy, and their websites are filled with tips on what to see, where to eat, and where to stay. They can handle bookings as well.

Unfortunately, the train fares are some of the most expensive in Europe, but there are ways to save money. Buying in advance, either online or at the ticket office for departure, saves a lot of money, often reducing the listed fares by half. The further in advance you book, the cheaper the prices get, and there are often family fares for those traveling with kids. Getting out into the country doesn't have to break the bank.

The best thing about all of these excursions is that they are all an easy day trip from London—no more than a 1.5-hour journey from one of the major rail stations. Staying overnight is recommended; once you get out of town, you'll be tempted to linger awhile. So get out of town! England awaits you.

PLANNING YOUR TIME

These excursions can be enjoyed in all seasons, but some times are better than others. You'll avoid the crowds if you go in winter, but you'll probably not want to be outside much. Places that have most of their attractions indoors, such as Oxford or Canterbury, are best at this time. Spring and summer are great for outdoor destinations, such as Salisbury Plain or any of the hikes, but the crowds get bigger as the weather improves, and the middle of summer can be a bit hot for hiking. Autumn is a good time, the crowds are thinner and there are some fine days, but it's best to pick a place that has both indoor and outdoor attractions because the weather can be unpredictable. St. Albans is a good choice. If it rains, go to the cathedral. If it's sunny, go visit the Roman ruins.

Bath

Bath is a beautiful Georgian city with a breathtaking countryside and a system of Roman baths and pump rooms designated as a World Heritage Site. Bath makes an alluring getaway from London and has been for centuries. The Romans originally took the waters here, and in the 18th century it again became a fashionable resort with many beautiful Georgian buildings preserved from that period. Bath is a compact town so it's easy to get around and see all it has to offer; when you're done, strike out into the countryside on two scenic but easy hikes.

The stained glass in Bath Abbey illuminates the interior with a thousand colors.

SIGHTS

BATH ABBEY AND HERITAGE VAULTS

Abbey Churchyard, 012/2542-2462, www.bathabbey.org

HOURS: Mon.-Fri. 9 A.M.-4:30 P.M., Sun. 1 A.M.-2:30 P.M. Nov.-Mar.

COST: Suggested donation £2.50

The Gothic spires of Bath Abbey loom over

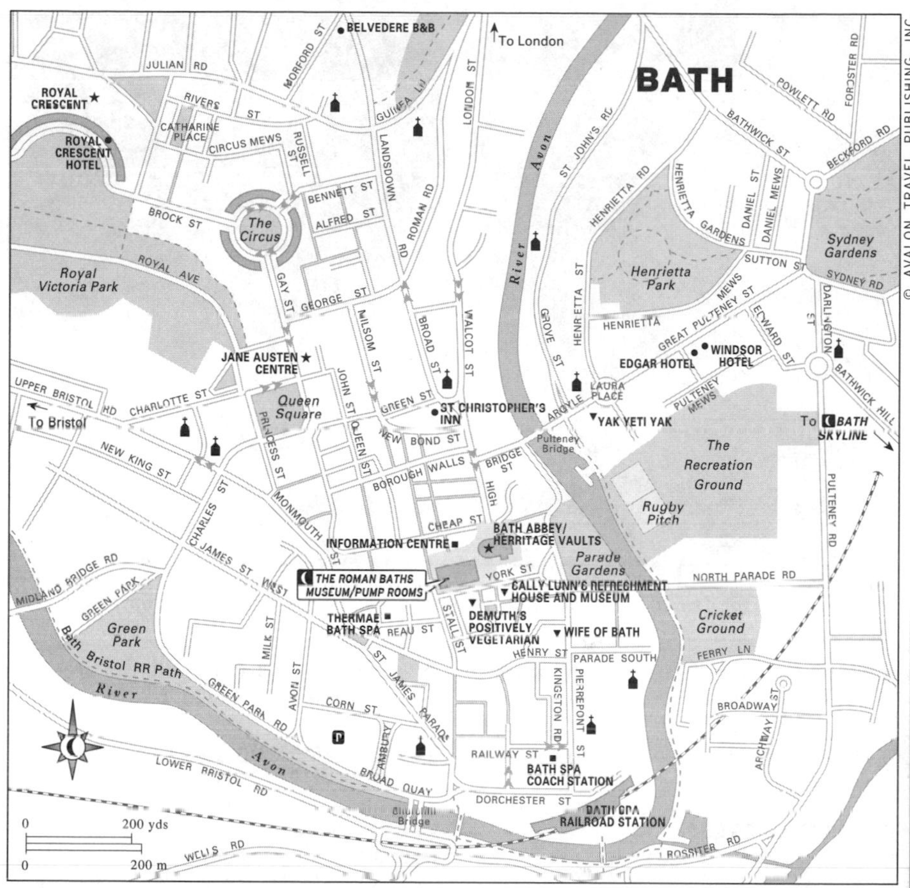

the city's skyline, providing an atmospheric backdrop to any stay. Begun in 1499, this is the last of the great Gothic cathedrals built in England and in many ways is a culmination of the style. Its great clear windows on the north and south walls soak the interior with light, while the intricate stained glass on the west and east ends are breathtakingly beautiful. When lit up at night it seems like a glowing jewel, and locals have dubbed it "The Lantern." A museum in the cellar traces the origins of Christian worship on the site from the 7th century to the present day.

JANE AUSTEN CENTRE

40 Gay St., Queen Sq., 012/2544-3000, www.janeausten.co.uk

HOURS: Daily 11 A.M.-4:30 P.M. Oct.-Feb., 10 A.M.-5:30 P.M. Mar.-Sept.

COST: Adults £5.95, seniors and students £4.50, children 6-15 £2.95, family£16

Fans of Jane Austen's society novels won't want to miss these exhibits. Austen lived for several years in Bath, and the peculiarities and social mores of its inhabitants shaped her perceptions and writing. Guides in period costume explain what it was like to live here in Jane Austen's

© MOIRA ALLEN

Bath is famous for its well-preserved Roman bathhouse and thermal, healing waters.

time and trace the history of high society in this first of English resorts. A Regency-style tea room offers refreshment and a gift shop sells books, Austen memorabilia, and reproductions of period lace and needlepoint.

NO. 1 ROYAL CRESCENT

1 Royal Crescent, 012/2542-8126, www.bath-preservation-trust.org.uk

HOURS: Tues.-Sun. 10:30 A.M.-5 P.M. Feb. 11-Oct. 28, Tues.-Sun. 10:30 A.M.-4 P.M. Nov. 1-26

COST: Adults £5, seniors and students £3.50, children 5-16 £2.50

Restored and furnished as it was in Georgian times, this sumptuous dwelling is part of a great sweep of town houses that are collectively a World Heritage Building. They were designed by John Wood the Younger and when completed in 1774 they became the swankiest address in the city. In fact, it still is. (In 2006, a house in the Crescent sold for £4.5 million.) The elegant interior is faithfully restored with period furnishings and conveys an excellent idea of what it was like to be ridiculously wealthy more than 200 years ago.

THE ROMAN BATHS MUSEUM AND PUMP ROOMS

Abbey Churchyard, 012/2547-7785, www.romanbaths.co.uk

HOURS: Daily 9:30 A.M.-4:30 P.M. Jan.-Feb., Nov.-Dec., daily 9:30 A.M.-5 P.M. Mar.-June, Sept.-Oct., 9 A.M.-9 P.M. July-Aug.

COST: Adults £10 (£11 July-Aug.), seniors and students £8.50, children 6-16 £6, family £28

The prime reason to come to Bath is this set of Roman thermal baths, the best preserved in the world and designated a World Heritage Site. When walking around its dim halls and central pool you get the feeling the Romans left 15 years ago, not 1,500. It's a real thrill to walk on the flagstones where Romans once walked and to see the waters in which they used to bathe. An excellent museum tells the story of the Roman town and bathhouse, and how it was sealed under later houses for centuries, keeping it preserved for today. It's absolutely a must for any history buff. An informative audio tour is included with admission.

THERMAE BATH SPA

Hot Bath St., 012/2533-1234, www.thermaebathspa.com

HOURS: Daily 9 A.M.–10 P.M.

COST: £19 for two hours, £29 for four, £45 for all day, treatments extra

The Romans came to Bath for its healing waters, and when Queen Anne stopped by in 1702 to cure her gout, she started a trend that lasted more than a century. Now people can come and again take the waters after the long-anticipated opening of this new spa. (It was a Millennium Project like the Dome in London, but it was delayed and way over budget and finally opened in 2006.) Two natural thermal baths allow guests to soak and relax, while other rooms offer massages, facials, and further treatments. Steam rooms and activity classes round out the day. A shop and café are on-site.

COUNTRY WALKS

BATH BRISTOL RAILWAY PATH

This 24-kilometer (13-mile) trail leading from Bath to Bristol is one of the most accessible walks. Built on the old tracks of the Midland Railway, it was abandoned in the 1960s and converted into a Railway Path between 1979 and 1986. The entire path is three meters (10 feet) wide and paved; it's wheelchair-accessible and popular with cyclists. To hire a bike, visit **Avon Valley Cyclery** (Bath Spa Railway Station, 012/2544-2442, www.bikeshop.uk.com/road.htm, 9 a.m.–5:30 p.m. Mon.–Sat.). The path is part of the National Cycle Network (011/7929-0888). Free maps of the trail are available from the information office in the train station.

The path officially starts at Brassmill Lane, 3 kilometers (2 miles) west of Bath city center, but in fact it joins a footpath and cycle route that starts at Churchill Bridge (or join it at Green Park). From Churchill Bridge head west, keeping the river to the left, until reaching Brassmill Lane; markers signify the start of the Railway Path.

Keeping on the path between the lane and the Avon River, head right (northwest) away from Bath. Almost immediately cross a small bridge across the Avon, then go under the A4 road and across another bridge, so that once again the river is to the left. The path is very well marked and impossible to miss.

From this point it's up to you how far to go, but keep in mind that the quickest way back is the way you came. The path meanders back and forth across the river (with accessible bridges each time) before departing from the river and going through pleasant countryside. Several pubs, restaurants, and picnic stops are along the way.

BATH SKYLINE

Like Rome, Bath is surrounded by seven hills. Unlike in Rome, much of the land on these hills is still nature reserve and makes for enjoyable hiking with wonderful views of the town and countryside. The Bath Skyline hike is 10 kilometers (6 miles), has several interpretive markers, and completes a circle, conveniently leading back to the start. To reach the path, walk up Bathwick Hill Road until the intersection with Cleveland Walk to the left. Here you will see the path leading off to the right. Path markers are white circles with a green arrow decorated with plants.

The trail leads through a field, offering admirable views, and meanders continuously over bridges, through gates and more fields, taking in Smallcombe Farm, Widcombe Hill (also known as MaCaulay Buildings), and the Rainbow Wood House. The view across Rainbow Wood fields is spectacular, so save some film for this part of the hike.

Further on the trail continues through scenic Bathampton Woods (stone was hauled down here on a tram to a former quarry; the grooves worn into some of the tracks are still visible) along the edge of the Bathwick Woods and eventully up to Sham Castle. This is a Victorian-era "folly," meaning a completely

© SEAN MCLACHLAN

The Bath Skyline walk ends near this fake castle, a Victorian-era "folly."

useless construction built for decoration. (Notice that the stone walls and turrets don't actually enclose anything—it's more like a movie set than a castle.) The path uses North Road and Clevedon Walk to terminate at Bathwick Hill, eventually coming full circle.

Note that the trail tends to meander and intersect with other paths, so be sure to look for the correct markers. For more information on the Bath Skyline hike, call 012/2583-3422 or visit www.nationaltrust.org.uk/bathskyline for a printable map.

RESTAURANTS

DEMUTHS POSITIVELY VEGETARIAN ££

2 N. Parade Passage, 012/2544-6059, www.demuths.co.uk

HOURS: Sun.-Fri. 10 A.M.-10 P.M., Sat. 9 A.M.-10 P.M.

A popular vegetarian restaurant just three minutes' walk from Bath Abbey, Demuths is a perfect pit stop while sightseeing. The interior is simple: Flowers decorate plain tables and white walls showcase a rotating collection of modern art. The menu caters to vegetarians and vegans and most of it is Fair Trade, organic, and bought from local farms. There's even an organic wine list. Meals come from all over the globe, with offerings such as Greek aubergine pie and *laksa lemak,* a Malaysian curry.

PUMP ROOM £££

Abbey Churchyard, 012/2544-4477, www.romanbaths.co.uk

HOURS: Open daily. Morning coffee: 9:30 A.M.-noon; Lunch: noon-2:30 P.M.; Afternoon Tea: 2:30-10 P.M.

Two centuries ago, the elite used to come here to be seen and to take their tea in the elegant Georgian dining room. It's a bit more egalitarian now, but the food is just as good with dishes such as char-grilled local asparagus and toasted almonds or Cornish smoked-trout salad—and it's still *the* place to go in Bath for tea. Fellows in 18th-century livery serve glasses of the famous Bath water (not to be confused with bathwater) for 50 pence—free if you've been in the Roman baths. There's free live classical and jazz music 7–10 P.M. in July and August.

SALLY LUNN'S REFRESHMENT HOUSE AND MUSEUM **££**

4 N. Parade Passage, 012/2546-1634, www.sallylunns.co.uk

HOURS: Mon.-Thurs. 10 A.M.-9:30 P.M., Fri.-Sat. 10 A.M.-10 P.M., Sun. 11 A.M.-9:30 P.M.

Sally Lunn was a Huguenot who fled persecution in France and moved here in the 1680s. Her house and museum is set in the oldest house in Bath, built around 1482. Everyone comes here to try the famous Sally Lunn Bun, a big, tasty bun dolloped with various sweet toppings such as jam, honey, or clotted cream. Besides the buns, there's a proper English tea and meals such as venison and beef casserole on a plate of bread. In the basement is a museum showing the kind of kitchen Sally would have worked in (adults 30 pence, free for everyone else).

WIFE OF BATH **££**

12 Pierrepont St., 012/2546-1745, www.wifeofbathrestaurant.co.uk

HOURS: Mon.-Sat. noon-2 P.M., 5:30-11 P.M., Sun. 5-10:30 P.M.

This cozy little Georgian basement has five separate dining rooms that make for an intimate evening. Choose from a variety of British and international dishes such as peppered lamb steak with a port and red currant jus, or penne pasta with a fennel, tomato, and blue-cheese sauce. The homemade puddings are especially popular with the locals. In good weather, sit out on the walled patio and admire the fountain. Both the interior and the patio are very romantic and a good place to take someone if you're looking to impress.

YAK YETI YAK **£**

12 Argyle St., 012/2544-2299

HOURS: Mon.-Sat. noon-2:30 P.M., 6-10:30 P.M., Sun. noon-2:30 P.M., 6-10 P.M.

The little cellar that houses this restaurant is decorated with photos and art of Nepal's stunning scenery. Nepali cuisine is a bit like Indian food, but heartier because of the country's mountainous and harsh climate. Vegetarians will have lots of choice, including *aloo tamar* (fermented bamboo shoots stir-fried with new potatoes, black-eyed peas, and vegetables), while meat-eaters will enjoy the Yak Yeti Yak (beef marinated with spices, onion, sweet pepper, and tomato). And where else in England are you going to get Nepali beer?

ACCOMMODATIONS

BELVEDERE BED AND BREAKFAST **£40-80**

25 Belvedere, 012/2533-0264, www.belvederewinevaults.co.uk

This town house was built in 1760 for a man who liked his wines. The large former wine cellar now acts as storage for the popular and trendy-looking bar serving tapas and other Mediterranean cuisine. Luckily, not much noise filters up to the rooms, which are all en suite and decorated with a combination of original features and modern rustic furniture. There are only four of them, however, so book early. A full English breakfast is included. The Belvedere is about 10 minutes' walk from the town center and has steep steps to the rooms, so it may pose problems for those with limited mobility.

EDGAR HOTEL **£40-80**

64 Great Pulteney St., 012/2542-0619, www.edgar-hotel.co.uk

Set in a row of Georgian era town houses, the Edgar's 18 rooms are en suite (shower only) and include a TV, hair dryer, and tea- and coffee-making facilities. A full English breakfast is included. The location is good—less than 10 minutes' walk to the town center but far enough away from any noise—and there are nice views of either the surrounding hillsides or the Georgian street. The service is efficient, but the decor is somewhat lacking; it seems all the atmosphere is on the outside.

ROYAL CRESCENT HOTEL **OVER £150**

16 Royal Crescent, 012/2582-3333, www.royalcrescent.co.uk

If you came to Bath to take the waters and feel like 18th-century nobility, stay here. The Royal Crescent Hotel is housed in an architectural jewel designed by John Wood the

Younger to house Bath's Georgian-era elite visitors. The whole complex is a World Heritage Building. The air-conditioned rooms are all individually designed and suites come with their own lounge. All rooms are en suite and come with little luxuries too numerous to list. A spa and gym are on-site, and there is a beautiful garden restaurant in back.

ST. CHRISTOPHER'S INN UNDER £40

9 Green St., local 012/2548-1444, international 020/7407-1856, www.st-christophers.co.uk

Backpackers stay at this popular hostel of the St. Christopher's chain to save money, socialize, and drink in the bar and chill-out room. The interior is clean and well maintained, but the crowd can be a bit raucous, although not overly so if you're used to staying in hostels. Rooms vary from twin beds to 12-bed dorms and a continental breakfast is included. You'll find a restaurant, Internet access, and laundry facilities on-site. The hostel is close to the center and the staff has loads of information on what to see and do around town.

WINDSOR HOTEL OVER £150

69 Great Pulteney St., 012/2542-2100

A converted Georgian town house with the interior matching the era of the exterior, this is one of the nicer hotels in Bath but it is beginning to show a bit of wear around the edges. All 14 rooms are en suite and come with a TV. Simple doubles are on the lower end of this price bracket, but the deluxe rooms get much more expensive. Service is good and free tea and coffee can be delivered to your room. A full English breakfast is included, but you must eat it in the reception area—how unusual for a hotel in this price bracket not to have a dining room!

PRACTICALITIES

GETTING THERE

First Great Western (084/5600-5604/2244, www.firstgreatwestern.co.uk), overseen by National Rail (084/5748-4950, www.nationalrail.co.uk), runs trains from Paddington Station to Bath Spa Station (corner of Dorchester and Manvers St., 084/5748-4950) for a 1.5-hour journey. Trains run at least twice an hour, starting at 5:43 A.M. and ending at 11:35 P.M. The first train leaves Bath Spa at 5:42 A.M. and service runs twice hourly until 10:52 P.M. On Saturdays the first train leaves Paddington at 6:30 A.M., and they run at least twice an hour until 11:30 P.M., while the first leaves Bath Spa at 5:42 A.M. and they run twice hourly until 10:52 P.M. On Sundays the first leaves Paddington at 8 A.M. and runs at least twice an hour until 11:30 P.M., while the first leaves Bath Spa at 7:52 A.M. and runs hourly until 9:42 P.M. The cost is £45 for a return. The railway station is about a quarter mile from the Abbey and Roman Baths.

There is also a **National Express** bus (087/0580-8080, www.nationalexpress.com) that leaves from Victoria Coach Station and takes a tiring 3.25 hours to reach the Bath Spa Station (corner of Dorchester and Manvers St., right opposite the railway station, 012/2546-6854), but it gives a more sedate look at some lovely countryside along the way. Coaches leave at least once an hour daily, sometimes three times in an hour, 7 A.M.–11:30 P.M. and cost £23.50. From Bath Spa, the first coach leaves at 3:40 A.M. and runs to 11 P.M. Make sure you don't get one that goes through Bristol or Swindon, as that will add 1–2 hours to your time. The bus station is about a quarter mile from the Abbey and Roman Baths.

If you're coming by car, take the A4 out of central London until you reach the M4 heading west, which you take to Exit 18, which gets you onto the A46 towards Bath/Stroud. The entire journey is 114 miles and takes about two hours.

GETTING AROUND

Bath is a fairly compact city and the well-preserved Georgian architecture makes walking a pleasing experience and public transport unnecessary.

Several tours are available, including

Bizarre Bath (012/2533-5124, www.bizarre-bath.co.uk, £7, students £5), a humorous 90-minute walking tour. **City Sightseeing** (012/2533-0444, www.citysightseeing.co.uk) runs 45-minute bus tours with live English and recorded multilingual commentary that gives a whirlwind look at all that Bath has to offer. Tours cost £9.50 for adults, £7.50 for students/seniors, and £5 for children. The first route leaves from High Street by Bath Abbey; the other leaves from the railway station. **Ghost Walks of Bath** (012/2535-0512, www.ghostwalksofbath.co.uk, adults £6, seniors, students, and children £5) meets at 8 P.M. every Friday in front of Garrick's Head pub and Theatre Royal on Barton Street. The **Great Bath Pub Crawl** (£5) runs at 8 nightly from Lambretta's Bar on North Parade and gives the history of various pubs in Bath, with plenty of chances to sample the wares (drinks not included in the price). By far the best value are the **free walking tours** (012/2547-4111, www.thecityofbath.co.uk) of Bath put on by the city and run by volunteers (who do not expect tips). These very informative tours last 90 minutes to two hours and meet outside the Pump Room in Abbey Churchyard (10:30 A.M. and 2 P.M. Sun.–Fri., 10:30 A.M. Sat.). There's a 7 P.M. walk on Tuesdays, Fridays, and Saturdays May–September.

To ply the waters of the Avon River, take a boat tour. **Bath City Boat Trips** (012/2548-0541, adults £6.95, seniors and students £5.95, children £4.95) runs from a pier on the east side of the river between Pulteney and North Parade bridges. Trips departs several times all day 11 A.M.–5 P.M. and last an hour. Interesting note: This is a different Avon than the one that flows through Stratford-upon-Avon. There are seven Avon rivers in Britain—the word means "river" in Old English—so this is actually the River River!

INFORMATION

The **Bath Tourist Information Centre** (U.K. only 090/6711-2000, overseas only 087/0444-6442, www.visitbath.co.uk) is in Abbey Chambers, Abbey Churchyard (just south of Bath Abbey) and is a good resource for information about the local area. It is open 9:30 A.M.–5 P.M. Monday–Saturday, 10 A.M.–4 P.M. Sunday October–May, and 9:30 A.M.–6 P.M. Monday–Saturday, 10 A.M.–4 P.M. Sunday June–September. A smaller office is at the train station.

Cambridge

Just 60 miles north of London lies the idyllic university town of Cambridge. With its Gothic towers, verdant gardens, and storied history, Cambridge is one of the more popular day trips from the capital. The university, founded in the 13th century, is divided into several colleges, each with its own character and history. In the town itself, winding streets and alleyways lead to atmospheric pubs, medieval churches, museums, and shops. Luckily for the visitor, Cambridge is compact and easily walkable. Punting on the River Cam will take the more adventurous into beautiful Cambridgeshire countryside.

SIGHTS

FITZWILLIAM MUSEUM

Trumpington St., 012/2333-2900, www.fitzmuseum.cam.ac.uk

HOURS: Tues.-Sat. 10 A.M.-5 P.M., Sun. noon-5 P.M.

COST: Free admission

Cambridge's biggest museum was founded in 1816 by the 7th Viscount Fitzwilliam of Merrion and is the art museum of the University of Cambridge. The ground floor includes ancient and Asian art and a medieval armory. Some of the highlights are Egyptian artifacts from the Amarna period and a good collection of illuminated manuscripts from the Middle Ages. The

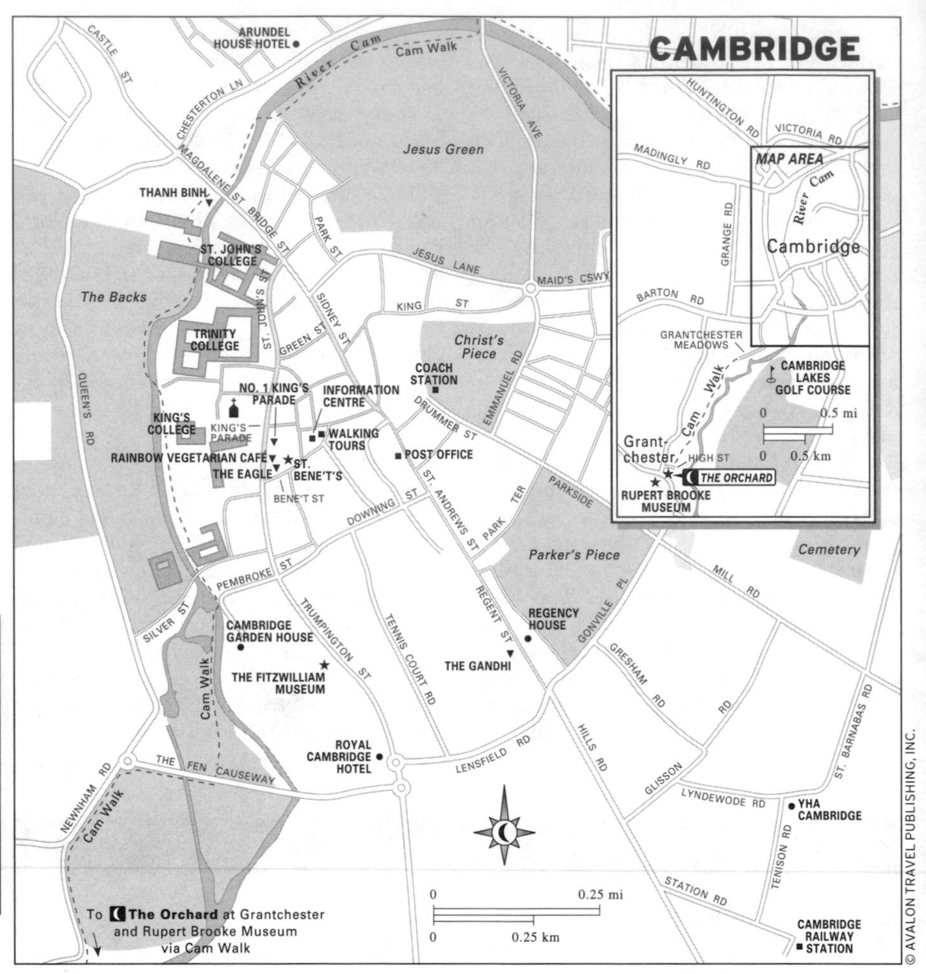

first floor has a large collection of European masters such as Rubens, Hogarth, Cezanne, and Picasso. An unusual aspect of the displays here is that most are simply hanging on the wall or on shelves as if they were the collection of some eccentric and vastly wealthy collector, which is exactly what much of this was. Unfortunately, someone stumbled on the stairs in 2006 and while trying to stop his fall managed to knock over and destroy a Ming vase. Luckily he was British, so there wasn't an international incident, but please be careful.

KING'S COLLEGE

Trinity St., 012/2333-8400, www.trin.cam.ac.uk

HOURS: Daily 10 A.M.–5 P.M.

COST: Adults £4.50, seniors over 65 and children £3

The most spectacular of Cambridge's many colleges is also one of the oldest, having been founded in 1441 by Henry VI. Visitors flock here to see the awe-inspiring chapel. After passing through the gatehouse, you'll find yourself in the large grassy Front Court with the chapel on your right. The Gibbs building (1724) stands before you with a massive Georgian facade of white Portland stone, now weathered to a gray that often matches the English skies. To the left is the Wilkins Building (1828), decorated with neo-Gothic spires and battlements. The chapel is the main attraction, however, with its twin spires visible from much of the city. Completed in 1547, it boasts a huge vaulted roof weighing 2,000 tons. Dizzying in its height and for the sheer beauty of its complex stone buttressing, this has to be one of the best architectural views in England. A series of 16th-century stained-glass windows tell the stories of the Bible, and the altar is decorated with the *Adoration of the Magi* by Rubens. The chapel is occasionally reserved for special events, so check the website for upcoming closures. During Easter term (late April–mid-June) the grounds are closed but the chapel is open.

PUNTING ON THE CAM

The River Cam

HOURS: Daily dawn-dusk

There's nothing quite as peaceful as punting a flat-bottomed boat on a canal through the lush British countryside on a lazy summer day. Boats generally seat 3–4 people, and the punter stands on the stern with a long pole and pushes along. To turn, gently push the pole through the water in the opposite direction from the one you want to go. You'll find about a dozen punting companies to choose from including Trinity College (012/2333-8483, daily 10:30 A.M.–5:30 P.M.), which has a Punt House right where the river passes the college. Prices are approximately £12 an hour, with a deposit required in case you punt off to parts unknown. To be even lazier on that lazy summer day, get someone else to do the work by joining one of the punting tours operated by most of these companies throughout the day. The swarms of touts who will intercept you countless times as you walk through the town will tell you all about them.

ST. BENE'T'S CHURCH

Benet's St., 012/2335-3903, www.stbenets.com

HOURS: Daily 8 A.M.-7 P.M., except when services are in session

COST: Free admission

The oldest of Cambridge's many churches, St. Bene't's was built by the Saxons around 1025 and dedicated to St. Benedict. The church has enjoyed the patronage of Corpus Christi College for centuries, and many of its priests are graduates of the college. Since 1946 it has been a Franciscan church. While it has been remodeled extensively in later centuries, much of the original stonework is still visible and makes for a rare example of Saxon architecture. The best feature of the original church is the tower, which you can climb to get photogenic views of town.

TRINITY COLLEGE

Trinity St., 012/2333-8400, www.trin.cam.ac.uk

HOURS: College: Daily 10 A.M.-5 P.M.; Wren Library: Mon.-Fri. noon-2 P.M., Sat. 10:30 A.M.-12:30 P.M. during term

COST: Adults £2.20, seniors, students, and children £1.30

Founded in 1546 by Henry VIII, Trinity College has graduated more than 30 Nobel Prize winners, but it was creating leading thinkers long before that prize was established. Sir Isaac Newton studied and then taught here 1661–1696. Architect Sir Christopher Wren designed the library in 1695, which is the main attraction beyond the ornate facades and statuary of the college buildings. The tall windows and white walls and ceiling bathe the interior with natural light, making a pleasing contrast to the dark wood furniture, much of it original. The collection of rare manuscripts includes an 8th-century copy of the *Epistles of St. Paul,* Newton's annotated first edition of the *Principia,* and A. A. Milne's manuscript of *Winnie-the-Pooh.* The admission price includes both the Wren Library and the college.

WALKING TOURS

Visitors Information Centre, The Old Library, Wheeler St., 012/2345-7574, www.visitcambridge.org

WILD WALKS: COUNTRYSIDE RAMBLES CLOSE TO LONDON

No countryside is more beautiful than England in good weather. The gently rolling hills, green pastures, and lush foliage of southern England are stirring and can imprint themselves in memory for the rest of one's days. It's highly recommended that you get out of London for at least one day and tromp through the paths and rural lanes of England.

The trick is, of course, to go in fair weather. As changeable as England's weather can be – sun one moment and rain the next – there's not much you can do except pack a raincoat, strike out, and hope for the best. Even if it does start raining, don't despair; it could just as easily become sunny again. If not, stop in a country pub and warm up beside the fire.

While the English countryside is beautiful, peaceful, and not terribly remote, you should take some basic safety precautions. Walks can be strenuous, with a lot of steep slopes, and hikers should be reasonably fit before heading out. Bring plenty of water, some food, a raincoat (preferably) or umbrella, waterproof shoes or hiking boots, and sunscreen. No matter the weather, bring all of these items. England's weather is terribly fickle and if it gets hot or rainy while you're in the countryside, there's no hotel to duck back into and change.

Also keep in mind that trails tend to run along private land, and in some cases, through it. If a trail runs through private land it is because the owner has agreed to its use, but the owner can withdraw permission if too many people litter or wander off the path. Please stay on the path, pack out any trash, and pick up any trash along the way. The Golden Rule of hiking is to leave the land as found.

Several organizations are dedicated to preserving the countryside and exploring it. **The National Trust** (www.nationaltrust.org.uk) is an independent charity with 3.4 million members that manages trails across the country, as well as archaeological sites, historic homes, and more. Its website is filled with information about its properties, most of which are open to the public and many of which are free. **English Heritage** (www.english-heritage.org.uk) is a government body that protects sites of historical importance. Since many of these sites are in the countryside, some trails come under their management. Its most famous property is Stonehenge, but it manages many historic sites and landscapes across the British Isles and provides information on them via its website. **English Nature** (www.english-nature.org.uk) is a government-funded body that promotes conservation of England's wildlife and natural features. It also publishes numerous books and pamphlets on the country's flora, fauna, and environment.

The Ramblers (www.ramblers.org.uk) is Britain's largest walking society (143,000 members) and hosts walks in every region. It also publishes a huge range of books and maps and helps maintain trails, shows them to others, and promotes country walking as a healthy pastime. **Best Walks** (www.bestwalks.com) is an excellent online bookshop that covers every region of the British Isles; its website is full of information about regional and themed walks.

In springtime, the English countryside bursts forth in bloom.

HOURS: Open daily 1:30 P.M.; Mon.-Sat. 10:30 A.M. and daily 2:30 P.M. July-Aug.; Mon.-Sat. 11:30 A.M. Oct.-Mar.
COST: Including King's College: Adults £8.50, children under 12 £4; Including St. John's College: Adults £6.50, children under 12 £4, children under 5 free

The two-hour tours operated by the Visitors Information Centre are very informative and a good way to learn a lot about the colleges and the city if you have limited time. The guides are very knowledgeable and field a barrage of questions with ease. They take you around central Cambridge, telling you the history of the town and colleges in great detail. Included in the price is admission to King's College and its famous chapel. When that college is closed, the tour goes to St. John's instead. The center offers other tours such as ghost tours, punting tours, and a popular "punt and a pint" tour. Special tours are occasionally organized, so check the website or call for details.

COUNTRY WALKS

CAM WALK TO THE ORCHARD AT GRANTCHESTER

Even if punting isn't your style, you can still enjoy this short hike along the river that ends at the charming little village of Grantchester and its famous tea house, the Orchard. It's only 2 kilometers (1.2 miles) each way and is level and easy to follow the entire length.

From the end of the little residential lane called Grantchester Meadows is a path heading into some woods and fields. From there it's clear sailing for a mile. The path at times wanders in woods, in fields at others, sometimes right next to the River Cam on the left (east), and at times a bit away from it. The walk is very quiet and peaceful. Punters glide their way across the river, birds and rabbits inhabit the fields, and there are several places to stop by the water and eat a snack or simply take in the view. It's amazing how quickly Cambridge is left behind and it feels like the middle of nowhere.

After a mile, a row of thatched-roof houses appears off to the right and away from the river; that's Grantchester. The path forks and heads toward the houses, but stay on the riverside path, continue through a gate, and take a right away from the river and up to High Street. Take a left at High Street and after about 125 meters (150 yards) is a sign for the Orchard.

THE ORCHARD AT GRANTCHESTER

The Orchard at Grantchester (45–47 Mill Way, Grantchester, 012/2384-5788, www.orchard-grantchester.com) is a splendid tea house set amid fruit trees. Lawn chairs, a sparkling stream, and high tea in the shade make for the perfect place to dream a vacation away. It's open 9:30 A.M.–7 P.M. daily in the summer and 9:30 A.M.–5:30 P.M. in the winter. Indoor seating is available, but the lawn chairs are much nicer, so come in good weather. A variety of teas are available, served with scones, jam, and that greatest of British culinary inventions, clotted cream. Lunch is available 11 A.M.–3 P.M. and includes a choice of sandwiches, soups, homemade bread, jacket potatoes, and ploughman's lunches. The pies and cakes are good too.

The Orchard was founded in 1897 and quickly became a favorite of students and residents in nearby Cambridge. Though close to town, it seems miles away and was considered a respectable destination for a day's outing. It became famous in 1909 when a young Cambridge graduate named Rupert Brooke moved to the village. He was already known to the local literati for his poetry and soon a literary circle grew up around him that included Virginia Woolf. The group, dubbed the "Neo-Pagans," was known for its fine writing and crazy social life. The free Rupert Brooke Museum on the Orchard grounds traces the life story of one of England's favorite 20th-century poets.

Grantchester is a little village and the Orchard is its only claim to fame, but it's worth wandering around to see small-town England. There are lots of traditional thatched-roof houses, a charming village church, and a couple of good pubs.

RESTAURANTS

THE EAGLE £

Benet St., 012/2350-5020

HOURS: Mon.-Sat. 9 A.M.-11 P.M., Sun. noon-11:30 P.M., food served Mon.-Fri. noon-2:30 P.M., 5-8:45 P.M., Sat.-Sun. noon-3 P.M.

A must-see for pub fans, the Eagle is close to the center of town and is a rambling place with lots of little nooks and crannies if you want to eat alone, and a friendly main area if you don't. It started serving the coach trade in the 15th century and became popular with American aviators from the nearby air base during World War II. Many of them wrote their names on the ceiling of the back room with candles and lighters, and you can still see their burnt scribbles. The kitchen offers all the usual pub fare, such as steak and kidney pie and fish-and-chips. Be aware that since this is a pub, children are allowed only in the courtyard, where there are several tables. Try to make it for the lunchtime Sunday roast.

THE GANDHI £££

72 Regent St., 012/2335-3942

HOURS: Mon.-Sun. noon-2:30 P.M. and 6 P.M.-midnight

Just five minutes from the center of town, The Gandhi serves a variety of Indian dishes in relaxed surroundings. You'll find all the usual kormas, vindaloos, and *jalfreezis* that you would expect from the Indian places in London but at a considerably cheaper price for the quality you get. Plenty of vegetarian options are on the menu.

NO. 1 KING'S PARADE ££

The Cellars, 1 King's Parade, 012/2335-9506, www.n1kp.com

HOURS: Mon.-Fri. noon-3 P.M., 6-11 P.M., Sat. noon-11 P.M., Sun. noon-3 P.M., 6-11 P.M.; Afternoon Tea 2:30-5:30 P.M.

This place is set in a medieval wine cellar opposite King's College—you can't get more atmospheric than this. The cuisine is a mix of traditional British and Continental favorites. The oak-smoked Scottish salmon is especially good, as are the English sausages with truffle oil. While there aren't any main courses for vegetarians, you can put together some starters and side dishes, such as grilled goat's cheese crostini and a warm bruschetta of tomatoes. Live blues and jazz start at 8 P.M. every Thursday night.

RAINBOW VEGETARIAN CAFÉ ££

9A King's Parade, 012/2332-1551, www.localsecrets.com

HOURS: Tues.-Sat. 10 A.M.-10 P.M.

Vegetarians will love this cozy little basement restaurant that serves some of the best veggie food in England, literally. Rainbow was named café of the year by the Vegetarian Society. Besides vegetarian food, it offers a good variety of vegan and gluten-free choices. The friendly service, heaping salads, and variety of internationally inspired dishes such as Thai curry make this a place to bring your non-veggie friends. Be warned that this place is popular, but the occasional long lines are a testament to its quality.

THANH BINH ££

17 Magdalene St., 012/2336-2456

HOURS: Tues.-Sun. noon-2:30 P.M., 6-9:30 P.M.

This popular downtown Vietnamese restaurant has quick service in nice but somewhat crowded surroundings. The meat dishes, especially the curried ones, are very good, as are the soups, which come with various savory sauces to give them that extra zip. Be careful of the more spicy dishes, though, as they are quite fiery. Note that while Thanh Binh does not have a liquor license, diners can bring their own from the wine shop right over Magdalene Bridge.

ACCOMMODATIONS

ARUNDEL HOUSE HOTEL £80-150

Chesterton Rd., 012/2336-7701, www.arundelhousehotels.co.uk

This Victorian terrace hotel sits right next to the River Cam and provides breathtaking views in spring, fall, and summer. While Arundel House has 103 rooms (decorated in a rather froofy pseudo-Victorian style) it's often full because of its popularity, so book well in advance. The rooms overlooking the river are best, but you might end up spending too much time staring out your window. A bar and restaurant are on-site and a continental breakfast is included. It's just a few minutes' walk from the center of town, so it's convenient too.

CAMBRIDGE GARDEN HOUSE £80-150
Granta Place, Mill Lane, 012/2325-9988, www.cambridgegardenhouse.com

A stay at the Cambridge Garden House is both convenient and pleasant. This modern hotel in the center of town has newly refurbished, spacious rooms set right next to the River Cam. Rooms facing the river offer nice views. The hotel has gardens where one can sit outside in fine weather. A restaurant, bar, pool, and steam room are on-site and a breakfast buffet is included. The Arundel is more traditional and this hotel is more modern, so take your pick. Both have good views and good locations.

REGENCY HOUSE £40-80
7 Regent Terr., 012/2332-9626, www.regencyguesthouse.co.uk

This Victorian town house near the center of town dates to the 1850s and overlooks a broad swath of parkland on one side and busy Regent Street on the other. Try to get a room on the park side or at least one on an upper floor to avoid any street noise. All rooms are modern in style and come with a full (and filling) English breakfast. Because of its central location, it's popular with visiting professionals and tourists alike. All in all, it's a good value close to the action.

ROYAL CAMBRIDGE HOTEL £80-150
Trumpington St., 012/2335-1631, www.forestdale.com

In an ornate row of Georgian terraced houses, this fine hotel is only a few minutes' walk from the city center. The bedrooms are larger than what you will become accustomed to in England and the service is impeccable. One big bonus is the eating and drinking facilities. The High Table Restaurant re-creates a traditional college dining experience, something far removed from American college caféterias. The decor is elegant, and the food is traditional British. The Kings Bar and Lounge provides old-style British surroundings for drinks and conversation.

YHA CAMBRIDGE UNDER £40
97 Tenison Rd., 012/2335-4601

The cheapest accommodation option in Cambridge is the YHA youth hostel near the railway station, about a 15-minute walk from the center of town. There are two, three, four, five, six, and eight beds per room set in a Victorian town house. Membership to the Youth Hostel Association is required, but a temporary membership is available for £3 per night. Breakfast is included and picnic lunches and dinners are available. You'll find Internet access, a bar, kitchen, common room, and laundry facilities on-site.

PRACTICALITIES

GETTING THERE

National Rail (084/5748-4950, www.nationalrail.co.uk) runs from London's Liverpool Street Station to Cambridge Railway Station (Station Rd., 084/5748-4950) and takes 1–1.5 hours depending on the train. The cost is £21 for a standard day return (£17.60 off-peak) and £8.80 for a standard day return for children 5–15 (£8.75 off-peak). On weekdays the first train leaves London Liverpool Street at 4:25 A.M. and the last at 11:58 P.M., while the first train leaves Cambridge at 4:48 A.M. and the last at 10:51 P.M. On Saturdays the first train leaves London at 5:58 A.M. and the last at 11:58 P.M., while the first train leaves Cambridge at 4:25 A.M. and the last at 10:51 P.M. On Sundays the first train leaves London at 7:58 A.M. and the last at 10:58 P.M., while the first train leaves Cambridge at 7:51 A.M. and the last at 10:51 P.M. These are the times for the most direct trains. Other, slower lines go to points in between and take much longer. The railway station is almost a mile from the center of town.

National Express (087/0580-8080, www.nationalexpress.com) runs buses from King's Cross and Liverpool Street to Cambridge Bus Station (Drummer St., 087/0608-2608) for £10.50 for a day return or £16 if you return on a later day. Seniors 60 and older and children 3–13 pay only £5.25 for a day return and £8 for an open return. On weekdays the service runs at least once an hour around the clock. On Saturdays the first bus from London leaves 8:30 A.M. and the last at 11:30 P.M., while the first bus leaves Cambridge at 5:55 A.M. and the last at 8:30 P.M. On Sundays the first bus leaves London at 3:20 A.M. and the last at 11:30 P.M., while the first bus leaves Cambridge at 1:35 A.M. and the last at 11:05 P.M.

Most trips are direct and take two hours, but be careful not to get one of the buses that stops at Stansted Airport or Milton Keynes Coachway, which can more than double the travel time. The direct buses are generally every hour on the half hour, but this can vary. The bus station is conveniently located right in the center of town.

To get to Cambridge from London by car, get onto the North Circular Rd./A406 to M11 north, and take Exit 13 on the left, which gets you onto A1303 and leads to Cambridge. The trip is 64 miles and takes about 1 hour and 15 minutes.

GETTING AROUND

Like all English towns, Cambridge has plenty of buses and taxis, but these aren't really necessary because it's so compact. In fact, a visit will be greatly enhanced by walking everywhere. You'll find plenty of pubs, restaurants, and cafés to rest weary feet, many with attractive views of the colleges. If taking a bus, get a map and schedule from the Tourist Information Centre. Taxis generally won't take passengers the short distances within the center of town, but you might want to get one to and from the train station, which will put you back only about £4. A cheaper option is to take bus C1 or C3 directly outside the station. These run every 10 minutes or so and can drop you off in the center of town for £1. Walking to town takes about 20 minutes and is a bit confusing, so don't be shy about asking for directions at the Tourist Information Centre in the station.

INFORMATION

The **Cambridge Visitors Information Centre** (The Old Library, Wheeler St., 087/1226-8006, www.visitcambridge.org) has a very helpful staff who will weigh you down with free brochures. The bookshop sells various guides and histories of the town and shire and the staff can book tours and hotels for you too. There's a smaller City Sightseeing Office at the train station, which gives out free maps, sells a nicer map, and makes bookings. Both offices are open 10 A.M.–5:30 P.M. Monday–Friday, 10 A.M.–5 P.M. Saturday, 11 A.M.–4 P.M. Sunday (closed Sundays in winter).

To save a bit of money, consider buying a Visitor Card for £2.50. It's available at the Visitors Information Centre and at various shops in town, or buy it through www.visitcambridge.org. The card gives discounts on walking and punting tours, theater tickets, dozens of businesses and restaurants, and entry to various sights (a complete list is on the website). The card is valid for a maximum of three weeks.

Canterbury

This famous pilgrimage center, immortalized by Chaucer's *Canterbury Tales* and the martyrdom of Thomas Becket, is less than 60 kilometers (35 miles) southeast of London, making an easy day trip. A plethora of good restaurants and affordable hotels makes this a good overnight option too. The famous cathedral, along with St. Martin's Church and St. Augustine's Abbey, together constitute a UNESCO World Heritage Site.

Canterbury was the stronghold of the Cantii, a tribe of Britons who gave their name to Kent, and who called their town Durovernon. When the Romans invaded in A.D. 43, they kept the name and made it into a regional center, part of the line of towns along Watling Street, running from the port of Richborough through Canterbury to London and northwest to Wroxeter. They built a theater, forum, baths, a city wall, and rich villas, parts of which can still be seen.

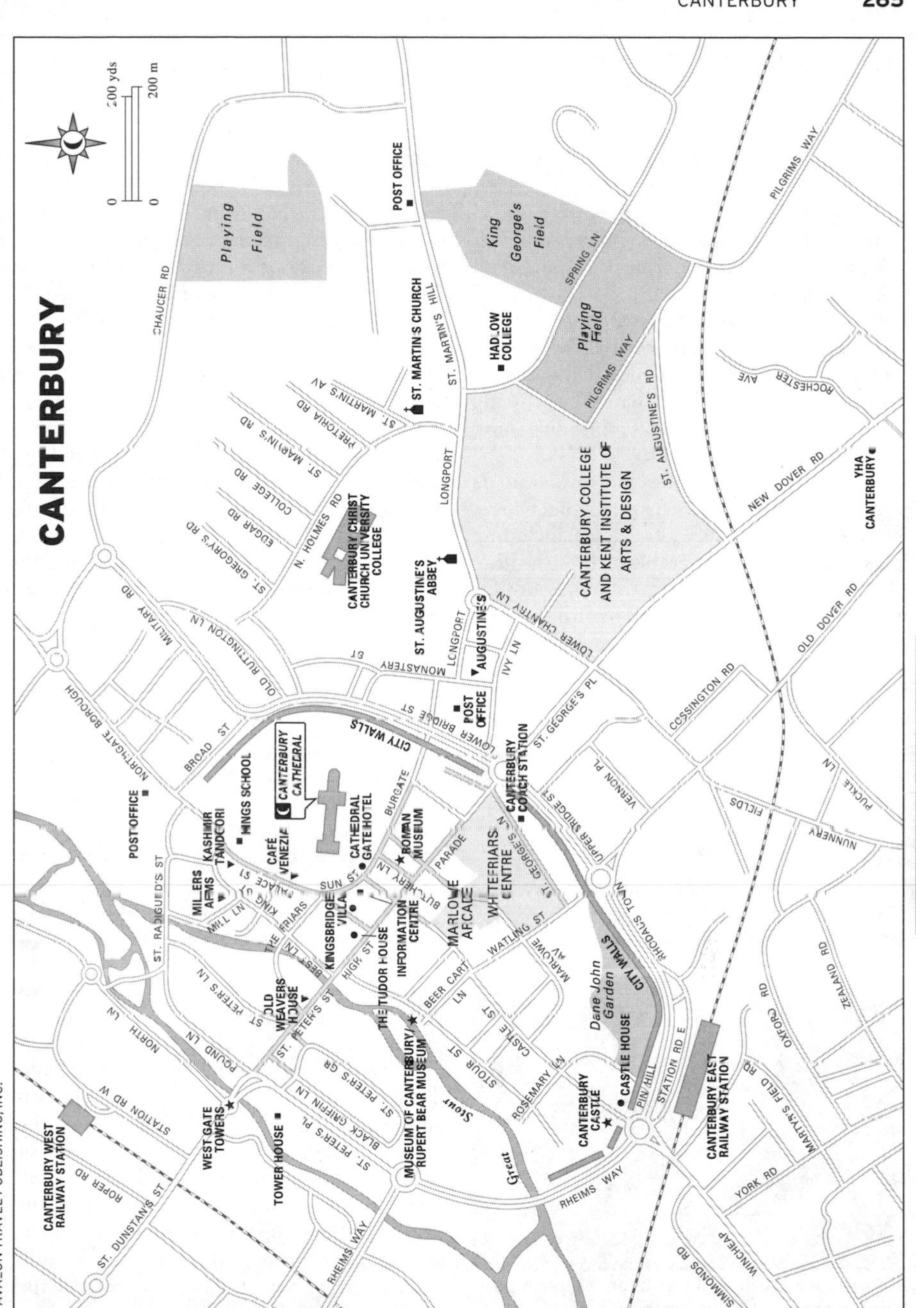
CANTERBURY
0
200 yds
0
200 m
Playing Field
POST OFFICE
King George's Field
CHAUCER RD
SPRING LN
PILGRIMS WAY
ST. MARTIN'S CHURCH
ST. MARTIN'S HILL
HADLOW COLLEGE
Playing Field
PILGRIMS WAY
ST. AUGUSTINE'S RD
ROCHESTER AVE
ST. MARTIN'S AV
PRETORIA RD
ST. MARTIN'S RD
COLLEGE RD
EDGAR RD
ST. GREGORY'S RD
N. HOLMES RD
CANTERBURY CHRIST CHURCH UNIVERSITY COLLEGE
LONGPORT
ST. AUGUSTINE'S ABBEY
CANTERBURY COLLEGE AND KENT INSTITUTE OF ARTS & DESIGN
ST. AUGUSTINE'S RD
NEW DOVER RD
YHA CANTERBURY
MILITARY RD
OLD RUTTINGTON LN
MONASTERY ST
LONGPORT
ST. AUGUSTINE'S
LOWER CHANTRY LN
IVY LN
OLD DOVER RD
NORTHGATE BOROUGH
BROAD ST
LOWER BRIDGE ST
POST OFFICE
CITY WALLS
CANTERBURY CATHEDRAL
KINGS SCHOOL
CANTERBURY COACH STATION
ST. GEORGE'S PL
COSSINGTON RD
VERNON PL
UPPER BRIDGE ST
FIELDS
NUNNERY
PUCKLE LN
POST OFFICE
KASHMIR TANDOORI
CAFÉ VENEZIA
CATHEDRAL GATE HOTEL
BURGATE
ROMAN MUSEUM
PARADE
WHITEFRIARS CENTRE
ST. GEORGE'S LN
MILLERS ARMS
PALACE ST
SUN ST
BUTCHERY LN
MILL LN
KING ST
ST. RADIGUND'S ST
THE FRIARS
KINGSBRIDGE VILLA
INFORMATION CENTRE
MARLOWE ARCADE
WATLING ST
MARLOWE AV
CITY WALLS
RHODAUS TOWN
BEST LN
HIGH ST
THE TUDOR HOUSE
BEER CART LN
Dane John Garden
ZEALAND RD
ST. PETER'S LN
OLD WEAVERS HOUSE
ST. PETER'S ST
CASTLE ST
CASTLE HOUSE
NORTH LN
POUND LN
ST. PETER'S GR
MUSEUM OF CANTERBURY/ RUPERT BEAR MUSEUM
STOUR ST
ROSEMARY LN
PIN HILL
STATION RD E
CANTERBURY EAST RAILWAY STATION
OXFORD RD
STATION RD W
WEST GATE TOWERS
TOWER HOUSE
BLACK GRIFFIN LN
ST. PETER'S PL
Great Stour
CANTERBURY CASTLE
MARTYR'S FIELD RD
CANTERBURY WEST RAILWAY STATION
ROPER RD
ST. DUNSTAN'S ST
RHEIMS WAY
RHEIMS WAY
YORK RD
WINCHEAP
SIMMONDS RD

Canterbury really came into its own in the Middle Ages when its large cathedral, the administrative and religious center of the church in England then and today, became a pilgrimage site. The most famous archbishop of Canterbury was Thomas Becket (1118–1170) who defied King Henry II when the king wanted to extend royal power over the church. When Henry complained, "Who will rid me of this turbulent priest?" four of his knights decided to do just that and hacked Becket to death with their swords. Henry claimed he never meant for Becket to be killed, and he did penance by sticking his head in a niche in the archbishop's tomb while monks whipped him.

The cathedral is the jewel in Canterbury's crown and the reason everyone comes here, but the town has plenty more to see, including preserved medieval streets bisected by the little River Stour. A Norman castle stands not far from the city center, parts of the Roman and medieval town wall still survive, and several museums explain the city's storied past.

Canterbury Cathedral has been a pilgrimage sight since the Middle Ages.

SIGHTS

CANTERBURY CASTLE

Gate St., 012/2737-8100

HOURS: Daily 8 A.M.-dusk

COST: Free admission

When William the Conqueror invaded England from Normandy in 1066, Canterbury gained the distinction of being the first town to submit without a fight. Apparently this didn't convince William of the citizens' reliability, because that same year he ordered a castle built near here. It was first constructed of wood on an artificial hill, still visible in the park just to the east, and in 1120 it was rebuilt on this spot in stone. Like the Tower of London, it incorporates part of the old Roman wall and features a large square keep. The keep is impressive and stands three stories tall with much of its architectural detail intact. Just to the south you can see the flint courses of the Roman wall, built in the 3rd century.

CANTERBURY CATHEDRAL

Cathedral Precincts, Burgate, 012/2776-2862, www.canterbury-cathedral.org

HOURS: Mon.-Sat. 9 A.M.-6:30 P.M. Easter-Sept., Mon.-Sat. 9 A.M.-5 P.M. Oct.-Easter, Sun. noon-2:30 P.M., 4:30-5:30 P.M. Precincts: Daily 7 A.M.-9 P.M.

COST: Adults £6, seniors, students, and children £4.50, family £14.50

There's been a church at this spot since A.D. 597, when St. Augustine founded one here to convert the pagan Anglo-Saxons. Like many early Christian churches, it was built upon the site of a pagan Roman temple to assert the dominance of the new faith. The church has been extensively rebuilt through the years, especially by the Normans in 1070 after a disastrous fire, and now sports a long nave and a soaring Gothic roof. The quire (which hosts a free evensong at 5:30 P.M. daily) shows skillful vaulting and some dazzling stained glass with Celtic knotwork. The final stop for pilgrims to this famous cathedral has long been the spot where Thomas Becket was martyred. There's a small chapel with the tomb of Becket and other worthies.

© SEAN MCLACHLAN

The gate to Canterbury Cathedral introduces the architectural splendor inside.

Also worth a look are the extensive crypts, with dark chapels, flickering candles, and the cathedral treasury. After seeing the church, be sure to visit the cathedral precincts, a quiet and relaxing series of gardens and squares that are soothingly beautiful in the fading light of evening. The cathedral is in big demand for weddings and other functions, so check www.canterbury.co.uk to make sure it's open.

MUSEUM OF CANTERBURY AND RUPERT BEAR MUSEUM

Stour St., 012/2747-5202

HOURS: Mon.-Sat. 10:30 A.M.-5 P.M., Sun. (June-Sept.) 1:30-5 P.M. (last admission 4 P.M.)

COST: Adults £3.30, seniors, students, and children £2.20, family £8.70

This kid-friendly local museum is housed in the medieval Poor Priest's Hospital, which still retains its oak-beam roof dating to 1373. Such a fine example of medieval craftsmanship makes the perfect backdrop to displays tracing the history of Canterbury from the age of the dinosaurs all the way to today. The life story of Canterbury's most famous resident, Thomas Becket, is given pride of place, as is the home-front struggle of Canterbury's citizens during the bombing in World War II. Several children's activities help interpret the artifacts, and there's a wing of the museum dedicated to Rupert Bear, one of England's favorite comic characters.

ROMAN MUSEUM

Butchery Ln., 012/2778-5575

HOURS: Mon.-Sat. 10 A.M.-5 P.M., Sun. (June-Oct.) 1:30-5 P.M. (last admission 4 P.M.)

COST: Adults £3, seniors, students, and children £1.85, family £7.60

This basement museum explains the development of Roman Durovernum through artifacts and re-created rooms, including a marketplace and house interior. The star attraction, however, is the section of a Roman house uncovered by a Luftwaffe bomb. One room had a heating system under the floor, a hollow area that would be heated by a nearby furnace. Also preserved is a hallway decorated with mosaics and leading to a bathhouse. For Rome fans it's not as good as the Verulamium Museum in St. Albans, but it's still worth a visit.

ST. AUGUSTINE'S ABBEY

Longport St., 012/2776-7345

HOURS: Daily 10 A.M.-6 P.M. Apr.-Sept., Wed.-Sun. 10 A.M.-4 P.M. Oct.-Mar.

COST: Adults £3.70, seniors and students £2.80, children £1.90

This abbey, now in a state of beautiful decay, was founded around A.D. 598 by St. Augustine, who brought Christianity to the mostly pagan people in Britain. It's the oldest Anglo-Saxon abbey in England and was the burial ground for the archbishops of Canterbury and the kings of Kent. The monks stayed busy converting the pagans and making the abbey a center of learning. It was the only abbey to survive the Viking invasions of the 9th century and thus became even more central to the religious life of the region, growing through the years until 1538, when Henry VIII dissolved religious houses across England and chose this one as a royal residence.

ST. MARTIN'S CHURCH

North Holmes Rd., 012/2776-8072 or 012/2745-3469

HOURS: Visitors: Tues. and Thurs. 10 A.M.-3 P.M., Sat. 10 A.M.-1 P.M.; Worship: Sun. 9 A.M.-6:30 P.M.

COST: Free admission

This little parish church, the oldest in England in continuous use, has origins shrouded in mystery. Some elements of the building may date to Roman times, and this has been a church since at least A.D. 597, when St. Augustine and his monks came to Canterbury. They worshipped here while building the famous abbey. While Augustine was famous (and made a saint) for preaching Christianity to the mostly pagan Anglo-Saxons, Queen Bertha of Kent was already using it as a church when he arrived. Her patronage was essential to Augustine's work.

WEST GATE TOWERS

St. Peter's St., 012/2778-9576

HOURS: Mon.-Sat. 11 A.M.-12:30 P.M., 1:30-3:30 P.M., Sun. 1:30-3:30 P.M.

COST: Adults £1.20, seniors, students, and children £0.70, family £2.80

Medieval towers still protect the west gate to the city and are home to an interesting little museum with medieval armor, dank prison cells, and an armory dating to the English Civil War. Some favorite bits are the murder holes, spaces in the floor where defenders could pour boiling water or other nasty surprises down on the attacking enemy. Contrary to popular belief, they didn't use boiling oil—that was too expensive—instead opting for the much cheaper but almost as uncomfortable boiling water.

RESTAURANTS

AUGUSTINE'S £££

1-2 Longport, 012/2745-3063, www.augustinesrestaurant.co.uk

HOURS: Daily noon-2 P.M., 6:30-9:30 P.M.

For fine dining in Canterbury, the European and British menu at Augustine's is a top choice. Several interesting selections come from the kitchen, such as wild French rabbit with kidney and liver pie. If eating cute little bunnies doesn't appeal, even though they taste so good, try one of the vegetarian options such as russet potato gnocchi with creamed parsnips and French chestnuts. This restaurant, in a Georgian house, seats only 20 people so reservations are recommended.

CAFFÉ VENEZIA ££

60-61 Palace St., 012/2778-7786, www.caffevenezia.co.uk

HOURS: Daily 8 A.M.-11 P.M.

This busy and informal Italian café keeps long hours for the locals who like their all-day breakfasts. It also offer *ciabattas* with various fillings and pizza, in case you've already had breakfast. Of course it serves a long list of pastas too, very well made and coming with or without meat, such as the cannelloni with spinach and ricotta cheese. The coffee is properly made too, which used to be a rarity in England, although now the British are waking up to what real coffee tastes like.

KASHMIR TANDOORI ££

20 Palace St., 012/2746-2050, www.kashmirtandoori.com

HOURS: Daily noon-2:30 P.M., 6 P.M.-midnight

This local favorite has been serving South Asian cuisine since 1966 and has won heaps of awards. If you try the cooking you'll know why. The balance of spices is masterful, emphasizing flavor over fire in a way that makes you appreciate South Asian cuisine as more than an endurance contest. It offers a variety of regional dishes, including the excellent and hard-to-find Bengal Masala (prawn, chicken, or lamb cooked with onion, tomato, pineapple, and fresh herbs). There's a good selection of vegetarian options and some nice South Asian beers on the menu. Highly recommended.

MILLERS ARMS ££

2 Mill Lane, 012/2745-6057, www.millerscanterbury.co.uk

HOURS: Food served daily noon-2:30 P.M., 6-9 P.M.

Enjoy traditional home-cooked English food in this pub owned by Shepherd Neame, one of the more popular brewers in Kent. The pub dates to 1826 and got its name from serving the workers of a nearby mill. While the menu is fairly pub standard—meat pies, fish-and-chips—it's cooked on the premises, not prepackaged like so much pub food, so you'll be getting traditional fare that's done right. Of course, plenty of Shepherd Neame ale is on tap, and there's a selection of other drinks.

OLD WEAVERS HOUSE **££**

1 St. Peters St., 012/2746-4660

HOURS: Daily 10 A.M.-11 P.M.

In a house dating to 1500 and set right next to the River Stour, this spacious restaurant has heaps of atmosphere and good food. The menu is mostly English, with such favorites as roast pies (including the tasty roast beef and lamb pie) enlivened with international offerings such as stir fry and pasta. Take a break from sightseeing here, get a table next to a window, and watch the boats go by on the river.

ACCOMMODATIONS

CASTLE HOUSE **£40-80**

28 Castle St., 012/2776-1897, www.castlehousehotel.co.uk

Set in a courthouse dating to the 1730s, this attractive bed-and-breakfast stands right next to the Norman castle and is a short walk to the center of town. The interior is decorated in a classic English style and some rooms receive an atmospheric view of the castle looming nearby. All rooms are en suite and are much larger than what you'll have resigned yourself to in London. Amenities include a TV, hair dryer, and tea- and coffee-making facilities. A detached cottage just behind the main hotel can house up to eight people, and there's a walled garden for all guests. A friendly, knowledgeable management and a full English breakfast make this a good choice.

CATHEDRAL GATE HOTEL **£80-150**

36 Burgate, 012/2746-4381

While this ancient hotel (serving pilgrims since 1438) is a bit tattered at the edges, it still manages to be slightly more expensive than the other places listed here. That's because it's got the best location of the lot, right next to the gate leading into the cathedral precincts. Make sure to get a room facing the cathedral and you'll be treated to splendid views every time you look out the window. Most rooms are en suite, and all come with a TV, and tea- and coffee-making facilities. There's a comfortable reading room too.

KINGSBRIDGE VILLA **£40-80**

15 Best Lane, 012/2776-6415, www.canterburyguesthouse.com

Part of this centrally located hotel incorporates the old Roman wall, but otherwise it's quite modern. All rooms are en suite and have a TV and tea- and coffee-making facilities. A full English breakfast is included, and the staff can do a vegetarian or vegan breakfast too. It's just a couple of minutes' walk from the cathedral, and it has a comfortable dining room and lounge if you just want to stay in for a bit.

THE TUDOR HOUSE **£40-80**

6 Best Lane, 012/2776-5650

This pleasant bed-and-breakfast is just what it advertises—a Tudor home complete with small-paned windows and a projecting upper story. The atmosphere can't be beat, and the fact that it has a back garden right next to the River Stour makes it even more attractive. While the house is 400 years old, it doesn't lack modern amenities. Most rooms are en suite and all come with TV and tea- and coffee-making facilities. It's also only a couple of minutes' walk from the cathedral.

YHA CANTERBURY **UNDER £40**

54 New Dover Rd., 087/0770-5744, www.yha.org.uk

The cheapest option for an overnight stay in Canterbury is this clean and bustling youth hostel in a Victorian villa. It offers everything from single rooms to 10-bed dorms, and included are a games room, Internet café, laundry and kitchen facilities, library, and TV lounge. Guests who aren't members of YHA must pay an extra £3 a night. It's not as centrally situated as the other places listed here, but it's still an easy walk to all the sights.

PRACTICALITIES

GETTING THERE

Canterbury has two railway stations: Canterbury West (Station Rd. at Shepherd's Gate, 084/5000-2222) and Canterbury East (Station Rd. at Henry Ct., 084/5000-2222). Both are an easy walk from the center of town and both are served by regular trains from London Victoria. Trains are run by **Southeastern Railway** (084/5000-2222, www.southeastern-railway.co.uk) and a day return costs £18.40. A train trip takes 90 minutes to two hours depending on how many stops that particular train makes. On weekdays the first train leaves London Victoria to Canterbury West at 6:10 A.M., with trains once or twice an hour until the last train leaves at 11:11 P.M. The first train from Canterbury West leaves at 7:47 A.M. to Victoria with trains once an hour until the last leaves at 7:34 P.M. On Saturdays the first train leaves Victoria at 6:18 A.M., with trains once or twice an hour until the final train at 11:11 P.M. The first train from Canterbury West leaves at 9:24 A.M. with trains once an hour until the last leaves at 5:24 P.M. On Sundays the first train leaves Victoria at 8:18 A.M. with trains at 18 minutes past the hour until the last leaves at 10:18 P.M. The first train from Canterbury West leaves at 7:52 A.M. with trains once an hour until the last leaves at 10:52 P.M., but the Sunday trains from Canterbury require transferring at Ashford International Station.

On weekdays the first train leaves London Victoria to Canterbury East at 6:41 A.M., with trains at least twice an hour until the last train leaves at 10:03 P.M. The first train from Canterbury East leaves at 6:14 A.M. with trains once or twice an hour until the last leaves at 10:22 P.M. On Saturdays the first train leaves Victoria at 6:41 A.M., with trains once or twice an hour until the final train at 10:03 P.M. The first train from Canterbury East leaves at 5:49 A.M. with trains once or twice an hour until the last leaves at 7:19 P.M. On Sundays the first train leaves Victoria at 8:03 A.M. with trains once or twice an hour until the last leaves at 10:03 P.M. The first train from Canterbury East leaves at 7:49 A.M. with trains once an hour until the last leaves at 10:19 P.M., but the Sunday trains from Canterbury require transferring at Ashford International Station. Note that some of the earliest and latest trains require a transfer at a station (which varies) along the route. This will be announced on the train, but check with the conductor if you're unsure.

National Express (087/0580-8080, www.gobycoach.com) runs a regular bus service from Victoria Coach Station to Canterbury Coach Station (St. George's La., 087/0243-3711), taking anywhere from 1 hour and 50 minutes to 2 hours and 20 minutes depending on how many stops that particular bus makes. A standard return costs £17.40, making it marginally cheaper than the train but also slower and less comfortable. On weekdays the first bus leaves London at 7 A.M. and then once an hour until the last leaves at 11:45 P.M. From Canterbury the first bus leaves at 5:20 A.M. and they run once an hour until the last bus at 10:50 P.M. On Saturdays the first bus leaves London at 11:30 A.M. and operates once an hour until the last leaves at 11:45 P.M. From Canterbury the first bus leaves at 11:50 A.M. and runs almost once an hour until the last bus leaves at 11 P.M. On Sundays the first bus leaves London at 7 A.M. and operates once an hour until the last leaves at 11:45 P.M. From Canterbury the first bus leaves at 5:40 A.M. and runs once an hour until the last bus leaves at 11 P.M. The bus station is a quarter mile from the cathedral.

To get to Canterbury from London by car, take the A102 out of town. Get onto the A2, then the M2, and then take Exit 7 for Canterbury. The trip is 62 miles and takes about 1 hour and 15 minutes.

GETTING AROUND

Canterbury is an old medieval town and as such it's very compact. Both train stations are only a few minutes' walk from the center, where all the sights are. Once you're within the old walls, the little medieval lanes can take you anywhere you want to go within a few minutes, with plenty of architecture and shops to see on the way. No public transport is needed within the city center, which is mostly blocked off to traffic anyway. It's definitely a very pedestrian-friendly town.

INFORMATION

The **Visitor Information Centre** (12–13 Sun St., 012/2737-8100, open 9:30 A.M.–6 P.M. Mon.–Sat., 10 A.M.–4 P.M. Sun.) has maps and booklets on Canterbury and Kent for sale and reams of free brochures. Regular tours, sponsored by **Canterbury Walks** (012/2745-9779, www.canterbury-walks.co.uk) depart from here at 2 P.M. daily April–October and 11:30 A.M. and 2 P.M. Monday–Saturday, 2 P.M. Sunday July–September. Tours run 90 minutes and cost adults £4.25, seniors, students, and children 12 or older £3.75, children under 12 £3, and families (two adults and three children under 12) £12.50. It also runs cathedral, museum, and coach tours. The Canterbury city government has a website at www.canterbury.gov.uk, and there's another helpful website for visitors at www.canterbury.co.uk.

Oxford

No other town is quite like Oxford. An important seat of learning since the 12th century, Oxford's famous university has graduated generations of scholars and members of government. And what a place to learn! Gothic architecture, cozy little bookshops, museums jam packed with the treasures of the world—it would be easy never to leave. While the atmosphere is studious, this is a college town too, so there's plenty of nightlife, especially at the numerous historic pubs. Though this is one of the larger towns, it's still compact enough to walk. With all the stunning architecture and a story on every corner, that's what you'll want to do anyway.

SIGHTS

ASHMOLEAN MUSEUM

Beaumont St., 018/6527-8000, www.ashmolean.org

HOURS: Tues.-Sat. 10 A.M.-5 P.M., Sun. noon-5 P.M.

COST: Free admission

Scholars at the University of Oxford have been gathering artifacts from the ancient world for centuries, and their accumulated collection is housed in this extensive museum. The collection of Egyptian artifacts is especially good, as are the European rooms, with rune stones and Tudor-period drinking flagons. One of the oldest artifacts here is a plastered human skull from Jericho dating to 7000 B.C., its shell eyes staring out creepily. The museum, open since 1683 and the oldest public museum in the world, is a bit of an artifact itself.

CHRIST CHURCH COLLEGE AND PICTURE GALLERY

St Aldgate's, 018/6528-6573, www.visitchristchurch.net

HOURS: Mon.-Sat. 9 A.M.-5 P.M., Sun. 1-5 P.M.

COST: Adults £4.70, seniors, students, and children £3.70

Cardinal Wolsey founded this college in 1524 and named it Cardinal College. This example of ecclesiastical modesty didn't last long, because Henry VIII renamed it Christ Church in 1546. Sir Christopher Wren, John Locke, Albert Einstein, and many other famous people studied here. The high points of this architectural jewel are the Great Hall (1539) and Tom Tower (1682), designed by Christopher Wren and which traditionally rings 101 times at 9:05 P.M. to give the students (who originally numbered 101) time to get back to the college before the gates shut for the night. Also worth a visit is the Picture Gallery, which has a stunning collection of Italian masters such as

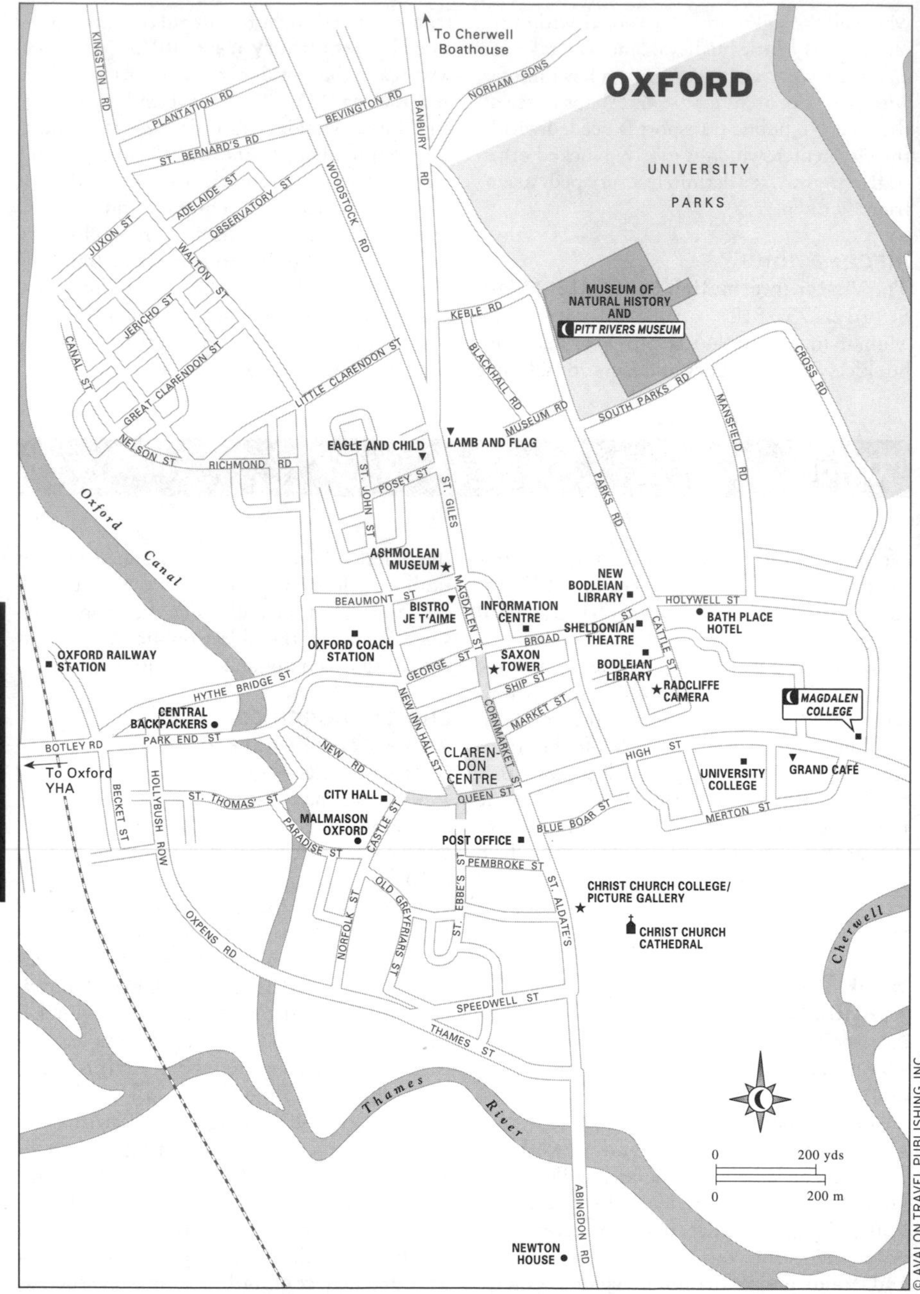

OXFORD
To Cherwell Boathouse
UNIVERSITY PARKS
MUSEUM OF NATURAL HISTORY AND
PITT RIVERS MUSEUM
LAMB AND FLAG
EAGLE AND CHILD
ASHMOLEAN MUSEUM
NEW BODLEIAN LIBRARY
BISTRO JE T'AIME
INFORMATION CENTRE
SHELDONIAN THEATRE
BATH PLACE HOTEL
OXFORD COACH STATION
SAXON TOWER
BODLEIAN LIBRARY
RADCLIFFE CAMERA
MAGDALEN COLLEGE
OXFORD RAILWAY STATION
CENTRAL BACKPACKERS
CLAREN-DON CENTRE
UNIVERSITY COLLEGE
GRAND CAFÉ
To Oxford YHA
CITY HALL
MALMAISON OXFORD
POST OFFICE
CHRIST CHURCH COLLEGE/ PICTURE GALLERY
CHRIST CHURCH CATHEDRAL
NEWTON HOUSE
Oxford Canal
Thames River
Cherwell
KINGSTON RD
PLANTATION RD
ST. BERNARD'S RD
BEVINGTON RD
BANBURY RD
NORHAM GDNS
WOODSTOCK RD
ADELAIDE ST
OBSERVATORY ST
JUXON ST
WALTON ST
JERICHO ST
CANAL ST
GREAT CLARENDON ST
LITTLE CLARENDON ST
NELSON ST
RICHMOND RD
KEBLE RD
BLACKHALL RD
MUSEUM RD
SOUTH PARKS RD
CROSS RD
MANSFIELD RD
PARKS RD
ST. JOHN ST
POSEY ST
ST. GILES
BEAUMONT ST
MAGDALEN ST
HOLYWELL ST
BROAD ST
CATTLE ST
GEORGE ST
SHIP ST
HYTHE BRIDGE ST
NEW INN HALL ST
CORNMARKET ST
MARKET ST
BOTLEY RD
PARK END ST
NEW RD
HIGH ST
QUEEN ST
BECKET ST
HOLLYBUSH ROW
ST. THOMAS' ST
PARADISE ST
CASTLE ST
BLUE BOAR ST
MERTON ST
PEMBROKE ST
ST. EBBE'S ST
ST. ALDATE'S
OLD GREYFRIARS ST
NORFOLK ST
OXPENS RD
SPEEDWELL ST
THAMES ST
ABINGDON RD
0 200 yds
0 200 m

Leonardo da Vinci and Michelangelo as well as works by Van Dyck and Dürer. Note that entrance to the Picture Gallery is separate from entrance to the college.

MAGDALEN COLLEGE

High St., 018/6527-6000, www.magd.ox.ac.uk

HOURS: Daily 1-6 P.M. (or dusk) Oct. 1-mid-June, noon-6 P.M. mid-June-Sept. 30

COST: Adults £3, seniors, students, and children £2

This college was founded in 1448 and sports beautiful Gothic spires, making it one of the most stunning groups of buildings in Oxford. The grounds are especially attractive, with a deer park and Addison's Walk winding through open fields that are bedecked with wildflowers in springtime. There are many fine buildings to see here, but one highlight is the Chapel (built in 1480) with its magnificent choir and beautiful stained glass. The Cloisters (finished in 1490) surround a large grass quad and give the feeling of being in a monastery. Since many of the students at the time were studying theology, they would have felt right at home. Above the college looms the Great Tower (finished in 1509), a landmark visible throughout much of Oxford and one of its most photogenic buildings. Note the hours are subject to change; check the website for precise opening hours.

MUSEUM OF NATURAL HISTORY

Parks Rd., 018/6527-2950, www.oum.ox.ac.uk

HOURS: Daily noon-5 P.M.

COST: Free admission

An interesting Gothic construction of steel and glass houses a large collection of the natural wonders of the world. Favorites include a dodo bird and dinosaur bones. In warm weather, head to the upper floor, where there's a beehive (cut off from the inside by glass) to see bees heading off to the local flower beds. Bees do a "dance" near the hive to tell other bees where the flowers are, and a device set into the wall helps interpret their movements so you can understand them too. This is a great stop for the kids; don't forget to visit the Pitt Rivers Museum in the same building.

PITT RIVERS MUSEUM

Access through Museum of Natural History, Parks Rd., 018/6527-0927, www.prm.ox.ac.uk

HOURS: Mon.-Sat. noon-4:30 P.M.

COST: Free admission

If you visit just one museum in England, see this one. Founded in 1884 by General Pitt Rivers and added to ever since, this collection of anthropological specimens is simply mind-boggling. Artifacts are packed in display cases dedicated to themes (such as Death or Music) rather than culture or time period. Under the cases are shelves that can be pulled out to view more artifacts. Ask for a torch (flashlight) from the reception desk to help you peer into the crowded cases. Dugout canoes hang from the ceiling, while shields and blankets adorn the walls. You could spend literally days in here and only scratch the surface; each visit gives a renewed appreciation for the diversity of human culture. The museum was undergoing renovation, which was due to be completed by the time this book goes to print.

SAXON TOWER

St. Michael at the North Gate, Cornmarket St., 018/6524-0940

HOURS: Mon.-Sat. 10 A.M.-5 P.M., Sun. noon-5 P.M.

COST: Adults £1.50, children 80 p

A rare example of Saxon architecture, this 11th-century tower offers fine panoramic views of the town, with Gothic spires rising over busy, winding streets. Be sure to check out the Treasury, a churchwarden's accounts from 1437, and a charter sealed by James I in 1612. The attached church dates to the 13th century and is also worth a look for its medieval stonework. This may be the oldest building in Oxford, but scholars aren't sure.

RESTAURANTS

BISTRO JE T'AIME £££

11 Wheatsheaf Yard, Blue Boar St., 018/6572-2473, www.bistrojetaime.co.uk

Most wouldn't expect to find a traditional French bistro in the middle of the quintessentially English city of Oxford, but here it is. The Bistro offers a small but select variety of meat,

EXCURSIONS

fish, and vegetarian dishes. The venison in port wine sauce is especially good, and vegetarians won't go wrong with the Provençal vegetables cooked in light puff pastry. On Monday evenings, the Bistro offers 50 percent off the à la carte menu. The wine list, of course, emphasizes the vintages of France.

CHERWELL BOATHOUSE **££**

Bardwell Rd., 018/6555-2746, www.cherwellboathouse.co.uk

HOURS: Daily noon-2:30 P.M., 6:30-10:30 P.M.

This restaurant/café overlooks the Isis River (actually the Thames, but it's called the Isis here) and serves modern English cuisine such as herb-crusted Hereford lamb with rustic Provençal, and *pave* of wild salmon with warm salad of beetroot, black pudding, and watercress. The wine list isn't very long, but it is reasonably priced—rare in restaurants in this country. In good weather the terrace is the place to be and the attached bar offers even closer views of the river. Reservations are recommended, especially on weekends.

EAGLE AND CHILD **£**

49 St. Giles, 018/6530-2925

HOURS: Mon.-Sat. 11 A.M.-11 P.M., Sun. noon-10:30 P.M.

One of the most famous pubs in England was home to the chancellor of the Exchequer during the English Civil War. It was also the meeting place for the Inklings, a writers' group that included C. S. Lewis and J. R. R. Tolkien. Photos of the Inklings adorn the walls of the room they used to meet in, and there are a few other little cubbyholes to hide away in. The food is standard pub fare, but it's home-cooked, not pre-made as in so many other pubs. A good selection of real ales is on tap too.

GRAND CAFÉ **££**

84 High St., 018/6520-4463

HOURS: Daily 9 A.M.-8 P.M.

This French café/restaurant offers French cuisine and good service, but the big draw is the interior, which is preserved like a Parisian café of the 1920s. Diners sit at antique marble tables between golden columns while sipping excellent coffee. Breakfast is served in the mornings, high tea and cream tea from 3 P.M., with various snacks and sandwiches throughout the day, including vegetarian options. The building is the site of the first coffeehouse in England, opened in 1651.

LAMB AND FLAG **£**

12 St. Giles, 018/6551-5787

HOURS: Mon.-Sat. 11 A.M.-11 P.M., Sun. noon-10:30 P.M.

Just across the street from the Eagle and Child stands the other great literary pub in town. Thomas Hardy used to drink here while writing *Jude the Obscure.* The pub is a former coaching inn dating to the 15th century, making it as old as some of the famous colleges. It contains much of its original fittings, including the charming little hidey-holes that the English of yesteryear used to like drinking in. (If you have a big group you might have to break up.) The food is typical but well-made pub fare.

ACCOMMODATIONS

BATH PLACE HOTEL **£80-150**

4-5 Holywell St., 018/6579-1812, www.bathplace.co.uk

Enjoy Oxford's Old World atmosphere? Then why not sleep in it? This group of 17th-century cottages around a little private courtyard has lots of charm. All rooms are en suite and are decorated in a simple but pleasing manner consistent with the period of the buildings. Amenities include a TV, tea- and coffee-making facilities, and fruit bowl. Another bonus is the location—it's right around the corner from several historic colleges.

CENTRAL BACKPACKERS **UNDER £40**

13 Park End St., 018/6524-2288, www.centralbackpackers.co.uk

This popular youth hostel is in the center of town and close to lots of nightlife, making for a rather boisterous crowd. Behind the bright-yellow door are facilities that include a dining room, lounge with Sky TV, kitchen facilities, laundry service, Internet access, and no curfew.

The staff is friendly, helpful, and has a good attitude. The dorms have four, six, eight, or 12 beds and while they can get a bit crowded, they are clean and well maintained. Families are welcome.

MALMAISON OXFORD **OVER £150**

3 Oxford Castle, 018/6526-8400, www.malmaison-oxford.com

Set in a converted castle prison, this has to be one of the most unusual hotels in England. The hallways still resemble those of a prison (but with more respectable people prowling the halls) but walls were knocked down to expand the cells, now beautified in a chic modern style. All rooms are en suite and come with a TV. A cool brasserie and bar are on-site, as is an exercise room. The hotel is close to the train station, but it's still a short walk into the center of town.

NEWTON HOUSE **£40-80**

82-84 Abingdon Rd., 018/6524-0561

Rather cramped rooms and a busy street are offset by a friendly and helpful staff serving great breakfasts. The hotel is a converted Victorian town house and has kept some of the original fittings. Not all rooms are en suite, but most provide a TV and tea- and coffee-making facilities. A full English or vegetarian breakfast is included. While not right in the center of town, it's only a 10 minute walk through a nice area and over a bridge, where you can see the Isis sparkling below.

OXFORD YHA **UNDER £40**

2A Botley Rd., 087/0770-5970, www.yha.org.uk

A clean if rather spare youth hostel close to the train station and a few minutes' walk from the town center, the Oxford YHA offers en suite private and dorm rooms holding up to six people, along with Internet access, a laundry service, cheap bicycle hire (great for seeing the lovely countryside all around the town), and kitchen facilities. A continental breakfast is included. It's a good place to meet other backpackers. Guests who aren't YHA members must pay an extra £3 a night to stay.

PRACTICALITIES

GETTING THERE

The most convenient way to travel between Oxford and London is via the **Oxford Tube** (018/6577-2250, www.oxfordtube.com), which is actually a bus and not the Tube. Buses depart every 12 minutes from early morning to evening and hourly from Grosvenor Gardens (opposite Victoria Rail Station), Marble Arch (Stop X), Notting Hill Gate (Stop N) and the Hilton Hotel at Shepherd's Bush. They arrive at the Oxford Coach Station (Gloucester Green, just off George St.). The trip takes 1 hour and 40 minutes and costs adults £14 return, seniors and children£7, and students £11. The station is right in the center of town.

National Express (087/0580-8080, www.nationalexpress.com) departs from Victoria Station to Oxford Coach Station at least twice an hour around the clock. The trip takes 1 hour and 40 minutes and costs adults £14 for a day return and seniors and children £7 for a day return.

National Rail (084/5748-4950, www.nationalrail.co.uk) runs trains from Paddington Station in London to Oxford Railway Station (Park End St., 084/5748-4950) once an hour at various times within the hour. The trip takes about 50 minutes and costs £25.50 for a day return. The first train leaves Paddington at 6:03 A.M. Monday–Friday and the last leaves at 9:48 P.M. From Oxford Railway Station the first train leaves at 6:38 A.M. and the last departs at 11:49 P.M. On Saturdays the first train leaves Paddington at 5:45 A.M. and the last leaves at 9:48 P.M., and from Oxford the first leaves at 7:26 A.M. and the last leaves at 10:35 P.M. On Sundays the first train leaves Paddington at 8:03 A.M. and the last leaves 9:37 P.M., and from Oxford the first leaves 10:26 A.M. and the last leaves 10:28 P.M. The train station is about half a mile from the city center.

To travel to Oxford from London by car, take the A501 west until it becomes the A40. Keep following the A40 until it merges with the M40, and take Exit 8 on the left to Oxford. The trip is 59 miles and takes 1 hour and 15 minutes.

GETTING AROUND

Oxford is a compact city with beautiful architecture and lots of hidden treasures, so it's best to hoof it. In the summer there are so many tourist buses on the roads that walking is often faster. Local buses run several routes around town and to nearby villages. The cost varies depending on how far you're going but is usually less than a pound within town. Check the Tourist Information Office for maps and schedules. There are also numerous taxi companies that can take you around town for a few pounds, such as **ABC Taxis** (6 Cowley Rd., 018/6577-0077).

INFORMATION

The **Oxford Information Centre** (15–16 Broad St., 018/6572-6871, www.visitoxford.org) is open 9:30 A.M.–5 P.M. Monday–Saturday and 10 A.M.–4 P.M. Sunday and has a good supply of information on local and regional sights. Official walking tours for the city leave from here. These tours are run by **Oxford Tours** (018/6572-6871, www.visitoxford.org) and depart daily at various times and with various themes, such as colleges, pubs, ghosts, and Inspector Morse. The college tour includes admission to the college. Not all colleges are open on any particular day, so it's luck of the draw which ones you see, but the tours are always informative and fun.

Another option is the **City Sightseeing Tours** (018/6579-0522, www.city-sightseeing.com), which runs a one-hour open-top bus tour of the city starting from Oxford Railway Station at 9:30 A.M. daily and then every 10–15 minutes after that. Hop on and hop off at various points of interest and listen to commentary in between. Tours cost adults £9.50, seniors and students £8.50, children aged 5–15 £4.50, and families (two adults and three children) £24.

The website www.oxfordcity.co.uk has lots of information on what to see and where to stay and eat.

Salisbury Plain

Stonehenge, the world's most famous prehistoric monument, stands on the ancient Salisbury Plain, but what many people don't realize is that it's part of a vast network of Stone Age monuments scattered across the plain and throughout the British Isles. Many visitors go only to Stonehenge, but Avebury is an even bigger megalithic (meaning "large stone") complex, and other monuments are also open to the public. Since they're all out in the countryside, getting there can be a bit tricky; your best bet is to take a tour. (For more information on England's prehistoric monuments, see the *Megaliths* sidebar.)

SIGHTS

AVEBURY

Avebury, Wiltshire, 016/7253-9250, www.nationaltrust.org.uk

HOURS: Monument open 24 hours, museum open daily 10 A.M.-6 P.M. Apr.-Oct., 10 A.M.-4 P.M. Nov.-Mar.

COST: Monument: Free; Museum: Adults £4.20, children £2.10

While Stonehenge gets all the glory, the megalithic complex of Avebury is actually much bigger. Completed near the end of the neolithic ("New Stone Age") around 2000 B.C., the main feature of this site is a stone circle 340 meters (1,115 feet) in diameter, enclosed by a ditch and encompassing the modern village of Avebury. Two smaller stone circles stood inside, and a double avenue of standing stones leads to a large concentric stone circle 2.4 kilometers (1.5 miles) away. Exploring this monument can take much of the day, but it rewards with atmospheric views and some great photo opportunities. You can find information, meals, and books in Avebury village or the museum.

SILBURY HILL

One mile west of West Kennet on A4, Wiltshire, www.english-heritage.org.uk

HOURS: Open 24 hours

COST: Free admission

This 40-meter-high (130 feet) artificial mound

The mysterious neolithic monument of Stonehenge stands on the windswept Salisbury Plain.

is the largest of its kind in Europe. It was constructed in stages from about 2800–2400 B.C. and contains almost 340,000 cubic meters (12 million cubic feet) of earth. Why a group of people would expend so much labor on such a project is a mystery unsolved by numerous excavations. Nobody seems to be buried in it (much smaller mounds often mark the graves of important people) and no buildings seem to have been on top of it. Unfortunately, recent erosion has meant that the hill has been made off-limits to visitors, but you can still stand in front of it and wonder. Silbury Hill is within sight of the West Kennet Long Barrow. Note: There are no facilities at this site.

STONEHENGE

Two miles west of Amesbury at junction of A303 and A344/A360, Wiltshire, 019/8062-4715, www.english-heritage.org.uk/stonehenge

HOURS: Daily: 9:30 A.M.–6 P.M. Mar. 16–May 31 and Sept. 1–Oct. 15, 9 A.M.–7 P.M. June 1–Aug. 31, 9:30 A.M.–4 P.M. Oct. 16–Mar. 15

COST: Adults £5, seniors and students £4.40, children £3

This famous prehistoric monument was constructed in several stages from the Neolithic to the Early Bronze Age, around 3,100–1600 B.C. The picturesque standing stones were once a lunar and solar observatory and may have had other functions. The "Heelstone," standing outside the circle, aligns with the sun as it rises at the summer equinox, and the sun shines right through the two upright stones and the lintel connecting them directly into the center of the monument. Researchers have found numerous other alignments, but there's a heated debate over whether these were deliberate or not. What's beyond argument is the vast amount of work needed to create such a place; some of the stones actually come from the Preseli Hills in Wales, about 250 kilometers (150 miles) away, and were probably shipped down a river before being dragged across the plains. A small café, museum, and bookshop are on-site.

WEST KENNET LONG BARROW

Less than a mile west of West Kennet on A4, Wiltshire, www.english-heritage.org.uk

MEGALITHS: ENGLAND'S STONE AGE WONDERS

People have been living in the British Isles for thousands of years, surviving by hunting game and collecting edible plants. By 4,000 B.C. Stone Age hunters and gatherers had settled down and started farming during the neolithic period ("New Stone Age"). The land was rich and they soon formed complex societies with a priest caste that studied the heavens to know the most propitious times for harvest and planting festivals. While their villages were small and made of wood and dried mud, they made spectacular monuments out of stone called megaliths (meaning "large stone").

Some megaliths feature several stones in a circle, the most famous of which is Stonehenge. There are also lone standing stones of various heights, often called menhirs. Menhirs come in rows too, like the avenues of standing stones that connect the stone circle sites at Avebury. To bury important members of their society, Neolithic farmers built chamber tombs or barrows, houses of stone put under artificial hills that sometimes erode away, leaving the large stones exposed. Those with a single chamber inside are often called dolmens, while those with several chambers for different burials, such as the West Kennet Long Barrow, are often called passage graves.

A few sites such as Stonehenge have become famous, but megaliths are far more common than many people realize. About 1,000 stone circles are in the British Isles, others are in Western Europe, and there are an estimated 50,000 dolmens in Europe as a whole.

Dolmens and passage graves are generally assumed to have been burials, since bones have been found in many of them. Standing stones are commonly believed to have been boundary markers, although the rows of menhirs are harder to explain. Stone circles are the biggest puzzle. Most researchers say they were religious sites, since the structures had no obvious practical purpose and many cultures expend huge amounts of energy to build sacred places. Others say they were meeting places for trade or government, although there may also have been a religious element. The Stone Age builders left no written record, so we can never know for sure, but one strong argument in favor of the religious interpretation is the sense of awe these monuments inspire. Religious buildings, from the massive temples of Egypt and the ornate Gothic cathedrals of Europe, down to the simplest Protestant church, are all created to take people out of their normal environment. It seems this emotion is important in creating a mood for worship.

So are stone circles the cathedrals of the Stone Age? Many researchers say yes and no. While they had an important role in religious life, they may have had a more practical purpose. Archaeologists have found that certain stones in a circle align with others to point to the rising or setting of the sun on the solstices and equinoxes. The sun's location on the horizon at sunrise and sunset changes according to the season, and knowing where it is in the sky can tell you the best time for planting and harvest, as well as provide a reliable calendar. Knowing these dates would have been very important to a complex society that relied on farming to support its villages, chieftains, and priests. Thus measuring the seasons was essential to preserving the social and economic order.

Other megaliths may have had astronomical alignments too. Researchers have discovered alignments in long barrows, so that the sun will shine on the back wall at certain times of the year, or a certain star will be visible through a sighting hole on an important date in the calendar. Astronomical alignments are difficult to prove, however. While major ones such as the summer solstice are pretty obvious, alignments with certain stars could easily be just chance. A good look at any modern building will produce astronomical alignments the builders never intended.

There are a number of misconceptions about megaliths, the most common being that they were built by the Druids. The Druids were a religious caste among the Celts from around the 2nd century B.C. to the 2nd century A.D., well after the megaliths were built. There's some evidence that the Druids *used* megaliths, however. Since Druidism was a faith closely linked with the landscape, Druids would surely have considered such evocative ruins sacred. Even today, a modern order of Druids celebrates the solstices at Stonehenge.

Other misconceptions are rooted in New Age beliefs. Some say primitive people couldn't have created such huge monuments and must have been helped by aliens from UFOs. Archaeologists have experimented with erecting large upright stones, such as the ones at Stonehenge, with primitive tools and while it's a lot of hard work, it isn't beyond the reach of Stone Age technology. Others believe megaliths are power centers for ley lines, channels of mystical energy crisscrossing the landscape. There's no evidence for this either, but adherents of various Earth-centered religions believe it is so and in the tricky workings of faith, it may be true for them. Many such people are leading the fight to save megaliths from threats of road expansion and similar "development," so if such a belief helps preserve these fabulous monuments, it's hard to argue against it.

Another persistent belief, often linked with the alien theory, is that an advanced civilization ruled much of the world in the distant past and left evidence of their technology on every continent. Once again, there's no evidence for such a civilization, and the sights such theorists point to as evidence vary widely in style and time period, from ancient stone circles to relatively recent Mexican pyramids. What this theory does have right, however, is that ancient peoples were very intelligent and advanced. Anthropologists studying preliterate cultures have found that such groups pass down amazing amounts of information orally through the generations. Without the distractions of the modern world, and with the strong motivations of maintaining a food supply and worshipping the gods, our ancestors were perfectly capable of building these fabulous monuments we are only beginning to understand.

Stonehenge, the most famous of the stone circles

EXCURSIONS

HOURS: Open 24 hours
COST: Free admission
This is one of the largest chambered tombs in Britain and was used for burials for 1,000 years. It was built around 3400 B.C.—earlier than Stonehenge—under a low earthen mound with large slabs of stone; there are five small chambers to hold the bones of the dead. Excavators found the remains of at least 46 individuals and evidence that the tomb was periodically cleared to make room for new occupants. The tomb is within sight of Silbury Hill and accessible via a short path on the south side of the highway. Note: There are no facilities.

PRACTICALITIES

GETTING THERE AND AROUND

Since Stonehenge is out in the countryside away from any population center, the best way to get there is by tour bus. Several companies offer trips and take in various other sights along the way, so compare each trip to find which is best suited for you. A longer tour that takes in two or more of these sights is preferable; this will give a good idea of the accomplishments of England's early inhabitants. (These tours take up most of the day anyway, so there won't be time for sightseeing back in London.) Make sure you're given plenty of time at each place. There's nothing worse than being rushed while you're busy gaping in awe.

Several London-based tour companies go to Stonehenge, many stopping at other sights in Salisbury Plain. **Astral Travels** (72 New Bond St., 087/0902-0908, www.astraltravels.co.uk) offers Stonehenge-access tours that take guests among the stones either before or after the monument is normally open to visitors. Tours take place up to six times a month, except for October and November, and cost adults £79 and children ages 3–16 £69. Its Stones and Bones tour visits both Avebury and Stonehenge and a few other monuments along the way, and costs adults £64 and children £59.

Best Value Tours (www.bestvaluetours.co.uk) offers tours to all four sights in the Salisbury Plain and includes an evening walk inside Stonehenge after regular closing time. Tours take place up to six times a month March–September and cost adults £65, children ages 3–16 £60.

Golden Tours (020/7233-7030, www.goldentours.co.uk) offers a tour to Stonehenge that also takes in Bath; the cost is adults £56, for seniors and students £51, and children ages 3–16 £46. A tour to Stonehenge, Bath, and Windsor costs adults £65, seniors and students £60, and children £55. There is also a tour that travels inside the stones and visits Bath too, which costs adults £64, seniors and students £59, and children £54.

The Stonehenge Tour Company (070/0078-1016, www.stonehengetours.com) offers daily tours from London. Its 5,000 Years in a Day tour takes in Stonehenge, Avebury, and other sights of interest. The cost is adults £64, children aged 3–16 £59.

The only public transportation available is to Avebury—and even this isn't direct. Take a **First Great Western** train (www.firstgreatwestern.com, 084/5700-0125) from London Paddington to the town of Swindon, then go to the bus station next door to catch a **Stagecoach** bus (www.stagecoachbus.com, 087/0608-2608) to High Street, Avebury. Avebury is a small village so you won't have trouble finding the site, which in fact surrounds it. The train takes 55 minutes and the bus takes 25 minutes. The first train departs at 5:43 A.M. and there's one at least once an hour until the last train leaves at 11:35 P.M. The bus service, however, only runs once an hour from 6:21 A.M. to 7:07 P.M. From Avebury, buses to Swindon leave once an hour from 7:29 A.M. to 8:24 P.M., and trains from Swindon leave at least once an hour from 5:27 A.M. to 11:21 P.M. **Traveline Southwest** (087/0608-2608, www.travelinesw.com) has a convenient online journey planner.

If you are traveling from London by car, you can reach Avebury by getting on the A4 west out of town and staying on it as it becomes the M4. Take Exit 16, which gets you on the A3102, and take the first exit to Hay Lane. Follow Hay Lane until exiting onto the A4361, which will take you right into Avebury. The route is 92 miles and takes about 1 hour and 45 minutes. Avebury is a good first stop, since you can enjoy the fantastic prehistoric site and buy pamphlets on Salisbury Plain before striking out to the other sites nearby.

INFORMATION

English Heritage (087/0333-1181, www.english-heritage.org.uk) manages Silbury Hill, Stonehenge, and West Kennet Long Barrow and offers visitor information at its website and on the phone. The **National Trust** (087/0240-3207, www.nationaltrust.org.uk) does the same for Avebury. Private tour companies also offer information, but the publications of English Heritage and the National Trust are better researched. Bookstores abound with titles on prehistoric monuments, some good, some bad, but the British Museum bookshop sells a good selection of well-researched titles.

St. Albans

A small town filled with history, St. Albans offers a relaxing refuge away from the bustle of London. People have been living here since prehistoric times, and here the Romans built their city of Verulamium, one of the largest cities in Roman Britain. The modern town is named after a 3rd-century Christian convert who was executed on the hill where the cathedral stands today to become England's first Christian martyr. His shrine became a pilgrimage site, and the town's location on the road heading north out of London made it important for trade and travel too. Several 17th- and 18th-century coaching inns are still in business today. Medieval and Tudor architecture, a beautiful park, and country walks make this an ideal weekend getaway.

SIGHTS

CATHEDRAL AND ABBEY CHURCH OF ST. ALBAN

Sumpter Yard, 017/2786-0780, www.stalbanscathedral.org.uk

HOURS: Daily 8 A.M.-5:45 P.M.

COST: Free guided tours

The crowning glory of any trip to St. Albans is a visit to its cathedral. Local legend says it is here that Alban, a citizen of Roman Verulamium, was executed sometime in the 3rd century A.D. for being a Christian. He had helped a fugitive priest escape by trading clothes with him, and when he was caught he was marched up to the top of this hill and beheaded, thus becoming England's first martyr. It's said that when the sword cut through his holy neck, the executioner's eyes popped out of their sockets! A Benedictine monastery was founded here in A.D. 793 by Offa, King of Mercia, and in 1077 work began on the abbey, using Roman bricks looted from

© SEAN MCLACHLAN

During the War of the Roses, priests painted both red and white roses on the Cathedral ceiling.

EXCURSIONS

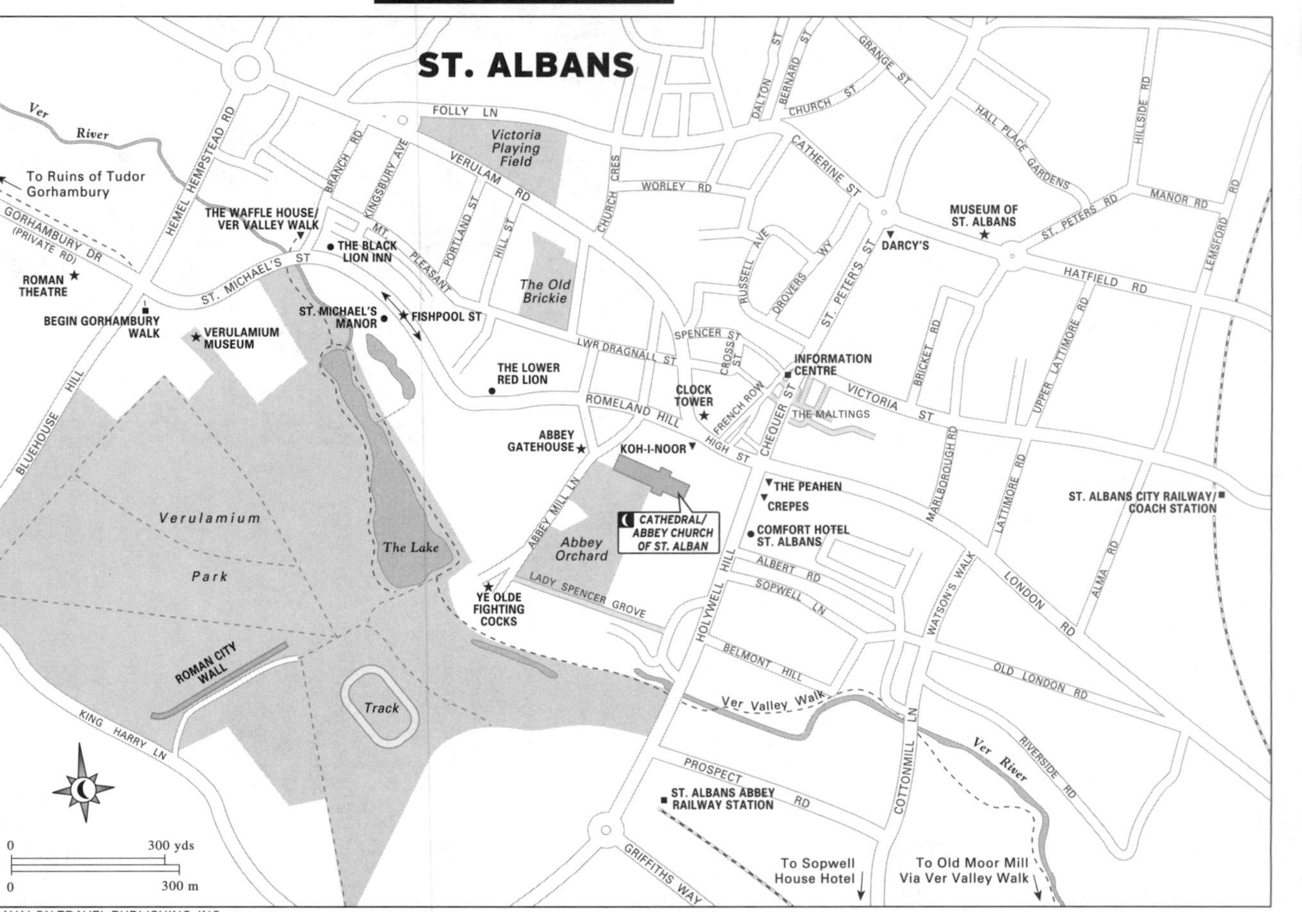
ST. ALBANS
Victoria Playing Field
The Old Brickie
The Lake
Track
Verulamium Park
Abbey Orchard
ROMAN CITY WALL
MUSEUM OF ST. ALBANS
DARCY'S
INFORMATION CENTRE
THE MALTINGS
THE PEAHEN
CREPES
COMFORT HOTEL ST. ALBANS
CLOCK TOWER
KOH-I-NOOR
CATHEDRAL/ ABBEY CHURCH OF ST. ALBAN
ABBEY GATEHOUSE
THE LOWER RED LION
YE OLDE FIGHTING COCKS
FISHPOOL ST
ST. MICHAEL'S MANOR
THE BLACK LION INN
THE WAFFLE HOUSE/ VER VALLEY WALK
VERULAMIUM MUSEUM
BEGIN GORHAMBURY WALK
ROMAN THEATRE
To Ruins of Tudor Gorhambury
GORHAMBURY DR (PRIVATE RD)
Ver River
Ver Valley Walk
ST. ALBANS CITY RAILWAY/ COACH STATION
ST. ALBANS ABBEY RAILWAY STATION
To Sopwell House Hotel
To Old Moor Mill Via Ver Valley Walk
LEMSFORD RD
MANOR RD
HILLSIDE RD
HATFIELD RD
ST. PETERS RD
HALL PLACE GARDENS
UPPER LATTIMORE RD
LATTIMORE RD
ALMA RD
LONDON RD
OLD LONDON RD
RIVERSIDE RD
MARLBOROUGH RD
WATSON'S WALK
COTTONMILL LN
BRICKET RD
VICTORIA ST
GRANGE ST
CHURCH ST
ST. PETER'S ST
CATHERINE ST
BERNARD ST
DALTON ST
DROVERS WY
RUSSELL AVE
CHEQUER ST
FRENCH ROW
CROSS ST
SPENCER ST
HIGH ST
ALBERT RD
SOPWELL LN
BELMONT HILL
HOLYWELL HILL
PROSPECT RD
GRIFFITHS WAY
WORLEY RD
CHURCH CRES
LWR DRAGNALL ST
ROMELAND HILL
ABBEY MILL LN
LADY SPENCER GROVE
FOLLY LN
VERULAM RD
HILL ST
PORTLAND ST
MT. PLEASANT
KINGSBURY AVE
BRANCH RD
ST. MICHAEL'S ST
HEMEL HEMPSTEAD RD
BLUEHOUSE HILL
KING HARRY LN
0 300 yds
0 300 m
© AVALON TRAVEL PUBLISHING, INC.

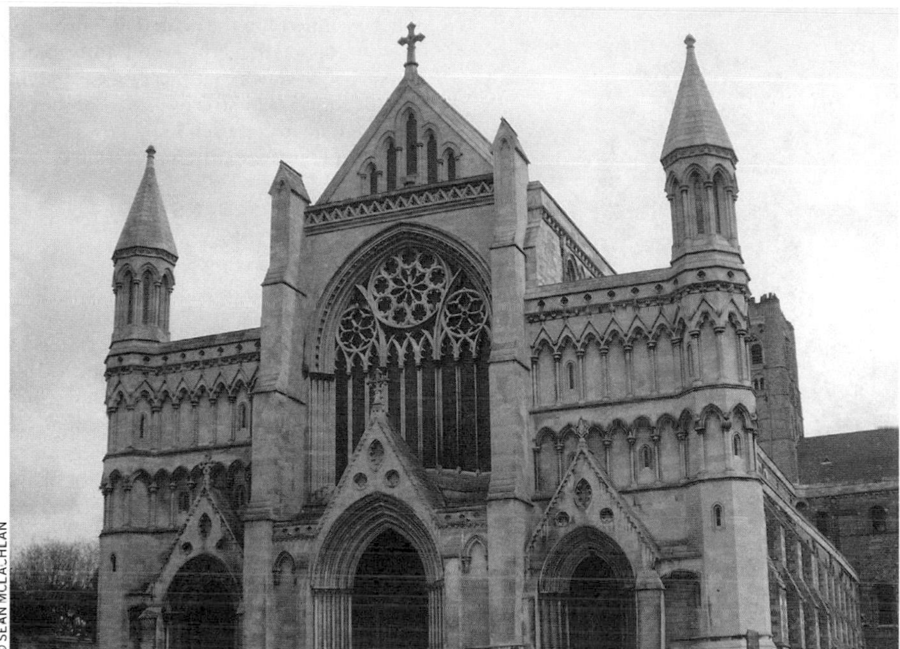

The Cathedral and Abbey Church of St. Alban incorporates more than a thousand years of architecture.

the old town. The cathedral's central square tower, built in the Norman style, dates to this time and is made of Roman bricks. The cathedral became a popular pilgrimage stop and was added onto in later years so that one can see various styles, including Gothic and modern, in its construction. At the east end, check out the shrine of St. Alban, made of Purbeck marble and dating to 1308. Inside rests a bone believed to be from the great saint himself. This cathedral is special in that some of its painted murals still survive, especially on the northern wall of the nave. Free guided tours run from 11 A.M. and 2:30 P.M. Monday–Friday, 11:30 A.M. and 2 P.M. Saturday, and 2:30 P.M. Sunday.

ABBEY GATEHOUSE

Sumpter Yard, 017/2786-0780

HOURS: Open 24 hours

All that remains of the great Benedictine Abbey of St. Alban, with its extensive lands and vineyards, are the cathedral and this gatehouse dating to 1360. The rest was sold off and eventually destroyed during the Dissolution—Henry VIII's great purge of church properties, which incidentally helped fund a major expansion of the Royal Navy and paved the way for England's domination of the seas. The Abbey Gatehouse is a picturesque old ruin with a Gothic arch in its interior. It was here that the monks defended themselves against the Peasants' Revolt in 1381. The building later became home to England's third printing press in 1479.

CLOCK TOWER

French Row, www.stalbansmuseums.org.uk

HOURS: Sat.-Sun. and bank holidays 10:30 A.M.-5 P.M. Easter-Oct.

COST: Adults 50 p, children 5-11 30 p, under 5 free

St. Albans was one of the first towns to get a clock tower, built sometime between 1402 and 1412, and it is now one of only two from that

The St. Albans clock tower, finished in 1412, still keeps time.

period remaining in the entire country. The 19.6-meter-tall (64 feet) tower makes an atmospheric backdrop to downtown, and the 92 narrow and winding steps lead to a fine view of the town, cathedral, and surrounding countryside. Don't forget to stop on the ground floor for the display of local history, and the upper floor to see the original bell set in the crude but functional woodwork of the period. The clock dates from 1866, although there has been a clock here since the tower was built.

FISHPOOL STREET

Fishpool St.

Take a stroll through the past along this remarkably preserved Tudor street. Most of the buildings are from the 17th century or earlier, with timber frames, small-paned windows, projecting upper story, and steep roofs. Occasionally you'll see brick Georgian buildings from the 18th century, notable for orderly rows of rectangular windows and the graceful symmetry of their architectural lines. There's no such symmetry in the older buildings; with 400 years of settling, the wood and plaster have warped so much that there isn't a straight line to be found. The street was part of the old coaching route to and from London, and many old inns and pubs are still in operation here.

MUSEUM OF ST. ALBANS

Hatfield Rd., 017/2781-9340,
www.stalbansmuseums.org.uk

HOURS: Mon.-Sat. 10 A.M.-5 P.M., Sun. 2-5 P.M.

COST: Free admission

This small but interesting museum traces St. Albans's storied past. The upper floor is dedicated to local history, with artifacts from Roman times onward, including a sample of the pilgrim's badges given out as mementos to the faithful who visited the shrine to St. Alban. The ground floor has interactive displays on life in earlier times; these are especially fun for children. A small pond and wildlife garden can be found behind the museum.

ROMAN THEATRE

Bluehouse Hill and Gorhambury Dr., 017/2783-5035,
www.romantheatre.co.uk

HOURS: Daily 10 A.M.-5 P.M. in summer, 10 A.M.-4 P.M. in winter

COST: Adults £1.50, seniors and students £1, children 50 p, children under 5 free

Explore the site of ancient Verulamium, where the foundations of many Roman buildings are laid bare. The outline of the theater, built around A.D. 140, can clearly be traced and a bit of the old stage still pokes out of the grass. It was probably on this spot that St. Alban was tried and found guilty of being a Christian. Around the theater stand the foundations of other buildings, such as shops and private homes, and the artifacts found in them have been put on display in the Verulamium Museum.

VERULAMIUM MUSEUM

St. Michael's St., 017/2775-1810,
www.stalbansmuseums.org.uk

HOURS: Mon.-Sat. 10 A.M.-5:30 P.M., Sun. 2-5:30 P.M.

COST: Adults £3.30, seniors, students, and children £2, children under 5 free, family £8

This extensive and fascinating museum showcases the finds from years of excavations in Verulamium. On display are mosaic floors, coins, tools, and other artifacts from Roman daily life. Several re-created rooms really bring the past to life, showing Romans hard at work or relaxing at home. There are video presentations and an electronic database of all the finds from the site, making this a great museum both for kids and serious historians. Nearby is the hypocaust building (free), preserving in situ a system of Roman central heating as well as a brilliant mosaic floor. Every second weekend of the month a group of re-enactors demonstrate their Roman military might. Check the website for details.

Oldest pub in England? There's been one at Ye Olde Fighting Cocks since the 8th century.

VERULAMIUM PARK

Bluehouse Hill, King Harry Ln., Fishpool St., and Holywell Hill, 017/2781-9366

The British are masters at creating beautiful parks, often screening them with trees so that you aren't even aware you're in the middle of a town or city. From the cathedral, take an easy walk downhill across green fields to a pond alive with waterfowl. From there the traces of the old Roman city wall are visible; beyond that there's a playground and lots of open space for picnicking, football games, or good honest lounging.

The Roman shops and theater of Verulamium still poke through the soil near St. Albans.

YE OLDE FIGHTING COCKS

16 Abbey Mill Lane, 017/2786 9152

Quaff a pint and enjoy some steak and Guinness pie in what could be the oldest pub in England. The octagonal central section dates to about 1400, but there may have been monks brewing on the site as early as A.D. 793. The pub gets its name from the cockfights that used to take place in one of its rooms; one of the stuffed champions is still on display. Cromwell is said to have spent the night here, with his horse occupying the bar area. More courteous guests are warned to watch their heads; the low roof beams are from the days when grown men stood barely above five feet.

COUNTRY WALKS

THE GORHAMBURY WALK

This walk travels through some wonderful rolling countryside along a paved and private road that is closed to all but a small amount of local traffic, so this is a good choice for those in a wheelchair or pushing a stroller. The entire walk is 8 kilometers (5 miles) round-trip. Please note that all the land, except for the ruins of Gorhambury, is on private property so please stay on the road. Information and a map are available from the St. Albans Tourist Information Centre, 017/2786-4511, www.stalbans.gov.uk.

The path starts from Verulamium Park, crosses Bluehouse Hill Road and enters the site of Verulamium. A small entrance fee allows access to the remains of the old Roman city, with its theater, shops, and houses. A half-kilometer up Gorhambury Drive, a thin strip of woodland appears on either side of the road. Look carefully to find a raised berm running within it. This is the overgrown Roman city wall, and the road now covers the site for Verulamium's northwest city gate. This road is of Roman origin and originally led all the way to Chester. Once past the strip of woodland, turn left to see another Roman remain, this time a defensive mound called The Fosse. This was an outer bulwark in front of the wall to give added protection for the city.

© ALMUDENA ALONSO-HERRERO

The Gorhambury Walk passes through the pastureland of local farms.

The road evetually turns southwest to the country estate of Gorhambury (open 2–5 P.M. Thurs. May–Sept.). All this land was the property of the Abbey at St. Albans, but the name comes from Geoffrey de Gorham, who was abbot of St. Albans 1119–1146. The land passed through several hands and is now owned by the Grimston family—aristocrats descended from Sir Harbottle Grimston, who helped get Charles II restored to the throne after the English Civil War. This stately home was designed by Sir Robert Taylor and finished in 1784 in a classical style. The interior is decorated with numerous family portraits, some up to 500 years old, as well as part of Sir Francis Bacon's library, and some beautiful Chippendale furniture.

Another half kilometer up the road are the picturesque ruins of the old Gorhambury house. It was once the home of Sir Nicholas Bacon, lord chancellor to Queen Elizabeth I and father of the famous Sir Francis Bacon. It was built in 1568 and later expanded when the queen stayed there and commented that it was too small. Apparently Sir Bacon didn't have much luck with contractors, because his house soon began to crumble and now stands as a very beautiful ruin. This is a good place to stop and have a picnic.

Beyond this point the road continues for another two kilometers, changing its name to Beechtree Lane and passing the site of a vanished Roman temple in the process, before coming to an underpass at the M10. If you're looking at a map, it may be tempting to get onto the Hemel Hempstead Road and take a shortcut back to St. Albans, but this is *not* recommended. There's no sidewalk and while walking on the grassy shoulder is possible, the way is often blocked by trees and bushes and rendered impassable. Once you reach the end of Beechtree Lane, turn back and retrace your steps, admiring the scenery once again.

© ALMUDENA ALONSO-HERRERO

Gorhambury, built 1777-1784, is an old-style British country estate.

VER VALLEY WALK

This walk follows the River Ver (actually not much more than a trickle in spots) through some scenic countryside, with the added bonus of starting and finishing at two historic mills. A northerly route runs from St. Albans to Redbourne, but the better-marked route runs south to Bricket Wood as described here. The total hike is 14 kilometers (9 miles) round-trip over easy terrain. The path is well drained and has no steep hills. The entire route is clearly marked not only by the path itself—which never fades to invisibility as many other English country paths have a habit of doing—but by signposts marked with a white circle around a yellow meandering arrow. From Bricket Wood, take a rural train line back to St. Albans. Note: The trail is also called the Alban Trail, so don't be confused by other markers with that name. Information and a map of this walk are available from the St. Albans Tourist Information Centre, 017/2786, www.stalbans.gov.uk.

The walk begins at Kingsbury Watermill, the first floor of which is the Waffle House restaurant. After visiting this 16th-century mill and its museum on the upper story, cross the bridge into Verulamium Park. The bridge may be as old as the human habitation of this area. When the Romans arrived in A.D., 43, there was already a causeway leading across the marshy land. The Romans, with their characteristic efficiency, built a road and bridge, which was rebuilt in medieval times to serve pilgrims visiting the shrine of St. Alban.

The walk continues through Verulamium Park to the river, where you'll have the pleasant company of the water and trees. From there it's easy sailing; the walk is marked quite clearly and the map will keep you on course. The walk leads through Ver Valley Meadows, the Park Street Roman villa, (nothing but a bare field now, but in the 1940s and '50s this was the site of a major archaeological excavation that revealed lots of interesting artifacts and two skeletons—all on display at the Verulamium Museum), and end at the Old Moor Mill, a functioning 18th-century mill run by a double waterfall on the River Ver. Historical records indicate that a mill stood here as long ago as A.D. 800. A nice pub on the premises serves the standard pub food and drinks.

After a well earned pint at the pub, retrace your steps or take a local train from Bricket Wood. Trains to St. Albans Abbey (not the city station, but right downtown) leave every 45 minutes Monday–Saturday, and hourly every Sunday. This is called the Abbey Flyer (084/5748-4950, www.abfly.org.uk). For a current schedule, check www.silverlink-trains.com on the Watford–St. Albans–Watford line. To reach the train station, head down the Mill's driveway and take a right (west) on Smug Oak Lane, continue to the end, and take a left (south) on Station Road, going just a few more steps before finding the station on the right.

RESTAURANTS

CREPES £££

15 Holywell Hill, 017/2784-6424

HOURS: Tues.-Fri. 6-10:30 P.M., Sat. 10:30 A.M.-11 P.M., Sun. 10:30 A.M.-10 P.M.

Traditional French decor and old American jazz make for an unusual atmosphere in this bustling little dining spot offering both crepes and galettes, a Breton pancake made with whole-meal buckwheat flour. The crepes come with various fillings, including the popular *traditionnel* stuffed with brie, bacon, walnuts, mozzarella, avocado, olives, and tomato. Nouveau cuisine this is not; the servings are generous and diners will leave quite full. Crepes stocks a range of French wines, beers, and ciders.

DARCYS £££

2 Hatfield Rd., 017/2773-0777, www.darcysrestaurant.co.uk

HOURS: Mon.-Sat. noon-2:30 P.M., 6-9:30 P.M., Sun. noon-3 P.M., 6-9 P.M.

Quality ingredients, a choice wine list, and contemporary European cooking distinguish Darcys as a fine dining experience that few small towns can boast. Patrons can choose between the courtyard or two dining rooms—one with dark red walls and another, brighter room—both of which are decorated with oil paintings. Dishes include such interesting combinations as chicken breast with mozzarella and pesto wrapped in proscuitto on crushed potatoes, and sea bass fillet with black olive tapenade on a chorizo and sun-blushed tomato couscous. Start or finish the evening with a drink in the lounge, a subdued, comfortable little place with excellent service.

KOH-I-NOOR ££

8 George St., 017/2785-5517/3602

HOURS: Daily noon-4 P.M., 6-11:30 P.M.

This Indian and Bangladeshi restaurant was the first to offer South Asian food in St. Albans when it opened in 1960, well before the current Asian food craze. It quickly became a local favorite and has remained so ever since. The 17th-century building has been remodeled in a country English style, but the focus is on the expertly prepared food. The chefs avoid the temptation of adding too much spice or ladening everything with cream, instead going for an authentic and subtle blend of spices that emphasizes flavor over fire. The menu includes quite a few seafood dishes, many made with king prawns shipped in from Asia. Reservations are recommended.

THE PEAHEN ££

14 London Rd., 017/2785-3669

HOURS: Mon.-Wed. 9:30 A.M.-11 P.M., Thurs.-Sat. 9:30 A.M.-midnight, Sun. 10 A.M.-10:30 P.M.

This combination bar and restaurant offers traditional British fare in a roomy dining area with views of the busy street outside. Dishes include Cumberland pork sausages with potato mash, and Heidi Pie stuffed with goat's cheese, roasted veggies, and sweet potato. It's all quite filling, the service good, and the beer list pretty lengthy. The Peahen has been popular with locals for many years and can get quite lively on weekend nights.

THE WAFFLE HOUSE £

St. Michael's Bridge, 017/2785-3502

HOURS: Daily 10 A.M.-6 P.M.

While waffles aren't exactly traditional British cooking, there couldn't be anything more traditional than the mid-16th-century water mill this restaurant is housed in. Indoor seating is set amid a display of old tools and photographs. Outdoor seating is right next to St. Michael's Bridge, where patrons will be serenaded by quacking ducks. The waffles are made with organic flour and eggs and come in a variety of flavors, such as pecan nut with butterscotch sauce or spiced fruit and banana. You can order ice cream on them too. Needless to say, it's very popular with local kids. The water mill itself is well worth a visit. The upper two floors of the structure are a museum, showing how the mill worked and revealing the simple but heavy machinery that ground farmer's grain into flour.

ACCOMMODATIONS

THE BLACK LION INN £40-80

198 Fishpool St., 017/2785-1786, www.theblacklioninn.com

Built in 1837, this former bakery now continues Fishpool Street's tradition of taking care of visitors. While the visitors come on trains now instead of stagecoaches, the inn still offers old-time hospitality. All rooms are en suite and the wooden beams and historic surroundings make for a very atmospheric stay. Archaeologists have discovered remains of a Roman alehouse from sometime between A.D. 60 and 250, making this the oldest pub site in England. The pub (open 11 A.M.–11 P.M. Mon.–Sat. and noon–10:30 P.M. Sun.) offers some fine real ales and is worth a visit even if you're not staying here. An on-site restaurant serves breakfast.

COMFORT HOTEL ST. ALBANS £40-80

Ryder House, 27 Holywell Hill, 017/2784-8849, www.choicehotels.com

In a late Victorian building right next to the cathedral and in the center of the shopping district, you'll be everywhere you want to be in this hotel. The rooms are modern, and what they lack in flair (think Holiday Inn) they make up for with affordability and location. There's a bar on-site, and the Six Degrees Restaurant serves good English cooking, but with the wealth of choices all around, you probably won't spend much time in the hotel.

LOWER RED LION £40-80

36 Fishpool St., 017/2785-5669, www.lowerredlion.com

The Lower Red Lion is, quite simply, the best value of any hotel I've tried in England. This old 17th-century coaching inn is still much as it was, and the three centuries' worth of hospitality shows in the helpful and friendly staff. It has seven rooms (only two of which are en suite) ranging in price £60–75, so book well in advance. A full English breakfast in a relaxed dining area is included. The pub (open 11 A.M.–11 P.M. Mon.–Sat. and noon–10:30 P.M. Sun.) offers seven—count 'em, seven!—real ales and serves some great pub grub. The combination of old architecture, honest English hospitality, a convivial pub, and home-cooked food offers an experience of England at its best.

ST. MICHAEL'S MANOR OVER £150

Fishpool St., 017/2786-4444, www.stmichaelsmanor.com

Elegance is the key word in this refurbished stately home, complete with a breathtakingly beautiful private garden and duck pond. The earliest parts of the home date to 1512, but the interior has been refurbished with modern amenities. The Georgian-era lounge makes for atmospheric tippling, and the conservatory overlooks the garden and pond. Each room is individually designed, some in English country style and others in modern, subdued Asian style. Darcy's, the hotel restaurant, offers impeccable service and fine European dining with occasional surprises from farther afield, such as kangaroo meat. The hotel often has special weekend rates at a considerable discount.

SOPWELL HOUSE £80-150

Cottonmill Lane, 017/2786-4477, www.sopwellhouse.co.uk

If you want to stay at a more modern hotel slightly outside of town, the Sopwell House is a good option. It's set right next to the Verulam Golf Course, home of the Ryder Cup, and amid beautiful gardens, so you won't see much except calming country greenery. The rooms are decorated in English country style and a few are equipped with a kitchenette and lounge. Two restaurants, a bar, and a free, fully equipped country club are on-site.

PRACTICALITIES

GETTING THERE

Trains leave King's Cross on the **Thameslink** (084/5748-4950, www.thameslink.co.uk) and take 20 minutes to reach the St. Albans City Station on Victoria Street, about half a mile from the city center. They run from King's Cross and back around the clock Monday–Saturday, several times an hour at peak periods. On Sundays the service stops at midnight. A return ticket costs £14.90. The **Silverlink** (084/5748-4950, www.silverlink-trains.com) route goes from Euston Station to the St. Albans Abbey Station at the bottom of Holywell Hill right in the center of town. This local, rural service takes 45 minutes and a return ticket costs £11.80. It runs only on weekdays, with trains departing Euston from 5:24 A.M.–9:04 P.M. and trains departing St. Albans Abbey Station from 6:21 A.M.–9:52 P.M.

While trains are much quicker and more convenient, you can also take the bus to St. Albans. **Green Line's** (www.greenline.co.uk, 087/0608-2608) 724 service runs from Heathrow Airport via Uxbridge on Belmont Road (Tube: Uxbridge) to St. Albans City Station and back, taking about 1 hour and 20 minutes. Since the City Station is a bit of a hike from the center of town, ask the driver if the bus continues to the town center. Many coaches stop near the town hall on St. Peter's Street. A return ticket costs £7 for a single. The service runs from Heathrow 6:25 A.M.–10:05 P.M. Monday–Saturday, and 9:20 A.M.–9:20 P.M. Sunday. From St. Albans City Station service runs 4:30 A.M.–8:28 P.M. Monday–Saturday, and 6:40 A.M.–9:14 P.M. Sunday. This bus also stops at St. Peter's Street at the center of town.

To get to St. Albans by car from London, take the A41 north and continue on it as it turns into the A1. Get on the M25 and then take Exit 22 to St. Albans. The trip is 22 miles and takes about 45 minutes.

GETTING AROUND

St. Albans is compact and highly walkable. All of the attractions mentioned here are within a few minutes' walk from each other. There is no need to take the local buses, but if you are loaded down with luggage when you arrive, the taxi stand outside the city station will get you a ride to the center of town for about £5. The Abbey Station does not have a taxi station, but it is already in the center of town.

INFORMATION

The **St. Albans Tourist Information Centre** (017/2786-4511, www.stalbans.gov.uk, open 10 A.M.–5 P.M. Mon.–Sat.) is on Market Place. It is well stocked with free pamphlets on local attractions and sell some interesting books on the area. It offers guided city walks at 11 A.M. and 3 P.M. Sunday April–October. There is an additional walk at 8 P.M. Wednesday July and August and a ghost walk the last Wednesday of each month. All walks start from the Tourist Information Centre and cost adults £2, accompanied children free.

Stratford-upon-Avon

Famous the world over as the birthplace of William Shakespeare, this town boasts many well-preserved Tudor homes dating to his lifetime. The main attraction, of course, is his home and that of Anne Hathaway, his wife. Theaters constantly perform his plays and there are some excellent performances here. The town is horribly touristy, however, and is so packed with people in high season that a visit can be quite frustrating. True devotees of the theater will grit their teeth and bear it, but for a relaxing day trip look elsewhere.

SIGHTS

ANNE HATHAWAY'S COTTAGE

Cottage Lane, Shottery, 017/8929-2100, www.shakespeare.org

HOURS: Mon.-Sat. 9 A.M.-5 P.M., Sun. 9:30 A.M.-5 P.M. June-Aug.; Mon.-Sat. 9:30 A.M.-5 P.M., Sun. 10 A.M.-5 P.M. Apr.-May and Sept.-Oct.; daily 10 A.M.-4 P.M. Nov.-Mar.

COST: Adults £5.50, seniors and students £4.50, children £2, family £13

The childhood home of Shakespeare's wife and the site of their courtship, this wonderfully restored thatched cottage gives a glimpse of life in the 17th century. A museum explains the history of the house and shows off some associated artifacts. Out back are gardens and a series of sculptures with Shakespearean themes. The property is in Shottery, one mile from Stratford-upon-Avon, and is reachable by foot or by regular shuttle buses from the center of town.

HOLY TRINITY CHURCH

Old Town, 017/8926-6316, www.shakespeareschurch.org

HOURS: Mon.-Sat. 8:30 A.M.-6 P.M., Sun. 12:30-5 P.M. Apr.-Sept., Mon.-Sat. 9 A.M.-5 P.M., Sun. 12:30-5 P.M.

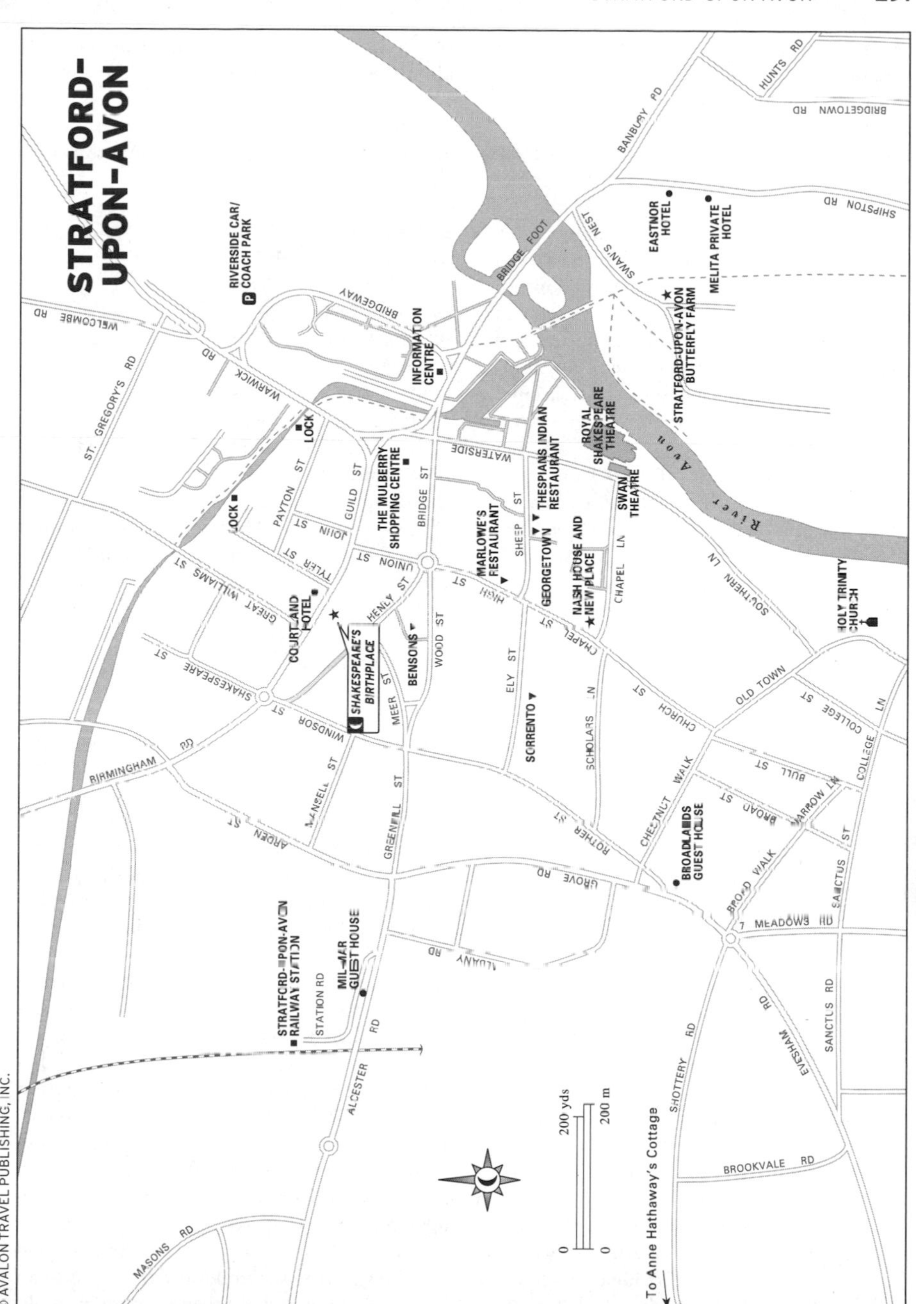
STRATFORD-UPON-AVON
RIVERSIDE CAR/ COACH PARK
WELCOMBE RD
ST. GREGORY'S RD
WARWICK RD
BRIDGEWAY
INFORMATION CENTRE
BRIDGE FOOT
BANBURY RD
HUNTS RD
BRIDGETOWN RD
SHIPSTON RD
EASTNOR HOTEL
MELITA PRIVATE HOTEL
SWAN'S NEST
STRATFORD-UPON-AVON BUTTERFLY FARM
ROYAL SHAKESPEARE THEATRE
River Avon
LOCK
PAYTON ST
GUILD ST
THE MULBERRY SHOPPING CENTRE
BRIDGE ST
WATERSIDE
THESPIANS INDIAN RESTAURANT
SWAN THEATRE
JOHN ST
TYLER ST
UNION ST
MARLOWE'S RESTAURANT
SHEEP ST
GEORGETOWN
NASH HOUSE AND NEW PLACE
CHAPEL LN
SOUTHERN LN
HOLY TRINITY CHURCH
GREAT WILLIAMS ST
COURTLAND HOTEL
HENLY ST
HIGH ST
CHAPEL ST
SHAKESPEARE'S BIRTHPLACE
BENSONS
WOOD ST
SHAKESPEARE ST
MEER ST
ELY ST
SORRENTO
SCHOLARS LN
CHURCH ST
OLD TOWN
COLLEGE ST
COLLEGE LN
WINDSOR ST
BIRMINGHAM RD
MANSELL ST
GREENHILL ST
CHESTNUT WALK
BULL ST
BROAD ST
NARROW LN
ROTHER ST
BROADLANDS GUEST HOUSE
ARDEN ST
GROVE RD
BROAD WALK
SANCTUS ST
MEADOWS RD
ALBANY RD
STRATFORD-UPON-AVON RAILWAY STATION
MILMAR GUEST HOUSE
STATION RD
ALCESTER RD
SHOTTERY RD
EVESHAM RD
SANCTUS RD
BROOKVALE RD
MASONS RD
0
200 yds
200 m
To Anne Hathaway's Cottage

Mar. and Oct., Mon.-Sat. 9 A.M.-4 P.M., Sun. 12:30-5 P.M. Nov.-Feb.

COST: Free admission, Shakespeare's Grave £1.50 adults, students and children 50 p

This parish church is home to the "weeping chancel," wherein Shakespeare is buried. The church first appears in records in A.D. 845, and parts of the present church date to 1210. Besides Shakespeare's grave, be sure to see the tomb of George Carew and Joyce Clopton, a magnificent piece of 17th-century funerary architecture complete with painted statues of the departed. This is an active house of worship, so maintain a respectful quiet; it will occasionally be closed during services.

NASH'S HOUSE AND NEW PLACE

Chapel St., 017/8929-1823, www.shakespeare.org.uk

HOURS: Mon.-Sat. 9:30 A.M.-5 P.M., Sun. 10 A.M.-5 P.M. June-Aug.; Daily 11 A.M.-5 P.M. Apr.-May and Sept.-Oct.; Daily 11 A.M.-4 P.M. Nov.-Mar.

COST: Adults £3.75, seniors and students £3, children £1.75, family £10

Shakespeare spent his retirement here in a home (now destroyed) next to this house of his granddaughter. Now a museum, it traces the history of the town before and after the life of its most famous resident. Tapestries and other furnishings from the Elizabethan era give an authentic touch. The site of Shakespeare's last home and property are preserved as a garden next to the house and include an Elizabethan knot garden and several statues of Shakespearean characters.

SHAKESPEARE'S BIRTHPLACE

Henley St., 017/8920-1823, www.shakespeare.org.uk

HOURS: Mon.-Sat. 9 A.M.-5 P.M., Sun. 9:30 A.M.-5 P.M. June-Aug.; Daily 10 A.M.-5 P.M. Apr.-May, Sept.-Oct.; Mon.-Sat. 10 A.M.-4 P.M., Sun. 10:30 A.M.-4 P.M. Nov.-Mar.

COST: Adults £7, seniors and students £6, children £2.75, family £17

The baby who would become the world's most famous playwright was born here in 1564. This was also probably the first house he lived in after marrying Anne Hathaway. The interior gives a good idea of what life was like at the time, and an exhibition at the visitors center (included in ticket) tells all about Shakespeare's life. Go here first to get grounded on the subject before exploring the town further. The gardens out back are lovely and planted with flowers mentioned in the Bard's plays.

STRATFORD-UPON-AVON BUTTERFLY FARM

Swan's Nest Lane, 017/8929-9288, www.butterflyfarm.co.uk

HOURS: Daily 10 A.M.-dusk in winter, daily 10 A.M.-6 P.M. in summer

COST: Adults £4.95, seniors and students £4.45, children £3.95, family £14.95

Take a break from the Bard with some butterflies. Hundreds of butterflies are here in an enclosed tropical garden and it's a lot of fun to see all these colorful little fellas fluttering around. There's also an insect zoo with caterpillars, an ant colony, and spiders. The scorpions are pretty creepy, and some of the caterpillar species are gigantic. This is a perfect way to cheer up kids suffering from museum fatigue.

THEATERS

It's no great shocker to say that there are plenty of theaters in Stratford-upon-Avon, served by a small army of actors and actresses. In brief these are: The Royal Shakespeare Theatre (Waterside, 087/0609-1110, www.rsc.org.uk), The Swan Theatre (Waterside, 087/0609-1110, www.rsc.org.uk), Civic Hall Stratford (Rother St., 017/8920-7100, www.civichall.co.uk), The Bacon Theatre (Dean Close School, Shelburne Rd., Cheltenham, 012/4225-8002, www.bacontheatre.co.uk), Everyman Theatre (Regent St., Cheltenham, 012/4257-2573, www.everymantheatre.org.uk), and The Loft Theatre (Victoria Colonnade, Royal Leamington Spa, 019/2674-2756, www.loft-theatre.co.uk), and Falstaff's Experience (Shrieves House Barn, 40 Sheep St., 087/0350-2770, www.falstaffsexperience.co.uk). All, of course, perform Shakespeare plays but they occasionally put on works by other playwrights. A good website showing schedules for all theaters can be found at www.shakespeare-country.co.uk.

RESTAURANTS

BENSONS £££

4 Bard's Walk, 017/8926-1116, www.bensonsrestaurant.co.uk

HOURS: Mon.-Fri. 10 A.M.-5:15 P.M., Sat. 8:30 A.M.-5:30 P.M., Sun. 10:30 A.M.-5 P.M.

This fine but reasonably priced restaurant offers breakfast, lunch, and tea. On the first floor of the Royal Shakespeare Theatre, it's perfect for pretheater dining. The menu features a fusion of modern British cuisine and a French patisserie. The meals incorporate local produce to make unexpected combinations, such as goat's cheese with caramelized onions and pine nuts served on toasted walnut bread. The high tea and champagne tea are very good. To start on the champagne early, order the champagne breakfast for two.

GEORGETOWN ££

23 Sheep St., 087/0755-7751, www.georgetownrestaurants.co.uk

HOURS: Daily noon-2:30 P.M., 5-11 P.M.

Malaysian food may not be generally associated with Stratford-upon-Avon, but this mix of Malay, Mandarin, and Tamil cooking reflects the culinary diversity of that country. The dining area is European formal, with meals served on fine crystal and china. For a cheaper option, try the £7.50 lunch special. The food is spicy, varied, and flavorful, with dishes such as Udang Bakar Kering (spicy pan-fried jumbo prawns in red onion sauce) and Pineapple Paradise (creamy fillets of cod served in a hollowed-out pineapple). There are plenty of vegetarian options and a good wine list.

MARLOWE'S RESTAURANT £££

18 High St., 017/8920-4999, www.marlowes.biz

HOURS: Bistro: Daily noon-2:15 P.M., 5:30-10:30 P.M.; Elizabethan Dining Room: Mon.-Fri. 5:30-10:30 P.M., Sat. 5:30-11 P.M., Sun. 7-9 P.M.

With silver service and oak paneling in a dining room dating to 1595, this is the place for atmosphere if you don't mind spending a bit of money. Since the room is from the same era as Shakespeare, it's a great option for getting into the mood before seeing one of the Bard's plays. Lots of other people have figured this out too, so reservations are recommended. The food is hearty country fare, such as corn-fed chicken and rich traditional puddings. You'll find a lounge with a toasty fireplace in winter where diners can have a drink, and a bistro open for lunch and dinner, though it's not as atmospheric.

SORRENTO ££

8 Ely St., 017/8929-7999

HOURS: Lunch: Tues.-Wed. 11:30 A.M.-1:45 P.M.; Dinner: Mon.-Sat. 5-10:30 P.M., Sun. by reservation only

This Italian restaurant offers an informal, unhurried atmosphere with somewhat formal decor (white pillars and real silverware) and traditional Italian cooking. The best way to start a meal is to sit down in a leather seat in the lounge and have a drink. Once you're seated, there's a good choice of pasta, meat, and seafood dishes. The proscuitto and melon starter was well done, and a good test for the restaurant since it's so easy to skimp with cheap ingredients—it didn't. The wine list emphasizes Italian vintages. There's also a dining area on the patio for fine weather.

THESPIANS INDIAN RESTAURANT ££

26 Sheep St., 017/8926-7187, www.thespiansindianrestaurant.co.uk

HOURS: Daily 5:30 P.M.-midnight

If you've had enough of Ye Olde English Fare, come here for some spicy northern Indian, Kashmiri, and Bangladeshi dishes. The menu is heavy on meat dishes (most Bengalis and Kashmiris are Muslim, so they eat meat) but there are some vegetarian options. For those who want to try a sampling of various dishes, order one of the *thalis*—sectioned trays that contain a sampler of what the restaurant cooks. The decor is rather simple, but it's a nice break from the Tudor (or imitation Tudor) overload everywhere else in town.

EXCURSIONS

ACCOMMODATIONS

BROADLANDS GUEST HOUSE £40-80

23 Evesham Pl., 017/8929-9181

If you want to stay right in the center of

Stratford's Old Town, this Victorian town house is a good option. It was completely refurbished in 2002 and is well maintained, with an English country-style decor and a very homey feel. All rooms are en suite and come with TV and tea- and coffee-making facilities. A full English breakfast is included. It's just a few minutes' walk to all the major sights, which will make you feel like a local.

COURTLAND HOTEL £40-80

12 Guild St., 017/8929-2401, www.courtlandhotel.co.uk

This Georgian town house in the center of Stratford offers refined 18th-century–style decor that's a welcome relief from the somewhat cutesy English country style common to most hotels in town. All rooms are en suite or have private facilities and are quite comfortable and well appointed. The Courtland is ideal for its nice atmosphere and superconvenient location, right behind Shakespeare's birthplace. You can't get much more central than this.

EASTNOR HOTEL £80-150

33 Shipston Rd., 017/8926-8115, www.eastnorhouse.com

Just a few minutes' walk from the center of town sits this bed-and-breakfast, a former Victorian home kept in its original style. The place is quite sociable, made more so by the beer garden and barbecue open to nonresidents and guests alike. The nicely appointed lounge doubles as a wine bar and offers a respite from the crowd, as well as (overpriced) Internet access. All rooms are en suite and come with TV, hair dryer, and tea- and coffee-making facilities. A full English breakfast is included.

MELITA PRIVATE HOTEL £40-80

37 Shipston Rd., 017/8929-2432, www.melitahotel.co.uk

Want to be close to the action? Then this 12-room bed-and-breakfast, just a five-minute walk from the center of town, is a good option. The Victorian building has kept its old-style ambience and features a lush garden that's great for getting away from the crowds. Sip tea amid the flowers and watch the birds twitter about the birdhouse. If it's raining, hang out in the Victorian-style lounge with its very un-Victorian TV. All the rooms are en suite and come with TV, hair dryer, and tea- and coffee-making facilities. A full English breakfast is included.

MIL-MAR GUEST HOUSE £40-80

96 Alcester Rd., 017/8926-7095

This little family-owned guesthouse less than a kilometer from the town center offers friendly service and extensive local knowledge. Many of the rooms feature a canopy bed, and all are decorated with bright floral designs typical of English country design. All rooms are en suite and come with a TV, hair dryer, and tea- and coffee-making facilities. A full English breakfast is included. This is a nice place to get away from the crowds clogging the center of town.

PRACTICALITIES

GETTING THERE

Chiltern Railways (084/5600-5165, www.chilternrailways.co.uk) runs hourly trains from Marylebone Station to Stratford-upon-Avon Railway Station (Station Rd., 084/5748-4950). Trips take a little over two hours and cost £25 for a day return. If you want to stay overnight, for just 30 pence more you can get a saver return valid for up to one month, but you have to leave London after 9:42 A.M. on weekdays or any train on weekends. On weekdays the first train leaves London at 8:04 A.M. and the last at 7:33 P.M., while the first leaves Stratford at 6:45 A.M. and the last at 7:09 P.M. On Saturdays the first leaves London at 8:54 A.M. and the last at 6:50 P.M., while the first leaves Stratford at 7:35 A.M. and the last at 7:50 P.M. On Sundays the first train leaves London at 8:40 A.M. and the last at 5:33 P.M., while the first leaves Stratford at 10 A.M. and the last at 8 P.M. On weekends the trains run only every two hours. The Stratford-upon-Avon (www.stratfordstation.co.uk) Train Station is on Alcester Road about 10 minutes' walk from the historic Old Town center.

National Express (087/0580-8080, www.nationalexpress.com) runs six coaches a day from Victoria Coach Station (020/7730-3466) that take anywhere from 2.5–5 hours depending on the bus. Tickets cost £16.50 for a day return or £19 for an economy return and must be used within three months. The buses end up at the Riverside Car and Coach Park on Bridgeway, right next to the Tourist Information Centre and near the center of town. Tickets for seniors and children cost £8.25 for a day return and £9.50 for an economy return. Buses leave London daily at 8:30 A.M. and the last at 11:30 P.M., while the first leaves Stratford at 2 A.M. and the last at 5:30 P.M. Stratford-upon-Avon's Riverside Bus Station is on Station Road and can be reached at 087/0609-6060 for the ticket office or 012/1634-2040 for customer service. Because the ride is so much longer and not much cheaper, the train is really the way to go.

To get from London to Stratford-upon-Avon by car, take the A501 out of town and keep on it when it turns into the A40. Merge onto the M40 and take Exit 15 to Stratford-upon-Avon. Take the first exit to get onto the A46, then get onto the A439, which turns into the A3400 and takes you right into Stratford-upon-Avon. The journey is 101 miles and takes about 1 hour and 45 minutes.

GETTING AROUND

Stratford-upon-Avon is a compact city, but movement is hampered by the vast throngs of tourists that flock here every summer. There's not much option but to walk, as the crowds fill the streets, mingling with traffic that isn't going any faster than the pedestrians. Shottery, the site of Anne Hathaway's cottage, is only a mile from town. Walk it, following the clearly marked signs, or ride a taxi for about £5 (for this price you can get anywhere within town if, for example, you don't want to walk from the train station).

INFORMATION

The **Stratford-upon-Avon Tourist Information Centre** (corner of Bridgefoot and Bridgeway, 087/0160-7930, www.shakespeare-country.co.uk, 9 A.M.–5 P.M. Mon.–Sat.) has the usual information. Another good website for information on what to see, and where to eat and stay, is www.stratford-upon-avon.co.uk.

Windsor

Less than an hour from central London stands the small town of Windsor, home to the impressive royal residence of Windsor Castle. Less than an hour's journey from London, this is one of the easiest and most popular day trips for overseas visitors. While the town can be a bit touristy, the castle is well worth a visit, and nearby Eton provides a glimpse into the public (private) school life of the country's elite.

SIGHTS

ETON

High St., Eton 017/5367-1177, www.etoncollege.com

HOURS: Daily 10:30 A.M.-4:30 P.M. Mar. 25-Apr. 19; Daily 2-4:30 P.M. Apr. 20-June; Daily 10:30 A.M.-4:30 P.M. July-Sept. 5; Daily 2-4:30 P.M. Sept. 6-Oct.

COST: Adults £4, seniors and children £3.20, £1 extra with tour

Eton has been educating England's best and brightest since it was founded by Henry VI in 1440 and it is still the country's most exclusive and prestigious public (private) school for boys today. Its historic connection to Kings College in Cambridge (which Henry VI also founded) means that many graduates have gone on to study there, although others have chosen archrival Oxford. The chapel also dates from the 15th century and features some interesting wall paintings and gorgeous stained glass. The Museum of Eton Life explains what the kids get up to in all these ornate buildings—and one thing they get up to is carving their names everywhere. You'll see graffiti

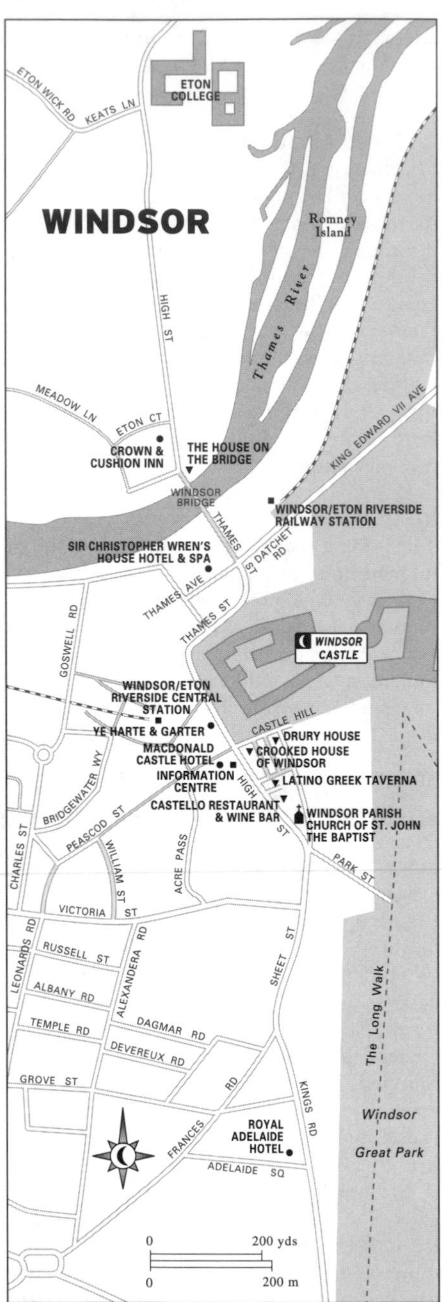

that's more than 400 years old on some of the walls. The informative tour is recommended, as there aren't any explanatory signs inside the school. Tours run at 2:15 and 3:15 P.M. daily and last an hour.

WINDSOR CASTLE

Castle Hill and High St., 020/7766-7304, www.windsor.gov.uk or www.royalcollection.org.uk

HOURS: Daily 9:45 A.M.-5:15 P.M. Mar.-Oct.; Daily 9:45 A.M.-4:15 P.M. Nov.-Feb.

COST: Summer: Adults £7, seniors and students £6, children £4, family £18; Winter: Adults £13.50, seniors and students £12, children £7.50, family £34.50

This impressive castle is one of the official residences of the queen, and she often spends her weekends here (tough life!). Built in 1070, it's the oldest and largest continually inhabited castle in the world. The first fort was a makeshift wooden affair on an artificial hill, commissioned by William the Conqueror along with dozens of other quick-and-cheap castles to assert his claim on England. The central round tower stands upon the site of this first castle, and surrounding it are several other towers, walls, and buildings. The oldest parts date to the reign of Henry II (reigned 1154–1189). In 1189, Prince (later King) John was besieged here by angry barons who eventually forced him to sign the Magna Carta, the first official limitation on the monarch's power. It was besieged again in 1216 during a similar confrontation. King Edward III (reigned 1327–1377) was born here and built much of the present structure. The castle was gradually remodeled into a more comfortable residence, although it briefly saw military action again during the Civil War and is still an imposing example of medieval military architecture.

One of the highlights is St. George's Chapel, an elaborately Gothic 15th-century medieval house of worship in which 10 monarchs have been buried and many more married. Other stops include Queen Mary's dollhouse, the extensive art collection with paintings by masters such as Holbein and Rubens, the armory hall, and the fine views of the surrounding countryside from atop the battlements.

© SEAN MCLACHLAN

The Queen spends many of her weekends at historic Windsor Castle.

Windsor Castle is one of those rare sights that's actually better to see in winter, because that's when the semi-state rooms are open. Built by George IV in the 1820s as living and socializing quarters for the royal family, they were meticulously restored after a fire in 1992 and include elegant furniture and giant oil paintings underneath elaborately molded plaster roofs. Together, these four rooms give a good idea what it was like to live as a royal in the castle during the 19th century.

An interesting footnote: Windsor Castle is not named after the House of Windsor (the royal family), but in fact the royal family is named after the castle. During World War I the royals decided their actual name, The House of Saxe Coburg-Gotha, sounded too German and changed it.

WINDSOR GREAT PARK AND THE LONG WALK

Windsor Great Park just south of Windsor Castle, access through Park St., 017/5374-3900

HOURS: Daily dawn-dusk

COST: Free admission

This giant park (about 4,800 acres) has been set aside for royal use since the 14th century, but it was used as hunting grounds by earlier Saxon kings. It's great for a picnic or a leisurely, photogenic stroll down The Long Walk, which runs nearly half a mile from the southern gate of Windsor Castle and used to be a promenade for the aristocratic set. Be careful in this park after dark because Herne the Hunter—a mysterious phantom rider with antlers and leading a pack of black hounds—has been known to ride by warning of imminent danger before disappearing.

WINDSOR PARISH CHURCH OF ST. JOHN BAPTIST

High St., Windsor

HOURS: Daily dawn-dusk

COST: Free admission

This church dates only to 1822, making it one of the younger buildings in the area, but it was built upon the foundations of a much older, medieval church and some of the worn gravestones from that era are preserved in the walls of the current structure. There's some lovely stained glass, but the two main attractions are the royal pews and a painting of the *Last Supper*. The pews were a gift from Princess Augusta, daughter of George III, and were used by her and George V and Queen Mary. Above the entrance to the church hangs a painting of the *Last Supper*. While it's masterfully done, nobody is quite sure when or where it was painted; one theory holds that it was by Franz de Cleyn (1588–1658).

RESTAURANTS

CASTELLO RESTAURANT AND WINE BAR ££

4 Church Lane, 017/5385-8331

HOURS: Daily noon-11 P.M.

The building that houses this Italian restaurant dates to 1423. Original oak beams crisscross the ceiling and walls and there doesn't seem to be a straight angle anywhere. The menu includes all the traditional favorites, such as pastas and pizzas, and the wine bar is well stocked with Italian and other vintages. For al fresco dining, step out onto a medieval cobblestone lane. Simple, reasonably priced food, good quantities, and served in a medieval setting—you might have to go to Rome to find this again.

CROOKED HOUSE OF WINDSOR ££

51 High St., 017/5385-7534, www.crooked-house.com

HOURS: Lunch: Mon.-Fri. 10:30 A.M.-6 P.M. Mar.-Oct., Mon.-Fri. 11 A.M.-5 P.M. Nov.-Feb., 10 A.M.-6 P.M. all weekends; Dinner: Wed.-Sat. until 10 P.M.

This little building, immediately noticeable for its distinct tilt, was built in 1687 but ran into trouble in 1718 when it was restructured with green oak. Builders take note: This is what happens when you use damp wood! The oak eventually dried, but it warped in the process. It's perfectly safe and now houses a charming little restaurant and tea room. The food is traditional British cuisine made mostly with organic, local produce, a testament to its membership in the Slow Food Movement. Go for simple sandwiches, such as the Scottish smoked salmon with avocado and cream cheese, or something more elaborate, such as the oven-roast pigeon with sweet potato. This should be your first choice for tea; it serves two dozen types of teas and several gourmet coffees.

DRURY HOUSE ££

4 Church St., 017/5386-3734, www.druryhouse.co.uk

HOURS: Daily 9:30 A.M.-5:30 P.M.

Locals have been eating here for more than a century. This is the oldest restaurant in town, but the building dates to 1645—a mere stripling compared to some of the aged structures sharing this tiny cobblestone street. It was the home of the Windsor Castle staff until they were booted in favor of Nell Gwyn, Charles II's mistress. The tunnel the two used for their trysts still runs to the castle, although it has now been blocked off. After absorbing the period atmosphere, tuck into some traditional British cooking such as the homemade pastries and pies. It also offers nice cream teas in the afternoon.

THE HOUSE ON THE BRIDGE £££

Windsor Bridge, 017/5386-0914, www.house-on-the-bridge.co.uk

HOURS: Mon.-Sat. noon-2:30 P.M., 6-11 P.M., Sun. noon-3:30 P.M., 6-10:30 P.M.

One of the finer restaurants in town, this roomy eatery combines international cuisine with a fine view of the Thames; try to get a table on the riverside veranda or terrace garden. The interior is less interesting, with minimal decoration but huge windows that emphasize the matchless location. The food is worth lingering over too, with a wide variety of meat and fish dishes—try the confit of duck with honey and apple sauce or roasted fillet of sea bass with mustard and chives. There are also a few vegetarian options, such as seasonal vegetable terrine with basil and tomato dressing. It's a good place to splash out.

LATINO GREEK TAVERNA ££

3 Church Lane, 017/5385-7711

HOURS: Daily 11 A.M.-11 P.M.

Simple, hearty fare from Greece is what's on the menu here. The filling souvlakis and Greek salads are recommended, but the Greek wine is a bit thin and tasteless. Luckily there's a well-stocked bar with plenty of other options. The interior, remodeled in 2006, is bright and cheery with wood floors and whitewashed walls, but eating out on the medieval cobblestone lane is much more atmospheric. Friday and Saturday nights bring live music and belly dancing.

ACCOMMODATIONS

CROWN AND CUSHION INN £40-80

84 High St., Eton, 017/5386-1531

If you feel like staying on the Eton side of the river, the Crown and Cushion Inn is your best bet. The location gets you close to the college, but you're also quite close to the river, making it an easy walk to all the Windsor sights. The building dates to the 15th century and retains much of its historic charm, with a Georgian facade and lots of original wood work. Some rooms are en suite, and all come with a television, hairdryer, and tea and coffee making facilities. There are only eight rooms, however, so book well in advance. A continental breakfast is included.

MACDONALD CASTLE HOTEL £150 AND UP

High St., 087/0400-8300, www.castlehotel-windsor.co.uk

You can't beat this place for historical flair. The building was a coaching inn in the 16th century, and was also used as a posting house in the Georgian period. For more flair, look out the window to see Windsor Castle rising majestically just a stone's throw away. All en suite rooms are decorated in a subdued, modern style and all come with a television, hairdryer, Internet access, and tea and coffee making facilities. A full English breakfast is included and there's a pricey restaurant onsite serving English cuisine and high tea.

ROYAL ADELAIDE HOTEL £80-150

46 Kings Rd., 017/5386-3916, www.meridianleisure.com

A Georgian building refurbished with modern amenities in 2006, the Royal Adelaide is ten minutes from Windsor Castle and overlooks the Long Walk, making it a bit out of the way of the tourist crush while still being convenient. The en suite rooms are decorated in dark, soothing browns and reds. Amenities include air-conditioning, wireless Internet, a hairdryer, television, and tea and coffee making facilities. A garden restaurant and terrace bar are onsite.

SIR CHRISTOPHER WREN'S HOUSE HOTEL AND SPA £150 AND UP

Thames St., 017/5386-1354, www.sirchristopherwren.co.uk

If you have a taste for history and fine architecture, this is your chance to stay in the home of one of England's greatest architects. Sir Christopher Wren, responsible for St. Paul's in London, the Guildhall in Windsor, and numerous other fine buildings, used this as his family residence. It's located right next to the river and close to all the sights in Eton and Windsor. The rooms overlooking the river are more expensive, but worth it. All rooms are en suite and come with a television, hairdryer, and tea and coffee making facilities. There's a nice restaurant with a terrace so you can eat and watch the boats pass by.

YE HARTE AND GARTER £80-150

High St., 017/5386-3426

Don't want to spend the money to get the views at the Macdonald Castle Hotel? Ye Harte and Garter is even closer and slightly cheaper, right opposite Windsor Castle with the towers looming practically outside your window. It's a Victorian building, but there was an inn of the same name in Shakespeare's day, mentioned in the *Merry Wives of Windsor*. All rooms are en suite and come with a hairdryer, television, and tea and coffee making facilities. A full English breakfast is included. Make sure to get a room facing the castle; while the hotel is nice enough on its own merit, the view is what really makes it special.

PRACTICALITIES

GETTING THERE

National Rail (084/5748-4950, www.national rail.co.uk) trains run from Waterloo Station to Windsor and Eton Riverside Railway Station (Datchet Rd., 084/5748-4950)in just under an hour. Standard day return tickets cost from £7.40. Monday–Saturday the first train leaves London Waterloo for Windsor at 5:05 A.M. and the last at 11:52 P.M., while the first train leaves Windsor for Waterloo at 5:51 A.M. and the last at 11:23 P.M. On Sundays the first train leaves Waterloo for Windsor at 6:44 A.M. and the last at 11:44 P.M., while the first train leaves Windsor for Waterloo at 6:59 A.M. and the last at 11:01 P.M. Trains elsewhere in the country often go to Windsor and Eton Central Railway Station (Thames St., 084/5748-4950). Both Windsor train stations are right in the center of town.

Green Line (087/0608-2608, www.greenline.co.uk,) runs buses on its 701 and 702 routes from Victoria Bus Station to downtown Windsor, stopping just opposite the parish church. Monday–Friday the first bus leaves London for Windsor at 7:45 A.M. and the last at 8:30 P.M., while the first bus leaves Windsor for Victoria at 7:12 A.M. and the last at 7:35 P.M. On weekends the first bus leaves Victoria at 9:45 A.M. and the last at 9:30 P.M., while the first leaves Windsor at 7:42 A.M. and the last at 7:35 P.M. Buses run hourly and take about 1 hour and 15 minutes. Day return tickets cost £9–11 depending on the time of day. Note that there is no actual bus station in the center of town, just the "Parish Church" bus stop along High Street.

GETTING AROUND

Windsor is compact enough that you can walk across it easily. The medieval cobblestone streets next to the castle are closed to traffic and are too narrow to accommodate vehicles. Two companies offer 40-minute trips along the Thames to Boveney Lock and Weir, passing Windsor Castle, Eton, and Brocas Meadows for some great photo opportunities.

French Brothers (River St., 017/5385-1900, www.boat-trips.co.uk) offers the cruise hourly 11 A.M.–4 P.M. February 10–March 30, half hourly 10 A.M.–5 P.M. March 31–October 28, and hourly 11 A.M.–4 P.M. weekends only November–December. The cost is adults £4.50, seniors £4.25, and children 3–13 £2.25. Salter's Steamers (1 Thames Side, 017/5386-5832, www.salterssteamers.co.uk) has been offering tours since 1858 and does the run at 11 A.M., noon, and 2, 3, and 4 P.M. daily. The cost is adults £4 and children £2 for children. Both companies offer other, special tours; see their websites for details.

City Sightseeing (017/0886-6000, www.city-sightseeing.com) offers open-top double-decker bus tours of Windsor and Eton lasting 50 minutes with recorded commentary. The cost is adults £7, seniors and students £6, children £3.50, and families (two adults and two children) £17.50. Tickets are valid for 24 hours and buses leave from Castle Hill at least once an hour and every 15 minutes in high season.

INFORMATION

The **Royal Windsor Information Centre** (information 017/5374-3900 or accommodations 017/5374-3907, www.windsor.gov.uk) is in the Windsor Royal Shopping Centre, just off High Street. It offers free town maps and sells various guides and maps of the town and surrounding area.

BACKGROUND

The Setting

GEOGRAPHY

London sits in a large, semicircular basin of clayey soil in southeast England that was once well-watered with several rivers. Most have now been channeled underground to make way for the city's inexorable growth, which has spread over more than 600 square miles. The main river still on the surface is the Thames, which cuts through London and is a major landmark as well as a transportation link and water source. The Thames flows eastward from Kemble 346 kilometers (215 miles) to the North Sea. It's a tidal river, meaning that water flows in and out of its lower reaches. If you stay on the Thames Walk long enough, you'll see narrow, stony beaches appear and then disappear along the edges of the water. To the north and south of the river are gentle hills, punctuated by the occasional larger eminence such as Primrose Hill, offering good vantage points from which to see the city.

CLIMATE

England has a generally mild climate, with an emphasis on the damp, and the weather on any

© SEAN MCLACHLAN

given day is notoriously fickle. What starts out as a sunny morning can soon turn overcast, and then rainy, before the clouds break up again and the sun comes out, only to go back to rain a little later.

July and August are the hottest months, with temperatures often in the 20s Celsius and sometimes in the 30s (low 70s–low 90s Fahrenheit). Occasional rainstorms are separated by long periods of sun. From September through November it's generally rainier and cooler, often ranging 10–15 degrees Celsius (50–60°F). Winter runs through February and temperatures rarely go below 5 degrees Celsius (41°F), but short days and precipitation (rarely snow, but often freezing rain, which is far more annoying) can make life miserable. Whole weeks can go by without seeing the sun, as the long nights give way to overcast days, quickly swallowed up by another winter night. Springtime usually starts in March and is very unpredictable, with temperatures generally between 11 and 15 degrees Celsius (50–60°F).

The key term that applies to London weather is *mildness*. The winters are rarely freezing, summers are rarely boiling (with the notable exception of the summers of 2003 and 2006) and the rain is usually not torrential.

That said, London can occasionally get some nasty bits of weather. On June 13, 2006, 1.5 inches of rain fell in less than an hour, the equivalent of a tropical monsoon. Flooding closed the Blackwell Tunnel for six hours, and a half dozen Tube stations also were closed. Even City Hall was evacuated. This sort of thing is rare, fortunately, but a weeklong drizzle is quite common. No matter what time of year you visit, assume that it's going to rain at least once during your stay and pack accordingly.

FLORA AND FAUNA

Because the land has been built upon for so many centuries, there isn't much unaltered nature within the city limits, but wildlife has a habit of breaking through. Foxes rummage through garbage bins in the middle of the night, seagulls and other waterfowl fly over the city or roost in the parks, and any bit of grassland left untended soon erupts into lush foliage.

Pelicans and other waterfowl wander St. James's Park.

Several parks have wild areas, Richmond Park and Hampstead Heath being two of the best. Here you can catch a glimpse of what the land must have been like before millions of people decided to move here. Herds of deer graze on long grass, wildflowers bloom next to the paths, and badgers skulk in the underbrush.

London's many parks abound in plant life, and a walk in the surrounding countryside will reveal even more. England has very fertile soil, and while London's soil is poorer than most English regions because of its high clay content, any spot that's left alone soon gets overgrown. Anyone interested in finding out more about the natural side of London should take a look at the *Parks and Scenic Squares* section in the *Recreation* chapter. Not only is there a great choice, but some of the most beautiful are close to or in the city center. There's even a wetlands sanctuary not too far from the center of town.

ENVIRONMENTAL ISSUES

The main problem facing London is its sheer size—7.5 million people in 33 boroughs makes for some serious governmental headaches. The metropolitan area has more than 12 million people. This vast city has its share of environmental problems too. Despite narrow, clogged streets, expensive petrol, and almost nonexistent parking, Londoners love their cars—so much so that the mayor, Ken Livingstone, had to slap on an extra tax (called the "congestion charge") in a moderately successful attempt to reduce traffic in the city center. The air is still pretty polluted, and you can feel the effect when coming back from the countryside or when jogging. Litter is another problem, although the city is pretty good at cleaning up.

The Thames was a major ecological disaster earlier in the 20th century and was virtually a dead river until a concerted cleanup campaign brought fish back to the waters and got rid of the worst of the toxins. While it's still not a place you want to go for a dip, it is safe to drink once it goes through a modern filtration system. In fact, much of London's water is from the Thames.

© SEAN MCLACHLAN

Unsung hero: Joseph Bazelgette saved countless lives by building London's first citywide sewer system.

History

London is situated in a basin that's well watered with a major river and several streams, but the soil was heavy with clay and not good for cultivation. Thus early farmers avoided it, although the usefulness of the Thames as a trade route meant there were always people passing through. Archaeologists have found a few scattered artifacts from this time, some of them apparently thrown into the Thames or nearby marshes as offerings to the gods. These include an ornate Celtic shield found in Battersea, now on display in the British Museum, and a few evocative wooden sculptures.

THE ROMAN ERA

Before the Romans arrived, there was nothing that could be called a town in the London area until A.D. 43, when the Emperor Claudius launched a successful invasion of the island. Julius Caesar had ventured here almost a century before, in 54 B.C., but while he wrote down some interesting observations and won several battles, he didn't stay.

Claudius, however, had come to conquer and colonize. The Roman legions quickly subjugated the divided Celtic tribes. Aulus Plautius, the first Roman governor of Britain, realized the strategic importance of the London basin and made it the capital of the province, naming it Londinium. He built a bridge close to where London Bridge stands today and Claudius himself passed through the city as he visited his new conquests. While the land wasn't great for farming, the river was a tidal one, making it easier for ships to come in and out. Londinium soon became a center for trade with the mainland Roman Empire.

There's an old stereotype that Roman Britain was on the fringes of the empire, a forlorn and half-forgotten backwater where nobody wanted to go. This is far from the truth. While Britannia was the most distant province from Rome, the land and its capital thrived. Londinium's forum, where people met for commerce and socializing, was the biggest outside of Italy, and its basilica, another common ground for meeting in the days before that type of building was used for churches, was second to none outside of Italy.

While the Roman legions were mighty, the Celtic tribes did not go quietly. The female leader Boudicca, ruler of the Iceni, waged war upon the Romans in A.D. 60, laying waste to St. Albans and other outlying towns before marching on Londinium and burning and looting it. The Romans counterattacked, and a titanic battle ensued in which thousands died. The Romans prevailed and Boudicca, despairing, poisoned herself. A local myth relates that the battle took place in the district of Battlebridge, and that the warrior queen is buried deep below Platform 7 of King's Cross Station.

Londinium was in the area now known as Square Mile, or The City, and a city wall encompassed that area. At its height the city had a population of about 25,000, making it one of the largest cities outside Italy, and it had rich villas, an amphitheater, and temples, including a temple to the mystery cult of Mithras. Sections of the city wall, Mithras temple, and amphitheater can still be seen.

Overextension, attacks by Germanic tribes and Persians, and numerous bloody coups gradually weakened the empire, and the province of Britain was abandoned in A.D. 410 so the army could concentrate on protecting wealthier provinces in mainland Europe. Londinium began to deteriorate, and within a couple of centuries the fine palaces and great public buildings had given way to the simple thatched huts of the Anglo-Saxons, who had migrated from Denmark and Northern Germany to fill in the power vacuum. They had

The Temple of Mithras was home to a faith that rivaled early Christianity in popularity.

© SEAN MCLACHLAN

Fragments of the old Roman wall remain in The City, also known as the Square Mile.

been hired for their reputation as fierce mercenaries to help protect the now-defenseless Romano-Britons, but they soon decided to take the land for themselves. A centuries-long struggle ensued, giving rise to the legend of King Arthur, who may have been a Romano-British war leader who had some success against the Anglo Saxons, although that success was only temporary.

THE ANGLO-SAXONS AND THE EARLY MIDDLE AGES

After the province was abandoned in A.D. 410, the economic system the Romans had put in place quickly collapsed. The land was soon divided among warring groups again, and there was no need for a commercial center. Londinium shrunk to a fraction of its former size, as the forum became choked with weeds and the splendid public buildings crumbled away.

But the city did not entirely die out. Some trade continued, and the strategic importance of this walled town next to the island's biggest river was obvious. The Anglo-Saxons found the Roman city too overgrown and filled with rubble and built a town slightly to the west, calling it Lundenwic ("London town"). The memory of this settlement is preserved in the street name Aldwych ("old town").

London languished during the early Middle Ages because in the rural and localized economy of England, with the land divided between petty warring states, there was no need for a big central city. When St. Augustine arrived in A.D. 601 to convert the pagans, the city had shrunk to practically a village, with only a few thatched-roof huts built within the ruins and the more prosperous trading center at Aldwych just to the west.

The wars between the petty states led to their gradual conglomeration into bigger kingdoms, but they were still too divided to prevent the town's looting by the Vikings twice in the 9th century. Eventually the Viking advance was stopped by Alfred the Great, King of Wessex and the first monarch to rule over something that resembled a united England. As the country slowly became unified, the mercantile network that had made London a major city in earlier times rekindled. Soon it became the main port for trade with France and the Low Countries, with merchants shipping out cloth in exchange for wine and other luxury goods. This had been going on since early Anglo-Saxon times, but now the trade really took off. London once again became an important city, although it still was a shadow of its Roman self.

THE MIDDLE AGES

The Norman king William the Conqueror invaded England in 1066 to dispute the accession of King Harold. Edward the Confessor, who died childless that year, had left a rather muddled legacy, and while many supported Harold's right to the throne, William had a strong claim too. The ruler of the Norman kingdom in Northern France and descendant of Vikings, William was Edward's cousin and had forced Edward to sign a document proclaiming him as Edward's heir. On the basis of this claim William sailed across the English Channel with an army and fought Harold's army at the Battle of Hastings. Harold fell with an arrow through his eye, his army was defeated, and the Normans set about conquering the countryside. This was the last time England fell to a foreign invader.

William immediately saw that London was the key to the kingdom. It was already the biggest Anglo-Saxon town and the major trade outlet for the island. He settled his local administration at Westminster, which Edward had made the royal seat, and continued Edward's work on the Benedictine monastery and church that is now known as Westminster Abbey. At that time Westminster was virtually an island, surrounded by marshes and connected to dry land only by a narrow bit of land now covered by the intersection of Birdcage Walk and Great George Street. This made it good for defense, important because the Anglo-Saxons kept up a spirited resistance for many years. Within days of his coronation as the new king of England, William ordered the construction of a castle to control the capital of his new land. At first it was a simple fort tucked into the corner of the old Roman walls, but by the late 1070s the famous White Tower, the nucleus of the present-day Tower of London, was completed. Moats and the old Roman walls made for an outer defense, but the massive square tower, built of white Caen stone from Normandy as a highly visible symbol of who was now in charge, was what made this fortification nearly impregnable. The tower, 90 feet high, went through several modifications but still stands as a fine example of early Norman architecture. This wasn't the end of the Normans' building program. Through the following decades they erected numerous churches, such as St. Bartholomew, and the first Westminster Hall, the original Palace of Westminster.

The Norman dynasty was replaced by the Plantagenet dynasty, which reigned 1154–1485, but London's building program continued, with additions such as Temple Church and, in 1176, London Bridge.

The bridge connected the two banks of the Thames and breathed new life into the South Bank. There had been a bridge in Roman times that had fallen into disrepair, and another that had been destroyed during the Viking invasions, but this new bridge was built of stone and would last for centuries. A great farmers market grew up on the south end of London Bridge, and this market survives as Borough Market today. To mark the increased stature of Southwark, a church, now called Southwark Cathedral, was erected as the first church in the Gothic style to be built in London. An odd side effect of the bridge was that its narrow arches slowed the flow of the river to the extent that in cold winters the river would freeze over, and Londoners would hold a Frost Fair on the ice. Vendors hawked food and ale while wealthy ladies and gentlemen got pulled about on sledges by their servants. One had to beware of breaks in the ice, however, and many people got a chilly dunking before they could be saved. The bridge lasted until 1831, when it was torn down and replaced by a larger London Bridge with wider arches. The river flowed more quickly again, and the Frost Fairs became another anecdote in London's long memory.

London had always been an entity unto itself. Far bigger than any other town, and controlling much of the foreign trade, it had the money to bankroll kings, or bankrupt them. London so dominated the finances of the kingdom that in 1215 the Mayor of London and the lords forced King John to approve the Magna Carta, which not only limited the power of the king but made the city independent and self-governing.

While London prospered as the seat of government and center of trade with Europe, it was not the nicest place to live. Streets were narrow and rarely cleaned, the air was hazy with wood smoke, and rats and lice were rife. In 1348 rats disembarking from foreign ships brought the bubonic plague to the city. It was spread by parasitic insects living on the rats, which would jump onto people and thus spread the infection. Crowded, unsanitary conditions and the lack of modern medicine meant the disease had free reign, and historians estimate a third of the city's population (and a third of Europe's entire population) died from what people called the Black Death.

The plague, while being a nightmare to anyone who had to live through it, was only a temporary setback. By this time London had become one of the main trading centers of Europe, shipping out fabrics of wool and silk, as well as wine, and importing a great deal of luxury goods from the continent and Baltic Sea. English shipbuilders were becoming renowned for their skill and more and more wharves appeared along both banks of the Thames. Other industries, both for domestic use and export, included various crafts. By the 13th century there were dozens of them, such as the drapers and goldsmiths, and between them they controlled much of the industry and finance of the capital. Parents apprenticed their sons at an early age to a member of one of these guilds, and the boy grew up learning the trade and eventually would become a full-fledged guild member himself. As shipping expanded, many of these craftsmen became venture capitalists and kings would rely on them through Acts of Parliament to fund wars and building projects. In a very real way, it was the money of London, not the king, which ruled England.

The Plantagenets were a long-lasting dynasty, but they never truly made England a unified nation because individual aristocrats were still very powerful. All that was to change under the Tudor dynasty, starting after Henry VII defeated Richard III at the battle of Bosworth in 1485. This was the culmination of the War of the Roses, a bitter civil war over succession to the throne between the Houses of Lancaster (whose emblem was a red rose) and York (which sported a white rose). Henry was of the House of Lancaster and Richard led the House of York. In the 30 years of fighting, execution, and exile, much of the nobility was killed or had their lands seized. While the aristocracy would remain a major player in English politics, the Tudors would be strong kings of a centralized and unified kingdom.

Their capital, of course, reaped the benefits. In 1500, shortly after the end of the war, the population stood at 75,000, but just 100 years later it would be 200,000, making it one of the largest centers of population in a region with few cities worthy of the name. Tudor London was a rollicking place, a center of trade but also of culture, as Southwark became home to a newfangled form of entertainment called the theater. Shakespeare and Marlowe wrote plays that bedazzled or scandalized their audiences, depending on their inclinations, and a host of lesser lights also saw their works performed. The theaters of the time were open to the air, with boisterous crowds, vendors hawking food and ale, and the actors shouting to be heard above the din. For those who wanted more traditional entertainment, there were cockfights and bearbaiting, in which a bear would be set upon by a pack of hounds, with everyone betting on how long the bear would last. One tale relates how a bear managed to kill all the dogs, and the crowd felt so ripped off (the people had all lost their bets, after all) that it threatened the organizers with bodily harm until another pack was sent in to finish the job.

The streets were no less chaotic. Most were narrow lanes that lacked cobblestones and when it rained they became mud slicks. Residents threw garbage and human waste out the windows of their wood-framed houses, and it was fortunate for the pedestrians that many Tudor buildings had upper stories that leaned out over the streets, almost touching those on the other side. It meant little light filtered through, and the smoke from cooking fires would coil through the streets, but at least it gave people a better chance of avoiding the unpleasant projectiles coming from above. This, by the way, is the origin of the custom of gentlemen's walking on the street side of their ladies, thus making them the targets of any nastiness. The custom continued long after tossing "night soil," as it was delicately called, was banned, because the streets remained muddy and passing carriages would spatter people with great globs of mire.

Even London Bridge was crowded, being lined with houses so that the road between was quite narrow. At turrets on the south end, the heads of criminals and traitors, preserved with pitch, were stuck on the ends of poles as a warning to those who would flaunt the law or plot against the sovereign.

For many, life in the capital was one of unending misery. Poverty and disease were rife, and those who resorted to crime could expect swift justice from an executioner's ax. Public executions were one of the great entertainments of the day, more dramatic than the theater and more exciting even than bearbaiting, because the victim was a human being. Mary Tudor upped the ante by burning more than 200 Protestants at Smithfield Market in the years 1554–1558, and later Queen Elizabeth I persecuted Catholics with equal vigor. This was to suppress Catholic resistance to the legacy of her father, Henry VIII, who broke from the Catholic Church both to get a divorce and gain more political independence. He created the Anglican Church, in practice little different from the Catholic Church except for one important fact—the king, not the pope, was its head. To make sure the church never got too powerful, he perpetrated the Dissolution, a seizure of all church property in the name of the crown. Some of the churches continued as Anglican houses of worship, but most of the monasteries, nunneries, and land was sold off to support Henry's numerous wars and his expansion of the Navy.

While London was a place of death, it was also a place of vibrant life. Scholars worked on scientific treatises and collected natural specimens and artifacts of previously unknown cultures from the captains of great merchant ships, who were just then beginning their voyages to find new lands. Arts and literature flourished, thanks to rich patronage and the development of the printing press. Fleet Street became a center for printers, who churned out cheap chapbooks and broadsheets of popular ditties and stories for an increasingly literate audience. The area remained a center for printing, and later for newspapers, until the end of the 20th century.

After Elizabeth died childless in 1603, James I became the first monarch of the Stuart dynasty. He was even more brutal toward the Catholics than his predecessors, and in 1605 a group of Catholics, among them the infamous Guy Fawkes, plotted to blow up the Houses of Parliament while it met in full session with James in attendance. They managed to rent a cellar below the building and filled it with gunpowder, but the plot was foiled and to this day across the United Kingdom, the effigy of Guy Fawkes is burnt on the night of November 5 to commemorate his arrest.

James's son, Charles I, came to power in 1625 and married a Catholic French princess. While this was good news to the Catholics in England, who had spent the last couple of generations in hiding, it didn't make him popular with the rest of his subjects. Charles loved continental Europe and hired the architect Inigo Jones to beautify London along the lines of the great cities of France and Italy. Instead of the crowded, smelly mess that London was, Jones imagined an open city with broad avenues and orderly parks. Jones laid out Covent Garden and Whitehall, and designed the

Queen's House in Greenwich, among many other projects.

This did little to improve Charles's popularity. His idea of the divine right of kings, meaning an autocratic rule over church and Parliament, didn't help either. Parliament objected to his heavy-handedness and Charles dissolved it three times, throwing the most rebellious ministers in prison. Charles ruled without a Parliament 1629–1640, but he was eventually forced to convene one to raise money for another of his costly and unsuccessful foreign wars, this time against the Scots, who didn't want the Anglican liturgy in their Presbyterian churches. The so-called Short Parliament, instead of giving him the money, drew up a long list of grievances and demanded he make peace with the Scots. He dissolved this Parliament too, the Scots promptly defeated his inadequate army, and he once again convened a Parliament. Later generations have dubbed this the Long Parliament, and for good reason; it wasn't going to let itself be dissolved. Its members forced the king to make numerous concessions, but eventually Charles had had too much and showed up in the House of Commons with an armed force. The populace rose up and Charles had to flee the city.

For the next four years, 1642–1646, supporters of the king and Parliament fought bitter battles across the land in what is now called the English Civil War. Oliver Cromwell, leader of the Parliamentary army, rose to power and when the war was over he had Charles beheaded in front of the Banqueting House, a building the king had ordered Inigo Jones to create for him.

Cromwell was the first commoner to rule England and the only one to rule with a written constitution. When he died the Restoration put royalty back in charge, and the House of Stuart would rule in England until 1714.

No battles occurred in London and the city survived the Civil War intact, but its luck was about to run out. In 1665, the plague visited London once again, and 100,000 people are estimated to have died. The next year a fire started in a bakery in Pudding Lane in the heart of the city. At first the city government didn't take the fire seriously, the lord mayor saying that it was "something a woman might piss out," but soon the fire got out of hand, with strong winds making it leap across narrow lanes to set thatched roofs ablaze. People fled with whatever possessions they could salvage. There was no fire department at the time, and those who did band together to fight the fire were too few and too poorly equipped for the challenge. The diarist Samuel Pepys watched the fire from Bankside on the south side of the river and witnessed, "one entire arch of fire from this to the other side of the bridge, and in a bow up the hill, for an arch of above a mile long." By the time the fire burnt itself out, 400 acres within the city walls had burned, and 63 acres outside, about 80 percent of the total area of London. St. Paul's and 87 other churches were destroyed, along with 44 livery halls, the Royal Exchange, the Guildhall, and 13,200 houses. Remarkably, only nine people are recorded to have died.

EXPANDING THE CAPITAL

The fire wasn't all bad. The plague had been abating for some time, but the fire finished it off. The government envisioned a new Continental-style city rising from the smoking ruins and made grand plans for it. They soon discovered, however, that individuals' property rights were too strong to overcome. Thus the modern streets of the city, with buildings that virtually all date to after 1666, still trace their old medieval paths. The government, however, forced the property owners to rebuild their houses with stone and brick, and while fires were still common, they never again got so out of hand.

There were other improvements too. Sir Christopher Wren was commissioned to rebuild the destroyed churches, including the present St. Paul's, considered his masterpiece. It was finished in 1710. His other surviving churches are also beautiful, and there are even a few pubs he built for his workmen that still serve pints today. Another Wren construction is the Monument, a tall pillar topped with gilded flames to commemorate the fire. It housed a laboratory for the Royal Society, the oldest scientific society in the world, and had an observatory on the top to view the stars.

To finance the rebuilding, the City Corporation got the power to tax imports and took closer control of the construction of new neighborhoods in the expanding city. One result of the new urban planning was the advent of the town square as an open space for traffic and pedestrians and also as a place for recreation. Bloomsbury Square was the first, being created shortly after the Great Fire, and many more would follow. While the square is commonly seen as part of the 18th-century Georgian style of town layout, it actually had its start in the 1660s.

Not even fire or a massive building project could slow down the economic growth of the city. By the end of the century, 69 percent of the kingdom's exports and 80 percent of its imports went through London. This created a need for financial institutions to deal with all the commercial transactions and to extend credit for more business ventures. The Bank of England was incorporated in 1694, the original £1.2 million in capital being raised through lotteries. Despite this odd way of creating a bank, the Bank of England became known for reliable and sober investments. Its checks, originally just handwritten pieces of paper, were as good as currency and soon the independently owned bank was favored with the job of minting the official coin of the realm.

THE GEORGIAN ERA

The 18th century was when London really came into its own. The rise of the Royal Navy as the master of the seas, and the rapid acquisition of new colonies on every continent, made London the capital of a vast global empire. The era, and its art and architecture, are generally referred to as Georgian, after the four King Georges who ruled 1714–1830. George I was the first king of the Hanover dynasty, which replaced the Stuarts after Queen Anne died childless.

The various Georges ruled over an empire that seemed almost invincible. Even George III's loss of the American colonies didn't make a serious dent in the empire's power, since it was still making plenty of money from its colonies in India, Africa, and elsewhere. Overseas trade created a need for credit even the Bank of England couldn't fill, and by the 1720s there were 13 banks in the city, mostly congregating around Fleet Street. They financed the ventures of an expanding empire and even funded the Army and Navy. More than ever before, London was now the place to be for those who wanted to become rich. There were occasional blips such as the South Sea Bubble, when speculators created hypervalued stocks for a company to develop South America. No projects were forthcoming, however, and the company eventually crashed, to the ruin of thousands of Londoners. Stricter banking laws stopped a repeat of the situation, but individual investors still could go bankrupt in the rough-and-tumble game of capitalism.

The great influx of wealth made London into a jewel of a city. The expansion and beautification that had started right after the Great Fire continued apace. New squares were laid out, learned societies were established, and new neighborhoods with streets lined with orderly houses sprung up on the edges of town. Culture bloomed. The British Museum was founded in 1753 in Bloomsbury, first as a private collection open to select members of society but eventually as a public museum. Over in Fleet Street, printers churned out countless newspapers and books to make London the publishing capital of the world. In 1755 they published the first dictionary of the English language, compiled by Dr. Johnson, the great commentator of his time who famously said, "When one tires of London, one tires of life." The rich patronized artists and musicians, and geniuses such as Gainsborough and Handel found inspiration here.

Yet all was not well for the majority of Londoners. Poverty and disease were still rife, and flocks of homeless children wandered the streets, trying to eke out a living as best they could. Many simply starved to death, while those of more means but equally bad luck found themselves bankrupt and ended up in debtors' prison. Dissatisfaction with the way society was progressing led to a high rate of crime and occasional riots. To deal with the first problem, the moneyed classes carried sidearms and turned their houses into urban fortresses. A look at the heavy locks on Dr. Johnson's House in The City will give the visitor a good idea of one man's fear of the mob.

The other problem, rioting, has proved equally impossible to solve. London is a city of riots, and every generation witnesses at least one or two. The greatest riot of them all occurred at London's zenith, when it was the center of the largest empire on Earth and perhaps was the wealthiest city on the planet. In 1778 Parliament passed the Catholic Relief Act, which protected Catholic priests from being thrown into prison and allowed Catholics to own and inherit land if they renounced the authority of the pope. Lord George Gordon created the Protestant Association and in 1780, 60,000 people marched to Parliament with a petition calling for the act to be cancelled. When they didn't get what they wanted, they set about burning Catholic homes and businesses, as well as Clink Prison and several other public buildings. The so-called Gordon Riots stopped only when troops were called in and shot nearly 300 rioters dead.

While the lack of any sort of social safety net was one reason for the suffering of the poor, they also brought it upon themselves through one of the great addictions of the age, gin. This cheap and potent brew became the favorite of the poor. Hogarth, the great engraver of his age, depicted *Gin Lane,* inspired by the area around St. Giles, north of Covent Garden. In it, the rabble is shown fighting and carousing, while a nearly unconscious mother doesn't notice as her baby falls over a ledge. Behind her a gin shop advertises, "Drunk for a penny, dead drunk for two pence, clean straw for nothing." By all accounts this apocalyptic scene wasn't much of an exaggeration. In St. Giles one in four houses sold gin, and countless people died or lost their jobs because of gin drinking. Hogarth's campaign against the evils of the drink helped push the Gin Law through Parliament in 1751, which required a license to sell gin and doubled the tax on it, a rare example of an artist actually affecting public policy.

THE 19TH CENTURY, LONDON'S GILDED AGE

London started the 19th century as a major urban center, and ended it as the largest city in the world. The 1801 census counted almost one million people, while the 1901 census counted more than 6.5 million. By the beginning of the 20th century, one out of every five people who lived in England and Wales lived in London, and the city had a greater population than the next biggest 18 English cities combined and was the undisputed center of the empire's financial might.

The cause of this massive explosion in numbers was due to growth in population in the countryside, where there wasn't enough work, and the steady immigration of people from all over the empire. Most came from Ireland, especially during the Potato Famine, and the country towns and villages of southern England. Their reasons for coming were pretty much the same as the reasons people move to London today–more work, better pay, and an interesting life.

Maintaining a city that was growing so rapidly posed some serious problems. Pollution from the coal plants powering the Industrial Revolution mixed with London's famous fogs to create smog, and for entire days the city would be shrouded in noxious yellow vapors. This problem plagued London for decades, but another one demanded more immediate attention, that of sewage disposal. Thames water, which was what everyone drank, was getting contaminated by raw sewage pumped out of houses. Outbreaks of cholera and other diseases were already causing concern, but the real change of heart came in what has become known as the Great Stink of 1858. Human and animal waste, mixed with piles of garbage, clogged up the Thames so much one hot summer that it became almost intolerable to get close to it. Members of Parliament hung thick curtains soaked in lime on their windows, but eventually the stink got so bad they had to arrange meetings farther from the river. The government finally gave money to institute higher sanitary standards and better sewage disposal. The new Metropolitan Board of Works built an ambitious sewage system, and the rate of water-borne diseases plummeted in the latter part of the century.

Another problem was transportation. Middle-class people were moving away from the pollution, noise, and crime of the city center and needed a way to get to work. In 1829 horse-drawn buses began to run regular routes, creating London's first public transportation. This was followed later in the century by an increasing number of railway lines, connecting outlying areas and distant towns to the center of the empire. Several bridges were thrown across the Thames and in 1863, the first line of the London Underground opened, running four miles from Paddington to Farringdon Street.

For much of the 19th century, the British Empire was ruled by Queen Victoria, who reigned from 1837 until her death in 1901—thus the whole era is often called "Victorian." The empire was at its height, with colonies around the world, and the old boast that "the sun never sets on the British Empire" was literally true. It was an exciting time, a time of a flowering in the arts and sciences. To celebrate this new era, Prince Albert, Queen Victoria's husband, hosted the Great Exhibition of 1851. More than 100,000 displays showcased the latest inventions and discoveries, and the profits were used to create the Science Museum and the Victoria and Albert Museum.

Progress was happening in people's daily lives too. Gas heating and lighting became common even in working-class homes by the end of the century, and the better hotels, followed by the houses of the wealthy, were soon lit by electricity. Better sanitation, better housing, and better medical care improved the lot of most Londoners.

Most, but not all. During the Victorian era journalists and missionaries became increasingly concerned about the fate of London's poorest residents, those who lived in crowded conditions in filthy slums. Pamphlets such as "The Bitter Cry of Outcast London" by the Reverend Andrew Mearns, and the innumerable publications by Charles Booth shocked the respectable public with their horrid tales of the crowded rooms, avoidable sickness, and immoral habits of the poorest of the poor. These reformers went "slumming," exploring the bad areas of town in much the same manner as the great explorers wandered through Darkest Africa or the Wilds of Asia (these florid descriptions always being capitalized for emphasis) and the tone of their writings are remarkably similar. The privileged classes began to think of the vast slums as an embarrassment in such an age of unrivaled wealth and power, as if they were a backwater colony on the capital's doorstep. The government cleared slums and replaced them with better housing, and numerous charities sprang up to help orphans, the aged, and the infirm.

But even the poorer classes who could find work didn't escape the misery. The demands of London's industry for more and more production led to the "sweat" system, in which workers were paid by the piece. A shirt factory, for example, would contract a middleman for a certain number of shirts, and the middleman would hire workers to make them, paying them less than the price the factory would pay him. Purchase wasn't guaranteed, if the work wasn't good or there was a temporary lull in demand, or if someone else supplied the factories first, the workers would get nothing. Even when business was good workers got poverty wages and eroded their health by working in crowded, poorly ventilated rooms for 12 or even 16 hours a day.

London's growth also created the need for a more centralized government. Most of the city's public affairs were in the hands of borough councils, so the quality of service varied widely depending on the neighborhood. In 1889 Parliament created the London County Council, the city's first directly elected government, although, like Parliament, it chose its own head. Mayors would not be elected until the year 2000. At first the LCC was pretty weak, but it gradually grew in responsibility and power.

For those with money, London was a wonderful place at this time. It became the fashion for country gentry to "come down for the season" to socialize, arrange marriages, make new business connections, and enjoy all London had to offer. Once the fox-hunting season was over in late March, rich families would arrive and stay in hotels until July. The richest would be presented at court, and people would jockey for invitations to the best parties and functions. Men would spend time at the gentlemen's clubs at Pall Mall, while their wives would shop at the new department stores such as Harrods. Grand theaters hosted musicals and plays, while more humble ones entertained the city's permanent residents. Parks offered relaxation, while the more studious could go to some of the greatest museums and art exhibitions in the world.

THE 20TH CENTURY AND BEYOND

The death of Queen Victoria was in many ways the end of an era. While the empire's sun had not yet set, the next 50 years would see its collapse and London's greatest transformation since the Great Fire of 1666.

At first everything seemed to be going along normally. At the turn of the 20th century London was the largest city in the world and it continued to expand and develop. In 1904 it got its first motorized buses, and within a decade the old horse-drawn buses were gone, and the double decker was a common sight. Business was booming and London seemed the center of civilization.

Then, in 1914, the heir to the Austro-Hungarian throne, the Archduke Franz Ferdinand, was assassinated by a Serbian nationalist in Sarajevo. Austro-Hungary invaded Serbia, which brought Russia into the war against them, and in turn brought Germany into war on the side of the Austro-Hungarians. Germany invaded France and Belgium, bringing England into the war. The network of alliances that had kept the peace for a generation now made most of the countries of Europe choose sides. As their colonies and allies joined in, the fighting raged from the fields of France to as far away as Africa and China, making it World War I. While the war seemed far away to Londoners at first, that wouldn't last as the casualties mounted and German Zeppelins bombed London. The damage was minimal, but the city had not been attacked since the Middle Ages and it came as a severe shock.

By the end of 1918 the war was over and millions were dead. While the war was a blow to the empire's economy, London had fared rather well, its industry making record profits. The interwar years saw London outpaced by New York, which took its place as the biggest city in the world. But London was still expanding, thanks to suburbs made accessible by lengthening Tube lines and the increased popularity of the automobile. Many middle-class families commuted to work now, returning from their city jobs to semidetached homes with yards. Inner-city Londoners, mostly working class, still lived in cramped flats or tiny row houses. Reform of the slum areas made slow but steady progress, thanks to the efforts of the London County Council, which built respectable (although still small) council housing. Now more and more poor families had running water in their homes and indoor bathrooms. The health of the poorer classes improved, although their standard of living was still far below that of the middle classes, who now enjoyed suburban living with gardens, electricity, and a multitude of diversions.

Those with leisure time had a lot to choose from. The BBC started radio broadcasts in 1922 and experimental television broadcasts in 1929. Film was popular, although many of the big hits came from Hollywood, and literature was going strong, led by such luminaries as Virginia Woolf and George Orwell.

The wide gulf between the haves and the have-nots led to a general strike in May of 1926. It started as a call for better pay in the coal industry, but it soon spread to all workers. London shut down for nine days as workers demanded fair pay, and the strike was halted only when the Army took over public transport and other essential services.

When Hitler invaded Poland in 1939, the British Empire was pulled once again into war. World War II would be even bloodier than the first and much more serious for London. Instead of clunky Zeppelins dropping inaccurate bombs, Londoners now faced the highly trained and technologically advanced Luftwaffe, and they later became the targets of V1 and V2 missiles. Hitler knew that London's docks were essential to Britain's war effort and pounded them unmercifully, but he also ordered the indiscriminate bombing of civilian neighborhoods, thinking he could make the people of London give up.

He was wrong. The Royal Air Force, greatly outnumbered, punched well above its weight and destroyed many German planes, prompting Prime Minister Winston Churchill to comment on what was called the Battle of Britain, "Never in the field of human conflict was so much owed by so many to so few." Antiaircraft batteries, often manned by men too old for active service, did their share too. Common images of this period are of civilians sleeping in

THE WORLD WARS AND THE BRITISH

The most tumultuous events for England in the 20th century have to be the two world wars. It is impossible to overestimate their effect on England's political, economic, and cultural fabric. The countless monuments to the war dead, in parks, factories, churches, even small streets, stand as eloquent testimony to the sense of loss the English feel at the horrors of the world wars.

It's hard for North Americans, who have never experienced warfare on their soil in living memory, to understand the deep impact that these two wars have had on the English psyche. World War I killed 733,000 U.K. citizens, soldier and civilian, including 670 in London. World War II killed 450,000, including about 30,000 in London. A whole generation of young men (and a considerable number of young women) were killed or maimed in the war, and this trauma echoes down the years.

World War I (1914–1918) was a real wakeup call to the British Empire. A little more than a decade before the British had fought the Boer War (1899–1902) against Dutch settlers for control of South Africa. Even though they won, the public was scandalized that 28,000 soldiers lost their lives. In World War I, there were battles in which the British Army sustained those sort of losses in a single day. The hell of the trenches became ingrained in people's minds through newspaper reports, books, the increasingly influential medium of film, and from the accounts of their friends and families.

It was in this war that London had its first experience with aerial bombardment. On May 31, 1915, a German Zeppelin dropped explosive and incendiary bombs on the Docklands and East End, killing seven people. More Zeppelin raids followed, and an angry postcard still preserved in a display in the Imperial War Museum rages against the indiscriminate bombing of civilians, something the world had not yet become accustomed to. Several other bombing raids followed, some using biplanes, and a total of 670 people lost their lives, including 160 in a single raid.

What London experienced in World War I was nothing compared to the devastation it suffered in World War II (1939–1945). The German air force, called the Luftwaffe, was one of the most technologically advanced of its day, and it mercilessly bombed London's industrial and transport centers, as well as civilian neighborhoods. Whole sections of the city were destroyed with fire bombs, including 130,000 homes and numerous historic buildings. Some buildings, such as St. Clement Danes church in The City, still bear scars from this war. The greatest scars, however, are the great swathes of the city that have no historic buildings. The atmospheric Tudor and Geor-

Tube stations and sending their children to the countryside. While both of these things happened, the majority of Londoners stayed put, helping to fight the fires and working in war industries. Older Londoners often reminisce of the time when everyone pulled together and pulled through.

After the war ended in 1945, the slow painful process of rebuilding began. Much of London's greatest architecture had been destroyed, including most of the Guildhalls, dozens of churches by Wren, Hawksmoor, and earlier architects, and countless private homes. While many of the churches were faithfully restored, other areas were blighted with giant concrete monstrosities of office and apartment blocks. The Luftwaffe ruined much of London, and real-estate developers, anxious for a quick fortune, did little to beautify the rubble. Now gray concrete facades stand next to graceful Victorian and Georgian frontages.

Postwar London was an architectural disaster, but it did rebound from economic hardship. The year after the war ended, Heathrow Airport opened and BBC resumed television broadcasts. Rationing was phased out as goods

gian houses, the ornate Victorian public buildings, were all turned to cinders, to be replaced in later years by ugly concrete structures or modern glass and steel constructions. The war not only killed many Londoners, it killed much of the atmosphere of their city.

These two conflicts also hastened the end of the British Empire, and indeed they helped hasten the end of European colonialism. Countries such as England and France were too devastated to have the strength to hold their overseas possessions, and they watched them quickly slip away. Europe had once owned much of the world, but by fighting among themselves they lost it.

Despite the horrors of both wars, the British look back upon them with pride and even fondness. They are justifiably proud of their role in fighting German aggression and of the bravery of their soldiers and civilians in those trying times. Londoners can be especially proud, since they bore the brunt of the civilian casualties yet managed to pull together. Older Londoners recall the civilian fire brigades putting out fires in neighbor's houses, or sleeping five to a room because their friends needed a roof over their heads. Everyone helped out, from the dockworkers who had to rebuild their workshops again and again, to the children who gathered scrap metal and rubber for the war effort. Londoners, indeed everyone in the United Kingdom, can look with nostalgia at a time when they were heroes and remind themselves with pride that they could do it again.

© SEAN MCLACHLAN

Memorials to WWI soldiers, like this one in Southwark, can be found all over London.

became more plentiful, and by the mid-'50s the docks, which had been damaged and repaired repeatedly during the war, served more than 1,000 ships a year, although its resurrection was only temporary, as the trucking and airline industries, and foreign ports, competed for more of the market share and England's manufacturing base began to dwindle. Financial life continued in The City, and industry in the suburbs took off like never before. The population of the city peaked at 8 million in 1951. It has since slipped somewhat in population, although if you count the metropolitan area it now numbers more than 12 million.

Meanwhile, the ethnic makeup of London enjoyed a renaissance of diversity. Starting in the late 1940s, large numbers of Caribbean people immigrated to London and other cities. They were joined by South Asians, and in later decades people from all over the world came to London in search of better lives. Many did not find it. Racism kept blacks and Asians from better jobs, and the council housing in which low-income families had to live was squalid and rife with crime. Riots flared in areas such as Brixton out of frustration for what felt like an intolerable situation.

More changes were afoot in the '60s, when youth culture took over. Centered around Carnaby Street, "Swinging London" was all about garish clothing, music, drugs, free love, and breaking old traditions. The Beatles, recording in Abbey Road Studios, fought it out with the Rolling Stones to be the biggest band. Another major change came in 1965 as London got a more coherent and extensive form of government called the Greater London Council to oversee the increasingly suburban city. At the same time, heavy industry began to leave the city, and by 1971, London's population had dropped from its high point of eight million two decades earlier to 7.5 million.

During the Tory rule of Prime Minister Margaret Thatcher (1979–1990), with its conservative fiscal policy that both gave and took ideas from Reaganomics, the stock market first faltered in recession. The loosening of industrial regulations led foreign firms to buy many of the major London banks and investment houses. The City, the heart of the United Kingdom's economic might, was no longer under its own control. The "Iron Lady," as many called her, fought a long battle with Ken Livingstone, leader of the Greater London Council, who wanted to reduce the cost of public transport and address the chronic unemployment in many boroughs. Thatcher, not liking anything even remotely resembling opposition, abolished the GLC in 1986.

That same year, Thatcher deregulated the Stock Exchange, setting off what Londoners call the Big Bang. Stock prices bloomed to unheard-of heights, and the wealthy found themselves wealthier than ever before. Property prices soared. The abandoned old Docklands were remodeled into lavish flats for the new rich. Bars, nightclubs, and exclusive restaurants sprouted like mushrooms, incidentally making London more attractive to the growing number of tourists that pumped even more money into the local economy.

It was not to last. Stock prices and property values faltered, and many found themselves unemployed. When Thatcher introduced the poll tax, in which people paid a flat tax instead of one based on wealth, there were riots in most major cities, including a large one in Trafalgar Square. Thatcher soon found her position untenable and gave way to her protégé John Major.

Major could do little to help the economy, and things went from bad to worse. In 1997 there was a general election and the Labour party won a majority in Parliament. Its leader, Tony Blair, became prime minister. Blair advocated "New Labour," which rejected the socialist ideas of the old Labour Party in favor of a market economy and privatization. The economy, especially the London economy, began to recover as the economic cycle rose again.

As if to prove his capitalist credentials, Blair invested millions in building projects for the new millennium, including the London Eye, Millennium Dome, Millennium Bridge, and the Tate Modern. The first two have since been sold off to private hands, with the Millennium Dome receiving special ire from Londoners'

© SEAN MCLACHLAN

The futuristic Millennium Dome, now called O2, was an expensive project, but stands empty.

for its vast cost overruns and apparent lack of purpose. More practical changes came that same year when Blair reintroduced the Greater London Council, which led to a reemergence of Ken Livingstone as a prominent political figure, and one who opposed Blair almost as much as he opposed Thatcher.

Another major change to how London was governed came in 2000, when Blair introduced elections for mayor for the first time in the city's history. He hoped a fellow member of the Labour Party would get the seat and one did, but unfortunately for him it was Ken Livingstone, an outspoken critic of his party's move to the center. Blair had arranged for another Labour man to run, so Livingstone ran as an independent, zipping around the city in a purple double-decker bus while broadcasting campaign promises through a megaphone. Livingstone has made a lot of political currency from criticizing the prime minister, with such easy shots as the Millennium Project and the war in Iraq, but he has struggled to govern because his office has no power to tax. He can create charges, however, and his congestion charge, which puts a hefty levy on any car driven into central London during the week, has helped calm the city's chaotic streets. Other plans, such as increased access for those with disabilities and more jobs, are stalled.

London today is perhaps unique among world capitals in that so little of its major businesses are owned by its citizens and yet it still dominates the economy. The industry of the 18th and 19th centuries waned throughout the 20th century until it has all but disappeared today. Banking, once the economic engine of British capitalism, is now mostly run by German and American companies. Other concerns, such as the insurance and auction houses, are still in British hands, and most of England's companies are based in London. Another major industry is tourism, pouring billions of pounds into the economy every year.

While it is no longer the capital of an empire, London still attracts immigrants from around the world, especially former British colonies. The most visible new communities in the past couple of decades have been South Asians and Eastern Europeans. Poles now serve many of the drinks at English pubs, and Indians run corner shops. The more fortunate of these groups have climbed their way up the corporate or professional ladders. This diversity makes London a fascinating place to wander around in, especially if you go to the outlying areas. New Kent Road in Southwark is home to a thriving Nigerian and Ethiopian community, and the Ethiopians have another community in Battersea. Afro-Caribbean people concentrate in Brixton and other areas, and South Asians dominate Brick Lane.

Such change has not come along without tensions. As in cities around the world, previous residents (often descended from immigrants themselves) feel threatened by the new arrivals. The British National Party, an openly racist party that would probably call itself fascist if it were really being honest, gained ground in the 2006 elections, winning many new council seats in London and doubling its number of seats nationwide. Racist graffiti and the occasional attack are a grim fact of life here, with Muslims being the target of choice.

Despite this, the vast majority of Londoners get along. The BNP made gains, it is true, but it still lags behind the two major parties and the Liberal Democrats and the Greens. Interracial couples are a common sight, and when groups of friends go out they often represent several different backgrounds. At the Chalk Farm secondary school, the 1,200 students speak 77 languages and hail from 55 countries. In 2006 they started using their lunch break to set up classes, and now kids are swapping Swahili and Polish lessons.

It's impossible to make any predictions about the future of this eclectic and vibrant city. Many say that it has lost its spirit, with the old architecture and old ways fading into the past, but I disagree. London has always been a center for immigrants, from the Danish Vikings who founded St. Clement Danes in the 9th century to the Indian Hindus who opened the Shri Swaminarayan Mandir in 1995, and each new group that has come to this city has made its own contribution. London had always been a place of change, with new buildings and parks appearing, but enough of the older areas surviving to give a taste of what came before.

Architecture

People have been living in the London area since the Stone Age, but London became a true city in Roman times nearly 2,000 years ago. While it lost a great deal in the Great Fire of 1666, some examples of Roman and medieval architecture survive. The vast majority of buildings, however, date from the 18th century to the modern day. While admiring the many fine buildings in the city, use this handy guide for figuring out how old they are.

ROMAN

When the Romans arrived they found a Celtic village along the Thames. Recognizing the strategic and commercial importance of the area, they founded the city of Londinium. Few remains exist from this time, except for a stretch of the old town wall in parts of The City, the biggest and best-preserved section being visible from a window in the Museum of London. The brickwork and large stones at the foundation are Roman, while the more regular masonry above it dates to the 13th century. Nearby are the foundations of Londinium's other survival, the Temple of Mithras, uncovered by a Luftwaffe bomb and moved to its present location to make way for a road.

SAXON

After the Romans left in A.D. 410, Londinium became a Saxon town. Most homes were of simple wood construction, but the Saxons built several stone churches. Some of the city's modern churches are built upon Saxon foundations.

One of the most clearly visible foundations is in the crypt under St. Bride's.

MEDIEVAL

As England became a nation, rather than a patchwork of warring kingdoms, the power and wealth of the king and church grew. Grandiose buildings sprang up across the country. Some of the best examples of medieval architecture are Westminster Abbey, the Palace of Westminster within the much newer Houses of Parliament, the Tower of London, and Southwark Cathedral. The styles take their inspiration from France, with lofty stone walls, Gothic arches, and intricately carved decorations. The simple folk still lived in wooden houses, and none of these remain.

TUDOR

The Tudor dynasty lasted 1485–1603 and saw the emergence of England as a major power. It was the era of Elizabeth and Shakespeare, a boom time for London, and inspired a flourishing style of building that emphasized thick wooden beams crisscrossing whitewashed walls. Often these beams have been painted over and are no longer visible except inside, where they hold up low ceilings and frame small doorways. Other aspects include steeply pitched roofs, tall chimneys, and mullioned windows (windows composed of small panes held together by wood or metal joins). Glassmakers hadn't yet figured out how to make large panes, so if you see a modern-sized window on a house, it's from the 18th century or later. Often Tudor-era buildings have upper floors that jut over the ground floor, which made the lanes of London quite dark. Some roofs were thatched instead of covered with wooden or ceramic tiles, but there are no original thatched roofs in London today.

Most of the Tudor city burned down in the Great Fire of 1666. While some buildings from the earlier city survived, time, subsequent fires, and the Luftwaffe took care of most of them. There is still a nice example at 13–14 Portsmouth Street in Covent Garden. It is called the Old Curiosity Shop because it inspired Dickens to write the novel of the same name. Built in 1567, it is one of the oldest surviving private buildings in the city and has been a shop for more than four centuries. Several pubs also date to this time, although they have been much changed by later generations. Check out The Old Bell and the Lamb and Flag for elements of Tudor architecture. Also see the marvelously reconstructed Globe Theatre on the South Bank, a faithful copy of the theater that showcased the Bard's plays when he was still alive. In the countryside you'll see many newer homes and pubs copying this timeless style.

© SEAN MCLACHLAN

The gateway to St. Bartholomew the Great Church is a rare survival of Tudor architecture.

BAROQUE

After the Great Fire, architects had a chance to reinvent London. A more elegant style inspired by mainland Europe emerged. Actually, this had been happening before the Great Fire, but the blank slate left by the destruction allowed architects to let their imaginations run wild. Baroque was essentially a rich man's or institutional style, and once you see a baroque building you'll know why. Elegant carved-stone facades, statues, domes, and towering columns don't come cheap. Some of the best baroque examples in London are churches, including St. Paul's. This jewel of British architecture is breathtaking in its ornate complexity, yet the strong soaring lines of the facade and dome give it a simple overall form.

GEORGIAN

The next great era of London architecture was 1714–1830 and is called the Georgian Period because of the four kings named George who ruled England during that time. This is when London truly came into its own. It was the capital city of an expanding empire and there seemed no end to the wealth coming into it.

The watchwords for Georgian architects were proportion and balance. The entire building, from the dimensions of the walls and the size of the windows, was set out on exact ratios. Everything ends up being made of rectangles, with the vertical lines being the long axis. This gives Georgian buildings a pleasing symmetry and a clean, orderly look. The surviving examples in London tend to be made of brick. Town houses for the wealthy were arranged in long rows, connected to make a single facade. Americans and Canadians will notice many of their colonial buildings take this style, and for a moment you might think you got on the wrong flight and ended up in Boston or Quebec City.

Entire Georgian streets and squares are still well preserved, so it's possible to be surrounded by the sights (if not the sounds and smells) of old London. Some of the best spots are in Bloomsbury, especially Bedford Square. There are many other areas of note, however, since Georgian buildings were built to last and are still in use across central London.

VICTORIAN

In the late 19th century, London boomed as it never boomed before. The empire was at its height and people flocked to London to make their fortune. Tastes were changing and people wanted more ornate brickwork and decorated

© SEAN MCLACHLAN

Elegant ironwork is a common feature on wealthier Georgian-era homes.

© SEAN MCLACHLAN

The Victoria Palace is a good example of ornate turn-of-the-20th-century theater architecture.

facades. It was also a time of heavy pollution because of the burning of massive amounts of coal for heating and industry, so the gaudy colors favored by Victorian architects, such as the ubiquitous red or yellow brick, had another purpose—they looked bright even with a good coat of soot.

It was a time of experimentation with a wide variety of styles competing for popularity, but they all shared a love for ornament. A look at the buildings of Tottenham Court Road will show you the sheer variety of decoration, from floral scrollwork to fake Grecian urns made of stone. Some experiments were downright bizarre, such as the Natural History Museum with its plant and animal motifs, creating a cathedral to life itself.

New materials led to new forms. Inexpensive steel and glass allowed for light, open spaces difficult to make with stone. The old railway stations, especially the terminal behind the Gothic Revival facade of St. Pancras Station, are superb examples of practical yet attractive steel construction.

As much as they looked forward, Victorians also looked back. Many Victorian buildings take their inspiration from earlier styles. The Palace of Westminster, which houses Parliament, is an example of Victorian Gothic Revival, also called neo-Gothic. Many businesses and private homes show a neoclassical style.

MODERN

As London entered the 20th century, it found itself facing tough times. Two world wars, the gutting of the city by German firebombing, and the disintegration of the British Empire made for serious challenges for British architects. In the period after the war, modernist styles such as brutalism came to the fore, with hulky slabs of concrete giving a reassuring if ugly security to the rebuilt city. To the contemporary eye much of this stuff looks cold and dirty, it doesn't age well, and present-day architects are doing better.

But it wasn't all grim and nasty. Experiments with steel and glass led to some sleek and lasting buildings, especially in commercial districts. Some iconic London buildings rose during this time, including the BP Tower and Centrepoint. Utilitarian and, to some eyes, plain, they nevertheless have become an integral part of the London skyline.

CONTEMPORARY

London is a city that constantly changes while keeping familiar patterns. The Docklands, once a thriving center of the sea trade, became derelict with the loss of British dominance in world shipping. But now it has been reborn as a center for shopping, office space, and entertainment. The shipping industry that created it is all but gone, but the area still attracts commerce. The City has also undergone a transformation, with many glittering new high-rises that look much the same as those in New York or Tokyo. Perhaps the most noticeable contemporary buildings are from the Millennium Project, which created the Millennium Bridge, the Millennium Wheel, and the Millennium Dome. The last of these three was an over-budget monstrosity

© SEAN MCLACHLAN

The new council building is one of the better examples of modern architecture in London.

that failed to draw visitors. The government took ages to sell the futuristic white dome with its spiky support towers because investors were too savvy to be weighed down with such a money pit. Some brave souls have finally bought it, renamed it O2, and plan to breathe new life into it as a concert venue. The whole affair was a mess from start to finish and people from all political parties lambasted Tony Blair and his friends for wasting so much tax revenue. But most Londoners like the other two creations. The Millennium Bridge is a cool span of metal connecting the Tate Modern with St. Paul's and combines chic with convenience. The Millennium Wheel, basically a giant Ferris Wheel with spaceshiplike pods instead of seats, is an overpriced attraction mainly for tourists, but it offers fantastic views and has become part of the London skyline.

Even on less ambitious projects, contemporary architects are taking advantage of advances in technology to experiment with form. Glass and steel are the rage, and an open look is favored over the concrete boxes of an earlier age. Architecture is alive and well in London, and it's only a matter of time before tastes change again and London is treated to a new era of building. Yet the structures from earlier times will remain, benefiting from a modern sensibility for preservation and a traditional British respect for the past.

Government and Economy

NATIONAL GOVERNMENT

England has always had a tradition of limited kingship with a dash of democracy, only recently widened to include more than a privileged few. Back in Anglo-Saxon days, the Witan, a group of nobles, bishops, and other important figures, would discuss affairs with the king, ratify public acts, and even choose the new king. As England developed into a medieval state, the lords made their voices heard by coming regularly to London to discuss the affairs of the day in the royal council. These powerful nobles eventually secured the Magna Carta from King John in 1215, guaranteeing that kings could not create any new taxes without their approval. The royal council became more of its own body after this and the Parliament was born. Later that century the Commons, meaning important but untitled merchants and landholders, also started to meet. The term "Parliamentum" was first used for a meeting in 1237, and although it did not become a standard word until the 14th century, this showed that the group was already beginning to think of itself as a formal body. Parliament began to sit (meet) on a regular basis, and after 1336 the Commons sat at every Parliament. While these wealthy commoners were often at odds with the titled gentry, they could find common cause in opposing the king. The struggle between king and Parliament was a tug-of-war lasting generations and depended on the political situation, the unity of the Parliament at the moment, and the strength of personality of the king. As the generations passed, Parliament gradually gained more power.

Kings often chafed under the growing restrictions of Parliament. Charles I's attempt to dissolve it was the spark that lit the bloody English Civil War, which lasted 1642–1646 and resulted in Charles losing his head. The rebels decided it was best to have a king, however, and the monarchy was restored in 1660, and wiser kings wielded power once again. In 1689 the English Bill of Rights made the kingdom a constitutional monarchy, securing rights for Parliament that have expanded as the days of kings and queens have waned. The representative body has met every year since, with the Commons getting greater power as the country became more democratic.

The lively debates and fractious political parties of this historic body have been the object of fascination for the British for centuries. Newspapers became filled with Parliamentary acts, and speeches and writing about the various factions and infighting became a full-time job for many aspiring writers. Early in his career, Charles Dickens covered the action for a paper called *The Mirror of Parliament*. The debates are just as lively now as they were then, and if you have a fast Internet connection, you can watch them online at www.parliamentlive.tv.

Despite being steeped in tradition (some officials still carry swords), Parliament has changed with the times. The first woman MP was Countess Constance Markiewicz from Ireland, elected in 1918, but as a member of Sinn Fein she did not take her seat. Now many women, as well as an increasing number of ethnic minorities, are winning seats. Another big change came in 1999 with Devolution. This created separate Houses of Commons for Wales, Scotland, and Northern Ireland. The unelected House of Lords has lost considerable power through the years, but it can still wield some might when it wants to, rejecting or amending bills that come to it from the House of Commons.

Above the ministers of Parliament is the prime minister, who is chief executive. He is also a member of Parliament, being the leader of the party with the most seats in the House of Commons. Ministers of Parliament are elected by popular vote, and as leader the prime minister is then asked to form a government by the monarch. Since Parliament handles both executive and legislative functions, there is no division between these two powers as there is in the United States. Prime ministers fall when there's either a vote of no confidence from Parliament or they fail to get Parliament to pass important legislation, which is a de facto vote of no confidence. Then a new member of the party takes over, or there may be early elections so the party can (it hopes) hold onto power with a new mandate from the people.

The current prime minister is Tony Blair, head of the Labour Party. He has advocated "New Labour," a business-friendly neoliberalism that has seen cuts to social services and the move to put many formerly state companies, such as the trains, partially or wholly in private hands. It appears that Blair may not stay in office long, however, as challenges from his own party because of his increasing unpopularity may soon force an election.

The other two major parties are the Conservatives (also called Tories) who advocate policies not far to the right of New Labour (but well to the left of the Republicans in the United States) and the New Democratic Party, a firmly left-of-center party that has always been in a minority but can occasionally make its voice heard in national politics. There are numerous other parties but they rarely have more than a few seats in Parliament, if that.

In recent years the power of the Parliament and the executive have been weakened somewhat by Devolution. Northern Ireland, Scotland, and Wales have all successfully agitated for their own parliaments and have taken over many of their own affairs. The United

Kingdom still exists, however, as decisions in important areas such as foreign affairs and defense are still decided in London.

THE MONARCHY

The United Kingdom is a parliamentary monarchy ruled (nominally) by a king or queen. Now that's Queen Elizabeth II, who succeeded to the throne in 1952. She was already married to Philip, Duke of Edinburgh, but since she is the offspring of the former king and he is not, it is she who rules. A hugely popular figure, Elizabeth turned 80 in 2006 but shows no signs of slowing down, keeping a whirlwind schedule of ribbon cuttings, meetings with foreign heads of state, charity functions, and sitting for 140 portraits (and counting). She has an uncanny knack of acting dignified without seeming arrogant or stiff, and she manages not to distract from public functions despite being the major center of attention. Her much less popular (and far less charismatic) son Charles is the heir to the throne.

The monarch has several formal powers, such as summoning and dismissing Parliament, and is the nominal head of the judiciary, head of the Church of England and Church of Scotland, commander-in-chief of the armed forces, and appoints all judges, diplomats, military officers, and archbishops. In reality, these posts are chosen by the prime minister, and Elizabeth rarely puts her foot down, at least in public.

The monarch has accrued various unusual powers and privileges through the centuries, such as owning all the dolphins, whales, and porpoises in U.K. waters, which is a good way to protect them from fishing. Traditionally the monarch's touch is supposed to cure various diseases, but there are no reports of Elizabeth trying this out.

CITY GOVERNMENT

The city is governed by a mayor who is elected every four years and a 25-member London Assembly, also elected every four years and which can accept or reject the mayor's budgets. Together these constitute the Greater London Authority. Beneath them are 32 borough councils, plus the City of London, a central neighborhood that has always had a slightly separate life because of its concentration of wealth and power. The current mayor of London, Ken Livingstone, was elected in 2000 and reelected in 2004. A progressive and a populist member of the Labour Party, he has caused controversy by openly criticizing Tony Blair on any number of issues and by passing congestion charges to discourage people from driving within central London. He has also worked on making London more wheelchair-accessible, less racist, and has sponsored many free events such as the annual Rise music festival.

The City of London (meaning the one neighborhood, not the city in general) is a truly special case, having its own annual elections for lord mayor. Like the monarchy, the job involves a lot of ceremony, but it also comes with a great deal of connections and clout. This figure can be important in that he or she welcomes foreign delegates, acts as a mediator between various factions, and fights for The City's interests against the Greater London Authority and the national government. The lord mayor also acts as a spokesperson for the business community and helps forge connections between government and business.

Because of its large population and power in the national economy, London is an important force in U.K. politics. The city has 74 ministers of Parliament, and it wields a great deal of influence because of its secure place as the largest and richest city in the country. People outside of London often complain that the city has too much say over national affairs, pushing the government to favor it over the countryside, but Londoners naturally see themselves as the center of the nation and don't understand what all the fuss is about.

ECONOMY

London is one of the major economic centers of the world, and it is responsible for a far greater share of its country's economy than most national capitals. More than a third of Britain's economy is within the city or its suburbs, most of its major companies are based here, and it is the center for banking, government, and law. With an annual economy of more than £120 billion, it is by far the country's most important city.

The largest sector of the economy is service, which employs about 85 percent of the workforce. Many work in the powerful financial services, including banking and insurance companies that are the powerhouse of the city's economy. Financial services bring in a net export earning of £19 billion a year, mostly from London offices. London is the greatest insurer in the world. Business is booming. More than half a million finance and business service jobs have been created since 1993. London's foreign-exchange market is responsible for a third of all global exchange, 43 percent of the global foreign equity market, and 70 percent of all trades in Eurobonds.

While London is the heart of the United Kingdom's economy, the heart of London's economy is The City, the old Square Mile that has been occupied since Roman times and that remains the nucleus of London's financial might to this day. A full 2.5 percent of the entire U.K. economy is generated within its office buildings. With all this money changing hands, it is not surprising that 75 percent of Fortune 500 companies have offices in London, most of them in The City.

Other important parts of the service economy include retail, media, and, above all else, tourism. The city gets more than 25 million tourists every year and the tourism industry employs more than 300,000 people. The city is the travel hub for English people and foreigners alike, with four airports and the nexus of rail and bus lines.

While London was once a great manufacturing center, this sector now amounts to only about 10 percent of the economy. As with other industrialized countries, much manufacturing has moved to cheaper labor markets overseas, but London is still a major producer of several products, mostly for the domestic market, including chemicals, electronics, printing and publishing, food and drink, and synthetic fibers.

But the economic picture is not all rosy. The mayor's office reported in 2005 that 43 percent of London's children live below the poverty

© LEAH BOYER

Abandoned warehouses still stand along the Thames, awaiting conversion into apartments.

line. There is also a shortage of such essential workers as teachers and nurses as rising costs of living and skyrocketing property values make it difficult for people in these professions to live in the city in which they work. This has led to the explosive growth of regional towns in counties such as Hertfordshire and Essex. These once-rural areas have seen a predictable rise in housing values, pricing locals out of the market while introducing new residents with few ties to their town and who work, play, and socialize almost exclusively in London.

So, while the wealthy and upper middle class having been seeing boom times in the past 20 years (allowing for unavoidable and periodic dips in the economy), the working class and regular middle class have been frustrated by a cost of living that far outpaces any rise in their salary.

The People

The London metro area has a population of 12 million, not counting the hundreds of thousands of commuters who pour into the city every weekday from outlying towns. London is also the main destination for immigrants and temporary workers seeking the good life the city has to offer. Thus London, with more than a sixth of the population of the United Kingdom (which stands at a little over 60 million), is a diverse, vibrant city that's always in a state of change and growth. London is one of the most ethnically diverse places in the world. Large numbers of just about all types of people can be found here, especially Eastern Europeans, South and East Asians, and Afro-Caribbean people.

Asians are major players in the London economy. The Greater London Authority estimated in 2004 that Asian businesses did more than £60 billion in trade a year, 13 percent of the city's total. There were nearly 39,000 Asian-owned businesses in the city, employing about 300,000 people, or 12 percent of the work force. When the English say "Asians" they are generally thinking of South Asians, such as Indians and Pakistanis, while when Americans use the term they generally mean East Asians, such as Japanese and Chinese. This reflects the origin of the Asian populations in the respective countries.

People of Indian extraction are the most acculturated to the British culture, and they are often referred to in government documents by the rather patronizing term "model minority." You will see many Indians in clubs and bars, and they are the most common group to choose interracial relationships. This does not, however, mean that they've tossed aside their own culture. Many still do *puja* at Hindu temples or go to dance clubs that play modern mixes of traditional Indian music, making for an interesting fusion between the old and new cultures. Just why the Indians have, in general, adapted so well to British society is a complex question. Part of it is that they are one of the older minority communities in the city, and part of it may be that the British influence in India was stronger than in many colonies.

The other major South Asian groups, Pakistanis and Bengalis, have also adapted to life in London, although they tend not to take on as much of the lifestyle. While the more religious Muslims frown upon what so many Londoners get up to on Friday and Saturday nights, many have done well by setting up shops or restaurants or getting work in offices. There's a close-knit Islamic community in London, with some giant mosques and many religious schools, the vast majority of which teach tolerance, despite what paranoid tabloids may say.

Another major immigrant group are Afro-Caribbeans, the local term for black people from the Caribbean. Many have been here for generations, while others are new arrivals. Afro-Caribbeans are a diverse group and have adapted to life in London in various ways. Many, especially those whose families have been here for a while, are fully integrated, while others stick close to their own neighborhoods. It's common to see Afro-Caribbeans in mixed relationships, but they tend to experience more racism than Indians do.

London's population grows by more than 10,000 every year, and this growth shows no sign of slowing. Much of this growth is through immigration, and while the above groups are the largest, there are also sizable communities of Africans, East Asians, Arabs, South Americans, and just about everybody else. It's even said that 1 percent of all Australians in the world live in London!

Such an unprecedented wave of immigration has not happened without a backlash. Many white Londoners complain that they are beginning to feel like foreigners in their own city. Comments such as "We've given it all away" or "England isn't English anymore" are common. This feeling is expressed not only by people who are racist, although there are plenty of those, but instead reflects a general dissatisfaction felt by many native English people about the direction their country is headed. It must be disconcerting growing up and seeing mostly white people on the Tube, with a sprinkling of South Asians and Afro-Caribbeans, and to take a Tube ride today and hear a dozen languages you don't speak, and a dozen more you can't even identify. Even some first- and second-generation immigrants say that immigration has gone too far.

On the other hand, a large number of English people enjoy the diversity their capital has to offer. Interracial dating is more common here than in the United States and Canada, and for the most part immigrants are at least tolerated. It seems that the majority of the younger people have accepted the new, more diverse England, if not welcomed it with open arms.

ENGLAND'S OLDEST MINORITY COMMUNITY

Black people have lived in England longer than there has been an England. There are records of Nubian merchants in Roman Londinium, and after the legions left some of them appear to have stayed. Since many white people in England are descended from Anglo-Saxons, Normans, and other later immigrants, this means there are a few black families who have been in England longer than the majority of white families.

Blacks are occasionally mentioned in medieval records, often being called "Moors." How many of these Moors were actually Muslims from North Africa as the name implies is difficult to tell, as most records mention them only in passing. The community grew larger because of one of early modern England's largest industries, the slave trade. The trade started in the 16th century, and some West African slaves came to London as early as 1555, but their numbers blossomed in the 18th century to serve the quickly growing empire.

Slaves were shipped to work the plantations of the West Indies and North America, and while few were used as laborers in England, they became popular as servants to the wealthy. Many were freed upon the deaths of their owners and settled into London life as laborers or shopkeepers. There are numerous references to marriages between black men and white women. Objections to this practice led Elizabeth I to make an early attempt to eject all black people from the kingdom, but it came to nothing and was not repeated as their numbers grew. Free blacks also arrived in London, usually as sailors on the many ships arriving daily from around the world.

London's black community remained a small one, probably fewer than 10,000 in 1800, increasing slowly with the addition of sailors from Africa or the West Indies, and occasional immigrants from England's colonies. One large influx came after the end of the American War of Independence. The British Empire had offered freedom to any American slaves who fought for the Crown, and true to its word, brought them back with the rest of the British Army.

While most blacks were working class and have disappeared from history, there were several important figures in the early days. Francis Barber, a liberated West Indian slave and Samuel Johnson's assistant and eventual heir, helped Johnson write the first English dictionary. The leading black intellectual of the 18th century was Ottobah Cugoano, a writer and abolitionist who was a member of the Sons of Africa, and early black antislavery group. Cugoano, a freed slave, amazed white Londoners by the depth of his education and his sharp wit and convincing arguments. His writings, which appeared in numerous books and newspapers, brought him the attention of such leading figures as William Blake and the Prince of Wales and were a major force in the abolition of slavery throughout the empire in 1807.

The community did not grow much until after World War II. On June 22, 1948, the SS *Windrush* docked in London and let off 492 Caribbean immigrants. Most settled in the south London neighborhood of Brixton, which is still mostly black today. They were taking advantage of the British Nationality Act, passed in 1948, which said that any citizen of a Commonwealth country or colony was free to move to Britain. More boats followed, and the influx of immigrants became even greater after 1952, when the United States passed the McCarran-Walter Act, blocking entry to people from the Caribbean. By the end of the '50s an estimated 100,000 had made London their new home. Others ventured to industrial cities or even small towns, changing the face of England forever. They came in search of work or were recruited by British companies. The London Transport Executive, for example, hired 2,000 people from Barbados to work as conductors and station workers. In the postwar boom, it was easy for Caribbean immigrants to find work, although pay was low, living conditions dismal, and the level of racism steadily increasing. The majority of the immigrants were educated and had held white-collar jobs back home, but they found themselves mostly relegated to working-class jobs in London, and there was a great deal of resistance to their working up the social and economic ladder. Advertisements for flats to rent often included the stipulation "No coloureds."

Thus Caribbean immigrants usually ended up in rather decrepit areas such as Brixton, Paddington, Hammersmith, and Notting Hill. This last neighborhood was the scene of violent race riots in 1958, when large mobs of young white men set upon lone black pedestrians. The attacks went on sporadically in various neighborhoods for a few weeks, injuring many blacks and promoting a climate of terror.

The riots prompted a call for equality that took on mass proportions in the '60s and '70s. While some in the community became radicals, the majority wanted simply to be an equal part of the society in which they worked and lived. Soon the black community adopted the term "Afro-Caribbean" to reflect their heritage, and art and community projects showcased their heritage and achievements.

The combination of racism, high unemployment, low pay, and lack of advancement for those who could find work led to widespread dissatisfaction and high levels of crime. The police, in a bid to lower crime in black areas, began to randomly stop and search (many would say harass) black pedestrians. This led to another riot, this time in Brixton, in 1981. Blacks violently protested police racism and many, including a fair number of white youths, used it as an excuse to loot and burn shops.

The Notting Hill Carnival, which has been running a celebration of Caribbean culture since 1966, was also the target of police harassment, leading to riots in 1975 and 1976, but in more recent years the police have had a lighter touch and there have been fewer conflicts and less crime.

History tends to remember the big events, the riots or the famous figures, but the real history of black London has been one of gradual progress. There's still racism, and it appears to be on the increase in recent years, but the black community is now better educated, better employed, and better integrated than ever before. The influx of African immigrants, mostly from West Africa or the Horn of Africa, has led to history repeating itself for those newcomers, but they too are making their mark in London. Black Londoners, whether African or Afro-Caribbean, are becoming leaders in the arts, business, and politics, and they add an important element to the city's culture.

CULTURE

Such a diverse population makes it hard to summarize what Londoners are like. While much of the focus in the media has been on immigration, most Londoners were born in the United Kingdom, and many of those have lived in London all their lives. Even those from elsewhere can quickly become adapted to the city, because one of the key characteristics of London culture is its ability to absorb newcomers. Stick around for a few months and complain about the public transportation and you'll be treated like an insider.

In general, Londoners are proud of their city and think of it as the center of everything in the United Kingdom, an attitude people in other towns resent, particularly because it's pretty much true. London *is* the center of the United Kingdom; most of the biggest concerts, festivals, and exhibits happen here, and most of the major businesses are based here, along with the offices of government. Special exhibitions at museums and galleries are always well attended and on Friday and Saturday nights the streets are filled with people taking advantage of London's spectacular dining and nightlife. Londoners always feel an urge to be part of the action. When there's always something happening, staying home makes you feel as if you're missing out.

The people live life at a faster pace here than in the rest of the country, and this is reflected in their overall behavior. People always seem to be in a rush, unless they've planted themselves at a café or pub, and they tend to ignore strangers. This doesn't mean Londoners are unfriendly, but they do generally lack the small-town warmth that characterizes so much of the rest of the United Kingdom. Still, if you catch them while they're keeping still they can be a welcoming and chatty people.

One stereotype of English people is that they're reserved and a bit shy. This is only partially true of the English in general and less true of Londoners in particular. The English have thought up various excuses to go out and meet one another to overcome their awkwardness in talking to complete strangers, the pub being only one of these. If you live in England for a while you will notice that there are innumerable clubs, societies, and organizations, all founded for the purpose of getting people with similar interests together in a social situation. The hikes or Morris dances or World War I lectures may be part of the enticement to join a particular club, but it seems the main purpose is to meet people. For the younger set, dance clubs are major meeting places, whether for "pulling" (flirting) or just having fun. The English *do* tend to be less chatty than North Americans, but they warm up quickly and once you become friends they are friends for life.

Londoners are of two minds about tourism. While most realize it's an essential part of London's economy, and the economy of the entire country, some don't like the huge numbers of foreigners tromping around the streets and taking photos. Many Londoners have told me they try to avoid the busy tourist areas such as Westminster and Covent Garden. There is, however, little open hostility toward tourists, and what hostility there is usually comes from some drunken yob who is looking for an excuse for a fight anyway, or some arrogant fellow who just wants to sneer at someone.

CONDUCT AND CUSTOMS

The English aren't radically different from North Americans when it comes to social mores. They tend to be a bit more formal, especially older people or professionals, but that wears away quickly once you get to know them. While they tend not to talk to strangers just out of the blue, if there's a context, such as being at the same nightclub or attending the same event (or being trapped in the same Tube) conversations can start easily.

Courtesy is important here, even in London, which has the reputation as the most impersonal city in the country. "Please" and "thank you" are vital, and "pardon" is important when bumping into people. The chorus of "pardons" during an average Tube ride can

PUB ETIQUETTE: THIS AIN'T NO BAR

Pubs are a cornerstone of British life. Most people go to them and many are regulars at their "local." Because of this, pubs are a great way to meet and learn about the English. Even if you don't drink you should go to some of the pubs listed in this book for their historic and cultural interest. Nobody objects to someone drinking a soda.

While much has been written about English reserve, this doesn't seem to apply to pubs. Generally people seated or standing at the bar are quite approachable, while those tucked away in a corner table either alone or in groups aren't looking for conversation.

Pubs have their own rules and etiquette. There are no queues, unlike everywhere else in England, but the barkeepers are adept at remembering who's first. When you walk in, catch the barkeeper's eye and he or she will be with you shortly. When ordering, don't forget to say "please." Politeness is de rigueur in all aspects of English society, but to barkeepers especially. If the folks behind the counter aren't swamped, feel free to ask for advice about what beer you should try.

Tipping is not required but is appreciated, and one nice tradition is tipping your barkeeper with a drink. Once they have served you and given the amount, you can ask, "And one for yourself?" at which point they will add a pint or half pint (usually a half) to your bill. If they're busy they might not get to your drink immediately, but once they do they'll be sure to thank you again. If they've been given too many pints already, or have a stern manager, they might politely refuse. Don't take it personally – they might work at a pub but they're still required to be sober.

It used to be the law that all pubs had to close at 11 P.M., a rule dating from World War I, when Parliament worried about the hazards of having hungover workers at munitions factories. Just before 11, the barman would ring a bell and shout "Last orders!" The law remained in place until 2005, when pubs were allowed to apply for permits to stay open longer. The permit is a pain to get and is not always granted. Sometimes pubs are refused as it would disturb the neighborhood. The pub closest to 10 Downing Street didn't get a late license for this reason, even though Tony Blair was the one to push the law through! Even if your pub closes at 11, you might experience a "lock-in," in which the pub "closes" and nobody is allowed in. Those already there can stay in and keep on drinking. I've generally seen lock-ins only at local pubs where the barkeeper knows most of the customers.

Even though everybody's drinking, most pubs are friendly and orderly places. Some establishments are rough, however, so you should beware. None are listed in this book, and it's usually pretty obvious which ones are bad by the shoddy look of the place and the large numbers of people wearing hooded sweatshirts.

So get out there and try a few pubs. It's very English (and Scottish and Welsh and *very* much Irish) and you're sure to have a good time.

Experience British culture at one of London's many pubs.

get a bit comical, but at least most people remember to say it. On the other hand, there can be some spectacularly rude people too, usually boors who are quick to fight—it's best just to ignore them. On the whole, the English are a polite people.

Like North Americans, people tend to shake hands upon being introduced, and the continental custom of greeting someone with a peck on each cheek is increasingly common among younger people. It tends to happen between men and women, and between women and women, who know each other at least fairly well. Many British do not do this at all, so it's best not to be the first to try it. Strangers never give a peck on the cheek. For that you'll have to go to Spain!

In most places, the English are pretty laid-back about table manners and are similar to North Americans in etiquette. Americans should try to avoid being the loudest people in the place. Americans generally speak at a higher volume than British people, so don't broadcast your conversation to half of England. Posh restaurants and wine bars are often quite formal, so it is expected that you will be on your best behavior. Some have dress codes such as "smart casual" (slacks and a decent shirt for men, the same or a nice dress for women) or "formal" (jacket and tie/evening dress) and these must be adhered to.

Another situation where the English are laid-back is at work. Coming late and leaving early are common, and there seems to be a lot of mucking about when they *are* at work. This can be a bit annoying if you're on a business trip but lots of fun if you've moved here for a job! While there's a bit of a lackadaisical attitude to work, the English tend to be fairly punctual otherwise. When people say they will meet you at 9, they will most often be there at the appointed time. If someone's late it's most often because of public transport. This can be a handy excuse if you're late yourself, and it helps that it is so often true.

One important aspect of British culture to be aware of is queuing—standing in line. "Thou shalt not jump the queue" is the 11th Commandment here, and people tend to make orderly lines for everything. It's a bit more chaotic in public transport and pubs, but people will usually give way if they think someone else is "first."

In all, the British are not so much different from North Americans. Add a bit more courtesy to your daily interactions and remember not to cut in line, and you'll navigate through the culture easily.

Religion

London has attracted immigrants from all over the world, so it is not surprising that every conceivable faith is represented here. According to the 2001 census, about 58 percent of Londoners identify themselves as Christian. The Catholic Church is the second-largest Christian community in the city, with many English and Irish members, and is growing because of immigration from Latin America and Africa. Methodist, Baptist, Congregationalist, Unitarian, and the Society of Friends churches are also prominent, and churches for just about any Christian denomination can be found in London.

An influx of South Asian immigrants in the late 20th century has added large and dynamic communities of Hindus, Sikhs, and Muslims, and their concentration in London means that the city is one of the most religiously diverse in the world. London is also host to many smaller communities of other faiths.

THE ANGLICAN CHURCH

About 60 percent of English Christians are Anglican. This church was formed between 1529 and 1536 when Henry VIII broke off from Catholic control, although English churches had been rankling under the rule of Rome for centuries before that. At first not

St. Martin-in-the-Fields in Trafalgar Square

much changed, the liturgy and church decoration staying virtually the same, but the growing influence of Protestantism soon made itself felt. Today one of the more visible differences between Anglicanism and Catholicism is the ordination of women, which was approved in 1975 although the first woman wasn't ordained until 1994.

There are no formal divisions within the church, but there is a distinct difference among individual churches as to how they worship. "High church" means those churches that adhere closely to Catholicism, with ornate altars, stained-glass windows, incense, and all the trappings of Roman religion, jokingly referred to as "smells and bells." "Low church" refers to those churches that are more Protestant in practice, with few and simple decorations and less pomp and circumstance in the ritual.

There is a heated debate within the Anglican Church over the status of homosexuals. The Archbishop of Canterbury, the head of the Anglican Church, has managed to keep most of the churches in the United Kingdom in line, but churches abroad, especially in North America, have gone into open rebellion by ordaining gay clergy. Some leading churches in London, such as St. Martin-in-the-Fields, are pressing for change in a less confrontational way.

ISLAM

After Christianity, Islam is the most popular religion in the city. About 8 percent of Londoners are Muslim, and more than a third of all Muslims in the United Kingdom live in the city. Mosques can be found in most immigrant neighborhoods, especially in the East End. The largest mosque is the London Central Mosque (www.iccuk.org) next to The Regent's Park. It's visible from a long way off because of its lofty minaret and golden dome. The main hall can accommodate up to 2,000 worshippers. The vast majority of British Muslims are moderate in their beliefs and were horrified and dismayed when some in their own community perpetrated the July 7, 2006, bombings. Unfortunately, a very vocal and visible minority who have not been able to adjust to life in the Western world have taken on a fiery brand of fundamentalism. They are the exception. Most London Muslims have been very tolerant of other faiths, although they look askance at what some of their fellow Londoners do on a typical Saturday night.

HINDUISM

Hindus first started coming to England in considerable numbers in the 19th century as students, and Hinduism is now a major faith here. About 4 percent of London's population is Hindu, and more than half of all Hindus in the United Kingdom live in London. Like Muslims, they have built many houses of worship and have pooled together to create a major one. The Shri Swaminarayan Mandir in Neasden, an ornately carved temple of white marble, is the largest Hindu temple outside of India. Hindus have faced little of the religious discrimination that Muslims do, although many Hindus complain of the racial discrimination all South Asians can suffer in this society.

OTHER FAITHS

Such a diverse population means that there is an equally diverse religious life in London and all faiths are represented here.

The Jewish community has a long history in London, having been present since the early Middle Ages and perhaps Roman times. While only 2 percent of London's population is Jewish, more than half of all the Jews in the United Kingdom live in London. In the 19th and early 20th centuries, Jews congregated in the East End, but many have since moved to other areas such as Golders Green.

Sikhs make up another 1.5 percent of the population. The majority of Sikhs are Punjabi, but members of other races have become increasingly interested in this faith. They are a very visible group because of the distinctive turbans the men wear and the high profile the organized Sikh community keeps by promoting outreach programs and cultural festivals.

Followers of other religions also add to the spectrum of beliefs. While most African immigrants are Christian or Muslim, some have maintained their traditional animistic religions. There are also a good number of Buddhists among the Asian population, and Buddhist practices find a following among the white and black communities as well. London is also home to a vibrant community of Wiccans and neopagans, who are trying to reconstruct and revive the pre-Christian beliefs of Europe. With three major occult bookshops in town and the occasional ritual at Stonehenge and the Temple of Mithras, it appears the old gods are not dead.

The census also revealed that about 16 percent of Londoners claim to have no religion, making atheism the second-largest "religion" in the city. Indeed, London seems to be in great part a secular society, especially among young whites, and the percentages of people saying they are from a certain religion must be taken with a grain of salt, since they may or may not regularly practice the faith they proclaim. Nevertheless, London is a great mixing pot for the world's religions.

Language

English speakers will, of course, have no trouble getting along in the country in which the language was born, but England has a great many dialects that can be strange to the unaccustomed ear. Numerous words also have different meanings on different sides of the Atlantic (see the *Glossary* section).

Other languages are well represented in London. Speakers of Punjabi, Hindi, Urdu, Spanish, German, Polish, and other major languages will often find people with whom they can share their native tongue. This can be a nice welcome when far from home and can lead to some fast friendships. Foreign-language tours and guidebooks are available at major tourist sights, and most major tour companies offer tours in a variety of languages. For example, both the Big Bus and The Original Tour have recorded commentary in several languages on their popular bus tours.

LEARNING ENGLISH

For those seeking to improve their English, London is full of language institutes offering classes of every length and level of proficiency. A good website listing London's many ESL schools is www.eslteachersboard.com. These institutes are often looking for teachers as well as students, so if you have a skill in a particular language and are in search of work, make the rounds. Universities, of course, are another good place to study English, although this isn't suited to the short-term visitor.

ESL TRAINING

Getting accredited to teach English as a Second Language (ESL) can open doors to jobs all over the world. Thousands of people of all ages make their living teaching English and can often boast of having worked on several continents. Others do it just as a short-term way of getting paid to see the world. Whether you are looking for a career or a fun job for a couple of years, there are several good schools that can get you prepared. There are three main kinds of certification, Teaching English as a Foreign Language (TEFL) and the more prestigious Cambridge Certificate in English Language Teaching to Adults (CELTA) and the Trinity Certificate in Teaching English to Speakers of Other Languages (CertTESOL). While all good schools offer TEFL certification, not all offer the other two. You can get through a TEFL in a few weeks, or even an intensive few days, but the CELTA and CertTESOL take longer, although they will get you better jobs in the long run. A good resource for finding schools in London is www.teflcourses.com. Costs, training time, and prestige of the schools vary widely, so shop around. A good website forum for ESL teachers is www.eslteachersboard.com, where you can get your questions answered by teachers who have already been through the system. Several places even offer TEFL courses in a long, grueling weekend of two 10-hour days.

LEARNING OTHER LANGUAGES

The vast number of language schools in London make it a good place to study before heading off to your next destination. You can learn virtually any language here, and what follows is just a sampling of schools for the most popular languages. Courses range in price depending on how long and intensely you study and the size of the class. Study materials may, or may not, be included in the price. Shop around before committing yourself to one. Embassies are a good starting point in your search.

One of the largest schools is **Cactus Language Training** (13 Marsham St. SW1, 084/5130-4775, www.cactuslanguagetraining.com, Tube: St. James's Park), which has courses in 15 languages, including French, German, Italian, Japanese, Mandarin, Portuguese, and Spanish. Class size averages eight students. For Italian, you may also want to try Affinitalia (Avalon Institute, 9 Great Newport St. WC2 020/8874-2926, www.affinitalia.co.uk, Tube: Leicester Square), a cultural organization promoting Italian culture. Those who want to learn Russian might want to try the **Russian Language Centre** (11 Coldbath Sq. EC1, 020/7689-5400, www.russiancentre.co.uk, Tube: Farringdon or Chancery Lane). Students of Arabic can go to the **Hammersmith and Fulham Adult Education Centre** (Macbeth St. W6, 020/8600-9191, Tube: Hammersmith).

ESSENTIALS

Getting There

BY AIR

Most visitors arrive to London by airplane. The city is served by several airports and with several hundred flights arriving every day from all over the world, there are no shortage of choices.

Because London is such a travel hub, there are plenty of opportunities to grab cheap fares from almost any destination. If money is an issue, avoid major holidays (including Easter) or the peak tourist season, mid-May–August. Flying in the off-season, during the middle of the week, or at inconvenient times can reduce your ticket price considerably. Either work through a travel agent, book through an airline's website, or try one of the bargain websites such as www.priceline.com or www.travelocity.com; for students there's **STA** (www.statravel.com) and **Council Travel** (www.counciltravel.com). Remember, it always pays to shop around.

Flying to London from the United States or Canada is pretty straightforward. There are regular, direct flights from major airports such as Chicago, Dallas, Los Angeles, New York, Toronto, Vancouver, and other cities. Flights from the West Coast take about nine hours, while flights from the East Coast take about seven hours. Try to get a direct flight. If you live in a smaller city or are getting a bargain ticket

this may not be possible, but a connection will lengthen your travel time by at least a couple of hours and seriously add to your jet lag.

There are numerous flights between London and major European cities. In fact, London is *the* center for budget flights to all over Europe. Sometimes you can get a ticket to Poland or Croatia or France for just a few pounds! Fares of less than £50 are common, and those less than £100 are routine. These tickets generally come with restrictions, such as you have to stay a minimum or maximum time, and the budget airlines that run these flights skimp on service (meals are rare, for example) in exchange for savings. Also look closely at which airports they are taking you to. Sometimes they dump you in an airport far from town and then gouge you on the shuttle fare. Also make sure all taxes and fees are included in the price. Budget carriers include **British Midland** (087/0607-0555, www.flybmi.com), **easyJet** (087/0600-0000, www.easyjet.com), **Monarch** (087/0040-5040, www.flymonarch.com), and **Ryanair** (087/0156-9569, www.ryanair.com). There are many more, and the situation is constantly changing, so shop around. Some carriers have limited routes. For example, Monarch goes only to Spain. Others, such as British Midland and esayJet, go all over Europe. The major airlines are getting into the budget game too and offer better service. **British Airways** (087/0850-9850, www.britishairways.com) offers many cheap flights to Europe. Good websites to check for last-minute fares are www.lastminute.com, www.travelocity.com, and www.bargainholidays.com. If you're flexible, you just might find yourself on the Adriatic Coast for less than the price of a meal at a good London restaurant.

London also has direct flights to major cities around the world, so if you're coming from outside North America or Europe, check with the airlines that go to your region.

Heathrow

If flying internationally, you will likely arrive at Heathrow, England's largest airport and the busiest in the world. It will be even bigger in 2008, when a fifth terminal is due to open. This massive but well-organized airport has the advantage of Tube and express rail links to the center of town.

Heathrow is easily accessible by Tube. The airport has two stations at the western end of the Piccadilly line, one for Terminals 1–3 and the other for Terminal 4. There are trains every few minutes from 5 A.M. (5:50 A.M. Sundays) to 11:45 P.M. (10:50 P.M. Sundays) and take about 50 minutes to get to and from central London. The cost is £3.80 for a one-way ticket to or from Zone 1, the zone for central London.

A faster, more expensive option is the **Heathrow Express** (084/5600-1515, www.heathrowexpress.com), which operates between Paddington Station and Heathrow. Tickets are available from machines at Heathrow or Paddington Station and cost £14.50 for a one-way trip and £27 for a return. Trains run from Paddington 5:10 A.M.–11:25 P.M. and run four times an hour between those times. Trains from Heathrow start from about 5:07 A.M. and run to 11:47 P.M. and four times an hour in between. The journey takes 15 minutes to Terminals 1–3 and 23 minutes to Terminal 4.

National Express (087/0580-8080, www.nationalexpress.com) runs a regular bus service at least twice an hour between Victoria Coach Station and Heathrow, taking about 40 minutes and costing £10 for a single and £15 for return. Services run from Heathrow 5:30 A.M.–9:30 P.M., and services run from Victoria 7:15 A.M.–11:30 P.M. The municipal bus service also operates to and from Heathrow and central London. It's not direct, and some buses can take well over an hour. One-way bus fare from Heathrow to anywhere in London is only £1.20, so if you're on a tight budget, this might be the way to go.

The fastest and most comfortable transportation between central London and Heathrow is the metered Black Cabs. They cost about £45 and can take about an hour depending on traffic.

Other airports also have express services. As with the Heathrow Express, you can buy tickets at machines in the airport or destination station.

Gatwick

Another popular airport is Gatwick, the second-largest airport in the United Kingdom. It is slightly farther away than Heathrow but still easily accessible with an express rail link and buses.

Gatwick Express (084/5850-1530, www.gatwickexpress.com) runs between Gatwick Airport and Victoria Station with a journey time of 30 minutes. Trains run from Victoria every 15 minutes 5 A.M.–11:45 P.M. and from the airport 5:50 A.M.–12:35 A.M. A few red-eye trains also run in the middle of the night. A one-way ticket costs from £14 and a return from £25. Gatwick Express allows you to buy tickets from the conductor with cash or credit card.

The **Thameslink** (084/5748-4950, www.thameslink.co.uk) connects Gatwick with King's Cross, Farringdon, London Blackfriars, London Bridge, St. Albans, and Luton and operates up to four trains an hour. Trips take around 50 minutes to King's Cross, 30 minutes to Victoria, and cost £8 single, £20 return. Both the Gatwick Express and Thameslink leave from the South Terminal. Don't worry if you're flying into or out of the North Terminal—there's a free monorail between terminals that takes only a couple of minutes.

National Express (087/0580-8080, www.nationalexpress.com) offers a bus service taking 90 minutes and costing £6.20 for a single and 11.40 return. Coaches run about once an hour around the clock.

A taxi to or from central London costs about £80 and takes about 90 minutes.

Stansted

London's third-biggest airport is Stansted, which is considerably smaller than the big two, but which is undergoing a major expansion and is set to become a third major airport servicing the city. It, too, has an express rail link from London and there are several bus options.

Stansted Airport has the **Stansted Express** (087/0000-0303, www.standstedexpress.co.uk), which takes abut 45 minutes to run between the airport and Liverpool Street Station, stopping off at Tottenham Hale on the way. Trains start from Liverpool Street Station at 4:55 A.M. Tuesday–Thursday and at 4:25 A.M. Friday–Monday. They end at 10:55 P.M. Monday–Wednesday and at 11:25 P.M. Thursday–Sunday. From Stansted they start at 6 A.M. Tuesday–Thursday and at 5:30 A.M. Friday–Monday. They end at 11:59 P.M. Monday–Thursday and at 12:30 A.M. Friday–Monday. There are trains twice an hour in the early morning and late evening and four times an hour otherwise. Tickets cost £15 one-way, £25 return.

There are two coach services to and from Stansted. **The National Express** (087/0580-8080, www.nationalexpress.com) A7 runs 24 hours a day at least twice an hour to and from Victoria Station and costs £10 single. Check its website for other locations it operates from, although Victoria Station is the most central. It takes about 90 minutes depending on the time of day. **Terravision** (012/7966-2931, www.lowcostcoach.com) runs an express service to and from Victoria that costs £8.50 for a single. It operates from Stansted 7:15–1 A.M. and from Victoria to Stansted 3 A.M.–11 P.M. Journeys on the express service take about 75 minutes.

A taxi ride to or from central London costs about £80 and takes about an hour.

Luton

If you are coming from Europe, you may fly into Luton. Situated 35 miles from London, it's a less convenient option, made worse by the general chaos in the terminal. Organization is poor, signage vague, and lines to the flights often intersect, so you might want to consider flying in somewhere different. Luton is very popular, however, because it is home to easyJet, one of the leading bargain airlines. Several other cheap carriers also use Luton, so if your budget is your prime concern, this may be your best option. There are regular buses from central London to Luton, as well as a rail link, although it doesn't go all the way to the airport and you still have to take a shuttle bus.

Thameslink takes 35 minutes to get from Luton Train Station to central London and at peak periods operates up to eight trains an hour, stopping at King's Cross, Farringdon, London Bridge, and Blackfriars. Single tickets are from £11.20 and returns are £30. There's a free and frequent shuttle service linking Luton Airport to Luton Train Station, which takes 10 minutes. **Green Line** (087/0608-7261, www.greenline.co.uk) offers coach (bus) service 3 A.M.–midnight at least twice an hour on its 757 line from Victoria Station via Brent Cross, Finchley Road, Baker Street, and Marble Arch. Tickets cost £9 one-way and £ 15 return and the journey takes 75 minutes. Another service is **easyBus** (www.easybus.co.uk), run by budget carrier easyJet. This minibus service goes to Baker Street and costs £8 single and £14 return. The first bus is at 4 A.M. and the last is at 12:20 A.M., and they are frequent 8:30 A.M.–8 P.M.

Taxis between Luton and central London can be quite expensive, but one of the cheaper ones is **Blueback** taxis (www.blueback.com), which charges £54.

London City Airport

Rarely used by anyone other than local professionals, London City Airport is about 9.5 kilometers (six miles) east of central London. London City Airport caters to business travelers with connections to 25 European destinations and is the quickest trip into town of any of the airports. It's reachable by Docklands Light Railway, from Canning Town on the Jubilee Line. The airport operates a shuttle bus from Canning Town and Liverpool Street stations. Several local buses also operate to and from all the airports.

To get there, take the Jubilee Line or Docklands Light Railway Service to Canning Town or Canary Wharf and then catch an Airport Shuttlebus. A taxi to or from central London costs about £20. The Black Cabs cost a whopping £80.

BY RAIL

The **Eurostar** (087/0518-6186, www.eurostar.com) is a fast, efficient train system with direct connections to Paris, Brussels, Lille, Euro Disneyland, Avignon, and the French Alps ski resorts from Waterloo International in London. From these destinations, especially Paris and Brussels, you can connect to more than 100 cities in mainland Europe.

The trains, which have uninterrupted journeys thanks to the Channel Tunnel, are clean, comfortable, and offer food and drink in special dining cars as well as trolleys that regularly go through along the aisles. Considering how quick some of the trips are (it takes less than three hours to get to Paris) the Eurostar is a better option than flying unless you can get one of the rock-bottom fares.

The trip between Paris and London is especially popular as it allows you to see two of Europe's great cities. Tickets range from £60 for a nonrefundable, nonexchangeable, round-trip Standard Value Fare to much more for flexible or same-day fares. For more on Paris, check out *Moon Metro Paris.*

If you are coming from another part of the British Isles, **National Rail** (www.nationalrail.co.uk, 084/5748-4950) operates trains between every major and most minor cities, as well as many smaller towns. It isn't the most efficient railway system in the world, so sometimes you'll have to make a connection or two, and delays are irritatingly common, but it's a comfortable way to get from point A to point B. Note that with privatization, many regions are served by private train companies now, but all the information is still available from National Rail.

BY BUS

If you're coming from elsewhere in Great Britain, you may arrive by bus. There are several bus connections from cities across England, Wales, and Scotland. **National Express** (087/0580-8080, www.nationalexpress.com), the largest scheduled coach service in Europe, has timetables and online booking on its website. Most of the long-distance buses go through Victoria Coach Station, which is a five-minute walk from Victoria Tube Station. The signage between the two is not very good, so keep a sharp lookout and feel free to ask a passerby.

Bus fares, like airfares, are often cheaper if you travel in midweek and/or book in advance. On some routes it is actually cheaper to buy two single fares than a round-trip fare. Why this is so remains a bit of a mystery, but it's good to keep in mind.

Eurolines (087/0514-3219, www.eurolines.com) is an association of bus companies operating from 52 Grosvenor Gardens (Tube: Victoria) with connections all over Europe. If you want to get to other European destinations, this is usually the cheapest way to go, but don't forget to check out the many bargain airfares from London. They might just be the same price and are much faster and more comfortable.

BY BOAT

A delightful if not quick way to get to and from London is by boat. There are several boat services linking the city to Ireland and mainland Europe. Fares vary widely depending on route, time of day/year, and whether you get a fixed or open return, so shop around.

For France the main companies are **P & O Stena Line** (087/0598-0333, www.posl.com), **Sea France** (087/0443-1653, www.seafrance.com). A faster option is a hovercraft operated by **Hoverspeed** (087/0870-1020, www.hoverspeed.co.uk).

For Ireland the main companies are **Irish Ferries** (087/0517-1717, www.irishferries.com) and **Stena Line** (087/0570-7070, www.stenaline.co.uk).

Ferries also operate between southern England and other European countries. *DG&G Travel Information Cruise and Ferry Guide* gives comprehensive coverage of sea routes and service providers for the region; it's available from DG&G Travel Information (080/0731-0163, www.dggtravelinfo.co.uk).

Getting Around

London has a convenient public transportation system that goes everywhere you want to go. Londoners complain that parts of the system can be a little slow and crowded, and all of it is more expensive than just about everywhere else, but on the whole London's public transport is quite good. Transport for London, the official organization overseeing it all, has an informative website at www.tfl.gov.uk with the latest news and fares. One of its pages features up-to-the-minute information about delays and problems at www.tfl.gov.uk/realtime and there's a handy journey planner at www.tfl.gov.uk/journeyplanner. It also operates a 24-hour hotline at 020/7222-1234. Please note that while the fares and information in this section were correct at press time, the details change constantly. You should use prices for comparison only, and it's best to check the TFL website before you arrive in London.

THE LONDON UNDERGROUND (A.K.A. THE TUBE)

London's famous Underground, popularly called the Tube, has been in running since 1863, making it the oldest subway system in the world. It's also the fastest and most convenient transport for tourists. There are 275 stations across London, 63 of them in central London, so there's a station near all the sights.

The system has 12 named and color-coded lines. For example, the Circle line is shown in yellow on all signs and maps, while the Northern line is shown in black. Be careful that you get on a train headed the right direction. The entrances to platforms are clearly labeled as Northbound, Southbound, Westbound, or Eastbound, with a map showing the stations in that particular direction. The sign on the front of the train shows the final destination. This is usually the last station on the line, but not always, so be aware of this if you're going to outlying areas. The ticket counters provide free information and maps.

Take a look at the Tube map in this guide. You can see that many of the lines intersect, so it's pretty easy to transfer from one line to another. Stations that have two or more lines intersecting can be quite large, so you might

The Tube goes to all main areas of interest.

have some walking to do. Also be aware that the Tube map has only a vague reference to actual geography. It was designed to be aesthetically pleasing and easy to use. Some tourists get tripped up by trying to guess where they are in relation to the surface by the relative location of the Tube stations.

The entire system is divided into six concentric zones, with Zone 1 at the center. The vast majority of attractions of interest to the visitor are in Zone 1, but Heathrow Airport is in Zone 6. Ticket prices depend on where you are going. A single (one-way) costs £3 for Zones 1 and 2. A day pass for Zones 1 and 2 costs £6.20 for peak times, and a three-day travel card for Zones 1 and 2 costs £15.40. A carnet (book of 10 tickets) for Zone 1 costs £17. If you are staying in London for a week, the best deal is the 7 Day Travelcard. This gives you unlimited access to the Tube, bus, Docklands Light Railway (excluding airport expresses), and one-third off Thames boat fares. It costs £22.20 for Zones 1 and 2. A monthly card costs £85.30. Children's fares are cheaper, as are tickets bought on off-peak times. Tickets that cover zones beyond Zone 2 cost more, but you will seldom need them unless you live here.

All tickets are available through machines and at ticket windows. Be careful when buying a carnet; the tickets will come out one at a time. Many visitors think the one ticket that comes out first is good for 10 trips. Wait until the rest come out! If you have a regular ticket, as opposed to an Oyster card, slip it in the slot at the front of the turnstile and pass through. Your ticket will then pop out a slot on the other side. Be sure to take it as you will need to put it in another turnstile to exit the station at your destination.

If you are staying in London for a couple of weeks or more, the cheapest option is the Oyster Card, which is a prepaid smartcard. You can buy as many fares or days as you need in advance, and you can put Travelcard and Bus Pass season tickets on them too. They're also quicker to use—you just slap them on the big yellow circles in front of the turnstiles beside the bus driver's seat and a scanning system reads it. Single fares are cheaper with an Oyster card than with cash and anyone can use it, which is convenient both for you and thieves, so keep it safe. Note that you can't use it and then hand it over the turnstile to your friend. It's timed so that it won't work that way. It's reusable, so when it runs out you can fill it up again by buying more credit. Your unused balance never expires. You can order an Oyster card online before you even get to London by going to www.oystercard.com or by calling 087/0849-9999.

Transport for London offers a few tips about traveling in the Tube:

1. Try to avoid rush hours, called "peak periods" here. The stations in the central part of the city get extremely crowded. I've missed a train a few times because I simply couldn't fit into the cars. It's not a good time to be dragging your luggage about.
2. If you are traveling with your luggage, no matter what the time, try to take up as little

space as possible. Backpackers should take their packs off.

3. On the escalators, stand to the right. This allows people who are in a hurry to pass you on the left.

4. Allow passengers off the train before boarding. It's safer and quicker. The train won't leave while people are still going to and fro.

5. Stand behind the yellow line on platforms. When boarding or leaving a train, mind the gap between the train and the platform. This is especially important for people with small children in tow.

6. The Tube is not air-conditioned and can get pretty hot in the warmer months, especially at peak times.

7. Practice basic safety precautions. Keep your bags with you at all times; otherwise either thieves or security will take them away. Pickpockets are common, so keep a hand on your valuables.

8. Please give up your seat to the elderly, those with disabilities, pregnant, or those carrying small children.

9. Keep your eyes and ears open for announcements of delays or line closures. The Northern line has been having an increasing number of delays because of technical errors, although a drastic revamping of the entire line should be finished by the time this book goes to print (but don't hold your breath). There are also frequent delays due to security concerns. Usually these are because some tourist has left a bag unattended. Police then have to close the line until they can determine what's going on. Please, for the sake of your fellow travelers (and your luggage, which might get destroyed by a bomb squad), don't leave any bags unattended.

BUSES

The bus system (www.tfl.gov.uk/buses/, 020/7222-1234) is a little more complicated to figure out than the Tube, but it has the advantage of allowing you to see the city as you go from one place to another. It's also cheaper. The buses are either "double-deckers," for which London is famous, or "bendies," massive one-story buses that bend in the middle. You can pick up a bus schedule at any of the major stations or from the driver. Riding in a double-decker is a lot of fun. Try to get a seat upstairs at the front; you'll be treated to a grand view. The bendies are nothing special, but they do get you from point A to point B.

Sadly, the old Routemasters, the original double-deckers with open entryways in the back so people could hop on or off, are all but gone, victims of European Union safety regulations. They are preserved only on Routes 9 and 15, the ones most often used by tourists.

A bus ride costs £1.50 for a single and £3.50 for a day pass. Keep in mind that a single is valid for only one ride on one bus; it doesn't count for a transfer. Holders of an Oyster card have to pay only £1 for a single and £3 for a day pass. The machine will automatically figure out if you've ridden more than once in a day and add on the charge accordingly, so you don't have to stop and inform the driver.

At busy bus stops you must buy tickets at the red dispensers provided. Note that they don't give change, so try to have the exact amount of coins. On less busy routes you can pay the driver, but once again you should have exact change as they are often short.

Most bus stops are provided with an index of destinations to help you figure out which bus is for you, as well as an electronic display showing the estimated arrival time of the next few buses. As most lines on popular routes run every 8–12 minutes, and there is often more than one line that will get you where you are going, you won't have to wait long.

Between midnight and 7 A.M., the Tube is closed and the day buses are replaced by night buses. These run on the same routes as their daytime brethren but carry the prefix "N" before their number. Not all routes are served by night buses, but the major ones are and many of them pass through Trafalgar Square, good news for visitors.

Buses stop only if you press the button requesting a stop or if there's someone waiting at

a double-decker on its way to Oxford Circus

a particular stop. Keep a sharp lookout for your stop so you don't go too far. Bus drivers are used to foreign visitors so feel free to ask them to stop at a particular place for you.

Most of the safety rules mentioned for the Tube also apply for the buses, with two added caveats. First, if you are traveling late at night, you may not want to sit alone on the top of a double-decker, as you could be a target for criminals. Second, be careful when going up or down the steps of a double-decker. Tourists and even locals have been known to tumble down at sudden stops. Use the handrails!

TRAIN

The **Docklands Light Railway** (020/7363-9700, www.tfl.gov.uk/dlr) is an increasingly popular option for Londoners living in parts east. It connects Bank and Tower Gateway stations and heads east to popular destinations such as Canary Wharf, Greenwich, Canning Town, and London City Airport.

The other major rail service within London is **Thameslink** (084/5748-4950, www.firstcapitalconnect.co.uk), which has stations at several central locations such as King's Cross, Farringdon, Barbican, Moorgate, City Thameslink, Blackfriars, and London Bridge. From there you can go north to St. Albans, Luton Airport Parkway, and Bedford, or head south to Gatwick and Brighton. A side line goes to Wimbledon via Elephant and Castle.

The safety rules outlined in the Tube section also apply for trains.

TAXIS

If you can spare the cash, taxis are a convenient way to get around town. Cabbies are often very knowledgeable about the city and current events and you can learn a lot from them. It seems immigrants in every city opt to become cabbies, and London is no exception. Taking a cab will give you a chance to chat with people from South Asia, the West Indies, and elsewhere.

At the taxi stands at rail stations, airports, and by the side of the road, use only the official black cabs, known as London Black Cabs. They are licensed and have to follow strict regulations. They are the only taxis allowed to prowl the streets courting customers. Other cab companies are allowed to take only phoned-in or Internet-booked rides. Just to make things confusing, not all Black Cabs are black anymore, since some have been painted with advertisements. The Black Cab drivers seem to be much more knowledgeable and courteous than drivers from other companies, although this can vary. The cabs carry five people, and some models carry six. They are all wheelchair-accessible and child seats are available. Unlike some of the other cabs, they are metered and so you know exactly what the fare is. You can tip the driver 10 percent but many people just round the fare up to the nearest pound, as long as that comes out to at least 50 pence extra. Cash and major credit cards are accepted.

Black Cabs all are metered and cost a minimum of £2.20, with an extra 20 pence for every 219 meters after the first 438 meters. This makes them the most expensive transport option, but they're also the quickest. The rate is the same whether you have one person or five with luggage, so it can be good value if you travel with more people.

The best way to get a cab is to go to one of the taxi stands outside a Tube or bus station, or by standing by a busy street and flagging one down. The yellow sign atop the cab will be lit if it's available, but at night many drivers keep their lights off so they can pick and choose whom they take. If you're trying to get a cab at night, try flagging down all of them.

You can also hire cabs for preset tours. Check www.londonblackcabs.co.uk or talk to one of the drivers for details. It's also possible to hire them for long journeys and golf excursions by hiring a cab at a daily rate. For a long journey, tour, or trip to the airport on short notice, call 079/5769-6673.

A whole army of licensed minicabs operates in the city, and they are generally cheaper than Black Cabs, although you have to go through the hassle of calling them. You can also walk into their offices if you happen to pass by one, and they'll get you a cab as soon as possible, which might be quite a long time if it's Friday or Saturday night.

There have been numerous criminal complaints about unlicensed cabs, varying from overcharging to sexual assault, so look for the white license clearly displayed on the back of the cab near the yellow license plate. While many unlicensed cab drivers are simply trying to make a living in a less-than-legal manner, there are more than a few bad apples among them so it's not worth the risk.

CAR

It is possible to hire (rent) a car in London, but it's far more trouble than it's worth. Parking is hard to find, roundabouts and left-side driving are confusing for foreign visitors, there's a pricey congestion charge to discourage people from driving in the first place, and the public transport is convenient enough that there's really no need. If you do want to hire a car, numerous companies have offices in the airports and advertise in the phone book.

CYCLING

Avid cyclists or those staying in town for a while may want to bike around London. While this is a quick and cheap way to get from one place to another, it does involve some inherent hazards. I would strongly advise against cycling in London unless you are used to riding in busy city traffic. Also be aware that you must lock up your bike at a proper bike stand; the police will remove it otherwise. This being a big city, if you *don't* lock up your bike, it will get removed by less official personnel. If you're riding at night make sure you are clearly visible by fitting your bike with a white light in front and a red one in back.

Despite these caveats, cycling is generally safe. Lots of Londoners get around this way,

Look for this sign when trying to park a bike.

so motorists are used to them. You must cycle on the far left, which doubles as the bus lane, and while it's a bit nerve-racking to have double-deckers looming a few feet in front of and behind you, they're piloted by the best drivers in the city and you should have no troubles with them. Getting in with a couple of other cyclists is a good idea as it increases your visibility, and talking to any of the city's innumerable bike messengers will land you expert advice on the best routes.

If you are willing and able to deal with city traffic, you can find a complete guide to cycling in London, and order a free cycle map, by going to www.tfl.gov.uk/cycling. You can register your bike for free at www.immobilise.com. If your stolen or lost bike is recovered, you will be contacted.

To rent a bike, check out the phone book for a multitude of options. One of the largest companies is The London **Bicycle Tour Company** (www.londonbicycle.com, 020/7928-6838). It provides a variety of bikes, which all come with an oh-so-necessary lock, as well as maps, route suggestions, and accessories. Regular bikes cost £3 per hour or £16 for the first day, £8 for the following days; tandem bikes cost extra. You can also rent by the month for £60. Accessories such as helmets (a smart idea) and lights (ditto) cost extra. Check out the website for links to cyclist organizations across the United Kingdom and Europe. They're a good way to meet like-minded people and have some fun.

RICKSHAW

Rickshaws came to the United Kingdom via India, where they are a major mode of transport in crowded cities. These aren't like the ones you see in old movies in which some poor fellow is trotting in front of you, pulling you and your baggage along; the modern rickshaws are actually bikes with a covered back bench that can fit two reasonably sized people. They're a fun way to get around town, and the drivers know the area well. Charges vary widely and you should agree on the fare

It's easy to walk London's tourist center.

before you go. It's acceptable to tip rickshaw drivers, and since they just pedaled your weight, their weight, the bike's weight, your friend's weight, and your shopping's weight from Big Ben up to the National Gallery through howling traffic and plumes of exhaust, you certainly should.

WALKING

Of course, you can always walk. Take a good look at the city map and plan out your day. You'll find that many attractions are close to each other and you can save a considerable amount of money by hoofing it. It's the best way to see London too. If you're going to the South Bank, especially recommended is a walk over one of the many bridges of the Thames. Tower Bridge is a historical sight in itself, and the ultramodern Millennium Bridge is convenient because it provides a direct route between the Tate Modern and St. Paul's. Be sure to bring an umbrella and, in the summer, a bottle of water.

Visas and Officialdom

CUSTOMS

Once you land at one of London's airports, you must go through customs. This is usually fairly straightforward. Nine times out of 10 the official will ask what the purpose of your visit is, you will respond "tourism" or "business," and he or she will stamp your passport and wave you through. Just don't mention that you may look for work or you might be turned away. That's something you have to arrange *before* you go. Extending your tourist visa is a little harder, and an extension is usually granted only if there's an emergency, such as if you are lying in a hospital somewhere. The easiest way to stay longer is to leave and come back. A quick weekend trip to Paris will do the trick. Don't overstay your visa or you may not be let back in.

TOURIST VISAS

If you are a citizen of Australia, Canada, New Zealand, South Africa, or the United States, you do not need to get a visa before you go to England. Simply show up with a valid passport and you will get a tourist visa for up to six months. Citizens of European Union countries and Switzerland can stay indefinitely. Since times can change, especially with the current security situation, it's always a good idea to call the British Embassy in your country and ask before you go.

STUDENT VISAS

If you're a student, a much easier way to stay in the country for a while is to come and study. This is best done through your university back home, which may already have a program in

London or at least could give you information on whom to contact. The British embassy in your home country will have all the information and forms. You will need to study full time, in other words, 15 hours a week or more. Citizens of EU countries do not need a student visa.

Students enrolled to study full time for at least six months get a passport stamp allowing them to work up to 20 hours a week during the term and any amount of work during holidays.

WORK VISAS

Getting a work visa for the United Kingdom can be a bit tricky, and it depends on your age, country of origin, and experience. Citizens of Switzerland and most EU countries do not need a work visa, but everyone else does.

U.S. citizens have a tough time getting a work visa unless they are being sponsored by a company that has already offered them a job, but U.S. college students and recent graduates (including permanent residents studying at U.S. universities) can get a six-month work visa. You must be at least 18 and studying full time in your home country. The visa is called a Blue Card and is available from **British Universities North America Club** (203/264-0901 or 800/462-8622, www.bunac.org). This program also covers Australians, Canadians, and New Zealanders.

Citizens from Commonwealth countries aged 17–27 are eligible for a Working Holiday Entry Certificate, allowing you to work a limited range of jobs and travel for up to two years. Applications are available from the British embassy in your home country. If your parent or grandparent was born in the United Kingdom, you can apply for a work permit on this basis. Check the embassy for details and an application form.

Numerous magazines and websites list jobs. A big help in getting work is to find a job agency, of which there are several listed in the London phone book. The reputable ones do not charge you, instead making their money from a fee the hiring company gives them. A good website is www.tntgrapevine.com, which lists job agencies and vacancies. Of course, all the papers list jobs, and the large Saturday editions have big sections for available positions. What they list depends on the paper, with tabloids listing working-class jobs and the *Financial Times* listing high-roller positions in The City.

If you do find work in London, you should try to get a National Insurance Number, qualifying you for free medical care. Call 084/5601-0142 to make an appointment. You need to bring your passport, three other forms of identification, and a letter proving you are employed or registered with a job agency. Once you have the card, call the National Health Service (NHS) for more information at 0845-4647 or look it up at www.nhs.uk, and it can provide you a list of doctors. Visits and birth-control pills are free, but you have to pay for medicine. Dental work costs money too, but the government picks up 25 percent of the bill.

Taxes are a bit of a pain in the United Kingdom, as they are everywhere else. All the forms you need are at www.hmrc.gov.uk. Taxes range from 10–40 percent depending on income and there's a threshold of £4,895 per year before you get taxed.

Please note that there are some dodgy employment agencies out there that prey on the unwary, especially those who don't speak good English or who aren't legally entitled to work. Watch out! Employment agencies are *not* allowed to retain your passport or any other document, and beware of high "processing fees." If you think you are being ripped off, call the police.

DRIVER'S LICENSES

If you have a valid driver's license, you can use it in the United Kingdom for up to a year before you have to get a local license. Local licenses are available by applying at the post office. If you plan on driving through several countries, get an International Drivers License, available in North America from the American Automobile Association. There's a fee but no test.

EMBASSIES, CONSULATES, AND HIGH COMMISSIONS

Your embassy can help with emergencies and can offer tips on getting student and working visas. Here's a list of selected foreign embassies in London:

Australia
Australia House
Strand WC2
020/7379-4334
www.uk.embassy.gov.au
Tube: Holborn

Canada
MacDonald House
1 Grosvenor Sq. W1
020/7258-6600
www.canada.org.uk
Tube: Bond Street

New Zealand
New Zealand House
80 Haymarket SW1
020/7930-8422
www.newzealandhc.org.uk
Tube: Piccadilly Circus

South Africa
South Africa House
Trafalgar Sq. WC2
020/7451-7299
www.southafricahouse.com
Tube: Trafalgar Square

United States
U.S. Embassy
24 Grosvenor Sq. W1
020/7499-9000
www.usembassy.org.uk
Tube: Bond Street

Following is a list of British embassies in other countries. If you have a simple question, it's best to check their websites as the phone lines are often horrendously busy. If you are already in the United Kingdom and have a question, either contact the embassy of your home country or contact the British Home Office at 087/0606-7766 or at www.homeoffice.gov.uk.

Australia
High Commission of the United Kingdom
Commonwealth Ave.
Yarralumla, Canberra, ACT 2600
02/6270-6666
www.uk.emb.gov.au

Canada
High Commission of the United Kingdom
80 Elgin St.
Ottawa, Ontario K1P 5K7
613/237-1530
www.britainincanada.org

New Zealand
High Commission of the United Kingdom
P.O. Box 1812
44 Hill St.
Thorndon, Wellington 1
04/924-2888
www.britain.org.nz

South Africa
British Consulate General
P.O. Box 500
Southern Life Centre
8 Riebeek St., 15th Floor
Cape Town, 8000
021/405-2400
www.britain.org.za

United States
Embassy of the United Kingdom
3100 Massachusetts Ave.
Washington, D.C. 20008-3600
General inquiries: 1-900/255-6685
Visa inquiries: 1-900/990-8472
www.britainusa.com

There are more than a dozen diplomatic offices in the United States, so check the website for the one closest to you.

Tips for Travelers

TOURS

Innumerable tour operators can take you around London's storied streets, so the list below is only a sampling of the most popular, as well as some lesser-known companies who give more personal attention and a unique insight into the city. The major tours are good if you are pressed for time and want to get a quick look at the town, but I strongly recommend going for the smaller companies, whose guides are often more knowledgeable and better able to tailor their tours to your particular needs. There's nothing like wandering around discovering the city on your own, and while major companies will whiz you around and give you a superficial *replacement* for individual travel, smaller companies and private operators will *enhance* your own explorations.

The Big Bus Company (48 Buckingham Palace Rd., 020/7233-9533, www.bigbustours.com), like its rival The Original Tour, runs open-top double-decker buses all around central London on three different lines. A ticket is valid for all lines. A selection of five walking tours, a much better way to see the city, come free with the price of a ticket, and you also get a free Thames cruise. If you go in person to its offices on Buckingham Palace Road, you can get discount tickets on selected shows and attractions. Tickets cost adults £20, children 5–15 £10.

The major bus tour company, **Gray Line Golden Tours** (4 Fountain Square, 123–151 Buckingham Palace Rd. SW1, 020/7233-7030, www.goldentours.co.uk), offers various themed tours of London, from historical to theater tours. It also offers numerous tours of sights outside of London, from one-day excursions to four-day tours and trips to Paris. Prices vary widely depending on the tour, but seniors, students, and children always pay less.

Cycling is a fun way to see the city. **London Bicycle Tour Company** (1A Gabriel's Wharf, 56 Upper Ground SE1, 020/7928-6838, www.londonbicycle.com) offers expert guides who will wheel you around various routes in the east or west part of the city. It also offers excursions and weekend trips. Bicycles and safety equipment are provided. The east and west city tours cost £16.95 and take 3.5 hours as they take you more than nine miles. Lots of fun, but with London traffic they're not for the faint of heart! On the other hand, if you are thinking of cycling in London, going with this outfit first will get you lots of good tips.

One of the more unusual tours you can take in London is via a big yellow amphibious craft that will drive you around town before plunging into the river and turning into a Thames cruise. **London Duck Tours** (55 York Rd. SE1, 020/7928-3132, www.londonducktours.co.uk) depart from Chicheley Street behind the London Eye and take you around the biggest sights of London. The combination of a bus tour and river cruise in the same vehicle is very convenient and a big hit with kids. Tours last 75 minutes and cost adults £17.50, seniors and children 13–15 £14, children 12 and under £12, and families (two adults and two kids under 12) £53.

One major tour company *does* give you an in-depth, personalized insight to the city. **The Original London Walks** (020/7624-3978 or 020/7794-1764, www.walks.com) offers a dizzying array of themed tours, all conducted by very qualified guides. The theater tours, for example, are led by actors and actresses from the London stage, while the historical walks are done by historians, not just some bloke who's read a couple of books. Tours have set meeting times and spots and you don't have to book, merely to show up on time. Visit the website or look for the ubiquitous white pamphlet. Tours cost adults £6, seniors over 65 and students £5, children under 15 free if accompanied by a parent.

Whether you decide to take its tours or not, **The Original Tour** (Jews Row SW18, 020/8877-1722, www.theoriginaltour.com) will be part of your visit; its open-top double-deckers are simply everywhere. Its 24-hour tickets allow you to use its hop-on, hop-off service, making your way between more than 80 stops. This allows you greater freedom than many other tour companies and lets you spend longer or shorter periods at places of your own choosing. Buses generally leave a particular stop every 15–20 minutes, and you can buy tickets on the bus. Live or recorded commentary (depending on the route) will keep you informed and free London activity packs help keep the kids entertained. There are four different routes and a ticket is valid on all of them; maps are available on the bus and the website. The buses use their own bus stops as well as regular bus stops, indicated by the words "The Original Tour" and a color code for the route. Tickets cost adults £18, children 5–15 £12, and families (two adults and three children) £72.

One of the major tour companies in London, **Premium Tours** (2nd Floor, Staple Inn Buildings South, Holborn WC1, 020/7404-5100, www.premiumtours.co.uk) offers air-conditioned guided bus tours of the major sights. It offers a variety of tours, the most popular being a full-day tour of the city that takes in the Tower of London, Buckingham Palace, a Thames cruise, a pub lunch (not included in the price), Westminster Abbey, and a choice of Harrods and tea at Kensington Palace or a flight on the London Eye. This costs adults £69 and children up to 16 £59 It also offers tours to popular destinations outside London. There's a free pickup service for many hotels.

GAY AND LESBIAN TRAVELERS

London is one of Europe's most gay-friendly cities, with Soho being the epicenter for gay culture and the gay rights movement. There are gay bars, clubs, and interest groups all over town, and gay travelers will have no trouble meeting like-minded individuals. Londoners are generally tolerant of homosexuals, especially in the center of town, and there are many openly gay public figures.

On a more official level, Mayor Ken Livingstone is a strong advocate for gay rights, in line with his populist politics. Several ministers of Parliament are gay, and not all of them are from the liberal parties, either. The Archbishop of Canterbury has made it clear that gays are welcome in the Anglican Church but has stopped short of sanctioning gay relationships or allowing clergy who are in such relationships.

The tolerance goes only so far, however. Some neighborhoods can be a bit unfriendly, if not downright hostile, but these are generally in residential areas of little interest to the visitor. Also be careful in pubs and bars outside of Soho, where someone might be looking for a fight and the crowd may not be so sympathetic. The Metropolitan Police has reported that homophobic hate crimes are, ironically, more common in areas where gays frequent than elsewhere.

TRAVELERS WITH DISABILITIES

Unfortunately, London poses a bit of a problem for people with mobility issues. Mayor Ken Livingstone has promised to make the city more accessible, but he's fighting a tough battle against listed buildings that can't be altered, a Tube system that has few wheelchair-accessible stations, and tiny lanes and sidewalks that are simply impossible. Many buildings, especially tourist attractions and hotels, have, however, installed ramps and other devices to improve accessibility.

For public transport, the most convenient are the Black Cabs, all of which are wheelchair-accessible. Few Tube stations are, and fewer still in the center. Of those stations of most interest to visitors, only Greenwich, Heathrow (all terminals), Kensington, Kew Gardens, London Bridge, North Greenwich, Richmond, Southwark, Westminster, and Wimbledon have step-free access between the street and the platform.

All buses and Docklands Light Railway stations are accessible and are therefore a better option than the Tube, but keep in mind that the sidewalks themselves are often obstacle courses for anyone in a wheelchair. Trains between cities are wheelchair-accessible, but it's best to call ahead to let the rail service know you're coming.

Because of recent legislation, all public buildings must now be wheelchair-accessible, although for some this means a cheap wooden ramp you have to ask someone to pull out for you. Listed buildings, because of their historic nature, can't be altered, and they are the worst to get into. Museums are generally easy to deal with, and London's theaters make a good effort toward accessibility. Headsets help the hearing impaired, and many venues have special sign-language performances, although England uses BSL (British Sign Language), which is different from ASL (American Sign Language). The Royal Opera House has subtitles for all performances, including ones in English. Most theaters are wheelchair-accessible but you must mention you want an accessible seat when you book your ticket.

Streets can also be a problem, especially older, narrow streets. Sidewalks come and go, curbs may or may not have been graded, and thick crowds make navigation difficult. For more information on disabled access in London, call Transport for London Access and Mobility at 020/7941-4600 or go to www.visitlondon.com and type "disabled" into the search engine.

SENIOR TRAVELERS

Seniors get discounts on public transport and many sights, can often finagle a discount at hotels (it never hurts to ask), and can qualify for reduced rates from some travel companies even before leaving home. What constitutes a senior citizen varies depending on the location, but people over 60, and certainly those over 65, usually qualify. Seniors must have proof of age, such as a driver's license or passport.

WOMEN TRAVELERS

London is generally a safe and enjoyable place for women, but there are some precautions to take. While some female visitors might attract unwanted attention in pubs, or the "accidental" contact with a stranger on a busy rail car, much of this is more pathetic than threatening.

Also be aware that the Tube gets less safe late at night, especially the farther you get from the center. Avoid standing on platforms or riding in carriages that have no one else in them, or only one or two men. Also, the usual caution against walking alone in dark streets late at night applies to London, especially on Friday and Saturday. Buses are a safer option; sit close to the driver and avoid the back or the upper story. Safer still is the licensed taxi.

Some resources for women travelers include **The Well Women Centre Marie Stopes House** (108 Whitfield St. W1, tel. 084/5300-8090 or 020/7574-7400 for general inquiries, info@mariestopes.org.uk, www.mariestopes.org.uk, Tube: Warren Street), which offers advice and procedures for contraception, abortion, and health screenings. Phone lines at **The Rape and Sexual Abuse Helpline** (tel. 084/5122-2331) are open noon–2:30 P.M., 7–9:30 P.M. Monday–Friday: 2:30–5 P.M. Saturday–Sunday.

ODDS AND ENDS

Besides essential documents such as your passport, there are several things you should take with you. If you have a university or senior citizen ID, bring it to get discounts on many attractions. Bring either a raincoat or an umbrella or both; chances are you'll use them. Don't forget your prescription or over-the-counter medications and toiletries. While anything you need is available in British pharmacies, you don't want to waste your vacation time figuring out which British brand of contact lens solution is the one for you. If you're lucky enough to have sunny spring or summer weather, you'll be thankful for having brought along some sunscreen. You'd be surprised at how quickly you can burn even in this northern clime. A water bottle is a good idea at any time of the year, because walking around all day will leave you thirsty. You can fill it up with tap water and save lots of money on drinks. A converter is also a good item to bring if you have any electrical items with you. Most decent hotels supply a hair dryer, but you might need a converter for your digital camera, iPod, or any other electrical item you might want to bring. (For more information on converters, see the *Electricity* section under *Weights and Measures* in the *Essentials* chapter.)

Health and Safety

London is a generally safe city, and the problems listed here are rare occurrences. This does not mean you should be unaware of your surroundings, however. As with any big city (or small town), London has its share of unseemly citizens.

EMERGENCY NUMBERS

To call the police, ambulance, or fire brigade, just dial 999 on any phone. The European standard number, 112, also works. The anonymous crime reporting hotline Crimestoppers allows callers to report crimes without fear of reprisal. It can be reached at 080/0555-111.

ALCOHOL AND DRUGS

Drinking is a big part of life here and it's easy to overindulge. Be aware that British beer is stronger than most American and Canadian brands and can sneak up on you. The mixed drinks can add up too. While a night on the town is lots of fun (and very English), use some common sense and know your limits. Illegal drugs, especially cannabis and ecstasy, are big in the club scene. Remember that these substances are *illegal,* despite the talk of decriminalization of cannabis. Those caught carrying or buying any illegal substances can get in serious legal trouble, and there are undercover agents are on the street.

CRIME

By far the most common crime tourists encounter is getting their pockets picked. Tourists are a magnet for pickpockets, since they're almost certainly carrying cash and credit cards. Pickpockets tend to congregate on busy train lines, where getting jostled by a stranger seems normal, and at tourist sights. Portobello Market is an especially bad area.

Pickpockets don't just go for wallets; they

The Metropolitan Police, dubbed "The Met," are a common sight in tourist areas.

also rummage around your day pack. Many tourists wear their day packs on the front to prevent this, but it doesn't help much; all it does is advertise that there's something in there worth stealing. The best thing to do is not carry anything valuable in your day pack. If you must put something important in there (such as a camera), shove it to the bottom under your spare clothes and snacks. At the worst, the crook gets away with a packet of Walkers Crisps and an old sweatshirt.

The best way to avoid getting your pocket picked is to have your wallet in your front pocket where it's harder for criminals to get at it. Purses should have both a clasp and a zipper, and you should hold them under the arm. Money belts, worn either under the shirt or on the waist (and always inside clothing) are a good place to store your passport and credit cards. In pubs and cafés, loop your bag around your chair leg so no one can grab it and run.

Be especially careful around pub closing time (11 P.M. Mon.–Sat., 10:30 P.M. Sun. for most establishments, although this is now changing with more liberal licensing laws). This is when you get to see the British at their worst. All the drinking establishments belch forth their besotted multitudes at the same time, filling the streets with raucous crowds that will occasionally pick fights or harass women. Ignore them and get away as quickly as possible. Days when there's a football match are especially bad. British hoodlums take their football seriously, and this is a good time to be an outsider.

With more and more pubs staying open late, and with nightclubs closing in the wee hours of the morning or at dawn, there can be a lot of rough characters anytime late at night. Try to walk in a group of people and avoid any altercations. If someone tries to goad you into a fight, ignoring the person and walking away (while watching your back) is usually the safest option.

Another worry is unlicensed taxi cabs. These tend to prowl around at night, especially at pub closing time. Avoid these cabs! There have been many criminal complaints varying from overcharging to outright theft and sexual assault. Do not get in a cab if it doesn't have a white license clearly showing.

There is also the occasional dishonest merchant. This is rare (although high prices aren't) but be aware. The official London Trading Standards Association is dedicated to making sure tourists and Londoners get a fair shake at the shops. Go to its website at www.lotsa.org.uk for some good advice. You can also download its helpful tourist information leaflet, "Making the Most of London." Consumer Direct is a group supported by the Department of Trade and Industry that gives advice on buyers' rights and the latest scams. Its website www.consumerdirect.gov.uk contains information mostly directed at residents, but it's worth a look. You can call the group at 084/5404-0506.

SCAMS

As with all areas with high tourist traffic, there are those who like to soak the tourists. The London Trading Standards Association warns of several scams.

Make sure taxi drivers start the meter when you get in. For any sort of tour, agree on a price beforehand. Also be aware while shopping. Street vendors may be selling fake, stolen, or faulty goods, just like back home. You will also see people on the street with huge placards advertising auctions, clearance, or liquidation sales. Usually you end up paying more than you bargained for and getting lousy merchandise in return.

Be especially wary of the auctions. There's a good chance they are setups and the only real customer is you. You may also be approached by charity workers on the street asking for donations. Most are legit, including the homeless people selling the *Big Issue* magazine. They should be wearing an ID tag and will be happy to provide contact information for their charity.

TERRORISM AND SECURITY

Terrorism is also an issue, especially after the July 7th, 2005, attacks on the subway and bus system. There have also been a few bombs by an IRA splinter group called the Real IRA in

AFTER THE ATTACKS: CONCERNS ABOUT SECURITY

During the morning rush hour of July 7th, 2005, a series of coordinated bomb blasts rocked London's public-transport system. At around 8:50 A.M., three bombs went off on different trains within a minute of each other. The first exploded in a train 100 yards from Liverpool Street Station. Another bomb ripped apart a train between Russell Square and King's Cross stations. More people died as a third bomb exploded on a train at Edgware Road Station. The fourth and final bomb exploded at 9:47 A.M. on the number 30 bus at Tavistock Square. The terrorist attacks left 52 dead and more than 700 wounded.

On July 31, there was another coordinated attack on London's bus and train system, but this time the bombs failed to work and nobody was killed.

The attacks were a major shock to the city. The threat of terrorism, here and everywhere, is a very legitimate concern, but you might consider taking a lesson from the Londoners themselves. There were no outbreaks of violence against the Muslim communities (several Muslims died in the attacks, just like at the World Trade Center), no mass panic, and no despair. Right after the July 7 bombings, the British Muslim Forum issued a fatwa (religious decree) forbidding suicide attacks and terrorism, saying they were against the teachings of Islam. The fatwa was read out in mosques across the country. Within days the number of commuters using the tube and buses was back at preattack levels. Londoners mourned, they were angry, they called for investigations, but they continued to live their lives.

This is because, in the end, there's not much you personally can do about terrorism. The best form of resistance is to not live your life in fear. That denies terrorists the only influence they have. One of the goals of the four suicide bombers was to disrupt the city's vital tourism industry. Don't let them. Don't let them affect your vacation. Don't let them affect any part of your life. It won't make them go away, but it will make them powerless.

recent years, as well as attacks by a solitary person against immigrants and homosexuals. While there really isn't any way to avoid terrorism, please be aware that London has tighter security than what most Americans and Canadians are used to. If you are driving into London or using the Tube, there's a chance you will have your bags searched. Some public buildings, and most government buildings, search *all* bags and make you go through a metal detector. Be cooperative and don't make jokes about there being a bomb in your bag. Security guards are not paid to have a sense of humor.

Since bombs are usually left in unattended bags, never, ever leave your bag unattended. If you see an unattended bag, don't touch it and go to the nearest official and report it. Don't be embarrassed; you won't get in trouble if it turns out to be nothing. It's better to be safe than sorry and you will be thanked for your vigilance. While airline security no longer allows bags to be locked, you can always pack a lock and use it once you are in the country.

ILLNESS

The visitor to London has few health worries. The tap water is drinkable, the food is sanitary except for the occasional dodgy fast-food stand, and the only thing you are likely to catch is a cold. No vaccinations are needed to visit the United Kingdom. The change in diet, along with tucking in large amounts of British food and beer, might create a few gastrointestinal problems, but simple over-the-counter medication will take care of that.

For emergency dental services, call the **Dental Emergency Care Service**

(020/7955-2186, 8:45 A.M.–3:30 P.M. Mon.–Fri.) There's also **Eastman Dental Hospital** (256 Gray's Inn Rd. WC1, 020/7915-1000, Tube: King's Cross).

One health issue to be aware of is sexually transmitted diseases, or STDs (here called STIs, or sexually transmitted infections), which have risen at an alarming rate in recent years. London clinics are having trouble dealing with the overload, while most people pretend the problem doesn't exist. Remember to exercise caution and engage in safe-sex practices as you would at home. Condoms are readily available in pharmacies and bathrooms.

For those under 25, the **Brook Centres** (080/0081-5023, www.brook.org.uk) offers free counseling, fact sheets, and condoms.

Hospitals

For minor health problems the pharmacies (called "chemists" here) can provide anything you need. The most common chain is **Boots.** All neighborhoods have at least one chemist open around the clock, and the hours for each should be clearly displayed on the front door. For more information on the National Health Service, check out its website at www.nhsdirect.nhs.uk.

If you have something serious enough that requires going to the hospital, here is a list of those with 24-hour emergency rooms. The hotel concierge, a policeman, or a taxi driver should know the closest one.

Charing Cross Hospital
Fulham Palace Rd. W6
020/8846-1234
Tube: Hammersmith

Chelsea and Westminster Hospital
369 Fulham Rd. SW10
020/8746-8000
Tube: South Kensington, then take bus No. 14 or 211

Guy's Hospital
St. Thomas St. SE1
020/7955-5000
Tube: London Bridge

Homerton Hospital
Homerton Row E9
020/8919-5555
British Rail: Homerton

Royal Free Hospital
Pond St. NW3
020/7794-0500
Tube: Belsize Park

Royal London Hospital
Whitechapel Rd. E1
020/7377-7000
Tube: Whitechapel

University College Hospital
Grafton Way WC1
020/7387-9300
Tube: Euston Square

INSURANCE

Travel insurance is always a good idea. Check with your health-insurance company to see if you are covered when you are out of the country. Citizens of European Union countries and people with work visas are covered by National Health Service, but make sure you have done the appropriate paperwork. Call NHS (0845-4647) for details.

EMOTIONAL SUPPORT

For those feeling depressed or suicidal, the Samaritans operate a 24-hour hotline to provide you a confidential, understanding, and helpful listener. They can be reached at 084/5790-9090 and online at www.samaritans.org. Check out the website for information on the more than 200 branches around the United Kingdom that offer face-to-face counseling, including several in London.

Money

CURRENCY

The United Kingdom uses pounds, the symbol for which is "£" One pound is divided into 100 pence. There are coins for 1, 2, 5, 10, 20, and 50 pence. Pounds come in coins of 1 and 2, and notes come in denominations of 5, 10, 50, and 100. When speaking, the British will often use "p" (PEE) for "pence," so "5 pounds, 20 p" means 5 pounds and 20 pence. Pounds are occasionally called "quid," but this slang term seems to be falling out of use, although it is not considered old-fashioned. Scottish pounds have the same value as British pounds and are legal tender in England. Most places take them without a fuss and they are all required to take them, despite grumpy signs to the contrary.

Major foreign currency such as dollars and euros are taken in some of the larger tourist sights and shops but usually at an unfavorable rate of exchange. Other places, such as The Orchard at Grantchester, proudly proclaim they take only pounds. The European Union and its currency, the euro, are quite sticky subjects with many British people, and much of their reluctance to merge more closely with the rest of Europe is based on their pride and confidence in the pound, so while they are part of the European Union, they haven't merged their currency with the euro. Since exchange counters abound in London, there is no need to try and foist off foreign currency where it isn't welcome.

CURRENCY EXCHANGE

Changing money is no problem in London. All banks can handle foreign currency, and in the tourist-heavy areas there are plenty of exchange counters. Banks offer a slightly better rate of exchange than money changers, but there will often be a longer line. It's best to look around a bit, asking how much money you will get for your dollars or euros after the exchange and commission. You can also change money at the airport or at some international airports back home, such as in Toronto or New York. For current exchange rates, go to www.x-rates.com. Type this URL carefully.

CREDIT CARDS AND ATMS

Credit cards are accepted in most shops and tourist locations. Hotels and rental agencies, of course, take most any type of plastic you may have, with MasterCard and Visa being more widely accepted than Diner's Club or American Express. You can also make cash advances at banks. The banks don't charge for this service, but they usually take only one type of card. HSBC takes MasterCard and Barclay's and Lloyds TSB take Visa. Debit cards are also widely accepted. Check your policy for your credit or debit card, as some providers charge a "foreign transaction fee." British credit cards are changing over to a chip system, making the older cards unreadable on the new machines. Mention that you have a foreign credit card and the clerk can type in the number manually or use one of the older machines.

ATM cards are handy to have. There are plenty of ATM machines (often called "cash points" here) in London, taking the major systems such as Cirrus, Star, Maestro, MasterCard, and Visa. Many businesses such as pubs will have one on the premises. While ATMs will give a good rate of exchange, they sometimes charge a fee, and your bank almost certainly will. ATMs at convenience stores and gas stations are more likely to charge a fee than those at banks, and all give you the option of backing out of the transaction before you're gouged. There are a couple of hitches with London ATMs. Most don't have alphanumeric pads, so if you memorized your PIN by letters you need to memorize the actual numbers before you go, and they accept numbers of up to only four digits, so if your PIN is more than four digits, change it before you go. Also, some banks don't allow you to withdraw from your savings account with foreign ATMs, so make sure you have plenty of money in your checking account. Before sticking your card into a machine, make sure at least one of the symbols on the ATM matches one of the symbols on the back of your card, or it can be eaten. Some ATMs aren't hooked up to any U.S. networks, so be careful. A quick trip to the bank manager will usually retrieve your card. An even stickier situation is if you type your PIN in wrong. Chances are the bank will consider it stolen and destroy it.

TRAVELER'S CHECKS AND MONEY TRANSFERS

Traveler's checks can be redeemed in all banks and exchange counters and in many hotels and shops. They also have the benefit of being replaceable if stolen. This is a safe way to carry money, but with ATMs so ubiquitous, there isn't much need for the old-fashioned traveler's check anymore.

Western Union is the quickest way to get a cash injection from home. It has several agents in central London and may be contacted at its U.K. offices at its toll-free, 24-hour number at 080/083-3833 or online at www.ukmoneytransfer.com. Also look for the familiar yellow sign at newsagents and chemists.

COSTS

The cost of a stay in London can vary widely depending on how much you eat out, how many sights you pay to go into, and what kind of accommodation and transport you choose. If you stay in a youth hostel dorm, cook all your own meals, walk everywhere, and go only to the free sights, you can squeak by on £25 a day, but if you're that cheap you should go to India, where your money will take you a lot further. A more reasonable budget is £75 a day, which will allow you to stay in a hotel, take the Tube, and eat out at cheap restaurants, but it doesn't allow for much shopping or many nights out on the town. At £100 or more a day life gets a lot more comfortable, and the sky is really the limit as far as how much you can spend beyond that. The best thing to do is look at the prices listed in this book and do the math yourself, and then add 50 percent because, after all, you're on vacation and you deserve to spend your hard-earned money.

TAXES

The British sales tax is called Value Added Tax (VAT) and comes out to 17.5 percent on everything except food, books, and kid's clothes. VAT is included in most prices, and restaurants are required to include it in their menu prices. It's possible to get this tax refunded, but certain conditions apply that make it almost more trouble than it's worth.

First, you must have spent less than a year out of the previous two years living in the United Kingdom before you make your purchase, and you must leave the European Union within three months afterward. Not all stores participate in the tax-return scheme (look for a sign saying Tax-Free Shopping or Retail Export Scheme) and those that do usually fix a minimum purchase level. If you satisfy all these criteria, ask for a VAT 407 form, fill it out, and present the purchase and the form to customs as you leave the country. Customs will then certify the form and you can send it back to the shop, which will then send you the refund, usually minus a service fee. As you can see, this whole process is really worth it only if you make some big purchases.

TIPPING

Tipping is not big here, but people will certainly appreciate a tip. In restaurants, a service charge is often automatically added to the bill, usually ranging 10–15 percent. If they don't add it, feel free to leave a similar amount for the waiter, although this isn't as necessary as it is in the United States or Canada. Taxi drivers do not generally expect a tip, but many riders round up to the nearest pound, as long as that comes out to at least 50 pence extra. Bartenders are not usually tipped, but they will gladly accept any spare coins you leave them. One nice thing you can do is to offer your bartender a drink. After you order ask, "And one for yourself?" and if he or she wants a drink the price of one will be added to your bill.

Doormen at swanky hotels also expect a tip, but they won't dump your luggage if you don't. Boat pilots will often ask for a tip if they give you running commentary while they take you around, but this is also not required.

In general, if the service makes you happy, you should return the favor. This is how these folks make their living, and staying chipper while dealing with their 43,518th tourist is a tough thing to do.

BARGAINING

In most cases you cannot haggle over prices. There are some exceptions to this rule, however, especially at markets. Whether you're buying antiques or cheap imports, if the sellers are on the street, they're more open to a bit of bargaining. Farmers markets usually aren't the place to haggle, but everyone haggles at the Brick Lane Flea Market or Portobello Antique Market. You can even haggle in antique stores, but it's best to know what you're buying beforehand or you'll be at a definite disadvantage.

DISCOUNTS

While London is expensive, there are plenty of ways to save a little. If you're a student, getting an International Student Identity Card from your university, Youth Hostel Association, or STA Travel will save you on admission charges and transport. Sometimes just a university ID from home will suffice. If you are studying in the United Kingdom or Europe, ask your institution how to get a local student card, which will be much more readily accepted.

There are also "concessions" at many sights, reserved for seniors, the unemployed, and those with disabilities. The amount you save and the actual criteria for gaining a concession changes from place to place, but it can't hurt to ask. Children get discounts too.

Another useful card is the **London Pass** (016/6448-5020, www.londonpass.com), which costs £12 or more a day and offers free entrance to more than 50 sights, including the major ones such as St. Paul's and the Tower of London. You also get to skip the line. This is very convenient, but you would have to be a busy tourist, going to at least one or two major charging sights a day, as opposed to the many free ones, to experience any real savings.

Maps and Tourist Information

London is always changing. There's a constantly renewing round of shows, exhibitions, and special events, and the quality of restaurants and hotels can fluctuate with time and changes in personnel. It's a good idea to drop into one of London's helpful tourist information centers early in your stay to pick up the latest information about what's on. You may want to get some specialized maps as well, especially if you have particular interests or plan to stay for a long time.

MAPS

The maps in this book will get you around London, but if you want a comprehensive atlas of the city there is no better source than the *London A-Z,* available in any souvenir shop, newsagent, or bookstore. Every London home seems to have one because it shows every street in the metropolitan area, with central neighborhoods given larger-scale maps. If you plan to go into outlying areas or will be settling down in London, this guide is essential.

A lot of other maps are available in London, but most aren't worth getting. The free maps offered by various bus tours generally lack detail and are hard to read. Maps are also for sale in vending machines in the Tube and at all the tourist sights, but once again they aren't as good as the maps in this book and the

London A-Z, so if you have one or both, you won't need anything else.

One exception to this are the specialized maps offered by the various tourist information centers. They show walking routes or tours of specific interest such as historic churches or literary landmarks. The majority of these are free and availability of particular titles can change, so ask at the nearest center to find out what they have to offer.

TOURIST INFORMATION

With tourism such a major part of the London economy, information on what to see and where to go is easy to come by. Some of the larger hotels and tour companies publish short guides to London, and everyone seems to have plenty of advice for the visitor. Keep a sharp lookout for brochures advertising shows, sights, and exhibitions. They can be found everywhere, from pubs to hotel lobbies, and can clue you in to special events or attractions you might not have heard of. The best sources for tourist information, however, are the official centers in various parts of the city. With up-to-date advice, trained staff, and plenty of free reading material, they can answer any question you may have. The centers are listed here, including a couple of local centers that concentrate on their boroughs but also have a fair amount of information on London in general.

The biggest and the best is **Britain and London Visitor Centre** (1 Lower Regent St. SW1, 087/0156-6366, www.visitbritain.org, 9:30 A.M.–6:30 P.M. Mon., 9 A.M.–6:30 P.M. Tues.–Fri., 10 A.M.–4 P.M. Sat.–Sun. 9 A.M.–5 P.M. Saturdays June–Sept., Tube: Piccadilly Circus). This center covers the whole of the United Kingdom as well as London and can handle bookings for flights, train rides, theater tickets, and it has a money changing counter too.

Conveniently located and expertly staffed, **City Information Centre** (St. Paul's Churchyard EC4, 020/7332-1456, www.cityoflondon.gov.uk, 9:30 A.M.–5 P.M. daily Apr.–Sept., 9:30 A.M.–5 P.M. Mon.–Fri., 9:30 A.M.–12:30 P.M. Sat. Oct.–Mar., Tube: St. Paul's) is run by the Corporation of London but stocks free information on all of London, and a fair amount beyond. It carries an especially good series of free walking guides.

Within sight of the *Cutty Sark,* it's hard to miss **Greenwich Tourist Information Centre** (2 Cutty Sark Gardens SE10, 087/0608-2000, www.greenwich.gov.uk, 10 A.M.–5 P.M. daily, Docklands Light Rail: Cutty Sark), with its detailed information and good free maps of Greenwich, as well as some information on London and England in general.

If you aren't too frazzled by your transatlantic journey, stop at **Heathrow Airport Tourist Information Centre** (Terminals 1, 2, and 3, 090/6866-3344, Tube: Heathrow Terminals 1, 2, and 3) for a quick primer on the attractions of London. It isn't supercomplete, but it can certainly get you started.

You can't beat the hours and convenience of **London Information Centre** (Leicester Sq., 020/7292-2333, www.londoninformation.org, 8 A.M.–midnight daily, Tube: Leicester Square). The staff here is very knowledgeable about London's sights, restaurants, and hotels. Because of its location, it's one of the busiest of the information centers, so expect to wait in line.

Attached to the popular bar Vinopolis, **Southwark Tourist Information Centre** (Vinopolis, 1 Bank End SE1, 020/7357-9168, www.visitsouthwark.com, open 10 A.M.–6 P.M. Tues.–Sun., Tube: London Bridge) concentrates on sights and events in Southwark, but it carries lots of information on the rest of London and England in general.

Waterloo Tourist Information Centre (Arrivals Hall, Waterloo International Terminal SE1, 020/7620-1550, www.londontouristboard.com, 8:30 A.M.–10 P.M. daily, Tube: Waterloo) is a perfect first stop if you enter London via this famous train station. While it isn't as comprehensive as the centers in Regent Street or Leicester Square, it's still a convenient and informative place and can get you headed in the right direction.

FILM AND PHOTOGRAPHY

The United States and Canada use the NTSC system for television, while the United Kingdom uses the PAL system. This means that videos and DVDs you buy in London may not play on your system at home. In addition, for DVDs, North America is in Region Code 1, while the United Kingdom is in Region Code 2. This can also block your use of DVDs, including computer DVDs, although most systems have a way of circumventing this and it's not illegal to do so. Most tourist shops sell in all formats to please their international clientele, but make sure you get the right one.

Quality film is available everywhere, and memory cards for your digital camera are easily found in any electronics shop, especially on Tottenham Court Road. The tourist kiosks tend to be overpriced, so try either a photo shop or Boots, a popular chemist (drugstore), or bring extra film and memory from home. The best film speeds for London's frequently overcast weather are ISO 200 or 400. Prices for just about everything are higher in England than in North America, so bringing what you need from home will save you time and money.

Some attractions have limitations on photography or don't allow flash. This is especially true with museums, as repeated flashes can fade the colors of priceless artwork. It's always best to ask before you click. Since video cameras don't flash, they are usually allowed, but once again it's best to check.

Of course, if you want a perfect image of something in the museum, you can usually get a postcard at the gift shop. These are taken by professional photographers under ideal conditions, so they always look just right. If you want to take a painting home with you, many museum gift shops offer full-size, high-resolution scans that look almost like the real thing.

Communications and Media

London is the media heart of England. Virtually all major newspapers, magazines, publishing houses, radio, and television stations are based here, so you will find an amazing variety of printed material and plenty on the boob tube and radio. The best sources for printed matter are the ubiquitous newsagents, which sell papers, magazines, and often snacks and alcohol. London is also the nexus of the British postal system, so your postcards will be on a plane headed for New York or Toronto in no time.

POSTAL SERVICES

Royal Mail (084/5722-3344, www.royalmail.com) handles the United Kingdom's postal service, and it is generally efficient and easy to deal with. There are post offices in most major tourist areas, easily spotted by their bright-red signs, and you'll find many more scattered about all neighborhoods, often attached to corner stores.

First-class domestic mail costs 32 pence or more if it's heavier than 20 grams, while a first-class letter to North America costs from 44 pence. Letters and postcards take around 3–5 days to get to North America, and they usually get to other locations in the United Kingdom by the next day. It also handles packages, with prices varying depending on weight and several levels of priority. If you are sending only paper materials, ask for a special book rate that will save you a considerable amount.

There's a poste restante service at the Trafalgar Square post office (24–28 William IV St. WC2, Tube: Charing Cross). The sender must put the receiver's name on it and "Poste Restante." The receiver must bring ID to pick it up. If you are outside London, you can have the letter addressed to "Poste Restante, TOWN NAME" and call Customer Services at 084/5722-3344 to find out which post office it will go to.

TELEPHONE, FAX, AND INTERNET

Using the phone in a foreign country can be a pain, but luckily all phone boxes come with clear instructions. Different cities have different area codes, with London's being 020. Other numbers come with various prefixes instead of an area code. 0500 or 0800 means it's toll-free, 0845 means that local call rates apply, even if you're calling long distance within the country, 0870 means that national call rates apply even if you're calling locally, and 09 is the most expensive, meaning that premium call rates apply (upward of 60 pence a minute).

To call within London, simply call the eight-digit number without the 020 area code. To call elsewhere in the United Kingdom, dial the area code and then the number. To call internationally, dial 00, then the country code, and then the phone number. To call the United Kingdom from abroad, you must dial your country's international access code, then the United Kingdom's country code of 44, then the area code (dropping the initial 0; therefore London is 20) and then the number. To call back home, dial the international access code 00, the country code, the area code, and the number.

For saving money on international calls, there is a bewildering array of international cards available at newsagents. The folks behind the counter will have information on all of them and can point you to the best one for your particular country. Note that you get more time if you call from a private phone than a public phone.

IMPORTANT TELEPHONE NUMBERS AND WEBSITES

Here are some important telephone numbers and websites you might need during your stay. Hotel reception and shops will have phone books in case you need something else, and www.yell.com has an online phone book.

Alcoholics Anonymous: 020/7833-0022
Black Cab Lost Property: 020/7918-2000
Collect Calls: 155
Directory Assistance: 118 118 or 118 500
Emergency Services (police, fire, ambulance): 999 or 112
International Directory Assistance: 153
International Operator: 155
Legal Services Commission: 020/7759-0000
Local and National Directory Assistance: 192
Local and National Operator: 100
National Health Service Direct: 020/7538-4449 or www.nhsdirect.nhs.uk
Rape Crisis Federation: 011/5900-3560 or 020/7837-1600
Relate (relationship issues): 084/5130-4016
Time: 123
Transport for London's Lost Property Office: 020/7486-2496

Heathrow Airport General Information: 087/0000-0123 or www.heathrowairport.com
Gatwick Airport General Information: 087/0000-2468 or www.gatwickairport.com
Stansted Airport General Information: 087/0000-0303 or www.stanstedairport.com
Luton Airport General Information: 015/8240-5100 or www.london-luton.co.uk
London City Airport General Information: 020/7646-0000 or www.londoncityairport.com

classic London phone booths

Copy shops and the larger hotels offer fax services at varying rates, with the copy shops generally cheaper. Many local libraries and some newsagents also offer fax services at cheap rates.

Internet Access

Most large hotels and youth hostels offer Internet access, but you'll find cheaper access in the innumerable Internet cafés. If you are near any sort of major attraction or main street you will have little trouble finding one. There are clusters of them along Charing Cross Road. Prices are usually about £1 an hour, but in outlying areas they can go as low as 50 pence an hour.

NEWSPAPERS

London is the home to a dazzling array of daily newspapers, their subject matter varying from financial analysis to the latest sex scandals. There are two main types of papers: the serious papers and the tabloids. Most papers have an extra-large edition on Saturdays (not Sundays as in North America), which contains various inserts such as a magazine and special sections on fashion, TV, or the arts.

Among the serious papers, one of the most popular is *The Guardian* (www.guardian.co.uk). Firmly left of center, its editorials eviscerate Labour and Conservative politicians alike, and it saves an especially acidic pen for a certain Republican president. The paper features extensive and in-depth national and international reporting, and a chunky Saturday edition with an excellent book review. *The Times* (www.timesonline.co.uk) is more conservative, while *The Daily Telegraph* (www.telegraph.co.uk) and *The Independent* (www.independent.co.uk) are more middle of the road. For economic news, the best source is the *Financial Times* (www.ft.com), which also covers national and international news.

And then there are the tabloids, noticeable for their big headlines and short words. They're perfect for finding out who is sleeping

London is home to a dazzling array of daily newspapers.

RADIO

The British Broadcasting Corporation, which started out as a group of radio pioneers in 1922, is a government-owned but surprisingly independent media outlet, and it has several stations offering every type of programming imaginable. London has a good selection of other stations as well. Here are some of the more popular:

BBC Radio 1 (98.8 FM), contemporary music
BBC Radio 2 (89.1 FM), oldies
BBC Radio 3 (91.3 FM), classical and drama
BBC Radio 4 (93.2 FM), news, drama, and talk
BBC London Live (94.9 FM), talk about London
Capital FM (95.8 FM), contemporary music
Choice FM (96.9 FM), soul
Classic FM (100.9 FM), classical
Jazz FM (102.2 FM), blues and jazz
Kiss 100 (100 FM), dance
News Direct (97.3 FM), news
Virgin (105.8 FM), contemporary music and news
Xfm (104.9 FM), independent/alternative
BBC Radio 5 (909 AM), sports and news
BBC World Service (648 AM, also several frequencies on shortwave), news and variety
Capital Gold (1548 AM), oldies

with and/or murdering who, and there's often a racy picture on that British institution, Page Three. While it's easy to give tabloids a derisive snort, they sometimes publish important investigative pieces, and the fact that they don't mind paying for information means whistle-blowers will often go to them first. *The Mirror* (www.mirror.co.uk), for example, once planted a fake bomb on a train transporting nuclear waste, and the *News of the World* (www.newsoftheworld.co.uk) photographed two convicted pedophiles filming children in a park. Another popular tabloid is *The Sun* (www.thesun.co.uk), while the *Daily Mail* (www.dailymail.co.uk) straddles the line between conservative paper and tabloid, giving a good insight to what a lot of fat white blokes think. A more cosmopolitan mix of news and tabloid sensationalism is the *Evening Standard* (www.thisislondon.co.uk), which focuses on London, especially the woes of its public-transport system and the mindless pretensions of its art scene.

As it's such a diverse city, there is a wealth of papers serving minority communities. For Jewish news, check out the weekly newspaper *The Jewish Chronicle* (www.thejc.com). For news from the Muslim world, there are several choices. The Arabic dailies are *Al Hayat* (www.daralhayat.com) and *Al Quds Al Arabi* (www.alquds.co.uk). There's also a Persian weekly called *Kayhan London* (www.kayhanlondon.com).

The better newsagents stock a wide variety of papers from across the United Kingdom and beyond. For extensive global news with a focus on the United States, check out the *International Herald Tribune* (www.iht.com), a Paris-based paper run by The New York Times Company. Papers from all other major countries, and many smaller ones, are easily available.

TELEVISION

The BBC was also a pioneering force behind television, having the first experimental station in the world in 1929, broadcasting sporadically to a tiny audience. World War II put a stop to television on both sides of the Atlantic for a time, and in the post-War reconstruction the United States leapt way ahead. The BBC didn't dawdle for long, however, and resumed regular broadcasts in 1946, a year after the end of hostilities and while much of London still lay in ruins.

There are now two stations, BBC1 and BBC2, which like the radio stations do not have commercials. There are also three independent, commercial stations, and cable or satellite can bring in much more. Newspapers carry listings of what's on, and you can also look on www.tvtv.co.uk.

BBC1 is the more popular of the two BBC TV stations, and it carries a range of movies and entertainment, especially reality TV, but also documentaries and news.

BBC2 is a bit more serious, with more of an emphasis on documentaries and news.

ITV is an independent channel carrying a full range of programming, from news to inane reality shows.

Channel Four is another independent channel and the most popular of them all. More entertainment-based, this station nevertheless has a respected news show and some excellent documentaries. After 10 P.M. it gets a little risque with "documentaries" of a different sort, such as interviews with swingers and fetishists in the name of sociology, but parents might want to change over to yet another World War II epic on BBC.

Channel 5's independent programming showcases a rather predictable blend of movies, entertainment, and news.

Weights and Measures

TIME ZONES

London and the rest of England are on Greenwich Mean Time (GMT), also known as Universal Time Coordinated (UTC). Late May–late October England is on British summer time, which is like the U.S. daylight saving time, and is one hour ahead of GMT. The world's time zones are all based on distances away from Greenwich. If you are coming from another European country, remember that England is one hour earlier than Western and Central Europe. As you land in London from North America, the pilot will announce the local time, which is usually eight hours ahead of the West Coast (Vancouver, L.A., etc.) and five hours ahead of the East Coast (Toronto, New York, etc.).

ELECTRICITY

England uses 240V AC, 50Hz. You will need an adapter if you want to bring any electric appliances. Look for one that converts from North American 120V with its two or three prongs, to the British 240V with three rectangular prongs. Converters are available both at home and in England. If you forget one, overpriced adapters are available in the airport and tourist shops, and cheaper ones in electronic stores, especially on Tottenham Court Road. Continental Europe uses 240V, but with two round prongs, so you'll need a different adapter.

MEASUREMENTS

The United Kingdom is stuck halfway between the metric system, invented by the French, and the old Imperial system, invented by the English but now used exclusively only by the United States. Most measures are shown in metric, but street signs show distances in miles, or both miles and kilometers. Measures for weight are often given in both, or just metric, but I've had butchers who didn't understand my order when I gave it in kilos. Beer is still measured in pints and half pints. Note that the glorious British pint is 0.568261 of a liter, while the U.S. pint is 0.473176 of a liter.

To complicate matters further, the weight of people and animals is often given in stone. A stone weighs 14 pounds and is always used in the singular. "I weigh 14 stone." In the old days, how much a stone weighed depended on the goods, so 10 stone of beef weighed differently from 10 stone of broccoli. But this unnecessarily complex system, like the old monetary system, is now a thing of the past, except for the term stone. Areas of land are given in hectares or acres, but usually not "square kilometers" unless discussing a large area.

RESOURCES

Glossary

The King's English, having had more than two centuries of separate development from Canadian and American English, has come up with some very different words and phrases that might not be familiar to the visitor. Below is a list, by no means complete, of some of the more common Englishisms that might trip you up.

abv alcohol by volume, displayed for all alcoholic beverages by law (look on the tap to see it for the beers at pubs)

Afro-Caribbean a common term for black people ("Black" is also used)

anorak a person obsessed with some obscure topic, so named because of the unstylish jacket train spotters and other such people wear (not to be confused with hoodie)

backbencher A minister of Parliament who is not prominent in his or her party, and tends to sit on the back benches, not participating in many debates; backbenchers occasionally rebel, however.

banger sausage ("Bangers and mash" are sausage and mashed potatoes)

bank holiday A national holiday, so called because even the banks close. Many tourist sights, and most pubs and restaurants, remain open on bank holidays.

bendie a long, single-story bus that bends in the middle

bespoke custom made. Many shops, especially tailors and jewelers, offer "bespoke service."

biscuit cookie

black economy work done on a cash basis to avoid paying taxes, also called "black money"

bloody A general explicative, but considered more low class than obscene. It generally translates to "very," as in "Bloody good show, that!" or used to increase the force of another word, as in "Bloody hell!"

BNP the British National Party, a conservative, anti-immigration party considered by many to be racist

bob a shilling (5p)

bobby a policeman

bonnet the hood of a car

boot the trunk of a car

bridle path a public country path for riders, cyclists, and hikers (also called a "bridle way")

chemist pharmacy or pharmacist

chav a lower-class white person who tries to dress like a black person

chips French Fries (there are no Freedom Fries in England)

The City the City of London; a neighborhood that was once Roman Londinium and still the economic center of the city (lower case) of London

coach a bus

cockney A resident of the East End of London. Also refers to that area's distinctive dialect.

copper a policeman

council housing Government subsidized, low-income housing. Also called "council estates" or "council flats."

crisps potato chips

cuppa a cup of tea

dead "very," as in the traffic sign "Dead Slow"

or the rather unappealing compliment "dead sexy"

dear expensive

DIY "Do It Yourself," usually referring to home repairs and improvement

Downing Street Term used to refer to the Prime Minister and his policies, in reference to his residence at 10 Downing Street. Also referred to as "Number 10."

fag a cigarette

first floor the floor above the ground floor, called the second floor in North America

fiver a £5 note

flat apartment

football soccer

fry up An English breakfast, which includes sausage, eggs, bacon, beans on toast, and often mushrooms or tomatoes. Greasy and wonderful!

give way yield

Great Britain the island made up of England, Scotland, and Wales (often shortened to "Britain")

half either a half pint, as in "give me a half, luvvie," or half past the hour, as in "half ten" (10:30)

to hire to rent

hoodie A sweatshirt with a hood, but also refers to the hooligans who often wear them (see *yob*). Not all people who wear hoodies are yobs, and not all yobs wear hoodies, but many make a strong correlation.

ironmonger a hardware store

Labour the Labour Party, the more liberal of the two major parties and as of this writing the governing party of England, with Tony Blair as Prime Minister

to let to rent, as in "a flat to let"

Lib Dem the Liberal Democratic Party, often called the Liberal Democrats, the third largest political party in England

license A license to sell alcohol. "Fully licensed" means the establishment can sell beer and hard liquor. "Late license" refers to an establishment that can serve alcohol after the traditional 11 P.M. closing time. "Off license" means a shop can sell alcohol but not serve it on the premises. Many convenience stores advertise they are "off license."

listed building A building of recognized historical or architectural value recognized by the Department of Culture, Media, and Sport. Grade I buildings are the rarest and are of exceptional interest. Grade II* designates buildings of more than special interest, while Grade II buildings are of special interest. There are about 370,000 listed buildings in the U.K. and there are limitations on how much they can be altered. A hotel in a "listed" building provides atmosphere, but may lack certain modern amenities such as disabled access.

loo the toilet

lorry a truck

The Met Metropolitan Police Authority

MP Minister of Parliament

mobile a cell phone

naff unstylish, lame

nanny babysitter

p pence, pronounced "pee"

peculiar An institution, usually a church, not run by the usual governing body. For example, St. Mary-le-Bow is a peculiar because it is under the jurisdiction of the Archbishop of Canterbury, rather than the Bishop of London. A royal peculiar is under the rule of the sovereign.

pissed drunk. The term "pissed off" can be used for being angry, but saying "I'm pissed" means you're drunk. One can also be "on the piss," which means you're drinking. "Taking the piss" means making fun of something or someone.

prat a fool

public convenience a public toilet

pudding dessert

punter gambler

quid a pound (of currency)

queue a line (to wait for something)

return round-trip (ticket, voyage, etc.)

roundabout traffic circle

rucksack backpack

sarnie sandwich

single one-way (ticket, voyage, etc.)

solicitor a lawyer

spliff a cannabis cigarette (illegal)

steady on! "hold up!" Used to stop someone from doing or saying something objectionable, often shortened to "steady!"

stone 14 pounds of weight. This old term is now used almost exclusively for weighing people and animals. It used to be that how much a "stone" weighed depended on the type of goods being measured, but virtually all measurements are now done in Imperial or metric. The term is always singular: "I weigh 12 stone."

subway pedestrian underpass

ta "thank you"

to take the piss to fool, lead on

tenner a £10 note

torch a flashlight

Tory a member of the Conservative Party, plural Tories

trainers sneakers

Tube the London Underground subway system

Union Jack the flag of the United Kingdom

United Kingdom the nation comprised of England, Northern Ireland, Scotland, and Wales, often shortened to U.K.

VAT Value Added Tax

Whitehall the national government, in reference to the government buildings at Whitehall

Yank A person from the United States. It can be used in a derogatory manner, but not always. Pay attention to the tone of voice, context, links with the word "bloody," and any objects being brandished in one's direction.

yob A violent, brutish, and usually drunken thug or bully often associated with football matches or cheap pubs. (See *hoodie.*)

zed the letter "Z"

Suggested Reading

As one of the great cities of the world, London has produced a wealth of literature. This section gives you a sampling of some of the best books about London. Included are novels set in the city that give some of its flavor from the earliest times to the present day, and nonfiction works that will help you understand the city better.

CULTURE

Ahmed, Iqbal. *Sorrows of the Moon: A Journey through London.* Coldstream. A moving voyage of discovery through the world of immigrants in London written by a Kashmiri who moved here in 1994. Ahmed reflects on his own experiences while interviewing sweatshop workers, nurses, doormen, and kiosk owners to paint a picture of London most visitors, indeed most British people, never get to understand. Sobering and enlightening.

Fox, Kate. *Watching the English: The Hidden Rules of English Behavior.* Hodder & Stoughton. An English cultural anthropologist studies her own people with insightful and often hilarious results. This is a very informative book to read before you go, as it will tell you all about the unspoken code of conduct that controls English society. As with any cultural theory, it is best not to take it too literally, however. People come in all varieties and the English are no exception. Still, this is a useful book and, rarely for the social sciences, very well written.

FICTION

Ackroyd, Peter. *The House of Doctor Dee.* A moody, atmospheric novel set both in the present day and in the Elizabethan period. A young man inherits a house once owned by the famous court mystic Doctor John Dee. Past and present begin to merge as the reader is taken from contemporary London to a time of dark superstition.

Ali, Monica. *Brick Lane.* Scribner. This enchanting debut novel traces the struggles of a Bengali woman trying to adjust to life in London and an arranged marriage. Sensitively and beautifully written, it shows a life most visitors to the city will never witness.

This novel launched Ali into instant fame and gave her the much-deserved reputation as one of Britain's best young novelists. Am I jealous? Oh, yes.

Dickens, Charles. While many of Dickins' novels take place in London, two are especially good at evoking the atmosphere and culture of his time. *Barnaby Rudge* is an overlooked classic set in the late 18th century during the Gordon riots, anti-Catholic and anti-Parliament riots that saw the burning of Newgate Prison. This book gives a look into the life of common people in the not-so-good old days. Dickens can transport the reader back in time with his descriptions of "long lines of poorly lighted streets... tall steeples looming in the air, and piles of unequal roofs oppressed by chimneys." *Sketches by Boz* is an early work of short sketches of people and places, from society drawing rooms to the horrors of debtor's prison. While it doesn't have the polish of some of his more famous books, it offers an insightful and often hilarious look at London life.

Doyle, Sir Arthur Conan. *Sherlock Holmes.* Most of the Sherlock Holmes mysteries take place in London, and the foggy streets and dirty dealings of the city in its heyday is admirably brought out in Doyle's prose. Seeing the city through Holmes's eyes is an interesting experience, as he is obsessed with the smallest detail. At times you'll think you're looking at a photograph rather than reading a story. An additional treat for Holmes fans is the fact that you can visit his "home" at Baker Street.

Waugh, Evelyn. *Brideshead Revisited.* Possibly the most nostalgic book in the English language, Waugh's masterpiece chronicles the decline of a noble family in the period between the two world wars. While this is not really a London novel, only a few scenes take place there, it's a wonderfully written study of a period in British history that saw great changes in all levels of society. The scenes of Oxford university life are interesting for those who plan to visit.

GENERAL INFORMATION

Geographer's A-Z Map Company. *London A-Z.* Distributed by Hunter Publishing. There is no way to compete with this authoritative tome. It covers all the streets in all the neighborhoods in London. If you are going to explore London beyond the confines of our book, you will want to have it on hand. Don't worry about buying it at home because it's for sale all over London. Even Londoners need this book to get around the winding streets of their city. An index to all streets, as well as Tube stations and sights of interest, make this a must-have for the serious walker.

Hampshire, David. *Living & Working in Britain: A Survival Handbook.* 4th edition. Survival Books, Ltd., 2004. The title pretty much says it all. If you are thinking of staying a while, this is a must-have source of information of all you need to know to live, work, and play in Britain. There are extensive and detailed sections on everything from getting a job to getting auto insurance. Make sure to get the fourth edition, as it has been extensively updated and expanded since the third edition.

Kamins, Toni. *The Complete Jewish Guide to Britain and Ireland.* St. Martin's Griffin, 2001. A concise and readable guide to Jewish heritage and resources in the British Isles. This book is especially strong in detailing history and kosher resources, and has a lengthy London section. It was published in 2001, however, so its listings are a bit out of date.

HISTORY

Ackroyd, Peter. *London: The Biography.* Anchor, 2003. This book is not a straight chronological history, but rather a meditation on London as a city and a symbol by one of England's greatest living writers. There is a great deal of history here, but names and dates take a back seat to the fate of criminals, the smells of Elizabethan streets, and the pomp of the Guildhall. Ackroyd makes the city come alive, as we walk beside him through the construction site of St. Paul's and the wards of Bedlam. At times effusive, his writing is as chaotic and eclectic as the city itself. If you love the city, you will love this book, and vice versa.

Glinert, Ed. *The London Compendium: A Street-by-Street Exploration of the Hidden Metropolis.* Gardeners Books, 2004. If you are going to buy any two books on London, buy the one in your hands and Glinert's captivating compendium of facts and anecdotes. Thumbing through this book is like taking another trip. It's great for planning a theme-based tour, such as a walk that includes sights of literary or political interest, or you can simply open it up while sitting on a bench and learn about the street and buildings around you.

Inwood, Stephen. *A History of London.* New York, NY: Carroll and Graf Publishers, 2000. Probably the most comprehensive single-volume work on the city ever written, this tome is 1136 pages long and packed with rich detail. Inwood writes a straight chronology with a great deal of information on social history. The prose can be a bit dry at times and getting through it all takes a lot of dedication, but it's sure to make you an expert.

Pepys, Samuel. *The Diary of Samuel Pepys.* Available in various editions, you probably want the abridged version for your luggage since the full text weighs in at more than 1000 pages. This diary of a city gentleman and womanizer who witnessed the plague and fire of 1665–1666 is memorable for its clear-eyed view of London life that manages to be both celebratory and jaded at the same time.

Wilson, A. N. *London: A Short History.* Phoenix, 2004. If you don't feel like wading through Inwood's magnum opus, try this quick history of the city. While it's just under 150 pages long, Wilson manages to pack in a lot of interesting facts about London and gives the reader a good general idea of its development, especially of its architecture.

MAGAZINES

The Big Issue
www.bigissue.com
You won't be in London long before you're approached by a homeless person calling out *Big Issue?* Selling this news and entertainment magazine provides them with a way to earn a living. Equally important, it breaks down the barrier between the haves and the have-nothings. It's quite common to get into a friendly chat once you've bought an issue. All legitimate vendors have ID tags and are not allowed to beg. Vendors say one of the toughest things about being homeless is how everyone pretends they're invisible. So please, if you don't want to buy an issue, smile, make eye contact, and say "no thank you."

The Economist
www.economist.com
This famous weekly magazine focuses on economic news and trends from around the world. It's jam-packed with information and ties cultural, political, and demographic trends into its analysis. Somehow they manage to write well enough to make business news *interesting.*

Granta: The Magazine of New Writing
www.granta.com
The leading literary journal in England, each quarterly issue is a full book of short stories, essays, reportage, and photo essays. The quality is consistently high and is a great source for reading some of the best contemporary British authors. There are occasional pieces from international writers as well. Editor Ian Jack has a regular column in the *Guardian Review of Books,* published on Saturdays.

The London Review of Books
www.lrb.co.uk
One of the leading book review magazines in the world, the LRB comes out twice a month and is full of erudite reviews of the latest books. Reviews tend towards more literary and academic works (it's a Dan Brown—free zone) and can teach you a great deal without having to

go out and buy the actual books. This is perfect for the chattering classes, and convenient because the LRB is a bit of a tome itself and it's difficult to get through one before the next one comes out.

Smoke: A London Peculiar
www.smokelondon.co.uk
This unusual literary magazine focuses on London and its public transportation system. The mixture of text, photography, the occasional poem and even drinking games makes it a lot of fun to read. There is some excellent work in here, mostly by unknown artists and writers, and their love and deep knowledge of the city shine through on every page.

Time Out London
www.timeout.com/london/
A weekly magazine featuring articles about arts and entertainment, but you'll really want it for the listings so you can find out what's on in music, theatre, museums, comedy, art, kids events, film, and gay and lesbian happenings. An essential resource if you plan on staying for a while.

Internet Resources

ACCOMMODATIONS

Gumtree
www.gumtree.com

This website was originally set up for Australians looking for a place to live, but is now used by just about everybody. A great resource for people looking to find short-term or long-term flatshares and bedsits in London. They even have a section for couch surfing!

Hostel World
www.hostelworld.com

A handy online reservation system for hostels in London and around the world. You can book by time, location, and prices. The site features profiles, photos, and user reviews of the city's many hostels. There is a limited selection of budget hotels and bed-and-breakfasts too.

Hotels of London
www.hotelsoflondon.co.uk

Another online booking site with hotels organized by neighborhood, making it easy to choose a place close to where you want to be. They also do theatre bookings.

Independent Hostel Guide
www.independenthostelguide.co.uk

A detailed listing of more than 300 hostels across the United Kingdom.

London Lodging
www.londonlodging.co.uk

This booking site not only does hotels, but also flat-shares, private apartments, and youth hostels.

London Tourist Board & Convention Bureau
www.londontouristboard.com

The tourist board has a huge amount of information on where to stay and what to do in London. Their annual list of inspected and approved accommodation, *Where to Stay and What to Do in London* is available for £4.99. For shoestring travelers, there's the (appropriately free) booklet *Where to Stay on a Budget*. Much of the information also appears on this website.

Visit London
www.visitlondon.com

The official site for London has special offers for budget and moderately priced hotels when you book online.

EMPLOYMENT

Any Work Anywhere
www.anyworkanywhere.com

An encyclopedic listing of jobs around the world, especially geared towards young travelers. Some of these odd jobs are truly odd: you might end up picking strawberries in a beautiful English field, or you might end up cleaning fish in some cannery. You can't fault the number of choices, however, and some of the more onerous jobs pay the best.

1rst 4 Jobs in London
www.1st4jobsinlondon.co.uk

Features links to many different job site and recruitment agencies and a search engine to find jobs listed onsite.

London Job Site
www.londonjobsite.com

This is a links site that connects to dozens of different job sites for London and the rest of England. Each site is described by the type of jobs it offers and the location of the work.

Londonjobs UK
www.londonjobs.co.uk

This job site features a search engine that matches your skills and desired location to available jobs. Type in a profile of yourself and you will receive appropriate job information automatically. Membership is required, but is free.

HISTORY

English Heritage
www.english-heritage.org.uk

English Heritage is the government body that oversees and preserves more than 400 of the nation's historic sights and buildings, including important and popular monuments such as Stonehenge. Their website is filled with historical and practical information on the places they manage, and has a handy events guide for London and beyond.

Time Travel Britain
www.timetravel-britain.com

An interesting site dedicated to historical travel in England, Scotland, and Wales. There are a large number of articles on London, including a few by yours truly, and a regular column on "Little-Known London." A good site to use as background reading before you go.

TOURISM

Art Fund
www.artfund.org

If you are staying a while and love art, you can save some money by joining the National Art Collections Fund. Annual dues cost £38 per person and gets you free admission to 200 galleries, museums, and historic houses, and significant discounts on most of the year's big shows, including those in all major London venues. The website has a handy list of what's on around the country.

City of London
www.cityoflondon.gov.uk

The official website of the City of London contains a wealth of information on attractions and upcoming events. While its focus is the City, it covers all London and even some attractions beyond the metropolitan limits.

Days Out Guide
www.daysoutguide.co.uk

Sponsored by National Rail, this site gives details on all sorts of excursions from London to southern England, many coming with money-saving offers if you go by rail.

Gay London
www.gaylondon.co.uk

A good online resource for the gay, bisexual, lesbian, and transgendered community, this website lists clubs, special interest groups, health resources, and everything else for the traveler or resident.

London Eating
www.london-eating.co.uk

London is constantly changing, and nothing changes as quickly as its restaurant scene. All it takes is a change of a chef or manager and a place can go from great to terrible, or the other way around. This book lists only restaurants I've eaten at and enjoyed, but things can change, so check out this website with its extensive coverage of London dining, including unedited and candid reader reviews. Tastes vary, so take any review with a grain of salt, but you can get some very useful tips from this website.

LondonTown.com
www.londontown.com

A commercial website chock full of information about sights, dining, and entertainment. Much of it is information that you already hold in your hands, but you can pick up some good advice here. You can also reserve discounted rooms directly with hotels through this site.

Park Explorer
www.parkexplorer.org.uk

An educational site covering the parks of London, their history and what to do in them. It's marketed towards school kids, but contains lots of useful information for adults too.

Saatchi Gallery
www.saatchi-gallery.co.uk

The website for the famous (or infamous, depending on your opinion of contemporary art) Saatchi Gallery has a handy guide to exhibitions in London. Very sporting of them to list what the competition is showing!

Ticketmaster
www.ticketmaster.co.uk

This is the major online ticket agency for shows and exhibitions in London, although there are many others. You can surf their site to find out what's on, but you should also check the website of the actual venue to see if you get a discount for booking directly through them.

Tripadvisor
www.tripadvisor.com

There are lots of travel review sites on the Internet, but this is my favorite. People write reviews of hotels, restaurants, and sights, giving you the latest tips on what's good and what's lousy. Take the reviews with a grain of salt, however, as people's tastes vary and there's a lot of random people who just want to sound off.

24 Hour Museum
www.24hourmuseum.org.uk

A virtual museum that comprehensively lists museums, galleries, and heritage sites across the U.K., along with information on temporary exhibits. If you are a museum or art junkie, give this a good read-through while planning your trip.

Visit Britain
www.visitbritain.com

An official website for tourism throughout Britain, it has huge amounts of detailed information on London. It is especially strong on accommodation.

Visit London
www.visitlondon.com
www.londontouristboard.com

This is the official site for London tourism and is packed with information on places to go and things to do. This is a good place to start your search because their many pages are filled with practical information. You can book hotels through this site as well.

TRANSPORT

Green Line
www.greenline.co.uk

This large bus company serves much of England and their website details their routes and timetables.

National Express
www.nationalexpress.com

The largest bus company in Great Britain, National Express goes just about everywhere. Their website details routes and itineraries and you can book online.

National Rail
www.nationalrail.co.uk

The government rail service crisscrosses the country with hundreds of routes. Many are now run by private operators, but all services are listed on this site, which can also handle bookings.

Transport for London
www.tfl.gov.uk/tfl/

The website for the city's central public transport planning team, this is filled with news and information about getting around London. Includes a handy Journey Planner to help you get around.

Index

CHURCHES

DE

F

G

H

MUSEUMS

N

OP

PARKS, GARDENS, AND SQUARES

QR

S

TU

VWXYZ

Acknowledgments

Writing up a huge city like London is impossible to do alone. I'd like to thank the many people, both friends and strangers, who gave advice and pointed the way to London's hidden gems. In particular I'd like to thank Payam and Paul for interesting titbits of history and tours of hidden corners of the City, Alan and Julie for some excellent recommendations for St. Albans, Stephen and Maria for advice on Soho, and the staff of the British Library for delving into their collections to provide me with reading material to further my education on the endless topic of the history and culture of London. A big thanks also goes out to all my housemates at 26 Searles Rd., that outpost of foreigners in Southwark. You're too numerous to mention, but you know who you are! Special mention goes to my housemates Chris and Michael for helping me with the gruelling task of researching the nightlife chapter. Thanks for the hazy memories, guys. Thanks to Moira, Dean, Michael, Almudena, and Leah for photos, and to Dean for proofreading the football section. Other neighbourhood regulars worthy of mention are Peter, who keeps the intersection clean when all others neglect it, and Smokey the fox, who brings a little wildlife into the urban landscape.

I'd also like to thank the staff at Avalon Travel publishing for all their help, Sabrina Young for sharp-eyed editing, Stefano Boni for advice on photos, Kat Smith and Albert Angulo for help with the maps, and Rebecca Browning for giving me the opportunity to do this book in the first place.

A very special thanks goes to my wife, Almudena Alonso-Herrero, who kept the home fires burning while I was off wandering the streets of London, and my son, Julián Alonso-McLachlan, who makes life so much more interesting. This book is dedicated to them.

Photo Credits

page 12: Shakespeare, Leicester Square © VisitLondon.com; The Tube © Purestock.com; Bishops of Winchester © VisitLondon.com; page 16: Big Ben © Purestock.com; Eros at Piccadilly © VisitLondon.com; Soho © VisitLondon.com; page 17: British Museum, Harrods, Portobello Road © VisitLondon.com; page 18: The Regent's Park, Camden Lock, Bank of London © VisitLondon.com; page 19: Islington © VisitLondon.com; Southwark Cathedral © Sean McLachlan; Royal Observatory Greenwich © VisitLondon.com; page 21: all © VisitLondon.com; page 22: © VisitLondon.com; page 23: © VisitLondon.com; page 24: © VisitLondon.com; page 25: Victorian streetlight and London Eye © VisitLondon.com; guards at Buckingham Palace © VisitLondon.com; Big Ben © Purestock.com; page 26: © VisitLondon.com; page 27: © Sean McLachlan; page 28: © Nigel Young; page 29: © British Museum; page 30: © VisitLondon.com; page 31: © VisitLondon.com

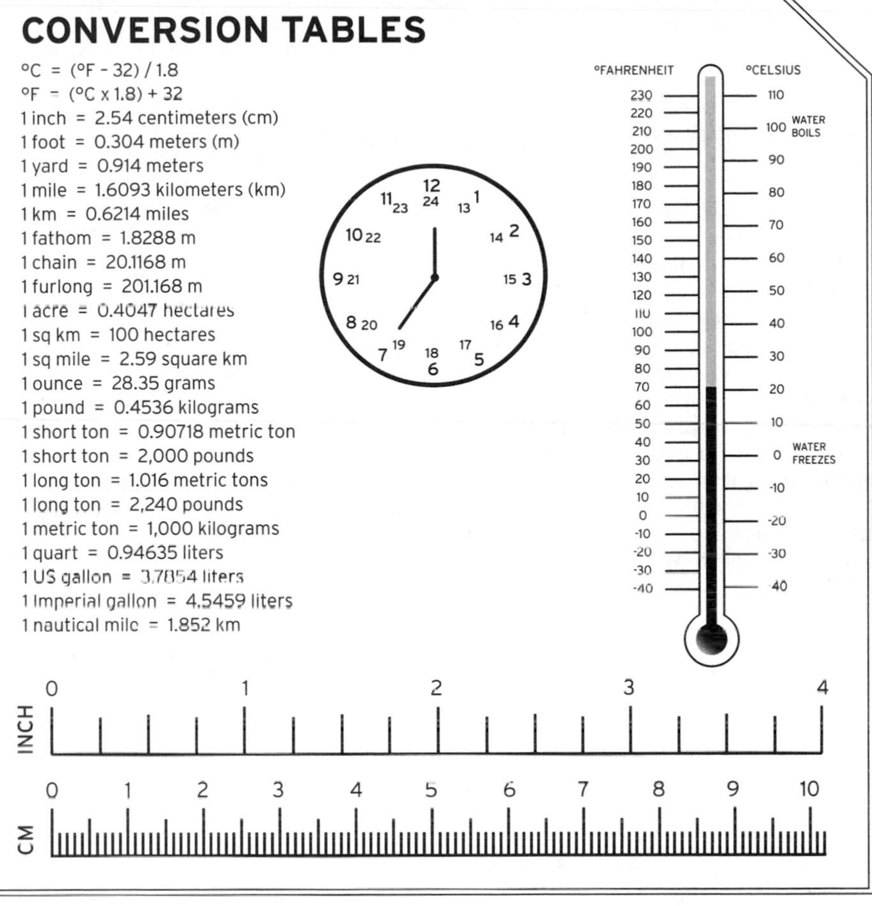

CONVERSION TABLES

°C = (°F - 32) / 1.8
°F = (°C x 1.8) + 32
1 inch = 2.54 centimeters (cm)
1 foot = 0.304 meters (m)
1 yard = 0.914 meters
1 mile = 1.6093 kilometers (km)
1 km = 0.6214 miles
1 fathom = 1.8288 m
1 chain = 20.1168 m
1 furlong = 201.168 m
1 acre = 0.4047 hectares
1 sq km = 100 hectares
1 sq mile = 2.59 square km
1 ounce = 28.35 grams
1 pound = 0.4536 kilograms
1 short ton = 0.90718 metric ton
1 short ton = 2,000 pounds
1 long ton = 1.016 metric tons
1 long ton = 2,240 pounds
1 metric ton = 1,000 kilograms
1 quart = 0.94635 liters
1 US gallon = 3.7854 liters
1 Imperial gallon = 4.5459 liters
1 nautical mile = 1.852 km

MOON LONDON

Avalon Travel Publishing
1400 65th Street, Suite 250
Emeryville, CA 94608, USA
www.moon.com

Editor: Sabrina Young
Series Manager: Kathryn Ettinger
Acquisitions Manager: Rebecca K. Browning
Copy Editor: Karen Gaynor Bleske
Graphics Coordinator: Elizabeth Jang
Production Coordinator: Elizabeth Jang
Cover Designer: Gerilyn Attebery
Map Editor: Albert Angulo
Cartographers: Aaron Darden, Kat Bennett, Suzanne Service, and Chris Markiewicz
Indexer: Greg Jewett

ISBN-10: 1-59880-040-X
ISBN-13: 978-1-59880-040-1
ISSN: 1934-5763

Printing History
1st Edition – May 2007
5 4 3 2 1

Front cover photo: Double decker busses driving past Big Ben © George Doyle / Getty Images

Title page photo: © Purestock.com

Printed in United States of America by Worzalla

KEEPING CURRENT

If you have a favorite gem you'd like to see included in the next edition, or see anything that needs updating, clarification, or correction, please drop us a line. Send your comments via email to feedback@moon.com, or use the address above.

MAP CONTENTS

Expressway
Primary Road
Secondary Road
Unpaved Road
Trail
Ferry
Railroad
Pedestrian Walkway

Highlight
City/Town
State Capital
National Capital
Point of Interest
Accommodation
Restaurant/Bar
Other Location

Airport
Mountain
Unique Natural Feature
Park
Golf Course
Parking Area
Church

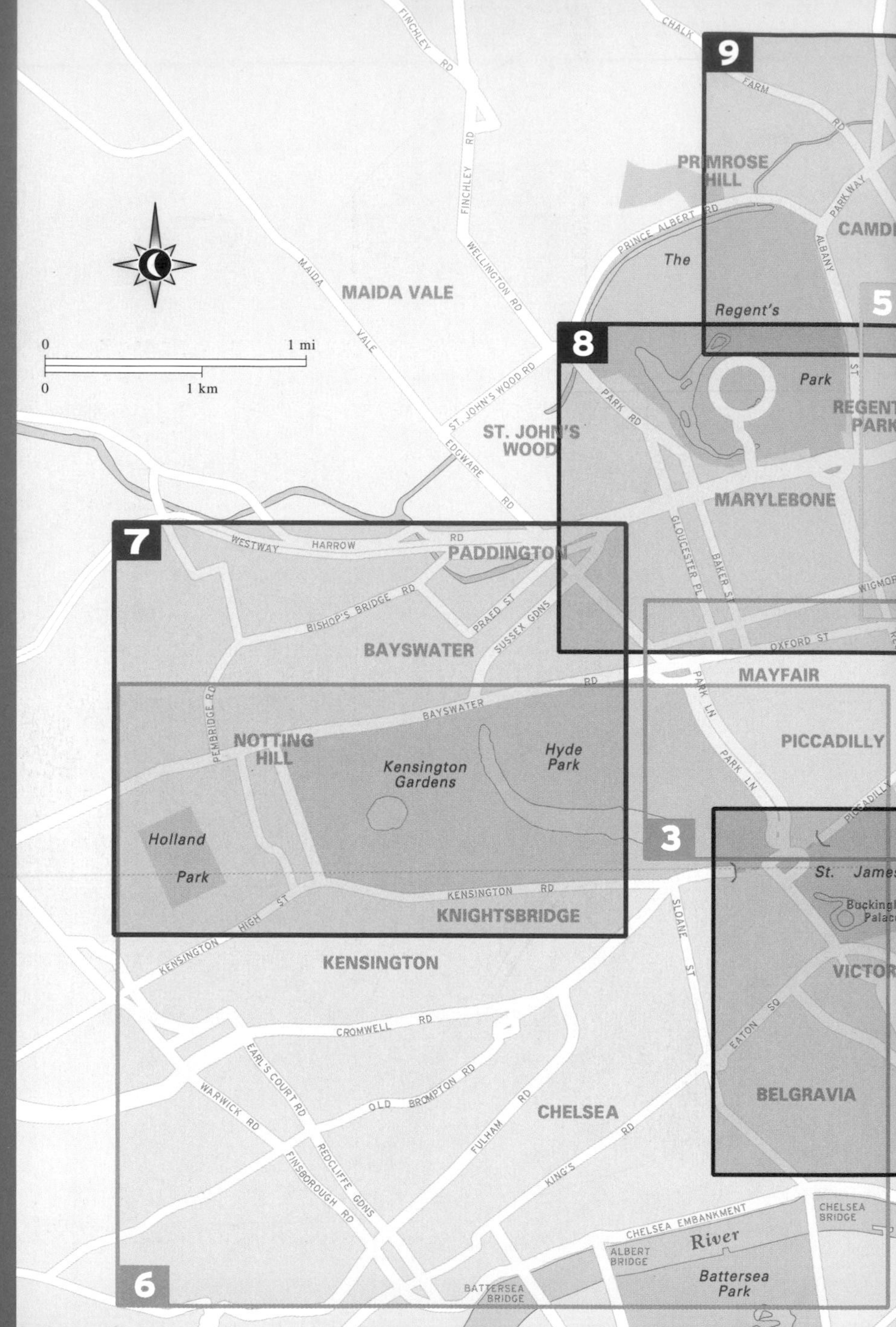
0
1 mi
0
1 km
MAIDA VALE
ST. JOHN'S WOOD
PRIMROSE HILL
CAMD
The Regent's Park
REGENT PARK
MARYLEBONE
PADDINGTON
BAYSWATER
MAYFAIR
NOTTING HILL
Kensington Gardens
Hyde Park
PICCADILLY
Holland Park
St. James
Buckingh Palace
KNIGHTSBRIDGE
KENSINGTON
VICTOR
BELGRAVIA
CHELSEA
River
Battersea Park
CHELSEA BRIDGE
ALBERT BRIDGE
BATTERSEA BRIDGE
CHALK
FARM RD
FINCHLEY RD
PRINCE ALBERT RD
PARK WAY
ALBANY
MAIDA VALE
WELLINGTON RD
ST. JOHN'S WOOD RD
EDGWARE RD
PARK RD
WESTWAY
HARROW RD
BISHOP'S BRIDGE RD
PRAED ST
SUSSEX GDNS
GLOUCESTER PL
BAKER ST
WIGMORE
OXFORD ST
BAYSWATER RD
PEMBRIDGE RD
PARK LN
PICCADILLY
KENSINGTON RD
KENSINGTON HIGH ST
SLOANE ST
EATON SQ
CROMWELL RD
EARL'S COURT RD
WARWICK RD
OLD BROMPTON RD
FULHAM RD
KING'S RD
FINSBOROUGH RD
REDCLIFFE GDNS
CHELSEA EMBANKMENT
9
8
7
5
3
6

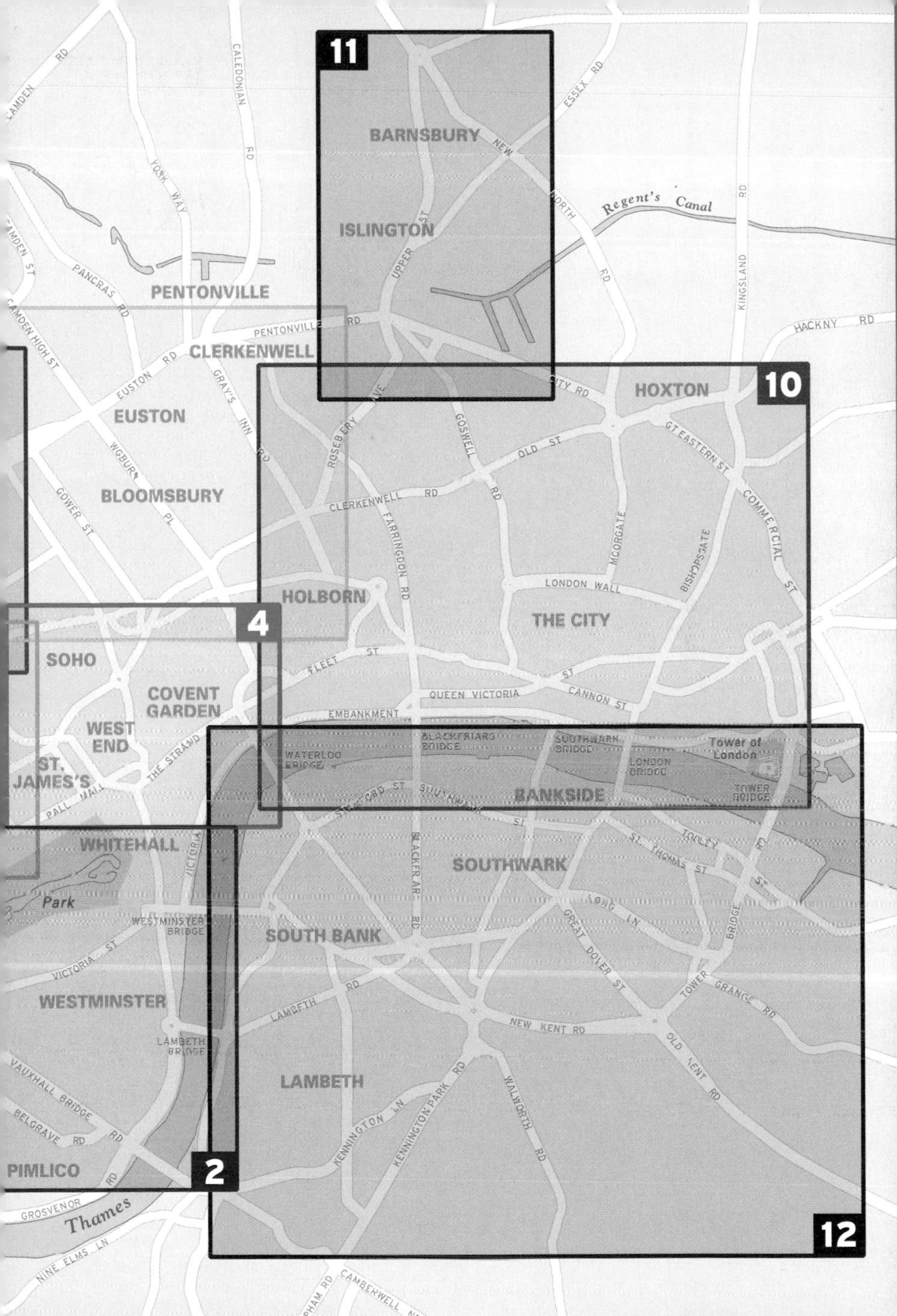

11
BARNSBURY
ISLINGTON
PENTONVILLE
CLERKENWELL
EUSTON
BLOOMSBURY
10
HOXTON
HOLBORN
THE CITY
4
SOHO
COVENT GARDEN
WEST END
ST. JAMES'S
BANKSIDE
Tower of London
WHITEHALL
SOUTHWARK
SOUTH BANK
WESTMINSTER
LAMBETH
2
PIMLICO
12
Thames
Regent's Canal
Park
CAMDEN RD
CALEDONIAN RD
ESSEX RD
YORK WAY
NEW NORTH RD
UPPER ST
CAMDEN ST
PANCRAS RD
CAMDEN HIGH ST
PENTONVILLE RD
EUSTON RD
GRAY'S INN RD
KINGSLAND RD
HACKNY RD
CITY RD
ROSEBERY AVE
GOSWELL RD
OLD ST
GT EASTERN ST
COMMERCIAL ST
WGBURN PL
GOWER ST
CLERKENWELL RD
FARRINGDON RD
MCORGATE
BISHOPSGATE
LONDON WALL
FLEET ST
QUEEN VICTORIA ST
CANNON ST
EMBANKMENT
BLACKFRIARS BRIDGE
SOUTHWARK BRIDGE
LONDON BRIDGE
TOWER BRIDGE
WATERLOO BRIDGE
THE STRAND
PALL MALL
STAMFORD ST
SOUTHWARK ST
TOOLEY ST
ST. THOMAS ST
VICTORIA ST
BLACKFRIARS RD
WESTMINSTER BRIDGE
LONG LN
GREAT DOVER ST
TOWER BRIDGE RD
GRANGE RD
LAMBETH RD
NEW KENT RD
OLD KENT RD
LAMBETH BRIDGE
VAUXHALL BRIDGE RD
BELGRAVE RD
KENNINGTON LN
KENNINGTON PARK RD
WALWORTH RD
GROSVENOR RD
NINE ELMS LN
CLAPHAM RD
CAMBERWELL NEW RD

SIGHTS

- 3 ST. JAMES'S PARK
- 5 THE CHURCHILL MUSEUM AND CABINET WAR ROOMS
- 6 BUCKINGHAM PALACE
- 7 CHANGING OF THE GUARD
- 8 QUEEN'S GALLERY
- 12 WESTMINSTER ABBEY
- 13 ST. MARGARET'S
- 15 BIG BEN
- 16 HOUSES OF PARLIAMENT
- 17 ROYAL MEWS
- 26 WESTMINSTER CATHEDRAL
- 40 TATE BRITAIN

RESTAURANTS

- 1 R. S. HISPANIOLA
- 11 PICKLES SANDWICH BAR
- 18 BANK WESTMINSTER
- 20 BISTRO 51
- 23 CINNAMON CLUB
- 27 FOOTSTOOL
- 41 TATE GALLERY RESTAURANT

NIGHTLIFE

- 22 THE ALBERT
- 30 EBURY WINE BAR AND RESTAURANT

ARTS AND ENTERTAINMENT

- 2 BANQUETING HOUSE
- 9 THE GUARDS MUSEUM
- 14 JEWEL TOWER

SHOPPING AND RECREATION

- 4 ST. JAMES'S PARK
- 24 COLLEGE AND LITTLE CLOISTER GARDEN
- 25 NOMAD ADVENTURE TRAVEL
- 32 CORNUCOPIA
- 35 PIMLICO ROAD MARKET

ACCOMMODATIONS

- 10 SANCTUARY HOUSE HOTEL
- 19 VANDON HOUSE HOTEL
- 21 51 BUCKINGHAM GATE
- 28 ROSEDENE HOTEL VICTORIA
- 29 LIME TREE HOTEL
- 31 MORGAN GUEST HOUSE
- 33 THE GRANGE ROCHESTER HOTEL
- 34 CITY INN
- 36 WINDERMERE HOTEL
- 37 NEW ENGLAND HOTEL
- 38 LUNA & SIMONE HOTEL
- 39 ASTOR VICTORIA HOSTEL

SEE MAP 3

SEE MAP 6

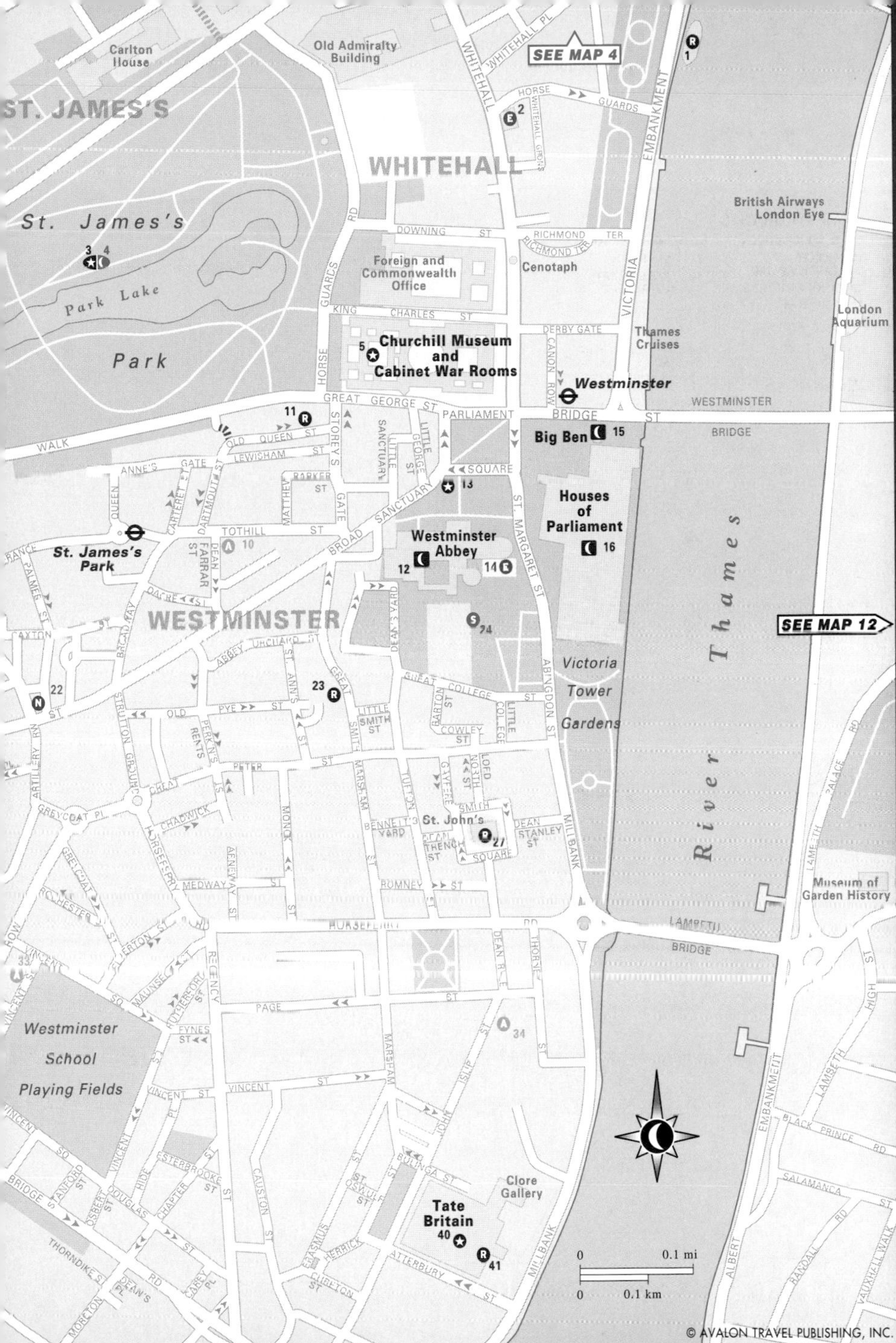

SEE MAP 4

SEE MAP 12

ST. JAMES'S

WHITEHALL

WESTMINSTER

Carlton House

Old Admiralty Building

St. James's Park

Park Lake

3 4

Foreign and Commonwealth Office

Cenotaph

5 Churchill Museum and Cabinet War Rooms

Westminster

Big Ben 15

Houses of Parliament 16

13

Westminster Abbey

12

14

24

10

11

St. James's Park

22

23

St. John's

27

Victoria Tower Gardens

River Thames

British Airways London Eye

London Aquarium

Thames Cruises

Museum of Garden History

Westminster School Playing Fields

Clore Gallery

Tate Britain

40

41

33

34

1

2

WHITEHALL PL

WHITEHALL

HORSE GUARDS

WHITEHALL GDNS

EMBANKMENT

DOWNING ST

RICHMOND TER

RICHMOND TER

KING CHARLES ST

DERBY GATE

CANON ROW

VICTORIA

HORSE GUARDS RD

GREAT GEORGE ST

PARLIAMENT SQUARE

BRIDGE ST

WESTMINSTER BRIDGE

WALK

OLD QUEEN ST

LEWISHAM ST

STOREY'S GATE

LITTLE SANCTUARY

LITTLE GEORGE ST

ANNE'S GATE

QUEEN

BARKER ST

MATTHEW

CARTERET ST

DARTMOUTH ST

TOTHILL ST

BROAD SANCTUARY

ST. MARGARET ST

FARRAR ST

DEAN

DACRE ST

PALMER ST

CAXTON

BROADWAY

DEAN'S YARD

ABBEY ORCHARD ST

ST. ANN'S ST

GREAT SMITH ST

GREAT COLLEGE ST

BARTON ST

LITTLE COLLEGE ST

COWLEY ST

ABINGDON ST

OLD PYE ST

STRUTTON GROUND

PERKIN'S RENTS

LITTLE SMITH ST

ARTILLERY ROW

PETER ST

MARSHAM ST

TUFTON ST

GAYFERE ST

NORTH ST

LORD NORTH ST

SMITH SQUARE

DEAN STANLEY ST

MILLBANK

GREYCOAT PL

GREAT PETER ST

CHADWICK ST

MONCK ST

BENNETT'S YARD

DEAN TRENCH ST

HORSEFERRY RD

AMBROSDEN AVE

ROMNEY ST

MEDWAY ST

GREYCOAT ST

ROCHESTER ROW

ELVERTON ST

REGENCY ST

DEAN RYLE ST

THORNEY ST

LAMBETH BRIDGE

VINCENT ST

MAUNSEL ST

RUTHERFORD ST

PAGE ST

FYNES ST

VINCENT SQ

VINCENT ST

JOHN ISLIP ST

ESTERBROOKE ST

BULINGA ST

ST. OSWULF ST

CAUSTON ST

HIDE PL

CHAPTER ST

DOUGLAS ST

OSBERT ST

STANFORD ST

BRIDGE PL

THORNDIKE ST

DEAN'S PL

MORETON

CAREY PL

ERASMUS ST

HERRICK ST

CURETON ST

ATTERBURY ST

ALBERT EMBANKMENT

LAMBETH PALACE RD

LAMBETH HIGH ST

BLACK PRINCE RD

SALAMANCA ST

RANDALL RD

VAUXHALL WALK

0 0.1 mi

0 0.1 km

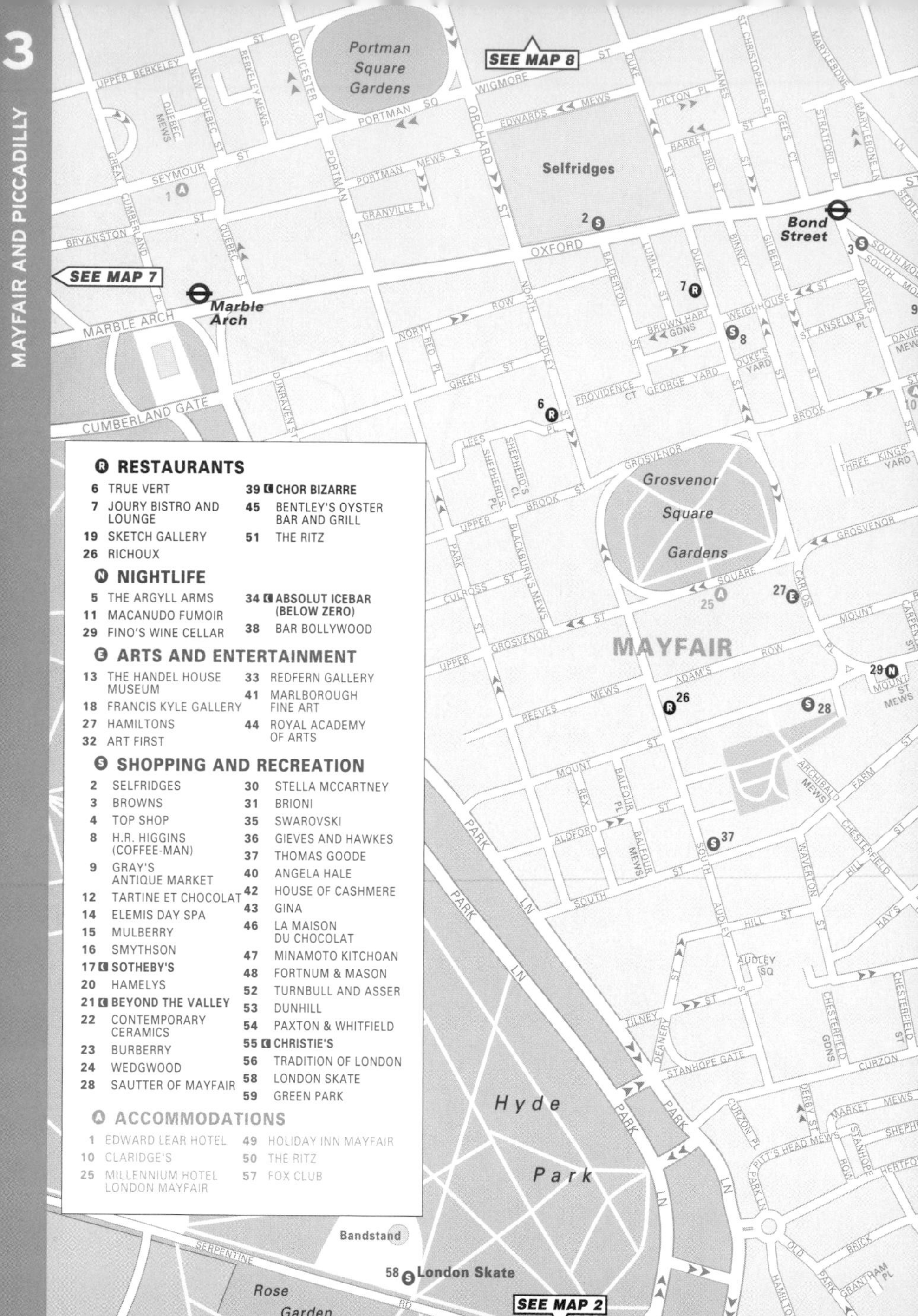
SEE MAP 8
SEE MAP 7
SEE MAP 2
Portman Square Gardens
Selfridges
Marble Arch
Bond Street
Grosvenor Square Gardens
MAYFAIR
Hyde Park
Bandstand
London Skate
Rose Garden
RESTAURANTS
6 TRUE VERT
7 JOURY BISTRO AND LOUNGE
19 SKETCH GALLERY
26 RICHOUX
39 CHOR BIZARRE
45 BENTLEY'S OYSTER BAR AND GRILL
51 THE RITZ
NIGHTLIFE
5 THE ARGYLL ARMS
11 MACANUDO FUMOIR
29 FINO'S WINE CELLAR
34 ABSOLUT ICEBAR (BELOW ZERO)
38 BAR BOLLYWOOD
ARTS AND ENTERTAINMENT
13 THE HANDEL HOUSE MUSEUM
18 FRANCIS KYLE GALLERY
27 HAMILTONS
32 ART FIRST
33 REDFERN GALLERY
41 MARLBOROUGH FINE ART
44 ROYAL ACADEMY OF ARTS
SHOPPING AND RECREATION
2 SELFRIDGES
3 BROWNS
4 TOP SHOP
8 H.R. HIGGINS (COFFEE-MAN)
9 GRAY'S ANTIQUE MARKET
12 TARTINE ET CHOCOLAT
14 ELEMIS DAY SPA
15 MULBERRY
16 SMYTHSON
17 SOTHEBY'S
20 HAMELYS
21 BEYOND THE VALLEY
22 CONTEMPORARY CERAMICS
23 BURBERRY
24 WEDGWOOD
28 SAUTTER OF MAYFAIR
30 STELLA MCCARTNEY
31 BRIONI
35 SWAROVSKI
36 GIEVES AND HAWKES
37 THOMAS GOODE
40 ANGELA HALE
42 HOUSE OF CASHMERE
43 GINA
46 LA MAISON DU CHOCOLAT
47 MINAMOTO KITCHOAN
48 FORTNUM & MASON
52 TURNBULL AND ASSER
53 DUNHILL
54 PAXTON & WHITFIELD
55 CHRISTIE'S
56 TRADITION OF LONDON
58 LONDON SKATE
59 GREEN PARK
ACCOMMODATIONS
1 EDWARD LEAR HOTEL
10 CLARIDGE'S
25 MILLENNIUM HOTEL LONDON MAYFAIR
49 HOLIDAY INN MAYFAIR
50 THE RITZ
57 FOX CLUB

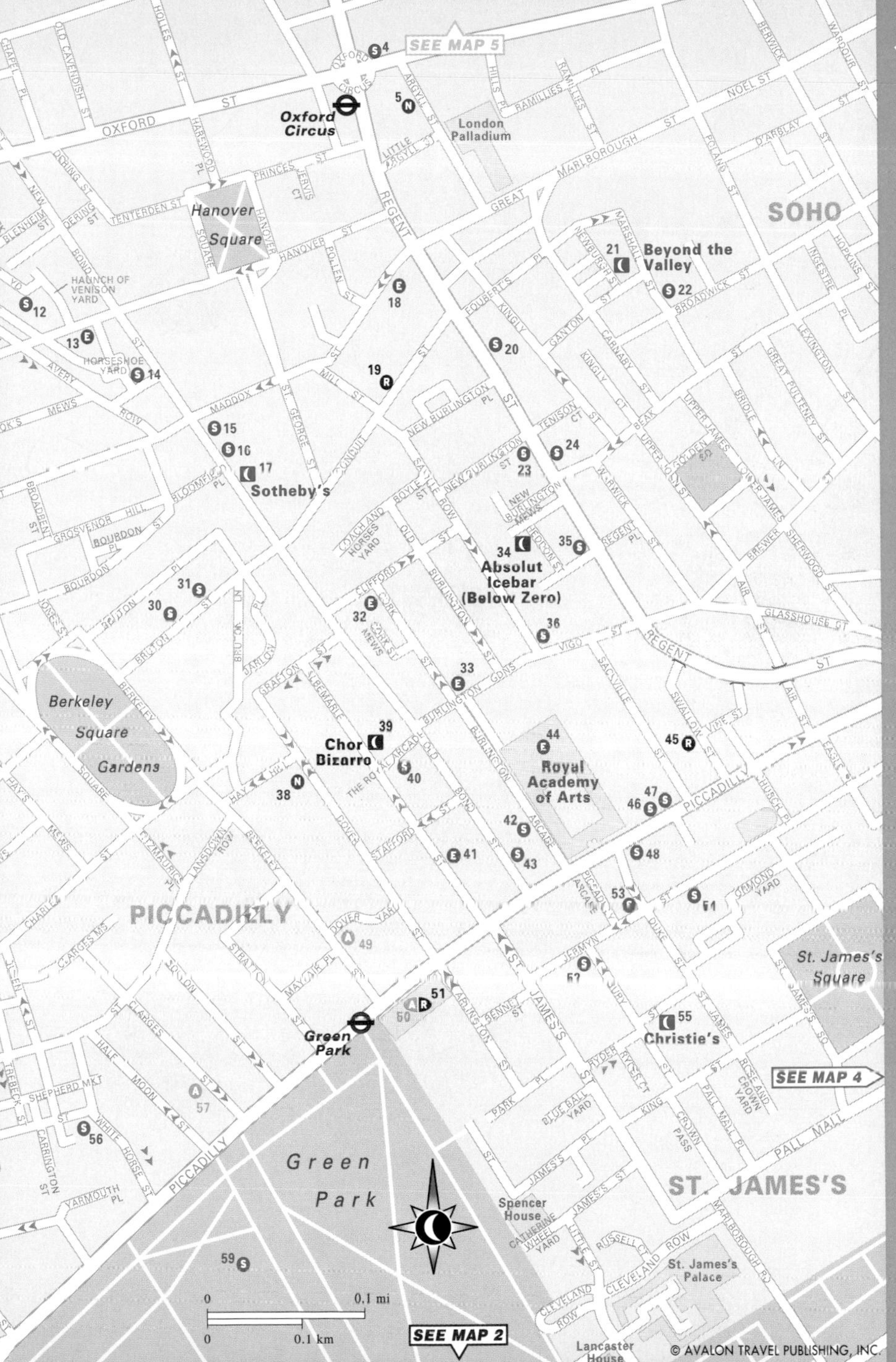
SEE MAP 5
Oxford Circus
OXFORD ST
London Palladium
GREAT MARLBOROUGH ST
NOEL ST
Hanover Square
REGENT ST
SOHO
Beyond the Valley
BROADWICK ST
HAUNCH OF VENISON YARD
HORSESHOE YARD
MADDOX ST
NEW BURLINGTON PL
MILL ST
CONDUIT ST
Sotheby's
GROSVENOR HILL
BOURDON ST
BRUTON ST
Absolut Icebar (Below Zero)
VIGO ST
GLASSHOUSE ST
Berkeley Square Gardens
Chor Bizarro
THE ROYAL ARCADE
Royal Academy of Arts
PICCADILLY
BURLINGTON GDNS
DOVER ST
ALBEMARLE ST
STAFFORD ST
JERMYN ST
ST. JAMES'S ST
Christie's
St. James's Square
SEE MAP 4
PALL MALL
ST. JAMES'S
Green Park
Spencer House
St. James's Palace
CLEVELAND ROW
MARLBOROUGH RD
Lancaster House
SEE MAP 2
0 0.1 mi
0 0.1 km
© AVALON TRAVEL PUBLISHING, INC.

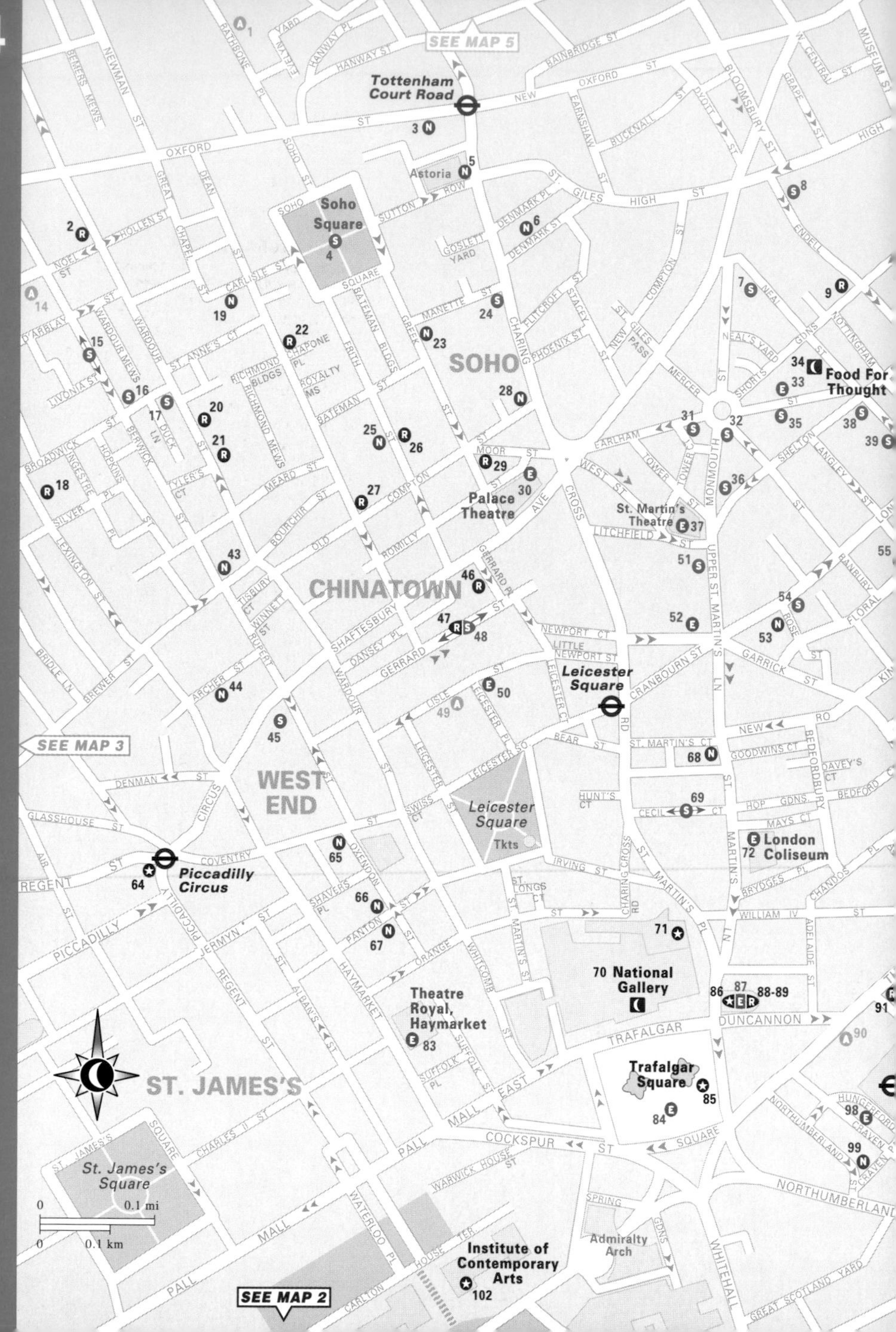
SEE MAP 5
Tottenham Court Road
Astoria
Soho Square
SOHO
Palace Theatre
St. Martin's Theatre
CHINATOWN
Leicester Square
SEE MAP 3
WEST END
Leicester Square
Tkts
Piccadilly Circus
London Coliseum
National Gallery
Theatre Royal, Haymarket
Trafalgar Square
ST. JAMES'S
St. James's Square
Admiralty Arch
Institute of Contemporary Arts
Food For Thought
SEE MAP 2
0 0.1 mi
0 0.1 km
OXFORD ST
NEW OXFORD ST
CHARING CROSS RD
SHAFTESBURY AVE
REGENT ST
PICCADILLY
HAYMARKET
PALL MALL
COVENTRY ST
WHITEHALL
NORTHUMBERLAND AVE
ST. MARTIN'S LN
UPPER ST. MARTIN'S LN
GERRARD ST
WARDOUR ST
DEAN ST
GREEK ST
FRITH ST
OLD COMPTON ST
GARRICK ST
CRANBOURN ST
JERMYN ST
DUNCANNON ST
WILLIAM IV ST
COCKSPUR ST
TRAFALGAR SQUARE
WATERLOO PL
CARLTON HOUSE TER
GREAT SCOTLAND YARD
BLOOMSBURY ST
NEAL ST
MONMOUTH ST
EARLHAM ST
SHORTS GDNS
NEAL'S YARD
ENDELL ST
HIGH HOLBORN
MUSEUM ST
BEDFORDBURY
ST. MARTIN'S PL

SEE MAP 1

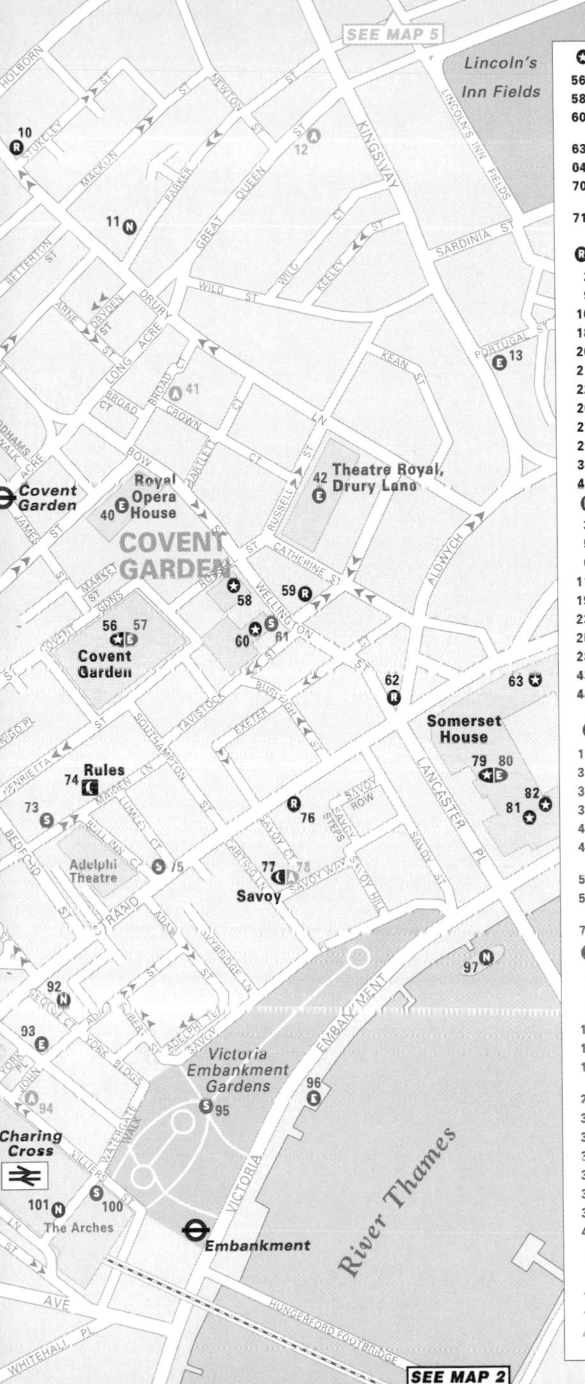

SEE MAP 2

SIGHTS

- 56 COVENT GARDEN
- 58 THEATRE MUSEUM
- 60 LONDON TRANSPORT MUSEUM
- 63 COURTAULD GALLERY
- 64 PICCADILLY CIRCUS
- 70 THE NATIONAL GALLERY
- 71 NATIONAL PORTRAIT GALLERY
- 79 SOMERSET HOUSE
- 81 GILBERT COLLECTION
- 82 HERMITAGE ROOMS
- 85 TRAFALGAR SQUARE
- 86 ST. MARTIN-IN-THE-FIELDS
- 101 INSTITUTE OF CONTEMPORARY ARTS

RESTAURANTS

- 2 MR. JERK
- 9 ROCK & SOLE PLAICE
- 10 SARASTRO
- 18 ANDREW EDMUNDS
- 20 BUSABA EATHAI
- 21 CASA DEL HABANO
- 22 HAMBURGER UNION
- 26 BAR ITALIA
- 27 PATISSERIE VALERIE
- 29 MAISON BERTAUX
- 34 **FOOD FOR THOUGHT**
- 46 NEW WORLD
- 47 GERRARD ST
- 59 REZ'S
- 62 AXIS RESTAURANT AND BAR
- 74 **RULES**
- 76 THE GRAND DIVAN, SIMPSON'S-IN-THE-STRAND
- 77 **SAVOY**
- 88 CAFÉ IN THE CRYPT
- 89 FLONDITZ
- 91 EXOTIKA

NIGHTLIFE

- 3 BLOW UP METRO
- 5 CLUB G-A-Y AT ASTORIA
- 6 12 BAR CLUB
- 11 GUANABARA
- 19 CANDY BAR
- 23 JAZZ AFTER DARK
- 25 RONNIE SCOTT'S
- 28 MOLLY MOGGS
- 43 MADAME JO JO'S
- 44 COMEDY CAMP/ BAR CODE
- 53 LAMB AND FLAG
- 65 COMEDY STORE
- 66 TOM CRIBB
- 67 COMEDY THEATRE
- 68 SALISBURY TAVERN
- 92 THE RETRO BAR
- 97 THE QUEEN MARY
- 99 THE SHERLOCK HOLMES PUBLIC HOUSE AND RESTAURANT
- 101 HEAVEN

ARTS AND ENTERTAINMENT

- 13 PEACOCK THEATRE
- 30 PALACE THEATRE
- 33 DONMAR WAREHOUSE
- 37 ST. MARTIN'S THEATRE
- 40 ROYAL OPERA HOUSE
- 42 THEATRE ROYAL, DRURY LANE
- 50 PRINCE CHARLES
- 52 PHOTOGRAPHERS' GALLERY
- 72 LONDON COLISEUM
- 80 SOMERSET HOUSE
- 83 THEATRE ROYAL, HAYMARKET
- 84 NELSON'S COLUMN
- 88 ST. MARTIN-IN THE FIELDS
- 93 PROUD GALLERY
- 96 CLEOPATRA'S NEEDLE
- 98 BENJAMIN FRANKLIN HOUSE

SHOPPING AND RECREATION

- 4 SOHO SQUARE
- 7 OFFICE
- 8 OASIS SPORTS CENTRE
- 15 BERWICK STREET
- 16 AGENT PROVOCATEUR
- 17 SOUNDS OF THE UNIVERSE
- 24 FOYLES
- 31 THE BEAD SHOP
- 32 DRESS CIRCLE
- 35 TIBET DREAMS
- 36 GROSVENOR PRINTS
- 38 CARLUCCIO'S
- 39 THE TEA HOUSE
- 45 FUNLAND
- 48 GERRARD STREET
- 51 THE CINEMA STORE
- 54 STANFORDS
- 55 THE TINTIN SHOP
- 57 COVENT GARDEN
- 61 PENHALIGON'S
- 69 CECIL COURT ROAD
- 73 AUSTRALIA/CANADA/ NEW ZEALAND/ SOUTH AFRICA SHOP
- 75 FRASER'S/ STANLEY GIBBONS
- 95 VICTORIA EMBANKMENT GARDENS
- 100 AFRICAN ENTERPRISES

ACCOMMODATIONS

- 1 RATHBONE HOTEL
- 12 KINGSWAY HALL HOTEL
- 14 YHA OXFORD ST.
- 41 THE FIELDING HOTEL
- 49 MANZI'S
- 78 SAVOY
- 90 THISTLE CHARRING CROSS
- 94 ROYAL ADELPHI HOTEL

SEE MAP 9
SEE MAP 8
SEE MAP 3
0 0.1 mi
0 0.1 km
SIGHTS
1 BRITISH LIBRARY
19 CHARLES DICKENS MUSEUM
35 BRITISH MUSEUM
51 SIR JOHN SOANE'S MUSEUM
RESTAURANTS
20 ARCHIPELAGO
23 PLANET ORGANIC
25 CAFÉ IN THE GARDENS
31 PARADISO
38 EVE'S SANDWICH BAR
39 MALABAR JUNCTION
44 BIBIMBAB CAFÉ
47 MY OLD DUTCH
50 NA ZDROWIE: THE POLISH BAR
NIGHTLIFE
18 THE LAMB
43 MUSEUM TAVERN
49 PRINCESS LOUISE
54 100 CLUB
55 BRADLEY'S SPANISH BAR
ARTS AND ENTERTAINMENT
7 CAMDEN PEOPLE'S THEATRE
8 ST. PANCRAS
9 THE PLACE
14 PERCIVAL DAVID FOUNDATION OF CHINESE ART
17 FOUNDLING MUSEUM
21 PETRIE MUSEUM OF EGYPTIAN ARCHAEOLOGY
28 OCTOBER GALLERY
29 DRILL HALL THEATRE
41 THE CARTOON MUSEUM
45 ST GEORGE'S
53 GETTY IMAGES
SHOPPING AND RECREATION
2 UNSWORTHS
6 LAURENCE CORNER
13 TAVISTOCK SQUARE
16 GAY'S THE WORD
22 HABITAT
27 RUSSELL SQUARE
30 PURVES & PURVES
32 BEDFORD SQUARE
36 QUINTO BOOKSHOP
37 LONDON REVIEW BOOKSHOP
40 GOSH!
42 PLAYIN' GAMES
46 ATLANTIS BOOKSHOP
48 MODEL ZONE
52 LINCOLN'S INN FIELDS
56 YMCA
57 ROYAL MILE WHISKIES
58 BOOKMARKS
59 JAMES SMITH & SONS
ACCOMMODATIONS
3 YHA ST. PANCRAS
4 ALHAMBRA HOTEL
5 ASHLEE HOUSE
10 MABLEDON COURT HOTEL
11 AVALON PRIVATE HOTEL
12 HARLINGFORD HOTEL
15 ALBANY HOTEL
24 AROSFA
26 HOTEL RUSSELL
33 THE MONTAGUE ON THE GARDENS
34 ASTOR MUSEUM INN
Euston
Euston Square
Goodge Street
Totenham Court Road
University College London
Petrie Museum of Egyptian Archaeology
Tavistock Square
Gordon Square Gardens
Bedford Square
British Film Institute
YMCA
TOLMERS SQUARE
CUMBERLAND
VARNDELL ST
MARKET
ROBERT ST
WILLIAM RD
LONGFORD ST
HAMPSTEAD RD
STANHOPE ST
NASH ST
DRUMMOND ST
EUSTON RD
GOWER ST
TOTTENHAM COURT RD
TORRINGTON PL
GOODGE ST
OXFORD ST
NEW OXFORD ST
BLOOMSBURY ST
GREAT RUSSELL ST
CHARLOTTE ST
WHITFIELD ST
EVERSHOLT ST
CARDINGTON ST
EUSTON SQ
UPPER WOBURN PL
WOBURN WALK
ENDSLEIGH GDNS
ENDSLEIGH ST
GORDON SQUARE
CHENIES ST
STORE ST
RIDGMOUNT GDNS
ALFRED MEWS
BEDFORD AVE
BAYLEY ST
MORWELL ST
ADELINE PL
PERCY ST
RATHBONE PL
BERNERS ST
NEWMAN ST
EASTCASTLE ST
HANWAY ST

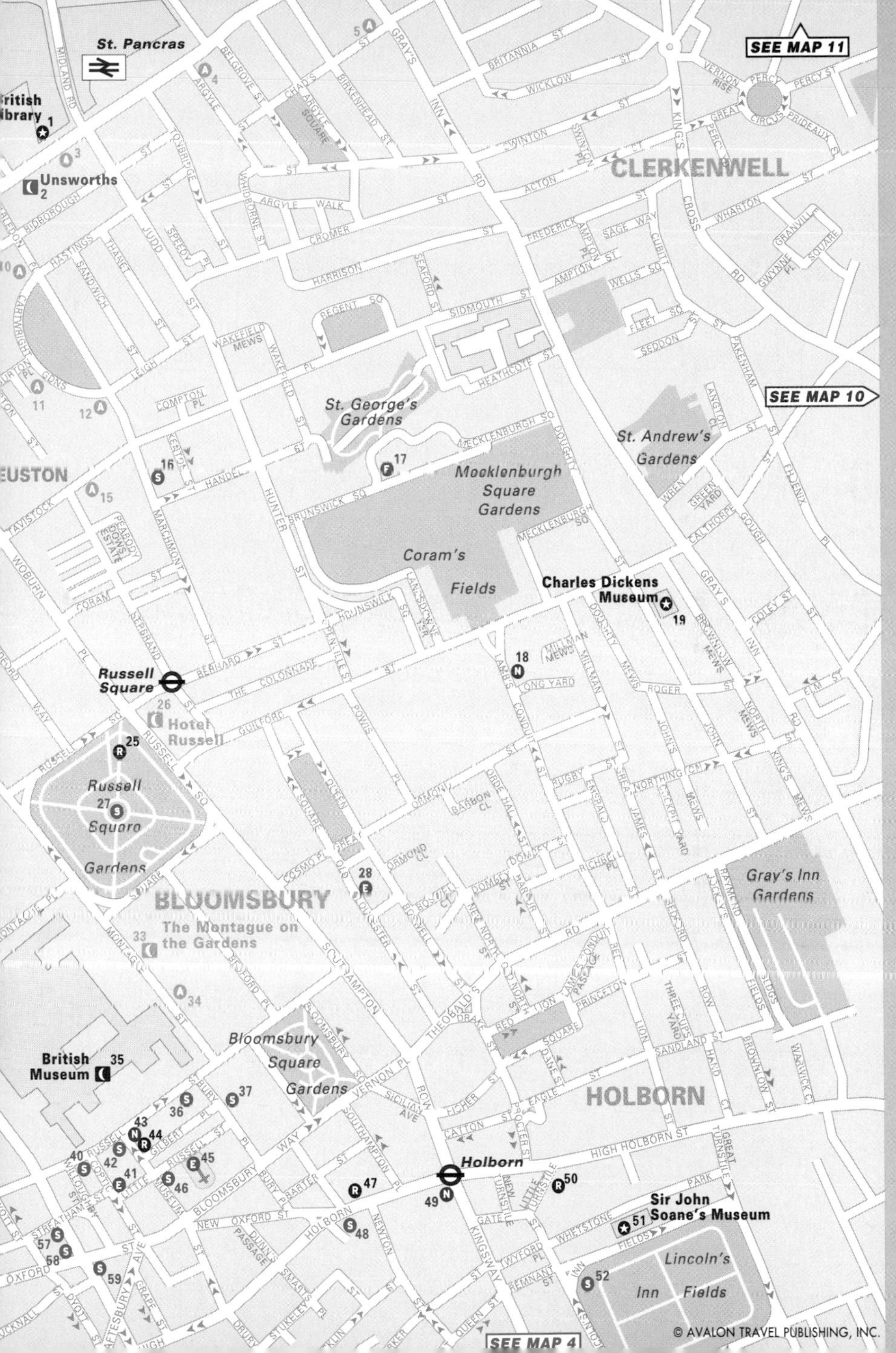
SEE MAP 11
SEE MAP 10
SEE MAP 4
St. Pancras
British Library 1
Unsworths 2
CLERKENWELL
EUSTON
St. George's Gardens
St. Andrew's Gardens
Mecklenburgh Square Gardens
Coram's Fields
Charles Dickens Museum 19
Russell Square
Hotel Russell
Russell Square Gardens
BLOOMSBURY
The Montague on the Gardens
Gray's Inn Gardens
British Museum 35
Bloomsbury Square Gardens
HOLBORN
Holborn
Sir John Soane's Museum
Lincoln's Inn Fields
© AVALON TRAVEL PUBLISHING, INC.

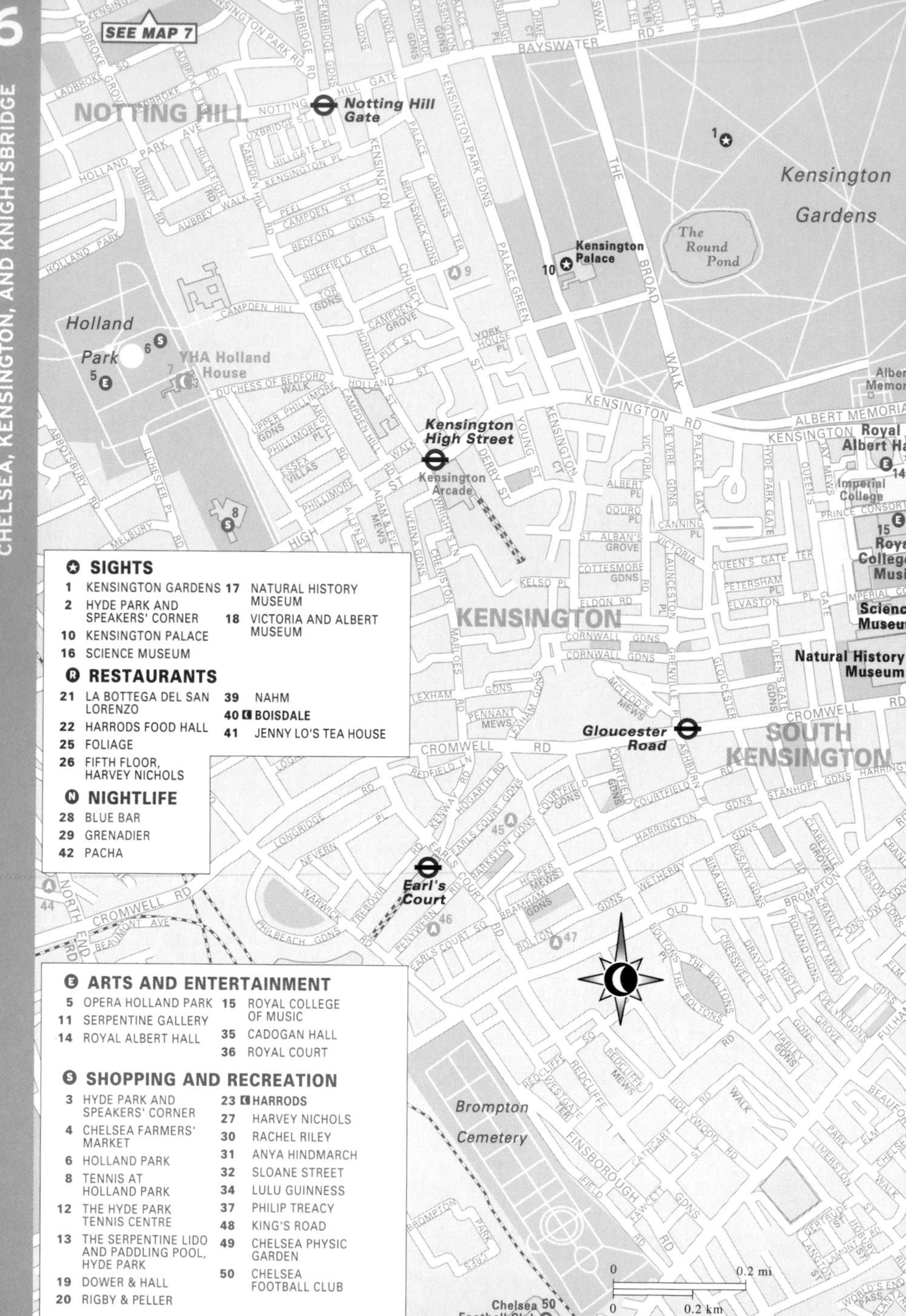

SEE MAP 7
NOTTING HILL
Notting Hill Gate
Kensington Gardens
The Round Pond
Kensington Palace
Holland Park
YHA Holland House
Albert Memorial
Kensington High Street
Kensington Arcade
Royal Albert Hall
Imperial College
Royal College Music
Science Museum
Natural History Museum
KENSINGTON
SOUTH KENSINGTON
Gloucester Road
Earl's Court
Brompton Cemetery
Chelsea Football Club 50
SIGHTS
1 KENSINGTON GARDENS
2 HYDE PARK AND SPEAKERS' CORNER
10 KENSINGTON PALACE
16 SCIENCE MUSEUM
17 NATURAL HISTORY MUSEUM
18 VICTORIA AND ALBERT MUSEUM
RESTAURANTS
21 LA BOTTEGA DEL SAN LORENZO
22 HARRODS FOOD HALL
25 FOLIAGE
26 FIFTH FLOOR, HARVEY NICHOLS
39 NAHM
40 BOISDALE
41 JENNY LO'S TEA HOUSE
NIGHTLIFE
28 BLUE BAR
29 GRENADIER
42 PACHA
ARTS AND ENTERTAINMENT
5 OPERA HOLLAND PARK
11 SERPENTINE GALLERY
14 ROYAL ALBERT HALL
15 ROYAL COLLEGE OF MUSIC
35 CADOGAN HALL
36 ROYAL COURT
SHOPPING AND RECREATION
3 HYDE PARK AND SPEAKERS' CORNER
4 CHELSEA FARMERS' MARKET
6 HOLLAND PARK
8 TENNIS AT HOLLAND PARK
12 THE HYDE PARK TENNIS CENTRE
13 THE SERPENTINE LIDO AND PADDLING POOL, HYDE PARK
19 DOWER & HALL
20 RIGBY & PELLER
23 HARRODS
27 HARVEY NICHOLS
30 RACHEL RILEY
31 ANYA HINDMARCH
32 SLOANE STREET
34 LULU GUINNESS
37 PHILIP TREACY
48 KING'S ROAD
49 CHELSEA PHYSIC GARDEN
50 CHELSEA FOOTBALL CLUB
0 0.2 mi
0 0.2 km

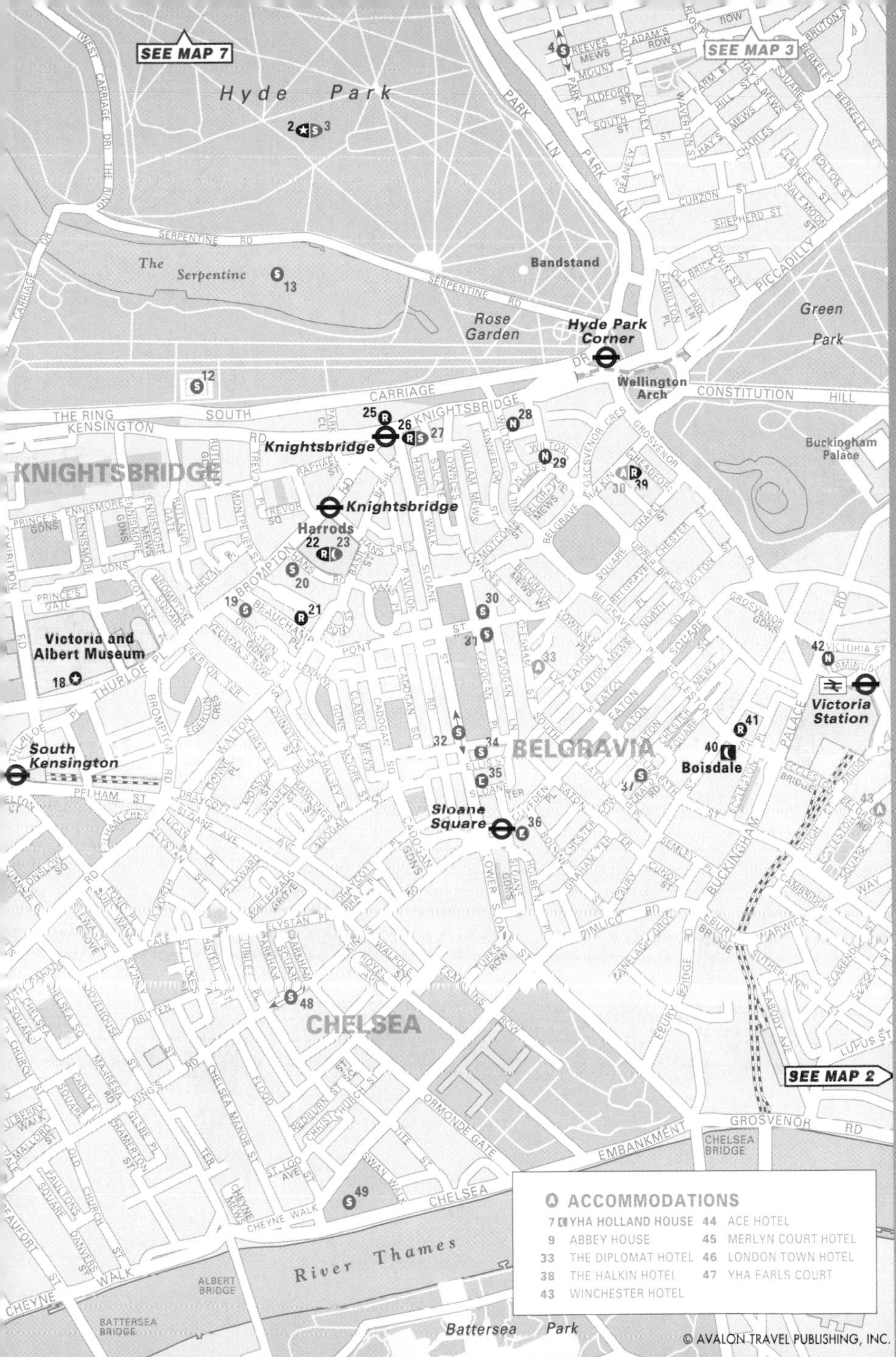

SEE MAP 7
SEE MAP 3
SEE MAP 2

Hyde Park
The Serpentine
Rose Garden
Bandstand
Hyde Park Corner
Wellington Arch
Green Park
Buckingham Palace
KNIGHTSBRIDGE
Knightsbridge
Harrods
Victoria and Albert Museum
South Kensington
BELGRAVIA
Boisdale
Victoria Station
Sloane Square
CHELSEA
River Thames
Battersea Park
Albert Bridge
Battersea Bridge
Chelsea Bridge

ACCOMMODATIONS

7	YHA HOLLAND HOUSE	44	ACE HOTEL
9	ABBEY HOUSE	45	MERLYN COURT HOTEL
33	THE DIPLOMAT HOTEL	46	LONDON TOWN HOTEL
38	THE HALKIN HOTEL	47	YHA EARLS COURT
43	WINCHESTER HOTEL		

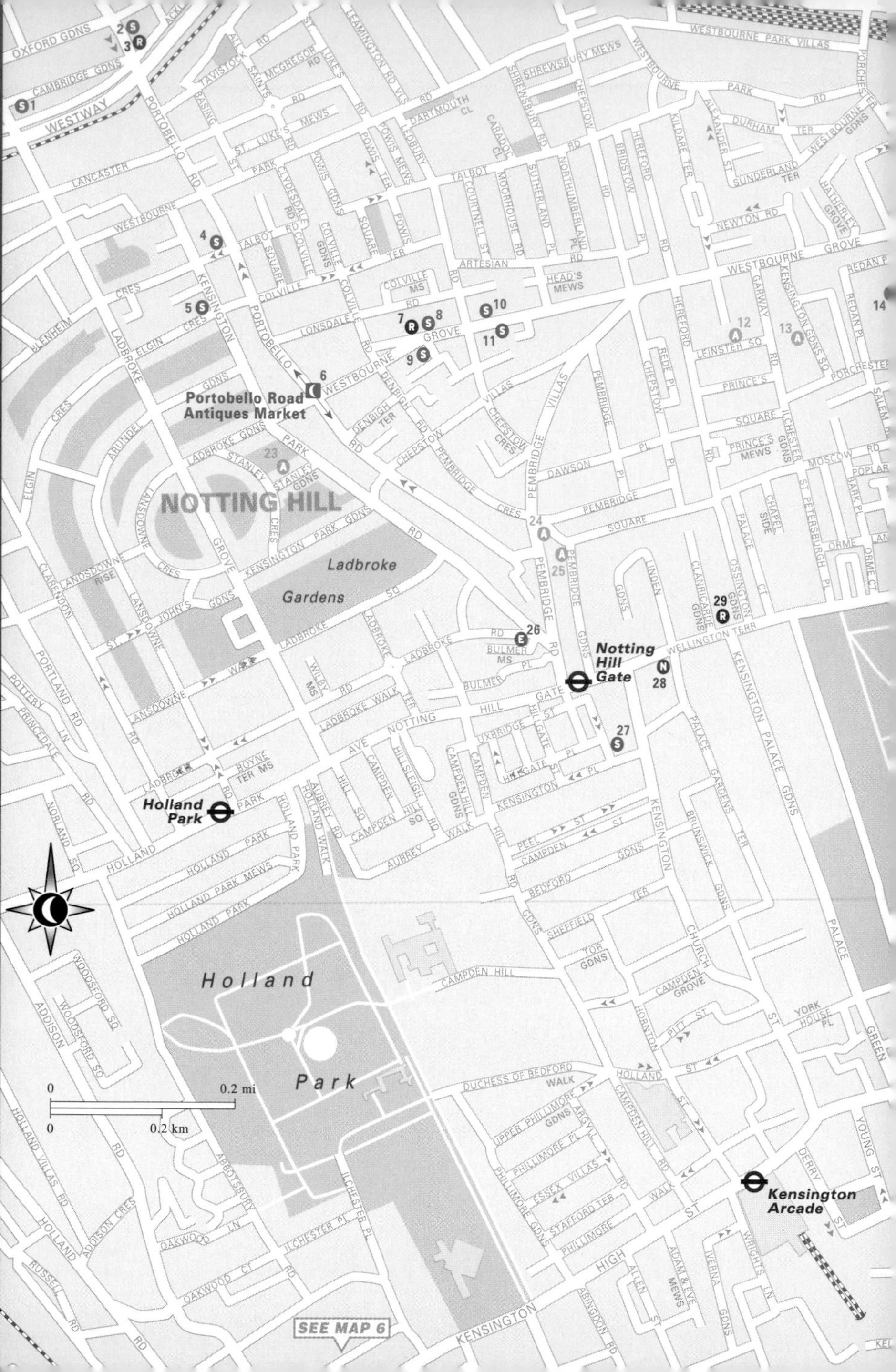
NOTTING HILL
Portobello Road Antiques Market
Ladbroke Gardens
Notting Hill Gate
Holland Park
Kensington Arcade
SEE MAP 6
0
0.2 mi
0
0.2 km
OXFORD GDNS
CAMBRIDGE GDNS
WESTWAY
WESTBOURNE PARK VILLAS
SHREWSBURY MEWS
LANCASTER
WESTBOURNE GROVE
TALBOT RD
COLVILLE
LONSDALE
ARTESIAN
HEAD'S MEWS
LEINSTER SQ
PRINCE'S SQUARE
MOSCOW RD
LADBROKE GROVE
PORTOBELLO RD
KENSINGTON PARK RD
PEMBRIDGE SQUARE
PEMBRIDGE VILLAS
CHEPSTOW VILLAS
DAWSON PL
STANLEY GDNS
LANSDOWNE CRES
CLARENDON RD
PORTLAND RD
POTTERY LN
PRINCEDALE RD
HOLLAND PARK AVE
NOTTING HILL GATE
WELLINGTON TERR
KENSINGTON CHURCH ST
KENSINGTON PALACE GDNS
CAMPDEN HILL
CAMPDEN HILL RD
HOLLAND ST
DUCHESS OF BEDFORD WALK
PHILLIMORE GDNS
KENSINGTON HIGH ST
ADDISON RD
HOLLAND VILLAS RD
ABBOTSBURY RD
ILCHESTER PL
OAKWOOD CT
WOODSFORD SQ
YORK HOUSE PL
DERRY ST
YOUNG ST
WRIGHTS LN

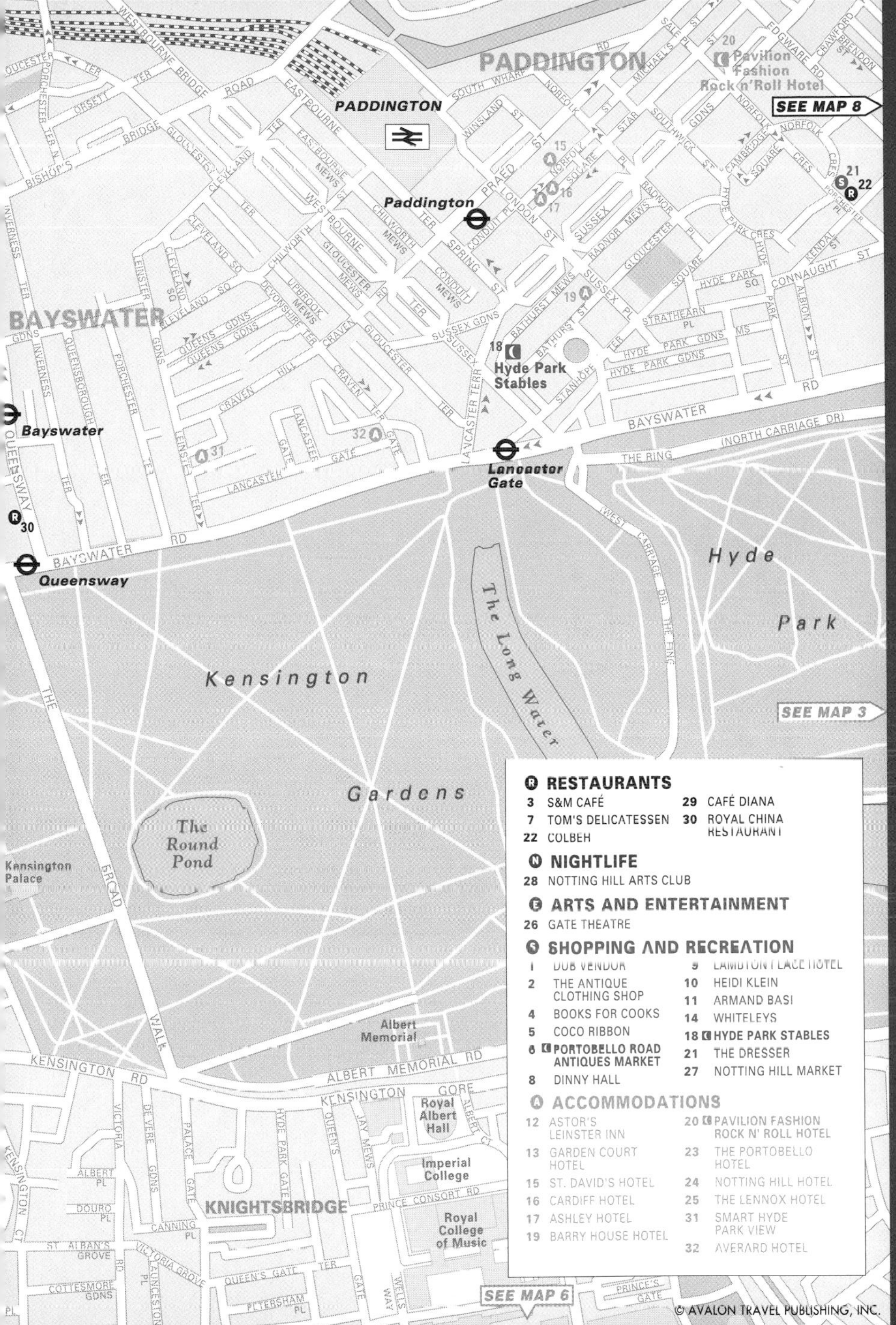
PADDINGTON
PADDINGTON
Paddington
BAYSWATER
Bayswater
Lancaster Gate
Queensway
Hyde Park Stables
Pavilion Fashion Rock n' Roll Hotel
SEE MAP 8
SEE MAP 3
SEE MAP 6
Hyde Park
Kensington Gardens
The Long Water
The Round Pond
Kensington Palace
Albert Memorial
Royal Albert Hall
Imperial College
Royal College of Music
KNIGHTSBRIDGE
BAYSWATER RD
KENSINGTON RD
ALBERT MEMORIAL RD
KENSINGTON GORE
PRINCE CONSORT RD
THE BROAD WALK
WEST CARRIAGE DR
(NORTH CARRIAGE DR)
THE RING
PRAED ST
EDGWARE RD
SUSSEX GDNS
WESTBOURNE TER
RESTAURANTS
3 S&M CAFÉ
7 TOM'S DELICATESSEN
22 COLBEH
29 CAFÉ DIANA
30 ROYAL CHINA RESTAURANT
NIGHTLIFE
28 NOTTING HILL ARTS CLUB
ARTS AND ENTERTAINMENT
26 GATE THEATRE
SHOPPING AND RECREATION
1 DUB VENDOR
2 THE ANTIQUE CLOTHING SHOP
4 BOOKS FOR COOKS
5 COCO RIBBON
6 PORTOBELLO ROAD ANTIQUES MARKET
8 DINNY HALL
9 LAMBTON PLACE HOTEL
10 HEIDI KLEIN
11 ARMAND BASI
14 WHITELEYS
18 HYDE PARK STABLES
21 THE DRESSER
27 NOTTING HILL MARKET
ACCOMMODATIONS
12 ASTOR'S LEINSTER INN
13 GARDEN COURT HOTEL
15 ST. DAVID'S HOTEL
16 CARDIFF HOTEL
17 ASHLEY HOTEL
19 BARRY HOUSE HOTEL
20 PAVILION FASHION ROCK N' ROLL HOTEL
23 THE PORTOBELLO HOTEL
24 NOTTING HILL HOTEL
25 THE LENNOX HOTEL
31 SMART HYDE PARK VIEW
32 AVERARD HOTEL
© AVALON TRAVEL PUBLISHING, INC.

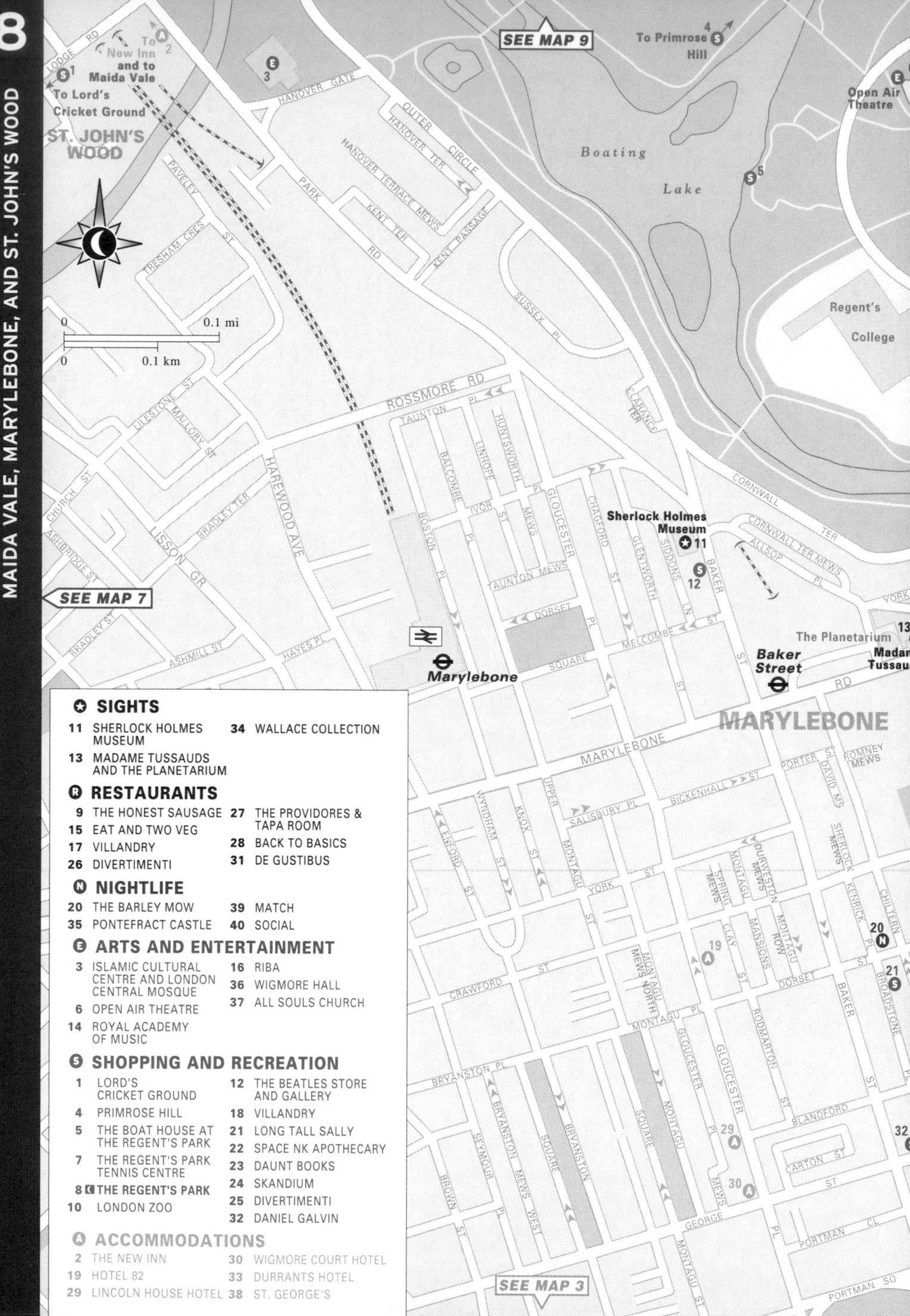

8
MAIDA VALE, MARYLEBONE, AND ST. JOHN'S WOOD
SEE MAP 9
SEE MAP 7
SEE MAP 3
To New Inn and to Maida Vale
To Lord's Cricket Ground
ST. JOHN'S WOOD
To Primrose Hill
Open Air Theatre
Boating Lake
Regent's College
Sherlock Holmes Museum
The Planetarium
Madame Tussauds
Baker Street
Marylebone
MARYLEBONE
0 0.1 mi
0 0.1 km
LODGE RD
HANOVER GATE
OUTER CIRCLE
HANOVER TER
HANOVER TERRACE MEWS
PARK RD
KENT TER
KENT PASSAGE
PAVELEY ST
TRESHAM CRES
SUSSEX PL
ROSSMORE RD
CLARENCE TER
CORNWALL TER
CORNWALL TER MEWS
ALLSOP PL
YORK
TAUNTON PL
BALCOMBE ST
LINHOPE ST
HUNTSWORTH MEWS
IVOR PL
TAUNTON MEWS
DORSET SQUARE
GLOUCESTER PL
CHAGFORD ST
GLENTWORTH ST
SIDDONS LN
BAKER ST
MELCOMBE ST
BOSTON PL
LILESTONE ST
MALLORY ST
CHURCH ST
ASHBRIDGE ST
LISSON GR
BRADLEY TER
HAREWOOD AVE
BRADLEY ST
ASHMILL ST
HAYES PL
MARYLEBONE RD
PORTER ST
ROMNEY MEWS
DAVID MS
BICKENHALL ST
SALISBURY PL
UPPER MONTAGU ST
WYNDHAM ST
KNOX ST
ENFORD ST
YORK ST
SPRING MEWS
MONTAGU MEWS
DURWESTON MEWS
SHERLOCK MEWS
KENRICK PL
CHILTERN ST
CLAY ST
MANSIONS
MONTAGU ROW
MONTAGU MEWS NORTH
CRAWFORD ST
DORSET ST
MONTAGU PL
RODMARTON ST
BROADSTONE PL
BRYANSTON PL
BRYANSTON MEWS WEST
BRYANSTON SQUARE
MONTAGU SQUARE
SEYMOUR PL
BROWN ST
BLANDFORD ST
CARTON ST
GEORGE ST
PORTMAN CL
PORTMAN SQ
MONTAGU ST
SIGHTS
11 SHERLOCK HOLMES MUSEUM
13 MADAME TUSSAUDS AND THE PLANETARIUM
34 WALLACE COLLECTION
RESTAURANTS
9 THE HONEST SAUSAGE
15 EAT AND TWO VEG
17 VILLANDRY
26 DIVERTIMENTI
27 THE PROVIDORES & TAPA ROOM
28 BACK TO BASICS
31 DE GUSTIBUS
NIGHTLIFE
20 THE BARLEY MOW
35 PONTEFRACT CASTLE
39 MATCH
40 SOCIAL
ARTS AND ENTERTAINMENT
3 ISLAMIC CULTURAL CENTRE AND LONDON CENTRAL MOSQUE
6 OPEN AIR THEATRE
14 ROYAL ACADEMY OF MUSIC
16 RIBA
36 WIGMORE HALL
37 ALL SOULS CHURCH
SHOPPING AND RECREATION
1 LORD'S CRICKET GROUND
4 PRIMROSE HILL
5 THE BOAT HOUSE AT THE REGENT'S PARK
7 THE REGENT'S PARK TENNIS CENTRE
8 THE REGENT'S PARK
10 LONDON ZOO
12 THE BEATLES STORE AND GALLERY
18 VILLANDRY
21 LONG TALL SALLY
22 SPACE NK APOTHECARY
23 DAUNT BOOKS
24 SKANDIUM
25 DIVERTIMENTI
32 DANIEL GALVIN
ACCOMMODATIONS
2 THE NEW INN
19 HOTEL 82
29 LINCOLN HOUSE HOTEL
30 WIGMORE COURT HOTEL
33 DURRANTS HOTEL
38 ST. GEORGE'S

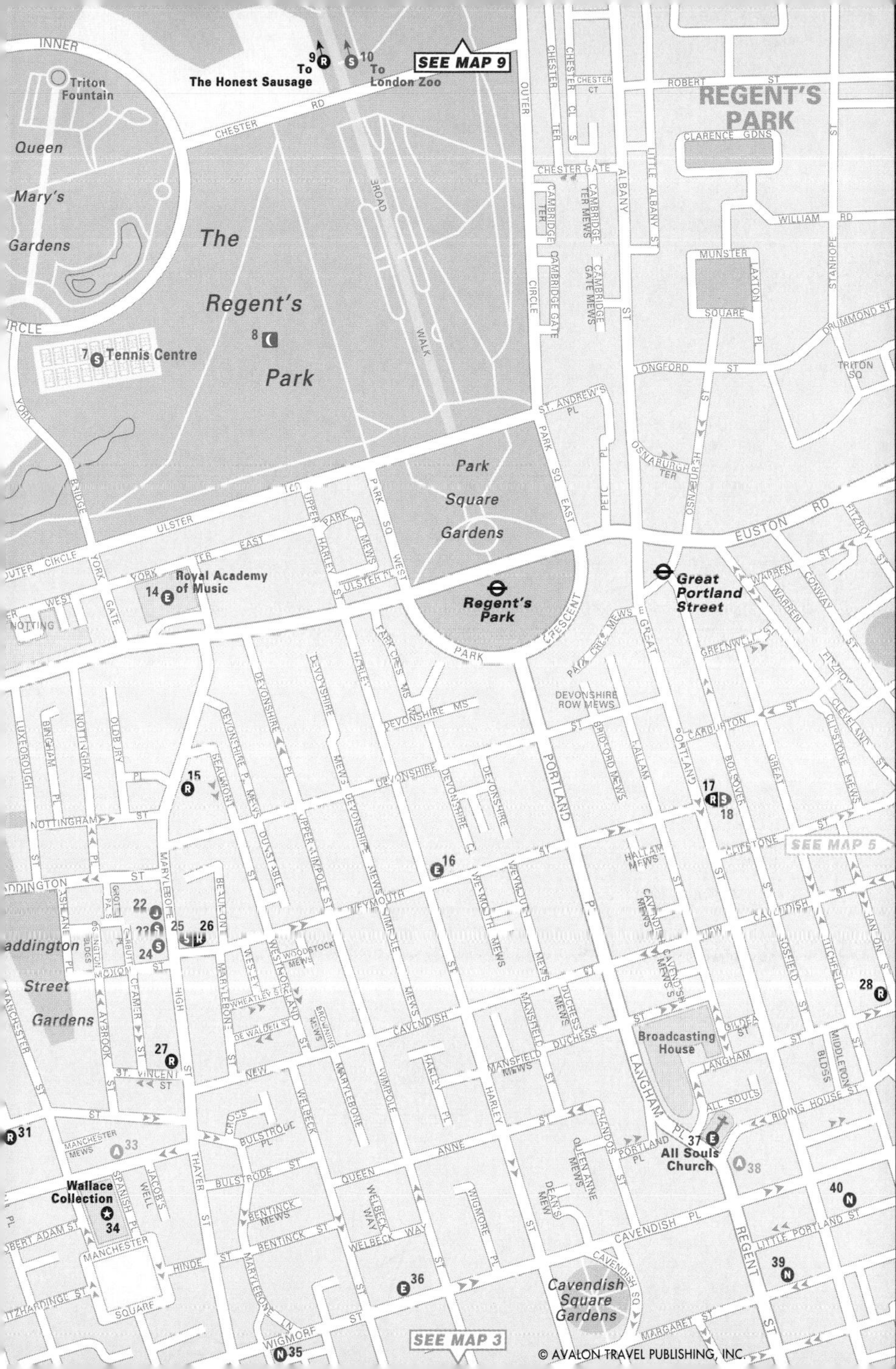

SEE MAP 9

9 R To The Honest Sausage
10 S To London Zoo

Triton Fountain
Queen Mary's Gardens
The Regent's Park
8
7 S Tennis Centre
REGENT'S PARK
Park Square Gardens
Regent's Park
Great Portland Street
14 E Royal Academy of Music
15 R
16 E
17 R S 18

SEE MAP 5

22 J
23 S
24 S
25
26 S R
Paddington Street Gardens
27 R
28 R
31 R
33
Broadcasting House
37 E All Souls Church
38
40 N
Wallace Collection
34
36 E
39 N
Cavendish Square Gardens
35 N

INNER CIRCLE
CHESTER RD
BROAD WALK
YORK BRIDGE
ULSTER TER
OUTER CIRCLE
YORK GATE
PARK SQ. EAST
PARK SQ. WEST
UPPER HARLEY ST
PARK SQ MEWS
ULSTER PL
EUSTON RD
PARK CRESCENT
PARK CRES MEWS E
CHESTER TER
CHESTER CL
CHESTER CT
CHESTER GATE
CAMBRIDGE TER
CAMBRIDGE TER MEWS
CAMBRIDGE GATE
CAMBRIDGE GATE MEWS
ALBANY ST
LITTLE ALBANY ST
ROBERT ST
CLARENCE GDNS
WILLIAM RD
MUNSTER SQUARE
LAXTON PL
STANHOPE ST
DRUMMOND ST
LONGFORD ST
TRITON SQ
ST. ANDREW'S PL
PETO PL
OSNABURGH TER
OSNABURGH ST
WARREN ST
CONWAY ST
FITZROY ST
GREENWELL ST
CLEVELAND ST
CARBURTON ST
DEVONSHIRE ROW MEWS
BRIDFORD MEWS
HALLAM ST
GREAT PORTLAND ST
BOLSOVER ST
GREAT TITCHFIELD ST
CLIPSTONE MEWS
CLIPSTONE ST
NEW CAVENDISH ST
HALLAM MEWS
CAVENDISH MEWS
BOLSOVER ST
HANSON ST
LUXBOROUGH ST
BINGHAM PL
NOTTINGHAM PL
OLDBURY PL
NOTTINGHAM ST
DEVONSHIRE PL
DEVONSHIRE PL MEWS
BEAUMONT ST
DEVONSHIRE MEWS
DEVONSHIRE ST
DEVONSHIRE CL
HARLEY ST
MARYLEBONE ST
DUNSTABLE MEWS
UPPER WIMPOLE ST
WEYMOUTH ST
WEYMOUTH MEWS
PADDINGTON ST
GROTTO PAS
CRAWFORD PAS
KENDALL PL
CHILTERN ST
HIGH ST
BEAUMONT ST
WESTMORELAND ST
WOODSTOCK MEWS
WHEATLEY ST
DE WALDEN ST
BROWNING MEWS
CAVENDISH ST
MANSFIELD ST
MANSFIELD MEWS
DUCHESS MEWS
DUCHESS ST
LANGHAM ST
LANGHAM PL
GILDEA ST
MIDDLETON BLDGS
RIDING HOUSE ST
ALL SOULS PL
CHANDOS ST
PORTLAND PL
QUEEN ANNE MEWS
QUEEN ANNE ST
DEAN'S MEWS
CAVENDISH PL
CAVENDISH SQ
LITTLE PORTLAND ST
REGENT ST
MARGARET ST
WIGMORE ST
WELBECK WAY
WELBECK ST
BENTINCK MEWS
BENTINCK ST
BULSTRODE PL
BULSTRODE ST
CROSS KEYS CL
THAYER ST
JACOBS WELL MEWS
SPANISH PL
MANCHESTER MEWS
MANCHESTER ST
MANCHESTER SQUARE
ST. VINCENT ST
AYBROOK ST
HINDE ST
ROBERT ADAM ST
FITZHARDINGE ST
NEW CAVENDISH ST

SEE MAP 3

9
CAMDEN TOWN
RESTAURANTS
5 COTTONS
9 CAMDEN LOCK MARKET
14 GREEN NOTE
20 CAFÉ CORFU
21 KAZ KREOL
NIGHTLIFE
4 BARTOK
6 BARFLY
8 JONGLEURS CAMDEN
13 EGG
15 DUBLIN CASTLE
18 JAZZ CAFÉ
ARTS AND ENTERTAINMENT
1 HIGHGATE CEMETERY
16 THE JEWISH MUSEUM
SHOPPING AND RECREATION
2 TALACRE COMMUNITY FITNESS CENTRE
7 NARROWBOAT TO LITTLE VENICE
10 CAMDEN LOCK
12 CAMDEN MARKETS
17 FRESH & WILD
19 CAMDEN COFFEE SHOP
22 ACUMEDIC CENTRE
ACCOMMODATIONS
3 CAMDEN LOCK HOTEL
11 HOLIDAY INN LONDON-CAMDEN LOCK
23 ST. CHRISTOPHER'S CAMDEN
24 SMART CAMDEN INN
To Highgate Cemetery
Kentish Town
Chalk Farm
CAMDEN TOWN
Camden Town
To Egg
Primrose Hill
London Zoo
The Regent's Park
Mornington Crescent
Oakley Square
The Honest Sausage
LEIGHTON RD
HOLMES RD
PRINCE OF WALES RD
KENTISH TOWN RD
ADELAIDE RD
CHALK FARM RD
CASTLE RD
HAWLEY RD
ROYAL COLLEGE ST
ST. PANCRAS WAY
CAMDEN HIGH ST
PARKWAY
JAMESTOWN RD
GLOUCESTER AVE
REGENT'S PARK RD
PRINCE ALBERT RD
DELANCEY ST
ARLINGTON RD
BAYHAM ST
PRATT ST
CAMDEN RD
HAMPSTEAD RD
EVERSHOLT ST
CROWNDALE RD
MORNINGTON CRES
OUTER CIRCLE
BROAD WALK
ALBANY ST
PARK VILLAGE EAST
0 0.1 mi
0 0.1 km
SEE MAP 8
© AVALON TRAVEL PUBLISHING, INC

To Arsenal Football Club

Highbury Fields

Paradise Park

Highbury and Islington

CANONBURY

BARNSBURY

Caledonian Road and Barnsbury

To Kandara Guest House

Essex Road

ISLINGTON

The Warwick Bar

Barnard Park

Afghan Kitchen

PENTONVILLE

Angel

Claremont Square

Middleton Square

RESTAURANTS

8 VIET GARDEN
14 METROGUSTO
15 OREGANO
19 AFGHAN KITCHEN
23 ART TO ZEN CAFÉ GALLERY
24 LOLA'S

NIGHTLIFE

6 THE HOPE AND ANCHOR
7 MEDICINE BAR
9 KINKY MAMBO
11 EMBASSY
16 THE WARWICK BAR
26 ELECTROWERKZ
28 SADLER'S WELLS

ARTS AND ENTERTAINMENT

2 ESTORICK COLLECTION OF MODERN ITALIAN ART
10 ALMEIDA THEATRE
13 KING'S HEAD THEATRE

SHOPPING AND RECREATION

1 ARSENAL FOOTBALL CLUB
3 NEW RIVER WALK
12 HAGGLE VINYL
17 FLASHBACK
20 RAU
21 CAMDEN PASSAGE
22 THE AFRICAN WAISTCOAT COMPANY
27 URBAN PAINTBALL GAMES

ACCOMMODATIONS

4 KANDARA GUEST HOUSE
5 ELENA HOTEL
18 HILTON HOTEL
25 JURYS INN

0 0.1 mi
0 0.1 km

SEE MAP 10

SIGHTS

- 2 GEFFRYE MUSEUM
- 10 BARBICAN
- 21 MUSEUM OF LONDON
- 22 GUILDHALL
- 23 GUILDHALL ART GALLERY
- 35 TEMPLE CHURCH
- 39 DR. JOHNSON'S HOUSE
- 45 ST. BRIDE'S
- 53 ST. PAUL'S CATHEDRAL
- 65 CEREMONY OF THE KEYS
- 66 **TOWER OF LONDON**
- 67 TOWER BRIDGE

RESTAURANTS

- 4 ABBAYE
- 5 SMITHS OF SMITHFIELD
- 15 BRICK LANE
- 26 K-10
- 27 GOW'S RESTAURANT AND OYSTER BAR
- 34 GAUCHO
- 41 YE OLDE CHESHIRE CHEESE
- 44 **PUNCH TAVERN**
- 48 LEON
- 54 JUST THE BRIDGE

NIGHTLIFE

- 3 TURNMILLS
- 6 **FABRIC**
- 13 THE DRUNKEN MONKEY
- 14 93 FEET EAST
- 40 YE OLDE CHESHIRE CHEESE
- 42 THE TIPPERARY
- 43 THE OLD BELL
- 47 THE BLACK FRIAR
- 56 YE OLDE WATLING
- 61 JAMAICA WINE HOUSE

ARTS AND ENTERTAINMENT

- 1 ST. LUKE'S
- 7 ST. BARTHOLOMEW THE GREAT
- 8 THE CHAMBERS GALLERY
- 11 BARBICAN
- 12 GUILDHALL SCHOOL OF MUSIC AND DRAMA
- 18 GOLDEN BOY
- 19 ST. SEPULCHRE-WITHOUT-NEWGATE
- 24 THE CLOCKMAKERS' MUSEUM
- 25 GUILDHALL ART GALLERY AND ROMAN AMPHITHEATRE
- 28 WHITECHAPEL ART FALLERY
- 30 ST. MARY-LE-STRAND
- 31 ST. CLEMENT DANES
- 33 PRINCE HENRY'S ROOM AND SAMUEL PEPYS EXHIBITION
- 36 TEMPLE CHURCH
- 37 ST. DUNSTAN-IN-THE-WEST
- 46 BRIDEWELL THEATRE
- 50 ST. MARTIN-WITHIN-LUDGATE
- 52 TEMPLE BAR
- 55 ST. MARY-LE-BOW
- 57 TEMPLE OF MITHRAS
- 58 BANK OF ENGLAND MUSEUM
- 63 MONUMENT
- 64 ST. MAGNUS THE MARTYR

SHOPPING AND RECREATION

- 9 IAN LOGAN DESIGN SHOP
- 16 BROADGATE ICE RINK
- 20 POSTMANS PARK
- 29 BBC SHOP
- 32 TWININGS TEA AND COFFEE MERCHANTS
- 38 LIPMAN AND SONS
- 49 T. M. LEWIN
- 59 THE ROYAL EXCHANGE

ACCOMMODATIONS

- 17 GREAT EASTERN HOTEL
- 51 YHA CITY OF LONDON
- 60 THREADNEEDLES
- 62 CLUB QUARTERS GRACECHURCH

SEE MAP 5
SEE MAP 4
SEE MAP 12